Cultural Anthropology

Cultural Anthropology

Asking Questions About Humanity

SECOND EDITION

Robert L. Welsch
FRANKLIN PIERCE UNIVERSITY

Luis A. Vivanco
UNIVERSITY OF VERMONT

New York   Oxford
Oxford University Press

Oxford University Press is a department of the University of Oxford. It furthers the University's objective of excellence in research, scholarship, and education by publishing worldwide. Oxford is a registered trademark of Oxford University Press in the UK and certain other countries.

Published in the United States of America by Oxford University Press
198 Madison Avenue, New York, NY 10016, United States of America.

For titles covered by Section 112 of the US Higher Education Opportunity Act, please visit www.oup.com/us/he for the latest information about pricing and alternate formats.

Library of Congress Cataloging in Publication Data
Names: Welsch, Robert Louis, 1950- author. | Vivanco, Luis Antonio, 1969- author.
Title: Cultural anthropology : asking questions about humanity / Robert L. Welsch, Franklin Pierce University, Luis A. Vivanco, University of Vermont.
Description: Second edition. | New York : Oxford University Press, [2018] | Includes bibliographical references and index.
Identifiers: LCCN 2017031718 | ISBN 9780190679026 (pbk. : alk. paper)
Subjects: LCSH: Ethnology.
Classification: LCC GN316 .W47 2018 | DDC 305.8—dc23
LC record available at https://lccn.loc.gov/2017031718

9 8 7 6 5 4 3 2
Printed by LSC Communications
Printed in the United States of America on acid-free paper

Robert L. Welsch:

To Sarah for her love and support, and to my students who have nudged me toward a broader and more complex view of the human condition and humanity's remarkable diversity.

Luis A. Vivanco:

To Peggy, Isabel, Felipe, and Camila for their love and support, and to my students who have taught me much about the importance of inspired teaching and learning.

Brief Contents

Contents

2 Culture:
Giving Meaning to Human Lives 31

3 Ethnography:
Studying Culture 55

4 Linguistic Anthropology:
Relating Language and Culture 81

6 Foodways:
Finding, Making, and Eating Food 137

7 Environmental Anthropology:
Relating to the Natural World 165

8 Economics:
Working, Sharing, and Buying 191

11 Gender, Sex, and Sexuality:
The Fluidity of Maleness and Femaleness 275

12 Kinship, Marriage, and the Family:
Love, Sex, and Power 301

13 Religion:
Ritual and Belief 329

15 Materiality:
Constructing Social Relationships and Meanings with Things 385

CLASSIC CONTRIBUTIONS: Daniel Miller on Why Some Things Matter 407

THINKING LIKE AN ANTHROPOLOGIST: Looking at Objects from Multiple Perspectives 403

ANTHROPOLOGIST AS PROBLEM SOLVER: John Terrell, Repatriation, and the Maori Meeting House at The Field Museum 393

Letter from the Authors

Dear Reader,

Imagine how people would react to you if the next time you went to the university bookstore you tried to haggle at the cash register for your textbooks. Or if the next time you caught a cold you explained to your friends that you were sick because a jealous person had hired a witch to cast a spell on you. In both cases, a lot of people would think you were crazy. But in many societies throughout the world, a lot of ordinary people would consider you crazy for *not* haggling or for *not* explaining your misfortunes as the workings of a witch.

Issues such as these raise some interesting questions. How do people come to believe such things? How are such beliefs reflected in and bolstered by individual behavior and social institutions in a society? Why do *we* believe and act in the ways *we* do? Such questions are at the core of the study of culture. The idea of culture is one of anthropology's most important contributions to knowledge.

The goal of our textbook is to help students develop the ability to pose good anthropological questions and begin answering them, our inspiration coming from the expression "99% of a good answer is a good question." We present problems and questions that students will find provocative and contemporary, and then use theories, ethnographic case studies, and applied perspectives as ways of explaining how anthropologists have looked at these topics over time. Our approach emphasizes what is currently known within the study of cultural anthropology and issues that continue to challenge anthropologists.

Central to the plan of this book are three underlying principles that guide our approach to cultural anthropology:

- An emphasis on learning how to ask important and interesting anthropological questions;
- Applying anthropology to understand and solve human problems;
- Respecting tradition, with a contemporary perspective.

Every chapter, every feature of the book has been written with these principles in mind. We have written a book about anthropology that draws on insights anthropologists have learned during the twentieth century. At the same time, with its cutting-edge content and pedagogy, this is a textbook that provides what students need for the twenty-first century.

For most students, an introductory course in cultural anthropology is the only educational exposure they will have to anthropological thinking. Most readers are unlikely to see anthropological thinking as relevant to their own lives unless we find a way to make it so. This book represents our endeavor to do just that.

Here's wishing you greater appreciation of cultural anthropology and a lifetime of cultural revelations to come.

Sincerely,

Robert L. Welsch

Luis A. Vivanco

About the Authors

Robert L. Welsch currently teaches cultural anthropology at Franklin Pierce University and previously taught for many years at Dartmouth College. He was affiliated with The Field Museum in Chicago for more than two decades. Trained in the 1970s at the University of Washington, at a time when anthropologists still focused mainly on non-Western village-level societies, and when cultural materialist, Marxist, structuralist, and interpretive theories dominated the discipline, Welsch has focused his research on medical anthropology, religion, exchange, art, and museum studies in the classic anthropological settings of Papua New Guinea and Indonesia, and the history of anthropology as a professional discipline. He is Associate Professor of anthropology at Franklin Pierce University.

Luis A. Vivanco teaches cultural anthropology and global studies at the University of Vermont, where he has won several of the university's top teaching awards. He was trained at Princeton University in the 1990s when post-structuralist perspectives and "studying up" (studying powerful institutions and bureaucracies, often in Western contexts) was becoming commonplace. Vivanco has worked in Costa Rica, Mexico, Colombia, and the United States, studying the culture and politics of environmentalist social movements, the media, science, ecotourism, and urban mobility with bicycles. He is Professor of anthropology and co-director of the Humanities Center at the University of Vermont.

Preface

What is cultural anthropology, and how is it relevant in today's world? Answering these core questions is the underlying goal of this book.

Cultural anthropology is the study of the social lives of communities, their belief systems, languages, and social institutions, both past and present. It provides a framework to organize the complexity of human experience and comprehend global cultural processes and practices. The practice of cultural anthropology also provides knowledge that helps solve human problems today.

Thinking Like an Anthropologist

Unlike textbooks that emphasize the memorization of facts, *Cultural Anthropology: Asking Questions About Humanity* teaches students how to think anthropologically. This approach helps students view cultural issues as an anthropologist might. In this way, anthropological thinking is regarded as a tool for deciphering everyday experience.

Organized Around Key Questions

Inspired by the expression "99% of a good answer is a good question," each chapter opens with a contemporary story and introduces key questions that can be answered by cultural anthropology. Each main section of a chapter is built around these questions. Through these unique chapter-opening and follow-up questions, students will see how classic anthropological concerns relate to contemporary situations. Additionally, this insight is reinforced by thought-provoking questions at the end of each section and "Reviewing the Chapter" features at the end of each chapter.

Solving Human Problems

At the heart of *Cultural Anthropology: Asking Questions About Humanity* is the belief that anthropology can make a difference in the world. We explain how anthropologists have looked at a wide range of human issues over time—mediating conflict, alleviating social problems, contributing to new social policies—exploring examples but also explaining challenges that still remain.

The Past Through a Contemporary Perspective

Cultural Anthropology: Asking Questions About Humanity represents our effort to close the gap between the realities of the discipline today and traditional views that are also taught at the introductory level. We believe that there is much to be gained, for ourselves and our students, by strengthening the dialogue between generations and sub-fields of anthropologists. We endeavor to bring classic anthropological examples, cases, and analyses to bear on contemporary questions.

Why We Wrote This Book

In view of how most academic work and life is organized and practiced today, our co-authorship is a somewhat unlikely collaboration. We come from different generations of anthropological training, teach at different kinds of institutions, do our research in opposite corners of the world, and work on different topics. Given the pressures and realities of regional and topical specialization within the discipline, we might not even run into each other at conferences, much less have reason to work together.

But as teachers concerned with sharing the excitement of anthropological findings and thinking with our undergraduate students, we have a lot in common. For one thing, we believe that there is strength in diversity, and we think our differing backgrounds are more representative of the breadth of the discipline and who actually teaches introductory courses in cultural anthropology. Because both of us feel that anthropological thinking is for everyone, we wrote this textbook to appeal to instructors who blend traditional and contemporary views of anthropology and teach students of many cultural backgrounds. We do this by treating the learning experience as a process of actively asking questions about real-world problems and applying theoretical insights to understand them, as nearly all anthropologists actually do.

Thematic Boxes

Four types of thematic boxes are used throughout the book to highlight key themes and principles. *Classic Contributions* boxes consider the history of anthropological thought on a particular topic and provide follow-up questions to promote critical analysis. *Thinking Like an Anthropologist* boxes invite students to exercise their own anthropological IQ by examining concrete ethnographic situations and formulating the types of questions that anthropologists typically ask. *Doing Fieldwork* boxes draw upon actual field projects to explore the special methods anthropologists have used to address specific questions and problems. Finally, *Anthropologist as Problem Solver* boxes describe cases in which anthropologists have applied disciplinary insights and methods to help alleviate social problems, mediate conflicts, and (re)define policy debates. These cases also provide insights into careers that take advantage of an anthropology background.

New in This Edition

Building on the successful approach established in the first edition, the second edition of *Cultural Anthropology* features a number of changes designed to keep the material up to date, relevant, and engaging for students. The following are the most visible changes.

- **A new chapter—"The Body" (Chapter 14)—that explores biocultural perspectives on health and illness.** Integrating new material with the most significant points from the first edition's chapters on biocultural concerns and medical anthropology, this new chapter shows students how the cultures in which we live shape our understandings and experiences of our bodies and minds, and our definitions and reactions to health and illness.
- **A thoroughly revised chapter—"Materiality" (Chapter 15)—on material culture.** Expanding on the discussion of material objects in the first edition, this chapter broadens its perspective to explore how and why objects have meaning and power to us in various cultural contexts, and it features a new section that examines issues related to the ownership of artifacts from other cultures.
- **New maps showing the locations of peoples and places discussed in each chapter.** Included near the beginning of each chapter, these new maps add context by helping students visualize where in the world the people and places under discussion are located.
- **A new map that highlights examples related to the processes and outcomes of globalization.** Located on the inside of the back cover, this map helps students quickly identify major discussions related to anthropologists' interest in how culture interacts with globalization processes around the world.
- **A new epilogue.** The final section in this book draws together important themes that run throughout the chapters—including the importance of appreciating human diversity, embracing a holistic perspective, and rejecting ethnocentrism—to help students recognize the many ways in which studying cultural anthropology can enrich their understanding of their world.
- **New chapter-opening stories drawn from real life.** New case studies exploring the ongoing Syrian refugee crisis (Chapter 5), the impact of the 2008 global financial crisis on foodways in Greece (Chapter 6), responses to climate change in the Marshall Islands (Chapter 7), the importance of social networks to entrepreneurs in China (Chapter 8), the 2014 Ebola outbreak in West Africa and the fear of the disease becoming widespread in the United States (Chapter 14), and the controversy surrounding the *Into the Heart of Africa* art exhibit in Canada (Chapter 15) help students relate major themes in each chapter to people's real-world experiences.
- **New thematic boxes.** New boxes draw students' attention to a wide variety of concerns that are important to American anthropologists today, including the social impacts of anthropological research (Chapter 1), collaborating with communities to preserve endangered languages (Chapter 4), tracking emergent forms of citizenship (Chapter 5), holistic approaches to fighting poverty (Chapter 8), (non)acceptance of trans people in America (Chapter 11), negotiating identity and culture in international adoptions (Chapter 12), and building and maintaining relationships with peoples whose cultural objects are on display in Western museums (Chapter 15).

In addition to these changes, we have also added new coverage of key topics in various chapters to ensure students receive a well-rounded introduction to cultural anthropology. These additions include the following:

- Chapter 1 features an expanded discussion of ethical obligations anthropologists must consider when conducting their research and sharing their findings.
- Chapter 2 provides a revised definition of culture as well as an expanded explanation of the authors' approach to culture in this book.

- Chapter 3 includes a restructured and expanded introduction to the skills and techniques anthropologists draw on when conducting fieldwork.
- Chapter 4 contains new sections on how anthropologists study language and the effects of new media technologies on language use.
- Chapter 5 provides new coverage of why people migrate and how migrants build and make use of social networks.
- Chapter 7 includes a new discussion of anthropologists' interest in the social dimensions of climate change.
- Chapter 8 features new explorations of cross-cultural perspectives on the significance of debt and the concepts of property and ownership.
- Chapter 11 features a thoroughly revised approach to gender, sex, and sexuality, focusing on the fluidity of maleness and femaleness.
- Chapter 12 includes new material on the study of cultural patterns in childrearing, and on international adoptions and the problem of cultural identity.
- Chapter 13 provides an in-depth analysis of the issues surrounding the 2015 attack on the offices of Charlie Hebdo in Paris, pointing out that such attacks are not merely the result of a "clash of civilizations."

Ensuring Student Success

Oxford University Press offers students and instructors a comprehensive ancillary package for *Cultural Anthropology*.

For Students
Companion Website

Cultural Anthropology: Asking Questions About Humanity is also accompanied by an extensive **companion website (www.oup.com/us/welsch)**, which includes materials to help students with every aspect of the course. For each chapter, you will find:

- **Learning objectives**
- **Chapter outlines** to help guide students through the chapter material
- **Interactive exercises** to engage students in fieldwork experience
- **A glossary of key terms** as a helpful reference for key concepts
- **Flashcards** to assist students in studying and reviewing key terms
- **Additional links** to websites providing supplemental information on the topics and ideas covered in the chapter
- **Additional recommended readings** that delve more deeply into the topics discussed in the chapter and that broaden student conceptions of what one can do with an anthropology degree
- **Self-grading review questions** to help students review the material and assess their own comprehension

For Instructors
Oxford University Press is proud to offer a complete and authoritative supplements package for both instructors and students. When you adopt *Cultural Anthropology: Asking Questions About Humanity,* you will have access to a truly exemplary set of ancillary materials to enhance teaching and support students' learning.

The **Ancillary Resource Center (ARC)** at www.oup-arc.com is a convenient, instructor-focused single destination for resources to accompany *Cultural Anthropology:*

Asking Questions About Humanity. Accessed online through individual user accounts, the ARC provides instructors with access to up-to-date ancillaries while guaranteeing the security of grade-significant resources. In addition, it allows OUP to keep instructors informed when new content becomes available.

The ARC for *Cultural Anthropology: Asking Questions About Humanity* includes:

- Digital copy of the **Instructor's Manual**, which includes:
  * A statement from the authors describing their pedagogical vision, clarifying the question-centered pedagogy, and offering advice on how to promote active learning in the classroom
  * Chapter outlines
  * Discussions of key controversies, which expand on the issues highlighted in the "What We Know" and "To Be Resolved" columns of the chapter-review tables
  * Key terms and definitions and summaries
  * Lecture outlines
  * PowerPoint slides
  * Web links and blogroll
  * In-class activities and project assignments
  * Suggestions for class discussion
  * Additional readings
  * Supplements to each box figure
  * Image bank
- A computerized **Test Bank** written by the authors and organized around principles from Bloom's Taxonomy for cognitive learning, including:
  * Multiple-choice questions
  * True/false questions
  * Fill-in-the-blank questions
  * Essay prompts
- **Ethnographic film clips** with supporting background and discussion questions for each clip, written by the authors, to explore and reinforce themes in the book.

Instructors may also order a complete **Course Management cartridge**. Contact your Oxford University Press Sales Representative for more information.

Acknowledgments

The authors would like to thank the many individuals who have supported this project from its inception to the final stages of production. The impetus for this book lies with Kevin Witt, who had an inspired vision for a new kind of anthropology textbook and the foresight to identify and support the team to write it. In its early stages while this project was with McGraw-Hill, development editors Pam Gordon, Nanette Giles, Susan Messer, and Phil Herbst each played an important role in shaping the manuscript.

At Oxford University Press, Sherith Pankratz, our acquisitions editor, and our two development editors, Thom Holmes (first edition) and Janice Evans (second edition), have managed this project and helped us further refine our vision with exceptional care and expertise. We would also like to thank associate editor Meredith Keffer for her extensive support, especially with the visual program. In addition, we would like to thank editorial assistant Larissa Albright, advertising and promotion product associate Marissa Dadiw, associate editor Andrew Heaton, editorial assistant Jacqueline Levine, and assistant editor Paul Longo for their helpful feedback on the headings. We would also like to thank permissions coordinator Cailen Swain. In production, we would like to thank designer Michele Laseau, production editor Lisa Ball, copy editor Gail Cooper, and proofreader Marianne Tatom. And last, but by no means least, we would like to acknowledge and thank our marketing team, including Tony Mathias, Frank Mortimer, Jordan Wright, and the other hardworking men and women who are marketing this book and getting it into the hands of the students for whom we wrote it. Although the sales and marketing teams often go unsung and unacknowledged by many authors, we know their work is critical to the success of a project like this one.

It is important to acknowledge and thank Agustín Fuentes of the University of Notre Dame, co-author of our general anthropology textbook, *Anthropology: Asking Questions about Human Origins, Diversity, and Culture* (published by OUP), who has helped shape our thinking on numerous dimensions of cultural anthropology.

We are grateful to Franklin Pierce University, the University of Vermont, Dartmouth College, the Hood Museum of Art, The Field Museum, the U.S. National Museum of Natural History (a branch of the Smithsonian Institution), the American Museum of Natural History in New York, the University of Costa Rica, and the National University of Colombia, all of whom have provided support in diverse ways. In particular, we appreciate the support and encouragement of Kim Mooney, President of Franklin Pierce University; Andrew Card, former President of Franklin Pierce University; Lynne H. Rosansky, Provost at Franklin Pierce; Kerry McKeever and Paul Kotila, Academic Deans at Franklin Pierce; and Jean Dawson and John Villemaire, Division Chairs of the Social and Behavioral Sciences at Franklin Pierce. At the University of Vermont, the Provost's Office and the Office of the Dean of the College of Arts and Sciences have provided important institutional support for this project.

Numerous librarians aided the development of this project at various stages, including Paul Campbell, Gladys Nielson, Amy Horton, Paul Jenkins, Leslie Inglis, Wendy O'Brien, Eric Shannon, Melissa Stearns, Lisa Wiley, and Jill Wixom at Frank S. DiPietro Library at Franklin Pierce University in Rindge, New Hampshire; Laurie Kutner at Bailey-Howe Library at the University of Vermont; Amy Witzel, Fran Oscadal, and John Cocklin at Baker Library at Dartmouth College; and staff of Alden Library at Ohio University in Athens, Ohio.

We want to especially thank our colleagues Kirk M. and Karen Endicott, Robert G. Goodby, Debra S. Picchi, Douglas Challenger, John E. Terrell, Robert J. Gordon, and Richard Robbins, all of whom have offered support, encouragement, and insights throughout the various phases of writing this book. Many other colleagues have contributed to this project in direct and indirect ways, including shaping our thinking about various anthropological topics, sparking ideas and being a sounding board about matters of content and pedagogy, and reading and responding to draft chapters. These colleagues include: at Dartmouth College, Hoyt Alverson, Sienna R. Craig, Brian Didier, Nathaniel Dominy, Seth Dobson, Dale F. Eickelman, Kathy Hart, Sergei Kan, Brian Kennedy, Kenneth Korey, Joel Levine, Deborah Nichols, and John Watanabe; and at the University of Vermont, Ben Eastman, Scott Van Keuren, Jennifer Dickinson, Teresa Mares, and Amy Trubek.

Several students at Franklin Pierce, the University of Vermont, and Dartmouth College have helped with research during the various stages of writing and rewriting. These include: Kristin Amato, Cory Atkinson, D. Wes Beattie, Kyle Brooks, Justyn Christophers, Michael Crossman, Matthew Dee, Brian Dunleavy, Catherine Durickas, Nathan Hedges, Kelsey Keegan, Saige Kemelis, Brian Kirn, Cooper Leatherwood, Adam Levine, Kevin Mooiman, Taber Morrell, Rebecca Nystrom, Shannon Perry, Keenan Phillips, Adam Slutsky, Scott Spolidoro, and Michael Surrett.

We want to thank our students at Franklin Pierce University and the University of Vermont who have test-driven both early drafts of this book as well as the first edition. Their feedback and insights have been invaluable. But in particular we want to thank Courtney Cummings, Kimberly Dupuis, John M. Gass, Kendra Lajoie, Holly Martz, Scott M. McDonald, Lindsay Mullen, and Nick Rodriguez, all of whom were students in AN400 at Franklin Pierce during the fall semester of 2012. Having used drafts of the text in their Introduction to Cultural Anthropology class, they reviewed all of the chapters in the book in focus-group fashion and offered useful insights about examples and writing in each chapter.

Last but certainly not least, we would like to thank our families for all the critical emotional and logistical support they have provided over the years to ensure the success of this project. Luis's children, Isabel, Felipe, and Camila, have aided us in various ways, from prodding questions about the book and anthropology to, at times, comic relief when we needed it. Our wives, Sarah L. Welsch and Peggy O'Neill-Vivanco, deserve our deepest gratitude for all their wise counsel over the many years this book was in development, and their ongoing support as we continue to improve it.

Manuscript Reviewers

We have greatly benefited from the perceptive comments and suggestions of the many talented scholars and instructors who reviewed the manuscript of the second edition of *Cultural Anthropology*. Their insight and suggestions contributed immensely to the published work.

Tara Deubel
University of South Florida

Christine Dixon
Green River College

Patrick Lathrop
Marist College

Ida Fadzillah Leggett
Middle Tennessee State University

David McCaig
Phoenix College

Melanie A. Medeiros
State University of New York at Geneseo

Andrew Nelson
University of North Texas

Donald Pollock
State University of New York at Buffalo

Leila Rodriguez
University of Cincinnati

Kathleen M. Saunders
Western Washington University

Michael E. Surrett
State University of New York College at Buffalo

David Syring
University of Minnesota Duluth

Laura M. Tilghman
Plymouth State University

Okori Uneke
Winston-Salem State University

Katherine Wahlberg
Florida Gulf Coast University

In addition, we would like to thank the reviewers whose thoughtful comments helped shape the first edition: Augustine Agwuele, *Texas State University*; Data D. Barata, *California State University, Sacramento*; O. Hugo Benavides, *Fordham University*; Keri Brondo, *University of Memphis*; Leslie G. Cecil, *Stephen F. Austin State University*; Carolyn Coulter, *Atlantic Cape Community College*; Matthew Dalstrom, *Rockford University*; Joanna Davidson, *Boston University*; Henri Gooren, *Oakland University*; Liza Grandia, *Clark University*; Ulrike M. Green, *Orange Coast College*; Shawn Dead Haley, *Columbia College*; Douglas Hume, *Northern Kentucky University*; Su Il Kim, *Metropolitan State College of Denver/Pikes Peak Community College*; Diane E. King, *University of Kentucky*; Frances Kostarelos, *Governors State University*; J. Christopher Kovats-Bernat, *Muhlenberg College*; Kuinera de Kramer-Lynch, *University of Delaware*; Scott M. Lacy, *Fairfield University*; Louis Herns Marcelin, *University of Miami*; Linda Matthei, *Texas A&M University, Commerce*; Faidra Papavasiliou, *Georgia State University*; Mark Allen Peterson, *Miami University*; Harry Sanabria, *University of Pittsburgh*; Elizabeth A. Scharf, *University of North Dakota*; Rocky L. Sexton, *Ball State University*; Carolyn Smith-Morris, *Southern Methodist University*; Victor D. Thompson, *University of Georgia*; James E. Todd, *Modesto Junior College/California State University, Stanislaus*; Susan R. Trencher, *George Mason University*; Neeraj Vedwan, *Montclair State University*; Jennifer R. Wies, *Eastern Kentucky University*; and Cherra Wyllie, *University of Hartford*.

Ancillary Co-Authors

Our sincere thanks also to the scholars and instructors who aided in the creation of the ancillary materials. Along with the textbook co-authors, they helped create high-quality additional resources specifically for this text:

Jason Fancher
Mt. Hood Community College

(Parts of the instructor's manual, PowerPoint slides, web links)

Meghan Ference
Brooklyn College, CUNY

(Portions of the test bank, interactive exercises, self-quizzes, additional readings)

K. Patrick Fazioli
Mercy College

(Web links, interactive exercises, additional readings)

Lola D. Houston
Burlington, Vermont

(Updates of the instructor's manual, PowerPoint slides, test bank, student materials)

Cultural Anthropology

Anthropology

Asking Questions About Humanity

Human beings are one of the world's most adaptable animals. Evolutionary history has endowed our species with certain common physical characteristics, instincts, and practices that have helped us to survive, even thrive, in every conceivable terrestrial environment. Yet no group of people is exactly like another, and as a species we exhibit tremendous variations across groups, and variations in our adaptations to the environment, our physical appearance, and our language, beliefs, and social organization.

Humans have always encountered groups of people who look different, speak unfamiliar languages, and behave in unexpected or unpredictable ways. Although sometimes hostility and wars have broken out between groups because of such differences, usually people have found ways to get along, often through trade and alliances. To be effective at establishing strong social and political bonds in spite of human differences has always required that people have a practical understanding of human variation.

Some of history's great travelers and explorers developed that practical understanding, among them the Venetian merchant Marco Polo (1254–1324), the Norman cleric Gerald of Wales (1146–1223), the Flemish Franciscan missionary William of Rubruck (1220–1293), the Moroccan traveler Ibn Batuta (1304–1368), and the Chinese admiral Zheng He (1371–1433). These individuals were all deeply interested in

---

⍦ **Intercultural Interactions.** In 1767, Captain Samuel Wallis and his crew were the first Westerners to reach Tahiti. Their first interactions were peaceful and included an exchange of gifts between Wallis and Queen Oberea. The cultural differences between Tahitians and the English raised many important questions about human differences and similarities, for both parties—the kinds of dynamics that interest anthropologists today.

other peoples, and their writings express sophisticated understandings of how and why the groups they encountered looked, acted, worshiped, and spoke as they did (Larner 1999; Bartlett 1982; Khanmohamadi 2008; Fazioli 2014; Harvey 2007; Menzies 2002; Dreyer 2007). Similarly, there is a rich historical legacy of intellectual thought about human variation. The great Chinese philosopher Confucius (551–479 BCE) wrote in two of his *Analects* some principles for establishing relationships with *yi* [yee], meaning cultural and ethnic outsiders. A generation later, the Greek historian Herodotus (484–425 BCE), in his multi-volume *Histories*, described the diverse peoples and societies he encountered during his travels in Africa, Southwestern Asia, and India, offering a number of possible explanations for the variations he observed across groups.

While all of these individuals were curious about other peoples and at times quite rigorous in their ways of thinking about human variation, they were not anthropologists as we think of anthropology today. They were not researchers asking systematic questions about humanity, and anthropology as a discipline did not emerge from their writings. Still, their various writings show that getting along with peoples from different cultures has always been important, a point that is sometimes lost on us in the United States, where our international prominence and our preoccupation with American exceptionalism may lead us to think that we don't need to understand people and cultures from other countries. But if we Americans want to be successful in dealing with people internationally in politics, trade, treaties, and global environmental or health policies, we need to understand in systematic ways people from other countries and the cultures that guide and motivate them.

These points lead us to our first question, the question at the heart of this chapter: *What is anthropology, and how is it relevant in today's world?* Embedded in this broader question are the following problems, around which this chapter is organized:

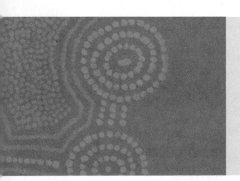

How did anthropology begin?

What do the four subfields of anthropology have in common?

How do anthropologists know what they know?

How do anthropologists put their knowledge to work in the world?

What ethical obligations do anthropologists have?

Anthropology is the study of human beings, their biology, their prehistory and histories, and their dynamic languages, cultures, and social institutions. Anthropology provides a framework for asking questions about and grasping the complexity of human experience, both past and present. Anthropology is about where humans have been, but it also provides knowledge that helps solve human problems today.

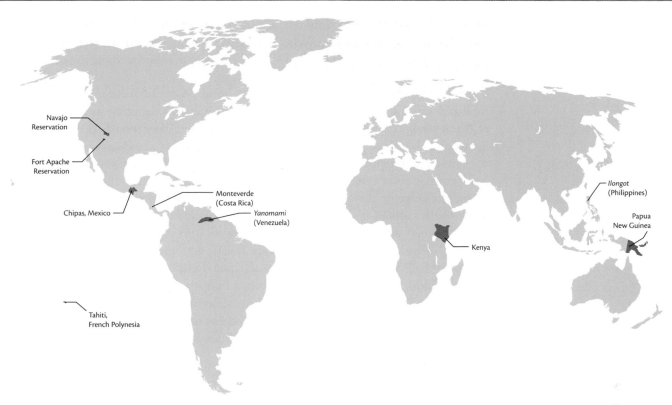

Figure 1.1 Select Peoples and Places Discussed in Chapter 1.

How Did Anthropology Begin?

During the nineteenth century, **anthropology** emerged in Europe and North America as an academic discipline devoted to the systematic observation and analysis of human variation. It was made possible once intellectuals and scholars had developed rigorous ways of comparing different species and people with different cultures. The Enlightenment or Age of Reason, which began in the early 1700s with the rise of modern science, demonstrated that careful observation and analysis could lead to understanding the natural world. While scholars observed differences among peoples living on the different continents, they did not attempt to explain these variations until their own societies had begun to change as a result of industrialization. Previously, cultural differences were assumed to be a given; cultural variation in the 1800s was thought to be essentially as it always had been. But as intellectuals began to notice that their own societies were changing because of the rise of factories, they realized that other societies around the world had also been changing.

Three key concerns began to emerge by the 1850s that would shape professional anthropology. These were (1) the disruptions of industrialization in Europe and America, (2) the rise of evolutionary theories, and (3) the growing importance of Europe's far-flung colonies with large indigenous populations whose land, mineral wealth, and labor Europeans and Americans wanted to control.

The Disruptions of Industrialization

Industrialization refers to the economic process of shifting from an agricultural economy to a factory-based economy. Industrialization disrupted American and European societies by bringing large numbers of rural people into towns and cities to work in factories. The rise of industrial towns and cities raised questions about how society was changing, including how a factory-based economy and the attendant growth of cities shaped society, government, residential patterns, and culture. These were the questions

- **Anthropology.** The study of human beings, their biology, their prehistory and histories, and their changing languages, cultures, and social institutions.

- **Industrialization.** The economic process of shifting from an agricultural economy to a factory-based economy.

that motivated great social thinkers, in particular German political economists Karl Marx (1818–1883) and Max Weber (1864–1920) and the French anthropologist-sociologist Émile Durkheim (1858–1917), each of whom influenced the rise of anthropology as a social scientific discipline.

At the beginning of the nineteenth century, most people in Western countries were rural and were usually engaged in farming. Factory economies affected such basic aspects of life as whom individuals would marry, what activities they would spend their days doing, and the role of religion in their lives. In the midst of these social and economic upheavals, anthropology developed as a discipline that sought to understand and explain how people in rural and urban settings organize their communities and how those communities change. It also led scholars to consider how industrialization affected peoples in European colonies in Africa, Asia, Latin America, and the Pacific Islands. Important new questions were posed: Why did these diverse societies organize their lives in the ways they did? Why had Native Americans and Africans not developed industrial societies as Europeans had? Why had the civilizations of China, India, and the Arab world developed social, political, and economic patterns distinct from those of Europeans? And why had these other civilizations not experienced industrialization as Europeans had? Asking about how European villages and cities were structured and how they perpetuated their cultures ultimately led to questions about how all sorts of non-Western societies worked as well.

The Theory of Evolution

- **Evolution.** The adaptive changes organisms make across generations.

A second key influence on the development of anthropology was the rise of evolutionary theory to explain biological variation between and within species. **Evolution** refers to the adaptive changes organisms make across generations. English naturalist Charles Darwin (1809–1882) developed a theory of how different species of plants and animals had evolved from earlier forms. The key mechanism of his evolutionary theory was what he called "natural selection," a process through which certain inheritable traits are passed along to offspring because they are better suited to the environment. Thus, in Darwin's view, in subtle ways nature was sorting out, or selecting, the forms best adapted for their environment.

- **Empirical.** Verifiable through observation rather than through logic or theory alone.

The idea of biological evolution was a remarkable notion for people used to thinking of species as fixed and stable. Religious scholars interpreted the book of Genesis in the Old Testament to suggest that God had created all of the natural species once at the time of creation and that no new species had been created since then. For Darwin, however, the question of the origin of species was not a religious one but an **empirical** one. It was a question that could be answered by observing whether species had changed and whether new species had emerged over time. From the findings of contemporary geologists, Darwin knew that many early species such as the dinosaurs had arisen and died out. For him, such changes were evidence that the natural environment had selected some species for survival and that extinction was the outcome for those not well suited to changing environments.

When Darwin published his groundbreaking work, *On the Origin of Species*, in 1859, he experienced a backlash, and few scientists accepted Darwin's ideas immediately. Indeed, as late as the 1920s, some biologists continued to be uncomfortable with the idea that species might change over time. But as the older generation left the scene, younger scientists recognized how easily this simple theory explained most kinds of biological variation both within and between species. Today, biologists and anthropologists no longer view biological evolution as controversial, and nearly all anthropologists and biologists accept evolution as the only way to explain the relationships among animal and plant species and the only way to explain why humans have the biological abilities and characteristics we can observe today.

Since Darwin's time, the broader scientific community has borrowed from his theory to produce a wave of new ideas involving evolution. Evolution seemed to provide a framework for studying both the biological and the cultural development of humans and their societies. Among biological anthropologists, the inheritance of physiological traits allowed science to understand the history of human origins and our relationship to other primates. Among early cultural anthropologists, evolutionary models seemed ideal for explaining how different societies had come to be as they were when Europeans encountered them for the first time. The notion of evolution allowed early anthropologists to rank societies along an evolutionary scale, ranging from more "primitive" forms of society with simpler technologies to more "advanced" forms of society that used more complex tools. Anthropologists today challenge such models of cultural evolution because this model does not fit the observed facts, but these early models motivated anthropologists to collect data from the so-called primitive societies before industrialization caused them to change or die out.

Colonial Origins of Cultural Anthropology

A third driving force behind anthropology was **colonialism,** the historical practice of more powerful countries claiming possession of less powerful ones. Although both China and Japan have had colonies, when we think about the development of anthropology, we usually think of colonialism as practiced by Europeans and North Americans. We can think of American domination over Indian lands as a form of colonialism, particularly when government policies moved Native Americans from the southeastern states to what is now Oklahoma, largely because white settlers wanted their land. Overseas, the colonial period flourished from the 1870s until the 1970s, and whites established mines, fisheries, plantations, and other enterprises using local peoples as inexpensive labor. Colonies enriched the mother countries, often impoverishing the indigenous inhabitants.

Colonized peoples everywhere had different cultures and customs, and their actions often seemed baffling to white administrators, a fact that these officials chalked up to their seemingly primitive or savage nature. Colonialists justified their actions—both philosophically and morally— through the **othering** of non-Western peoples, a process of defining colonized peoples as different from, and subordinate to, Europeans in terms of their social, moral, and physical norms (Said 1978). Early anthropologists contributed to othering through the creation of intellectual labeling and classification schemes that were sometimes little more than negative stereotypes (Tuhiwai Smith 2012). At the same time, early anthropologists were developing new social scientific methods of studying non-Western societies, primarily to inform colonial officials how to govern and control such radically different peoples.

Most Europeans and Americans expected their colonial subjects to die out, leading to the urgent collection of information about tribal societies before it was too late. Well into the 1920s, anthropologists pursued an approach known as the **salvage paradigm**, which held that it was important to observe indigenous ways of life, interview elders, and assemble collections of objects made and used by indigenous peoples because this knowledge of traditional languages and customs would soon disappear (Figure 1.2). Of course, today we know that while some Indian tribes, especially along the east coast of North America, largely died out, many other groups have survived and grown in population. But these Native American cultures have had to adjust and adapt to the changing American landscape and all the changes that Americans of different national origins have brought to the continent.

- **Colonialism.** The historical practice of more powerful countries claiming possession of less powerful ones.

- **Othering.** Defining colonized peoples as different from, and subordinate to, Europeans in terms of their social, moral, and physical norms.

- **Salvage paradigm.** The paradigm that holds that it is important to observe indigenous ways of life, interview elders, and assemble collections of objects made and used by indigenous peoples.

Figure 1.2 The Salvage Paradigm. Efforts to document indigenous cultures "before they disappeared" motivated anthropologists and others—including well-known American photographer Edward S. Curtis, who took this picture of an Apsaroke mother and child in 1908—to record the ways of traditional people.

Anthropology as a Global Discipline

By the end of the nineteenth century, anthropology was already an international discipline, whose practitioners were mainly based in Western Europe and the United States. Although they had some shared concerns, anthropologists in particular countries developed specific national traditions, studying distinct problems and developing their own styles of thought. Throughout the twentieth century, anthropology began to emerge in many regions other than Europe and the United States. Many students in colonial territories had attended European and American universities where they learned anthropology, and these students brought anthropology back home. In these countries, anthropology often focuses on practical problems of national development and on documenting the minority societies found within the country's borders. Today, anthropology is a truly global discipline with practitioners in dozens of countries asking many different kinds of questions about humanity.

• •

THINKING CRITICALLY ABOUT ANTHROPOLOGY

Can you think of something you do at your college or university that feels "natural" but is probably done somewhat differently at another college? Consider, for example, how your experiences in high school classes may have led you to expect something different from your college classes.

• •

What Do the Four Subfields of Anthropology Have in Common?

Anthropology has traditionally been divided into four subfields: cultural anthropology, archaeology, biological anthropology, and linguistic anthropology (Figure 1.3).

Cultural anthropology focuses on the social lives of living communities. Until the 1970s, most cultural anthropologists conducted research in non-Western communities, spending a year or two observing social life. We call this kind of research *anthropological fieldwork*. These anthropologists learned the local language and studied broad aspects of the community, recording information about people's economic transactions, religious rituals, political organization, and families, seeking to understand how these distinct domains influenced each other. In recent decades, they have come to focus on more specific issues in the communities they study, such as how and why religious conflicts occur, how environmental changes affect agricultural production, and how economic interactions create or maintain social inequalities. Today, anthropologists are as likely to study modern institutions, occupational groups, ethnic minorities, and the role of computer technology or advertising in their own cultures as they are to study cultures outside of their own.

Archaeology studies past cultures, by excavating sites where people lived, worked, farmed, or conducted some other activity. Some archaeologists study prehistory (life before written records), trying to understand how people lived before they had domesticated plants and animals, or trying to reconstruct the patterns of trade or warfare between ancient settlements. Two themes have been traditional concerns of prehistoric archaeology: (1) the transition from hunting and gathering to agriculture and (2) the rise of cities and states, when complex social, political, and economic institutions arose, along with occupational specializations, social class distinctions, and the emergence of early political forms that resemble states.

• **Cultural anthropology.** The study of the social lives of living communities.

• **Archaeology.** The study of past cultures, by excavating sites where people lived, worked, farmed, or conducted some other activity.

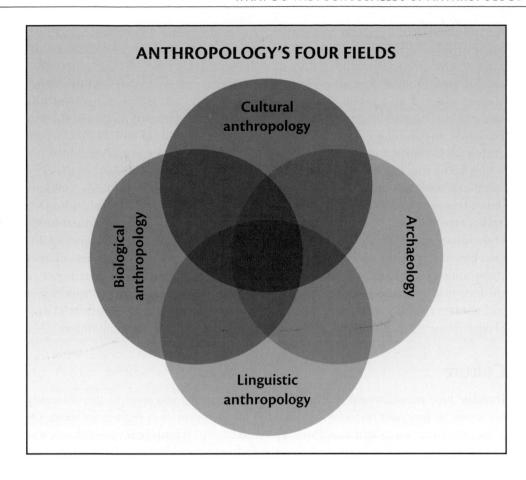

ANTHROPOLOGY'S FOUR FIELDS

Cultural anthropology

Biological anthropology

Archaeology

Linguistic anthropology

Figure 1.3 Anthropology's Four Fields.

Another branch of archaeology is historical archaeology, in which archaeologists excavate sites where written historical documentation about the sites also exists. The goal is to find physical evidence in the ground that will supplement or verify what we know about a community or society based on written records. Interestingly, historical archaeologists often find that few people actually lived as described in their diaries and other historical documents. For example, excavations on American cotton plantations have added a great deal to what we already know about the living conditions of slaves on plantations, information that does not generally appear in written records because the lives of slaves and poor white farmers were rarely documented in more than cursory ways.

Biological anthropology (also called *physical anthropology*) focuses on the biological aspects of the human species, past and present, along with those of our closest relatives, the nonhuman primates (apes, monkeys, and related species). A mainstay of biological anthropology has been the attempt to uncover human fossils and reconstruct the pathways of human evolution. By the 1950s and 1960s, biological anthropologists expanded into the study of human health and disease and began to look at the nonhuman primates (especially monkeys and apes) to determine what is part of our basic primate biology and what comes with culture. Biological anthropology is currently a field of many specializations; researchers still explore human evolution, health and disease, and primate behavior, but they also study human genetics, how social stress impacts the body, and human diet and nutrition.

Linguistic anthropology studies how people communicate with one another through language, and how language use shapes group membership and identity. Linguistic anthropologists also look at how language helps people organize their cultural beliefs and ideologies. These anthropologists have traditionally studied the categories that indigenous people use in their own languages, attempting to understand how they classify parts of their social and natural worlds differently from peoples in other societies.

- **Biological anthropology.** The study of the biological aspects of the human species, past and present, along with those of our closest relatives, the nonhuman primates.

- **Linguistic anthropology.** The study of how people communicate with one another through language and how language use shapes group membership and identity.

Anthropology is by nature an interdisciplinary discipline. Its subfields cross into many other academic disciplines across the social and natural sciences. Cultural anthropologists, for example, often draw on sociological and psychological approaches, and for some projects they rely on historical and economic data as well. Most archaeologists need to understand the principles of geology, including stratigraphy (the study of the layering of rock) and geochronology (the dating of rocks and fossils). Biological anthropology draws heavily on biological subfields of morphology (which deals with the form and structure of organisms), cellular biology, and genetics.

One thing that keeps such diverse subfields together is a shared history. In the early twentieth century, anthropology became organized into the four subfields we know today, from a shared evolutionary perspective. Archaeologists and cultural anthropologists, especially in North America, generally see themselves as asking similar kinds of questions about human cultures. The major difference is that cultural anthropologists can observe cultures as they are lived, while archaeologists can only reconstruct these cultures from what they have left behind. Another reason for the persistence of the four-field approach is that anthropologists share certain fundamental approaches and concepts, which they agree are important for making sense of humanity's complexity. These include culture, cultural relativism, diversity, change, and holism.

Culture

Imagine how people would react to you if the next time you went to the university bookstore to buy your textbooks you tried to haggle at the cash register for them. Or if the next time you caught a cold you explained to your friends that your sickness was caused by someone's jealousy, and that the jealous person had hired a witch to cast a spell on you. In both cases, most people would think you are crazy. But in many societies throughout Africa, Asia, Latin America, the Pacific, and other regions, a lot of ordinary people would think you are crazy for *not* haggling or for *not* explaining your misfortunes as the workings of a witch.

- **Culture.** The taken-for-granted notions, rules, moralities, and behaviors within a social group.

Every human group has particular rules of behavior and a common set of explanations about how the world works. Within the community, these behaviors and explanations feel totally natural; which is to say, self-evident and necessary. People who behave differently are strange, wrong, maybe even evil. What feels natural to us may seem totally arbitrary to another group of people, because the rules and explanations vary from one group to another. In anthropology, the term **culture** refers to these taken-for-granted notions, rules, moralities, and behaviors within a social group that feel natural and suggest the way things should be. (See also our discussion about definitions of culture in Chapter 2, on pages 33–41.)

The idea of culture is one of anthropology's most important contributions to knowledge. It is also one of anthropology's oldest concepts, its first use commonly credited to British anthropologist Edward Burnett Tylor in the 1870s. In "Classic Contributions: Edward Burnett Tylor and the Culture Concept," we examine his original definition of culture.

Anthropologists believe that people have culture in two senses: the general and the particular. Culture in the general sense refers to humans' possession of a generalized capacity, even necessity, to create, share, and pass on their understandings of things through culture. From this point of view, the development of culture is *the* defining feature of our species' evolutionary history, and thus of great relevance to the subfield of biological anthropology.

Culture in the particular sense refers to the fact that people live their lives within particular cultures, or ways of life. For example, although the "American way of life" is actually culturally diverse, with differences across regions, social classes, and ethnic groups, most Americans share very similar beliefs about such things as the value of a formal education, what kinds of clothes women and men should wear to the office, and what side of the road to drive on. Archaeologists, linguistic anthropologists, and

Classic Contributions

Edward Burnett Tylor and the Culture Concept

LIKE OTHER ANTHROPOLOGISTS of the latter half of the nineteenth century, Edward Burnett Tylor believed that the social and cultural differences of humanity could be explained as the product of evolutionary forces. Tylor's primary intellectual concern throughout his career was developing an evolutionary sequence that would explain how people evolved from a state of what he called "primitive savagery" to more "advanced" levels of civilization. In his book *Primitive Culture*, published in 1871, he advanced his argument that humans are subject to evolutionary forces in all aspects of their lives, including what he called "culture," offering the now-classic definition presented here. Although contemporary uses of the term *culture* have changed since Tylor's definition—mainly because anthropologists today reject Tylor's evolutionary perspective—Tylor's definition is important because it provided a basis for the scientific study of culture that has been central to the discipline ever since.

Edward Burnett Tylor.

Culture or Civilization, taken in its wide ethnographic sense, is that complex whole which includes knowledge, belief, art, morals, law, custom, and any other capabilities and habits acquired by man as a member of society. The condition of culture among the various societies of mankind, in so far as it is capable of being investigated on general principles, is a subject apt for the study of laws of human thought and action. . . . [I]ts various grades may be regarded as stages of development or evolution, each the outcome of previous history, and about to do its proper part in shaping the history of the future. (Tylor 1871:1)

Questions for Reflection

1. How is this definition different from or similar to the notion of culture you had before taking an anthropology course?

2. Tylor believed that people acquire culture as members of a society. But how, specifically, might someone acquire his or her culture?

cultural anthropologists tend to study people's lives in the context of a particular culture. In Chapter 2 we explore the concept of culture more deeply, but here it is important to know that when anthropologists use the term *culture* they are nearly always referring to ideas about the world and ways of interacting in society or in the environment in predictable and expected ways.

Cultural Relativism

All human lives are constantly embedded in and shaped by culture. Anthropologists, of course, also carry with them basic assumptions about how the world works and what is right or wrong, which typically become apparent when one is studying a culture that makes completely different assumptions. One possible response to the gap in understanding that comes with being in another culture is **ethnocentrism**,

• **Ethnocentrism.** The assumption that one's own way of doing things is correct, and that other people's practices or views are wrong or ignorant.

is increasingly practiced by women and members of many ethnic and racial minority groups. In the United States today, in fact, women constitute the majority of professional anthropologists. Around the world, decolonization of former colonies has brought once-excluded indigenous peoples and members of internal minority groups into universities where many have studied anthropology, further expanding the kinds of backgrounds and perspectives represented in the global discipline.

Holism

• **Holism.** Efforts to synthesize distinct approaches and findings into a single comprehensive interpretation.

In bringing together the study of human biology, prehistory, language, and social life under one disciplinary roof, anthropology offers powerful conceptual tools for understanding the entire context of human experience. The effort to synthesize these distinct approaches and findings into a single comprehensive explanation is called **holism**. It is American anthropology that has strived to be the most holistic. This was a legacy of German-born Franz Boas, long considered the founder of American anthropology, through his work in the American Anthropological Association and at Columbia University in the early twentieth century. His student Alfred Kroeber once described four-field anthropology as a "sacred bundle" (Segal and Yanagisako 2005).

In the discipline's early years, it was possible for individuals like Boas, Kroeber, and some of their students to work in all four subfields, because the body of anthropological knowledge was so small. But within several decades, the expansion of the discipline and increasing specialization within its branches forced anthropologists to concentrate on a single subfield and topics within subfields, a continuing trend today. In the face of specialization and calls to "unwrap the sacred bundle" (Segal and Yanagisako 2005)—that is, have the subfields go their separate ways—anthropology has struggled to retain its holistic focus.

And yet many anthropologists are deeply dedicated to holism, citing its ability to explain complex issues that no single subfield, much less any other social science, could explain as effectively (Parkin and Ulijaszek 2007). In "Doing Fieldwork: Conducting Holistic Research with Stanley Ulijaszek," we highlight how one anthropologist conducts research in a holistic fashion. Working together, the subfields draw a compelling holistic picture of a complex situation. So how do anthropologists actually come to know such things? We turn to this issue in the next section.

• •

THINKING CRITICALLY ABOUT ANTHROPOLOGY

Can you suggest ways that you may learn how people in your town or city view college students from your campus?

• •

How Do Anthropologists Know What They Know?

Anthropology employs a wide variety of methodologies, or systematic strategies for collecting and analyzing data. Some of these methodologies are similar to those found in other natural and social sciences, including methods that involve the creation of statistics and even the use of mathematical models to explain things. Other methods aimed at describing cultures very different from our own are more closely allied with the humanities.

Doing Fieldwork
Conducting Holistic Research with Stanley Ulijaszek

STANLEY ULIJASZEK IS a British anthropologist who has been conducting research for several decades in the swamplands of coastal Papua New Guinea, an island state in the Southwest Pacific. In recent years, he has turned his attention to an interesting question: in this difficult landscape that is unsuited to agriculture, how do people acquire a sufficient, safe, and nutritious food supply? To answer this question properly requires substantial knowledge of the human biology, prehistory, and culture of coastal New Guinea.

🌱 **Cultivating Nutrition from the Sago Palm.** *(Top)* Transforming the pith of the sago palm into food is a complex process. First the pith must be chopped out of the trunk and pulverized using simple cutting and pounding tools. *(Bottom)* Next, the starch must be leached from the dense mass of fiber using a frame made from the base of the leaf stalk in which the starch is pounded with water to release and strain the edible starch, leaving the inedible fiber behind in the frame. Later the sago flour is collected from a basin where it has settled.

At the center of this story is the sago palm, a palm tree that grows abundantly in swamps. Its stem contains starch, a staple food for the people who cultivate it. People cook sago in long sticks resembling dense French bread, eating it with a bit of fish. Sago is not a great staple food; it is 99.5% starch, making it an excellent energy food, but it has few other nutrients. Worse, perhaps, is that sago is toxic when eaten uncooked or improperly prepared. Its toxicity threatens people with a specific genetic mutation that does not allow the red blood cells to carry the toxins out of the body, a mutation common among coastal New Guinea populations. Thus, because of this toxicity, eating sago presents a risk to these coastal people (Ulijaszek 2007).

It turns out, however, that this same genetic mutation confers some resistance to malaria, a mosquito-borne infectious disease common in the tropics. The key to protecting the people while releasing the nutritional energy of sago is to separate the starch from the pith at the center of the sago palm by washing and straining it, then cooking the starch, all of which reduces its toxicity to safe levels. Archaeological evidence indicates that people in this region figured out this process at least 6,000 years ago, which is when they began leaving behind their hunting-and-gathering way of life to take up agriculture. Ulijaszek concludes that they adapted sago for human consumption by detoxifying it, which in turn allowed people's genetic mutation to survive, thus providing some resistance to malaria in this difficult environment. People then continued to pass on the genetic trait of malarial resistance.

Ulijaszek's research addresses an interesting puzzle about how humans can successfully adapt to a challenging natural environment, and how those changes are intertwined with genetic factors like the resistance to malaria. To put the pieces together, Ulijaszek drew on the evidence of cultural and linguistic anthropology, gained by observing how people cultivate, process, consume, and talk about sago. He also drew on archaeological evidence of sago production that goes back thousands of years, not necessarily by conducting the excavations himself, but by relying heavily on the evidence archaeologists working in that area had produced. He also drew on evidence about the genetic make-up of local populations drawn from blood samples and genetic analyses.

(continued)

Doing Fieldwork (continued)

Questions for Reflection

1. How do you think Ulijaszek's findings would have differed if he had relied only on the evidence of cultural anthropology? Archaeology? Biological anthropology?

2. Do you think Ulijaszek's approach would be applicable to a study of low-fat diets in the United States? How would you apply it?

The Scientific Method in Anthropology

- **Scientific method.** The standard methodology of science that begins from observable facts, generates hypotheses from these facts, and then tests these hypotheses.

Anthropology often uses the **scientific method**, the most basic pattern of scientific research. The scientific method is quite simple. It starts with the observation of a fact, a verifiable truth. Next follows the construction of a hypothesis, which is a testable explanation for the fact. Then that hypothesis is tested with experiments, further observations, or measurements. If the data (the information the tests produce) show that the hypothesis is wrong, the scientist develops a new hypothesis and then tests it. If the new tests and the data they produce seem to support the hypothesis, the scientist writes up a description of what he or she did and found and shares it with other scientists. Other scientists then attempt to reproduce those tests or devise new ones, with a goal of disproving the hypothesis (Figure 1.5).

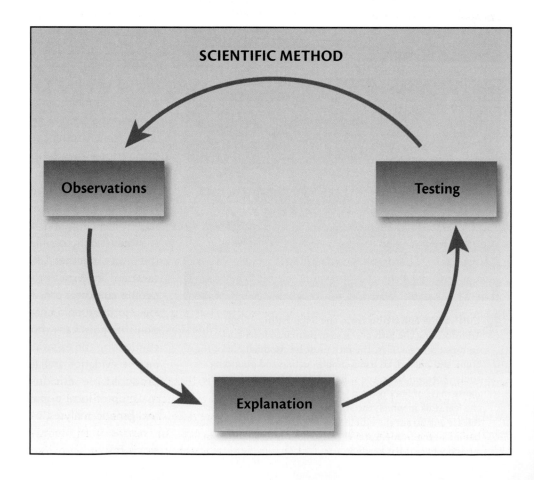

SCIENTIFIC METHOD

Observations

Testing

Explanation

Figure 1.5   The Scientific Method. The process is circular, not linear.

Note that this way of doing things is a method, not the pursuit of ultimate truths. The goal of the scientific method is to devise, test, and try to disprove hypotheses. Life's big questions—"Why are we here?" "Why is there evil in the world?" and so on—are *not* the goal of science. At best science can provide a reasonable degree of certainty only about more limited questions—"Do the planets revolve around the sun?" "Do mold-encrusted bagels cause people to get sick?" "How did our species develop the traits we now have?" and so on. Scientists regularly disagree among themselves, often passionately. Researchers with differing backgrounds and orientations ask different types of questions and look at data in different ways. Scientists tend to see such debates as beneficial to the practice of science because the more questions asked, the more observations made, and the more tests conducted, the more knowledge is produced.

Theories Guide Research

Theories, which are tested and repeatedly supported hypotheses, are key elements of the scientific method. A **theory** not only explains things, it also helps guide research by focusing the researcher's questions and making the findings meaningful. It is important to note that while many Americans assume that a theory is some wild hunch or guess, when scientists in the natural and social sciences use the term *theory*, they mean a carefully constructed hypothesis that has been tested and retested. There is rarely any guessing involved.

● **Theory.** A tested and repeatedly supported hypothesis.

Quantitative Data Collection

Building and testing hypotheses and theories requires data. Anthropology's subfields employ a number of techniques for gathering and processing data. Some of these techniques use **quantitative methods**, which classify features of a phenomenon, count or measure them, and construct mathematical and statistical models to explain what is observed. Most quantitative research takes place in the subfields of biological anthropology and archaeology, although some cultural and linguistic anthropologists use quantitative techniques as well.

● **Quantitative method.** A methodology that classifies features of a phenomenon, counting or measuring them, and constructing mathematical and statistical models to explain what is observed.

As an illustration of quantitative research, consider the work of Agustín Fuentes, a biological anthropologist at the University of Notre Dame with whom we've co-authored a book (Welsch, Vivanco, and Fuentes 2017). His research examines the nature of human–monkey interactions, and how, when, and why disease-causing agents, such as viruses, get passed between these species. Fuentes and his team (including many undergraduate anthropology students) observe monkeys and humans interacting in Bali, Singapore, and Gibraltar. In each location, they record quantitative details about interactions: who interacts, how many individuals interact, the length of interactions, whether interactions are aggressive or friendly, whether physical contact between species occurs, and whether food is involved in the contact. They interview humans at the locations, sometimes using surveys or administering questionnaires, and collect detailed physical information about the landscape inhabited by the people and the monkeys. They also take blood or fecal samples from both the monkeys and the humans, analyzing them for pathogens and parasites. All these variables are considered independently and then compared statistically to see what patterns emerge. Fuentes has discovered that human–monkey interactions vary depending on the species of monkey, human cultural patterns, gender differences in the humans, and sex differences in the monkeys.

Qualitative Data Collection

Anthropologists also employ **qualitative methods**, in which the aim is to produce an in-depth and detailed description of social behaviors and beliefs. Qualitative research usually involves interviews with people as well as observations of their activities. Research data come in the form of words, images, or objects. In contrast with quantitative methods, qualitative research does not typically use research instruments like

● **Qualitative method.** A research strategy that produces an in-depth and detailed description of social behaviors and beliefs.

surveys or questionnaires. The research instrument is the researcher himself or herself, whose subjective perceptions and impressions of the subject matter also become the basis for knowledge. The **ethnographic method**, which involves prolonged and intensive observation of and participation in the life of a community, is a qualitative methodology and is a hallmark of cultural anthropology.

Luis Vivanco, one of this book's authors, is a cultural anthropologist who uses qualitative methods to ask how global environmentalism affects people's relationships with nature in Latin America. In one of his research projects, he conducted more than 20 months of research in Monteverde, Costa Rica, a rural community bordering a tropical cloud forest and renowned worldwide as a site of conservation and ecotourism. He interviewed local farmers, environmental activists, ecotourists, and scientists, usually on multiple occasions, sometimes with a tape recorder and notepad and other times in informal conversations at the local grocery store or in some other public setting (Figure 1.6). Working as a volunteer in a nature preserve, he listened to how its managers and the ecotourists talked about tropical rain forests. He collected newspaper clippings and reports from local environmental groups and took pictures of people doing things. His fieldnotes, recordings, images, documents, and personal experiences with environmental activists and farmers have helped him understand environmentalism to be a complex arena of social conflict where people struggle not just over how to protect nature, but also over how to deal with rapid social changes caused by globalization (Vivanco 2006).

The Comparative Method

Unlike other scientists, anthropologists do not conduct experiments or make predictions. Instead, anthropologists use the **comparative method** (Kaplan and Manners 1972:42–43). The comparative method allows anthropologists to derive insights from careful comparisons of two or more cultures or societies. The actual "method" is nothing like a precise recipe for research, however, but a general approach. This approach holds that any particular detail of human behavior or any particular social condition should not be seen in isolation, but should be considered against the backdrop of the full range of behaviors and conditions in their individual social settings.

The research of cultural anthropologist Robert Welsch, this book's other author, illustrates how anthropologists can use the comparative method. Welsch has conducted extended ethnographic research both in Papua New Guinea and in Indonesia

• **Ethnographic method.** A research method that involves prolonged and intensive observation of and participation in the life of a community.

• **Comparative method.** A research method that derives insights from a systematic comparison of aspects of two or more cultures or societies.

Figure 1.6   Monteverde Bus. In his research on environmentalism in Costa Rica, Luis Vivanco explored the social dynamics of environmentalism and ecotourism. This focus led him to spend a lot of time among ecotourists, such as the ones shown here arriving in Monteverde by bus.

(Welsch 2006). One of his research projects explicitly made use of comparative research strategies to understand the social and religious meanings of masks and carved objects in three societies along the Papuan Gulf of New Guinea. To conduct his comparative study, Welsch studied museum collections holding the masks, pored over published and unpublished accounts of the people who collected the masks, and interviewed older villagers about their traditional practices (Figure 1.7). He learned that although these three societies used the same kinds of objects, their differing decorative styles suggested differences in the social purposes for which each society used the objects. In one society, similarity in designs minimized differences between clans to create group cohesion in war. In another, the designs supported social competition among clans within the village. And in the third, the way men displayed these decorative boards gave a visual recognition of each man's social networks and where men in his clan had married.

When Anthropology Is Not a Science: Interpreting Other Cultures

Not all anthropologists characterize what they do as science. Prominent British anthropologist E. E. Evans-Pritchard (1902–1973) pronounced in 1961 that anthropology should be grouped with the humanities, especially history, rather than natural sciences (Evans-Pritchard 1961). Describing other people, he argued, requires an understanding of their inner lives and beliefs that no scientific methodology can grasp. His view was that the complexity of social behavior prevents any completely objective analysis of human culture.

These days most cultural anthropologists agree with this position. They disregard the scientific ideal of the researcher's detachment from the subject of study: the belief that researchers are not supposed to talk about what they feel and experience, or how emotions and experiences influence what they learn and know (Fabian 2001). The work of American anthropologist Renato Rosaldo (b. 1941), who studied head-hunting in a Filipino society called the Ilongot [Ill-**lahn**-goht], illustrates this point of view. When Rosaldo (1989) asked the Ilongots to explain why they take heads, they explained that when a loved one dies, their grief turns to rage, and the only way to vent that

Figure 1.7   Boards Inside a Longhouse at Naharo. Robert Welsch visited many longhouses to discuss ritual carvings and their meaning as part of his comparative analysis of art and its social contexts in traditional societies of the Papuan Gulf. This image shows boards he was discussing with elders and their families in Naharo village.

rage and get on with life is to take the head of a traditional enemy. Rosaldo initially dismissed this explanation, assuming there had to be a "deeper" social purpose for head-hunting, such as creating group cohesion or allowing young men to prove their worthiness for marriage by showing they could kill an enemy.

Then, Rosaldo's wife, Shelly, also an anthropologist, died in an accident during fieldwork in the Philippines, and his own devastating loss generated a similar combination of grief and rage. While he was adjusting to Shelly's death, Rosaldo could grasp emotionally what the Ilongot were getting at. Dealing with the death opened his eyes to the force of emotions in social life, something he and most other anthropologists had never really considered. Rosaldo (1989) realized that his training as an anthropologist, which emphasized scientific detachment, accounted for his initial dismissal of Ilongot notions of head-hunting. He concluded that his other interpretations of head-hunting were not wrong, they just gave him an incomplete picture of why the Ilongot did it. He also concluded that building ethnographic knowledge is an open-ended process: as an ethnographer's own life experiences and knowledge change, so do his or her insights into other cultures.

Ethnographers know other cultures from particular points of view. Although they strive to see things from many perspectives—the perspectives of the many people they interview and observe—anthropologists' insights are always partial; indeed, only some of many possible interpretations of culture. But anthropologists do not just try to understand the world of culture and other human concerns, they also intervene in it in practical ways, which is an issue we explore next.

● ●

THINKING CRITICALLY ABOUT ANTHROPOLOGY

How might you use a comparative perspective even if you visit only one country while on vacation? Consider the other cultural contexts you have experienced and how these might provide a comparative framework for experiencing a novel society and culture.

● ●

How Do Anthropologists Put Their Knowledge to Work in the World?

Anthropological research is relevant and useful for addressing many social problems. At some point in their careers, most anthropologists get involved in work with practical, real-world concerns, applying their research skills and knowledge to the creation or implementation of policies, the management of social programs, the conduct of legal proceedings, or even the design of consumer products.

Applied and Practicing Anthropology: The Fifth Subfield?

Practical applications are such an important component of anthropology that some anthropologists consider them the "fifth subfield." These practical applications include those of **applied anthropology**, anthropological research commissioned to serve an organization's needs, and those of **practicing anthropology**, the broadest category of anthropological work, in which the anthropologist not only performs research but also gets involved in the design, implementation, and management of some organization,

● **Applied anthropology.** Anthropological research commissioned to serve an organization's needs.

● **Practicing anthropology.** Anthropological work involving research as well as involvement in the design, implementation, and management of some organization, process, or product.

process, or product. One reason some consider these two enterprises a fifth subfield is that the numbers of anthropologists doing these things has swelled in recent decades as university budget cuts have diminished job opportunities in academia.

Not all anthropologists, however, agree with the "fifth subfield" idea, because it implies that putting anthropological knowledge to work is not something that is done in the other subfields. Moreover, the "fifth subfield" notion sets up a false dichotomy between academic (or theoretical) and practical (or applied) work, which have often been intertwined throughout the history of the discipline (Field and Fox 2007).

Putting Anthropology to Work

Putting anthropological skills and knowledge to work is a challenging enterprise, not least because of tensions it creates with some anthropologists who feel that "we should never forget that a commitment to improving the world is no substitute for understanding it" (Hastrup and Elass 1990:307). In spite of the challenges, however, anthropologists have effectively put their discipline to work addressing difficult social, health, and educational problems, as the following snapshots demonstrate.

Mary Amuyunzu-Nyamongo: Bringing Cultural Knowledge to Health Programs in Kenya

Like many other anthropologists, Kenyan anthropologist Mary Amuyunzu-Nyamongo (Figure 1.8) works on pressing social and health problems confronting her country. She is currently executive director and co-founder of the African Institute for Health and Development, an organization that provides research and training on the social dimensions of debilitating illnesses in Kenya, including HIV/AIDS. One of the problems Amuyunzu-Nyamongo has studied is the lack of detailed knowledge of local communities that is necessary to make health programs work. Amuyunzu-Nyamongo collected the local knowledge from insights about people's health beliefs and practices through qualitative research. For example, during a campaign to control mosquito-borne illness in a coastal village, government officials wanted to conduct blood screenings to identify levels of infection. They told schoolchildren to tell their parents to get screened, which failed. Amuyunzu-Nyamongo knew that in this culture, male heads of households control decision-making. She organized a meeting where the issue of screenings was introduced to these men. Once the men became involved, the screenings became successful (Amuyunzu-Nyamongo 2006).

Figure 1.8 Cultural Anthropologist Mary Amuyunzu-Nyamongo.

Davina Two Bears: Applied Archaeology on the Navajo Reservation

Because archaeologists often encounter burials when they excavate prehistoric Indian sites, American Indian communities have often found themselves at odds with archaeologists over the question of what to do with the human remains uncovered. Some Indians object to any excavation at all. But the work of Navajo archaeologist Davina Two Bears (2006; Figure 1.9) runs counter to the expectations many people may have about the inherent tensions between Indians and archaeologists. For several years now, she has worked with the Navajo Nation Archaeology Department, which emerged in 1988 from the Navajo Nation Cultural Resource Management Program. As both an archaeologist and a cultural resource management professional for the Navajo tribe, she advises on potential damage to archaeological sites that might be caused by road construction or building projects. Two Bears uses her professional archaeological training to prevent damage to ancient sites, which many Navajo people view as deserving great respect. Two Bears identifies and records the locations and characteristics of sites. When proposed projects would damage archaeological sites, Two Bears and her colleagues try to identify alternative locations. She feels that although she has been professionally trained, her

Figure 1.9 Archaeologist Davina Two Bears.

work is more an extension of what Navajos have always done in protecting their ancestors and their ancestors' special sites.

James McKenna: The Naturalness of Co-sleeping

In much of the Western world, it is considered "healthy" for an infant to sleep in a crib, alone, for long stretches during the night. When a baby wakes frequently or wants to sleep alongside the parents, many see the child as too dependent and not doing well. In our society we also have many deaths from sudden infant death syndrome (SIDS), in which infants die in the night for unknown reasons. After decades of examining how humans and their infants share social and physical space, biological anthropologist James McKenna (1996; Figure 1.10) and his colleagues developed an explanation for how and why many SIDS deaths occur in the United States. They collected biological and evolutionary evidence to demonstrate that the advice of the medical establishment and many popular parenting books is plain wrong.

Through their intensive studies of sleeping mothers and infants around the planet, McKenna and his colleagues found that the frequent stirring of young infants, nursing, and the carbon dioxide and oxygen mix created by bodies close together are important aspects of the healthy development of human babies. The physical closeness to the parent not only fosters the healthy development of the child's body, but also facilitates feelings of well-being in both mother and child. McKenna's research showed that co-sleeping assists with the infant's development and dramatically reduces the risk of SIDS.

Figure 1.10   Biological Anthropologist James McKenna.

Marybeth Nevins: Supporting the Sustainability of Endangered Languages in Arizona

There are an estimated 6,800 languages spoken in the world today, but many experts expect a great number of them to be gone within the next century. In the face of this problem, linguistic anthropologists have tended to dedicate themselves to the task of documenting endangered languages before their last speakers die. But in recent years, many linguistic anthropologists have also begun to work directly in efforts to protect and maintain endangered languages. Marybeth Nevins (Figure 1.11), of Middlebury College in Vermont, is one such anthropologist. Nevins, who has conducted her research in Arizona on the Fort Apache reservation and with the Susanville Indian Rancheria in California, is critical of the idea that academic linguists can be "superheroes" who come to "save" the local language (Nevins 2013). One problem is that preserving something so dynamic and changing as language is more difficult than many academics are prepared to admit. Another is that many local language speakers, such as the Apache with whom Nevins works, respond with ambivalence to academic outsiders, whom they see as claiming a privileged authority over their language. In addition, as Nevins explains, in any community of speakers there are distinct cultural dynamics at work that lead to conflicting attitudes toward the language and its use. These matters are further complicated by competing networks of families, religious groups, and political factions that claim authority in and over the language. Nevins argues that instead of promoting what academic linguists determine to be "proper" ways of preserving language, linguists and other language professionals should approach programs as open-ended exchanges with other members of a language community and support efforts that keep the language in use and relevant to community life. This approach, which she says is driven by the value of "sustainability" (as opposed to "revitalization" or "preservation"), requires outsiders to temper their own ideas about how to maintain the language, by listening to ways that indigenous language users themselves perceive and represent their linguistic heritage.

These snapshots offer a small sample of the range of ways anthropologists put their discipline to work. As we discuss in the next section, anthropology—whether practical or academic in its orientation—raises important ethical issues.

Figure 1.11   Linguistic Anthropologist Marybeth Nevins.

● ●

THINKING CRITICALLY ABOUT ANTHROPOLOGY

Compare how an anthropologist and an engineer might each approach a problem involving where to situate a bridge or highway in a heavily populated area.

● ●

What Ethical Obligations Do Anthropologists Have?

Issues of **ethics**—moral questions about right and wrong and standards of appropriate behavior—are at the heart of anthropology, in two senses. First, anthropologists learn about how and why people in other cultures think and act as they do by researching their moral standards. Anthropologists often find these things out in the process of adjusting themselves to a culture's rules of ethical behavior. Second, doing anthropology itself involves ethical relationships between researchers and others, raising many important and complex issues about the ethical conduct of anthropological research and practice. Ethics in anthropology—the moral principles that guide anthropological conduct—are not just a list of dos and don'ts. Nor are they simply cautionary tales of research gone awry. Ethics are organically connected to what it means to be a good anthropologist (Fluehr-Lobban 2003).

Ethical matters tend to reflect the issues and events of the day. For example, the issue of anthropologists working as spies for the U.S. government—a contentious practice during and after World War I—is no longer a front-burner issue, mainly because anthropologists today routinely reject clandestine research. The reason anthropologists reject work as spies overseas is that doing so puts all anthropologists under suspicion. Ethical issues also change because new topics of study emerge. In recent years, for example, anthropologists have begun considering the ethics of conducting research in cyberspace and of using new scientific techniques to study and control human DNA. The discipline also faces challenges about its ethics from outsiders, particularly indigenous groups who have challenged archaeologists over how they handle artifacts and sensitive community matters.

Here we consider three issues of common ethical concern that all anthropologists are obliged to consider: doing no harm, taking responsibility for one's work, and sharing one's findings.

Do No Harm. But Is That Enough?

The Nuremberg trials after World War II revealed that Nazi scientists had conducted harmful experiments on people in concentration camps. Scientists responded by establishing informal ethical codes for dealing with research subjects. But in 1974 news of the abuse of medical research subjects in the United States led the Congress to pass a law preventing unethical research with human subjects (Figure 1.12). This new law required all research institutes and universities where research was conducted to establish an Institutional Review Board (IRB) to monitor all research involving human subjects. Medical, scientific, and social science organizations, including anthropological organizations, published codes of ethics emphasizing the importance of avoiding harm to people and animals who are the subjects of research.

"Do no harm" continues to be a bedrock principle in anthropology's primary code of ethics, the American Anthropological Association's Principles of Professional

● **Ethics.** Moral questions about right and wrong and standards of appropriate behavior.

Responsibility (see inside front cover). Anthropologists routinely explain to people involved in their research any risks their participation might carry, and they obtain these people's "informed consent" to participate. Anthropological publications avoid sharing confidential information and commonly disguise informants' identities, in case those individuals could be targeted for harm because of what they say.

Some anthropologists believe the principle of "do no harm" is not enough, however. They assert that anthropologists also have a moral imperative to go further by doing good, for example, by working for social justice and the alleviation of suffering in powerless and marginalized communities (Scheper-Hughes 1995; Fluehr-Lobban 2003). This is the position of **action anthropology** (sometimes also known as "advocacy anthropology"), an approach developed in the 1940s and 1950s by anthropologist Sol Tax (1907–1995) that directly addresses issues of social injustice. Tax, who taught in Chicago, sent his students directly into that city's poor neighborhoods to study miseries like ill health, unemployment, and political disempowerment, and to work collaboratively to improve community welfare.

Proponents of action anthropology argue that their approach effectively supports the empowerment of marginalized people, while providing opportunities for research into the obstacles to improving human welfare (Scheper-Hughes 1995; Bennett 1996). Critics commonly charge that this position compromises scientific rigor (Harris 1968). The debate remains unsettled, and, as a result, taking a position of advocacy for research subjects is considered to be a researcher's choice, not a professional obligation (Fluehr-Lobban 2003:240).

- **Action anthropology.** An approach to anthropological research that seeks to study and, at the same time, improve community welfare.

Take Responsibility for Your Work. But How Far Does That Go?

The primary ethical responsibility of anthropologists is to the people, species, or artifacts they study. Whether it is a pottery shard, a baboon, or a person, anthropologists are expected to side with their subjects. This does not mean that an archaeologist is expected to throw himself or herself in front of a bulldozer to prevent an archaeological site from being destroyed, or a cultural anthropologist to take up arms in defense of informants threatened by police or military. Rather, it means that anthropologists should take whatever action is possible when their subjects are threatened, short of

Figure 1.12   Scandal at Tuskegee. Between 1932 and 1972, the U.S. Public Health Service studied syphilis among white and black men. When scientists learned they could treat syphilis with penicillin, they gave the drug to the white men, but not the black men. This abuse precipitated reform in the use of humans as research subjects in the United States.

doing something illegal or that would cause serious harm to themselves or others. Such action might include helping prepare legal paperwork necessary to stop a bull-dozer and therefore conserve the threatened artifacts.

What complicates this principle is that anthropologists are also responsible to other parties. For example, anthropologists also have a responsibility to the public, including the obligation to disseminate the findings of their research—even when certain findings might lower public opinion about a group of people. Anthropologists also have respon-sibilities to the sponsors who fund their research and to the discipline itself, including its standards of integrity and openness. In "Thinking Like an Anthropologist: Should Anthropologists Take Responsibility for the Influences They Have on the Societies They Study?" we examine yet another dimension of anthropological responsibility.

Share Your Findings. But Who Should Control Those Findings?

Historically, anthropologists took blood samples, did long-term ethnographic research, and excavated archaeological sites with little concern for those who might object to these activities, especially in indigenous communities. But during the past several de-cades, there has been a global sea change in favor of indigenous rights. After seeing their graves robbed and cultural resources taken for so long without their permission—often in the name of science—native peoples have claimed and been winning legal rights to control their heritage and cultural property. For example, in the United States, the 1991 Native American Graves Protection and Repatriation Act (NAGPRA) legally re-quires the repatriation of any funerary objects, sacred objects, and skeletal remains to their respective peoples. Some archaeologists and biological anthropologists initially challenged this law, insisting that their claims to scientific knowledge have higher value than native claims of cultural heritage. Nowadays, most researchers are happy to follow the law and routinely collaborate with native communities affected by their research.

But questions over who should control anthropological data and knowledge are often problems of ethics, not law. For cultural anthropologists, the issue of control often relates to questions about who should define the research problem and preserve the data—the anthropologist or the subjects of research. Traditionally, the anthropolo-gist has controlled those things, but communities have increasingly challenged anthro-pologists to provide them with research skills and information produced by research so they can continue to use them to their benefit after the anthropologist leaves.

For biological anthropologists, issues of control over bodily samples like DNA, blood, and hair can grow especially sensitive and contentious. For example, the U.S. government recently claimed patent rights to the DNA of a man from Papua New Guinea because of his apparent immunity to certain cancers, in hopes that new therapies could be developed from studying his DNA. Many indigenous rights groups have decried this patent and other efforts to claim ownership of samples from living people, believing that living beings should not be privatized, owned, or turned into commercial products. Where people are mistrustful of what happens to the samples taken from their bodies, biological anthropol-ogists have been forced to clearly explain the intentions of their research and accept limits on what they can do with those samples.

● ●

THINKING CRITICALLY ABOUT ANTHROPOLOGY

If you were studying a local Head Start program with few resources and observed problems with local funding for the facility, what "action anthropology" projects might you suggest to help the organization?

● ●

Thinking Like an Anthropologist

Should Anthropologists Take Responsibility for the Influences They Have on the Societies They Study?

ANTHROPOLOGISTS BEGIN THEIR research by asking questions. In this box, we want you to learn how to ask questions as an anthropological researcher. Part One describes a situation and follows up with questions we would ask. Part Two asks you to do the same thing with a different situation.

PART ONE: THE SOCIAL IMPACTS OF ANTHROPOLOGICAL RESEARCH

One of the biggest controversies to rock anthropology in recent decades focused on the work of American anthropologist Napoleon Chagnon with an Amazonian tribe called the Yanomami. Thanks to a series of books and films Chagnon made about them during the 1970s and

A NEW YORK TIMES NOTABLE BOOK
WITH A NEW AFTERWORD

Darkness in El Dorado

HOW SCIENTISTS AND JOURNALISTS DEVASTATED THE AMAZON

"My guess is that [the book] will become a classic in anthropological literature, sparking countless debates over the ethics and epistemology of field studies."
—JOHN HORGAN, *New York Times Book Review*

PATRICK TIERNEY

Tierney's *Darkness in El Dorado*.

1980s, the Yanomami are among the world's best-known tribal people, and Chagnon himself became somewhat of an academic celebrity. Generations of college students have learned about the relentlessly aggressive dynamics of Yanomami life, thanks to Chagnon's depiction of them as the "fierce people" (Chagnon 1968). But during the past decade and a half, Chagnon's work has come under intense scrutiny because of claims that it seriously harmed the Yanomami.

The scrutiny began with the work of an investigative journalist named Patrick Tierney who claimed that Western scientists, anthropologists, and medical researchers had abused the Yanomami. In a high-profile magazine article and a book published in 2000—*Darkness in El Dorado: How Scientists and Journalists Devastated the Amazon*—Tierney described how Chagnon in particular had treated the Yanomami in an unethical manner and distorted his findings about them. Some of Tierney's claims were proven to be unfounded, one of them being that Chagnon and colleagues made a measles epidemic worse by vaccinating the Yanomami against the disease.

But other claims are more difficult to dismiss. One such claim is that the image Chagnon created of the Yanomami as fierce and violent is a crude misrepresentation, and perhaps more of a reflection of Chagnon's confrontational personal style and belief in the innateness of violence in humans than an accurate representation of the Yanomami. A second is that Chagnon manipulated his data to prove that more violent men had more offspring, which could support his claim that violence was genetically programmed into the society. A third is that Chagnon actually exacerbated conflicts by giving away machetes to his friends, which gave them an unfair advantage over their neighbors, inspiring even greater levels of violence. Further, according to Tierney, when gold was discovered on Yanomami lands, Chagnon never publicly objected to the use of his work to justify violence against the Yanomami by goldminers and to hinder the creation of a Yanomami reserve.

The American Anthropological Association (AAA)—the main professional society of anthropologists in the United States—responded to these allegations by setting up a task force to examine them, a process that exposed

(continued)

deep divisions among anthropologists. Some anthropologists came to Chagnon's defense, while others feared that Chagnon's unethical research practices and misrepresentations had compromised the integrity of the whole discipline. In its final report, published in 2002, the AAA task force asserted that Chagnon had indeed represented the Yanomami in harmful ways, and that he had not received informed consent or government permission to do some of his work. In 2005, however, the AAA voted to rescind its previous acceptance of the report, not because of anything in the report itself, but because the AAA had violated its own policy prohibiting the adjudication of ethics violations by getting involved in the first place. Concerns over the lasting impacts of these allegations on the integrity of the discipline persist even today.

What questions does this situation raise for anthropological researchers?

1.   Are anthropologists responsible for how others use their research?

2.   Should anthropologists place the welfare of their subjects over the success of their research?

3.   Are anthropologists responsible for the negative social impacts of their fieldwork practices and findings?

4.   Are there ways of doing research that are mutually beneficial to the anthropologist and the subjects of the research?

PART TWO: ANTHROPOLOGY STUDENTS AND ETHICAL RESPONSIBILITIES

As a student of anthropology, you may be confronted with ethical dilemmas about the effects of your work. You may also find that you have conflicting responsibilities in your work. For example, it is possible that you will be asked to conduct basic research, such as studying a club or fraternity on campus, or a social setting or group in the community. During the course of your research, you may witness an illegal activity—such as alcohol use by a minor, drug dealing, or vandalism of school property. What questions would you ask about this situation as an anthropological researcher? (Sample questions can be found at the end of this chapter. There is no single set of correct questions, but some questions are more insightful than others.)

Conclusion

Ever since the 1850s, anthropologists have been asking questions about and developing perspectives on human societies past and present. Their expertise is on culture, diversity, how and why social change happens, the dynamics of human biology, and the ways people communicate with each other. The four subfields of anthropology—cultural anthropology, archaeology, biological anthropology, and linguistic anthropology—sometimes come together to offer powerful conceptual tools for understanding the whole context of human experience, an approach called *holism*. Featuring an impressive range of methodological tools—sophistication with theory, quantitative methods, qualitative methods, and the comparative method—anthropology as a discipline offers highly relevant insights into today's complex and ever-changing world.

But because anthropology deals with people, their bodies, and cultural artifacts meaningful to people, nearly everything anthropologists study invokes ethical concerns. Throughout this book we consider the ethics and application of anthropological research as we explore the aims, approaches, and findings of the discipline. But let us begin our journey toward an understanding of anthropology with a fuller discussion of the concept of culture.

KEY TERMS

Reviewing the Chapter

Chapter Section	What We Know	To Be Resolved
How did anthropology begin?	During the nineteenth century, the rise of industrialization, the influence of evolutionary theory, and colonial contact with less-industrialized cultures led to the discipline of understanding how cultures operate and interact.	Anthropologists are still fascinated—and challenged—by the contrasts and changes in culture worldwide as a result of globalization.
What do the four subfields of anthropology have in common?	Anthropologists in all subfields share certain fundamental approaches and concepts, including culture, cultural relativism, diversity, change, and holism.	Some anthropologists continue to debate the idea that the subfields, with their distinct methods and specialized research interests, belong together in the same discipline.
How do anthropologists know what they know?	Anthropology has a strong relationship with the scientific method: all anthropologists use theories, collect data, and analyze those data.	While most cultural anthropologists reject the possibility of a completely objective analysis of human culture, other subfields of anthropology, such as archaeology and biological anthropology, are thoroughly committed to the scientific method.

How do anthropologists put their knowledge to work in the world?	All four of the subfields have both theoretical and applied aspects. Applied research uses the insights of anthropological theory to solve problems.	Most anthropologists see an anthropological approach as providing a better way of understanding people from different backgrounds than that of any other discipline, but anthropologists continue to disagree among themselves about how to apply that understanding to address human problems.
What ethical obligations do anthropologists have?	Issues of ethics—moral questions about right and wrong and standards of appropriate behavior—are at the heart of anthropology.	Certain ethical issues have no easy resolution, such as the ideal that anthropologists should do no harm; the question of how to resolve sometimes-conflicting responsibilities anthropologists have to different groups; or the question of how and with whom anthropologists should share their findings.

Readings

Numerous books examine the historical emergence and intellectual history of anthropology. One of the best is the 2007 book *A New History of Anthropology*, edited by Henrika Kuklick (Malden, MA: Wiley-Blackwell).

....

The 2005 book *Anthropology Put to Work*, edited by Les Field and Richard G. Fox (Oxford, UK: Berg Publishers), offers an introduction to both the opportunities and the disciplinary, social, and political complexities involved in applying anthropological expertise.

....

For a detailed exploration of the primary ethical concerns and dilemmas involved in anthropological research across the subfields, see the 2013 book *Ethics and Anthropology: Ideas and Practice*, by Carolyn Fluehr-Lobban (Walnut Creek, CA: AltaMira Press).

....

The 2007 book *Holistic Anthropology: Emergence and Convergence*, edited by David Parkin and Stanley Ulijaszek (New York: Berghahn Books), provides a contemporary perspective on the development of cross-subfield collaborations dedicated to the notion of holism. For a critical perspective on

that desire for holism, see the 2005 book *Unwrapping the Sacred Bundle: Reflections on the Disciplining of Anthropology* (Durham, NC: Duke University Press), edited by Daniel Segal and Sylvia Yanagisako.

....

Renato Rosaldo's 1989 book *Culture and Truth: The Remaking of Social Analysis* (Boston, MA: Beacon Press) is a classic text that reflects critically on cultural anthropology's complicated relationship with the sciences and objectivity.

....

SUGGESTED ANSWERS TO "THINKING LIKE AN ANTHROPOLOGIST"

Use these examples as a guide to answering questions for other "Thinking Like an Anthropologist" boxes in the book.

1. Does withholding information about illegal activities compromise the integrity of the discipline?
2. Would you be obliged to tell your professor everything you've found out through research, or can and should some information be held back?
3. Should loyalty to one's peer group transcend loyalty to one's university, or the discipline of anthropology?
4. How could you protect the identity of your informants?

Culture

Giving Meaning to Human Lives

IN 2005, THE BODY that governs intercollegiate sports in the United States, the National Collegiate Athletic Association (NCAA), banned teams with American Indian names and mascots from competing in its postseason tournaments. Clarifying the ruling, an official stated, "Colleges and universities may adopt any mascot that they wish. . . . But as a national association, we believe that mascots, nicknames, or images deemed hostile or abusive in terms of race, ethnicity or national origin should not be visible at the championship events that we control" (National Collegiate Athletic Association 2005). The ruling affected a number of schools with competitive sports programs, including Florida State ("Seminoles"), University of North Dakota ("Fighting Sioux"), and University of Illinois ("Fighting Illini").

The ruling concluded decades of pressure from American Indians, students, and others who have argued that these mascots stereotype and denigrate Indian traditions. As one Oneida woman expressed, "We experience it as no less than a mockery of our cultures. We see objects sacred to us—such as the drum, eagle feathers, face painting, and traditional dress—being used, not in sacred ceremony, or in any cultural setting, but in another culture's game" (Munson 1999:14). Moreover, most Indian activists point out that the same institutions and states that use Indian symbols are the very places where white people stole Indian lands, forcibly moving Indian people to much less desired areas on reservations. To Indians, the mascots seem to be just another

Mascot Chief Illiniwek. Chief Illiniwek performs during a University of Illinois football game. In 2007, after a long controversy, the university retired the mascot.

attack on the Indian cultures that non-Indians have tried to eliminate for several centuries.

Outraged students, alumni, and political commentators have countered that these mascots honor Indian traditions, pointing to the strength and bravery of Native Americans they hope to emulate in their teams. They also point out that the mascots are part of venerable traditions, part of the living cultures of their universities. Abandoning their mascots is like turning their backs on a part of their own cultural heritage.

This battle of words over college mascots has brewed for decades, with participants on both sides making claims, sometimes exaggerated, about the other side's motivations or intentions. Yet each side in the controversy calls into play an issue of deep concern to them that divides the participants into two opposed groups, each with a radically different interpretation of the issue that often views the opposing point of view as irrational or wrong. In that respect, this conflict is a cultural one.

The word *culture* is widely interpreted in society. To some it refers to aspects of popular culture such as art, music, fashion, theater, and other forms of self-expression and creativity. An even broader definition of culture encompasses the many elements of society often associated with ethnicity, from flags and banners to ethnic costumes, songs, and styles of cooking.

The concept of culture is also at the heart of anthropology. But anthropologists interpret culture differently from these uses of the term and provide it with its most foundational and scientific definitions. *Culture*, as anthropologists use the term, is a concept that refers to the perspectives and actions that a group of people consider natural, self-evident, and appropriate. These perspectives and actions are rooted in shared meanings and the ways people act in social groups. Culture is, as we will see, a uniquely human capacity that helps us confront the common problems that face all humans, like communicating with each other, organizing ourselves to get things done, making life predictable and meaningful, and dealing with conflict and change. From an anthropological perspective, culture is a central component of what it means to be human.

The culture concept provides a powerful lens for making sense of what people do, why they do it, and the differences and similarities across and within societies, a point that leads to a key question: *How does the concept of culture help explain the differences and similarities in people's ways of life?* Embedded in this broader question are the following problems, around which this chapter is organized:

What is culture?

If culture is always changing, why does it feel so stable?

How do social institutions express culture?

Can anybody own culture?

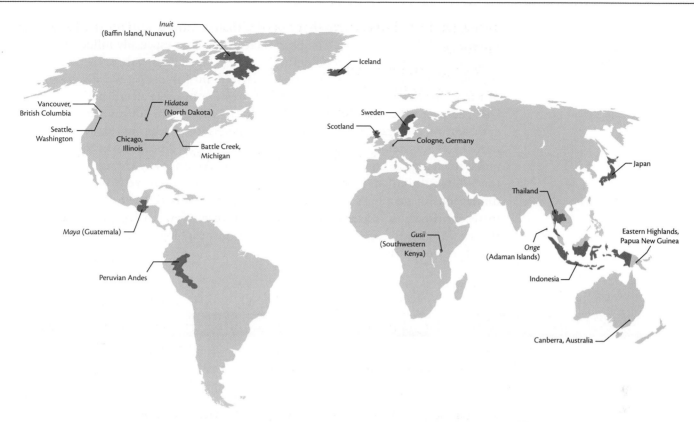

Figure 2.1 Select Peoples and Places Discussed in Chapter 2.

In this chapter, we present an overview of how anthropologists approach culture and explain why this approach is so relevant to understanding human beliefs and actions. We also offer a definition of culture that informs and shapes the rest of this textbook. We start with the key elements that all anthropologists accept as central to any definition of culture.

What Is Culture?

Culture has been defined in many ways by anthropologists, and there are nearly as many approaches to studying it as there are anthropologists. This lack of agreement does not frustrate or paralyze anthropologists. In fact, most anthropologists see this diversity of perspective as the sign of a vibrant discipline.

What is most striking about how different anthropologists define culture in somewhat different ways is that most of these definitions share a number of features. Culture is learned. It uses symbols. It is dynamic and is integrated with daily experience. It shapes people's lives. It is also shared by groups of people, who by following its rules and guiding principles construct it anew for each new generation. In addition, culture makes us feel that the ways we do things are correct or natural. We explore each of these elements of culture in turn.

Elements of Culture

English scholar Sir Edward Burnett Tylor (1832–1917) was a founding figure of cultural anthropology. He offered the first justification for using the word *culture* to understand differences and similarities among groups of people. He defined culture as "that complex whole which includes knowledge, belief, art, morals, law, custom, and any other capabilities and habits acquired by man as a member of society" (1871:1).

Two aspects of Tylor's definition, especially that culture is *acquired* (today we say *learned*) and that culture is a "complex whole," have been especially influential.

Since Tylor's time, anthropologists have developed many theories of culture, the most prominent of which are summarized in Table 2.1. We discuss many of these theories in later chapters, and we explore in more detail how they have changed over time. One of the most important changes in cultural theory is that early anthropologists tended to see cultures in societies with simple technologies as more fixed and stable than anyone does today. We now know that every culture is quick to change as conditions around it change. Another key change is that since the 1960s cultural anthropologists have focused more intensively on the symbolic dimensions of people's social lives. These approaches have led to more emphasis in recent times on interpretive theories of culture. Nevertheless, across all these theories, there are seven basic elements that anthropologists agree are critical to any theory of culture.

TABLE 2.1   PROMINENT ANTHROPOLOGICAL THEORIES OF CULTURE

Theory	Period	Major Figures	Definition
Social evolutionism	1870s–1910s	Edward Burnett Tylor (1871), Herbert Spencer (1874), Lewis Henry Morgan (1877)	All societies pass through stages, from primitive state to complex civilization. Cultural differences are the result of different evolutionary stages.
Historical particularism	1910s–1930s	Franz Boas (1940), Alfred Kroeber (1923), Edward Sapir (1921)	Individual societies develop particular cultural traits and undergo unique processes of change. Culture traits diffuse from one culture to another.
Functionalism	1920s–1960s	Bronislaw Malinowski (1922)	Cultural practices, beliefs, and institutions fulfill psychological and social needs.
Structural-functionalism	1920s–1960s	A. R. Radcliffe-Brown (1952)	Culture is systematic, its pieces working together in a balanced fashion to keep the whole society functioning smoothly.
Neo-evolutionism	1940s–1970s	Leslie White (1949), Julian Steward (1955)	Cultures evolve from simple to complex by harnessing nature's energy through technology and the influence of particular culture-specific processes.
Cultural materialism	1960s–1970s	Marvin Harris (1979)	The material world, especially its economic and ecological conditions, shapes people's customs and beliefs.
Cognitive anthropology	1950s–1970s	Ward Goodenough (1965), Roy D'Andrade (1995)	Culture operates through mental models and logical systems.
Structuralism	1960s–1970s	Claude Lévi-Strauss (1961, 1949/1969)	People make sense of their worlds through binary oppositions like hot–cold, culture–nature, male–female, and raw–cooked. These binaries are expressed in social institutions and cultural practices like kinship, myth, and language.
Interpretive anthropology	1970s–present	Clifford Geertz (1973), Victor Turner (1967), Mary Douglas (1966), Roy Wagner (1975)	Culture is a shared system of meaning. People make sense of their worlds through the use of symbols and symbolic activities like myth and ritual.
Post-structuralism	1980s–present	Pierre Bourdieu (1977), Renato Rosaldo (1989), James Clifford, George Marcus, and Michael M. J. Fischer (Clifford and Marcus 1986; Marcus and Fischer 1986)	Not a single school of thought, but a set of theoretical positions that rejects the idea that there are underlying structures that explain culture. It embraces the idea that cultural processes are dynamic, and that the observer of cultural processes can never see culture completely objectively.

Culture Is Learned

Although all human beings are born with the ability to learn culture, nobody is born as a fully formed cultural being. The process of learning a culture begins at birth, and that is partly why our beliefs and conduct seem so natural: we have been doing and thinking in certain ways since we were young. For example, the Onge [ahn-**gay**], an indigenous group who live in the Andaman Islands in the Indian Ocean, learn from a very early age that ancestors cause periodic earthquakes and tidal waves, a fact that is as given to them as it would be strange to you, who were not raised with such beliefs. When these natural events occur, the Onge have a ready-made explanation for how the world works. It helps guide their responses so that they do not have to learn how to deal with these things anew every time they occur. Anthropologists call this process of learning the cultural rules and logic of a society **enculturation**.

Enculturation happens both explicitly and implicitly. Your student experience illustrates how both explicit and implicit enculturation processes have shaped you. Throughout your schooling, your teachers have explicitly taught you many things you need to know to be a productive member of society: to write, to analyze a text, to do mathematics, and so on (Figure 2.2). But you have also learned many other things that are more implicit; that is, not clearly expressed. The more implicitly learned lessons in your school years included obedience to authority and respect for social hierarchy. You learned these lessons from sitting in class. In the typical classroom, chairs face forward in rows so the teacher, who represents authority, can control your attention and movement. Bells and announcements over the loudspeakers also regulate your activities and the flow of your day. By the time you reach the university, these patterns are so ingrained that you take them for granted. As a result, you know more or less exactly what to do when you walk into a university classroom without thinking about it. But that does not mean enculturation has stopped. It will, in fact, continue throughout your life. You might notice that you are also involved in enculturation, explicit and implicit, as a student at your university, as you learn its specific traditions, which might include creating loyalty to certain mascots and other university symbols.

- **Enculturation.** The process of learning the cultural rules and logic of a society.

Culture Uses Symbols

Clifford Geertz (1926–2006) was one of the best-known American anthropologists of recent years. He proposed that culture is a system of **symbols**—a symbol being something that conventionally stands for something else—through which people make sense out of the world. Symbols may be verbal or nonverbal. Symbols are things that people in a given culture associate with something else, often something intangible, such as motherhood, family, God, or country. To illustrate this point, Geertz posed an interesting question: How do we know the difference between a wink and a twitch (1973:6–7)?

As movements of the eye, winks and twitches are identical. But the difference between them is enormous, as anyone who has experienced the embarrassment of taking one for the other can attest. A twitch is an involuntary blink of the eye, and generally speaking carries no symbolic significance. A wink, however, communicates a particular message

- **Symbol.** Something—an object, idea, image, figure, or character—that represents something else.

Figure 2.2   Do You Get It? You were enculturated to read from left to right. But when speakers of the Hebrew language are taught to read, such as those who might read this cartoon from a Hebrew language newspaper, they begin on the right and move left.

to a particular someone, and it takes a lot of implicit knowledge, first, to decide if it is a wink or a twitch, and second, to understand what it communicates.

To tell the difference and interpret any possible meanings, we must quickly consider a number of questions: Is there intent? What is the intent—conspiracy, flirtation, parody, ridicule, or something else? Would it be socially appropriate for this person to wink at me, and under what conditions? Underlying our considerations, which may barely rise to the surface of consciousness, is a shared system of meaning in which we and the winker participate that helps us communicate with and understand each other. Interestingly, what sounds like a complex computational process when broken down into these many decision points actually comes quite naturally to the human mind. This is because of the human capacity for learning with symbols and signs that otherwise have little meaning outside of a given culture.

Geertz's concept of culture, often called the **interpretive theory of culture**, is the idea that culture is embodied and transmitted through symbols. This fundamental concept helped anthropologists clarify the symbolic basis of culture, something virtually all anthropologists take for granted today. Because culture is based on symbols, culture is implicit in how people think and act, so they rarely, if ever, recognize culture for what it is; it is simply natural to them. In fact, people express culture in *everything* they do—playing games, speaking a language, building houses, growing food, making love, raising children, and so on (Figure 2.3). The meanings of these things—and the symbols that underlie those meanings—differ from group to group, and, as a result, people do things and organize themselves differently around the world. These differing meanings are what make the Balinese Balinese, Zapotecs Zapotecs, and Americans Americans.

- **Interpretive theory of culture.** A theory that culture is embodied and transmitted through symbols.

Cultures Are Dynamic, Always Adapting and Changing

In a globalized world with high levels of migration across cultural borders, communication flowing in all directions, and social and ethnic mixing, it is often impossible to say with any certainty where one culture or social group ends and another begins. As a result, many anthropologists today talk less about culture as a totally coherent and static system of meaning and more about the *processes* through which social meanings are constructed and shared.

Attention to cultural processes yields another insight: culture is *dynamic*. Cultural processes are adaptive, helping people adjust to the dynamic worlds in which they live. At the same time, social groups are not uniform or homogeneous, because not everybody interprets the events of everyday life in the same way, nor do they blindly act out scripts already laid out for them to perform. So cultural processes are emergent, fluid, and marked by creativity, uncertainty, differing individual meaning, and social conflict. Relations of power and inequality also permeate cultural processes. For example, no social group in the United States is composed of people who are absolutely equal, despite Americans' insistence that we all have equal opportunity. Some people seem to be natural leaders, perhaps because of their charm, intelligence, or wealth. People who are leaders of a group, like the most influential students in your dorm, can help others accept burdensome rules or help develop ways to evade them, whereas someone who is less a leader or trendsetter will have much less influence in shaping the culture of the same dorm. And university administrators and resident advisors (RAs) on dormitory floors know that their direct power over student behavior is limited to imposing or enforcing a few rules. But we all know that some RAs

Figure 2.3   It's Like Getting a Joke. When a popular comedian like Trevor Noah tells a funny joke, most of us barely think about what makes it so funny. Like other examples of culture Geertz discussed, we just "get it."

can influence their dorm residents better than others, even though everybody knows that colleges and universities have it in their power to expel students for violating basic rules. When conflicts emerge in such settings, those with much less "official" power may have more influence on the people involved. In the same way, understanding the changing culture of any group requires understanding who is powerful and how they come by this influence.

Culture Is Integrated with Daily Experience

As cultural beings, how we relate to the world seems natural to us, transparent, obvious, inevitable, and necessary. Our sense of passing time, for example, might contrast sharply with people's sense of time in other cultures. In Western cultures, we think of time as an entity that moves from past to present to future. This concept—an element of culture—has a critical influence on our daily lives, because it helps us organize and regulate our activities every day. It also motivates us to make plans, since this concept of time leads us to believe that time must be used or it will be lost.

Our values and beliefs are shaped by many integrated elements of life experience that can be grouped under the term *culture*. The foods we eat, the jobs we have, the clothes we wear, how we worship, the way we behave toward others on the street—these and other aspects must work well together to keep a culture fully functional. Understanding that culture comprises a dynamic and interrelated set of social, economic, and belief structures is a key to understanding how the whole of culture operates.

The integration of culture across these domains leads to expectations that are specific to a given social group. For example, white middle-class American parents think it is "natural" for their babies to sleep in single beds, often in their own rooms (Small 1998:116–118). They believe that sleeping with their babies creates emotional dependence. In our society, which prizes personal independence and self-reliance, such dependence seems damaging to the child. American couples often think of their own bed, the parents' bed, as a place of privacy and sexual intimacy where children do not belong. Other societies find these ideas strange and exotic. The Gusii of Kenya, for example, think it is "natural" to sleep with their babies, not to mention hold them constantly during waking hours, precisely because they *want* them to grow up to be dependent on others. For them, proper human behavior means constantly relying on other people.

How we sleep also demonstrates that activities you might think of as "natural"—that is, biologically based, as sleeping is, and therefore universally the same for all humans—are actually culturally patterned. Culture helps shape the basic things all humans must do for biological survival, like eating, sleeping, drinking, defecating, having sex, and so on. There is no better illustration of this fact than food preferences. As omnivores, humans can eat an enormous range of foods. But many Americans' stomachs churn at the thought of eating delicacies like rotten shark flesh (Iceland), buffalo penis stew (Thailand), or dogs (East Asia) (Figure 2.4).

No other animal so thoroughly dwells in artificial, or human-made, worlds of its own creation. Anthropologists stress that a **cross-cultural perspective** (analyzing a human social phenomenon by comparing that phenomenon in different cultures) is necessary to appreciate just how "artificial" our beliefs and actions are. A cross-cultural perspective demonstrates the incredible flexibility and plasticity of the human species—human belief and practices come in all shapes and forms.

• **Cross-cultural perspective.** Analyzing a human social phenomenon by comparing that phenomenon as manifested in different cultures.

🌱 **Figure 2.4 Yummy . . . Or Not.** A meal of insect larvae might make some Americans vomit or retch, which shows how powerful cultural beliefs are: they actually provoke a biological response to something that is perfectly digestible, if not healthy and delicious.

Culture Shapes Everybody's Life

White middle-class North Americans tend to believe they have no culture, in the same way that most people feel they have no accent. But just as people from Dallas, Boston, or Oklahoma City may each feel they have no accent, they are likely to feel their culture is not very distinctive either. They will probably feel that they possess the most mainstream aspects of American culture, even though each of the others, not to mention people from Los Angeles, Honolulu, or Seattle, will almost certainly feel that they have a fairly distinctive accent and an equally distinctive culture that varies from mainstream "American culture." These are understandable reactions to the transparency and naturalness of culture.

But the other side of the coin is the tendency to view minorities, immigrants, and others who differ from white middle-class norms as "people with culture," as compared to people who have what they understand as a fairly generic American culture. In the United States, these ideas are tied to social and institutional power: the more "culture" in this sense of the term one appears to have, the less power one wields; the more power one has, the less one appears to have culture (Rosaldo 1989). This power of mainstream culture over ethnic cultures is about the relationships of power and inequality that we mentioned earlier. In fact, by differing from mainstream patterns and norms, a group's culture becomes more visible to everyone. It is in this sense that groups with the most obvious cultures tend to be the least powerful.

Culture Is Shared

The notion that culture is shared refers to the idea that people, through their participation in social groups, make sense of their worlds and order their lives. Culture is not a product of individual psychology or biology, nor is it reducible to either individual psychology or biology. As a result, anthropologists generally accept that purely psychological and biological explanations of human experience are inadequate. Until recently, most anthropologists thought about culture as being transmitted and participated in through face-to-face networks in real communities. But, as every student knows, today we can participate in social groups virtually through the Internet, suggesting that the dynamics of creating shared cultures are shifting.

• **Cultural construction.** The meanings, concepts, and practices that people build out of their shared and collective experiences.

An individual's comprehension of anything is always based on what his or her group defines collectively as proper and improper. Anthropologists commonly refer to such definitions as **cultural constructions**, which refers to the fact that people collectively "build" meanings through common experience and negotiation. In the debate over college mascots, for example, both sides collectively "constructed" the significance of these images and symbols for both American Indians and colleges through their debates, protests, and discussions. A "construction" derives from past collective experiences in a community, as well as lots of people talking about, thinking about, and acting in response to a common set of goals and problems.

Cultural Understanding Involves Overcoming Ethnocentrism

One of the key features of culture is that it makes us feel that the ways we do things are correct; that is, that we do things—or think things out—in the "right" way and everybody else thinks and does things wrongly. As we mentioned in the previous chapter, feeling that everyone else does things the wrong way and that our way of doing things is right is called *ethnocentrism*. You may think of this process as a community-wide form of egocentrism. But for anthropologists, who like all other humans have a culture, ethnocentrism presents a major problem. How can we as anthropologists overcome our own ethnocentric biases to view any other culture or group of people objectively? Going and living with a community provides access to understanding what other people do, say, think, and believe, but if we are constantly judging their society and how it does things by our own goals, morals, and understandings we cannot ever understand them in their own terms.

From the beginning of cultural anthropology in America, anthropologists have argued that the only way to understand other cultures is in terms of that other culture's own goals, ideas, assumptions, values, and beliefs. The concept of *relativism*, by which we interpret and make sense of another culture in terms of the other culture's perspective, using their own goals, values, and beliefs rather than our own to make sense of what people say and do, is a central means of overcoming ethnocentrism, and it is a major feature of the anthropological perspective on culture.

But understanding another culture in its own terms does not mean that anthropologists necessarily accept and defend all the things people do. Even though the job of an anthropologist is not to judge other cultures but to learn to understand how and why other peoples do things as they do, anthropologists still carry basic values as individuals and as members of a particular society. A relativistic perspective is simply a useful tool that can help anthropologists overcome ethnocentrism and begin to see matters from the point of view of another culture.

A number of anthropologists, in fact, advocate a "critical relativism," or taking a stance on a practice or belief only after trying to understand it in its cultural and historical context. Critical relativism also holds that no group of people is homogeneous, so it is impossible to judge an entire culture based on the actions or beliefs of a few. For example, many North Americans practice male circumcision, which other societies consider abhorrent, including people in the German city of Cologne who banned circumcision in 2012 as a human rights abuse. There is even a small but growing social movement in the United States that condemns the practice along similar lines. But when people from other societies or members of this movement criticize this practice, they are not condemning our entire culture. Similarly, anthropologists can take critical perspectives on particular cultural practices and beliefs without indicting an entire culture as if it were a homogeneous entity (Merry 2003).

Another motive for advocating critical relativism is that, in an extreme form, cultural relativism can be a difficult position to uphold. It can lead to **cultural determinism**, the idea that *all* human actions are the product of culture, which denies the influence of other factors like physical environment and human biology on human action. Some critics also argue that extreme relativism can justify atrocities like genocide, human rights abuses, and other horrific things humans do to one another. For some background on the origins of relativism in anthropology, see "Classic Contributions: Franz Boas and the Relativity of Culture."

- **Cultural determinism.** The idea that all human actions are the product of culture, which denies the influence of other factors like physical environment and human biology on human action.

Defining Culture in This Book

Although all anthropologists agree that these seven elements of culture are critical to any definition, in their research different anthropologists emphasize or interpret these elements differently, which contributes to the diversity of culture theories expressed in Table 2.1. So while we, too, accept the importance of these key elements to any definition, we do approach culture throughout this book in a particular way. In Chapter 1, we defined culture as the taken-for-granted notions, rules, moralities, and behaviors within a social group that feel natural and suggest the way things should be. Building on this broader definition, here we can define culture with even more precision as *those collective processes through which people construct and naturalize certain meanings and actions as normal and even necessary*. Whatever particular ways any group of people does things, to members of that group those ways seem like the only sensible ones—they seem natural, obvious, and appropriate—even though other people might only scratch their heads, perplexed, in response to them. No matter how much our culture changes during our lifetimes, our reactions to the people and things around us always seem normal or natural. Of course, it only seems this way to us and to those who share our culture. Those cultural processes are, in fact, quite artificial, as they are constructed by humans.

Classic Contributions
Franz Boas and the Relativity of Culture

GERMAN-BORN FRANZ BOAS (1858–1942) was a pioneer anthropologist and the major figure responsible for establishing anthropology in America. Although he had a doctorate in physics, he became interested in studying non-Western cultures while conducting research on Baffin Island (today part of the Canadian territory of Nunavut) on the color of ice and sea water. He befriended many Inuit (so-called Eskimos) and learned that they thought about the world differently; for example, they did not distinguish between the colors green and blue. From these conversations, he learned a valuable lesson that would be at the heart of his work for the rest of his life: to learn about another people's perspective, one has to try to overcome one's own cultural framework. This perspective has come to be known as cultural relativism.

✿ **Franz Boas posing for a museum display about the Hidatsa at the American Museum of Natural History.**

The data of ethnology prove that not only our knowledge, but also our emotions are the result of the form of our social life and the history of the people to whom we belong. If we desire to understand the development of human culture we must try to free ourselves of these shackles. This is possible only to those who are willing to adapt themselves to the strange ways of thinking and feeling of primitive people. If we attempt to interpret the actions of our remote ancestors by our rational and emotional attitudes we cannot reach truthful results, for their feeling and thinking were different from ours. We must lay aside many points of view that seem to us self-evident, because in early times they were not self-evident. It is impossible to determine a priori those parts of our mental life that are common to mankind as a whole and those due to the culture in which we live. A knowledge of the data of ethnology enables us to attain this insight. Therefore it enables us also to view our own civilization objectively. (Boas 1940:636, translated from the original German, published in 1889 as Die Ziele der Ethnologie)

Questions for Reflection

1. Do you think it is really possible, as Boas said, "to free ourselves of these shackles" (our own self-evident points of view)? Why and how? If you do not think it is possible, why not?

2. Do you think we can know what our self-evident points of view are? How?

Our more precise definition of culture emphasizes that culture is not a static set of rules, or a totally coherent system of symbolic beliefs that people "have" or "carry" like a toolbox that gets passed down from generation to generation, which have been rather common views of culture among anthropologists. Culture, in fact, is more dynamic, emergent, and changing than these views allow, as cultures intermingle due to cross-border interconnections such as migration, global media, economic globalization, and other such dynamics of our contemporary world. Moreover, culture is emergent and even unstable, responding to innovation, creativity, and struggles over meaning. The power of our definition is that it presents culture as a dynamic and emergent process based on social relationships, leading anthropologists to study the ways cultures are created and recreated constantly in people's lives.

Another element of our approach is that it can help us understand "the way society becomes deposited in persons" in the form of lasting dispositions, norms, and tendencies (Bourdieu 1977; Navarro 2006:16). This notion is closely associated with the French scholar Pierre Bourdieu, who called these dispositions and norms a "habitus." When we approach culture in this way, we can begin to recognize that culture is "created through a social, rather than individual process leading to patterns that are enduring and transferrable from one context to another, but that also shift in relation to specific contexts and over time." Culture, thus, "is not fixed or permanent, and can be changed under unexpected situations or over a long historical period" (Navarro 2006:16).

This view presents culture as less material and stylistic than Tylor understood it to be, and less a statement about the enduring power of traditions that many American anthropologists emphasized during the first half of the twentieth century. We can use an ordinary laptop as a metaphor to explore how these views of culture differ from our own. Your laptop has an operating system, which is the interface of hardware and software necessary to run programs and files. We can think of humans as similarly having an operating system, but that system is not, in itself, culture; it is merely the capacity to have culture. In our species, that capacity is a product of our evolution. As Tylor understood it, culture was a digital file sitting on our desktop or in some file folder. The early twentieth-century view of culture as an enduring tradition builds on this understanding by acknowledging that this file can be changed at any moment as we revise and rewrite sections of the essay of our lives, yet the basic form persists each time we open one of these saved versions. All three of these components—the hardware (our brains and bodies), the software (our mental faculties), and the file (culture as an enduring tradition)—are important to anthropologists, but in our view they are not in themselves "culture."

Adapting this analogy to our view of culture, we see different cultures as the individual programs we can run on our laptop with the operating system we are using. Our operating system is capable of running multiple programs, each of which performs certain tasks in its own ways. (You might think of one culture as Word, another as Excel, another as PowerPoint, and so on.) Moreover, these "programs" are always changing in small ways, as they respond and adjust to changing conditions.

Throughout this chapter, and in subsequent chapters, we will illustrate how our definition of culture works. But this definition does raise an immediate question: If culture is a dynamic process, why doesn't it always feel that way to people? We deal with this question in the next section.

• •

THINKING CRITICALLY ABOUT CULTURE

How can an understanding of the complexities of culture help us make sense of the day-to-day world in which we live? Give an example from your life to illustrate your answer.

• •

If Culture Is Always Changing, Why Does It Feel So Stable?

Imagine how chaotic life would be if you could not expect the same rules and processes for interacting with others from one week to the next. People need cultural stability. If we always had to stop and think about changes in the rules of social interaction, we could not function in our society. The very power of culture is that its processes feel totally natural and simultaneously predictable. Yet the previous section defined culture in a way that emphasizes its processes as dynamic and emergent. So how does something feel stable if it is so dynamic?

The concept of enculturation—the idea that people have been doing or believing things for much of their lives—only partly explains why culture feels so stable. There are numerous other features of culture—symbols, values, norms, and traditions—that help explain the sense of stability that people feel about it.

Symbols

One way of approaching the issue of cultural stability and change is by examining symbols. Leslie White, a prominent American anthropologist, once said that the symbol is "the origin and basis of human behavior" (1949). Human life, in all of its social and material dimensions, is symbolically constituted (Sahlins 1999:400). A symbol, as we have already said, is something that conventionally stands for something else. The relationship between the symbol and what it refers to is arbitrary, based on no particular rhyme or reason (Figure 2.5). Symbols can be more than just images or concepts, however; people also use their bodies as symbols. In Japan, for example, bowing is a form of greeting, but depending on how low one bows, the gesture may also symbolize respect, apology, gratitude, sincerity, remorse, superiority, or humility.

A society will store its conventional meanings in symbols because their meanings tend to be stable. But symbols and their meanings can and do change, sometimes dramatically. For example, during the Spanish conquest of the Peruvian Andes during the sixteenth century, the Spaniards carried banners of their patron saint, Santiago Matamoros, to ensure victory over the Indians. The Indians quickly absorbed Santiago into their native religion. They identified Santiago as their own god of thunder and lightning, Illapa, who they believed changes forms. To the Indians, Santiago symbolized the power of their own mountain gods and encouraged resistance against the Spaniards (Silverblatt 1988).

Figure 2.5 Love, Affection . . . and Toilets. Symbols are arbitrary. In the United States and several other countries, the heart conventionally symbolizes love and affection. But in rural Sweden and other parts of Scandinavia, people also associate the heart with outhouses, or rustic toilets (Lonely Planet 2014).

- **Values.** Symbolic expressions of intrinsically desirable principles or qualities.

Values

Studying values also helps us understand how change and stability are so closely related. **Values** are symbolic expressions of intrinsically desirable principles or qualities. They refer to that which is moral and true for a particular group of people. For example, "Mom" and "apple pie" symbolize American core values (values that express the most basic qualities central to a culture), such as patriotism or loyalty to country. In the United States, "Mom" expresses the purity of selfless sacrifice for the greater good. "Apple pie," a common food since colonial times, expresses Americans' shared heritage. Of course, not everybody eats apple pie and not every mother is loyal to her family, much less sacrifices herself for the greater good. The point is not that these ideals reflect what actually happens in the real world. Rather, they orient thinking about one's obligations as a citizen, like putting aside differences with other Americans and being willing to sacrifice oneself for love of family and country.

Values are conservative in that they conserve prevailing ideas about social relations and morality. Yet this does not mean that a community's values do not change. Nor does it mean that within a society or community people will not have opposing values. It is not even uncommon for people to hold conflicting values simultaneously.

- **Norms.** Typical patterns of actual behavior as well as the rules about how things should be done.

Norms

While values provide a general orientation for social relations, norms are more closely related to actual behavior. **Norms** are typical patterns of behavior, often viewed by participants as "the rules" of how things should be done. In our society, for example, it would be unimaginable to try to haggle over the price of toothpaste at the grocery store, because everyone expects you to pay the listed price. But in many other societies, especially in the Arab world and in Indonesia, the norm is just the opposite: no matter how small the item, it is considered rude *not* to haggle. In such places, taking the first asking price disrespects the seller. For more expensive items, such as a digital camera, buyers and sellers may expect to haggle over the price for an hour. The norm is for the starting price to be three to five times the item's actual worth, and buyers may break off negotiations and leave the shop two or three times so the buyer can run after them, bringing them back into the shop with a lower price.

Norms are stable because people learn them from an early age and because of the social pressure to conform. Norms also tend to be invisible (we are usually not conscious of them) until they are broken, as visitors to a different society or even city often find when they do things the "wrong" way. In Chicago, for example, pedestrians at a stoplight rarely pay much attention to a "Don't Walk" light; many people cross the street whenever they see a break in the traffic. But in Seattle, the social norm is different. People wait for the light to change to "Walk" before crossing the street, even in the rain and even when there is no traffic. When people from Seattle visit Chicago, they are pushed and bumped by other pedestrians rushing to cross the street. When Chicagoans visit Seattle, they tend to cross against the light while Seattleites wait patiently at the corner, scowling at the norm-breaking visitors. The scowl provides a **social sanction**, a reaction or measure intended to enforce norms and punish their violation. To avoid this public display of disapproval, Chicagoans in Seattle quickly learn to follow the norm. Long-established norms may eventually become **customs**, which have a codified and lawlike aspect.

Traditions

Tradition usually refers to the most enduring and ritualized aspects of a culture. People often feel their traditions are very old, which justifies actions that make no logical sense in contemporary times. With such justifications, individuals and groups go to great lengths to protect their traditions. The controversy between American Indians and NCAA schools over mascots with which we opened this chapter illustrates how powerful such traditions can be.

But anthropologists are careful not to assume that traditions are as old as people may say, because appearances can be deceiving (Hobsbawn and Ranger 1983). For example, Scottish people often celebrate their identity with bagpipes and kilts made from tartans, plaid textiles that comprise stripes of different widths and colors that identify the wearers' clans. But these traditions, while indeed venerable, are not actually ancient. As a matter of fact, these objects, and the sense of a distinctive tradition they symbolize, emerged only during the eighteenth and nineteenth centuries (Trevor-Roper 1983). An English iron industrialist designed the kilt as we know it for his workers in the late 1700s. As the kilt caught on in the Scottish highlands, textile manufacturers began producing distinctive plaids to expand sales and found willing buyers among clan chiefs. The chiefs wanted to distinguish themselves and their ancestry as unique, so they adopted particular designs. When England's King George IV made a state visit to Scotland in 1822, the organizers heavily promoted the use of kilts and tartans to enhance the pageantry of the visit. This occasion legitimized highlands culture and established the look as a national institution. The power of tartans comes not from their antiquity, but from their association with the clans that have long been central to Scottish highlander social life. Figure 2.6 shows another example, drawn from Japanese culture, of a similarly recent and flexible tradition.

Such examples demonstrate that what we take as timeless and authentic examples of tradition may be quite recent innovations. But knowing that a particular tradition

- **Social sanction.** A reaction or measure intended to enforce norms and punish their violation.

- **Customs.** Long-established norms that have a codified and law-like aspect.

- **Tradition.** Practices and customs that have become most ritualized and enduring.

Figure 2.6   Sumo Wrestling in Japan. Like the use of tartans in Scotland, Sumo wrestling in Japan feels ancient, although key features of it—such as the practice of awarding one person the championship—are less than 100 years old.

is a recent invention does not mean people are any less protective of it (just ask defenders of American Indian mascots on college campuses; most mascots came about only during the early twentieth century).

Historically, anthropologists have emphasized that culture is "shared" among a group of people, implying a kind of uniformity and stability in culture. Clearly, people need a relatively stable and common base of information and knowledge in order to live together. But these different aspects of culture—symbols, values, norms, and traditions—are features that seem stable and common even though they may not be shared by everybody in a society. There is another reason culture feels stable. It is that culture is expressed through social institutions, a theme we turn to next.

THINKING CRITICALLY ABOUT CULTURE

Most students think it is easy to identify the symbols, values, norms, and traditions that support other people's practices. But they find it more difficult to think about their own daily practices in the same terms. Use any of your own daily practices to illustrate how these four features of culture reinforce your own behavior.

How Do Social Institutions Express Culture?

● **Social institutions.** Organized sets of social relationships that link individuals to each other in a structured way in a particular society.

The **social institutions** of any society are the organized sets of social relationships that link individuals to each other in a structured way in that society. These institutions include patterns of kinship and marriage (domestic arrangements, the organization of sex and reproduction, raising children, etc.), economic activities (farming, herding, manufacturing, and trade), religious institutions (rituals, religious organizations, etc.), and political forms for controlling power. Each culture has its norms, values, and traditions for how each of these activities should be organized, and in each case they can vary greatly from one society to another because each society has a different culture.

Let us consider how mid–twentieth-century anthropologists approached culture's relationship to social institutions. Then we will consider how changes in these institutions can shape cultural patterns, which ultimately transform the social institutions themselves.

Culture and Social Institutions

From the 1920s to the 1960s, the dominant answer to the question of how culture is expressed in social institutions was that culture is like the glue that holds people together in ordered social relationships. Associated with British anthropologists Bronislaw Malinowski and A. R. Radcliffe-Brown, this theory, known as **functionalism**, holds that cultural practices and beliefs serve social purposes for society, such as explaining how the world works, organizing people into roles so they can get things done, and so on. Functionalists emphasize that social institutions function together in an integrated and balanced fashion to keep the whole society functioning smoothly and to minimize disruptive social changes.

- **Functionalism.** A perspective that assumes that cultural practices and beliefs serve social purposes in any society.

As an illustration of functional analysis, think back to the case of the Onge, the people who believe their ancestors make earthquakes and tidal waves. A functionalist would focus on how Onge beliefs about their ancestors explain how the natural world works, and on how these beliefs in turn help shape and are shaped by the Onge's migratory hunting-and-gathering existence. Working together with other structures of Onge society, such as political organization, economics, kinship, and so on, these beliefs contribute to the maintenance of an ordered society.

For functionalists, cultures were closed, autonomous systems. But even at its height of popularity, critics insisted that functionalism's vision of culture was *too* stable. In fact, not all societies function smoothly, and functionalism's static view of culture could not explain history and social change. One of Britain's most prominent anthropologists, E. E. Evans-Pritchard, famously broke with functionalists in 1961 when he said that anthropology should not model itself on the natural sciences but on humanistic disciplines, especially history with its processual focus.

In spite of its shortcomings, functionalism has left important legacies, especially that of the **holistic perspective**, a perspective that aims to identify and understand the whole—that is, the systematic connections between individual cultural beliefs, practices, and social institutions—rather than the individual parts. This does not mean contemporary anthropologists still see a society as wholly integrated and balanced. Rather, the holistic perspective is a methodological tool that helps show the interrelationships among different domains of a society, domains that include environmental context, history, social and political organization, economics, values, and spiritual life. Thus, the life of a community becomes expressed through the social relationships among its members, organized as they are through their social institutions. To understand how changes in cultural values can lead to changes in social institutions, consider the relationship between diet, industrialization, and sexual deviance in America during the nineteenth and early twentieth centuries.

- **Holistic perspective.** A perspective that aims to identify and understand the whole—that is, the systematic connections between individual cultural beliefs, practices, and social institutions—rather than the individual parts.

American Culture Expressed Through Breakfast Cereals and Sexuality

Let us begin by posing a simple question: Why do so many Americans prefer cereal for breakfast? Most of us today prefer cereal because it is part of a "healthy and

Figure 2.7   The Effects of Masturbation, Circa 1853.
This image comes from a book called *The Silent Friend* about the "horrors of masturbation." At the time, common wisdom held that masturbation would lead to insanity.

nutritious diet" (the standard industry line) or because of its convenience. In any event, eating cereal for breakfast has become a social norm for tens of millions of Americans. It builds on positive cultural values attributed to health and on the symbolism of "healthy food = a healthy body." But corn flakes were invented in the nineteenth century as a cure for sexual deviance, masturbation being the most worrisome.

Nineteenth-century religious leaders considered masturbation an abomination, and the emerging scientific disciplines of psychiatry and surgery claimed that masturbation caused shyness, hairy palms, jaundice, insanity, cancer, and murderous behaviors (Figure 2.7). From 1861 to 1932, the U.S. Patent Office issued some two dozen patents on anti-masturbation devices to prevent boys from masturbating, among them a safety pin to close the foreskin of the penis, various kinds of male chastity belts, and an electric bell attached to the penis that would notify parents if their son got an erection during the night. As recently as 1918, a U.S. government brochure advised new parents to prevent their babies from masturbating by tying their hands and legs to the sides of their cribs. Circumcision became the most commonly performed surgery in the United States based on the view that it prevented masturbation.

John Harvey Kellogg (1852–1943), the inventor of corn flakes, was a physician from Battle Creek, Michigan. He was a nutritional enthusiast and a follower of the health food movement of vegetarian and dietary reformer Sylvester Graham (1794–1851), who had developed graham flour used in graham crackers. Kellogg became director of a Seventh-day Adventist sanitarium in Battle Creek, where he built on Graham's ideas, inventing corn flakes and various granolas as food for his patients (Figure 2.8). Both men were concerned with health and sexuality—they especially abhorred masturbation, which they attributed to animalistic passions that were enhanced by a rich, meaty, or spicy diet. Both believed that bland but healthy foods were the way to soothe these volatile and unhealthy sexual urges (Money 1985).

Of course, their solution to the perceived problems of sexual passion was based on the symbols of passion being "fiery," which they thought could be quenched (symbolically) with bland cereals. None of these efforts was very effective in preventing masturbation, of course, and no one defends them for that purpose anymore. But these assumptions were enough to create corn flakes and graham crackers. The meanings we give to eating cereal and masturbation have changed as our lifestyles and diets have changed. In fact, an increasing number of medical professionals embrace masturbation as good for mental health.

During the nineteenth century, the American breakfast, like the rest of the American diet, was a hearty meal of meat, eggs, fish, biscuits, gravy, jams, and butter. Although farmers worked off the calories in their fields, as America became more urban, such rich meals became a sign of prosperity, just as the ideal body type was full-bodied for both men and women. But as American culture began to value healthy eating early in the twentieth century, industrial cereal makers, like C. W. Post and Kellogg's brother William, took advantage of this connection between cereals and good health to market their creations as nutritious foods. By the 1920s, the American diet had shifted dramatically, along with the ideal body type becoming much thinner. The result was an increased demand from consumers for convenient and tasty breakfast cereals, spawning a giant breakfast cereal industry associated with good taste and health rather than with preventing sexual deviance.

Figure 2.8 Happiness Is Wellness in the Bowels. John Harvey Kellogg's Battle Creek Sanitarium, opened in 1876, served corn flakes, granolas, and yogurts to promote good bowel health. There was also an enema machine that could pump 15 gallons of water through a person's bowel in seconds. Kellogg's sanitarium was a popular and fashionable vacation destination.

In answering our initial question about why many Americans prefer cereal for breakfast, we see interrelationships between separate domains like beliefs (about sexual morality, good health), social institutions and power (expert knowledge, medical practices), and daily life (changes in labor organization and economic life, dietary preferences). This is the holistic perspective.

We also see the integration of specific domains. For example, beliefs about sexual morality are intertwined with institutions of social authority, such as sanitariums and medical disciplines like psychiatry and surgery, and those institutions in turn regulate people's sexual relationships. Similarly, changes in people's economic relationships and work habits help shape and are shaped by their ideas about what is good to eat. At any historical moment, these domains feel stable because they are reflected in the other domains, even though some may be highly transitory and dynamic. The values, norms, and traditions in one domain are buttressed and supported by values, norms, and traditions in many other domains.

And herein lies the power of a cultural analysis: it shows how doing something that feels totally "natural" (pouring yourself a bowl of cereal in the morning) is really the product of intertwined "artificial" (or culturally constructed) processes and meanings. In "Thinking Like an Anthropologist: Understanding Holism" we present a scenario to illustrate how simple innovations can lead to changes in social institutions.

Thinking Like an Anthropologist
Understanding Holism

ANTHROPOLOGISTS BEGIN THEIR research by asking questions. In this box, we want you to learn how to ask questions as an anthropological researcher. Part One describes a situation and follows up with questions we would ask. Part Two asks you to formulate your own questions based on a different situation.

PART ONE: INTRODUCING CASH CROPS TO HIGHLAND NEW GUINEANS

When anthropologist Ben Finney (1973) studied coffee as a cash crop in the Eastern Highlands of Papua New Guinea, he observed that some younger men planted large fields in coffee and some had become coffee buyers. In the years since Finney's field research, many of these men became very successful coffee planters and buyers. Several acquired whole fleets of Isuzu and Toyota trucks, which they used to bring coffee beans to local warehouses and to coastal cities (Westermark 1998).

On the face of it, this program was dramatically successful in introducing a valuable cash crop to a region that had known only subsistence horticulture. But a holistic approach illustrates that coffee also brought important social consequences for Highland communities.

In the 1950s, an Australian colonial ban on tribal warfare opened up large tracts of no-man's-land between formerly hostile groups. Colonial officers brought coffee seedlings for villagers to plant in this formerly useless land. Some Highlanders planted coffee; others rejected the whole idea, saying, "What good is coffee? You can't eat it and pigs can't eat it either," pigs being an especially important form of wealth in Highlanders'

political and economic lives. Most of the village leaders and prominent elders continued planting sweet potatoes and tending pigs as they always had. The pigs ate surplus sweet potatoes and were used in feasts and ceremonial exchanges with friends and rivals in other villages. Men with extensive exchange networks became village leaders called "big men." Big men achieved prominence and influence over others from their own hard work, assisted by the hard work of their wives and female relatives in the gardens. Traditional subsistence farmers made fun of their coffee-planting neighbors.

But after seven years, the coffee trees began to bear fruit, and the officers showed the coffee planters how to pick, process, and sell the beans. The young coffee planters now had larger sums of cash than people had ever seen. Coffee profits increased as more and more trees matured. Unexpectedly, younger men found themselves with money that they would have had to work for months or years on a coastal plantation to earn.

These young coffee growers used this money to achieve social status because they, unlike the old men, had access to all sorts of imported goods in the stores. In some cases, the prestige of these new big men was even greater than that of the older big men. Suddenly, everyone wanted to become a coffee planter, but after seven or eight years, nearly all of the open land was already planted in coffee.

Elimination of tribal warfare and the introduction of coffee did not eliminate the big man political system or the cultural logic upon which it is based. But a holistic perspective shows that it did have important ramifications throughout the society.

What questions does this situation raise for anthropological researchers?

1. How did Highland society change as a result of coffee?
2. What were the unexpected effects of introducing coffee on this small-scale egalitarian society?
3. Which effects were positive? For whom were they positive? Who experienced negative consequences from the introduction of coffee?

PART TWO: INTRODUCING SMARTPHONES TO AMERICAN COLLEGE STUDENTS

Consider the relatively recent rise in the use of smartphones by high school and college students. As recently as ten or fifteen years ago, most students were forced to use a landline if they wanted to talk to their friends, which usually meant that they were calling from home. Nowadays, growing numbers of students have their own smartphones,

Women process coffee in a local factory in Highland Papua New Guinea   Although men initially planted coffee as a cash crop, as the economy has begun to modernize, some farmers built factories for roasting and bagging the roasted coffee as we see here.

not just for making phone calls, but for taking pictures, surfing the Internet, texting, and so on. Students use their smartphones in a variety of ways not possible on their parents' landlines. These mobile devices have brought lifestyle changes for young people that might be considered unexpected effects when cell phones were initially introduced.

Using a holistic approach, think about some of the changes that smartphone use and texting have introduced into the lives of high school and college students. What questions would you ask about this situation as an anthropological researcher? (Sample questions can be found at the end of this chapter.)

THINKING CRITICALLY ABOUT CULTURE

Anthropologists feel that holism is one of the key aspects of culture because it links together lots of things that people in other disciplines do not routinely think about. Use an example of an object in daily life to show how it is holistically linked to other aspects of American life. (Consider, for example, an item you use in your classes—such as a book, a pencil and paper, or an iPad—to show how this object is linked to or breaks from our past but is connected to many other things in our lives.)

Can Anybody Own Culture?

As we have defined culture, the question of "owning culture" may appear to make little sense. How can somebody own the collective processes through which people construct and naturalize certain meanings and actions as normal and necessary? For the most part, owning culture is about power relations between people who control resources and (typically) minority communities who have been kept outside the mainstream. At one level, nobody can own culture, but many will claim the exclusive right to the symbols that give it power and meaning.

The debate over sports teams' Indian mascots is only one example of a conflict over who has the right to use, control, even "own," symbols, objects, and cultural processes. This conflict is related to the phenomenon of **cultural appropriation**, the unilateral decision of one social group to take control over the symbols, practices, or objects of another. Cultural appropriation is as old as humanity itself. The fact that people adopt ideas, practices, and technologies from other societies demonstrates the fluidity of social boundaries and partly explains why societies and cultures are changing all the time.

Yet cultural appropriation also often involves relationships of domination and subordination between social groups. For American Indians, for example, the pressure to assimilate into the dominant white Euro-American society has coincided with the dominant society's appropriation of Indian cultural symbols. That appropriation goes beyond the use of Indian images as sports mascots and includes, among other examples, kids "playing Indian," New Age religion's imitation of Indian spirituality and rituals, Hollywood's endless fascination with making movies about Indians, and even the use of the Zia Pueblo sun symbol on the New Mexico state flag (Strong 1996; Brown 2003). While some Indians do not mind, others find these uses of Indian symbolism degrading

• **Cultural appropriation.** The unilateral decision of one social group to take control over the symbols, practices, or objects of another.

Anthropologist as Problem Solver
Michael Ames and Collaborative Museum Exhibits

FOR SEVERAL DECADES, indigenous activists in the United States and Canada have criticized museums for mishandling sacred indigenous artifacts and displaying objects without the permission of tribal leaders. Until the 1990s, most museums paid little attention to these concerns. They rarely sought indigenous input into museum exhibits, and when they did, it was usually long after planning for an exhibit was complete.

In the United States, the passage of the Native American Graves Protection and Repatriation Act (NAGPRA) in 1990 changed the playing field substantially. The law provides a framework for the return of human remains, burial goods, and religious objects to tribes that can demonstrate a direct connection to them (Brown 2003). At first, museum professionals worried that their collections would be cleaned out by Indian claims. But for the most part, museums and Indian tribes have made concerted efforts to find effective solutions to these problems. Anthropologists have played key roles as mediators and advocates—for both museums and Indians—in many of these situations.

One pioneer in creating a partnership between native communities and museums in Canada was Michael M. Ames (1933–2006), who was the director of the Museum of Anthropology (MOA) at the University of British Columbia in Vancouver from 1974 until 1997. Ames made several changes in the relationships between museums and their publics, including museum visitors and native peoples. While he was director of the MOA, he put all of the museum's ethnographic collections on display in visible storage so that the ordinary visitor could see everything in the collection. This was a striking shift for a museum, but nothing compared to his efforts in the 1990s to establish a new relationship between the MOA and the local First Nations—as Indian communities are referred to in Canada. He pioneered collaborative exhibitions in the museum.

Two proposed exhibitions dealt with archaeological material excavated on the lands of First Nations communities. Early in the planning process, Ames contacted tribal leaders from the communities, who agreed to participate and wanted to do so fully in managing the exhibitions and interpreting the objects displayed. The tribal leaders insisted on meaningful consultation at every stage of the process, including selection of objects, the final design of the exhibition, the interpretation of each object, installation, promotion, and exhibit maintenance.

▼ **Michael Ames and Margaret Mead.**

Tribal leaders became so involved in developing these exhibits that some museum staff feared that the MOA was giving up its scholarly role altogether. After extensive negotiations with tribal leaders facilitated by Ames, First Nations communities acknowledged that museum professionals were experts in research, interpretation, and exhibition design. But they asked that this expertise be used toward the Indians' educational goals (Ames 1999:46). For example, even though the objects displayed were prehistoric and archaeological, they had contemporary relevance for the native groups involved. Ames (1999:48) suggests that these archaeological pieces "have a powerful resonance for the living descendants and thus in a very real sense are contemporary as well as prehistoric" objects, especially since these prehistoric objects and sites are part of their historical record and thus part of their assertion of continuing sovereignty over their territories. These objects have current meaning in much the same way that documents and historic sites from the American Revolution have ongoing meaning for Americans.

Ames's efforts to have real participation by native groups in the museum's exhibitions have changed the museum's relationships with native communities throughout British Columbia. These communities feel that every object in the museum from their area is part of their own cultural patrimony. Museums may hold them, but they do so in trust for the native communities, who made, used, and continue to value these objects. Ames's work helped build bridges where previously there had been little more than suspicion toward anthropologists and museum professionals.

Questions for Reflection

1. From the perspective of museum curators, what might be lost if they make indigenous peoples partners in an exhibition?

2. What are the possible benefits to the museum of accepting indigenous input?

3. Even though museums may purchase cultural artifacts from members of indigenous communities, who really owns these objects?

and simplistic, because they ignore the realities of Indian communities and traditions, or because nobody asked permission to use the culturally meaningful objects and symbols.

Some of these conflicts have taken shape as dramatic protests, as in the 2002 case of Australian Aboriginal activists who removed the coat of arms at the Old Parliament House in Canberra, Australia. These activists declared that images of the kangaroo and emu (a large, flightless Australian bird resembling an ostrich) on the national seal are the cultural property of Aboriginal people (Brown 2003). Other conflicts have happened in courts, such as the highly publicized lawsuit Zia Pueblo brought against the State of New Mexico in 1994, formally demanding reparations for the use of the Zia sun symbol in the state flag (Figure 2.9).

Anthropologists have not escaped indigenous scrutiny and criticism for claiming expertise about native cultures. Anthropologist Kay Warren (1998), for example, studied the rise of the Pan-Maya ethnic movement in Guatemala. When she gave an academic presentation on Maya political activism, Maya intellectuals and political leaders in attendance responded by challenging the right of foreign anthropologists even to study Maya culture. As Warren points out, indigenous movements like Pan-Mayanism reject the idea that anthropological knowledge is neutral or objective. They insist that doing anthropology raises important political and ethical questions: Who should benefit from anthropological research? Why do the people studied by anthropologists not get an opportunity to help define and evaluate research projects?

Figure 2.9   The Cause of Indigenous Rights. Indigenous groups forced the United Nations to establish the Permanent Forum on Indigenous Issues in 2000. The forum's goal is to address the human, cultural, and territorial rights of indigenous peoples around the world.

Responding to such questions, a number of anthropologists like Warren have modified how they do cultural research, including inviting the subjects of their research to be collaborators in all stages of the research, from the definition of the study all the way through to publication. In "Anthropologist as Problem Solver: Michael Ames and Collaborative Museum Exhibits," we explore how one anthropologist collaborated with indigenous people in the creation of museum exhibitions.

● ●

THINKING CRITICALLY ABOUT CULTURE

Discuss whether people from one culture could "own" a dance—like the samba from Brazil—that originated with people from another ethnic group. Could anyone own a style of pop music?

● ●

Conclusion

At the heart of all anthropological discussions of culture is the idea that culture helps people understand and respond to a constantly changing world. As we have defined it, culture consists of the collective processes through which people construct and naturalize certain meanings and actions as normal and even necessary. Based on symbols and expressed through values, norms, and traditions, culture offers a relatively stable and common base of information and knowledge that helps people live together in groups. A holistic perspective on culture illustrates how different domains of a society interrelate. But culture is also dynamic, responding to innovation, creativity, and struggles over meaning.

In spite of the many difficulties involved in studying culture, it is more important than ever to understand culture, what it is, and how cultural processes work. The big and urgent matters of our time have cultural causes and consequences. These matters range from the problems posed by development and change for indigenous groups and heated conflicts about social identity over mascots and traditions on college campuses, to others like terrorism, environmental degradation and sustainability, ethnic diversity and racial conflict, religious intolerance, globalization, and health care. As you read this book, you will learn how anthropologists use cultural perspectives to understand, explain, and even contribute to resolving problems related to these matters.

KEY TERMS

Cross-cultural
    perspective   p. 37

Cultural appropriation   p. 49

Cultural construction   p. 38

Cultural determinism   p. 39

Customs   p. 43

Enculturation   p. 35

Functionalism   p. 45

Holistic perspective   p. 45

Interpretive theory of
    culture   p. 36

Norms   p. 42

Social institutions   p. 44

Social sanction   p. 43

Symbol   p. 35

Tradition   p. 43

Values   p. 42

Reviewing the Chapter

Chapter Section	What We Know	To Be Resolved
What is culture?	Culture is a central component of what it means to be human. Culture involves the processes through which people comprehend, shape, and act in the world around them.	Although most definitions of culture emphasize common themes, anthropologists have never agreed on a single definition of culture.
If culture is always changing, why does it feel so stable?	Cultural processes are emergent, fluid, and marked by creativity, uncertainty, differing individual meaning, and social conflict. Yet culture is also remarkably stable.	Anthropologists continue to debate which is more important—dynamism or stability—in explaining how culture works in people's lives.
How do social institutions express culture?	A holistic perspective enables anthropologists to understand how different social institutions and domains of a society are interrelated.	Anthropologists continue to debate how and why social institutions in any society change.
Can anybody own culture?	The phenomenon of cultural appropriation illustrates the tensions between cultural change and stability, and it raises important ethical and political questions about anthropological knowledge itself.	Anthropologists continue to debate over which research and collaborative strategies are most effective to respond to the ethical and political issues raised by the creation of anthropological knowledge about culture.

Readings

For an overview of different theories of culture in anthropology and how and why they differ across schools of thought within the discipline, see Adam Kuper's *Culture: The Anthropologists' Account* (Cambridge, MA: Harvard University Press, 2000). In this book, Kuper actually expresses deep skepticism about the centrality of the culture concept to anthropology, and he illustrates why anthropologists continue to debate what culture means.

For an intellectual history of the development of the culture concept in anthropology and its place in the discipline during the early twentieth century, the essays in George Stocking's book *Race, Culture, and Evolution: Essays in the History of Anthropology* (Chicago, IL: University of Chicago Press, 1968) are classics and remain relevant today.

The book *Who Owns Native Culture?* by anthropologist Michael Brown (Cambridge, MA: Harvard University Press, 2003) is a highly readable account of the vexing legal, ethical, and methodological issues involved in questions about who owns native cultural symbols and heritage.

SUGGESTED ANSWERS TO "THINKING LIKE AN ANTHROPOLOGIST"

Use these examples as a guide to answering questions for other "Thinking Like an Anthropologist" boxes in the book.

1. How has cultural life on campus changed because of smartphones?
2. Are there unexpected effects of introducing smartphones into college life?
3. How has the proliferation of smartphones changed college students' patterns of communication with their parents and friends?
4. Are people more connected socially than they were before?
5. Are there ways that people are less connected socially?
6. Does smartphone use have any impact on the ways university classrooms operate?

Ethnography

Studying Culture

YOU DON'T HAVE TO TRAVEL far and wide to study culture, and anthropologists have long studied the social lives of people in their home countries and communities. One such study was conducted during the 1980s and 1990s in East Harlem, a neighborhood in New York City, by American anthropologist Philippe Bourgois. East Harlem is largely cut off from mainstream America, if not from the very city in which it exists. Its residents, who are largely Puerto Rican, are isolated because of language and educational barriers, unemployment, poverty, and ethnic segregation. Bourgois, who had previously conducted research on Costa Rican banana plantations, lived in East Harlem to study how people experience this marginalization and how they make a living in an economy that does not seem to want them.

Bourgois soon discovered that the neighborhood was saturated with crack cocaine, which came to the market in the 1980s. Over the next four years, he spent hundreds of nights on the street and in crack houses, building trust with dealers and addicts. He tape-recorded and carefully transcribed many of his conversations with them, recorded their life histories, and visited with their families. He attended parties, family reunions, Thanksgiving dinners, and New Year's Eve celebrations. He heard many stories about being

Life in Spanish Harlem. Ethnographic methods have been used to study the lives of many distinct societies and communities, including communities within the United States. For example, ethnographers have studied the lives of residents of East Harlem, New York City, such as those pictured here playing dominoes on the sidewalk.

excluded from mainstream jobs in midtown Manhattan, and thus falling back on crack as dealers or users. He documented the many self-destructive behaviors that so often accompany addictions. At times, the research was dangerous for Bourgois.

Bourgois found that census records and other official documents gave an inaccurate picture about wealth and poverty in East Harlem, because they did not account for the thriving underground drug economy. Studies by other social scientists were no more helpful, because they typically confirmed the stereotype that poor people in the inner city deserve their poverty, in large part because of their drug-related illegal activities. But during his conversations and interviews, Bourgois was stunned to learn that people who run crack houses work much like any business owner pursuing the American dream. As he wrote, "They are aggressively pursuing careers as private entrepreneurs; they take risks, work hard, and pray for good luck. They are the ultimate rugged individualists braving an unpredictable frontier where fortune, fame, and destruction are all just around the corner" (Bourgois 1995:326).

Such insights came to Bourgois only because, as an ethnographic fieldworker, he participated in the lives of the crack dealers over a long period. Never a crack user himself, Bourgois got to know dealers and users personally in ways that almost no one who sets American policy about poverty and drug use does. And he came away with an appreciation of the community's all-too-American aspirations, even when mainstream opportunities and employment had been denied to them.

For those of you accustomed to stereotypes of anthropologists working in far-flung corners of the world with non-Western people, Bourgois's research might seem surprising. In fact, until the 1970s, the typical path of the anthropologist was to seek an out-of-the-way place where cultural differences appear most pronounced. Today, cultural anthropologists are as likely to do fieldwork among advertising executives, factory workers, transnational migrants—or, in this case, urban drug dealers and users—as we are to live in villages in remote settings. Bourgois's five years of ethnographic research involved a longer stay in "the field" than most anthropologists spend. But the distinctive methods he used were essentially the same as those of any cultural anthropologist 50 years ago who was studying people's lives in small villages in Africa, Latin America, or Oceania. At the heart of all of these research projects is a central goal: to learn about people who live in cultural circumstances different from our own. It leads us to ask: *How do anthropologists learn about other ways of life?* Embedded within this question are several more specific questions around which this chapter is organized:

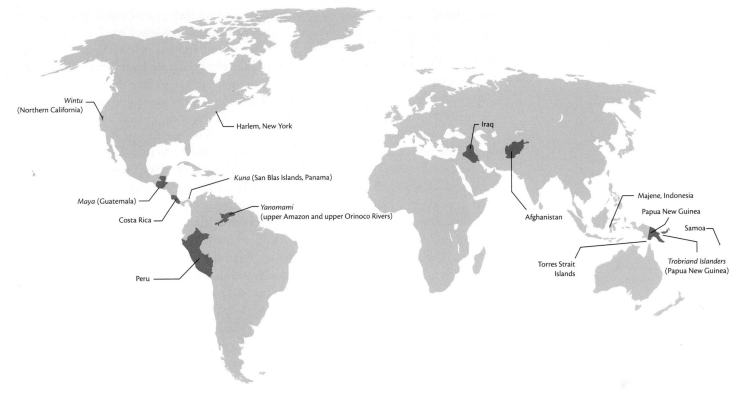

Figure 3.1   **Select Peoples and Places Discussed in Chapter 3.**

What distinguishes ethnographic fieldwork from other types of social research?

How do anthropologists actually do ethnographic fieldwork?

What other methods do cultural anthropologists use?

What unique ethical dilemmas do ethnographers face?

Ethnographic research methods have been around for the better part of a century because they have proven to be an effective tool for helping anthropologists gather the kind of information they require to understand social complexities and the inner lives and beliefs of people. We begin by examining what traditional ethnographic research is all about.

What Distinguishes Ethnographic Fieldwork from Other Types of Social Research?

In popular culture, an aura of mystery has long surrounded the question of what cultural anthropologists do. In part, this is because anthropology is generally less well known than other social scientific fields such as economics, psychology, or political science. But even anthropologists can sometimes find it difficult to define precisely how they collect and produce data. Graduate students preparing to do their research still hear, with an awkward humor, advice such as what the American anthropologist Cora Du Bois (1903–1991) heard before she went off to study the Wintu Indians of Northern California: "Carry a stick as the dogs are vicious," and "Take plenty of pencils and paper" for taking notes (Goldschmidt 2000). Anthropologists are well advised to take the right equipment along to do fieldwork in a foreign culture. But to focus only on equipment suggests that the persons giving the advice do not know enough about the culture to offer anything more significant. Cultural anthropologists do research by building personal relationships over a long period, and it is difficult to tell a student how to do that with people who are culturally different. Thus, although cultural anthropology shares some methods with other social sciences, it also has its own distinctive and effective methodological tools.

In general, social scientists gather data or information about human beings and the social, economic, political, and psychological worlds they inhabit. They use methods that are either quantitative (e.g., statistical) or qualitative (e.g., descriptive and interpretive). Although most anthropologists use quantitative data, cultural anthropology is the most qualitative of the social sciences. Anthropologists are distinct in that they are more holistic, traditionally studying all aspects of social life simultaneously, rather than limiting themselves to a single dimension of people's lives, such as economic, political, psychological, or religious dimensions. Anthropological researchers have also found that long-term immersion in a community (for a year or more) as well as an open mind yield insights they would never achieve had they started with preconceived ideas about the relationships among social, economic, political, and religious institutions.

Fieldwork

- **Fieldwork.** Long-term immersion in a community, normally involving firsthand research in a specific study community or research setting where the researcher can observe people's behavior and have conversations or interviews with members of the community.

We call this long-term immersion in a community **fieldwork**. It is *the* defining methodology of the discipline, to the point that pioneer British anthropologist C. G. Seligman (1873–1940) once observed that fieldwork is to anthropology what blood was to the martyrs of the early Church (McGee and Warms 2013:762). During fieldwork, anthropologists become involved in people's daily lives, make observations and ask questions about what people are doing, and take notes on those observations and interactions. Being involved in people's lives for an extended period of time is critical to the method, generating insights we would not have if we simply visited the community a few hours a day, to administer a survey or questionnaire, or to conduct a brief interview. As virtually every anthropologist will tell you, people may say one thing but then go and do something completely different. Sticking around helps us put what people say in context.

Fieldwork also helps us achieve one of our discipline's central goals, which Clifford Geertz (1973) once described as deciphering "the informal logic of everyday life," which is to say, trying to gain access to the implicit assumptions people make and the tacit rules they live by. Most Americans, for example, assume that drug dealers have a set of values that differs from their own, but Bourgois's long-term involvement with them suggests otherwise, even if their style of talking and their way of interacting with one another differ from those of other Americans. By immersing ourselves directly in community activities, we can observe what is important to the community, what community members discuss among themselves, and how these matters are intertwined with social institutions. This approach can yield rich insights about people's behaviors, actions, and ideas, insights that the people themselves might not notice or understand, as we explore in "Thinking Like an Anthropologist: Fieldwork in an American Mall."

Seeing the World from "the Native's Point of View"

Living for a long period of time as a researcher—a year or more—in an unfamiliar community in order to observe and record cultural differences emerged as a standard

Thinking Like an Anthropologist
Fieldwork in an American Mall

ANTHROPOLOGISTS BEGIN THEIR research by asking questions. In this box, we want you to learn how to ask questions as an anthropological researcher. Part One describes a situation and follows up with questions we would ask. Part Two asks you to formulate your own questions based on a different situation.

PART ONE: OBSERVING THE USE OF SPACE IN THE AMERICAN SHOPPING MALL

We've all been to a shopping mall, but have you ever stopped to consider how people actually use malls? Anthropologist Paco Underhill (2005) has spent his career studying the American shopping mall and advising retail businesses on how to use space to sell products to the American consumer. From his observations, it is clear that visiting a mall is a socially patterned experience, although visitors may not realize how their actions are being shaped by others.

Underhill begins his research on a mall, perhaps surprisingly, in the parking lot. There, he observes the possible entrances to the mall and the fact that, from the outside, the shopper can see little of what is inside. Landscaping is minimal, as is any other attraction that might keep the would-be shopper outside, so visitors stream into the building. The goal of the mall, Underhill infers, is to get people inside to begin spending money.

Once people enter, Underhill observes, they need time to slow down and adjust to the space of the mall, so shops are rarely placed at the entrances; instead, these spaces are rented to doctors, accounting firms, and other businesses whose customers require appointments. After leaving this "decompression area," visitors come to the excitement of the mall proper: shop after shop with brightly colored merchandise pouring out into the hallways to attract attention.

Unlike the halls of a hospital or an office building, those at the mall are extra wide. Underhill seeks to understand what goes on in these spaces that requires room for two broad lanes of foot traffic, often separated by stalls, carts, and tables filled with merchandise. While most people pop in and out of the many shops, others stop to look at the shop windows and the merchandise that lies on tables or hangs along the way. Still others—particularly during cold or stormy weather—power-walk alone or in pairs, getting their exercise.

Underhill pays close attention to the people in these hallways and what they do, taking careful notes of his observations. He notes their ages and sexes, whether they walk by themselves or with others, who those others might be (children? parents? friends?), and whether these patterns change by day of the week and time of day. Entering the food court, Underhill observes the types of restaurants, the ways people interact with those restaurants, the kinds of

⬇ **Inside an American Shopping Mall.**

Thinking Like an Anthropologist (continued)

shops near them, and how long people linger before return-ing to shopping. Underhill then turns his attention to the restrooms, observing where they are located, which is often hidden away in distant corners and corridors, intended not to affect the shopping experience negatively.

As Underhill wanders in and out of the large anchor stores, he makes other observations. Merchandise is piled up in the entryways, some on sale, some seasonal. He ob-serves what grabs people's attention, getting them to slow down and pause. He observes how and where stores place different kinds of products, which influences how people move through the store and what they are likely to see (and possibly purchase even though they did not come to buy that particular thing).

Underhill's research shows that by looking at the archi-tecture and observing closely the flow of shoppers through it, we can sense what kinds of behavior the store managers had hoped to encourage, what behaviors they might have hoped to discourage, and how people actually make use of these semi-public spaces.

The experience of walking through the mall with Paco Underhill raises important questions for anthropological researchers, such as the following:

1. What might an anthropologist learn about the use of space from watching and observing what people do as opposed to interviewing them?
2. How can an anthropologist check the inferences he or she might make about the goals of store managers?
3. What should a fieldworker focus on when making observations?

PART TWO: OBSERVING THE USE OF SPACE IN THE COLLEGE LIBRARY

CONSIDER THE LIBRARY at your college or univer-sity. Most libraries have a variety of tables, desks, and study carrels. The stacks may be open, or students may need to show their ID cards to get inside. Audiovisual materials may be accessible to everyone in the student body, or professors may put some videos or DVDs on reserve. Modeling your work on Paco Underhill's, what kinds of questions would you pose to orient your observations of a college library?

i

field methodology after 1914 and led to profoundly new kinds of understandings of native peoples. It had become clear that living in the community did not by itself guarantee cultural relativism—that is, understanding a native culture on its own terms—nor did it promise that the researcher could overcome his or her ethnocen-trism and cultural bias. But it increased the likelihood that the anthropologist could get some sense of the world in terms that local people themselves understood.

Of course, nobody ever gets into another person's mind or shares another person's exact thoughts. Even in our own community, we rarely understand fully how classmates, neighbors, colleagues, roommates, or teammates think about a certain topic. Moreover, even when we think we understand how someone thinks or how someone might react to a particular situation, a similar but new situation often produces a different and un-expected reaction. Moreover, if we talk about two seemingly different reactions, we can nearly always understand that the two were triggered by different conditions or contexts.

As an illustration of this point, think about how politicians respond to scandals. If the scandal is perpetrated by an elected official in another party, politicians often react with harsh criticism, but when someone in their own party is involved in a scandal, they rarely seem to make a fuss. It is tempting to write off this behavior as paradoxical or hypocritical, but a more accurate view is that their moral outrage is situational, condi-tioned by the context of who is involved, how well they know them, and perhaps how much impact the incident might have on a party's outcome in the next election.

Now put yourself in an anthropologist's shoes. As outsiders we might initially think that our informants can be similarly paradoxical. But after some time and effort to see things in terms of local context, things people say and do begin to make sense, and we generally feel we are beginning to move beyond what anthropologists call an **etic perspective** (an outside observer's perspective on a culture) and see the world from an **emic perspective** (a cultural insider's perspective on his or her culture). Long before these terms came to be used, anthropologist Bronislaw Malinowski referred to the emic perspective as "the native's point of view" and asserted that it lay at the heart of the ethnographic method he claimed to have invented when he famously pitched his tent on the beach near the houses of Trobriand Islanders (Figure 3.2), as we discuss in "Classic Contributions: Bronislaw Malinowski on the Ethnographic Method."

- **Etic perspective.** An outside observer's perspective on a culture.

- **Emic perspective.** A cultural insider's perspective on his or her culture.

Avoiding Cultural "Tunnel Vision"

Most people assume that their own way of doing things is inherently better than everyone else's. No matter how much we think we understand the world better than anyone else, we can never understand others' reactions until we see the world from their point of view. We face a similar problem when we first interact with people from another culture. Their reactions to nearly everything seem foreign and strange, and our own cultural "tunnel vision"—unquestioned tacit meanings and perspectives drawn from our own culture that prevent us from seeing and thinking in terms of another culture's tacit meanings and perspectives—can lead to ethnocentrism. But as we get to know them and see more of their culture, their reactions seem less puzzling and unexpected, even reasonable. We do not usually start thinking the way they do, and we will often continue to feel that their way of doing things is peculiar or even wrong, but we will gradually come to accept their reactions as making sense in terms of the local culture. Until we can make sense of the local cultural logic, we will inevitably use tunnel vision to understand another culture, complete with all its ethnocentric biases.

Of course, people in other societies are ethnocentric as well. They feel that their way of doing things; their moral, ethical, and legal codes; and their ways of thinking about the world are correct, while everyone else's are flawed. In other words, they have their own tunnel vision. When anthropologists attempt to see the world "from the native's point of view," we are not claiming that the other culture's way of thinking is necessarily better than our own. But by understanding the native's point of view, we are attempting to unravel the cultural logic within which actions that are unthinkable in our own society become commonplace in another culture.

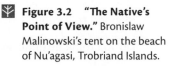

Figure 3.2   "The Native's Point of View." Bronislaw Malinowski's tent on the beach of Nu'agasi, Trobriand Islands.

Classic Contributions
Bronislaw Malinowski on the Ethnographic Method

🌿 **Bronislaw Malinowski sits on a canoe chewing betel nuts with a white trader and one of his Trobriand Islander informants, 1918.**

POLISH-BORN ANTHROPOLOGIST Bronislaw Malinowski (1884–1942) was the leading figure in British social anthropology between the First and Second World Wars. Before Malinowski, nearly all anthropological fieldwork consisted of regional surveys, and researchers stayed for only short periods in any one community, rarely learning the local language. Malinowski turned this all on its head. Between 1914 and 1917, he spent some 18 months in Omarakana in the Trobriand Islands of Papua New Guinea, in the process realizing that the best way to understand native life was to live with native people. In this excerpt from his best-known book, *Argonauts of the Western Pacific*, Malinowski outlines his basic approach to fieldwork, later celebrated as the "ethnographic method":

Soon after I had established myself in Omarakana, I began to take part, in a way, in the village life, to look forward to the important or festive events, to take personal interest in the gossip and the developments of the small village occurrences; to wake up every morning to a day, presenting itself to me more or less as it does to the native. I would get out from under my mosquito net, to find around me the village life beginning to stir, or the people well advanced in their working day according to the hour and also to the season, for they get up and begin their labours early or late, as work presses. As I went on my morning walk through the village, I could see intimate details of family life, of toilet, cooking, taking of meals; I could see the arrangements for the day's work, people starting on their errands, or groups of men and women busy at some manufacturing tasks. Quarrels, jokes, family scenes, events usually trivial, sometimes dramatic but always

significant, formed the atmosphere of my daily life, as well as of theirs. It must be remembered that as the natives saw me constantly every day, they ceased to be interested or alarmed, or made self-conscious by my presence, and I ceased to be a disturbing element in the tribal life which I was to study, altering it by my very approach, as always happens with a new-comer to every savage community. . . .

Also, over and over again, I committed breaches of etiquette, which the natives, familiar enough with me, were not slow in pointing out. I had to learn how to behave, and to a certain extent, I acquired "the feeling" for native good and bad manners. With this, and with the capacity of enjoying their company and sharing some of the games and amusements, I began to feel that I was indeed in touch with the natives, and this is certainly the preliminary condition of being able to carry on successful field work. (Malinowski 1922:7–8)

Questions for Reflection

1. Up to the time that Malinowski came to stay with them, few of the islanders had had more than a quick glimpse of a white man. What was it about Malinowski's way of living that led the islanders to begin to take Malinowski for granted and to pay little attention to him?

2. As newcomers to any community might do, Malinowski made many mistakes breaching or violating the local etiquette. How do you think he turned this situation to his advantage?

3. How did Malinowski go from simply pitching his tent next to the houses of the islanders to beginning to look at events from the "native's point of view"?

4. Do you think he understood the native's view completely, on every topic? Why or why not?

For example, when Philippe Bourgois (1995) studied the lives of crack dealers in East Harlem, he recognized that addiction had taken a toll on the lives of many of his informants. He did not use crack himself, and he did not believe that using crack is a good thing. Nevertheless, to understand the lives of his informants, he had to suspend his tunnel vision—that is, the perspectives that so many Americans share about those who sell and use crack cocaine, and the judgments that arise from those perceptions. Fieldwork was key to getting at that understanding. So what is actually involved in doing ethnographic fieldwork? In the next section, we explore this question.

THINKING CRITICALLY ABOUT ETHNOGRAPHY

Just spending time in the field, making observations, and speaking with locals are not enough to shake an anthropologist out of his or her own cultural tunnel vision. Why not? What are some other ways you can think of for an anthropologist to avoid cultural tunnel vision?

How Do Anthropologists Actually Do Ethnographic Fieldwork?

In cultural anthropology, fieldwork is more than a matter of simply collecting data. It is a core practice that integrates the primary philosophical elements of the discipline—especially a commitment to holism, cultural relativism, and ethical behavior—into a single frame of inquiry. One's experience and success in it, as well as where it is actually done, can strongly shape one's anthropological career and identity, by defining one's expertise in the anthropological community. Fieldwork relies less on a set of prescribed technical procedures or formulas than it does on a range of skills and techniques an anthropologist can draw on, depending on the context. At the heart of this approach to creating data and knowledge are participant observation, interviews, and note-taking.

Participant Observation: Disciplined "Hanging Out"

Participant observation is a key element of anthropological fieldwork. It is a systematic research strategy that is, in some respects, a matter of just hanging out. One of the things that distinguishes anthropologists from college students—who also do a lot of hanging out—is that anthropologists record much of what transpires while we are hanging out. In the field, we are also in a social position that is very different from what we are normally accustomed to, and we must work hard to build rapport and friendships in a community where we have no friends (Figure 3.3). Establishing rapport requires a lot of discipline, as well as acceptance of local customs and practices, however peculiar, unfamiliar, or uncomfortable.

Participant observation makes the anthropologist a professional stranger. Neither pure observation nor pure participation, it has been compared to living on the edge of a razor (Delaney 1988). As observers, anthropologists cannot remove themselves from the action. Yet giving in to participation too easily prevents one from noticing subtleties of behavior and learning to intuit their significance. Too much participation

• **Participant observation.** The standard research method used by cultural anthropologists that requires the researcher to live in the community he or she is studying to observe and participate in day-to-day activities.

Figure 3.3   Building Rapport in the Field. Finding ways to "fit in" is always a key concern of anthropologists, and sometimes wearing appropriate clothing helps. In addition, an anthropologist can build rapport by demonstrating that he or she respects local customs and culture. Here coauthor Robert L. Welsch wears traditional Mandarese clothing, including a silk sarong, batik shirt, and cap to attend a wedding reception near Majene on the island of Sulawesi in Indonesia.

- **Intersubjectivity.** The realization that knowledge about other people emerges out of relationships and perceptions individuals have with each other.

- **Informants.** Any person an anthropologist gets data from in the study community, especially a person who is interviewed or who provides information about what the anthropologist has observed or heard.

- **Interview.** Any systematic conversation with an informant to collect field research data, ranging from a highly structured set of questions to the most open-ended ones.

is sometimes referred to as "going native," because the researcher stops being an engaged observer and starts to become a member of the community.

Some years ago, anthropologist Johannes Fabian (1971) suggested that any notion that an anthropologist in the field is collecting "objective" data misses the point of the discipline. The data anthropologists bring home in their field notebooks were not out there to be gathered like blackberries; they were created by the relationships between an anthropologist and the people with whom he or she interacts in the field. The anthropologist observes things in the field setting, observes them a second or third time, and later inquires about them, gradually pulling together an enriched sense of what he or she has observed. Both the anthropologist and the people he or she works with have been actively creating this synthesis that becomes field data. For Fabian such observations and understanding are neither objective nor subjective but the product of **intersubjectivity**, which means that knowledge about other people emerges out of relationships individuals have with each other.

The traditional term for a fieldworker's subjects is **informants**, which generally refers to the people an anthropologist gets data from. But this term does not necessarily capture the subtlety of Fabian's point, because it may describe only one kind of relationship an anthropologist has in a community. Some anthropologists find other terms more appropriate to describe people with whom they have these relationships, including "collaborators" (evoking a shared enterprise in exploring culture), "interlocutors" (evoking ongoing conversations), and "consultants" (evoking advice shared by experts).

Interviews: Asking and Listening

Participant observation gives us many insights about how social life in another society is organized, but it is up to us as anthropologists to find systematic evidence for our perceptions. So another key goal of fieldwork is to flesh out our insights and gain new perspectives from **interviews**, or systematic conversations with informants, to collect data.

There are many kinds of interviews, ranging from highly structured, formal ones that follow a set script, to unstructured, casual conversations (Table 3.1). Anthropologists use structured interviews to elicit specific kinds of information, such as

TABLE 3.1	CHARACTERISTICS AND NATURE OF DIFFERENT KINDS OF INTERVIEWS		
Kinds of Interviews	Nature of Interview	Clear Focus for Interview	Kind of Fieldnotes
Interview schedule	Questions are read from a printed script exactly as written to all subjects of the interview. Often used for survey data collection. Researcher has decided ahead of time what is important to ask.	Yes	Interview schedule form
Formal/structured interview	Interviewer has a clear goal for the interview and writes down the informant's answers or tape-records the interview. Often used for survey data collection. Researcher has decided ahead of time what is important to ask.	Yes	Transcript of answers or of questions and answers.
Informal/open-ended interview	Interviewer has a focus for the interview but may not have a clear goal of what information he or she wants from the interview. While the researcher may begin with certain questions, he or she develops new questions as the interview proceeds. The interviewer may have a notebook present, but most of the time is spent in conversation rather than writing notes.	Sometimes	Preliminary notes that outline the discussion, which the researcher later uses to write up a full description of the context and content of the discussion.
Conversation	Resembles an ordinary conversation, and notebooks are not present. The anthropologist might ask certain questions, but the flow is highly conversational. Afterward, the anthropologist jots a few notes so he or she can remember the topics discussed, or goes somewhere private to write up more detailed raw notes that can be fleshed out later.	No	Headnotes and jot notes, which the researcher later uses to write up a full description of the context and content of the discussion. Notes often include topics to follow up on in future interviews or conversations.
Hanging out (participant observation)	Involves spending time with members of the community in gender- and age-appropriate ways. Hanging out may involve helping with fishing, cooking, planting, or weeding in rural or traditional societies, or playing in some pickup sport like basketball or soccer. It could involve hanging out in a local coffee shop, diner, or bar, or in a work environment such as an office or lunchroom. Anthropologists may occasionally make jot notes, but most of the time they record details in their notes later, when people are not around.	No	Headnotes and jot notes, which the researcher later uses to write up a full description of the context and content of the discussion. Notes often include topics to follow up on in future interactions.

terms for biological species, details about the proceedings of a village court case, or the meaning of symbols and behavior in rituals (Figure 3.4). Anthropologists might also conduct systematic surveys, such as a village census or a survey of attitudes about an event, using carefully structured interviews so that all informants are asked the same questions and their responses are thus comparable. In an **open-ended interview**, or unstructured interview, informants discuss a topic and in the process make connections with other issues. Open-ended questions usually encourage informants to discuss things the anthropologist wants to hear about, or that informants find especially meaningful.

The questions an anthropologist asks during an interview depend on the situation and the information he or she is seeking. Researchers often draw questions from theories and background literature, from an advisor or other colleague, or from simple curiosity. These questions change during fieldwork as we experience and confront new cultural realities. A solid education prepares us to ask insightful questions. As the expression goes, "Ninety-nine percent of a good answer is a good question." For example, anthropologists find that questions posed to elicit a "yes" or "no" answer are almost always unproductive. Our goal is, quite simply, to get people talking, not to get them to provide simple, short answers. The more they talk, the more people tell us about the cultural logic they use in their daily lives that they may not even be conscious of.

- **Open-ended interview.** Any conversation with an informant in which the researcher allows the informant to take the conversation to related topics that the informant rather than the researcher feels are important.

Figure 3.4   Interviews in the Field. Interviews take place in all kinds of settings, from the most formal and sterile, such as an office, to informal settings like this one, in which coauthor Luis Vivanco (left, holding plants) interviews an environmental activist in rural Costa Rica who is showing him an agricultural demonstration project.

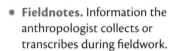

- **Fieldnotes.** Information the anthropologist collects or transcribes during fieldwork.

- **Headnotes.** The mental notes an anthropologist makes while in the field, which may or may not end up in formal fieldnotes or journals.

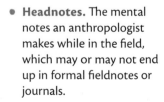

Scribbling: Taking Fieldnotes

Much of the time in the field is spent scribbling **fieldnotes**, which are written records of information that the anthropologist collects. Some of this scribbling happens in the ebb and flow of everyday life, as we jot down notes in conversation with others, or when a festival, ritual, or some other structured activity is taking place. Usually these scribbles are only shorthand notes made in small, unobtrusive notebooks and often referred to as "jot notes" that remind us of a conversation or observation we can document more fully later (Figure 3.5). Unlike your professors, most people are not comfortable when somebody opens a notebook and starts writing notes about what they are saying or doing. But with time and plenty of explanation about what we plan to do with the information, people become accustomed to it. Anthropologists have an ethical commitment to share our reasons for doing research with our informants openly, and explaining our goals often helps build rapport with informants.

Many anthropologists bring out a notebook only when they are conducting structured interviews and surveys. We also write down many details after the fact, or after we have had a chance to reflect more deeply on something. It is simply too difficult to capture everything taking place or being said in the moment. Every day—early in the morning, during the evening, or whenever we tear ourselves away from the flow of everyday life—we write up the details about what we did, who we spoke with, what struck us as odd or puzzling, and the context in which we saw or heard about certain things. A lot of us keep diaries in which we express personal frustrations, and keep what anthropologist Simon Ottenberg referred to as **headnotes**, which are the mental notes we make while in the field (Sanjek 1990:93–95), all of which can prove to be useful later.

Writing fieldnotes takes great discipline. It is also absolutely essential because, as one anthropologist has written, "If it's not written down, it didn't happen" (Sanjek 1990). Think about it. You are in the field for at least a year. Once you get back home, settle in, organize and analyze all your fieldnotes, think about what you want to write, think about it again, and then write it, *several years* may have passed.

These techniques—of becoming involved in people's lives, getting them to talk, and taking notes about it—enable anthropologists to pursue a major goal of fieldwork, which is to see the world from the point of view of the people who are the subjects of

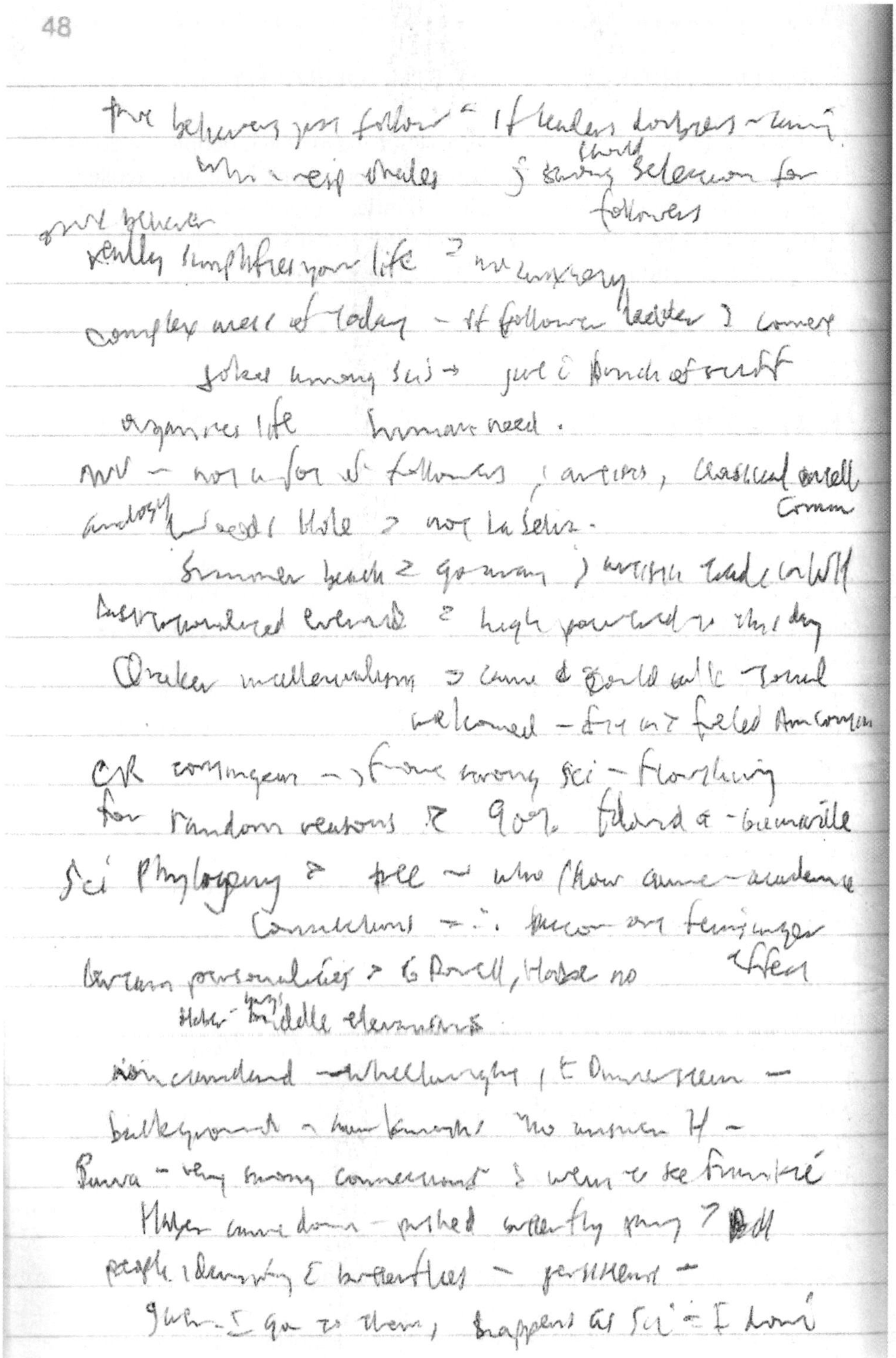

48

Figure 3.5 An Anthropologist's Fieldnotes. Pictured here is a page of fieldnotes from Luis Vivanco's fieldwork in Costa Rica during the 1990s and early 2000s. Every anthropologist develops their own particular way of taking notes.

research. Importantly, not every ethnographer will necessarily experience and record the same things, even in the same community. Fieldworkers have differences in backgrounds, personalities, social identities, theoretical inclinations, and perceptions that affect what they will observe, how people in a community will interact with them, and how they will interpret the data they collect. Every fieldwork project is, to a high degree, a very unique and individual experience. As such, some projects require researchers to use other methods to collect their data. What are these other methods? We explore this question in the next section.

What Other Methods Do Cultural Anthropologists Use?

- **Human Relations Area Files (HRAF).** A comparative anthropological database that allows easy reference to coded information about several hundred cultural traits for more than 350 societies. The HRAF facilitate statistical analysis of the relationship between the presence of one trait and the occurrence of other traits.

Although participant observation and unstructured, open-ended interviews are the core research methods for cultural anthropologists, some projects require additional strategies to understand social complexity and the native's point of view. Some of the most important of these methods include the ones we review here: the comparative method, the genealogical method, life histories, ethnohistory, rapid appraisals, action research, anthropology at a distance, and analysis of secondary materials.

Comparative Method

Since the beginning of the discipline, anthropologists have used the comparative method, which we defined in Chapter 1 as a research method that involves making a systematic comparison of aspects of two or more societies. The first American anthropologist, Lewis Henry Morgan, for example, sent letters to people all over the world, requesting lists of kinship terms in local languages. From these scattered reports, he conducted a comparative study of kinship terminologies around the world, which he published as *Systems of Consanguinity and Affinity of the Human Family* (1871). Early anthropologists also used comparative data to establish models of how they believed the cultures of modern Europe had evolved from so-called primitive societies.

The comparative method is still relevant in anthropology today. For example, anthropologists studying globalization use a version of the comparative method called "multi-sited ethnography," which involves conducting participant observation research in many different social settings. Another kind of comparative research strategy is exhibited by the **Human Relations Area Files (HRAF),** a database that collects and finely indexes ethnographic accounts of several hundred societies from all parts of the world. Each paragraph in the database has been subject-indexed for a wide variety of topics, such as type of kinship system or trading practices. This indexing allows researchers to conduct statistical analyses about whether particular traits appear to be randomly associated or whether they are regularly found together in human cultures (Figure 3.6).

Figure 3.6   Opening Page of HRAF's Website.

Genealogical Method

The **genealogical method** was developed by English anthropologist William H. R. Rivers in 1898 during the Cambridge Anthropological Expedition to the Torres Strait Islands, which lie between Australia and New Guinea (Figure 3.7). Rivers was studying visual perception among the Torres Strait Islanders and observed that the islanders had an unusually high incidence of mild colorblindness. To understand whether colorblindness was genetically passed only in certain families or was a more generalized trait, Rivers needed to discern the relationships between the islanders.

The task was at first confusing, because Torres Strait Islanders used terms that Rivers interpreted as "mother," "brother," and "grandfather" for a much wider variety of people than just the relatives Euro-Americans refer to with these terms. Rivers developed a simple but systematic way of classifying all kin according to their relationship to his informants. This was essentially a system of notation—for example, using "MBD" to refer to the mother's brother's daughter—that allowed him to classify how islanders were related. This methodology was widely used during the past century and became a key tool for understanding all sorts of relationships in nonindustrial societies, where political, economic, and

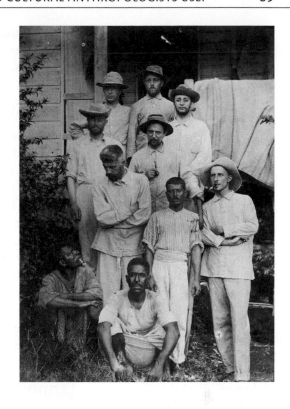

- **Genealogical method.** A systematic methodology for recording kinship relations and how kin terms are used in different societies.

Figure 3.7 Members of the Cambridge Anthropological Expedition to the Torres Strait Islands. (*Top*) W. H. R. Rivers (*standing left, wearing glasses*), A. C. Haddon (*standing in front of Rivers, looking down*), C. G. Seligman (*top right, with a pipe and glasses*), linguist Sidney Ray (*standing center, holding a pipe*), and Charles Wilkin (*standing front right*). Each studied different aspects of life on the Torres Strait Islands, but their conversations provided a holistic view of the culture. (*Bottom*) An anthropological record card used in the 1898 Cambridge expedition to the Torres Straits. Anthropological guides such as this asked for anthropometric measurements, general assessments about how a particular community did things, or what they believed.

social institutions are based on kin relationships. It is increasingly used in hospitals today to understand patients' genetic predisposition to certain diseases, such as breast and ovarian cancers.

Life Histories

- **Life history.** Any survey of an informant's life, including such topics as residence, occupation, marriage, family, and difficulties, usually collected to reveal patterns that cannot be observed today.

Understanding the **life histories** of informants has been an important tool for anthropologists in understanding past social institutions and how they have changed. During the 1920s, American anthropologists developed life histories as part of their fieldwork on Indian reservations, because the questions they were studying had to do with the American Indian societies before they had been profoundly transformed by contact with white American society. Anthropologists quickly recognized that by interviewing elders about their lives, they could get an understanding of how life was before contact.

Life histories reveal important aspects of social life, such as whether or not the society being studied has changed dramatically. As people develop, become adults, mature, and grow old, people take on different roles in society and in its social institutions. By recording the life histories of a number of individuals, the anthropologist can build an image of how a person's age influences his or her role in the community and how typical social roles unfold over a lifetime.

Ethnohistory

- **Ethnohistory.** The study of cultural change in societies and periods for which the community had no written histories or historical documents, usually relying heavily on oral history for data. "Ethnohistory" may also refer to a view of history from the cultural insider's point of view, which often differs from an outsider's view.

Ethnohistory combines historical and ethnographic approaches to understanding social and cultural change. The approach has been most important in studying non-literate communities, where few written historical documents exist, and those documents that do exist can be enhanced with archaeological data and ethnographic data such as life histories.

Ethnohistorians are also interested in how societies understand and recount the past. The concepts of history and how to tell it may differ from one society to another. Western history is linear, reflecting a view of time as marching through past and present straight toward the future. But Mayan societies, for example, view time as cyclical—which is to say, repeating itself during regular periodic cycles—so their notion of history is different from that in the Western world. And as societies have changed over the past century, museum collections have become another source of data about historic conditions.

Rapid Appraisals

While typical anthropological studies involve an extended stay of a year or two in the field community, some field projects—including many applied anthropological studies—do not have time for many months of fieldwork and require answers to focused research questions within a month or two. In such cases, what is an anthropologist to do?

- **Rapid appraisal.** Short-term, focused ethnographic research, typically lasting no more than a few weeks, about narrow research questions or problems.

The only solution is to use a focused research strategy known as a **rapid appraisal**, sometimes jocularly referred to as "parachute ethnography" because the researcher drops in for a few weeks to collect data. Such focused fieldwork requires a general knowledge of both the region and the topic under investigation. This kind of research requires that the anthropologist have considerable field experience to begin with, so she or he knows to focus on the features that distinguish the community under study from other, similar ones (Figure 3.8).

Action Research

One criticism of all social scientific research—not just ethnography—is that research often benefits the researcher more than it benefits the subjects of research. Even if the

Figure 3.8 Short-Term Ethnography. Some projects have no time for long-term field research. Applied anthropologist Anthony Oliver-Smith investigates the impact of an earthquake in Peru.

researcher publishes a study at the end, it may advance his or her career more than it improves the conditions of the people being studied. This problem is especially acute for disenfranchised communities, where the gap between a community's needs and a researcher's own personal interests may be greatest. Policy makers have even used reports about a marginalized or underserved community to justify their limited efforts to help the community.

In the 1950s, prominent American anthropologist Sol Tax began advocating action anthropology, or research committed to making social change (see Chapter 1). He encouraged anthropologists to offer voluntary help to disenfranchised communities in airing their grievances and solving their collective problems. Tax believed in the importance of inserting one's political values into anthropological research and of treating research subjects as equal partners (Bennett 1996). Today, some anthropologists use a variant of action research methods by promoting the involvement of community members in formulating the research questions, collecting data, and analyzing the data. Often called **participatory action research**, it is based on the idea that marginalized people can and should do much of their own investigation, analysis, and planning (Chambers 1997). This approach not only aims to place the researcher and subjects on a more even plane; it also encourages researchers to share their methods so people can act to improve their own social, economic, and political conditions.

Anthropology at a Distance

While "parachute anthropologists" may not have much time in a field setting, at other times, anthropologists have no way of getting into the field at all. In times of war or political repression, for example, an anthropologist may be unable to conduct fieldwork in a particular setting. As a result, the researcher may choose to conduct interviews with people who are from the community but who live elsewhere. Such studies can be thought of as anthropology at a distance.

One famous example is Ruth Benedict's research on Japanese society and culture during the Second World War, *Chrysanthemum and the Sword* (1946). Because the United States was at war with Japan, Benedict could not visit Japan, so she interviewed Japanese living in the United States and read widely in the published literature about that country and its customs. The result was a solid account of Japanese culture as it was in the 1890s, when most of her Japanese informants had left Japan for California.

- **Participatory action research.** A research method in which the research questions, data collection, and data analysis are defined through collaboration between the researcher and the subjects of research. A major goal is for the research subjects to develop the capacity to investigate and take action on their primary political, economic, or social problems.

Analysis of Secondary Materials

- **Secondary materials.**
Sources such as censuses, regional surveys, or historical reports that are compiled from data collected by someone other than the field researcher.

- **Primary materials.**
Original sources such as fieldnotes that are prepared by someone who is directly involved in the research project and has direct personal knowledge of the research subjects.

Anthropologists also use both published and unpublished materials to learn about other people's lives. For example, we can learn a great deal from media clippings, government reports, scientific studies, institutional memos and correspondence, and newsletters. These materials, called **secondary materials** because they are not **primary materials** (which are produced by the researcher him- or herself), provide yet another level of context for what we observe and learn in interviews. Like historians, though, anthropologists must read documents critically, paying attention to who wrote them, what their author's motivations (thus biases) might have been, and any other factors that may have influenced the writing and distribution of the document.

Many anthropologists make provisions to donate their fieldnotes to an archive, such as the National Anthropological Archives at the Smithsonian Institution, and these notes can become a form of secondary materials (Figure 3.9). Margaret Mead, for example, deposited most of her fieldnotes at the Library of Congress, where many younger anthropologists have pored over her notes from Samoa, New Guinea, Bali, traditional Omaha lands in the Midwestern United States, and other field sites (Figure 3.10). Some, however, feel that their fieldnotes could harm their informants and thus lodge those notes at an archive with the provision that they may not be consulted for 20 or 50 years. Still others say that once everything useful from their notes has been published, the notes should be destroyed to prevent harm to their informants or misunderstandings. But when fieldnotes exist, they nearly always contain data that can help us understand the culture of the people studied as well as the perspective of the anthropologist who created the notes.

For the most part, anthropologists developed the methods described here to help them study village settings in out-of-the-way places. These methods especially made sense when applied in non-Western communities, because they were effective at helping anthropologists gain critical insights into cultures radically different from their own. But as anthropologists have increasingly focused their research on communities in their own countries, they have been confronted by social groups whose cultures do not always differ so much from their own. Next we consider how anthropologists can study their own societies.

Figure 3.9   The National Anthropological Archives. Besides fieldnotes written by anthropologists, the National Anthropological Archives hold many things collected by anthropologists in the past. Here, anthropologist Jake Homiak (*right*) and Achu Kantule from the San Blas Kuna community of Panama (*left*) examine a map of the Kuna sacred landscape drawn around 1925 by Kantule's grandfather. It was collected by anthropologist John Peabody Harrington, who was a field ethnologist for the Smithsonian's Bureau of American Ethnology during the early 1900s.

Figure 3.10 Preservation of Ethnographic Data. Anthropologists Margaret Mead and Gregory Bateson, who were married at the time, typing up their fieldnotes in their quarters on the Sepik River of Papua New Guinea. Most of Mead's fieldnotes are at the Library of Congress.

Special Issues Facing Anthropologists Studying Their Own Societies

An important reason anthropologists can understand other cultures is that, when we go overseas or work with a community different from our own, the differences between our culture and theirs are immediately obvious. The effect of being a proverbial "fish out of water," struggling to make sense of seemingly senseless actions, heightens our sensitivities to the other society's culture. These sensitivities allow us to ask questions and eventually understand what seems obvious to members of the other community. What happens if we try to do this work within our own society?

When we understand the language and already have well-formed views about people's behavior and attitudes, being a "professional stranger" becomes more difficult. We are more likely to think we know what is going on and miss the local particularities that make people's actions sensible. A common technique to overcome these limitations is to study social conflicts, because when people are complaining or making allegations against others, their informal logic emerges quite clearly. For example, when anthropologist Laura Nader wanted to understand how American culture deals with relatively minor injustices—such as when a product breaks and consumers have a difficult time getting it fixed—she studied hundreds of consumer complaint letters received by her brother, the nationally prominent consumer rights activist Ralph Nader. In these letters, Laura Nader found people asserting their basic values about fairness and accountability.

It is important to remember as well that anthropology has always been an international discipline, conducted by people from many different countries outside of Europe and North America. In nonindustrialized countries where poor and/or indigenous populations are common, the goals of anthropology have often been closely aligned with national development needs, such as researching the health conditions of rural and poor people to improve government programs. Some anthropologists have also taken an activist stance such as fighting for minority rights, a theme we explore in "Anthropologist as Problem Solver: Alcida Rita Ramos and Indigenous Rights in Brazil."

It is important to recognize that indigenous people also practice anthropology themselves. As one Maya ethnolinguist has observed, indigenous peoples often conduct anthropological research as a way of speaking not just *about* their own societies, but *for* their own societies: "Our dominators, by means of anthropological discourse,

Anthropologist as Problem Solver
Alcida Rita Ramos and Indigenous Rights in Brazil

BRAZILIAN ANTHROPOLOGIST Alcida Rita Ramos (1990, 2000) has been championing the rights of indigenous Brazilian Indians for many years. She argues that anthropology in Brazil has a different "feel" from anthropology as practiced by Americans or Europeans. When American or European anthropologists study Amazonian tribes, they often overlook the harshness of the Indians' contact with mainstream Brazilian society, spending many more pages on the traditional cultural practices than on the cultural contact that destroys so many indigenous communities today. As a result, Ramos argues, American anthropologists tend to romanticize Indian culture. Brazilian anthropologists, in contrast, are deeply invested in writing about the intercultural strife that faces Amazonian tribes and are equally engaged in activist efforts to protect those tribes.

🌱 **The Yanomami of Brazil.** Yanomami Indians have suffered a great deal from the steady intrusion of more than 50,000 Brazilian peasants onto their traditional territory. The top photo shows Yanomami villagers; the bottom photo shows an example of land encroachment by Brazilian peasants.

In recent decades, anthropologists like Ramos have needed to get permission from the Brazilian government to conduct research among indigenous peoples in the Amazon. The 1970s, when Ramos began research there, was a period when the authoritarian Brazilian regime had lightened its restrictions on domestic and foreign anthropologists, allowing them to go into indigenous areas. The government even allowed anthropologists to help them create development programs for these areas. Many Brazilian and foreign researchers helped, suggesting the formation of a Yanomami Park that would shield the indigenous people from the onslaught of Brazilian developers who wanted to cut down portions of the rain forest and replace them with agricultural areas.

By the 1980s, the government had decided to support industrial interests and clamped down on anthropological research in the Amazon. Then, in 1987, gold was discovered in the Yanomami region, an area that straddles the Brazil–Venezuela border. Some 50,000 poor Brazilian prospectors and miners flocked to the area, disrupting the Yanomami economy, diet, and way of life. Prohibited from visiting the Yanomami, anthropologists could not see the effects of malnutrition caused by economic disruption. When images of the local tragedy were broadcast on TV, the situation became a national scandal, and the Brazilian government allowed anthropologists to assist.

Ramos was among those who insisted on getting involved. She gave numerous interviews to reporters, criticizing the government for its inaction and pleading that the Brazilian peasants be removed from Yanomami territory. In this way, the Yanomami became a symbol of exotic peoples in danger of extinction at the hands of the Brazilian government. Ramos helped raise awareness in the international community, which also exerted pressure on the Brazilian government. Ramos also offered herself as an expert witness in legislative inquiries and court cases. While she has not been able to reverse the depredation of Yanomami lands and resources, she has been one of the loudest voices advocating for the interests of the Yanomami on the national political stage. This approach to anthropological research and scholarship is highly valued at her university, and she believes her work as an activist anthropologist is no less important than her academic contributions.

Questions for Reflection

1. How might an activist anthropologist justify his or her approach to more theoretically minded anthropologists?

2. Given that she lacked government support for her views and had no direct power to control the situation among the Yanomami, what kinds of tools and strategies do you think Ramos might have used to influence conditions among the Yanomami?

3. If a researcher practices activist anthropology, should she or he maintain a teaching position at a university? Are the two roles compatible? How?

have reserved for themselves the almost exclusive right to speak for us. Only very recently have we begun to have access to this field of knowledge and to express our own world" (Alonso Camal 1997:320). For example, the Pan-Maya ethnic movement in Guatemala, which is led by linguists (like the one just mentioned) who have studied anthropological theory and methods, aims to assert a research agenda and methods derived from and relevant to Maya social interactions and worldviews. This anthropology is often in direct tension with that of other national and foreign anthropologists because one of its central goals is to support the political claims and self-determination of a particular indigenous group (Warren 1998).

Although issues like indigenous rights are highly political, for anthropologists, what often underlies their involvement is the feeling of an ethical commitment to a certain group or issue. In our last section, we explore in more detail the ethical issues facing ethnographers.

● ●

THINKING CRITICALLY ABOUT ETHNOGRAPHY

Because the methods associated with action anthropology involve explicitly political commitments, some critics view them as less "objective" than some of the other methods described in this chapter. How would you respond to such a claim?

● ●

What Unique Ethical Dilemmas Do Ethnographers Face?

When Philippe Bourgois decided to conduct research among crack dealers and users in East Harlem, he knowingly entered a situation in which he would witness illegal activities that could put him and his informants at great risk. One central ethical dilemma he confronted was ensuring that he did not betray the people who trusted him. His commitment to protecting their interests was tested every day, since the dealers and users he interviewed would be subject to arrest, prosecution, and prison if he uncovered their identities to authorities (Figure 3.11).

Unlike Bourgois, most anthropologists do not set out to study illegal activities, in part because of the risks both to themselves and to their informants. But all anthropologists, nevertheless, face certain common ethical dilemmas, no matter where they conduct

Figure 3.11   Philippe Bourgois in East Harlem.
Bourgois's research with crack dealers and users required great sensitivity to the interests of his informants, most of whom were engaged from time to time in illegal activities. But his presence in a predominantly Puerto Rican community led police to stop him frequently on the street because they assumed that the only reason a young white man would be in East Harlem would be to buy drugs.

their research. As we discussed in Chapter 1, these dilemmas arise in relation to anthropologists' commitment to do no harm, considerations about to whom anthropologists are responsible, and questions about who should control anthropology's findings. Here we explore how such issues play out in the specific context of ethnographic research.

Protecting Informant Identity

Social research can affect its subjects in powerful ways. For example, when living in a community, anthropologists often learn about matters that their informants would prefer to keep secret from other members of their community. Disclosure of these secrets may lead to social isolation of an informant, contention in the community, or even criminal investigation, as Bourgois knew all too well in East Harlem.

Disclosure of any kind of objectionable behavior or medical condition can cause difficulties or harm to informants and members of their family or community. For example, many communities around the world stigmatize HIV/AIDS, alcohol use, and certain sexual practices. In some settings, such as in countries with repressive governments, simply talking with a foreign researcher may harm an informant by casting doubt on his or her loyalty or patriotism.

In order to do no harm, anthropologists need to conceal the identities of everyone they have interviewed, and sometimes they must also conceal content. Typically we use pseudonyms for informants in published accounts, but we might also change details to further disguise an informant's identity. In her monograph on Samoa, for example, Margaret Mead (1928) changed details about characteristics of the adolescent girls she interviewed so nobody, even within the small community she studied, could identify the girls. She was especially concerned about informants who had admitted to having had premarital sex, which Mead knew some older Samoans would disapprove of.

The Limits of Anthropology's First Amendment Protections

In some respects, anthropological fieldwork resembles the work of journalists in that we interview people to learn what is happening in a community. But anthropologists differ from journalists in several important ways. First, anthropologists tend to stay in a community gathering field data for a long time, and most anthropological data come directly from participant observation and interviews with informants. In contrast, journalists often get their information secondhand and rarely stay on assignment for more than a few days or weeks.

Second, in the United States, anthropologists have no constitutional protections, such as those provided to reporters under the First Amendment, that allow them to conceal their informants or the sources of their data. This means that, while anthropologists are obligated to protect their informants, their fieldnotes, tape recordings, and photographs are nevertheless subject to a subpoena from a court should the police or some similar legal authority show cause that one should be issued.

Who Should Have Access to Fieldnotes?

Generally anthropologists work hard to protect their fieldnotes from scrutiny, mainly because those notes inevitably contain information that was given in confidence. When anthropologists publish excerpts, they do so in short passages that give the flavor of the field experience or of an interview. The purpose is not to reveal an informant's secrets. Most of us feel that our fieldnotes are too personal, private, and fragmentary for public dissemination, and if they are published on the Internet, they have nearly always been heavily edited.

In some communities, informants insist they should have access to and control of anthropological fieldnotes, since they helped create the data and should therefore benefit from it (Brown 2003). This situation can create a dilemma for the anthropologist.

On the one hand, many anthropologists share the sentiment that their research should benefit the community. On the other, they know that many communities are divided into factions, so raw data turned over to the community can benefit some and harm others. In situations where an anthropologist agrees to share fieldnotes, he or she negotiates with community members what will be shared.

Anthropology, Spying, and War

Anthropologists ask prying questions and seem to stick their noses into many aspects of people's lives, which has led many anthropologists to be accused of spying. Anthropological research does bear some similarities to the work of spies, since spying is often a kind of participant observation. When anthropologists conduct participant observation, however, we are ethically obligated to let our informants know from the outset that we are researchers. As researchers, our primary responsibility is to our informants, not government agencies or the military.

Yet many anthropologists have used their anthropological skills in service to their countries. For example, during World War II, a number of anthropologists assisted with the war effort. As mentioned earlier in this chapter, Ruth Benedict studied Japanese culture from interviews with Japanese people living in the United States. Sir Edmund Leach assisted the British government in Burma, and E. E. Evans-Pritchard used his knowledge of the Sudan to mobilize the war effort against Germany there (Geertz 1988). David Price (2002) has explored American anthropologist Gregory Bateson's wartime work with the OSS (Office of Strategic Services)—the predecessor to the Central Intelligence Agency (CIA). Bateson willingly used his anthropological insights about how to influence tribal peoples in order to ensure they sided with the Allies. In later years, Bateson came to view his wartime service with regret because he had inadvertently assisted in the ill treatment, manipulation, and disempowerment of native peoples.

More recently, controversy swirled around the use of anthropological researchers in the U.S. wars in Iraq and Afghanistan. After the terror attacks of September 11, 2001, some anthropologists like Murray Wax and Felix Moos (2004) asserted that every American anthropologist has a moral obligation to help fight terrorism. A handful of anthropologists agreed and joined a new U.S. military program called the Human Terrain System (2007–2014), which placed a non-combatant social scientist with combat units to aid officers in gathering information and working with local communities in Iraq and Afghanistan. This program was based on the reasonable assumptions that the U.S. military had little knowledge or experience in these foreign cultures, and that military success required the insights provided by cross-cultural research (McFate 2005). But the American Anthropological Association—with the strong support of the vast majority of its members—condemned this program and its use of anthropology, recognizing the dilemma that Bateson's experience suggests, that anthropologists may end up helping the state act against minority groups by providing cultural insights

CRITICAL THINKING ABOUT ETHNOGRAPHY

In addition to disguising the identity of specific informants, anthropologists often disguise the identity of a village or community to protect it from scrutiny by outsiders. But individuals and even whole communities sometimes object to anthropologists' efforts to maintain their anonymity. How do you think an anthropologist should respond to such a situation?

that can harm or disadvantage members of those groups. Many anthropologists also worried that the military use of anthropology in one place would undermine the trust local communities elsewhere place in anthropological researchers, compromising the trust and rapport all anthropologists strive to create with their informants.

Conclusion

Anthropologists have used the ethnographic methods of participant observation and open-ended interviews for about a century and have developed systematic ways to get holistic data that are accessible to few other social scientists. Such methods were tested and developed as research strategies in remote, non-Western communities. But for the past few decades, anthropologists have shown that the same methods are effective for studying modern American culture, even the culture of urban drug dealers.

Participant observation provides rich insights because it emphasizes a holistic perspective, direct experience, long-term participation in people's lives, and responsiveness to unexpected events. And, as Bourgois has shown, the insights that come from living in a community and participating in its daily life often yield unexpected and startling findings. For example, many other social scientists have studied the problem of drug use in urban minority neighborhoods. Few, however, have recognized, as Bourgois did, that although most drug dealers lack the benefits that many college students take for granted, many still pursue the American dream as active and energetic entrepreneurs.

Anthropologists use other methods besides participant observation and interviews, including the comparative method, the genealogical method, collecting life histories, ethnohistory, and rapid appraisal. Each of these research strategies is effective in tackling different research questions where participant observation may not be possible. And, as always, cultural anthropologists have an ethical responsibility to protect their informants from coming to any harm as a consequence of their research.

KEY TERMS

Emic perspective   p. 61

Etic perspective   p. 61

Ethnohistory   p. 70

Fieldnotes   p. 66

Fieldwork   p. 58

Genealogical method
    p. 69

Headnotes   p. 66

Human Relations Area Files
    (HRAF)   p. 68

Informant   p. 64

Intersubjectivity   p. 64

Interview   p. 64

Life history   p. 70

Open-ended interview
    p. 65

Participant observation
    p. 63

Participatory action
    research   p. 71

Primary materials   p. 72

Rapid appraisal   p. 70

Secondary materials
    p. 72

Reviewing the Chapter

Chapter Section	What We Know	To Be Resolved
What distinguishes ethnographic fieldwork from other types of social research?	Anthropology's most important advances emerged once anthropologists started to conduct fieldwork, living in the communities of the peoples they were studying for long periods of time. Fieldwork provides rich and nuanced insights about the cultural logic of social life and cultural practices because it offers the researcher a chance to see what people do, not just what they say.	Although nearly all anthropologists accept that immersive fieldwork is a reliable research method, scholars in other disciplines, particularly economics, political science, and psychology, do not accept it as reliable because it seems to them subjective.
How do anthropologists actually do ethnographic fieldwork?	Becoming involved in people's lives through participant observation, asking people questions through interviews, and then taking notes about it all are the ethnographer's most important research techniques.	No two ethnographers are likely to produce the same interpretation of any culture. Fieldworkers have distinct individual backgrounds that affect their interpretations as well as how others in a community might interact with them.
What other methods do cultural anthropologists use?	Anthropologists draw on the comparative method, the genealogical method, life histories, ethnohistory, rapid appraisals, action research, anthropology at a distance, and the analysis of secondary materials. The choice of method depends on the context, the research questions, and the particular socioeconomic conditions of the community under study.	Anthropologists still prioritize ethnographic fieldwork methods, and when anthropologists use other methods, they can sometimes struggle to define what is uniquely "anthropological" about their work.
What unique ethical dilemmas do ethnographers face?	In the past few decades, anthropologists have increasingly attempted to help their study communities by assisting with locally defined goals and by standing up for the rights of individuals in these communities. Generally, anthropologists recognize that their primary ethical obligation is to protect the interests of their informants.	While anthropologists increasingly take on dual roles as academic and applied anthropologists, many disagree about whether we can do both simultaneously. In addition, efforts to protect our informants are now well established, but questions still persist as to who owns ethnographic data.

Readings

There are many useful introductions to ethnographic methods, but Michael Agar's *The Professional Stranger: An Informal Introduction to Ethnography* (second edition, San Diego, CA: Academic Press, 1996) is a classic resource for the beginning student. There are also numerous historical analyses of the development of ethnographic methods, and among them George Stocking's edited volume *Observers Observed: Essays on Ethnographic Fieldwork* (Madison, WI: University of Wisconsin Press, 1983) is one of the most important.

....

For a resource for exploring the intellectual and theoretical issues involved in the practice of writing and analyzing fieldnotes, see *Fieldnotes: The Makings of Anthropology*, edited by Roger Sanjek (Ithaca, NY: Cornell University Press, 1990). A more practical guide to writing and analyzing fieldnotes is *Writing Ethnographic Fieldnotes*, by Robert Emerson, Rachel Fretz, and Linda Shaw (second edition, Chicago, IL: University of Chicago Press, 2011). If you are looking to get some concrete experience with ethnographic fieldwork methods, see co-author Luis Vivanco's book *Field Notes: A Guided Journal for Doing Anthropology* (New York: Oxford University Press, 2017).

....

To explore debates over anthropological involvement in the U.S. wars in Iraq and Afghanistan, begin with Montgomery McFate's 2005 article "The Military Utility of Understanding Adversary Culture" (*Joint Force Quarterly* 38:42–48). The author helped design and strongly supported the Human Terrain System program. Critical reactions against that program and the broader involvement of anthropologists in war are many, including David Price's 2011 book *Weaponizing Anthropology: Social Science in Service of the Militarized State* (Petrolis, CA: AK/CounterPunch Books), and Roberto González's 2009 *American Counterinsurgency: Human Science and the Human Terrain* (Chicago: Prickly Paradigm Press).

....

subordinate to her, or worse, like a child. He felt Linda was trying to limit his freedom as an adult and as a man.

Josh and Linda speak the same language, yet they were clearly talking past one another. In their case, the same words—"I'll have to check with Josh (or Linda)"—meant very different things to each person. What explains the miscommunication? While the expression "Women are from Venus and men are from Mars" overstates the situation, in American culture, men and women do live in somewhat different worlds. We have different expectations of each other, expectations that help shape how we use language. If Linda were more direct, people would consider her harsh, aggressive, and unladylike. Josh's directness, however, would typically be considered a sign of his strength, independence, and maturity, the supposed ideal for a man in American culture. Taking this a step further, we can see how American patterns of gender inequality are built into how we use language. In some settings—the workplace, say—Linda's concern for preserving good social relationships could appear as a sign of weakness, dependence, and uncertainty, limiting her ability to climb the corporate ladder.

This perspective on language leads us to ask a question at the heart of anthropology's interest in language: *How do the ways people talk reflect and create their cultural similarities, differences, and social positions?* Embedded within this larger question are the following problems, around which this chapter is organized:

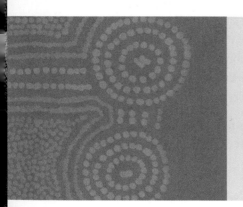

How do anthropologists study language?

Where does language come from?

How does language actually work?

Does language shape how we experience the world?

If language is always changing, why does it seem so stable?

How does language relate to power and social inequality?

Language is one of the most rule-bound and structured aspects of human culture. Yet, ironically, language is also one of the least conscious and most dynamic aspects of culture. Language helps us make sense of the world around us, and our use of language both marks and reinforces social hierarchies and gender differences within a society. Before we get into these kinds of subtleties, however, it is important to understand how anthropologists approach the study of language, as well as where language comes from in the first place.

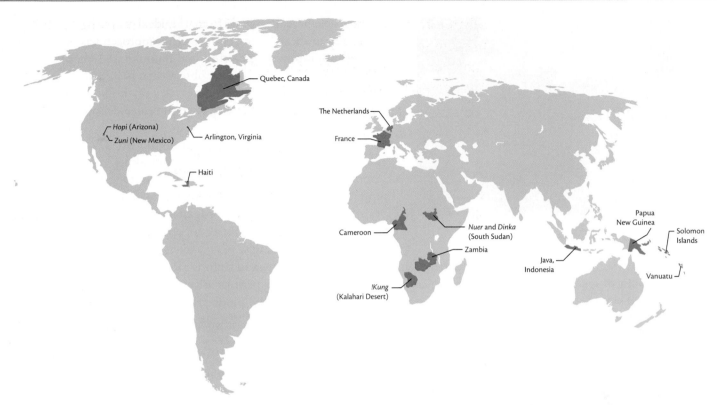

Figure 4.1 Select Peoples and Places Discussed in Chapter 4.

How Do Anthropologists Study Language?

Linguistic anthropologists, like cultural anthropologists, work directly with their informants or research subjects. Thus, much of their research involves fieldwork, building rapport with informants, and long periods of immersion in another culture. But the specific field strategy that a linguistic anthropologist adopts will depend on the kind of questions he or she is asking about the use of language in a particular culture.

In the early decades of the twentieth century, anthropologists saw language as central to understanding culture. Franz Boas (1911) and his team of researchers who were studying the tribes of the northwest coast of North America in the late 1890s published many texts transcribed in their original Indian languages along with English translations. They insisted that the categories and concepts encoded in Native American myths and stories were distinctive of local cultures. They pioneered a tradition—expanded by Boas's student Edward Sapir—that has come to be called **anthropological linguistics**, the branch of linguistics that later influenced the development of linguistic anthropology. In referring to this period, the American linguist and anthropologist Harry Hoijer (1961:110) suggested that anthropological linguistics "is devoted in the main . . . to the languages of people who have no writing" (see also Teeter 1964; Voegelin 1965). Anthropological linguists of this period conducted systematic analyses of languages; for example, examining how verbs are constructed and inflected, how words are formed, and the range of meaning for particular words. The methods they used generally followed those of descriptive linguistics (see below).

In the 1960s and 1970s, linguistic anthropologist Dell Hymes (1962, 1972, 1973) pioneered a new anthropological approach to language that distinguished the ways

• **Anthropological linguistics.** The study of language from an anthropological point of view.

Figure 4.2   Dennis Tedlock.

- **Ethnography of speaking.** The study of how people actually use spoken language in a particular cultural setting.

- **Ethnopoetics.** A method of recording narrative speech acts—including oral poetry, stories, and ritual use of language—as verses and stanzas in order to capture the format and other performative elements that might be lost in written prose.

that people actually speak from the ideal ways that people are supposed to speak in any culture. This approach has been called the **ethnography of speaking** (see Bauman and Sherzer 1974). This approach uses participant observation that focuses on listening to what people say, the register they say it in, the words they use, and what they are hoping to communicate—both intentionally and unintentionally.

Linguistic anthropologist Dennis Tedlock (1972, 1988, 1993) also focused on the ethnography of speaking. In his work, he emphasized the technical aspects of recording precisely what an informant or research subject utters, including the pauses, the mistakes, and the specific word choices. He looked at all speech acts as performances, and used an approach that has come to be known as **ethnopoetics**, which refers to a method of recording narrative speech acts in the form of verses and stanzas rather than as prose paragraphs in order to capture the format and other performative elements that might be lost in written prose. For example, Tedlock (1999) pioneered ways of recording Zuni stories and ritual texts as spoken by tribal elders. The hallmark of his groundbreaking work was his recording of not just the words being said, but also as many variables as he could, including silences, pauses, timbre, volume, and tone. For native speakers of the language, these variables would be perceived intuitively (Figure 4.2).

Over the last two decades or so, many linguistic anthropologists have sought to understand how people use language to mark and communicate social position in the community. These researchers are interested in how language is gendered, how language helps establish patterns of dominance and subordination, and how one person in a community can use a language cue to influence others. One applied example concerns how political advisors for national political parties sometimes use linguistic anthropological research, focus groups, and political polling of potential voters to determine which words and phrases are likely to have the greatest appeal for voters. Several years ago, the Republican pollster and linguistic researcher Frank Luntz (2007) introduced a new way for Republicans to talk about the estate tax, a tax on the wealth (the estate) of a person who dies. Republicans wanted to eliminate the estate tax, which affected only the wealthiest 2% or so of all Americans. To muster the support of the 98% of all voters who would not benefit from this change in tax law, Luntz suggested calling the tax not the "estate tax," a term that most Americans didn't understand, but rather the "death tax," a term that suggests the government is taxing the act of dying, something that 100% of the population will eventually experience. After making the change in terminology, opposition to the death tax soared. Luntz typically uses focus groups as a methodology for learning about how ordinary people in the community understand and perceive words, phrases, and concepts. As his research suggests, it is not the specifics of what a politician says that matter, but what people think they hear him or her saying.

THINKING CRITICALLY ABOUT LANGUAGE

Why do you think most people are unaware of how they actually use language? If you listen carefully to the patterns of speech of your friends or roommates, can you identify how they say commonplace things differently from one another? From your different professors?

Where Does Language Come From?

A **language** is a system of communication consisting of sounds, words, and grammar. This simple definition emphasizes three features: (a) Language consists of sounds organized into words according to some sort of grammar; (b) language is used to communicate; and (c) language is systematic. But where does language come from? We can begin to answer this question in two ways: one is evolutionary, having to do with our biological heritage; the other is historical, related to how languages have developed over time.

- **Language.** A system of communication consisting of sounds, words, and grammar.

Evolutionary Perspectives on Language

The simple fact that we are able to make sounds and put them into meaningful sequences suggests three different biological abilities that both link us to and separate us from nonhuman animals. First is the ability to make linguistic sounds using the mouth and larynx. Second is the ability to reproduce these sounds in an infinite variety of ways to produce an equally diverse range of thoughts. Third is the ability to generalize one set of sounds to a whole class of objects or behaviors, by being able to apply one string of sounds to a group of similar objects. To what extent do we share these capabilities with other animals?

There are clearly examples in which an animal appears to talk. Animal behaviorist Irene Pepperberg worked for several decades to train her famous African grey parrot Alex (1976–2007) to make simple sentences using symbolic concepts of shape, color, and number. Alex could pick out and identify a series of shapes and select the one with the right color. He could also count the number of objects when asked to do so. Alex's ability to use language was quite rudimentary compared to human speech, but it suggests that the critically important ability to use basic symbolic thinking was not exclusive to primates. The importance of this fact was recognized by the *New York Times*, which published an obituary for him (Carey 2007). But the question remains: Do animals really talk?

Call Systems and Gestures

Most animals cannot talk because they do not have a larynx. Yet most animals use sounds and movements of the body to communicate. Anthropological linguists refer to these sounds and movements as **call systems**, which are patterned forms of communication that express meaning. But why is this communication not language? There are four major reasons:

- **Call systems.** Patterned sounds, utterances, and movements of the body that express meaning.

1. *Animal call systems are limited in what and how much they can communicate.* Calls are restricted largely to emotions or bits of information about what is currently present in the environment. In contrast, language has few limitations on the kind or amount of information it can transmit.
2. *Call systems are stimuli-dependent, which means an animal can communicate only in response to a real-world stimulus.* In contrast, humans can talk about things that are not currently happening in the real world, including things and events in the past or future.
3. *Among animals, each call is distinct, and these calls are never combined to produce a call with a different meaning.* In contrast, the sounds in any language can be combined in limitless ways to produce new meaningful utterances.
4. *Animal call systems tend to be nearly the same within a species, with only minor differences between call systems used in widely separated regions.* In contrast, different members of our species speak between 5,000 and 6,000 different languages, each with its own complex patterns.

Figure 4.3   Koko with Penny Patterson.

Humans are evolutionarily distinct from other animals in that we developed not just the biological capacity to speak through a larynx, but the brain capacity to combine sounds to create infinite symbolic meanings. Both abilities form the basis of human language.

Teaching Apes to Use Sign Language

It is clear that some apes have the ability to communicate, beyond the limits of a call system, as researchers who have attempted to teach American Sign Language (ASL) to apes demonstrate. A well-known example is a chimp named Washoe, who grew up in captivity but heard no spoken language from her human caregivers, R. Allen Gardner and Beatrice Gardner. The Gardners instead used ASL whenever they were with her, and Washoe learned over 100 signs that had English equivalents. Even more striking, she was able to combine as many as five signs to form complete, if simple, sentences (Gardner, Gardner, and Van Cantfort 1989). Similarly, Penny Patterson (2003) worked with a female gorilla named Koko, who has learned to use more than 2,000 signs and can also combine them in short sentences (Figure 4.3).

Chimpanzees and gorillas clearly have the cognitive ability to associate signs with concepts and then to combine them in original ways, comparable in some respects to the linguistic ability of a toddler. Such capabilities are not surprising among our nearest relatives in the animal kingdom, given evolutionary patterns among apes that favored the development of cognitive and social complexity. At the same time, it is helpful to remember that our human evolutionary lineage split from those of gorillas and chimpanzees over 7 million years ago. It is almost certain that fully human language involving the possibility of creating more or less infinite combinations of signs and meanings emerged long after this split.

Several anthropologists have nevertheless challenged whether apes like Washoe and Koko actually demonstrate any innate linguistic ability (Wallman 1992). These critics argue that the two apes are extremely clever and have learned to respond to the very subtle cues of their trainers, in much the way that circus animals learn remarkable tricks and know when to perform them. But as linguistic anthropologist Jane Hill (1978) has noted, most of these critics have never worked with apes.

Whatever the case, studies of apes using sign language do suggest that our capacity for language may have begun to emerge with our ancestral apes. Most likely, from a rudimentary ability to associate meaning with signs and gestures, full-blown language evolved as human cognitive abilities became more complex.

Historical Linguistics: Studying Language Origins and Change

Historical linguistics focuses on how and where the languages people speak today emerged. This approach uses historical analysis of long-term language change. The approach began in the eighteenth century as **philology**, which is the comparative study of ancient texts and documents. Philologists like the German Jacob Grimm (1822), best known for his collections of fairy tales, observed that there were regular, patterned differences from one European language to another. To explain these patterns, he hypothesized that English, German, Latin, Greek, Slavic, and Sanskrit all came from a common ancestor. As speakers of languages became isolated from one another—perhaps because of migration and geographical isolation—the consonants in the original language shifted one way in Sanskrit, another way in Greek and Slavic languages, in a different direction in Germanic and English, and yet another way in

- **Philology.** Comparative study of ancient texts and documents.

- **Proto-language.** A hypothetical common ancestral language of two or more living languages.

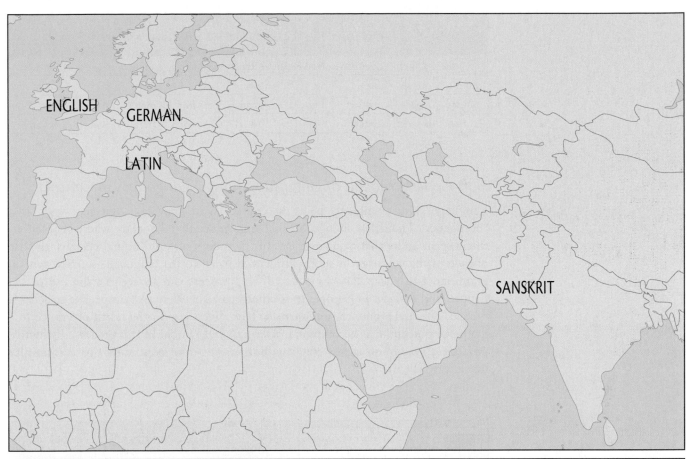

INDO-EUROPEAN INITIAL CONSONANT	ENGLISH	GERMAN	LATIN	SANSKRIT
*p	foot	Fuß	pes	pet
*p	father	Vater	pater	pita
*d	two	zwei	duo	dva
*d	tooth	zahn	dens	dan
*k	hundred	hundert	centum	satam
*k	heart	Herz	cor	
*k	hound	Hund	canis	sua

Latin and the Romance languages, all of which came to be known as Grimm's Law (Figure 4.4). The supposed common ancestor language, which became extinct after these divergences took place, is called a **proto-language**.

Genetic Models of Language Change

Contemporary historical linguists call Grimm's approach "genetic," since it explores how modern languages derived from an ancestral language. To identify languages that have a common ancestry, historical linguists identify **cognate words**, which are words in two or more languages that may sound somewhat different today but would have changed systematically from the same word (Table 4.1). As groups of speakers became isolated from one another for geographic, political, or cultural reasons, consonants, vowels, and pronunciation diverged and eventually resulted in new, mutually unintelligible languages. For example, German, Dutch, and English are descended from the same proto-Germanic language, but speakers of these three languages cannot usually understand each other unless they have studied the other language.

Figure 4.4   Grimm's Law.
Early Indo-European forms using *k* in Greek, Latin, and Irish shifted to *h* in the Germanic languages of English, German, Danish, and Norwegian. This figure offers examples of this shift (as well as the shift from *p* to *f* and from *d* to *t*) across Sanskrit, Latin, German, and finally English. Other examples of the shift from *k* to *h* include head and heart.

- **Cognate words.** Words in two languages that show the same systematic sound shifts as other words in the two languages, usually interpreted by linguists as evidence for a common linguistic ancestry.

TABLE 4.1		EXAMPLES OF COGNATE WORDS IN INDO-EUROPEAN LANGUAGES						
English	Dutch	German	Norwegian	Italian	Spanish	French	Greek	Sanskrit
three	drei	drei	tre	tre	tres	trois	tri	treis
mother	moeder	mutter	mor	madre	madre	mère	meter	matar
brother	broeder	bruder	bror	fra	hermano	frère	phrater	bhrator

Non-Genetic Models of Linguistic Change: Languages in Contact

Languages also change by being in contact with another language, which is a "non-genetic" model of change. Such change generally takes place where people routinely speak more than one language. In the speech of multilingual persons, the use of each of the languages is subtly influenced by the other language's sounds, syntax, grammar, and vocabulary. Evidence of this process can be seen in the use of the flapped and trilled *r* in Europe. In southern parts of Western Europe, the trilled *r* is typical, but this pronunciation seems to have given way in the north of France to a uvular or guttural *r*, as is common in German and Dutch. In this process, distinctive pronunciations move across language boundaries from community to community like a wave (Figure 4.5).

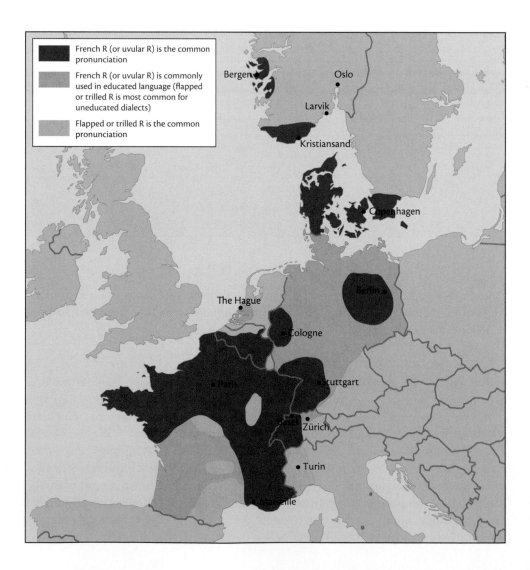

Figure 4.5   The Wave Theory of Language Change. Uvular, trilled, and flapped *r* in European languages. Note that pronunciation patterns sweep across language boundaries from French to German and even to Scandinavian languages.

Now that we have some understanding about the emergence of language, we can consider how language actually works.

THINKING CRITICALLY ABOUT LANGUAGE

How would you respond to a friend who claims that his or her dog understands English because it responds to English words in regular and predictable ways? What do examples like this tell us about language generally?

How Does Language Actually Work?

Over the past century, linguists and linguistic anthropologists have studied the majority of the world's languages and found that each is highly structured. Moreover, most people are largely unaware of the structure of their language until someone makes a mistake. Even then, they do not always know what is wrong, they just know the sentence sounded wrong.

To explain such reactions, the Swiss linguist Ferdinand de Saussure (1916, 1986) suggested a distinction between the structure, or formal rules, of a language (*langue*) and the way in which people actually speak a language (*parole*). Distinguishing between *langue* ("language") and *parole* ("speech") allows linguists to separate the rules and expected usage of language from what people actually say. The distinction is useful because it helps us realize that the rules we use to produce the sounds, word formation, and grammar as native speakers of a language can differ from how we actually speak, which is as much a social and cultural phenomenon as it is a function of language's structure. Here we explore how language is formally structured, which is the field of descriptive linguistics, and then the social contexts of language use, which is the field of sociolinguistics.

Descriptive Linguistics

The study of *langue*, or the formal structure of language, is called **descriptive linguistics**, which refers to the systematic analysis and description of a language's sound system and grammar. Linguists distinguish among three types of structure in language: (a) **phonology**, the structure of speech sounds; (b) **morphology**, how words are formed into meaningful units; and (c) **syntax**, how words are strung together to form sentences and more complex utterances, such as paragraphs. (High school grammar classes mostly focus on morphology and syntax.) All languages have predictable phonological, morphological, and syntactic structures. Next, we take a closer look at phonology and morphology.

Phonology: Sounds of Language

Linguists typically identify the distinct sounds of a language by marking systematic contrasts between pairs or groups of sounds. The majority of both these sounds and the contrasts appear in many of the world's languages, and yet each language has its own unique pattern of sounds. When linguists listen to natural language, such as when people talk un-self-consciously in ordinary conversations, they identify "minimal pairs," which are pairs of words that differ only in a single sound contrast.

- **Descriptive linguistics.** The systematic analysis and description of a language's sound system and grammar.

- **Phonology.** The systematic pattern of sounds in a language, also known as the language's sound system.

- **Morphology.** The structure of words and word formation in a language.

- **Syntax.** The pattern of word order used to form sentences and longer utterances in a language.

Consider, for example, the initial sounds in the English words *pan*, *ban*, and *man*. Three sounds, [p], [b], and [m], distinguish these three words, while the other sounds in these words are the same. Thus, [p], [b], and [m] are considered to be distinct sounds in English.

Linguists often group distinct sounds based on how they are formed. For example, the consonant sounds [b], [d], [g], [p], [t], and [k] are known as "stops" because they are all made by an occlusion, or stopping, of the airstream through the oral cavity or mouth. In addition, [b], [d], and [g] are distinguished from [p], [t], and [k] in that they are "voiced," or formed by the vibration of the vocal cords (glottis) at the Adam's apple. Similarly, the voiced consonants [m], [n], and [ng] are grouped together into the category of "nasals" because they are all formed by allowing the air to pass through the nasal cavity. An example of a consonant sound that does not occur in English is the click (one of which is denoted by the symbol !) sound used by Southern African peoples like the !Kung. While most speakers of any language are not fully aware of how they form the different sounds they use when speaking, linguists recognize that sound systems are surprisingly systematic.

Another interesting way to think about phonology is to consider **accents** and **dialects**, which are regional or social variations of a single language. Sometimes the variation occurs between generations or among people of different social classes. Part of the distinctive sound of these forms of speech results from differences in "intonation," the pattern of rising and falling pitch, but careful analysis of the sounds usually shows that accents and dialects also have systematic differences in their respective sound systems.

Up to the 1970s, linguists assumed that American English was becoming increasingly homogeneous. It seemed that, owing to schools or to national broadcasts on television and radio where the accent is standardized, regional dialects would disappear. In fact, variation in sound systems across America seems to be greater now than ever before. The sociolinguist William Labov (1990; Labov, Ash, and Boberg 2006) observed in the 1980s that language change in the sound system of American English was concentrated in the cities. He also noted that sound change was most pronounced between generations in the same communities. Such findings suggest a much stronger role for peer groups in the transmission of linguistic forms than linguists had previously noticed.

Morphology: Grammatical Categories

The elements of grammar—tense, word order, which genders are marked, and so on—are also structured. Just like cultural patterns, grammatical patterns learned during childhood feel extremely natural to native speakers in any language, even though the same forms and structures would seem quite unnatural to speakers of most other languages. A couple of examples—the first looking at tenses, the second at pronouns—will illustrate how varied even the most basic grammatical categories can be.

English-speakers tend to assume that there are only three natural tenses: past, present, and future. But not all languages use this same set of tenses, and some languages do not even require that tense be unambiguously marked in any particular sentence. For example, the Ningerum language of Papua New Guinea uses five tenses: present, future, today-past, yesterday-past, and a-long-time-ago-past. Events that happened earlier in the day receive a different tense marking from those that happened yesterday or the day before. Similarly, events that happened several weeks, months, or years ago take a different tense marking. In contrast, Indonesian has no regular tense marking in its verbs but uses adverbs or other time references to emphasize when something has happened or will happen.

American English has fewer pronouns than many other languages. We distinguish between singular and plural, among three persons (first, second, and third), and

- **Accent.** A regional or social variation in the way a language is pronounced (e.g., an Alabama accent).

- **Dialect.** A regional or social variety of a language in which the vocabulary, grammar, and pronunciation differ from those of the standard version of the language (e.g., African American vernacular English).

among three cases (subjective, objective, and possessive). If we consider only person and number, we have six basic pronouns, plus two extra pronouns for gender marking in the third-person singular (*he, she,* and *it*). This set of pronouns does not even begin to exhaust the possible pronoun distinctions that could be used. In French, for example, the second person singular pronoun ("you") takes two forms: *tu* (an informal, intimate form) and *vous* (a formal form). The Awin language of Papua New Guinea has singular, dual, and plural forms of its pronouns, meaning "you" (one person), "you two," and "you" (more than two).

Such basic examples illustrate some of the wide range of possibilities that arise in natural languages. Each configuration suggests certain distinctions that represent meaning encoded in the language's grammar. But such patterns do not alone create meaning.

Figure 4.6 One of the Most Common Signs in American Life. Even without words on it, we all know the meaning of this sign.

Sociolinguistics

Sociolinguistics is the study of how sociocultural context and norms shape language use and the effects of language use on society. Sociolinguists accept whatever form of language a community uses—which de Saussure referred to as *parole*—as the form of language they should study.

When one examines the actual speech (*parole*) used in any community, one often finds that different people may use the same grammar and sound system (*langue*), but the actual sentences they make (*parole*) often carry different assumptions and connotations. This is because meaning emerges from conversation and social interaction, not just from the formal underlying rules of language. We can see how sociocultural context shapes meaning by looking at signs, symbols, and metaphors.

- **Sociolinguistics.** The study of how sociocultural context and norms shape language use, and the effects of language use on society.

Signs

Signs are words or objects that stand for something else, usually as a kind of shorthand (Figures 4.6 and 4.7). They are the most basic way to convey meaning. A simple example is the ordinary traffic sign that tells motorists to stop at an intersection. The colors, shapes, and designs used in such signs are largely arbitrary; when highway signs were invented early in the twentieth century, engineers could have selected any shape or color for the stop sign. The choice was not totally arbitrary, however, because Americans feel red is more dramatic than yellow or blue, and it may well have been associated with fire departments before the automobile.

Symbols

Symbols, which we introduced in Chapter 2, are basically elaborations on signs. When a sign becomes a symbol, it usually takes on a much wider range of meanings than it may have had as a sign. For example, most colleges and universities in America have mascots and colors associated with their football teams. A mascot, such as a wildcat or panther, is a sign of the team, but mascots also readily become a symbol for the whole school, so that the wildcat represents all of the distinctive features of the institution and its people. But note that symbols work because signs themselves are productive, capable of being combined in innovative and meaningful ways.

Anthropologist Sherry Ortner (1971) distinguished three kinds of key symbols, or culturally powerful symbols. These are summarizing symbols, elaborating symbols, and key scenarios.

Figure 4.7 The Productive Use of Signs Around the World. The image of a red circle with a line crossing through it is recognized in many cultures as signifying "no." On this notice board in front of a business in Papua New Guinea, the "no" sign is placed over an image of a betel nut to communicate a ban on the sale and thus chewing of betel nut. When chewing betel nut, a common practice in Papua New Guinea, one needs to spit out bright red spittle frequently.

Figure 4.8 Making Use of a Summarizing Symbol. The Marine Corps War Memorial in Arlington, Virginia, pictured here is based on the famous photograph "Raising the Flag on Iwo Jima" by Joe Rosenthal. The image of Marines raising the flag has become a symbol of the American struggle for freedom.

Figure 4.9 An Elaborating Symbol to Make Sense of Social Relations. Dinka cattle have various kinds of markings and colors, which the Dinka use to make sense of social differences in their community.

Summarizing symbols sum up a variety of meanings and experiences and link them to a single symbol. An example is the American flag, which many Americans see as summarizing everything good about America, especially such things as "democracy, free enterprise, hard work, competition, progress, national superiority, freedom, etc." (Ortner 1971:1340; Figure 4.8).

Elaborating symbols explain and clarify complex relationships through a single symbol or set of symbols. Elaborating symbols work in exactly the opposite way from summarizing symbols, because they help us sort out complex feelings and relationships. For example, the cow is an elaborating symbol among the Nuer and Dinka peoples of South Sudan. For these herding groups, cows are used for bride wealth (see Chapter 12), and people spend an extraordinary amount of time thinking about their cows, their coloration, their body parts, and the like. The Nuer and Dinka think of the cow as resembling the body of society with its varied and interlinked parts. By talking about cows, they can talk about social relations within the community (Figure 4.9).

The key scenario differs from the other two kinds of symbols because it implies how people should act. A common American key scenario is the Horatio Alger myth. In Horatio Alger's many novels, this scenario often involves a young boy from a poor family who works hard to become rich and powerful. It does not matter that most of us will not become these things; the scenario has meaning for how we feel about and evaluate hard work and persistence.

Metaphors

Metaphors are implicit comparisons of words or things that emphasize the similarities between them, allowing people to make sense of complex social relations around them. For example, in our culture, we "metaphorize" ideas as food, as in "this textbook gives you *food* for thought, and some things to *chew* over, although you probably can't *stomach* everything we tell you here." Another example is how we metaphorize love as a disease, as in "he got over her, but she's got it bad for him, and it broke her heart" (Sheridan 2006:54).

Through signs, symbols, and metaphors, language thus reinforces cultural values that are already present in the community. Simultaneously cultural norms and values reinforce the symbols that give language its power to convey meaning. Such relationships between language and culture raise a very interesting and old question: Do speakers of different languages see the world differently, just as people from different cultures might? We turn to this issue in the next section.

THINKING CRITICALLY ABOUT LANGUAGE

How might paying attention to the metaphors and symbols we use in our daily language allow us to frame important issues in more or less appealing ways? Consider, as an example, the use of the term *downsizing* rather than *firing* in employment contexts.

Does Language Shape How We Experience the World?

Most Americans generally assume that the world is what it is, and our experience of it is shaped by whatever is actually happening around us. But as we saw in Chapter 2, our culture predisposes us to presume some features of the world, while other people's cultures lead them to assume something different. For many decades, anthropologists and linguists have been debating a similar point in relation to language: Does the language we speak shape the way that we perceive the physical world? According to the Sapir–Whorf hypothesis, which we examine next, it does.

The Sapir–Whorf Hypothesis

In the 1920s, linguistic anthropologist Edward Sapir (1929) urged cultural anthropologists to pay close attention to language during field research. Recognizing that most non-European languages organized tense, number, adjectives, color terms, and vocabulary in different ways from English, French, or German, he argued that a language inclines its speakers to think about the world in certain ways because of its specific grammatical categories. We explore this hypothesis further in "Classic Contributions: Edward Sapir on How Language Shapes Culture." It is anthropology's first expression of **linguistic relativity**, which is the idea that people speaking different languages perceive or interpret the world differently because of differences in their languages.

Sapir's student Benjamin Lee Whorf (1956) expanded on Sapir's work. Whorf had studied the language of the Hopi Indians and found that his knowledge of the grammars of European languages was of little help in understanding Hopi grammar. He concluded that people who speak different languages actually do—are not just "inclined to," as his teacher Sapir would have said—perceive and experience the world differently. By the 1950s, linguistic anthropologists saw the ideas of Sapir and Whorf as related and began referring to them as the "Sapir–Whorf hypothesis." Let us illustrate the hypothesis with one of Whorf's best examples, the lack of tenses in Hopi.

- **Linguistic relativity.** The idea that people speaking different languages perceive or interpret the world differently because of differences in their languages.

Hopi Notions of Time

Whorf studied Hopi language and concluded that it lacked tenses like those we have in English. Hopi uses a distinction not expressed grammatically in European languages, which he called "assertion categories." These include (1) statements that report some fact (e.g., "he is running" or "he ran"); (2) declaration of an expectation, whether current or past (e.g., "he is going to eat" or "he was going to run away"); and (3) statements of some general truth (e.g., "rain comes from the clouds" or "he drinks only iced tea"). These three assertion categories do not overlap and are mutually exclusive. When translating these Hopi concepts into English, most people will use our tenses (past, present, and future), partly because we have to express tense in English to make a sentence, and partly because this is the only convenient way to express these different types of assertions in English.

Whorf argued that the structure of the Hopi language suggested different ideas to Hopi than translations of that language would to English-speakers. He also linked these grammatical categories to Hopi "preparing" activities that surrounded certain rituals and ceremonies, arguing that "To the Hopi, for whom time is not

Classic Contributions
Edward Sapir on How Language Shapes Culture

THE LINGUISTIC ANTHROPOLOGIST Edward Sapir (1884–1939) was the only professionally trained linguist among the students of Franz Boas, a founder of American anthropology. Sapir believed that language "provided the ethnographer with a terminological key to native concepts, and it suggested to its speakers the configurations of readily expressible ideas" (Darnell and Irvine 2006). In this excerpt, we see Sapir's strongest statement about how language shapes the cultural expectations of the individual speaker:

❦ **Edward Sapir.**

It is an illusion to think that we can understand the significant outlines of a culture through sheer observation and without the guide of the linguistic symbolism which makes these outlines significant and intelligible to society. . . .

Language is a guide to "social reality." Though language is not ordinarily thought of as of essential interest to the students of social science, it powerfully conditions all our thinking about social problems and processes. Human beings do not live in the objective world alone, nor alone in the world of social activity as ordinarily understood, but are very much at the mercy of the particular language which has become the medium of expression for their society. It is quite an illusion to imagine that one adjusts to reality essentially without the use of language and that language is merely an incidental means of solving specific problems of communication or reflection. The fact of the matter is that the "real world" is to a large extent unconsciously built up on the language habits of the group. No two languages are ever sufficiently similar to be considered as representing the same social reality. The worlds in which different societies live are distinct worlds, not merely the same world with different labels attached. . . . We see and hear and otherwise experience very largely as we do because the language habits of our community predispose certain choices of interpretation. . . . From this standpoint we may think of language as the symbolic guide to culture. (Sapir 1929:209–210)

Questions for Reflection

1. Can you think of an example, either from your native language or from another language you know, in which language predisposes you to think in certain ways?

2. How does thinking of language as a "symbolic guide to culture" affect how you think about culture?

a motion but a 'getting later' of everything that has ever been done, unvarying repetition is not wasted but accumulated" (1956). Americans, in contrast, might see repetitive actions before a celebration as a sapping of effort or as inefficiency (Figure 4.10).

Since Whorf's death in 1941, several linguists have challenged his interpretation of Hopi grammar. Malotki (1983), for example, argues that Hopi does, in fact, have tenses that resemble English tenses. Malotki's claims have not gone unchallenged,

Figure 4.10 A Hopi Ceremony of Regeneration. Tendencies in language are reflected in and reinforced by social action, such as this ritual that emphasizes regeneration and the recycling nature of the world.

but if true, such a finding would call Whorf's example into question, although not necessarily his theory of the relationship between language and culture. Moreover, in the time between Whorf's and Malotki's research, Hopi have become more knowledgeable and conversant in English, suggesting that if the Hopi language now has tenses, these may be evidence of language change since the 1930s.

Ethnoscience and Color Terms

In the 1960s, anthropologists began to explore how different peoples classified the world around them, focusing on how people conceptually group species of plants and animals or other domains, such as planets or colors. The study of how people classify things in the world became known as **ethnoscience** (see Chapter 7). These studies began with a very different set of assumptions about the relationship between language and culture from those accepted by Sapir and Whorf. These scholars assumed that the natural world was a given, and that all human beings perceived it in the same way. Differences in classification were simply different ways of mapping categories onto empirical reality.

For example, anthropologists Brent Berlin and Paul Kay (1969) analyzed the color terms of more than 100 languages and found that basic color terms are consistent across languages. For example, if a language has only two basic color terms, they are terms for dark (black) and light (white). But if a language has three terms, they are black, white, and red. The third term is never green, blue, purple, or orange. An example of a language with three basic color terms is Lamnso, spoken in the Central African country of Cameroon (see Figure 4.11). If a fourth color is present, then the terms are black, white, red, and blue/green. Some anthropologists suspect that these patterns are universal and may have to do with the way our optic nerve responds to light of different wavelengths (Figure 4.11).

This universal pattern does not disprove the Sapir–Whorf hypothesis, but it does suggest there are limits on the extent to which language shapes our experience of

• **Ethnoscience.** The study of how people classify things in the world, usually by considering some range or set of meanings.

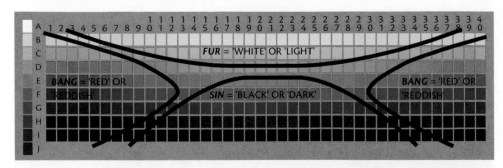

Figure 4.11   The Munsell Color Chart. The Cameroon language of Lamnso has three basic color terms that center on the colors called *sin*, *fur*, and *bang*, which we would gloss as *black* (or *dark*), *white* (or *light*), and *red* (or *reddish*), respectively. But as we can see from the plot of these three color terms on a standard Munsell color chart, our sense of black, white, and red is not at all typical of the range of colors included in each of these Lamnso terms.

the world. Indeed, other studies have shown that when informants with limited numbers of basic color terms are given paint chips displaying a wide range of colors, they can distinguish among the different colors, but they classify the chips into groups that correspond to their basic color categories. Thus, it seems that people who speak different languages do not actually see colors differently, they just classify them differently.

Is the Sapir–Whorf Hypothesis Correct?

By the late 1960s, ethnoscience had largely dismissed the Sapir–Whorf hypothesis as having no significance for understanding human cognition. The most powerful argument against the idea that our language shapes our thought is that we have no way of knowing for sure what cognitive processes are involved when we use language in different ways. All we have is the language, which is where we started in the first place, plus our own researcher's intuition (Pinker 1994).

Today, most anthropologists accept what has come to be called the "weak" or "non-deterministic" version of the linguistic relativity argument, which suggests (much as Sapir wrote) that the language habits of a community lead people to think about the world in certain ways and not others. Such a reading of the Sapir–Whorf hypothesis supports the idea that some ways of thinking are guided by the language we use, while others are not.

There are implications here for language change. Over the long term, such suggested ways of thinking would lead to a preference in each language for some kinds of linguistic change over others. If we take a rather static view of language, this issue might lead us to believe that languages are very stable, slow to change; and yet throughout this chapter we have suggested that language is dynamic. Let us now consider how language can constantly be changing, yet seem so stable.

• •

THINKING CRITICALLY ABOUT LANGUAGE

How might the coarse slang used in daily conversations by college and university students be interpreted differently by parents or grandparents?

• •

If Language Is Always Changing, Why Does It Seem So Stable?

A striking paradox in linguistics is that, like culture, language constantly changes, yet most people experience their own language as stable and unchanging. We tend to notice the changes only when we hear other people in our communities using words, pronunciations, or grammatical forms that differ from our own. Usually national policies come into play to enforce or support the use and stabilization of certain linguistic forms over others, leading to language change within a strong framework of stability.

Linguistic Change, Stability, and National Policy

The increase of commerce, communication, and migration around the world over the past few centuries has produced new environments for language change. Colonial powers such as Great Britain, France, and Spain learned about new plants, peoples, and ways of living in their far-flung colonies. In the Americas, these powers also introduced slave labor from Africa, resulting in the blending of diverse African cultures, which were also blending with diverse Native American cultures. These societies developed dynamic new languages, such as creole and pidgin languages, and implemented national language policies, in some cases to stabilize rapid linguistic change.

Creole and Pidgin Languages

In the Americas, local colonized societies developed hybrid languages that linguists call **creole languages**, languages of mixed origin that developed from a complex blending of two parent languages. A prominent example is the language commonly spoken in Haiti that combines several African languages with Spanish, Taíno (the language of Caribbean native peoples), English, and French.

In Asia and the Pacific, these hybrid forms have generally been called **pidgin languages**, which refers to a mixed language with a simplified grammar that people rarely use as a mother tongue, but to conduct business and trade. In the independent Melanesian countries of Vanuatu, the Solomon Islands, and Papua New Guinea, for example, local forms of Pidgin that combine various local languages and English have become national languages along with the colonial languages of English or French. In all three countries, the ability to speak Pidgin has a positive social status.

National Language Policies

Different countries have tried to control language change through the creation of national language policies. Short of making one particular regional dialect the national language, however, countries have found it nearly impossible to dictate what language or what form of the national language the public will speak. Three examples— taken from the Netherlands, France, and Quebec (Canada)—demonstrate different approaches to controlling processes of language change.

In the Netherlands during the twentieth century, Dutch linguists recognized that pronunciation and vocabulary had changed so much that spelling no longer reflected how people pronounced words. Dutch linguists recommended that spelling be changed to keep up with changing language use, and twice in the twentieth century, the ruling monarchs, Queen Wilhelmina and Queen Juliana, issued royal decrees changing the official spelling of Dutch words to parallel actual use. The Dutch approach is quite tolerant of changing language.

- **Creole language.** A language of mixed origin that has developed from a complex blending of two parent languages and exists as a mother tongue for some part of the population.

- **Pidgin language.** A mixed language with a simplified grammar, typically borrowing its vocabulary from one language but its grammar from another.

Figure 4.12   Mock Language and Exoticization. The American firm that produces LeSportsac uses mock French words to exoticize its products.

Figure 4.13   Defending Quebecois from Anglicization. In Quebec, store signs must display French, and any English they contain must not be more prominent than the French.

In contrast, the French spent much of the twentieth century trying to preserve traditional French words that were being replaced by English loans, such as *le hamburger*. The French parliament has passed several laws restricting English words from formal French documents, and prominent leaders have spoken out against the use of foreign words in proper French. But such laws have had little effect on the everyday speech of French people—especially the young, who readily borrow from English when discussing music, the arts, film, and anything trendy (Figure 4.12).

French Canadians in the Province of Quebec have been considerably more successful in preserving Quebecois (the form of French spoken in Quebec) against the pressure of English-speaking Canadians, who have historically considered English to be the superior language. Although government officials throughout Canada must be bilingual in English and French, the Province of Quebec conducts all government business primarily in French. To stem the tide of Anglicization (the creeping influence of English), the provincial parliament passed laws that require signs in public places to be in French. If English is also used, the English text cannot be longer or larger than their French translations (Figure 4.13). In this case, language use coupled with nationalist control of the provincial parliament has encouraged the use of French throughout the population of Quebec.

Language Stability Parallels Cultural Stability

As the situations of language use in France and Quebec demonstrate, the potential loss of a native language can be a critical issue for a group of people. In such cases, people view the use of a particular language not just as a means of communication but as integral to their cultural identities and worldviews. As a result, the preservation of language and culture are often seen to go hand in hand.

The connection between cultural stability and the ongoing use of language is an especially critical one for many indigenous peoples around the world, who are striving to protect their languages and distinctive ways of life in face of rapid social change. In many cases, the cultural disruptions created by rapid social changes such as colonization and globalization have undermined the use of native languages. As a result, many indigenous groups around the world are facing what scholars call "language death," referring to the dying out of many minority languages. Some linguists argue that nearly half of the world's 5,000 or 6,000 languages are in jeopardy of dying out within a century (Hale 1992).

In many cases, government actions have systematically set the stage for native language death by discouraging younger members of the community from using their indigenous language in favor of the national language. For example, in the United States, the Bureau of Indian Affairs sent many American Indians to schools where, until the 1970s, they were prohibited from using their native languages and were taught that their languages were inferior. The effect has been that many Indians stopped using their native tongues, and most indigenous North American languages are spoken by only small numbers of older people.

Many scholars believe that these dramatic losses will have considerable impact on the world's linguistic diversity, even as new languages are created all the time. And because of the close relationship between language and culture, the world's cultural diversity will suffer as well. As our discussion of the Sapir–Whorf hypothesis suggests,

Doing Fieldwork
Helping Communities Preserve Endangered Languages

WITH ABOUT 1,000 different languages—roughly one-sixth of all known languages—the island of New Guinea is one of the most linguistically diverse regions on earth. The vast majority of the island's distinct languages have very small numbers of speakers, often fewer than two or three hundred, which is not enough to protect these languages from extinction.

Linguistic anthropologist Lise Dobrin (2008) conducted fieldwork among the Mountain Arapesh in the Sepik region of Papua New Guinea, where a small community she calls Apakibur was attempting to preserve their language. In particular, community members were concerned because most of their youth were learning Tok Pisin, one of the country's four official languages, as their primary language. Dobrin notes that the language of daily life is no longer one of the Arapesh dialects, as it would have been in the 1930s when Margaret Mead conducted research in the same region. Today, the youngest speakers of Arapesh are in their 50s, while everyone speaks Tok Pisin.

Describing the Arapesh as an "importing culture," Margaret Mead (1934:159–160) had noted that villages in the Sepik region might change languages within a generation or two. Other researchers have observed the sort of language shift predicted by Mead across the region, including in some coastal Arapesh villages that were abandoning Arapesh in favor of one of the unrelated Austronesian languages (Welsch 2013).

Like many American anthropologists, Dobrin did not want to impose her own views about the value of the indigenous Arapesh language or whether it should be saved. She recognized that the language people spoke should be up to them, not an anthropologist on a year's field visit. She also recognized that for communities to maintain their endangered languages, they needed to feel empowered, but she found that the Arapesh-speakers she worked with, like most Papua New Guineans, felt their communities were the "last place" when viewed from the perspective of global wealth and power. How was it possible to feel empowered when all of the forces with either wealth or power who had so much gave so little to them and expected villagers to empower themselves? The symbolic message was that the Arapesh were unworthy.

Wanting to engage with foreign anthropologists, the Arapesh people of Apakibur asked Dobrin to participate in a program that they had established to save their language from extinction. They felt that their program was failing because it had received very little input from outsiders. Dobrin observed that by helping the community with their language program, she encouraged a sense of reciprocal exchange that required both her and the community to maintain efforts to keep the program going. She argues that, in Melanesia, outsider engagement in such programs is not a reimposition of colonial control, but a productive engagement built on an intercultural moral exchange that is present in all Melanesian exchange systems. By participating as an outsider, she was adding to the excitement and interest of the language program for Arapesh youth. Reflecting on her experiences, Dobrin encouraged all anthropologists and linguists to "embrace opportunities to participate in culturally appropriate relationships of exchange" as a way of addressing the growing problem of language extinctions (Dobrin 2008:317–318).

Questions for Reflection

1. Why would an anthropologist's involvement in a program to preserve an endangered language not be seen by Arapesh as a reimposition of colonialist control?

2. What significance should we give to the fact that people throughout much of Melanesia seek, rather than reject, involvement with the West?

3. Do fieldworking anthropologists and linguists have a responsibility to leave their study communities unchanged? Do they have an obligation to participate in the affairs of their host community?

Preserving an Endangered Language. Linguistic anthropologist Lise Dobrin works with language teacher Matthew Rahiria to transcribe a recording of the Arapesh language.

language is the primary medium through which people experience the richness of their culture, and loss of language suggests a genuine loss of a culture's fullness. In response to such concerns, many linguistic anthropologists have turned their attention to helping indigenous communities save their traditional languages; in "Doing Fieldwork: Helping Communities Preserve Endangered Languages," we examine an example from Papua New Guinea.

As we have seen in this section, issues of language stability and change are closely tied to questions of domination, control, and resistance, a theme we explore in more detail in our final section.

• •

THINKING CRITICALLY ABOUT LANGUAGE

What is it about our language that makes it feel so personal and so much a part of us? How is it that our language actually changes so seamlessly as we hear and adopt new words and expressions?

• •

How Does Language Relate to Power and Social Inequality?

Anthropological linguists established long ago that language use influences the cultural context and social relationships of its speakers. But in recent years, they have become especially attuned to issues of power and inequality in language use, specifically how language can become an instrument of control and domination. We explore these issues here by introducing the concept of language ideology.

Language Ideology

• **Language ideology.** Widespread assumptions that people make about the relative sophistication and status of particular dialects and languages.

The concept of **language ideology** refers to the ideologies people have about the superiority of one dialect or language and the inferiority of others. A language ideology links language use with identity, morality, and aesthetics. It shapes our image of who we are as individuals, as members of social groups, and as participants in social institutions (Woolard 1998). Like all ideologies, language ideologies are deeply felt beliefs that are considered truths. In turn, these truths are reflected in social relationships, as one group's unquestioned beliefs about the superiority of its language justifies the power of one group or class of people over others (Spitulnik 1998:154). In the accompanying "Thinking Like an Anthropologist" box, we explore how the use of mock Spanish by Anglo-Americans in the United States reflects and reinforces the impression of social inferiority of Latinos.

Gendered Language Styles

In our daily interactions, men and women often experience miscommunication, as Josh and Linda did in the vignette at the beginning of this chapter. Typically, each speaker feels that she or he has expressed things correctly and that the other speaker is at fault. When a man feels that his way of speaking is better and that a woman's is wrong, a language ideology about gendered use of language has come into play.

Thinking Like an Anthropologist
Exploring Relationships of Power and Status in Local American Dialects

ANTHROPOLOGISTS BEGIN THEIR research by asking questions. In this box, we want you to learn how to ask questions as an anthropological researcher. Part One describes a situation and follows up with questions we would ask. Part Two asks you to formulate your own questions based on a different situation.

PART ONE: MOCK SPANISH IN THE AMERICAN SOUTHWEST

Anthropological linguist Jane Hill (1993, 1998), who lives and teaches in Arizona, noticed that Anglo residents of southwestern states who were monolingual speakers of English incorporated a large number of Spanish words and phrases into their everyday speech. Hill notes that these borrowings are not just random uses of Spanish or Spanish-like words in English, but they are often used in jokes or in contexts intended to be humorous. Usually such utterances are grammatically incorrect both in English and in Spanish. Hill describes these utterances as "mock Spanish."

Speakers and hearers can only get jokes in mock Spanish if they already assume that Mexicans or Mexican Americans have traits that are viewed as negative in mainstream Anglo culture. Although Hill found that working-class whites used and understood some mock Spanish jokes, she feels that the most productive use of mock Spanish is found among middle- and upper-income, college-educated whites. Indeed, the domain of mock Spanish is to be found in the university seminar, in the boardroom, or the country club. For Hill, mock Spanish serves as a covert form of racism in which the jokes or utterances implicitly disparage Latinos, simultaneously identifying the speaker and hearers as

members of different social classes. To many listeners, these jokes may not seem overtly racist, and some easily dismiss them as merely providing evidence that the speaker has lived around Spanish-speaking people, or as harmless jokes.

Examples of mock Spanish include such words and phrases as "no problemo," "cojones" used as a euphemism for the vulgar English "balls," "mucho" used to mean "much," and "numero uno" and its mock Spanish variants like "numero ten-o," as well as more seeming benign words such as "amigo" and "comprende?" Hill suggests that it is the seemingly innocuous nature of these mock Spanish forms that creates a powerful racist distinction between the Anglo-speaker as superior and the Mexican American as inferior.

Hill's findings raise important questions for anthropological researchers, such as the following:

1. How does language use serve to create or at least reinforce social distinctions?
2. What is it about the use of mock Spanish that allows Anglo-Americans who are monolingual in English to feel superior to their Spanish-speaking neighbors?

PART TWO: LANGUAGE USE ON YOUR CAMPUS

On your campus, students and faculty most likely use colloquial words and phrases that your parents and surrounding community members would probably not understand. What kinds of questions could you pose about how this colloquial dialect draws boundaries between different groups of people, or how it enhances and builds on distinctions between social groups, social classes, ethnicities, and the like?

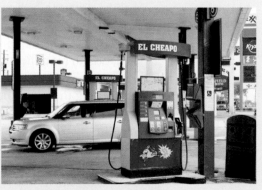

☙ **Mock Spanish.** In the example on the left, the mock Spanish term *Beerveza* is being used to advertise Miller Chill beer. On the right is another type of mock Spanish, in this case arrived at by Hispanicizing an English word ("cheap") that doesn't exist in Spanish. In these examples, mock Spanish marks Hispanic Americans, their culture, and their language as inferior.

Despite what your high school English teachers may have told you, there is no "proper" way to speak English or any other language. From the anthropological perspective of language ideology, there are only more and less privileged versions of language use. This is to say, language use either legitimates an individual or group as "normal" or even "upstanding" or defines that individual or group as socially inferior. Consider, for example, the findings of a classic study in sociolinguistics that explores how gendered expectations of how women speak English in our culture can reflect and reinforce the idea that women are inferior to men. In her research, Robin Lakoff (1975) described how "talking like a lady" involved the expectation that a woman's speech patterns should include such things as tag questions ("It's three o'clock, *isn't it?*"); intensifiers ("It's a *very* lovely hat!"); hedge ("I'm *pretty* sure"); or hesitation and the repetition of expressions, all of which can communicate uncertainty and were largely absent in expectations about men's speech. Lakoff argued that the social effects of speaking in this way can marginalize women's voices in contexts like a courtroom or a workplace, where speaking in a way that implies uncertainty—even if the speaker is not intentionally expressing uncertainty—can undermine a woman's testimony (as in a court of law) or trustworthiness (as in a workplace). Such situations, she suggested, are used to justify elevating men to positions of authority over women.

Lakoff herself recognized that some men may communicate in female-preferential ways, and not all women use the patterns just described, since language ideologies are not hard-and-fast for every speaker. Indeed, more recent research of email communications between men and women (Thomson, Murachver, and Green 2001) suggests that men and women can actually be quite flexible in their use of gendered language styles, changing these depending on whom they are talking to. As a result, men may use female-preferential language when interacting with a woman, and women may use more typically male language patterns when interacting with a man, further suggesting that language ideologies do not always exercise total control over how people speak.

Language and Social Status

As we saw with gendered language, language ideologies are closely tied to the creation of social differences. They are also closely tied to the creation and maintenance of social status. Let us see how this works in a particular society by considering language and social status among the Javanese, for whom language use reflects and reinforces a highly stratified and unequal society.

The people of the Indonesian island of Java are among the most status-conscious people on earth. In any social setting, one person has a higher social position, while the other has a lower status. Politeness—and through it, social position—is expressed in Javanese in nearly every sentence. Nearly every word takes on a different form in each of three different "registers" (varieties or levels of speech used by people of a certain social status or social class): *Ngoko* (informal speech), *Madya* (intermediary register), and *Karya* (polite speech). Throughout Java, every sentence marks the speaker's social status in relation to his or her listener, both by choice of vocabulary and by the pronoun used to refer to the listener. Most verbs and many nouns have at least three different forms representing the lower, intermediate, and polite registers. Younger people use the more polite words with their elders, and peasants or other low-status people use the more polite forms with nobles. But elders and nobles usually respond with informal word forms. In Java, the vocabulary used in any conversation differs for speaker and hearer.

As the linguist Robbins Burling (1971) noted, poorer and low-status people may know only the lowest and crudest register of Javanese, while higher-status people are conversant with a much wider range of registers. Using these registers, with their different choices of words, helps Javanese sort out a wide variety of social positions beneath theirs (see Table 4.2).

TABLE 4.2	THE THREE BASIC REGISTERS OF JAVANESE THAT MARK SOCIAL STATUS							
	Are	you	going	to eat	rice	and	cassava	now?
3 (high)	menap	sampéjan	bade	neḍa	sekul	kalijan	kaspé	samenika
2 (middle)	napa	sampéjan	adjeng	neḍa	sekul	lan	kaspé	saniki
1 (low)	apa	kowe	arep	mangan	sega	lan	kaspé	saiki

Note: All three registers are Javanese, but the vocabulary changes depending on a person's social class. Elites use the highest register with higher-ranking people. They use the second register with one another, and the lowest register with servants. Servants use the highest register with high-status people but the lowest register within their families. Unlike in English, there is no neutral register; a speaker must mark social position.
Source: Adapted from Burling (1971:82–87).

Language and the Legacy of Colonialism

In places like sub-Saharan Africa, nineteenth-century European colonial powers introduced their own language as the official language, in large part because they viewed indigenous languages as socially inferior to their European languages. When the countries of this region acquired independence, many of these languages became one of several national languages. As a way of building a national identity, many newly independent nations have had to decide which of their many vernaculars to select as their official language or languages. In Zambia, for example, which gained independence from Great Britain in 1964, the government recognized seven of the most important of its 73 local languages, plus English, as national languages, since nearly everyone in Zambia knows one or another of these languages. In theory, each is equal to the others, but in practice they are not, as listening to Zambian radio broadcasts reveals (Spitulnik 1998).

Although all eight of Zambia's official languages are given air time, English dominates the airwaves, both in the number of hours per week it is used and in having a more sophisticated and cosmopolitan content. Certain of the more widely spoken indigenous local languages also get more air time than minority languages. Over the past decades, broadcasters have presented to their ethnically diverse listening public what they feel are appropriate topics in each of the different languages, such as themes related to subsistence farming for certain language groups considered less sophisticated, and themes related to business and politics for others deemed linguistically superior. These broadcasting decisions have shaped how the public evaluates each indigenous language, presenting some as more sophisticated than others, but all as less sophisticated than English. In this case, broadcasts not only become models of language hierarchy in Zambia but also reinforce hierarchical views of different languages and the ethnicities associated with them.

Language and New Media Technologies

We can also see language ideologies at work in debates over changes in language use accompanying the proliferation of texting and communication through social media sites. Some older Americans have expressed dismay at the ways young Americans use their smartphones and other electronic devices to communicate with their friends. Text messaging on portable devices encourages a simplified spelling, so common phrases are often abbreviated, as in "Where R U?" (for "Where are you?"), "LOL" (for "laughing out loud"), and "OMG!" (for "Oh my God!"). Dozens of new abbreviations and new terms, as well as an ever-growing palette of "emoji," have entered the vocabulary of young Americans in recent years, a large percentage of which can be traced back to text messaging and online platforms such as Twitter, Snapchat, Instagram, and even Facebook. Technology has always influenced our language by introducing new terms, new abbreviations, new ideas, and new ways of doing things. As we discussed before, we should expect such changes because language is dynamic, always adjusting to the new conditions that people encounter. But do these modern devices change the way people actually speak, aside from adding new vocabulary and simplifying spelling? And, perhaps more significantly, do they degrade the language as so many older Americans fear?

At the heart of the concern over this new use of language is the idea that it makes its users seem "dumb" and incapable of using proper spelling. But while we may assume that new terms and spellings are the most important changes that new technology brings, the more significant changes are probably found in how texting and online communication change our grammar, particularly in the areas of morphology and syntax. For example, social media sites have introduced a number of new verbs derived from nouns and nouns derived from verbs. The noun *friend* is now commonly used as a verb, as in "I *friended* you on Facebook"; with the addition of the prefix *un-*, it has also been transformed into a verb with the opposite meaning, as in "If you don't like my posts, you can *unfriend* me." The noun *tweet* has taken on a new meaning ("a message posted on Twitter") and similarly been transformed into a verb, as in "I'm going to tweet to my followers." Yet these sorts of changes are not unprecedented; they arose from the same need that led to the use of *gift* as a verb—"My mother re-gifted that ugly bowl to Aunt Sally last Christmas."

Thanks to new media technologies, syntactic changes have also become more widespread in the American language. One common example is the overcorrection of *me* to *I*, as in constructions like "he gave it to John and I" or "they showed Sarah and I around the property." (In both cases, the objective form *me* is traditionally considered to be correct.) Undoubtedly, there are multiple causes contributing to such changes, including the shift away from formal teaching of grammar in schools, and the rise of 24-hour cable news programs that require hour upon hour of unscripted screen banter, which would never pass muster with editors in print media like the *New York Times* or the *Chicago Tribune*. Yet new media technologies have quickened the pace at which changes to the "rules" of grammar become more acceptable.

New media technologies have also introduced much broader changes in the tone of public discourse by allowing online users of many blogs, forums, and news services to post comments anonymously. Unlike Facebook, which makes it difficult for users to post anonymous comments, many sites, including Twitter, allow for anonymity. As a result, users of such sites often feel freer to "troll" other users who express views that they do not approve of. During the 2016 political campaigns, for example, Twitter became a key forum for political communication and led to unprecedented levels of uncivil discourse, anonymous personal attacks, and libel.

Of course, these examples illustrate that language is dynamic, constantly responding and adapting to changing circumstances, without our ever really noticing that it is changing. But it is important to always remember that efforts to declare any use of language to be "correct" or more desirable than any other use—such as when older Americans complain about the "improper" use of language among young people—is evidence of language ideology at work.

• •

THINKING CRITICALLY ABOUT LANGUAGE

Students often feel they will never be able to participate in the professional lives of their advisors because their advisors and other professors seem to speak a language that many students do not understand. Of course, they are speaking English, but they use many complex words that few students know. How does language in this situation become a tool of control and power over students?

• •

Conclusion

The capacity for language is one of the central features that distinguish humans from other animals. Whatever the particular language being spoken, human languages are universally structured and rule-bound, as descriptive linguistics demonstrates, and they change in fairly uniform ways, as historical linguistics tells us. But to end there—with the idea that language is something that all humans have access to and use in the same ways—misses the crucial facts that sociocultural contexts and norms shape language use and that the use of language has important impacts on everyday social relationships. To separate language from culture leads to an impoverished understanding of *both* language and culture.

This point, of course, is one that Sapir and Whorf made many decades ago when they advanced the idea that particular languages guide ways of thinking and acting. We can see a more updated illustration of the relationship between culture and language—and perhaps a more recognizable one to all of us—in the vignette that opens this chapter, in the different ways that Josh and Linda communicate with each other. Their particular miscommunication is not the result of a universal human situation in which women and men cannot understand each other, but the product of a particular culture that expects girls and women to speak in some ways, and boys and men in others. On its own, this insight is interesting and reveals something about how our culture socializes us to communicate in certain ways.

But we should not forget the social consequences of language use, especially when certain ways of talking and expression imply the correctness or superiority of one group, gender, or social class, and the incorrectness or inferiority of another. The broader point here is that language has great power to shape not just our meanings and comprehension of the world but our experiences as social beings as well.

KEY TERMS

Accent   p. 90

Anthropological linguistics   p. 83

Call system   p. 85

Cognate words   p. 87

Creole language   p. 97

Descriptive linguistics p. 89

Dialect   p. 90

Ethnography of speaking p. 84

Ethnopoetics   p. 84

Ethnoscience   p. 95

Language   p. 85

Language ideology   p. 100

Linguistic relativity   p. 93

Morphology   p. 89

Philology   p. 86

Phonology   p. 89

Pidgin language   p. 97

Proto-language   p. 86

Sociolinguistics   p. 91

Syntax   p. 89

Reviewing the Chapter

Chapter Section	What We Know	To Be Resolved
How Do Anthropologists Study Language?	Linguistic anthropologists generally use participant observation to study how people use language in their everyday lives.	Some linguistic anthropologists disagree on how much emphasis should be placed on the study of paralinguistic cues such as pauses, changes in pitch and volume, and gestures.
Where Does Language Come From?	Animals do not have language, but some primates have a rudimentary ability to use signs, which is a necessary but not sufficient condition for language to develop.	Although most linguistic anthropologists accept both genetic and non-genetic models, the relative importance of these models remains unclear, and we currently have no unified models that draw on both.
How Does Language Actually Work?	Language is systematic, but most descriptive linguistic models are static and do not express the dynamic nature of language.	By and large, linguistic anthropologists have not found historical models of language change to fully explain why particular sound systems or grammatical patterns have taken the forms they do.
Does Language Shape How We Experience the World?	Meaning is conveyed through symbols, but particular meanings have their roots in the social processes of daily life.	Although the structures of language vary widely in different languages, anthropologists and linguists have never reached a consensus about whether the structure of language actually shapes the ways we perceive the world.
If Language Is Always Changing, Why Does It Seem So Stable?	Languages are always changing in small ways as sound systems gradually change and as new words are borrowed from other languages or created anew.	Although anthropologists recognize that languages change as cultures change, there is no current consensus about how these changes emerge.
How Does Language Relate to Power and Social Inequality?	A language ideology links language use with identity, morality, and aesthetics. It helps us imagine the very notion of who we are as individuals, as members of social groups and categories, and as participants in social institutions.	Despite efforts of governments to control their populations by shaping language policies, creole and pidgin forms of languages are far more important than was thought to be the case half a century ago. Yet anthropologists do not have a full understanding of the precise conditions under which a creole or pidgin language can assert its own importance.

Readings

William A. Foley's book *Anthropological Linguistics: An Introduction* (Malden, MA: Blackwell, 1997) provides a general introduction to linguistics from an anthropological perspective. A more classical approach to the basics of language and its relation to culture was published by Edward Sapir in his 1921 book, *Language: An Introduction to the Study of Speech* (New York: Dover Publications, 2004).

Linguistic anthropologist George Lakoff has published several books dealing with the symbols and metaphors that provide meaning in the words and phrases we hear. One of his classic studies is *Metaphors We Live By* (Chicago, IL: University of Chicago Press, 1980), co-written by Mark Johnson.

....

A key survey of how governments create and promote nationalism through language policy can be found in Bambi B. Schieffelin, Kathryn A. Woolard, and Paul V. Kroskrity's book *Language Ideologies: Practice and Theory* (New York: Oxford University Press, 1998).

....

One of the best introductions to gendered speech can be found in Deborah Tannen's *Talking from 9 to 5: How Women's and Men's Conversational Styles Affect Who Gets Heard, Who Gets Credit, and What Gets Done at Work* (New York: W. Morrow, 1994).

....

Globalization and Culture

5

Understanding Global Interconnections

DURING EARLY SEPTEMBER OF 2015, media outlets around the world fixated on the tragic image of a young boy whose body had washed up on a Mediterranean beach in Turkey. The boy was a Syrian refugee named Alan Kurdi, who drowned when the overcrowded boat he and his family were on capsized as they left Turkey for a nearby Greek island. His family had hoped that in Greece they might be able to gain visas that would allow them to resettle with relatives living in Canada.

Although images and news stories of desperate refugees flooding into Europe had become increasingly common during the year—in 2015 alone, over 1.3 million people requested legal asylum in a European country—this particular image stood above the rest. It poignantly signaled that a full-blown humanitarian crisis was happening, the magnitude of which had not been seen in Europe since the Second World War. European political leaders were scrambling to handle the flow of refugees, provoking sharp tensions between themselves and harsh reactions from anti-immigrant voices within their own countries. But the young boy's death generated special anguish and shock. Donations to international organizations that support refugees surged, and half a world away in Canada, candidates in the ongoing campaign for prime minister were forced to discuss their country's role in coordinating an international response to the crisis.

 An Influx of Refugees   Syrian refugees, such as those pictured here crammed on a boat, have been making harrowing trips across the Mediterranean to escape civil war in their country. These trips have taken many lives and sparked intense debate throughout Europe about how many refugees should be allowed to stay.

Taking stock of the European refugee situation, the leader of the International Rescue Committee, David Miliband, observed that large-scale displacement of people is a persistent feature of the contemporary world. As he told reporters, "This is not a blip. The forces that are driving more and more people from their homes—weak states, big tumults within the Islamic world, a divided international system. . . . None of these things are likely to abate soon" (Kambas and Bronic 2016). The plight confronting Syria, a mostly Arab country in the Middle East, is an especially acute illustration of these problems. What began as an internal conflict in 2011 between the government and pro-democracy protestors has escalated into a multi-sided war involving armed groups backed by Turkey, Russia, France, the United States, various Persian Gulf states, Iran, and militant Islamist groups that draw their fighters from many countries. The current war is, in important respects, the latest manifestation of a century-long history in the Middle East in which armed conflict and foreign manipulation contribute to territorial disruption and the creation of refugees.

The Syrian war has led to the displacement of as many as 11 million people, half the country's pre-war population. Although Syrians are the largest group of new refugees arriving in Europe, the vast majority of displaced Syrians are internal refugees or have gone to neighboring countries, including Jordan and Turkey. In those two countries, Syrians have faced a complex mixture of belonging, exclusion, and containment (Merabet et al. 2016). Jordan has a long history of taking in refugees, often with the support of the United Nations. Since the beginning of the war, it has allowed Syrians with clan ties in Jordan to apply for legal asylum. Increasingly, however, it has sought to keep out Syrian Palestinians or push them into refugee camps, reflecting a history of fraught relations between the monarchy and Palestinians. Meanwhile in Turkey, which has taken in upward of 2 million Syrians as temporary "guests" (which prevents them from applying for legal asylum), Syrians have faced considerable anti-Arab prejudice and discrimination. Syrian Kurds such as Alan Kurdi's family, who have cultural and family ties to the Kurdish minority (which has long been denied cultural and linguistic rights in Turkey), have been singled out by political leaders for special vilification.

Most people around the world have little direct knowledge of or connection to the Syrian conflict and its refugees. But globally circulating images of this struggle and the people it has displaced have had powerful emotional, social, and even political effects in distant places. The cross-border flow of people in and out of Syria and the role of foreign interests in shaping and responding to the refugee crisis also confirm that this story is not simply a regional or local one, but one with complex globalized dimensions. These sorts of international connections influence more than just Middle Eastern wars and refugee crises, of course. Today, many aspects of people's lives everywhere are intertwined with globalization and cross-border interconnections.

Globalization raises compelling opportunities and dilemmas for anthropologists who have for so long studied culture as a local phenomenon. One question

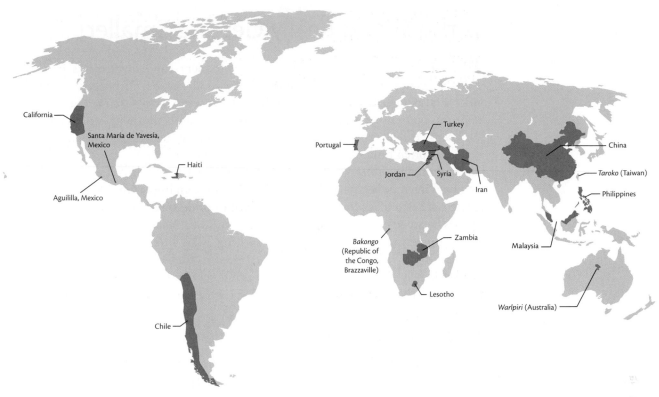

Figure 5.1   **Select Peoples and Places Discussed in Chapter 5.**

stands at the core of anthropological interest in globalization: *What do intensive global interconnections mean for understanding cultural processes in the contemporary world?* Embedded in this larger question are several problems, around which this chapter is organized:

Is the world really getting smaller?

What are the outcomes of global integration?

Doesn't everyone want to be developed?

If the world is not becoming homogenized, what is actually happening?

How can anthropologists study global interconnections?

We aim to deepen your understanding of culture as a dynamic process by showing its importance for understanding contemporary global processes. For anthropologists, globalization is not simply a matter of cultural homogenization. It is a process that illustrates how people create and change their cultures because of their connections with others. Not everybody participates equally in these diverse kinds of global connections, which means we also have to consider power relationships and social inequality.

Is the World Really Getting Smaller?

Asian hip-hop in London . . . American retirement fund investments in a South Korean steel conglomerate . . . Indian "Bollywood" movies in Nigeria . . . Mexican migrants cooking Thai food in a North Carolina restaurant—each of these situations confirms our sense that the world is getting smaller and cultural mixing is on the rise. This sense extends to anthropologists, who recognize that the people whose lives we study are often profoundly affected by global interconnections, migratory flows, and cultural mixing. During the past several decades, understanding how those processes of global interconnection affect culture has become an important issue for all anthropologists. For a discipline that has long tried to understand the differences and similarities between human groups and cultures, the idea that the world is getting smaller might suggest that the differences are melting away. But is the world really getting smaller? To answer this question, we first need to understand what globalization is. Unfortunately, defining globalization is, as one scholar has observed, like eating soup with a fork (Nederveen Pieterse 2004). Why is this so?

Defining Globalization

Defining globalization is a challenge for two reasons. First, different academic disciplines define globalization differently because they study different things. Economists focus on investment and the activity of markets, political scientists on international policies and interactions of nation-states, and sociologists on non-governmental organizations (NGOs) and other international social institutions. But there is a second problem. Is globalization a general *process* or a *trend* of growing worldwide interconnectedness? Is it a *system* of investment and trade? Is it the *explicit goal* of particular governments or international trade bodies that promote free trade? Or is it, as some say, "globaloney," something that does not actually exist at all (Veseth 2005)?

- **Globalization.** The widening scale of cross-cultural interactions caused by the rapid movement of money, people, goods, images, and ideas within nations and across national boundaries.

Anthropologists define **globalization** as the contemporary widening scale of cross-cultural interactions owing to the rapid movement of money, people, goods, images, and ideas within nations and across national boundaries (Kearney 1995; Inda and Rosaldo 2002). But we also recognize that social, economic, and political interconnection and mixing are nothing new for humanity. Archaeological and historical records show that humans have always moved around, establishing contacts with members of other groups; and that sharing or exchanging things, individuals, and ideas is deeply rooted in human evolutionary history.

- **Diffusionists.** Early twentieth-century Boasian anthropologists who held that cultural characteristics result from either internal historical dynamism or a spread (diffusion) of cultural attributes from other societies.

Early American anthropologists also recognized these facts. Franz Boas and his students Alfred Kroeber and Ralph Linton developed a theory of culture that emphasized the interconnectedness of societies. The Boasians thought of themselves as **diffusionists**, emphasizing that cultural characteristics result from either internal historical dynamism or a spread (diffusion) of cultural attributes from one society to another (Figure 5.2). Later, beginning in the 1950s, Marxist anthropologists like Eric Wolf argued against the isolation of societies, suggesting that non-Western societies could not be understood without reference to their place within a global capitalist system, which reaches across international boundaries with abandon. And yet, until the 1980s, such themes of interconnectedness rarely interested most cultural anthropologists.

Mainstream anthropology was locally focused, based on research in face-to-face village settings. But as encounters among societies have seemed to intensify, anthropologists have realized that paying attention only to local settings gives an incomplete understanding of people's lives. It also gives an incomplete understanding of the causes of cultural differences. As we will see, differences often emerge not in spite of, but *because of*, interconnections.

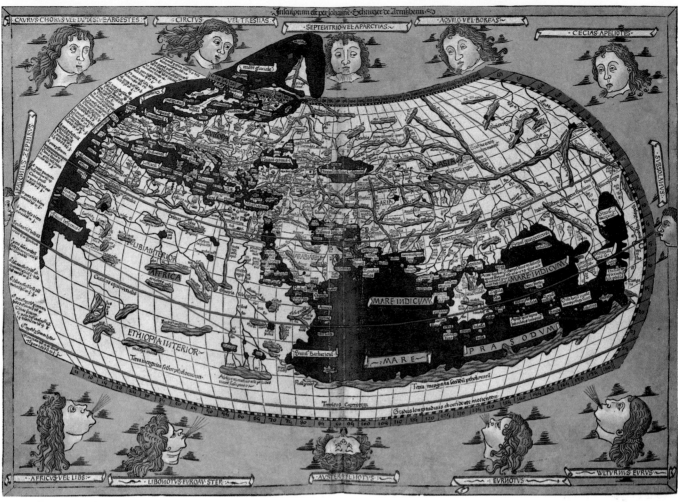

Figure 5.2 A Global Ecumene. The Greeks referred to an "ecumene" as the inhabited earth, as this map shows. Much later, anthropologist Alfred Kroeber (1876–1960) used the term to describe a region of persistent cultural interaction. The term became current again in the 1980s and 1990s as anthropologists adopted it to describe interactions across the whole globe.

- **Transnational.** Relationships that extend beyond nation-state boundaries but do not necessarily cover the whole world.

The World We Live In

How do anthropologists characterize the world in which we live today? Several factors stand out, including the scale of human interconnections and a growing awareness of these interconnections (Nederveen Pieterse 2004). But even if we acknowledge the intense interconnections, anthropologists know that these changes hardly mean everybody is participating equally in the same globalizing processes. Furthermore, the word "globalization," unfortunately, tends to make us think of the entire globe, exaggerating the scale and expanse of financial and social interconnections, which, while great, are typically more limited and often more subtle than the word implies. Indeed, some anthropologists prefer the term **transnational** to describe the circulation of goods and people instead of the word *global,* because *transnational* imagines relationships that extend beyond nations without assuming they cover the whole world (Basch, Schiller, and Blanc 1993). Whatever the case, it is useful to think of globalization as indicating persistent interactions across widening scales of social activity in areas such as communication, migration, and finances.

Communication

At the heart of globalization are rapid increases in the scale and amount of communication taking place. With smartphones, the Internet, and email accessible in most parts of the world, it is clear that the scale of contact has made a quantum leap forward

Figure 5.3   An Explosion in Mobile Phones. Seven billion people, or 95% of the world's population, now live in an area covered by a mobile network. This connectivity, which was unimaginable even a generation ago, has had important consequences for people everywhere, including these young Aboriginals of the Taroqo tribe in Taiwan.

- **Migrants.** People who leave their homes to live or work for a time in other regions or countries.

- **Immigrants.** People who enter a foreign country with no expectation of ever returning to their home country.

- **Refugees.** People who migrate because of political oppression or war, usually with legal permission to stay in a different country.

- **Exiles.** People who are expelled by the authorities of their home countries.

over the past generation. Such rapid and much more frequent communication means that people in very remote places can be in contact with people almost anywhere on the globe (Figure 5.3). Never before has this capability been possible.

But access to these innovations is generally distributed unevenly. In 2016, for example, more than half the world's population (53%) did not use the Internet. Africa was the least connected, with 75% of that continent's people offline. In contrast, only 21% of Europeans were offline (International Telecommunication Union 2016). As a result, some observers—to highlight real inequalities of access—prefer to talk about the globalization of communication in terms of wealth and poverty.

Migration

Another key feature of the changing scale of globalization is the mobility of people. Whether **migrants** (who leave their homes to live or work for a time in other regions or countries), or **immigrants** (who leave their countries with no expectation of ever returning), or **refugees** (who migrate because of political oppression or war, usually with legal permission to stay), or **exiles** (who are expelled by the authorities of their home countries) (Shorris 1992), people are on the move. According to the United Nations, the number of international migrants—people living in a country other than the one in which they were born—reached 244 million in 2015, which was a 41% increase from the year 2000 (United Nations 2016). Nearly two-thirds of those international migrants live in Asia or Europe, but the United States is the single country with the largest number of international migrants—47 million (Figure 5.4). These movements of people bring larger numbers of people in contact with one another, offering many possibilities for intercultural contact.

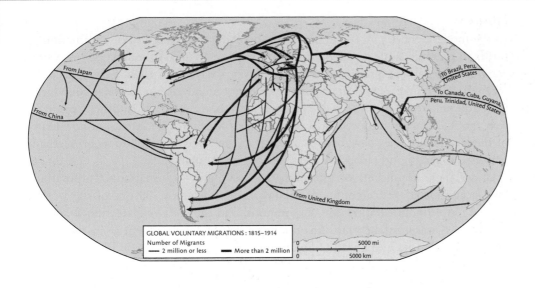

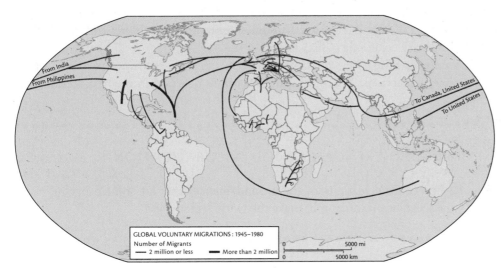

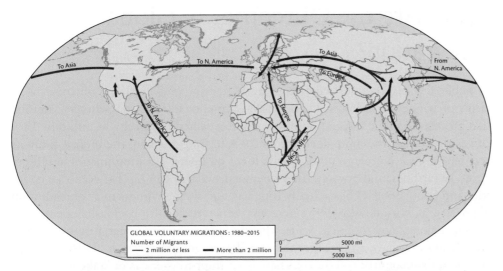

🌿 **Figure 5.4 Global Voluntary Migrations.** These three maps show dramatic differences in the directions of migratory flows. During the European colonial era, Europeans were motivated to migrate out of Europe because of opportunities in the colonies (*top map*). After the Second World War, decolonization saw a reversal in the flow, as non-Europeans and non-U.S. Americans began moving into Europe and the United States in search of new opportunities for themselves (*middle map*). Today, most migrants stay within the same major region of the world in which they are born (*bottom map*).

Finance

In the modern era, financial globalization involving the reduction or elimination of tariffs to promote trade across borders began in the 1870s. Although the two world wars disrupted those processes, the past 70 years have seen their reemergence. In recent decades, finance and the rapid movement of money across national boundaries have allowed corporations to move factories from one country to another. A generation ago, U.S. factories moved their operations to Mexico and China, but now many of these same factories have been shuttered and relocated to Honduras or Vietnam because of rising hourly labor costs in Mexico and China.

Under these conditions of globalized capital, many transnational corporations have accumulated vast amounts of capital assets. Currently, 69 out of the world's 100 largest economic entities are corporations, and the rest are countries. Walmart, the world's largest retailer, ranks as the tenth-largest economic entity in the world, just behind Canada and ahead of Spain (Global Justice Now 2016). Because powerful corporate interests often influence the policies of governments, some see in this situation a movement of power away from nation-states (Korten 1995). But this economic growth and trade are also highly uneven. "Thinking Like an Anthropologist: Understanding Global Integration Through Commodities" explores the complexities of contemporary economic globalization.

Such analyses raise a key question: Who benefits from and who pays the costs of global interconnections? We turn to this important question in the next section.

• •

THINKING CRITICALLY ABOUT GLOBALIZATION

Beyond communications, migration, and finance, what are some other culturally significant forces that make the world feel smaller?

• •

What Are the Outcomes of Global Integration?

In public debates, the most common way of framing globalization's outcomes is in terms of winners and losers. Globalization's promoters focus on winners, arguing that greater economic integration brings unprecedented prosperity to millions. They cite evidence that the more open a country is to foreign trade, the more rapidly its economy grows (Norberg 2006). Critics focus on losers, invoking images of refugee crises, sweatshops, and poverty. They offer evidence that the gap between rich countries and poor countries has actually widened, and we are witness to a "globalization of poverty" (Chossudovsky 1997). In recent years, a nationalist backlash has emerged, evident among some political leaders in the United States, Great Britain, France, and Russia who have argued that the real "losers" in globalization are the working classes in their countries whose jobs have been shipped overseas or "taken" by newer immigrants. In the face of such arguments, it is useful to remember that all sides are often discussing fairly narrow economic policy questions related to free trade, labor conditions, outsourcing of jobs, and so on. These are important issues, but they tend to ignore the cultural nuances of global interconnections, which include inequality, confrontation, domination, accommodation, and resistance.

Thinking Like an Anthropologist
Understanding Global Integration Through Commodities

ANTHROPOLOGISTS BEGIN THEIR research by asking questions. In this box, we want you to learn how to ask questions as an anthropological researcher. Part One describes a situation and follows up with questions we would ask. Part Two asks you to formulate your own questions based on a different situation.

PART ONE: THE T-SHIRT ON YOUR BACK

Concepts like the "global economy," "economic integration," even "globalization" are pretty abstract. Here, by considering the common t-shirt as a concrete example of economic globalization, we can show how your life is touched by seemingly remote and abstract economic, social, and political forces.

The things people want and need depend increasingly on the interactions of numerous institutions, individuals, states, and corporations, many of which are anonymous to consumers. To understand these diffuse interconnections, it is helpful to start with a concrete object that circulates through and between these actors. All objects have "biographies"; that is, particular life stories and trajectories. You can learn a lot about a social system—especially global integration—by following the trajectory of an object such as a t-shirt: who produced it, how it has changed hands, who has used it, and the uses to which it has been put (Kopytoff 1986).

Let us begin in the most obvious place, the tag on your shirt. Chances are pretty good it says "Made in . . ." followed by an exotic port of call: Bangladesh, Malawi, Malaysia, the Philippines, Mexico, or maybe China, which since 1993, has been the world's largest producer and exporter of clothing, about 30% of the world's share. Each year, Americans buy about one billion garments from China, four for every U.S. citizen (Rivoli 2005:70).

To tell the full story of your t-shirt, though, we have to get the whole picture, which includes understanding the commodity chain, or the linked elements—labor, capital, raw materials, etc.—that contribute to the manufacture of a commodity. Quite likely, your t-shirt originated in a cotton field around Lubbock, Texas. The United States has dominated cotton production markets for two hundred years, thanks largely to our ability to be highly productive while controlling labor costs. Before the Civil War, slavery kept these costs down; now, tractors and government subsidies do. Raw cotton is then shipped off, quite likely to China, to be made into thread and cloth, and then, if it does not stay in China to be manufactured into a t-shirt, off to somewhere else to be cut and sewn. The manufacturer then sells the t-shirts to a distributor, probably a U.S.-based business, and

Chinese Garment Factory. T-shirts are made in this garment factory.

maybe after changing hands once again for silk-screening, it goes to the retailer who sells it to you.

But let's keep going. After you wear it for a while, you might toss it in the trash, where it finds its way into a landfill. Or you might donate it to a used clothing charity bin like those in the parking lots of some grocery stores. The charities themselves rarely handle your clothing, but in turn sell it to companies like Ragtex or Savers that sort, bundle, and ship used clothing in 1,000-pound bales to sub-Saharan Africa (the largest market for used U.S. clothing), Eastern Europe, East Asia, or Latin America. A whole new series of wholesalers and small traders take over from there (Veseth 2005).

In these markets, people rarely think of these clothes as cast-offs or rags, as we do. For example, in Zambia, in southern Africa, where anthropologist Karen Tranberg Hansen (2000) has researched the local trade in used clothing, people call this clothing *salaula*, which means "opportunity," "choice," and "new chances." At the same time, the arrival of so many inexpensive t-shirts and other clothing to places like Zambia undermines the local clothing industry, which cannot compete with the low cost of these used items.

What questions does this situation raise for anthropological researchers?

1. Is the supply chain that created your t-shirt really "global"?
2. Why are t-shirt production facilities no longer in the United States, and why are these facilities in the places they are?

(continued)

Thinking Like an Anthropologist (continued)

3.   Who are the different actors who participate in the processes of manufacturing and using your t-shirt, both before and after you own it?

4.   What are the consequences for local people of this global trade in t-shirts?

PART TWO: CHILEAN TABLE GRAPES

In industrialized economies like the United States and Europe, food is also quite likely to come from far away. This is especially true of fruits and vegetables, which can be harvested in the Southern Hemisphere during the American winter when domestic fruits and vegetables are not available in the United States. Chile is a major exporter of fruits to the United States and Europe, because its summer harvests coincide with the winter off-season in the northern hemisphere. If you wanted to understand global economic integration through table grapes such as those produced in Chile, what questions would you ask as an anthropological researcher?

Colonialism and World Systems Theory

- **World systems theory.** The theory that capitalism has expanded on the basis of unequal exchange throughout the world, creating a global market and global division of labor, dividing the world between a dominant "core" and a dependent "periphery."

For several decades, **world systems theory** has provided the social sciences with an important theoretical lens for understanding global inequality. Developed by economic historians André Gunder Frank and Immanuel Wallerstein, world systems theory rejects the idea that global interconnections are anything new, identifying the late fifteenth century as the beginning of a new capitalist world order that connected different parts of the world in new ways. During this historical period, according to world systems theory, the expansion of overseas European colonies was enabled by and rooted in the creation of a global capitalist market. This market was based on unequal exchange between a "core" (the home countries) and a "periphery" (the rest of the world). The core (the winners) developed its economy by exploiting the periphery (the losers), whose role was to provide labor and raw materials for the core's consumption. European colonial institutions and authority secured capitalism's ability to extract labor and natural resources from the periphery. The result is the periphery's long-term poverty, under-development, and dependency on the core. Anthropologists have made a particular contribution to world systems studies by posing a question other social scientists had not: How has this world system affected the native peoples and cultural systems of the periphery?

In his influential book *Europe and the People Without History*, anthropologist Eric Wolf took on this question. Wolf argued that long-distance trade and cultural interaction were around long before the development of capitalism, but that the expansion of European colonialism and capitalism drew non-European people into a global market, in which, as producers of commodities, they were to serve the cause of capital accumulation as a subordinate working class (Wolf 1984:352–353). These processes disrupted, even destroyed, many societies (Bodley 1999).

But Wolf rejected the customary divisions we make between "West" and "non-West." He insisted that people in the periphery also have helped shape the world system, because they have not responded passively to capitalist expansion. In fact, they have often resisted it. These are the common people usually ignored by the victorious elites when they wrote their histories. Wolf argued that we need to pay close attention to the peripheral people's active role in world history. As we explore in "Classic Contributions: Eric Wolf, Culture, and the World System," Wolf's argument challenged not only popular stereotypes of indigenous people as isolated and passive, but also anthropology's bias toward the local; that is, the traditional ethnographic focus on villages and other small groups.

Because world systems theory focused on the rise of capitalism as a global system, this macro-level perspective did not readily lend itself to ethnographic research of smaller communities and non-global economics. But the theory helped anthropologists better explain the historical emergence and contemporary persistence of uneven development patterns around the world and has been of critical interest to scholars of **postcolonialism**, the field that studies the cultural legacies of colonialism and imperialism. It has also helped anthropologists understand the linkages between local social relations (families, kin networks, communities) and other levels of political-economic activity, like the regional, national, and transnational.

- **Postcolonialism.** The field that studies the cultural legacies of colonialism and imperialism.

Cultures of Migration

One of world systems theory's key assertions is that the same conditions that produced an unbalanced world order have also generated territorial displacement and population flows, especially to supply labor for capitalist needs. Social scientists, including sociologists, geographers, and economists, have tended to study global migratory flows in terms of the structural **push-pull factors** that shape an individual's decision to migrate. These factors could include poverty, violent conflicts, political uncertainties, and others that "push" individuals to migrate from their home countries, and factors like economic possibilities and social and political opportunities that "pull" them to host countries (Massey et al. 1993).

Anthropologists take such structural factors into account when studying migration. But detailed ethnographic studies of migrant-sending and migrant-receiving communities, as well as of migrants themselves, have revealed a greater level of complexity to these processes than a simple push-pull model allows (Brettell 2003). For example, when they migrate, individuals rarely act in social isolation. Their decision to migrate is often made by members of a household who consider its resources, the varying talents and abilities of its members, community traditions such as whether there is a history of migration, and the relative strength of opportunities in the destination (Kearney 1996; Cohen 2004). Not all individuals in a community have equal access to migration, either, because certain social groups—for example, relative economic elites, or members of a certain gender or ethnic group—sometimes have greater ability to be mobile than others.

- **Push-pull factors.** The social, economic, and political factors that "push" people to migrate from their homes and that "pull" them to host countries.

Moreover, migrants typically move within and between social networks, made up of kin and other social connections, that shape their choice of destination. These social networks help support new migrants, and they also sustain the flow of migrants; as Massey et al. (1993: 449) observe, "Each act of migration itself creates the social structure needed to sustain it. Every new migrant reduces the costs of subsequent migration for a set of friends and relatives, and some of these people are thereby induced to migration, which further expands the set of people with ties abroad." Reconnecting with those social networks is often a high priority for involuntary migrants, such as the Syrian refugees described at the outset of this chapter, especially since governments and bureaucracies that manage refugees often ignore the importance of these social ties in successful adaptation to a new place.

In some circumstances, social networks are so spatially extended that migrants participate in a **transnational community**. Roger Rouse (1991) documented this phenomenon while studying the effects of migration on the rural Mexican village

- **Transnational community.** A spatially extended social network that spans multiple countries.

Classic Contributions
Eric Wolf, Culture, and the World System

ERIC WOLF (1923–1999) studied issues of power, inequality, and politics in Latin America. He insisted that anthropologists and other social scientists needed to discover "a history that could account for the ways in which the social system of the modern world came into being" (1984:ix). He was interested in the origin and workings of peasant and tribal societies, but always in relation to the powerful governmental and business interests that so often kept peasants poor. In this selection, Wolf presents why anthropologists should view most societies over the past 500 years as societies linked to other societies, often with tragic consequences for some of the people involved.

Eric Wolf.

While some anthropologists thus narrow their focus to the ever more intensive study of the single case, others hope to turn anthropology into a science by embarking on the statistical cross-cultural comparisons . . . drawn from large samples of ethnographically known cases. . . .

What, however, if we take cognizance of processes that transcend separable cases, moving through and beyond them and transforming them as they proceed? Such processes were, for example, the North American fur trade and the trade in native American and African slaves. What of the localized Algonkin-speaking patrilineages, for example, which in the course of the fur trade moved into large nonkin villages and became known as the ethnographic Ojibwa? What of the Chipeweyans, some of whose bands gave up hunting to become fur trappers, or "carriers," while others

continued to hunt for game as "caribou eaters," with people continuously changing from caribou eating to carrying and back? . . . What, moreover, of Africa, where the slave trade created an unlimited demand for slaves, and where quite unrelated populations met that demand by severing people from their kin groups through warfare, kidnapping, pawning, or judicial procedures, in order to have slaves to sell to the Europeans? In all such cases, to attempt to specify separate cultural wholes and distinct boundaries would create a false sample. These cases exemplify spatially and temporally shifting relationships, prompted in all instances by the effects of European expansion. If we consider, furthermore, that this expansion has for nearly 500 years affected case after case, then the search for a world sample of distinct cases is illusory. (Wolf 1984:17–18)

Questions for Reflection

1. What happened about five hundred years ago that changed the relations between societies from what they had been?

2. Why does Wolf feel that most societies have been in touch with Europeans and others outside of their society for the past five hundred years?

3. How would you explain to your younger brother or sister why Wolf feels anthropologists should not view societies as bounded and unconnected to other societies?

Figure 5.5 Migration and Social Status. The Zapotec village of Santa María de Yavesía, in the southern Mexican state of Oaxaca, has experienced migration to the United States and other parts of Mexico for decades. One way migrants demonstrate their success and show new social status is by building nice new homes and having them painted in bright colors.

of Aguililla [ah-gee-**lee**-uh]. As a result of out-migration, Aguilillans were scattered across multiple outposts and settlements in urban Mexico and the United States. Nevertheless, community members still felt that they were members of a single social unit, and they maintained close social, kin, and economic ties through regular phone contact and movement of individuals between settlements, and by ensuring that important decisions were made collectively. Rouse found that what bound Aguilillans together, even across national boundaries, was not a nostalgic tie to their home village, but a close connection to the migratory circuit itself (Figure 5.5).

Cultural attitudes, perceptions, and symbolic values also shape migration, creating what anthropologists call a **culture of migration**. Through migration, people generate new meanings about the world, their home, and themselves. In many places where migration is prevalent, it is viewed as an important—even necessary—rite of passage into adulthood, a means to elevate or maintain social status, and an experience in which new social identities are formed (Nagengast and Kearney 1990). For example, in her fieldwork among Portuguese migrants in Portugal, Brazil, France, and North America, Caroline Brettell (2003) found that the concept of "the emigrant" holds a powerful symbolic meaning in people's ideas about what it means to be Portuguese. It shapes and reinforces Portuguese people's national constructions of themselves as tolerant and worldly people who have been proactive in shaping the conditions of the modern world, and it forms the basis of a strong ethnic identity in countries where Portuguese people have settled.

- **Culture of migration.** The cultural attitudes, perceptions, and symbolic values that shape decision-making processes around, and experiences of, migration.

Resistance at the Periphery

The expansion of the capitalist world system generated greater cross-border movement, but it also met with resistance from the peripheral peoples affected. Anthropologists have devoted considerable attention to this resistance, finding examples that range from open rebellion and mass mobilizations to more subtle forms of protest and opposition.

Many forms of resistance may not be obvious to us, because they are rooted in culturally subtle forms of expression. For example, in one factory in Malaysia studied by anthropologist Aihwa Ong (1988), spirit-possession episodes have erupted, disrupting work and production goals. According to the factory women of Malaysia, the facility violated two basic moral boundaries: close physical proximity of the sexes, and male managers' constant monitoring of female workers. Young female workers, who as Muslims are expected to be shy and deferential, believe these two factors force them to violate cultural taboos that define social and bodily boundaries between men and women. They also believe that the construction of modern factories displaces and angers local spirits, who then haunt the toilets. For the women, these transgressions combine to provoke spirit possession, in which the women become violent and loud, disrupting work in the factory. Spirit possession episodes help the women regain a sense of control over both their bodies and social relations in the factory (Ong 1988:34). Such resistance interests anthropologists because it shows how people interpret and challenge global processes through local cultural idioms and beliefs.

Globalization *and* Localization

- **Localization.** The creation and assertion of highly particular, place-based identities and communities.

Perhaps greater global integration also creates opportunities for local cultures to express themselves more vividly. This is a phenomenon that some anthropologists call **localization**, and it is the flip side, or a side effect, of globalization. Localization is the creation and assertion of highly particular, place-based identities and communities (Friedman 1994). It is evidenced by the rise of autonomy movements among Hawaiian separatists and other indigenous groups throughout the world that seek self-determination; nationalist and ethnic movements like that of the Basques in Europe; and other movements engaged in reinforcing local control; for example, by encouraging community-supported agriculture and the use of local currencies (Friedman 1994). Each of these movements seeks to revive and protect local identities and places in the face of greater economic and cultural integration within a nation or a transnational network.

Other evidence of localization lies in people's patterns of consumption, which is a common way people express their local identities and ways of being. In our own society, people choose certain clothing and shoe brands because they believe it says something about them as individuals: their social status, lifestyle, and outlook on the world, in particular (see Chapter 8). People in other countries do this, too, but because of local culture and history, patterns of consumption can communicate very different things.

For example, among the Bakongo in the Republic of the Congo, a former French colony in Central Africa, poor Bakongo youths in urban shanty towns of the capital city, Brazzaville, compete with each other to acquire famous French and Italian designer clothes (Figure 5.6). Calling themselves *sapeurs* (loosely translated as "dandies"), the most ambitious and resourceful go to Europe, where they acquire fancy clothes by whatever means they can. By becoming hyper-consumers, *sapeurs* are not merely imitating prosperous Europeans. Europeans may believe that "clothes make the man," but Congolese believe that clothes reflect the degree of "life force" possessed by the wearer (Friedman 1994:106). The *sapeur*'s goal is not to live a European lifestyle; his goal is to accumulate prestige by linking himself to external forces of wealth, health, and political power. In highly ranked Congolese society, the poor Bakongo urbanite ranks lowest. By connecting to upscale European fashion trends, the *sapeur* represents an assault on the higher orders of Congolese society who normally dismiss him as a barbarian.

Whether Malay factory women, Congolese *sapeurs*, or for that matter, ourselves, people continue to define their identities locally. What is different today from previous generations, perhaps, is that people increasingly express their local identities through their interaction with transnational processes, such as communications, migration, or consumerism, and with institutions, such as transnational businesses. In today's world, people participate in global processes *and* local communities simultaneously. But they rarely participate in global processes on equal footing, because of their

 Figure 5.6   Bakongo *Sapeur*. The *sapeur's* engagement in both transnational fashion worlds and local processes of social stratification destabilizes any strong local–global dichotomy.

subordinate place in the world system or in their own countries. Nevertheless, many anthropologists feel that to identify them in stark terms as *either* winners *or* losers of global integration greatly simplifies the complexity of their simultaneous involvement in globalization and localization processes.

As these examples show, people can be accommodating to outside influences, even while maintaining culturally specific meanings and social relations, whether because of defiance or because they actively transform the alien into something more familiar (Piot 1999). In these circumstances, cultural differences exist not in spite of, but because of, interconnection. But it still seems difficult to deny that so many millions of people are striving to become developed and pursue lifestyles similar to those of middle-class Americans.

● ●

THINKING CRITICALLY ABOUT GLOBALIZATION

Who should define who is a winner or loser in the processes of global integration? What kinds of criteria (financial, social, political, etc.) do you think are most appropriate for defining such a thing?

● ●

Doesn't Everyone Want to Be Developed?

Long before the current globalization craze, discussions about global integration were often framed as the problem of bringing "civilization" (Western, that is), and later economic development, to non-European societies. But the question we pose here—Doesn't everyone want to be developed?—has no easy answer. Ideas differ about what development is and how to achieve it, so first we must ask: What is development?

What Is Development?

In 1949, U.S. President Harry Truman gave his inaugural address, in which he defined the role of the United States in the post–World War II world, when the West confronted the Communist nations. He said, "We must embark on a new program for making the benefits of our scientific advances and industrial progress available for the improvement and growth of the underdeveloped areas" (Truman 1949). He defined two-thirds of the world as "underdeveloped" and one-third as "developed." Truman believed that if poor people around the world participated in the "American dream" of a middle-class lifestyle, they would not turn toward Communism (Esteva 1992).

The Cold War is over, but development is still with us. It is a worldwide enterprise that was never solely American. Many European nations give aid to their former colonies. The stated goals of this aid range from expanding capitalist markets through trade and new building to alleviating poverty, improving health, and conserving natural resources. Key actors include the United Nations, the government aid agencies of most industrialized countries, lending agencies like the World Bank, and NGOs like CARE International.

Contemporary international development still aims to bring people into the "modern" world and correct what it identifies as undesirable and undignified conditions like poverty and the lack of modern conveniences. And, just as in the colonial era, "advanced" capitalist countries still provide the economic and social models for development.

But there is ambiguity to the concept of development. Is it a means to a particular end? Or is it the end itself? Who defines the shape and course of development? More important for our purposes, development has an ambiguous relationship with cultural diversity. Is its goal to foster the unfolding potential and purposeful improvement of people—from their own local cultural perspective? Or is it a program of forced change that is eliminating cultural diversity to create a world ordered on the universal principles of capitalist societies? Is it an effort to remake the world's diverse people to be just like us?

There are two distinct anthropological approaches to development: **development anthropology** and the **anthropology of development** (Gow 1993). While development anthropologists involve themselves in the theoretical and practical aspects of shaping and implementing development projects, anthropologists of development tend to study the cultural conditions for proper development, or, alternatively, the negative impacts of development projects. Often the two overlap, but at times they are in direct conflict.

Development Anthropology

Development anthropology is a branch of applied anthropology. It is a response to a simple fact: many development projects have failed because planners have not taken local culture into consideration. Planners often blame project failures on local people's supposed ignorance or stubbornness (Mamdani 1972). But it is often planners themselves who are ignorant of local issues or set in their ways. Projects are more likely to meet their goals when they are fine-tuned to local needs, capacities, perspectives, and interests.

A classic example recognized by many anthropologists is the work of Gerald Murray on deforestation in Haiti. In the 1970s and 1980s, the U.S. Agency for International Development (USAID) invested millions of dollars in Haitian reforestation projects that consistently failed (Murray 1987). Poor farmers resisted reforestation because it encroached on valuable croplands. Worse yet, aid money directed to farmers kept disappearing in the corrupt Haitian bureaucracy. Murray saw that planners misunderstood the attitudes and needs of local farmers, not to mention the most effective ways to get the resources to them. He suggested a different approach. Planners had conceived of this project as an environmental one. He convinced USAID instead to introduce it to farmers as planting a new cash crop, and to avoid involving

- **Development anthropology.** The application of anthropological knowledge and research methods to the practical aspects of shaping and implementing development projects.

- **Anthropology of development.** The field of study within anthropology concerned with understanding the cultural conditions for proper development, or, alternatively, the negative impacts of development projects.

the Haitian bureaucracy. Farmers would plant trees along the borders of their lands, allowing crops to continue to grow (Figure 5.7). After several years, they could harvest mature trees to sell as lumber. It was a very successful project: within four years, 75,000 farmers had planted 20 million trees, and many discovered the additional benefits of having trees on their land.

Development anthropologists often think of themselves as advocates for the people living at the grassroots—the poor, small farmers, women, and other marginalized people—who could be most affected, negatively or positively, by development but who lack the political influence to design and implement projects (Chambers 1997). As a result of pressure from anthropologists and other social activists, governments and major development organizations like the World Bank began to commission social impact studies to understand the potential impacts of their projects, and to try to alleviate the negative effects on local populations. Today, many anthropologists work in development agencies, both internationally (such as in USAID) and domestically (in community development organizations). One indication of how successful anthropologists' contributions to development have been is that the current director of the World Bank, Dr. Jim Yong Kim, is an anthropologist (see Chapter 8).

And yet there are limits to what anthropologists can do. Policy makers and development institutions may not pay attention to their advice. Or the anthropologist may not have enough time to fully study a situation before having to make recommendations (Gow 1993).

Anthropology of Development

Some anthropologists have supported the work of development anthropology by analyzing the social conditions that might help projects succeed. Other anthropologists have examined the development enterprise itself, and challenged its unpredictable and often harmful impacts on local cultures. These critics argue that no matter how well-intentioned the developers are, the outcome of most development projects is to give greater control over local people to outsiders, or the worsening of existing inequalities as elites shape development projects to serve their own political and economic interests (Escobar 1995). They also charge that the notion of development itself is ethnocentric and paternalistic (Escobar 1991).

Anthropologist James Ferguson applied some of these perspectives in his study of the Thaba-Tseka Rural Development Project. This project was a World Bank and U.N. Food and Agriculture Organization (FAO) project that took place between 1975 and 1984 in the southern African country of Lesotho (Ferguson 1994). Its goal was to alleviate poverty and increase economic output in rural villages by building roads, providing fuel and construction materials, and improving water supply and sanitation. But the project failed to meet its goals.

Ferguson argued that intentional plans like this one never turn out the way their planners expect, because project planners begin with a distinctive way of reasoning and knowing that nearly always generates the same kinds of actions. In this particular case, the planners believed that Lesotho's problems fit a general model: its residents are poor because they are subsistence farmers living in remote and isolated mountains, but they could develop further if they had technical improvements, especially roads, water, and sanitation.

But, according to Ferguson, this perspective has little understanding of on-the-ground realities. He noted that people in rural Lesotho have been marketing crops and livestock since the 1840s, so they have already been involved in a modern capitalist economy for a long time. They are also not isolated, since they send many migrants to and from South Africa for wage labor. In fact, most of the income for rural families comes from family members who have migrated to South Africa.

Figure 5.7   Haitian Farmers Planting Saplings for Reforestation.

Ferguson's point is that people in rural Lesotho are not poor because they live in a remote area and lack capitalism; they are poor because their labor is exploited in South Africa. But by viewing poverty as a lack of technical improvements in the rural countryside, the project failed to address the socioeconomic inequalities and subordination that are the underlying causes of poverty in rural Lesotho. All of this misunderstanding led to one major unexpected consequence: the arrival of government development bureaucrats to put the development project's technologies in place undermined the power of traditional village chiefs. Ferguson concluded that development exists, not to alleviate poverty, but to reinforce and expand bureaucratic state power at the expense of local communities.

Not all anthropologists, especially those working in development, are comfortable with such critiques. Some counter that we cannot sit on development's sidelines, that we have a moral obligation to apply our knowledge to protect the interests of the communities we study. Others argue that critics ignore the struggles within development institutions that indicate that there is not simply one discourse of development but a variety of perspectives among developers (Little and Painter 1995). Still others insist that development is less paternalistic and more accountable to local communities than it has ever been (Chambers 1997).

These debates remain unresolved, but now that we have some background, we can begin to answer the bigger question: Do people really want to be developed? The answer often depends on how much control over development processes people will have.

Change on Their Own Terms

In indigenous and poor communities around the world, it is not uncommon to hear variations on the following phrase, originally attributed to Lilla Watson, an Australian Aboriginal woman: "If you have come here to help me, you are wasting your time. But if you have come here because your liberation is bound up with mine, then let us work together." According to this perspective, outside help is not automatically virtuous, and it can undermine self-determination. Some scholars view this basic desire—to negotiate change on one's own terms—as a fundamental challenge to development's real or perceived paternalism and negative effects on local culture (Rahnema and Bawtree 1997). As confirmation of that fact, they point to the explosion of grassroots social movements throughout the Third World that challenge capitalist development schemes and seek alternatives such as social justice and environmental sustainability (Escobar, Alvarez, and Dagnino 1998).

Understandably, in the face of forced change, people want to conserve the traditions and relationships that give their lives meaning. This point is one of the keys to understanding culture in the context of global change. Culture helps people make sense of and respond to constant changes in the world, and it is itself dynamic. But culture also has stable and conservative elements, and different societies have different levels of tolerance for change, both of which mean that cultural change is not a uniform process for every society. This situation of uneven change partly explains why we see the persistence of cultural diversity around the world in spite of predictions that it would disappear.

● ●

THINKING CRITICALLY ABOUT GLOBALIZATION

Are anthropologists ethically obligated to help communities develop if members of the community want their help?

● ●

If the World Is Not Becoming Homogenized, What Is Actually Happening?

Like the previous question about whether everyone wants to be developed, this one has no simple answer. Anthropologists are divided on this question. The interaction of culture with political, economic, and social processes is complex, and in many ways, the world's material culture and associated technologies are becoming homogeneous. Anthropologists who study these processes pursue one form of cultural convergence theory or another. Other anthropologists see people all over the world using aspects of modern technology in their own ways and on their own terms. These scholars use an approach called "hybridization theory." In this section, we examine the strengths and relevance of both theories.

Cultural Convergence Theories

In the 1960s, the famous media scholar Marshall McLuhan suggested that the world was becoming a "global village" in which cultural diversity was in decline. Many social scientists agree. British philosopher and social anthropologist Ernest Gellner, for example, believed that the spread of industrial society created a common worldwide culture, based on similar conditions of work within the same industry. Making t-shirts in a factory, for example, is going to be similar whether situated in Honduras, Tanzania, or Vietnam. Gellner wrote that "The same technology canalizes people into the same type of activity and the same kinds of hierarchy, and . . . the same kind of leisure styles were also engendered by existing techniques and by the needs of productive life" (1983:116–17). Gellner's view was that local distinctions and traditions will gradually fade as Western ideas replace those in non-Western communities.

Another version of convergence theory envisions a worldwide convergence of consumer preferences and corporate practices, invoking the image of "McDonaldization." Advocates of this version assert that the principles of the fast-food restaurant—efficiency (quick service at a low cost), calculability (quantity over quality), predictability, tight control over production, and using technology over human labor—characterize American society and, increasingly, the rest of the world (Ritzer 1996).

Still another variation on this theme imagines "Coca-Colonization," alternatively called "Westernization" or "Americanization." This model proposes that the powerful and culturally influential nations of the West (especially the United States) impose their products and beliefs on the less powerful nations of the world, creating what is known as **cultural imperialism**, or the promotion of one culture over others, through formal policy or less formal means, like the spread of technology and material culture.

The appeal of these theories is that they address the underlying causes of why the world feels smaller, as well as how rich societies systematically exploit poor societies by drawing them into a common political-economic system. They also appear to explain the appearance of a common **world culture**, based on norms and knowledge shared across national boundaries (Lechner and Boli 2005; Figure 5.8).

But many anthropologists disagree with the basic assumptions convergence theorists make about culture, and in fact most proponents of convergence are not anthropologists. As we discussed earlier in this chapter, the fact that people might consume the same goods, wear the same clothes, or eat the same foods does not necessarily mean that they begin to think and behave in the same ways. A major limitation of convergence theories is that they underestimate variability and plasticity as key features of human culture and evolutionary history (Nash 1981).

- **Cultural imperialism.** The promotion of one culture over others, through formal policy or less formal means, like the spread of technology and material culture.

- **World culture.** Norms and values that extend across national boundaries.

Figure 5.8   World Culture and the Olympic Games. The Olympic Games is a quintessential global event: currently 205 countries participate in the Olympic Games, even more than are members of the United Nations. Drawing on certain core values—competitiveness, internationalism, amateurism, etc.—they foster an awareness of living in a single world culture.

- **Hybridization.** Persistent cultural mixing that has no predetermined direction or end-point.

Hybridization

An alternative theory that many anthropologists prefer is **hybridization**, which refers to open-ended and ongoing cultural intermingling and fusion. While the convergence theories imagine a world based on or moving toward cultural purities, hybridization emphasizes a world based on promiscuous mixing, border crossing, and persistent cultural diversity (García Canclini 1995; Piot 1999).

Hybridization has several aliases, including syncretism and creolization. Anthropologists have usually applied the word *syncretism* to the fusion of religious systems; *creolization* is most commonly used to mean the intermingling of languages. Still another metaphor is the notion of "friction," which anthropologist Anna Tsing (2005) employs: just as rubbing two sticks together creates light and heat, the coming together of diverse and conflicting social interactions creates movement, action, and effects. Tsing's broader assertion is that globalizing processes produce important effects around the world, but that these effects are rarely predictable, given the particularities of how people situated in their local cultures relate to those effects. Debates continue over the relative usefulness of each of these terms. But anthropologists recognize that each revolves around a common theme: the synthesis of distinct elements to create new and unexpected possibilities.

One compelling example is how the Warlpiri [Warl-**peer**-ee] Aborigines, hunter-gatherers in the remote Central Desert of Australia, have interacted with and ppropriated visual mass media since the 1980s. During the past century of contact with Europeans, the Warlpiri had maintained their distinctive culture and language, but when televisions and video cameras began circulating among them, many observers began to worry that the introduction of mass media would destroy their culture.

But the Warlpiri turned this alien technology toward more familiar ends, by incorporating the genre of film and the activity of filmmaking into their own traditions of storytelling. In Warlpiri settlements, viewing a video is a social event where people participate and collaborate in ways that are similar to how they view their traditional sand paintings or tell stories. Warlpiri people view films in socially appropriate kin groups, on video players that are collectively owned and shared according to traditional patterns. They also make films to tell their traditional stories. Their films are often disappointing to and misunderstood by Western audiences because of the slow and subtle way they unfold, taking their meaning from the Warlpiris' own cultural style and aesthetic criteria. The camera pans slowly across a landscape, and the long, still shots seem empty of meaning to Westerners. But the Warlpiri examine these films closely for the important stories they are supposed to reveal, with the camera tracking locations where ancestors, spirits, or historical characters are believed to have traveled (Michaels 1994:93). In short, the Warlpiri use this global technology to express their own local traditions and worldviews, borrowing from the outside world what they want to maintain or even revitalize of their own. In the process, they have hybridized Western media technologies and imagery (Figure 5.9).

Hybridization theory does have its critics. Some argue that cultural mixing is merely a superficial phenomenon, the real underlying condition being convergence. Others charge that all the talk about boundary-crossing and mixture ignores the fact that boundaries—national, social, ethnic, and so on—have not disappeared (Friedman 1999). At the heart of this criticism is the charge that hybridization theory ignores

Figure 5.9 Hybridity and Warlpiri Media. Warlpiri people of northern Australia have taken to watching and producing their own films. Their cinematic productions reflect particular social dynamics and perspectives, in the process hybridizing a Western technology and its practices.

real political and economic power and inequalities. Others assert that convergence and hybridization are not mutually exclusive, but that both are happening in multiple places at the same time.

Although these debates can be contentious, for a discipline historically accustomed to studying culture from a local vantage point (the stereotype of the anthropologist in a village), there is widespread consensus that taking on big questions like these opens up exciting new possibilities for research.

● ●

THINKING CRITICALLY ABOUT GLOBALIZATION

Can you identify any examples of cultural hybridization in your community? How does the example you came up with connect to transnational dynamics and processes?

● ●

How Can Anthropologists Study Global Interconnections?

Nowadays, nearly every anthropologist accepts that it is impossible to make sense of local cultural realities without some understanding of the broader political, economic, and social conditions that also shape people's lives (Kearney 1995). The problem is that anthropologists have typically conducted their studies in a single field site (a village, community, tribe, or district), while the transnational or transregional connections may be very far away. So how can anthropologists simultaneously study a local phenomenon in a community and the national or international factors and forces shaping that community?

Defining an Object of Study

Some anthropologists, such as Eric Wolf, have defined their object of study as the world system itself. They focus on the role of culture in that system. Others who take a global system more or less for granted have focused on specific components within that system, especially objects, money, and ideas that "flow" and "circulate" around it (Appadurai 1996), or the "cosmopolitan" people (journalists, urbanites, world travelers) who move within and through it (Hannerz 1992). And still others contend that in a transient world, the migrant offers the most productive object of study (Kearney 1995; García Canclini 1995).

But some reject the notion of a unified global system altogether. These anthropologists propose investigation of what Tsing (2000:348) describes as "interactions involving collaboration, misunderstanding, opposition, and dialogue" between transnational and local actors. A key component of this approach is learning how people find meaning in their places within broader political, economic, and cultural systems.

Each of these approaches raises questions about the adequacy of anthropology's most distinctive methodological tool, ethnographic research. Understood as intensive participation and observation in the everyday life of a single place during an extended period, ethnographic research has yielded incredibly rich insights into how people live

Doing Fieldwork
Tracking Emergent Forms of Citizenship with Aihwa Ong

SINCE THE 1980s, Malaysian-born anthropologist Aihwa Ong of the University of California, Berkeley, has studied the interaction between globally circulating ideas and practices—especially transnational capitalism, industrialization, and neoliberal policies promoting free markets—and local cultures and politics in the Pacific Rim. One of her key contentions is that Asian societies' experiences of globalization are not simply reproductions of ideas and practices transplanted from the West, but a complicated mixture of the local and the global in which new and emergent forms of social life and politics become possible and take shape. In order to support this contention, Ong has drawn on traditional site-based ethnographic fieldwork—such as her interviews and participant observation research with Muslim women factory workers in Malaysia, discussed before—as well as multi-sited research; that is, using a

research strategy that moves across and through different social and political spaces in order to understand large-scale linkages and processes.

One theme on which Ong has conducted multi-sited research is the changing ideas about national belonging and rights of citizenship in the Pacific Rim. These changes are subtle and complex, requiring fieldwork strategies that involve tracking and following ideas and practices surrounding citizenship as they circulate across and between different social settings in different countries. This style of research does not aim to study globalization or the world system in its totality; rather, its goal is to identify interconnections and configurations that link geographically and socially dispersed settings in culturally meaningful ways. Ong's research strategies have included fieldwork following elite Chinese business people as they

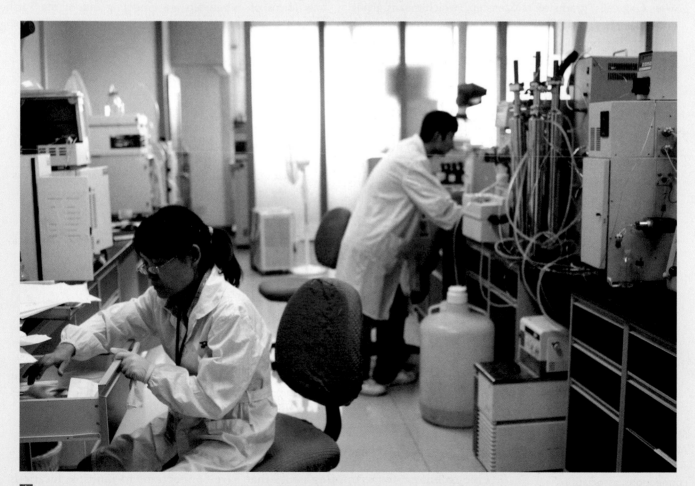

🌱 **Workers in a bioscience lab in Singapore, one of the settings of Aiwha Ong's multi-sited fieldwork.**

(continued)

Anthropologist as Problem Solver (continued)

travel back and forth between Asia and the U.S. West Coast; participant observation and interviews among professional workers in Shanghai, China; fieldwork in Cambodian refugee communities in California; and participant observation in high-tech bioscience companies in Singapore. She has also interviewed government officials, workers, business leaders, labor activists, and others who have diverse interactions with these different communities.

This transient method has provided important perspectives on complex changes in socio-political and cultural notions of citizenship. Ong argues that, as states have opened their borders to attract the flow of capital, technology, investment, and workers, they have been forced to be flexible in their conceptions of territorial sovereignty, or what aspects of their national space they are willing to control and regulate. The drive to be globally competitive has led some states—such as Singapore and Malaysia—to pursue what Ong calls "graduated citizenship," which means giving different rights to different groups (Ong 2006). For example, to ensure the productivity of low-wage workers for transnational corporations, these states will encourage the importation of foreigners to work as maids or factory workers with few formal protections, create policies that weaken labor unions, and use the police or military to enforce discipline on laborers. At the same time, mobile expatriate workers in high-tech fields may receive citizen-like privileges, incentives, protections, and benefits to ensure they bring their skills and knowledge to the economy (Ong 2006). In these circumstances, Ong suggests, the broader emphasis on skills, knowledge, and entrepreneurialism is replacing the idea of citizenship as a bundle of rights and obligations.

In addition, wealthy elites have developed their own conceptions and practices of "flexible citizenship," which involves manipulating the immigration laws of different countries to protect their wealth and security (Ong 1999). For example, Ong found that wealthy Chinese families practiced a strategy of flexible citizenship in which they might buy a house in a city like San Francisco or send their children to an elite American college, even as their businesses continue to be based in China or Southeast Asia. Their goal was not to seek citizenship in the sense of professing a national allegiance, but as a way to protect their wealth and economic assets. In the United States, this attitude generated controversy among upper-middle-class whites who lived in the same neighborhoods, and Chinese business elites found themselves in an unfamiliar position of having to navigate complicated racial politics.

In exploring these broader transformations in citizenship in the Pacific Rim, Ong has emphasized that Asian experiences of globalization are rooted in deep complexities of regional history and culture, and are not a simple matter of reacting to Western development patterns. The fact that these new forms of citizenship are emerging out of the Pacific Rim reflects Asian agency and participation in the ongoing creation of global capitalism.

Questions for Reflection

1. What would Ong have gained if she had stayed in one place to do her research on emergent forms of citizenship? What would she have lost?

2. What do you think are some of the practical problems facing an anthropologist who wants to conduct multi-sited research?

3. Do you think that multi-sited research raises any particular ethical issues?

and make sense of their lives. Yet most ethnographers also assume that, to learn about a community, one should stay in one place. But what if the community or the issues one wants to study extend beyond that place?

- **Multi-sited ethnography.** An ethnographic research strategy of following connections, associations, and putative relationships from place to place.

Multi-Sited Ethnography

One technique for examining issues that have connections to multiple locations is to use **multi-sited ethnography**, which is a strategy of following connections, associations, and putative relationships from place to place (Marcus 1995). Its goal is not a holistic representation of the world system as a totality. Rather, it seeks to track cultural themes as they express themselves in distinct places and settings that are typically connected in some concrete way. Its goal is to describe relationships and connections among these different places. In this sense, multi-sited ethnography offers a comparative method. Comparisons emerge from juxtaposing phenomena that were once thought "worlds apart" (Marcus 1995:102). "Doing Fieldwork: Tracking Emergent Forms of Citizenship with Aihwa Ong" considers how one anthropologist has taken advantage of the opportunities multi-sited ethnography presents for studying culture in transnational contexts.

Multi-sited fieldwork has been productive for studying transnational phenomena like environmentalism and other social movements, the media, certain religious societies whose membership extends across the borders of many countries, and the spread of science and technology. As the object of anthropological research has expanded to include topics like these, more and more anthropologists are doing multi-sited research. Multi-sited research is not appropriate for every research topic, but it is now becoming a common anthropological research strategy.

THINKING CRITICALLY ABOUT GLOBALIZATION

Can you identify any practical difficulties or ethical dilemmas involved in multi-sited research that might be different from traditional ethnographic research in a single community setting?

Conclusion

No anthropologist can claim to have easy answers to the dilemmas, dislocations, and problems raised by globalization. But anthropological research can provide critical perspectives on how and why people relate to large-scale social, economic, and political changes in the ways they do.

As we have established in this chapter, culture helps people make sense of and respond to constant changes in the world, which is itself dynamic. But cultural change is not a uniform process. There are many reasons for this. Different societies have differing levels of tolerance toward change, and some are more protective of their cultural traditions than others. In addition, as the story about Warlpiri creating media demonstrates, people can be open to outside influences even while maintaining culturally specific meanings and social relations. They do this by actively transforming the alien into something more familiar. Even more important, perhaps, is that not all people participate in global processes on equal terms. Their position within broader political-economic processes and regional dynamics helps shape their consciousness and experience of global cultural integration. The complexities of migration demonstrate this point in general ways, and the crisis surrounding Syrian refugees described in the opening of this chapter does so in more specific ways.

The socioeconomic and political inequalities associated with globalization are one reason that cultural diversity continues to exist in the world. But there is another key reason. It is that cultures are created in connection with other cultures, not in isolation, as many anthropologists had previously thought. This is not to say that there are not certain elements that make the world feel smaller, including empirical changes in communications, migration, and finances. But does this mean we live in a global village as Marshall McLuhan once claimed? Only if we think of a village as a place in which diversity, and not uniformity, is the defining feature of that village.

KEY TERMS

Anthropology of
   development   p. 124

Cultural imperialism   p. 127

Culture of migration   p. 121

Development
   anthropology   p. 124

Diffusionists   p. 112

Exiles   p. 114

Globalization   p. 112

Hybridization   p. 128

Immigrants   p. 114

Localization   p. 122

Migrants   p. 114

Multi-sited ethnography
   p. 132

Postcolonialism   p. 119

Push-pull factors   p. 119

Refugees   p. 114

Transnational   p. 113

Transnational
   community   p. 119

World culture   p. 127

World systems theory
   p. 118

Reviewing the Chapter

Chapter Section	What We Know	To Be Resolved
Is the World Really Getting Smaller?	It is impossible to make sense of local cultural realities without some understanding of the broader political, economic, and social conditions that also shape people's lives.	Anthropologists do not have easy answers for the cultural, economic, and political dilemmas raised by globalization.
What Are the Outcomes of Global Integration?	Not everybody participates equally in the diverse kinds of interconnections that make up globalization, and taking globalization seriously means taking power relationships and social inequality seriously.	While some anthropologists emphasize the destructive and dominating effects of global capitalism's spread for many non-Western societies, others have argued that expressions of resistance, creative localization, and migration are meaningful and important responses.

Doesn't Everyone Want to Be Developed?	Development raises complex and politically charged issues about socioeconomic and cultural change for anthropologists and the indigenous and poor communities that are the target of development initiatives.	Anthropologists are deeply divided over the positive and negative impacts of development, and they continue to debate the merits and drawbacks of anthropological involvement in development and other projects that promote globalization.
If the World Is Not Becoming Homogenized, What Is Actually Happening?	Globalization is a complicated matter that illustrates how people create and change their cultures, not in isolation, but through connections with others.	Although many anthropologists accept that globalization is a process primarily of hybridization, others argue that it is a process of cultural convergence, and some argue that it is a complex mixture of both.
How Can Anthropologists Study Global Interconnections?	Multi-sited ethnography is one approach for tracking cultural themes as they express themselves in distinct places and settings, and it seeks to identify concrete connections between those places and settings.	Anthropologists continue to debate whether or not multi-sited research is as effective for understanding culture as traditional community-based ethnographic methods.

Readings

The Anthropology of Globalization: A Reader, edited by Jonathan Xavier Inda and Renato Rosaldo (second edition, Malden, MA: Blackwell, 2007), offers a broad overview of the history, topics, and debates in the anthropological study of globalization, including essays on themes such as migration, the creation of transnational identities, and the movement of goods and capitalist economic structures across political, economic, and cultural boundaries. For a more specific discussion of anthropological approaches to migration, see Caroline Brettell's *Anthropology and Migration: Essays on Transnationalism, Ethnicity, and Identity* (Walnut Creek, CA: Altamira Press, 2003).

....

Although he is not an anthropologist, Pico Iyer has written a book—*The*

Global Soul: Jet Lag, Shopping Malls, and the Search for Home (New York: Vintage, 2001)—that offers a fine-grained description of many of the cultural dilemmas and situations that draw anthropological attention about global processes. Anthropologist Michael Jackson's book *At Home in the World* (Durham, NC: Duke University Press, 1995) offers a rich ethnographic and philosophical counterpart to Iyer's book, juxtaposing the author's own global travels and sense of uprootedness with how Australian Warlpiri construct a concept of home as hunter-gatherers who move across large geographic distances.

....

Many anthropologists have written noteworthy ethnographic monographs exploring the intersections of culture and globalization. Among the

more thought-provoking are Anna Lowenhaupt Tsing's book *Friction: An Ethnography of Global Connection* (Princeton, NJ: Princeton University Press, 2005), which examines how global institutions and interactions shape the problems facing Indonesian rain forests and indigenous peoples; Charles Piot's *Remotely Global: Village Modernity in West Africa* (Chicago, IL: University of Chicago Press, 1999), which explores how village life among the Kabre of Togo is shaped by a complex mixture of local traditions and colonial and postcolonial histories; and Aihwa Ong's *Neoliberalism as Exception: Mutations in Citizenship and Sovereignty* (Durham, NC: Duke University Press, 2006), which is described in the "Doing Fieldwork" box in this chapter.

....

Foodways

Finding, Making, and Eating Food

THE 2008 GLOBAL FINANCIAL CRISIS hit Greece especially hard, producing political, economic, and social turmoil that has continued to the present. Although the crisis began in Wall Street financial markets, it exposed deep problems in the Greek economy, including the fact that the government was doing a poor job of collecting taxes—especially from the wealthy—and had been paying for its extensive welfare programs with international loans. As global financial markets weakened, international lenders grew alarmed about Greece's high foreign debt levels, and they shut Greece off from further borrowing. By 2010, the country was headed toward bankruptcy, so the International Monetary Fund (IMF), the European Central Bank, and the European Commission organized a series of bailouts. The bailouts required the government to implement neoliberal reforms and austerity measures, including deep cuts in public spending on social welfare programs and pensions, the privatization of public services, a sharp increase in taxes, and an overhaul of the economy to increase exports and encourage foreign investment. As a result, the Greek economy shrank, unemployment shot up, poverty rates grew, and millions turned out in the streets to protest the bailouts—which went to pay international lenders, not into the Greek economy directly—and the politicians who had not only agreed to the bailouts, but neglected to take responsibility for any of the economic problems.

Yogurt and Politics. This Greek lawmaker gets back into her car after protestors threw yogurt at her face while she was attempting to reach Parliament. The protest, which took place in 2011, was part of a 48-hour general strike against the government for its austerity measures related to the financial bailout.

In the midst of this turmoil, concerns around food have gained special significance. For many, simply getting food is a major problem. Food prices have increased, shortages in staples have occurred, and incomes have shrunk or disappeared, leaving many people struggling to feed themselves and their families. In cities, the number of people seeking free meals at soup kitchens has grown dramatically, and increasing numbers of people have turned to growing their own food on their patios and on reclaimed urban lots (Partalidou and Anthopoulou 2016). In rural areas, where people often have greater access to land and the ability to produce at least some of their own food, the concerns have been somewhat different, though no less pressing. On the island of Kalymnos, for example, where big multinational supermarket chains had recently arrived and began changing people's food-shopping habits, the crisis spurred many people to return to local grocers because, unlike the impersonal supermarkets, they will sell on credit (Sutton 2011).

But food also has powerful symbolic and moral significance, and the idiom and imagery of food have become important ways for people to express their discontent about what is happening to their country. For example, in describing why ordinary Greeks should accept the controversial bailouts, Deputy Prime Minister Theodoros Pangalos used a food metaphor: "We all ate together," which means something like "We're all in this together." In response, protestors in the streets chanted, "You lying bastard! You're so fat you ate the whole supermarket!" Meanwhile, throwing yogurt on the heads of government officials and police in public has become an important symbolic expression of indignation and ridicule. Referred to as *yaourtoma* [yo-ur-**toh**-mah], throwing yogurt on others carries special moral and cultural resonance in Greek society. The yogurt, which is made from strained sheep's milk, has strong associations with Greek identity and, as a common rural food, traditional Greek values. In the 1960s, rebellious urban youths began throwing yogurt on bystanders to express their discontent with those traditional values, and the practice was outlawed. But in the past few years, *yaourtoma* has returned and gone mainstream, as have calls to decriminalize it. Frustrated people feel it is one of the few tools at their disposal to get the attention of officials who agreed to the IMF policies that run counter to the *Greek* vision of a just society, in which a competent government provides welfare to all of its citizens (Vournelis 2011).

- **Foodways.** Structured beliefs and behaviors surrounding the production, distribution, and consumption of food.

This situation offers a brief glimpse into the political-economic and cultural contexts of one particular country's **foodways**, or the structured beliefs and behaviors surrounding the production, distribution, and consumption of food. Foodways are dynamic, and changes in food habits and production systems are happening not just in Greece, but all over the globe. These changes, which are playing out in distinct ways in different places, reflect a variety of interconnected issues and widespread challenges that involve too much or too little access to food, diet-related diseases, and the environmental and social consequences of the shift to industrial agriculture.

Figure 6.1 **Select Peoples and Places Discussed in Chapter 6.**

Yet, in spite of changing foodways in a global economy, there is still tremendous cultural variation in how people relate to food. This variation exists not just in how and why people obtain or raise certain foods, but in how and why they consume them.

Central to anthropology's interest in food is the question around which this chapter is organized: *Why do we eat the things we eat?* Embedded in this larger question are the following problems, around which this chapter is organized:

Why is there no universal human diet?

Why do people eat things that others consider disgusting?

How do different societies get food?

How are contemporary foodways changing?

Food is a fundamental aspect of culture: we organize our productive and social lives around it; reach out to friends, families, and enemies with it; find both pleasure and disgust in it; define social status and identity through it; get sick and die from it. Anthropologists bring a holistic perspective to the study of food and foodways, meaning that we focus on the complex interactions between human nutritional needs, ecology, cultural beliefs, industry, and political-economic processes. We begin by exploring the diversity of things people eat.

Why Is There No Universal Human Diet?

As a species, humans are omnivores, which means we eat both plants and animals. Our actual everyday diets usually come from a limited range of foods, determined by what is available, by dietary restrictions, and by what we have learned to prefer as individuals and as members of a particular social community. But most humans can eat a tremendous variety of things because the human diet evolved to be extremely fluid and adaptable.

Human Dietary Adaptability and Constraints

Six million years ago, our nonhuman primate ancestors were largely tree-dwelling frugivores (fruit-eaters), following an evolutionary past that helped make them biologically suited to a plant- and fruit-rich diet. A pivotal evolutionary shift came some 1.8 to 2 million years ago as certain primates began to consume meat more regularly and in larger quantities, developing increasingly sophisticated tools to expand their diets. Sometime around 400,000 years ago, this dietary shift was supported by the ability to use fire for cooking, which breaks down tendons and toxins in meats. Human teeth, chewing muscles, and digestive organs got smaller, and greater access to high-quality protein supported the evolution of greater complexity in the human brain. All of these factors contributed greatly to the adaptability of our species. With no primary prescribed diet, and with large brains, fire, and tools at our disposal, our species could branch out to many different environments, from the arctic tundra to tropical rain forests, savannas, and deserts.

Humans do have certain biologically constrained nutritional needs, and we will get sick and die if we do not meet them. Some of these requirements include having sufficient calories, water, vitamins, lysine, and iron. But in different societies, people get differing amounts of these vital nutrients. The differences can be staggering because of factors such as whether a diet is based principally on meat or plant foods, whether a group is cut off from nutritious foods for economic or political reasons, or whether a particular food is available in the natural environment. For example, people living in the Tibetan plateau historically have suffered high rates of goiter, an enlargement of the thyroid gland, because their environment and diet lack a natural source of iodine, which is essential to keeping the thyroid in good health. In other cases, however, a population has developed biological adaptations to the lack of certain nutrients in their environments. One example is the Inuit, who live in icy northern latitudes. For obvious climatic reasons, the traditional Inuit diet is very low in plant carbohydrates, which is a basic source of energy for most human populations. To get their daily calories, the Inuit eat mostly animal fat and protein. They have a metabolic adaptation that allows them to efficiently transform the amino acids in animal protein into glucose, a key energy source for the body (Lieberman 1987).

In spite of the sheer diversity of things humans *can* eat, the food we *actually* eat does seem to follow somewhat reliable patterns. Anthropologist Sidney Mintz (1992) observes that, except in a handful of unusual cases of people who eat only plants *or* only animals, the typical human meal forms a common core-legume-fringe pattern: a core, consisting of a complex carbohydrate (the starchy seeds of grasses or tubers) that provides the caloric basis of a meal, a legume like beans or a small piece of meat that provides a small amount of protein, and a fringe that provides flavor (Figure 6.2).

Figure 6.2   Dinner in Costa Rica and Ethiopia. The core-legume-fringe pattern is generally not consciously apparent to eaters. But the pattern is more or less the same around the world: a dominant carbohydrate core, a smaller amount of protein, and fringe foods to provide flavor.

This meal serves both biological needs, providing us with key nutrients, and cultural needs, such as providing taste and flavor. When it comes to human diets, culture and biology interact in complex ways.

Cultural Influences on Human Evolution: Digesting Milk

The evolution of dietary flexibility in our species resulted from a complicated mix of biological and cultural processes. One illustration concerns something many North Americans take for granted: the ability to digest milk. Looking at all human populations across the globe, however, being able to digest milk is a rare thing.

All mammalian babies produce an enzyme called lactase that allows them to digest lactose, a simple sugar found in their mothers' milk. For the majority of the world's human population, lactase production ceases before adulthood, and drinking fresh milk or eating dairy products can create symptoms of lactose intolerance, such as bloating, diarrhea, and cramps (Wiley 2004, 2011).

Only a few populations have developed the ability to digest lactose in adulthood, notably Northern Europeans (from whom many North Americans trace their ancestry), South Asians, and herders in the Middle East, the Arabian Peninsula, and sub-Saharan Africa. People in these societies have a condition called **lactase persistence**, which refers to the ability to continue producing lactase in adulthood. People who do not have this trait are lactase impersistent, meaning they are unable to produce lactase in adulthood.

Lactase persistence is a genetically regulated trait, but it is made possible by a particular cultural environment (Wiley 2004). Domestication of animals, especially in the Middle East by 12,000 years ago, set the stage for lactase persistence, because fresh milk was constantly available to those adults with the genetic mutation that allowed them to take advantage of the nourishment milk provides. Other cultural factors today, such as the central role of milk production in the domestic economy and the belief that the consumption of dairy products is a healthy practice, also support lactase persistence (Wiley 2004).

In the United States, we see these cultural factors in the high profile of the dairy industry and in the advice we give to young children to drink their milk so they will grow up to have strong bodies. Few Americans know about biological variations in the ability to digest milk, and both the federal government and the dairy industry appear to sanction this lack of awareness, routinely telling us that cow's milk is indispensable to healthy bones and brain development. This message remains strong even though as much as 25% of the American population is lactase impersistent.

Around the world there is no evidence that *not* drinking milk or *not* eating dairy products has created developmental or bone density problems among lactase impersistent populations, who get their calcium, fat, and proteins from other sources (Wiley 2004) (Figure 6.3). But we still assume that the ability to digest milk and other dairy products is the norm.

The milk example shows how flexible human bodies are in responding to their natural and cultural environments, depending on what is available and appropriate to consume. There is no universal human diet, because our dietary physiology is open-ended, leaving our needs to be defined and fulfilled partly by the specific natural environments in which we find ourselves, and even more

- **Lactase persistence.** Continuation of lactase production beyond early childhood that allows a person to digest milk and dairy products.

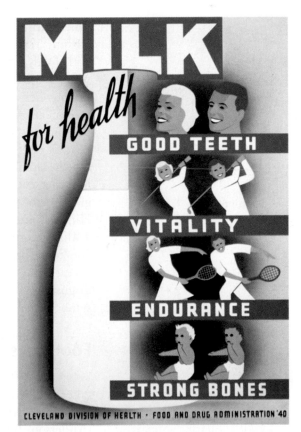

Figure 6.3 Drink Milk for Health? Participants in the anti-milk movement argue that milk consumption contributes to health problems like heart disease and obesity. They also point out that the majority of the world's population does not suffer from bone density problems, because they get their calcium from other sources.

so by the particular societies in which we live. The cultural shaping of dietary particulars is so extreme that one group of people will eat things that another group considers disgusting, which is a theme we explore in the next section.

• •

THINKING CRITICALLY ABOUT FOODWAYS

Although humans are able to adapt to different environments to get the nutrition they need, not all human diets are optimal for human health. Can you think of examples of human dietary practices that do not maximize health? Why do people maintain dietary practices that can make them sick or even die?

• •

Why Do People Eat Things That Others Consider Disgusting?

One exciting aspect of traveling to another country is the opportunity to eat the local cuisine. Yet many travelers face the common concern that they will be presented with foods they find strange or downright revolting, as travelers to Iceland might when offered the local delicacy of *hákarl*, or rotten shark flesh; as visitors to Thailand might when offered buffalo penis stew; or as visitors to Zambia might when offered caterpillars and other insects. These things are not only delectable to certain people but also reasonable sources of calories, proteins, and vitamins. The same sense of disgust, of course, can be experienced by people from other places who find the things North Americans eat to be revolting. For example, many people around the world find cheese to be gross (it is, after all, intentionally spoiled secretions from an animal's glands), and others find our love of beef hamburgers and steaks horrifying (such as Hindus from India who consider cows sacred).

That one group of people finds some things delicious that others consider disgusting goes to the heart of how much culture shapes the foods we desire to eat, when and how we eat them, and why we eat them. As we will see in this section, ideas about what is disgusting—or delicious—to eat are closely tied to processes of cultural construction, symbolism, group identity, and cultural change.

Foodways and Culture

When we talk about the relationship between food and culture, anthropologists take a holistic perspective on foodways, which are the structured beliefs and behaviors surrounding the production, distribution, and consumption of food (Anderson 2005). The foodways perspective recognizes that food is both a tangible substance that provides nutrition and a conduit of symbolic meaning and social relationships. Although the actual use of the term *foodways* is relatively new in anthropology, the holistic approach it emphasizes is in fact not at all new to the discipline. In "Classic Contributions: Audrey Richards and the Study of Foodways," we explore how one British social anthropologist pioneered the holistic analysis of foodways.

Classic Contributions
Audrey Richards and the Study of Foodways

Audrey Richards with harvesters in Zambia.

BRITISH SOCIAL ANTHROPOLOGIST Audrey Richards (1899–1984) is best known as a founder of the field of nutritional anthropology, which studies the relationship between human nutritional needs, ecological conditions, and what people actually eat (Anderson 2005). Because of Richards's influence, nutritional anthropologists today approach eating holistically, exploring how biology, health concerns, ecology, political-economic processes, and most of all, culture, shape people's relationships with food. In this selection, drawn from her classic 1939 book *Land, Labor, and Diet in Northern Rhodesia: An Economic Study of the Bemba Tribe,* Richards justifies a holistic perspective on what we now call foodways.

The study of . . . magico-religious attitudes to different foods must be an essential part of any nutritional survey as well as a record of the people's digestive theories and their beliefs as to the correct feeding of infants and the sick.

But if social values and nutritional dogmas shape a people's food habits, it is their economic institutions that enable them to produce their supplies. Here again the anthropological approach to diet problems is seen to be a very important one. Agricultural and pastoral activities are governed by cultural rules, some based on empirical knowledge and some on magico-religious beliefs. These vary from tribe to tribe, even in areas where environmental conditions are very similar.

Food is everywhere produced by co-operative action and it is on the success of their social organization that different people's diets depend. Man works to produce sufficient or surplus victuals under the urge of a number of economic incentives and these are culturally defined in each tribe. Distribution is a question of the utmost importance among peoples living for the most part on perishable foods, and it is their different legal systems and principles of social grouping that enable them to share their supplies between the different members or classes of the community. All these social and economic factors directly affect the production and consumption of food in a native area. (Richards 1939:8–9)

Questions for Reflection

1. What do you think Richards meant when she referred to the "magico-religious attitudes to different foods"? Why do you think these are important to understanding a society's foodways?

2. Richards said that the production and distribution of food are also culturally defined. Can you think of an example from our own society that illustrates her point?

Foodways Are Culturally Constructed

Foodways are culturally constructed in that they are always surrounded by cultural beliefs and governed by systematic rules and etiquette. These rules regulate what and how people hunt and gather; what plants they raise and how they harvest them; how and with whom they share and prepare food; and how and with whom they consume it. These rules, all culturally constructed, differ from one society to the next.

For example, those of us who get our food from supermarkets tend to think of food as material, impersonal, and dissociated from the producer and its natural environment. In contrast, the Hua, who live in the Eastern Highlands of Papua New Guinea, believe that food possesses mystical dynamism, vitality, and danger (Meigs 1997). For the Hua, the act of eating unites them with the individual who produced or shared food with them and invigorates them with the vital essences of the organisms they are consuming. They believe that because food is so spiritually powerful, humans are susceptible to its influences. The Hua have devised many rules governing who can handle, share, and eat certain foods. Some of these rules—for example, rules that do not allow women or men to eat certain foods—strengthen the social distinction between male and female. Other rules, such as those that require certain foods to be shared, build stronger bonds among members of the same clan, village, and gender.

Foodways Communicate Symbolic Meaning

In every society, food is a rich source of meaning, and people use it to communicate specific messages. Particular foods and meals can draw people together, especially when people share and consume foods that symbolize concepts like home, family, or conviviality. When you are traveling and become homesick, the yearning for certain "comfort foods" is not just a desire for a familiar taste; it is a desire to feel connected to things that are symbolically important to you, such as your home and family.

But food can just as easily communicate division and unequal power relations, as with so-called sumptuary laws that limit consumption of certain items along class lines. For example, in Renaissance England, the Parliament passed a law that allowed "gentlemen" to eat two courses of meat and fish during a meal, but restricted their servants to only one course of meat during the day (Figure 6.4).

The use of food as a form of symbolic communication is so pervasive that some anthropologists, such as Mary Douglas and Claude Lévi-Strauss, have suggested that food operates with logic similar to that of language. English anthropologist Douglas, for example, observed that an English formal dinner takes on a certain precise order, just like a sentence: appetizers, soup, fish, and so on, to dessert (Anderson 2005:110; Douglas 1966). Douglas also wrote about food taboos, which are prohibitions on eating certain foods. She argued that these are especially important modes of symbolic communication. For example, in her analysis of Jewish dietary laws that prohibit the consumption of pork, Douglas concluded that abiding by these taboos was a means through which ancient Israelites symbolically communicated their religious piety (Douglas 1966). And French anthropologist Claude Lévi-Strauss famously observed that food is good to think, not just eat. The anthropological theory of **structuralism**, which he established, argues that the human mind creates meaning and understanding by making patterned oppositions and contrasts. For example, all cultures make a distinction between food that is raw and food that is cooked, which on a symbolic level means that all cultures draw a distinction between nature and culture (Lévi-Strauss 1969b). The act of cooking marks the transition from nature to culture, easing the opposition between them and contributing to the meanings that people give to food.

● **Structuralism.** An anthropological theory that people make sense of their worlds through binary oppositions like hot–cold, culture–nature, male–female, and raw–cooked. These binary oppositions are expressed in social institutions and cultural practices.

☘ **Figure 6.4   Sumptuary Laws, Circa 1500s England.** These laws reflected and strengthened everyone's awareness of the advantaged position of aristocrats at a time when the European preference for meat eating allowed it to symbolize aristocracy.

Foodways Mark Social Boundaries and Identities

Food preferences, etiquette, and taboos also mark social boundaries and identities. As anthropologist Carole Counihan (1999:8) has observed, "One's place in a social system is revealed by what, how much, and with whom one eats." Eating practices might mark gender differences, as when men and women eat different foods. They might mark ethnic or regional differences, as when particular groups identify themselves closely with certain foods. Or they could mark profession or class status, as when certain individuals consume certain foods identified with their social station (Lentz 1999). These social markers are closely related to differing notions of **taste** that may exist between or within groups. Taste can refer to both the physical sensation on the tongue (as in "This crab cake tastes good") and social distinction and prestige (as in "Her consumption of fine wine shows she has good taste") (MacBeth 1997).

Every society has a notion of the "perfect meal," which typically reflects people's culturally acquired tastes and is closely identified with their social identity as a group. For example, German anthropologist Gerd Spittler (1999) found that, among the Kel Ewey Tuareg [kell **eh**-way **twar**-egg] nomads who live in the Sahara desert region in northern Mali, West Africa, the perfect meal is simple and always the same for everybody, regardless of their relative wealth. Breakfast is a drink made of cheese, dates, and the grain millet, stirred in water. Lunch and dinner are millet prepared in the style of polenta and sprinkled with soured camel's or goat's milk. Spittler theorizes that Tuareg prefer these types of meals because these foods identify them as a people who provide a stable diet for all its members in a precariously dry environment. These Tuareg view variety in the diet—something that many of us take for granted—as a characteristic of people who must be so desperately poor and hungry they are forced to eat anything they can find.

Changes in taste and food preferences are often linked to broader changes in social differentiation, such as an increasing social stratification within a population. Middle- and upper-class urban dwellers in Ghana, for example, tend to prefer drinking factory-produced bottled beer to sorghum beer, which is common in the villages. Drinking bottled beer allows members of the middle and upper classes to distance themselves symbolically from poor and illiterate village dwellers, and it identifies them with the prestige of modern institutions (Lentz 1999).

One of the most significant ways food shapes social differentiation is in the ways it mediates relationships between men and women. In many societies, producing, sharing, and eating food is a highly gendered experience (Counihan 1999). In "Thinking Like an Anthropologist: Food Preferences and Gender," we explore how gender differentiation helps organize women's and men's distinct preferences for food.

- **Taste.** A concept that refers to the sense that gives humans the ability to detect flavors, as well as the social distinction associated with certain foodstuffs.

Foodways Are Dynamic

Because foodways are so bound up with people's identities, it is easy to assume that people always hold onto them tightly. In some cases, foodways are remarkably persistent. For example, the diet in region of Andalucía in southern Spain is about the same as it was during Roman times: crusty bread, olive oil, eggs, pork, wine, cabbage, herbs, onions, and garlic (Anderson 2005:163).

But foodways change for many reasons. Environmental changes, like overhunting or overfishing, change what is available. Or people may begin to identify certain foods with good health, such as the reputation beef held among North Americans during the mid–twentieth century, but which in recent decades has given way to new ideas about the healthiness of a diet based on vegetables, soy products, and whole grains. Or formerly expensive foods, like white bread and processed sugar, become

Thinking Like an Anthropologist
Food Preferences and Gender

ANTHROPOLOGISTS BEGIN THEIR research by asking questions. In this box, we want you to learn how to ask questions as an anthropological researcher. Part One describes a situation and follows up with questions we would ask. Part Two asks you to formulate your own questions based on a different situation.

PART ONE: FOOD PREFERENCES AMONG THE YAO OF THAILAND

In all societies, maleness and femaleness are associated with certain foods, bolstered by social rules and etiquette that govern what men and women can and cannot eat (Counihan 1999). As a result, people learn to prefer the foods that are appropriately identified with their gender. Consider, for example, the case of the Yao people, who are farmers living in the forested mountains of northern Thailand. Yao men prefer raw meat and blood, spiced with chili pepper and fragrant leaves of mint, basil, and dill (Hubert 1997). When men get together as friends to socialize, they drink alcohol and snack on grilled bits of meat and offal. The men view their food preferences as a sign of their virility. In contrast, women are expected to show a slight repulsion toward raw meat and blood. Yao believe that if women prepare or consume these foods they will experience illness and conflict with their husbands. Their preference is for soft, boiled, tender, and bland foods, like rice-based meals and stews. They also prefer fruits, which in Yao culture symbolize femininity.

These food preferences are difficult to comprehend without a broader understanding of Yao cosmology and concepts of space and gender (Hubert 1997). Yao connect particular foods to particular spaces in the cosmic order, and in turn connect these foods and spaces with either women or men. Their notion of the cosmos is like a set of concentric circles. The smallest circle, in the center, is the civilized space of the home. The next ring out is the "swiddens"—the fields they cultivate—which they consider to be semi-wild. The third ring represents the forest, which is a wild and dangerous space. Finally, the outer ring, which encompasses all the others, is the otherworld, a space beyond the pale of the living, which is inhabited by ancestors and other spirits. Women and their foods—which are the staple foods everyone, male and female, eats on a daily basis—are associated with the inner circle. Men and their foods—especially raw and grilled meats—are associated with the "wilder" outer rings of swidden and forest. Raw meats are prepared only on special occasions, such as a wedding banquet or sacrifice to the ancestors.

In Yao cosmology, the more foods are cooked or the closer to home they are produced, the more they are considered civilized. Raw and bloody foods are stronger and more dangerous. This arrangement reflects and reinforces ideas about the qualities of maleness and femaleness. Women should be mild, polite, and civilized, working primarily in or near the home. In the space of the home, men are expected to be polite as well. But they also go into the wild and dangerous space of the forests to hunt animals and collect useful plants, and as a result, they are permitted, even expected, to be virile and at times less civilized.

What questions does this situation raise for anthropological researchers?

🌱 **Are These American Foods Gendered?**

1. What are Yao qualities of maleness and femaleness?
2. What are the qualities of female foods and what are the qualities of male foods?
3. How do people learn to prefer one food to another?
4. Are there cultural rules about who can prepare certain foods and how they prepare them?
5. How do ideas about gender-appropriate foods relate to other notions of gender-appropriate behavior?

PART TWO: FOOD PREFERENCES IN NORTH AMERICA

In North America, we identify certain meals and foods with men, such as steaks, hamburgers, beer, and fried foods. But Americans also increasingly label these foods "unhealthy" and assume that most men have unhealthy diets. Alternatively, we identify "light" and "healthy" foods with women, such as fresh fruits and vegetables, and especially salads. While there are exceptions to these patterns, most of us take these distinctions for granted.

What questions would you ask about this situation as an anthropological researcher?

inexpensive because of new industrial processing techniques. Or changes in family dynamics force changes in eating habits, such as in North America where women's increasing involvement in the workforce has helped fuel the rapid rise of convenience foods such as frozen dinners and takeout (Anderson 2005:165–68).

People construct their own foodways, but never independently of broader social dynamics or economic contexts. This is especially true of societies involved in geographically dispersed trading networks. For example, around Aitape on the north coast of Papua New Guinea, sago (starch from the sago palm) and smoked fish are the staple foods for everyone, whether they live on the mainland or on small offshore islands. But only mainland villagers have direct access to sago palms, which grow in abundance in swampy areas. The islanders enjoy an abundance of fish but have no sago or other vegetables. Islanders exchange smoked fish and other goods for foods like sago, yams, and bananas grown on the mainland. Even though the communities that constitute this trading system are scattered across a large geographical area, they are nevertheless intimately connected and reliant on each other.

Foodways are also dynamic because they are subject to the influence of large-scale political-economic processes such as cross-border trade and globalization policies, which can shape and disrupt people's diets and access to food in important ways (Watson and Caldwell 2005). We saw this in our discussion of Greece at the beginning of this chapter. But consider as well the example of the Middle East, where bread has long been an important source of low-cost sustenance. In Egypt, it is so important that the word for bread, *aish*, also means "life." Like many other Middle Eastern countries, Egypt does not produce enough wheat domestically to meet demand; in fact, it is the world's largest wheat importer, and most of the wheat it imports comes from the United States. When global grain prices spiked in 2007 and 2008, the price of bread rose 37%, which had dire consequences for the 40% of Egyptians who live below the poverty line (Zurayk 2011). The government responded, as it often did, by increasing subsidies for bread to lower the cost to consumers. But factors beyond Egypt's control caused food costs to continue to rise, and by 2011, popular frustration spilled out into the streets. In the protests, images of bread were common—indeed, many observers thought that these were "bread riots" that had been happening periodically since the 1980s (Zurayk 2011). But it turns out that bread was a catalyst that opened the door

Figure 6.5   Bread and the Arab Spring. The imagery of bread loaves was common in the protests that erupted in Tahrir Square (Cairo, Egypt) in 2011 and fueled the Arab Spring. Bread has long been used during riots as a political symbol to express discontent with government policies. In 2011, protestors were angry about policies that failed to protect citizens from the negative impacts of broader globalization processes, as well as the lack of opportunities to participate in political processes.

to broader expressions of discontent with government policies in areas beyond just food policies, and these protests eventually brought the whole government down. The success of the Egyptian protests inspired people throughout the Middle East to challenge their regimes in what is now known as the Arab Spring (Figure 6.5). Clearly, when a people rely on a staple food that becomes too expensive or out of reach, it can contribute to major societal unrest.

Examples such as this raise a basic, yet critical, question: How do people actually get their food in the first place? This is a longstanding interest in anthropology, and we turn to it in the next section.

THINKING CRITICALLY ABOUT FOODWAYS

What is your idea of an ideal meal? Beyond its flavor, why is this food so good in your opinion? What does it communicate to you and others? Are there any special expectations about who should prepare it and how? When and with whom do you typically eat it? Why do you think some people, like you, really like this meal, while others do not?

How Do Different Societies Get Food?

Whether a society's foodways are successful or not depends on a combination of environmental, economic, and historical conditions that shape how the community gets its food. Anthropologists call the social relationships and practices necessary for procuring, producing, and distributing food **modes of subsistence**. There are four major modes:

- **Modes of subsistence.** The social relationships and practices necessary for procuring, producing, and distributing food.

1. Foraging, or the search for edible things;
2. Horticulture, or small-scale subsistence agriculture;

3. Pastoralism, which means the raising of animal herds;
4. Intensive agriculture, or large-scale, often commercial, agriculture.

For the past several thousand years, intensive agriculture has furnished most people with most of their food supplies. But foraging, horticulture, and pastoralism are still important dimensions in many of the world's diets. Not only do these three modes persist in the contemporary world, but they also demonstrate the range and flexibility of human approaches to procuring and producing food. Societies are rarely committed to a single mode of subsistence, but often combine two or more modes. We explore each mode in turn.

Foraging

Foraging refers to searching for edible plant and animal foods without domesticating them. Hunter-gatherers, who obtain their subsistence through a combination of collecting foods and hunting prey, are called "foragers." Because of their limited storage and transportation technologies, most foragers live mobile lives, traveling to where the food happens to be, rather than moving the food to themselves (Bates 1998).

A common stereotype about foraging is that it is a brutal struggle for existence. This stereotype is inaccurate, because in reality foragers tend to work less to procure their subsistence than people who pursue horticulture or pastoralism. For example, Richard Lee found that !Kung San (also known as Ju/'hoansi) hunter-gatherers of the Kalahari Desert in Southern Africa spent less than 20 hours per week getting food (Lee 1969). Although some hunter-gatherer groups work more hours per week, none of them routinely work the equivalent of a 40-hour week as people in agricultural and industrial societies typically do. Anthropologist Marshall Sahlins (1972) used Lee's data to suggest that hunter-gatherer societies are the "original affluent society" because they had more leisure time than people in most other societies. Sahlins did not define affluence in terms of material possessions, as many of us might think of it, but in terms of how much free time hunter-gatherers have compared to everyone else in the world. In addition, Sahlins's idea of affluence reflects hunter-gatherers' view that their natural environments are not harsh (as we might view them), but are always providing for their needs, even in times of objective scarcity such as drought (Bird-David 1992).

It is all too easy to view foraging communities as a peculiar survival of our Paleolithic past, since humans lived this way for 99% of our history. But contemporary foragers tend to inhabit extreme environments where horticulture or pastoralism are not feasible, such as the desert, the arctic tundra, or certain rain forests. There is plenty of ethnographic evidence that most contemporary foragers often integrate some gardening or herding into their hunting-gathering strategies. Many have also had trading relationships with food-producing communities, especially to obtain carbohydrates (Spielmann and Eder 1994). For example, the foraging Okiek (oh-**kee**-eck) of Kenya obtain more than half their calories from domesticated garden vegetables grown by neighboring settlers, which they trade for goods collected in forests, such as honey and fruits. The trade networks in which foragers participate can even have a global reach. For example, during the nineteenth century, San hunter-gatherers in Southern Africa hunted elephants and gathered the tusks to feed the booming global trade in ivory to produce piano keys (Gordon 2005).

One of the main questions surrounding foragers is why they persist in a world of food producers (Spielmann and Eder 1994). Why do they not turn to agriculture? Remember first that the foraging life is not as brutal a struggle for existence as stereotypes about it suggest. Foragers tend to give up their mode of subsistence only because they are forced to give it up. One explanation is that increased population density

• **Foraging.** Obtaining food by searching for it, as opposed to growing or raising it.

Figure 6.6   !Kung San Fighting for the Right to Hunt.
In Botswana, Bushmen have faced eviction from their traditional hunting lands. They have organized protests to raise awareness about their plight.

within foraging groups, which brings greater competition for plants and game, causes foragers to settle in one place and grow a reliable food source. Another explanation is the over-exploitation of a resource base by neighboring non-foraging people or foreign corporations. For example, the deforestation that accompanies the work of Japanese lumber companies has put major pressure on foraging communities in Southeast Asian rain forests, forcing them to settle because they can no longer live nomadically.

Foragers are typically ethnic minorities, and often they are treated in discriminatory ways by neighboring agricultural and herding peoples who view them as social inferiors. Sometimes maintaining a foraging existence is a form of resistance and a way of avoiding subordination to stronger groups (Dentan, Endicott, Gomes, and Hooker 1997; Gordon 2005). For example, some San foragers have fought to keep foraging, which they view as means to maintain their social independence. They have also become politically active in recent years, seeking to gain rights over territory that they see as the key to their survival (Figure 6.6).

Horticulture

Horticulture is the cultivation of gardens or small fields to meet the basic needs of a household. It is sometimes referred to as "subsistence agriculture," which means cultivation for household provisioning or small-scale trade, but not investment (Bates 1998). Horticulturists tend to be sedentary, living in one place. Horticulture emerged some 12,000 years ago with domestication, which gave humans selective control over animal and plant reproduction. Domestication increases the amount of predictable or reliable food energy that humans can get out of a piece of land (Bates 1998:70) (Figure 6.7).

The primary goal of horticulture is to feed a single household, resulting in certain characteristics. First, farmers cultivate only small plots and employ relatively simple technologies (hand tools like knives, axes, and digging sticks, for example) that have low impact on the landscape. Horticulture relies heavily on human labor and energy. Horticulturists have relatively small yields and are vulnerable to crop failures and soil depletion, and so they tend to rely on several plots of land scattered over a large area. Many horticulturalists also rely partly on hunting and products traded from other groups, particularly foragers who provide wild game, fruit, and nuts, to round out their diets.

The most common form of horticulture is **swidden agriculture**, or slash-and-burn agriculture. In some geographic areas, such as the tropics, swidden agriculture is the most effective mode of agriculture because burning releases nutrients into the soil. Tropical soils are nutrient-poor because most nutrients reside in the vegetation, and heavy rainfall washes nutrients out of the soil. By clearing a patch of forest and burning the vegetation, farmers create ash that fertilizes the soil. A farmer can use such a plot for several years (between three and seven or so, depending on local climate and soil conditions), usually planting 10 to 20 different crops that mature or ripen at different times. These garden plots often imitate the ecological diversity and structure of the rain forest itself, with some plants living in the understory shade, others in the twilit middle level, and others in the sunny top. By the time the crops are all harvested the soil is depleted, and the farmer will move to another plot to repeat the process. Old plots lie fallow so nitrogen-fixing bacteria in the soils can regenerate the soil and trees and shrubs can grow. If there are no other pressures, such as population growth or new settlers coming to a rainforest area, a farmer might not return to work one

- **Horticulture.** The cultivation of gardens or small fields to meet the basic needs of a household.

- **Swidden agriculture.** A farming method in tropical regions in which the farmer slashes and burns a small area of forest to release plant nutrients into the soil. As soil fertility declines, the farmer allows the plot to revert to forest and regenerate nutrients to the soil.

Figure 6.7 Horticulture in Papua New Guinea. *(a)* Mixed garden enclosed in a fence in the lowland Ningerum area; *(b)* Freshly planted sweet potato mounds in Highland New Guinea; *(c)* A married couple in their mature sweet potato garden.

of these fallow plots for several decades, rotating between several plots of land over a long period of time. Slash-and-burn agriculture tends to work best when population densities are low, because the land requires long fallow periods.

The shift from foraging to horticulture was not a matter of people "discovering" that seeds grew into plants, shrubs, and trees. Early foraging peoples knew more about these natural processes than most of us do today, because they lived within these complex natural environments. According to Danish economist Ester Boserup (1965), full-time horticulture takes more work than foraging, and foragers would never have shifted to planting crops unless forced to because a group's population was growing. Boserup theorized that, with growing numbers of mouths to feed, foragers would have started planting some crops, gradually becoming more settled and less nomadic. Although anthropologists still debate details of this theory, it has helped explain the role of population growth and technology in the transition from foraging to horticulture.

Pastoralism

Pastoralism is the practice of **animal husbandry**, which is the breeding, care, and use of domesticated herding animals such as cattle, camels, goats, horses, llamas, reindeer, and yaks (Bates 1998). Rather than raising animals for butchering as food, pastoralists mainly consume their milk and blood and exploit their hair, wool, fur, and ability to pull or carry heavy loads. This approach allows them to get more out of the animal in the long run. Pastoralists typically occupy the landscapes beyond the reaches of productive agricultural lands, especially arid scrublands where irrigation cannot reach (Figure 6.8).

While some pastoralists are sedentary, others live as nomads, moving themselves and their herds in search of grazing lands. One form of nomadic pastoralism is **transhumance**, or regular seasonal movement from one ecological niche to another. For example, during the dry season, the Maasai of Kenya move their cattle to areas

- **Pastoralism.** The practice of animal husbandry.

- **Animal husbandry.** The breeding, care, and use of domesticated herding animals such as cattle, camels, goats, horses, llamas, reindeer, and yaks.

- **Transhumance.** Regular seasonal movement of herding communities from one ecological niche to another.

Figure 6.8   Saami Reindeer Herder. The Saami, who live in northern Scandinavia, are pastoralists who live from reindeer herding.

● **Horizontal migration.** Movement of a herding community across a large area in search of whatever grazing lands may be available.

where there are permanent waterholes, and during the rainy season, to grazing lands that are normally dry (Igoe 2004). A different form of nomadic pastoralism is **horizontal migration**, which refers to movement across a large area in search of whatever grazing lands may be available. The Bedouins of the Arabian Peninsula, for example, move their herds across many thousands of square miles, making use of whatever scant vegetation might be available in this arid environment, periodically congregating at permanent water holes for short periods (Bates 1998).

Because a livestock herd can do quick, even irreparable, damage to vegetation in arid landscapes, this mode of subsistence requires the constant movement of herds (Igoe 2004). This movement is typically coordinated between herd-owning households. At the heart of this system is common ownership of land and social institutions that ensure herders do not sacrifice the fragile environment for short-term individual gains. These social institutions include livestock exchanges to redistribute and limit herd size, punishments for individuals who diverge from planned movement patterns, and the defense of rangeland boundaries to ensure that neighboring pastoral groups cannot invade with their own livestock (McCabe 1990). When these institutions work successfully, pastoralism is an effective mode of subsistence, providing people with a stable source of nutritious foods (milk, blood, and meat) without irreversibly destroying the fragile landscape.

In recent decades, certain pressures have forced some nomadic pastoralists to settle and abandon their mode of subsistence semi-permanently. Causes include drought, famine, livestock diseases, loss of common property, and the political turmoil of civil wars, such as in the Sahelian countries of Sudan and Somalia (Fratkin 2003). Also, a number of governments and development aid agencies view pastoralism as primitive or a sign of underdevelopment and have tried to encourage or even force pastoralists to settle by digging wells and building villages for them, or by dividing up common lands and privatizing them to exploit the resources "more rationally." But most of these schemes have had disastrous social, economic, and ecological consequences for pastoralist communities because they disrupt the mobility and collective control of resources that are so critical to effective pastoralism (Stiles 1993).

Intensive Agriculture

While the goals of horticulture and pastoralism are to feed families, the goal of intensive agriculture is to increase yields to feed a larger community. There are a number of approaches to **intensification**, which refers to processes that increase yields (Bates 1998). These include the following:

- *Preparing the soil*, with regular weeding, mulching, mounding, and fertilizing;
- *Using technology*, which can be simple, such as a harness or yoke that allows a farmer to use horses or oxen to plow a field; complex, such as a system of canals, dams, and water pumps that provide irrigation to an arid landscape; or very complex, like a combine harvester, a machine that harvests, threshes, and cleans grain plants like wheat, barley, and corn;
- *Using a larger labor force*, such as in Asian rice farming, which sustains the nutritional and energy needs of large populations and provides many people with employment (Geertz 1963);
- *Managing water resources*, which can range from the practice of adding pebbles to fields to retain soil moisture (as ancient Pueblo dwellers of North America did), to the use of large-scale and sophisticated irrigation systems implemented by modern states;
- *Modifying plants and soils*, through selective breeding of plants to produce better yields, reduce the time needed to mature, or create a more edible product, as farmers have done for major grains like maize, rice, and wheat (Bates 1998).

Intensification carries certain trade-offs. On one hand, it solves an important human problem, which is how to provide food for a large number of people, including those who do not work directly in food production. It also provides a relatively steady supply of food, though famines can still happen. For thousands of years, intensive systems around the world have provided large communities with a stable source of nutrition and energy and, many archaeologists insist, have made possible the rise of cities and states with their complex social organization.

On the other hand, intensification can create new problems, especially environmental ones. By rearranging ecosystems to achieve greater control over natural processes, intensive agriculture is vulnerable to declining environmental conditions. For example, clearing a hillside to plant crops, build terraces, or install waterworks may increase productivity in the short run, but these can lead to the erosion of topsoils, lowering of water tables, concentration of salts in soils, the silting up of waterworks, and so on. Farmers may not notice declining environmental conditions immediately, because these are often long-term effects. Eventually, however, farmers may have to work harder just to maintain the same level of productivity. Such is the case in California's Imperial Valley, where decades of irrigation to aid the production of vegetables for sale throughout the United States market have created salt concentration in the soil, worsening overall soil quality (Bates 1998).

Industrial Agriculture

The most intensive form of agriculture is **industrial agriculture**, which applies industrial principles to farming. Key principles include specialization to produce a single crop, and the obtaining of land, labor, seeds, and water as commodities on the open market (Figure 6.9). This form of agriculture is characteristic of highly industrialized and post-industrial economies in which only 1% to 5% of the population engages in farming. Many proponents of industrial agriculture claim it is the only way to feed a burgeoning world population, although there is enormous global inequality in terms

- **Intensification.** Processes that increase agricultural yields.

- **Industrial agriculture.** The application of industrial principles to farming.

Figure 6.9   Factory Farms in the Twenty-first Century. In the United States, most of the farms that produce meat, eggs, and dairy products are organized on industrial principles. These farms create economies of scale to reduce costs and maximize profits.

- **Green Revolution.** The transformation of agriculture in the Third World, beginning in the 1940s, through agricultural research, technology transfer, and infrastructure development.

of how its benefits are distributed. It is closely associated with the **Green Revolution**, an initiative born after the Second World War in which scientific research has been applied to the expansion and intensification of crop production in the Third World. The Green Revolution has spread the use of "super crops" developed from new genetic strains and grown with the use of synthetic chemical inputs, in many places tripling or quadrupling crop yields (Bates 1998).

Through the use of machines and other technologies, industrial agriculture harnesses sources of energy such as steam power and petroleum, vastly increasing the scale of productivity. It is very energy-intensive—about one-fifth of all energy consumption in the United States goes toward sustaining industrialized foodways (Mark 2006)—and, compared with other subsistence strategies, inefficient, because it uses many more units of energy (in nonrenewable resources) than it produces (in calories the food yields). Technology-based farming has also redefined our notion of what agricultural work is. On some farms, such as those that produce grains like corn and wheat, farming now means tending to huge machines that provide nearly all the actual farm labor (Bates 1998). As a result of mechanization, a small rural labor force (in the United States, less than 2% of the total population) can produce so much food that one of industrial agriculture's greatest economic problems is *over*-production.

Industrial agriculture also requires very specific environmental conditions in order to be successful. Creating these conditions requires heavy inputs of synthetic chemical fertilizers, pesticides, and large amounts of water. These inputs have various effects on ecosystems, including pollution of waterways and rivers with phosphate from fertilizers, poisoning of groundwater with pesticide residues, and depletion of water supplies. Over the long run, this approach undermines soil quality, and as soil quality declines, industrial farms become even more dependent on synthetic fertilizers.

Today, biotechnology is also a common feature of industrial agriculture, providing farmers not only with "improved" high-yield seeds and fertilizers—beyond anything the Green Revolution ever created—but with crops that are pest- or pesticide-resistant or that ripen within a set time frame. These high-tech developments are expensive to purchase, so it is either large landowners or giant agricultural corporations who benefit most from industrial agriculture.

Because of industrial agriculture, foodways around the world are changing quickly, as we discuss in the next section.

THINKING CRITICALLY ABOUT FOODWAYS

Even though most of us probably get our food from a supermarket, can you identify examples of other modes of subsistence in our own society? How and why do these multiple modes of subsistence persist? Can you identify situations in which people combine modes of subsistence?

How Are Contemporary Foodways Changing?

Industrial agriculture and dynamics like globalization are fueling major changes in foodways around the world. In some countries, financial pressures are forcing farmers to switch from raising traditional crops that can feed local communities to producing non-traditional crops that can be exported for cash. For example, the World Bank has encouraged countries such as Costa Rica, Honduras, and Colombia to produce houseplants, flowers, melons, and other highly specialized commodities that can be sold to foreign markets. The goal is to generate foreign revenue that the countries can then use to pay back their World Bank loans and to invest in domestic development. Similar trends exist in the United States, where government policies favor industrial agriculture over small-scale or subsistence-oriented production (McDonald 1993). For example, in the so-called "Corn Belt" (the dozen or so Midwestern states that dominate corn production), family farms have largely been replaced by a handful of heavily government-subsidized agribusiness conglomerates that are able to produce enormous quantities of grain for export and for industrial processing into food. Industrially produced corn is a key ingredient in virtually all processed foods, and it is a major source of feed for livestock.

In response to these and other significant changes in foodways, anthropologists have turned their attention to situations like the interactions between community-level and industrial food systems, labor conditions in factory farming, and causes of local food insecurity. Many of these issues meld into public health concerns, and there, too, anthropologists are focusing on relevant issues such as the relationship between food and urban development policies that contribute to diet-related diseases. A key concern is how changes in contemporary foodways have contradictory and uneven effects on people, producing a situation that food-systems scholar Raj Patel (2008) refers to as "stuffed and starved."

Contradictory Patterns in India's Changing Foodways

We can see a powerful illustration of these contradictory patterns in India's changing foodways. In recent decades, India has experienced a rapid explosion in the number of people suffering from diabetes, currently at about 63 million (Kleinfield 2006; IANS [Indo-Asian News Service] 2014). Most of these people suffer from type 2 diabetes, a chronic disease of high blood sugar that can lead to blindness, heart failure, and limb amputations. The development of type 2 diabetes is linked to obesity, diets based on calorie-dense processed foods, and sedentary lifestyles. In India, it is a disease of the prosperous and overnourished, mainly afflicting the country's burgeoning population of urban middle-class professionals.

Simultaneously, about 300 million people in India are undernourished, and 42% of children under the age of five suffer from malnutrition (Yardley 2012). Many of these people live in rural areas, where for thousands of years small farmers have produced grains and vegetables for household consumption. But India's government has yielded to pressures from industry and encouraged a shift to industrial agriculture based on biotechnology and genetically modified organisms, fertilizers, and pesticides. Promising access to global markets and big profits, this industrial agriculture dictates a type of farming that transforms rural lands into expansive farms that produce export cash crops, such as cotton and soy, rather than food for local consumption.

This shift has been difficult for many of India's small farmers. Having to purchase expensive seeds, fertilizers, and pesticides to accommodate the new methods, many

Figure 6.10 Indian Farmer Suicides. Caught in a trap of indebtedness to keep up with the increasing industrialization of agriculture in rural India, tens of thousands of farmers have committed suicide in recent years.

- **Food security.** Access to sufficient nutritious food to sustain an active and healthy life.

- **Obesity.** Having excess body fat to the point of impairing bodily health and function.

- **Overweight.** Having an abnormally high accumulation of body fat.

farmers have gone deeply into debt. Even when global prices go up, many farmers can barely make ends meet because their interest payments are so high. And when global prices drop, farmers become vulnerable to debt collectors and the social stigma of defaulting on their loans. The ecological costs are also high. Cash crops attract new insect pests, so farmers have applied more pesticide. Overuse of pesticide has poisoned waterways, destroyed soils, and killed off natural predators that traditionally control pests. Even worse, many pests have become pesticide resistant. During the past two decades, the combined factors of increasingly dismal harvests, indebtedness, and the shame of defaulting on loans have come crashing down on the most vulnerable farmers, leading tens of thousands—at its high point (2002–2006), as many as 17,500 a year—to commit suicide by drinking the very pesticide that contributed to their woes (Sharma 2004; Patel 2007) (Figure 6.10).

As industrial agricultural development has spread across India, most affected farmers have lost control of their production and now work as laborers or tenant farmers for large agribusinesses, most of whose production is for export to industrialized countries. Thus, there is little rice, grain, or vegetables available for the local population (Patel 2007). These conditions have undermined local **food security**, which refers to access to sufficient nutritious food to sustain an active and healthy life. As we will see in "Anthropologist as Problem Solver: Teresa Mares and Migrant Farmworkers' Food Security in Vermont," concerns over what happens to rural people's food security when their foodways industrialize have become an important area of anthropological research and application.

Industrial Foods, Sedentary Lives, and the Nutrition Transition

As noted, industrialized foodways can affect people's health in negative ways. One dimension of this problem is the role industrial foods have played in the dramatic global rise of people who are overnourished, as reflected in growing global rates of **obesity** and of **overweight**. There are now more people in the world who are suffering the effects of overnourishment—estimated at 1 billion overweight and 475 million obese people—than people classified as undernourished, estimated at 875 million (Food and Agriculture Organization of the United Nations [FAO] 2012; International Obesity Task Force 2013). Because obesity and overweight can cause chronic diseases—diabetes and heart disease among them—health officials and researchers consider them to be among the most serious public health crises facing the world.

Obesity is a complex metabolic syndrome, or combination of medical conditions, that is related to non-genetic factors like maternal health and diet during pregnancy, and environmental conditions. For example, an individual whose mother smoked or received insufficient nutrition during pregnancy may have a higher likelihood of developing obesity later in life. New research also links obesity to the presence of certain environmental toxins that have disruptive effects on endocrine production. Some individuals may be genetically predisposed to gain weight more easily than others, but it is also clear that obesity tends to develop in a person who eats a lot of food while expending little energy (Ulijaszek and Lofink 2006).

Anthropologist as Problem Solver
Teresa Mares and Migrant Farmworkers' Food Security in Vermont

KNOWN FOR ITS high-quality cheeses and as the home of the iconic ice cream brand Ben & Jerry's, Vermont has long enjoyed a reputation as an idyllic agrarian landscape full of milk cows. But dairy farming is a difficult, year-round job with unreliable financial returns due to fluctuations in the price of milk. The activity has shifted in the past 60 years from being managed primarily as small-scale family-run operations to what is now a highly mechanized industry made up of a small number of large farms. Not able to rely on locals, who no longer want to work on these farms, the Vermont dairy industry has increasingly staked its survival on the employment of low-wage migrant farmworkers, most of them undocumented laborers from southern Mexican states like Chiapas, Veracruz, and Oaxaca.

University of Vermont food anthropologist Teresa Mares, who studies how the diets and foodways of Latino/a immigrants change as a result of migration (Mares 2014), set out to research ethnographically what the lives of these farmworkers are like and how their dietary patterns have changed now that they work on dairy farms. She quickly found out through interviews with farmworkers and immigrants' rights advocates that working on a dairy farm in rural Vermont is a stressful and isolating experience. These farmworkers rarely get away from their places of work because they are afraid of being deported. Moreover, they have limited access to transportation to travel the long distances from the farms to the nearest towns.

Mares conducted a "Community Food Security Assessment" of these farmworkers, which is a U.S. Department of Agriculture survey that measures household access to food, food availability and affordability, and community food production resources. The results showed that something most of us take for granted—the ability to go to a supermarket to get nutritious food—is almost impossible for these farmworkers, who have to rely on others to do the shopping for them, usually their employer or someone else who lives on or near the farm. These trips are often irregular, and miscommunication between Spanish and English speakers is a common problem, resulting in hunger due to inconsistent access to any food, much less food that is culturally familiar and affordable.

There are multiple ironies to this situation, the most obvious one being that the very people producing an iconic food product themselves suffer from food insecurity and hunger. Another irony is that most of these people left their homes in rural Mexico in the first place because of food insecurity brought on by the kinds of globalizing factors now opening jobs for them in Vermont's dairy industry. Among

🌱 Teresa Mares.

🌱 A Pastoral Vermont?

(continued)

Anthropologist as Problem Solver (continued)

these factors is the 1994 North American Free Trade Agreement (NAFTA), which displaced southern Mexican farmers who could not compete with cheaper American imports of Midwestern corn and milk from various dairy states, including Vermont.

Recognizing an opportunity to address an acute problem and to create new opportunities for collaborative research with colleagues in other fields like agriculture and health, Mares worked with her university's extension office and community volunteers to create a program that would make seeds, tools, and technical guidance available to farmworkers so that they could plant their own vegetable and herb gardens on the dairy farms. Mares met regularly with farmworkers participating in the program, interviewing them at length about issues such as their knowledge about gardening techniques, what kinds of foods they liked to eat, their cooking patterns, and their household spending patterns. She also worked alongside them in gardens and kitchens—hoeing soils, transplanting seedlings, making meals, etc.—which are useful vantage points from which to observe their actual food practices.

This research has produced detailed ethnographic insights into how farmworkers cope with food insecurity and struggle to maintain food practices that are meaningful to them, as well as the successes the program has made in improving the farmworkers' food security. It has also been useful to the people who run the program, who have used Mares's data to assess the effectiveness of the program and to improve its delivery as they begin to address other issues of food insecurity in rural Vermont.

Questions for Reflection

1. Review the USDA's Community Food Security Assessment Toolkit (available online at https://www.ers.usda.gov/publications/pub-details/?pubid=43179). How do the data this toolkit elicits differ from the data one might gather from participant observation? In what ways do the two types of investigation complement each other?

2. What kinds of ethical dilemmas accompany research with a community like undocumented farmworkers?

Social factors influence how much food people eat and contribute directly to the production of obesity and overweight. These factors include the presence of other individuals at a meal, television viewing, portion size, cultural attitudes toward body fat, and learned preferences (Ulijaszek and Lofink 2006). Consider how powerful just one of these factors—television viewing—can be: in the United States during the 1990s, a child watched, on average, 10,000 television advertisements for food per year, with 95% of those foods being sugared cereal, sweets, fast food, and soft drinks, all of which are fattening (Brownell 2002). Or consider portion sizes, which food corporations have increased to enhance profitability. Twenty years ago, for example, the average bagel was 3 inches in diameter and 140 calories. Today it is 6 inches and 350 calories!

Scholars have also traced the current worldwide rise of obesity and overweight to a global **nutrition transition**, the combination of changes in diet toward energy-dense foods (high in calories, fat, and sugar) and a decline in physical activity. These changes in diet are related to an abundant, secure, and inexpensive food supply, which is the very definition of success for industrial agriculture. But this success is double-edged, because the result is a food supply of relatively low nutritional quality, offering processed grains, fats, and refined sugars instead of fruits, vegetables, whole grains, and lean meats—the foods on which we thrive as a species. The other major change is the movement worldwide since the mid–nineteenth century of massive numbers

● **Nutrition transition.** The combination of changes in diet toward energy-dense foods (high in calories, fat, and sugar) and declines in physical activity.

of people away from rural areas, where they tend to lead physically active lives, to cities and suburbs, where they lead more sedentary lives and have more transportation options. For example, in 1900, only about 10% of the world population lived in cities. Today it is 50%, and rates of urbanization continue to be high around the world.

Both of these factors also explain why the problem of obesity is a problem not just in wealthy countries like the United States, but also in poor countries. As we saw earlier, the importation of inexpensive foods from industrialized countries into poorer ones affects the economic accessibility of foods as well as local diets. Because small-scale farms, which produce locally grown and nutrient-rich food, can rarely compete with the low-cost foods of transnational agribusinesses, many small-scale farms shut down their operations. With fewer farms to support rural livelihoods, people then migrate to urban areas where they tend to be less physically active.

The Return of Local and Organic Foods?

Widespread concern over access to healthy foods is currently driving an explosion of interest in **sustainable agriculture** (farming based on integrating goals of environmental health, economic productivity, and economic equity), organic foods, and local food production, especially among consumers in Europe and the United States, who live in the heart of industrialized agriculture. During the past decade and a half, farmers' markets have reappeared in many American cities and suburbs to support local production. Community-supported agriculture, in which neighbors buy shares in a local farm and receive its produce, has also proven to be a viable business model for a growing number of small farmers.

Researchers are also challenging the assumption that industrial agriculture consistently produces more, if not also better, food than traditional systems of farming do. A study of small farms in 52 countries found that when farmers adopted certain techniques of **agroecology** (the integration of the principles of ecology into agricultural production), their average yields rose 93%, increases that were greater than what the farmers could have achieved by using industrial methods of production (Pretty 2002). These agroecological techniques emphasize organic production and, instead of turning to synthetic fertilizers and pesticides sold by international conglomerates, involve the integration of natural processes such as nutrient cycling, nitrogen fixation, and soil regeneration, as well as the introduction of natural enemies of pests. These farming practices also incorporate the knowledge and skills of the local farmers, who typically have a superior understanding of local ecological conditions (Pretty 2002).

There are also important cultural dimensions to these efforts at localizing food, according to anthropologist Amy Trubek, who has studied local food movements in France and the United States. Trubek (2008) explains that the new interest in local foods taking the United States and a number of other countries by storm has its origins in the French ideal of *gout de terroir* ("taste of place"), which refers to the connection between locally based farming and cooking practices and the quality of a food's flavor. Being able to identify the origins of a food and know particular details about the land on which it was produced and the practices of the farmer who produced it, Trubek argues, is an important new way of expressing social discernment around food and drink. It also aligns closely with support for local and traditional methods of food production, such as organic and small-scale production. Trubek suggests that what is happening is itself a process of globalization, as the ideal of eating "the taste of place" is being spread around the globe through food television channels and other media.

- **Sustainable agriculture.** Farming based on integrating goals of environmental health, economic productivity, and economic equity.

- **Agroecology.** The integration of the principles of ecology into agricultural production.

The Biocultural Logic of Local Foodways

Although foodways are dynamic, people have a pretty stable concept of an appropriate diet that reflects their understanding of proper foods, good taste, and nutritional requirements. It is relatively stable because our biological requirements of adequate energy and nutrition and the cultural requirements of meaning and satisfaction are themselves fairly stable. Underlying these facts is a simple biocultural logic: if a diet works, if it provides sustenance and meaning, then people are unlikely to drop it completely when something new comes along. People integrate new foods and cuisines into their existing dietary practices all the time, but since this biocultural logic of local foodways is also integrated into the production, preparation, and sharing of food, overnight change is unlikely.

The biocultural logic of foodways is also related to the reason people do not automatically adopt industrial methods to increase productivity. The cultural logic underlying industrial agriculture is to create never-ending productivity and accumulation of profit. But many people around the world do not share this cultural logic. Their goal is to meet their basic subsistence needs, based on a cultural logic of sufficiency and adequacy. As long as population densities remain low, foraging, horticulture, pastoralism, and some forms of small-scale agriculture require a much smaller investment of work and financial investment, while providing adequate nutrition and energy.

• •

THINKING CRITICALLY ABOUT FOODWAYS

There is perhaps no more consequential issue for the future of human environmental and bodily health than the changing dynamics of foodways in the contemporary world. What role do you think anthropologists of food should play in the issues of changing foodways? What specific kinds of knowledge or interventions do you think are most appropriate for anthropologists to consider?

• •

Conclusion

Returning to where we opened this chapter, with the complex dynamics of Greek foodways, we have to recognize that at the heart of that situation is a critical point: what and how people eat, the foods they find or grow, and how they share and prepare those foods are patterned and interlocking issues (Pottier 1999:25–26). The fact that each of these elements is subject to diverse pressures, including financial crises and other broader patterns of global interactions, means that changes in foodways are always complicated. Or consider India, where alarming numbers of people are developing diabetes from overnourishment and sedentary lifestyles, while others, particularly those living in rural areas, are confronting poverty, starvation, and ecological ruin. Each of these processes is related to certain aspects of Indian society and history, but each is also a consequence of that country's involvement in broader global changes that affect the production, distribution, and consumption of food. Because these global dynamics also affect many other countries, Greece and India are not alone in confronting rapidly changing foodways.

But even as foodways are dynamic, we also know that there are certain relatively stable characteristics of human foodways, as can be seen with modes of subsistence. The simplest mode of subsistence is foraging, in which hunter-gatherers collect wild fruits, nuts, tubers, and greens and hunt for animals. As populations grew and the land could no longer provide sufficient food for communities, people began producing their own crops with simple horticulture, small fields for family-based subsistence. Some of these producers specialized into pastoralists, who tended herds, and intensive agriculturalists. Intensive agriculture was the first mode of subsistence able to feed people not engaged in food production, allowing for the rise of cities and states. With increasing mechanization, industrial agriculture has developed, with its potential for large yields per acre but fewer farmers and important consequences for the environment, food security, and people's health.

The panorama of human relationships with food is broader than that of any other species, based on the highly fluid and adaptable aspects of our human dietary biology. But this does not explain why we eat the things we eat. The answer to that question has to do with the fundamental role of culture and political-economic processes in shaping how people meet their basic nutritional and energy needs.

KEY TERMS

Agroecology   p. 159

Animal husbandry   p. 151

Food security   p. 156

Foodways   p. 138

Foraging   p. 149

Green Revolution   p. 154

Horizontal migration
p. 152

Horticulture   p. 150

Industrial agriculture
p. 153

Intensification   p. 153

Lactase persistence
p. 141

Modes of subsistence
p. 148

Nutrition transition
p. 158

Obesity   p. 156

Overweight   p. 156

Pastoralism   p. 151

Structuralism   p. 144

Sustainable agriculture
p. 159

Swidden agriculture
p. 150

Taste   p. 145

Transhumance   p. 151

Reviewing the Chapter

Chapter Section	What We Know	To Be Resolved
Why Is There No Universal Human Diet?	There is no universal human diet because our dietary physiology is open-ended, leaving our needs to be defined and fulfilled partly by the specific natural environments in which we find ourselves, and even more so by the particular societies in which we live.	Anthropologists are still trying to understand the complex interactions between human biological evolution, histories of food production, and the development of food preferences.
Why Do People Eat Things That Others Consider Disgusting?	Cultural processes strongly shape which foods we eat, when and how we eat them, and why we eat them.	Anthropologists continue to work through how cultural attitudes and social practices surrounding food relate to social categories and dynamics such as class, race, ethnicity, and gender.
How Do Different Societies Get Food?	Humans have developed four general modes of subsistence—foraging, horticulture, pastoralism, and intensive agriculture—each of which carries certain social and environmental trade-offs and opportunities.	Anthropologists are working to understand how and why foragers, horticulturalists, and pastoralists persist in a world increasingly dominated by industrial and other forms of intensive agriculture. They are also investigating the pressures on these modes of subsistence.
How Are Contemporary Foodways Changing?	Industrial agriculture's rapid expansion around the globe is related closely to unequal political-economic relationships, creates new environmental and health risks, can diminish food security, and has important biocultural consequences. The effects of these pressures can be quite contradictory, leading to some groups being "stuffed" and others being "starved."	Anthropologists of food are relatively new to public health policy discussions about critical issues like food security and obesity, and they have just begun to define the anthropological dimensions of these issues.

Readings

There are many books, produced mostly by ecological anthropologists, on the diverse modes of subsistence described in the third section of this chapter. A useful introduction to that diversity is Daniel Bates's textbook *Human Adaptive Strategies: Ecology, Culture, and Politics* (third edition, Boston, MA: Allyn and Bacon, 2005), which does a good job not only of describing the social and ecological details of each individual mode of subsistence, but also of explaining how each mode is affected by contemporary global political-economic dynamics.

....

An excellent overview of the relationship between food and culture can be found in Eugene Anderson's *Everyone Eats: Understanding Food and Culture* (New York: New York University Press, 2005). It pairs well with Raj Patel's book *Stuffed and Starved: The Hidden Battle for the World Food System* (Brooklyn, NY: Melville House Press, 2008), which offers a culturally informed perspective on the globalization of industrialized foodways.

....

Andrea Wiley's book *Re-Imagining Milk: Cultural and Biological Perspectives* (New York: Routledge, 2011) offers a fascinating biocultural analysis of milk, explaining how and why cow's milk has become such a powerful marker of cultural identity for some people, even though most people in the world cannot consume it without great discomfort.

....

Carole Counihan and Penny Van Esterik's edited volume *Food and Culture: A Reader* (third edition, New York: Routledge, 2013) is a classic compilation of essays by many of the top figures in the anthropology of food.

....

Amy Trubek's book *The Taste of Place: A Cultural Journey into* Terroir (Berkeley, CA: University of California Press, 2008) offers close ethnographic description of local food movements around Europe and the United States, with a particular focus on how these movements develop ways for people to talk about the relationship between the taste of a food and where it comes from.

....

Environmental Anthropology

7

Relating to the Natural World

GIVEN CURRENT PATTERNS of climate change, the Micronesian country of the Marshall Islands will probably be submerged by the end of this century. Consisting of five islands and 29 coral atolls spread across 750,000 square miles of the central Pacific Ocean, the country's 70 square miles of land sit just a few feet above sea level. Consequently, rising seawaters represent an existential threat to the islands, adding another layer of woe in a region long fractured by the disruptions of European colonialism, the militarization of the Pacific during the Second World War, and most notoriously, U.S. nuclear and missile testing that has made the Marshall Islands, according to a 1956 report by the U.S. Atomic Energy Commission, "by far the most contaminated place in the world" (Cooke 2009: 168). The human and environmental costs of this testing have been high, with whole areas of land and ocean being declared off-limits, and many people experiencing health problems resulting from exposure to nuclear fallout.

The Marshallese are already feeling the effects of climate change, including intensified drought and flooding. Climate change raises many pressing questions for the country's 53,000 people, the most obvious being where they will go as their homes disappear. Under current international law, they cannot gain status as refugees because the legal category "refugee" applies only to people displaced by

The Challenge of Climate Change in the Marshall Islands.   Climate change has intensified flooding in the low-lying Marshall Islands. In this instance, a king tide was energized by a storm surge, leading to the flooding of Majuro, the capital atoll.

persecution, not to those displaced by an environmental problem like climate change.

One of the ironies of this situation, at least from a Marshallese perspective, is that the environmental problems facing them are not of their making. Indeed, the people living in the Marshalls since about 2,000 BCE developed strategies for living sustainably in a challenging environment where natural resources like fresh water, arable land, and fisheries are scarce, and extreme weather events such as droughts, tsunamis, earthquakes, and hurricanes are common. Marshallese food-production systems take these ecological conditions into account. For example, the traditional agricultural practice of growing taro, an important tuber in the Marshallese diet, in "humidity pockets" (pits dug in the ground and lined with layers of plants, organic mulch, and coral rubble) simultaneously reduces consumption of fresh water and increases food production in nutrient-deficient soils (Bridges and McClatchey 2009). Another traditional strategy, which is still in use today, is to designate a reef or an island, or parts of one, as *mo*, which means "prohibited" or "taboo." Such areas are under the control of high-ranking chiefs who regulate access. These chiefs might grant permission to harvest an area only for a special feast or in times of famine. Other customs limit the harvest of crabs and fish to certain times of year and prohibit the harvesting of females with eggs, to ensure the resilience of wild populations (Tibon n.d.).

Another important strategy has been to distribute the environmental risks of living on islands by scattering food production sites and trading with other islands. Like other Micronesians and Polynesians, the Marshallese were, until fairly recently, highly sophisticated seafarers who made voyages of sometimes thousands of miles in sailing canoes to participate in trading networks, using maps made of sticks, specialized knowledge of ocean currents and swell patterns, weather and tide forecasts, astral constellations, and close observation of wildlife behavior to navigate (Genz 2011).

But as a result of globalization patterns, almost no society in the world today relates to its environment or manages its resources in isolation, and the Marshallese are no exception. Recognizing that climate change is threatening their islands, the Marshallese have taken a global role in arguing for more sustainable relations with the natural world. For example, Kathy Jetnil-Kijiner, a Marshallese poet and activist, made a passionate appeal for action at the 2014 United Nations Climate Summit. In her keynote address, she described the Marshallese as "a proud people" who "don't want to leave" their islands, without which they feel they are "nothing" (Jetnil-Kijiner 2015)

The dilemmas facing Marshall Islanders lead us to the question at the center of **environmental anthropology**, the field that studies how different societies understand, interact with, and make changes to the natural world: *Why do some societies have sustainable relations with the natural world while others seem to be more destructive of their natural environments, and what sociocultural factors are driving environmental destruction in the contemporary world?*

● **Environmental anthropology.** The field that studies how different societies understand, interact with, and make changes to the natural world.

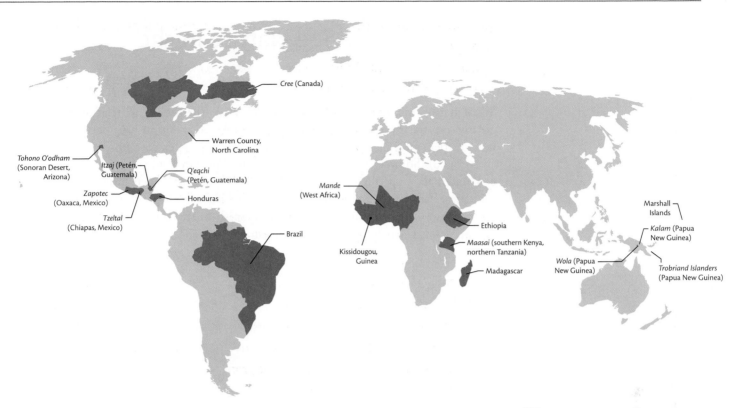

Cree (Canada)

Warren County,
North Carolina

Tohono O'odham
(Sonoran Desert,
Arizona)

Itzaj (Petén,
Guatemala)

Q'eqchi
(Petén, Guatemala)

Zapotec
(Oaxaca, Mexico)

Honduras

Tzeltal
(Chiapas, Mexico)

Brazil

Mande
(West Africa)

Ethiopia

Kissidougou,
Guinea

Maasai (southern Kenya,
northern Tanzania)

Madagascar

Marshall
Islands

Kalam (Papua
New Guinea)

Wola (Papua
New Guinea)

Trobriand Islanders
(Papua New Guinea)

Embedded in this broader question are the following problems, around which this chapter is organized:

Figure 7.1 Select Peoples and Places Discussed in Chapter 7.

Do all people see nature in the same way?

How does non-Western knowledge of nature relate to science?

Are industrialized Western societies the only ones to conserve nature?

How do social and cultural factors drive environmental destruction?

Because different groups of people view the natural world differently, they also have different environmental management practices. Studying the environmental beliefs, knowledge, and practices of different societies has long been a major concern at the heart of cultural anthropology. These issues have traditionally been studied in the settings of small-scale, non-Western societies where beliefs, knowledge, and practices differ markedly from Western views and practices. But in recent years, as global concern with environmental degradation, climate change, and the loss of biodiversity has mushroomed, environmental anthropologists have also been paying close attention to the effects of global economic changes on human–nature relations, the impacts of pollution and nature conservation initiatives on certain groups, and what sustainability means for different people. We begin by exploring how a people's environmental values and behaviors emerge from particular ways of thinking about the natural world.

Do All People See Nature in the Same Way?

What nature means to people and how they see themselves in relation to it vary greatly around the world. Consider, for example, the relationships between indigenous settlement and natural ecosystems in southern Mexico and Central America (Figure 7.2). Some of these areas, such as the Yucatán Peninsula, the Petén region of Guatemala, and the Miskito Coast of Nicaragua, have been inhabited for many centuries. These lowlands provided Indians of the region productive environments in which to live. After the arrival of the Spanish in the 1500s, they were safe areas for indigenous people because the Spanish conquerors found the tropical heat and

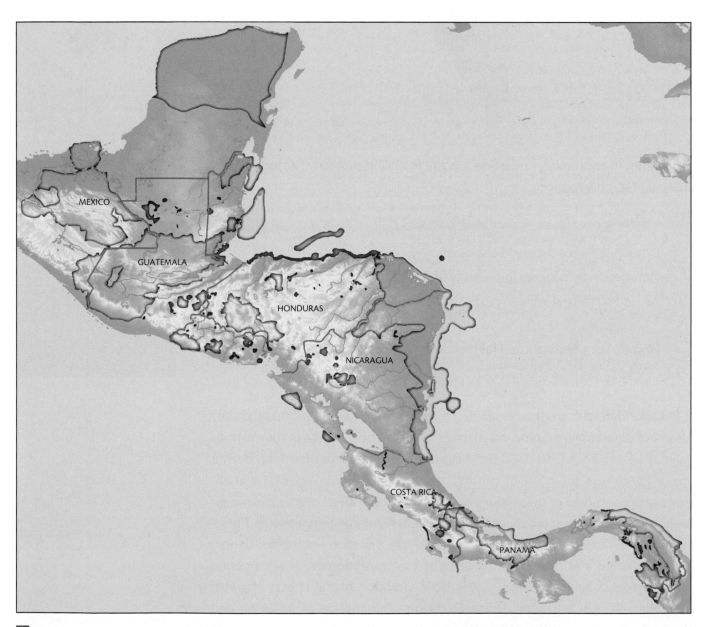

Figure 7.2   Linkages Between Biological and Cultural Diversity. The areas outlined in red on this map mark zones where indigenous populations live and where intact biodiverse ecosystems can be found in Central America and southern Mexico. This map is a simplified version of a map produced by the Center for the Support of Natives Lands and originally published in *National Geographic*, which superimposed the distribution of cultural diversity and the distribution of biological diversity in this area.

diseases undesirable (Lovgren 2003). Why did the indigenous people not simply cut the forest down for fields, as European settlers did in other parts of the New World? One reason was their low population density and subsistence economies based on swidden agriculture in which fields go back to forest to lie fallow after harvesting. But economic practices alone do not explain good stewardship; for that we need to understand the indigenous people's views of their environment. As Ken Rapp of the Center for the Support of Native Lands observed, "It's part of their belief system. They don't see a division between nature and man" (Lovgren 2003).

The Human–Nature Divide?

A good example of a group whose belief system fits with what Rapp described is the Itzaj, a Maya group that has lived in the Petén tropical lowlands of Guatemala since pre–Spanish contact times (Figure 7.3). According to Itzaj beliefs, humans and nature do not occupy separate realms; there is both real and symbolic reciprocity and communication between plants, animals, and humans. For example, forest spirits called *arux* ("masters of the wind") continually monitor people, and they play tricks on those who cut down too many trees or kill too many animals (Atran 2001:169). Those who show respect by not wantonly destroying plants and animals receive help from the *arux*, who will lead people to animals they are hunting or to useful trees (Atran 2001:169). It is not accidental that Itzaj agricultural practices respect and preserve the forest.

These ideas are quite alien to most of us in North America, but not all forms of Western thinking inherently divide humans from nature. The medieval Italian friar St. Francis of Assisi, for example, put all creatures more or less on the same plane as humans. Nevertheless, Western thought does tend to emphasize detachment, if not opposition, between humans and nature. This detachment can be seen in the metaphor of "natural resources," in which we see nature as an object for humans to possess, control, exploit, and manage. The ancient Greek philosopher Aristotle's notion of the Great Chain of Being, which proposed that all living beings exist in hierarchical order with humans (who were thought to be closest to God) at the top, provides an early basis for this metaphor. Western science later refined the idea of human dominion over "lower" beings. The English philosopher Sir Francis Bacon,

Figure 7.3 The Petén Region of Lowlands Guatemala.
Historically, people in the Petén have been swidden agriculturalists living in small settlements. Today, logging and tourism development are creating new economic opportunities—as well as ecological pressures—for communities.

- **Environmental determinism.** A theory that attempts to explain cultural characteristics of a group of people as a consequence of specific ecological conditions or limitations.

- **Ecological anthropology.** The specific vein with environmental anthropology that studies directly the relationship between humans and natural ecosystems.

- **Ecosystem.** Natural system based on the interaction of non-living factors and living organisms.

- **Cultural landscape.** The culturally specific images, knowledge, and concepts of the physical landscape that help shape human relations with that landscape.

the sixteenth-century originator of the scientific method, said that the "purpose of science was to restore to man the dominion that had been lost by the fall [from Eden]" (Thomas 1983:27). This view, that nature should be harnessed to make the world a better place for humans, is the basis of seeing nature as a resource (Igoe 2004:78).

Some Western philosophical traditions have emphasized an even starker separation between humans and nature, viewing nature as an independent force outside of humans that shapes the very characteristics of their societies. This position extends back at least to the ancient Greeks. In his work *Historiae,* the renowned historian Herodotus (484–425 BCE) argued that biophysical factors shaped human events and societies, declaring, for example, that Scythians were aggressive and fearsome warriors because of their struggle to survive in a barren desert environment. This idea is an early version of **environmental determinism**, the theory that nature and environmental conditions shape the characteristics and lifeways of a group of people. Some cultural anthropologists have promoted a version of environmental determinism, such as American anthropologist Marvin Harris (1979), who argued in the 1970s that customs develop as a direct way of regulating limited resources, acquiring protein for sustenance, controlling populations, and adapting to local ecological conditions.

The notion that nature plays a shaping role in human cultural life became broadly accepted within **ecological anthropology**, the specific vein within environmental anthropology, prominent between the 1960s and 1980s, that studied directly the relationship between humans and natural ecosystems. But many other environmental anthropologists believe that an extreme deterministic position leaves humans and nature divided, virtually in opposition, and that there is in fact less of a stark division between people and nature and more of a give-and-take in which people's lives are affected by nature but people also shape nature to fit their own interests. Indeed, contemporary ecological science supports this second position, recognizing that humans have dramatic and subtle effects on their environments, acting as a "keystone species"—predators who regulate animal populations and the functioning of **ecosystems**, which are natural systems based on the interaction of non-living factors and living organisms (Stoffle, Toupal, and Zedeño 2003).

Figure 7.4   Mother Nature as Metaphor. An example of a metaphor of human–nature relatedness is "Mother Nature," a concept that is familiar in many cultures and that remains popular in North America and Europe today. It represents nature as a living force with feminine qualities of procreation and nurturing, and it is an example of an "adult–child caring" metaphor that exists in many societies (Bird-David 1993).

The Cultural Landscape

For anthropologists, however, one of the problems with purely ecological analyses of human–nature relations is that they do not account for the abstract ideas people have about landscapes and other ideas that shape and guide their actions. One way to think of these abstract ideas is through the concept of a **cultural landscape**, which consists of the culturally specific images, knowledge, and concepts of the physical landscape that affect how people will actually interact with that landscape (Stoffle, Toupal, and Zedeño 2003:99). For example, the Itzaj consider nature to be an extension of their social world, full of spirits that influence their everyday lives. As a result, they are less likely to wantonly destroy the landscape in which they live, because doing so would destroy their very selves. Clearly, different social groups can hold distinct, even conflicting, ideas and images of the same landscape, because it is just as easy to imagine another view (that many North Americans might hold) of that same landscape as a place with useful resources—tropical hardwoods, for example—to exploit.

Key to understanding the cultural landscape is the idea that people use metaphors to think about their natural environments, and these metaphors are connected to social behavior, thought, and organization (Bird-David 1993:112; Figure 7.4). For example, in many hunting and gathering societies, people use metaphors of personal relatedness—sexuality, marriage, or family ties—to describe human–nature relations. An illustration of this notion is from the Cree who live throughout northern Canada, who describe hunting through sexual metaphors. The hunter "courts" the prey, whether moose, bear, or caribou, using magic and songs to "seduce" it. Hunters describe the kill as sexual intercourse, and its result (the corpse) is believed to be the joint product of hunter and prey. The male hunters, and the women who prepare the corpse to be eaten, are expected to show great respect to the prey (especially by using all parts of the corpse), because they see killing animals as ensuring the reproduction of both humans and animals. In this metaphoric way, the Cree think of animals as "married" to humans.

Metaphors are always complex, and different people may not understand them in the same ways. Nevertheless, metaphors offer insights into a community's cultural landscapes that symbolize the society's feelings and values about its environment. Anthropologists recognize that these metaphors also provide the intellectual and moral foundations upon which people construct more systematic environmental knowledge.

• •

THINKING CRITICALLY ABOUT ENVIRONMENTAL ANTHROPOLOGY

People's images and metaphors of human–nature relatedness reflect and communicate their attitudes toward nature and act as important guides to action. Besides "natural resources" and "Mother Nature," can you think of other metaphors of human–nature relatedness in our society? How do you think those metaphors relate to people's actual interactions with nature?

• •

How Does Non-Western Knowledge of Nature Relate to Science?

Environmental anthropologists try to describe the traditional knowledge that different societies have of their natural environments, recognizing that all knowledge systems about nature, including science, are culturally based. This goal dates back to the beginnings of anthropology as a discipline. For example, during his years among the Trobriand Islanders (1915–1918), Bronislaw Malinowski was keenly interested in people's knowledge of gardening, canoe building, and navigation. From observing these activities, he concluded that "primitive humanity was aware of the scientific laws of natural process" as well as magical processes, and went on to add that all people operate within the domains of magic, science, and religion (1948:196).

American anthropologist Paul Radin reached a similar conclusion from his fieldwork with Native Americans and wrote about it in his 1927 work *Primitive Man as Philosopher,* observing that "it is manifestly unfair to contend that primitive people are deficient either in the power of abstract thought or in the power of arranging these thoughts in a systematic order, or, finally, of subjecting them and their whole environment to an objective critique" (1927:354). In their time, these were highly controversial claims. Malinowski was implying that modern knowledge operated partly on non-scientific principles of magic and religion (which the West looked down upon as features of "less civilized" societies), and both were claiming that non-Western people could be scientific, too.

Do native knowledge systems have scientific validity? Malinowski reasoned that if knowledge is born of experience and reason, and if science is an activity characterized by rationality, then indigenous knowledge is part of humankind's store of scientific knowledge (Nader 1996:7). Since his time, anthropologists have demonstrated that scientific attitudes and methods of validation—close observation, experimentation, and analysis—are not unique to the West (1996:8). It is also the case that modern sciences have borrowed extensively from non-European societies. Key concepts and methods in mathematics, for example, are derived from India and the Arab world; some agricultural products and techniques from the pre-Columbian Americas; and technologies such as the magnetic needle and gunpowder from China (Harding 1994:347). So other societies have what we think of as scientific attitudes and practices. One key difference that distinguishes many non-Western knowledge systems from Western sciences, however, is that they are not necessarily viewed as distinct realms of knowledge, being integrated into people's spiritual beliefs, social practices, and individual identities, while in the West people tend to think of science as separate from all these things, as its own special domain of knowledge.

Ethnoscience

- **Ethnoscience.** The study of how people classify things in the world, usually by considering some range or set of meanings.

Early interest within environmental anthropology concerned with knowledge in non-Western societies was called **ethnoscience** (see also Chapter 4, on p. 95). During the 1960s, when ethnoscience was at its peak influence, ethnoscientists aimed to describe and understand the conceptual models and rules with which a society operates, following Malinowski's call for anthropologists to see the world from the "native's point of view" (Sturtevant 1964:100). They began by comparing the systems of classification used by the different peoples they studied.

Classification systems are reference systems that group things or ideas with similar features. Examples include plant and animal taxonomies, kinship terminologies, color schemes, and medical diagnoses. Classification systems create a common intellectual framework that people use to work with the natural world and communicate with each other.

The Linnaean classification system is what the scientific discipline of biology uses to classify all living organisms into species. Closely related species belong to the same genus, and related genuses are grouped into families, and so on. Brent Berlin, who studied **ethnobiology** (indigenous ways of naming and codifying living things) of the Tzeltal Maya [**schell**-tall **my**-yah], has argued that the Tzeltal and most societies for whom we have data divide living things into groups based on shared morphological characteristics as the Linnaen system does (Berlin 1973). Based on these findings, Berlin concluded that all human classification systems were basically reflective of an underlying cognitive structure of the human brain that organizes information in systematic ways—in other words, that all human minds more or less think alike.

- **Ethnobiology.** The subfield of ethnoscience that studies how people in non-Western societies name and codify living things.

But numerous challenges to Berlin's conclusions exist, based largely on the observation that some societies use non-morphological characteristics to classify plants and animals. For example, the Kalam people of the Papua New Guinea highlands do not consider the cassowary, a large flightless bird, as a bird. They also distinguish it from bats, which they put in the same category as birds. The Kalam classification system gives cassowaries a special taxonomic rank that places them close to humans (Bulmer 1967). Kalam mythology identifies cassowaries as sisters and cousins to Kalam men, and the Kalam place special restrictions on hunting them. The special taxonomic status of these creatures not only results from their unexpected physical characteristics (a bird that cannot fly) but also reflects certain social categories and relationships.

Another challenge comes from the existence of societies in which classification is a highly dynamic and unstable affair. For example, the Wola, who also live in the highlands of Papua New Guinea, have a system of classification that leaves much room for disagreement. In itself, such disagreement is not especially surprising: people often disagree with one another when they classify natural phenomena, because different people have different knowledge (Sillitoe 2002:1162). But the extent of disagreement in Wola is such that it can undermine the entire classification system. People regularly disagree over the identification of particular animals, devise their own names and categories based on personal experiences, and even dispute the structure of taxonomy itself. Confronting this system, environmental anthropologist Paul Sillitoe argues that the Wola have a taxonomy less in the Greek sense of a *taxis* (arrangement) of natural phenomena for intellectual purposes, than an arrangement in the political sense of being a way of talking through and settling differences (Sillitoe 2002:1169). The main purpose of their taxonomy is not to provide certainty, Sillitoe believes, but to keep people talking to each other, working out the issues and disputes that arise in everyday life. This situation is especially important for a society like the Wola, which has a non-hierarchical political order and has no political authority to settle disputes.

Traditional Ecological Knowledge

In environmental anthropology, ethnoscience's interests these days tend to focus on **traditional ecological knowledge**, which consists of indigenous ecological knowledge and its relationship with resource-management strategies. One of the more important findings of this field is that many ecological relations recognized by indigenous peoples are not known to Western science. One reason for Western unfamiliarity is that this knowledge often involves species that are endemic to remote regions and do not exist elsewhere. Indigenous knowledge also sometimes makes connections that Western science does not make. For example, many indigenous groups in the Americas make a distinction between domesticated and wild chili peppers. Groups such as the Tohono O'odham [Toe-**hoh**no Oh**oh**-dom] people of the Sonoran Desert in the American Southwest use a term akin to "bird peppers" for the wild ones, and when asked, they will name certain birds that consume those chilies and disperse their seeds. Ethnobiologist Gary Paul Nabhan designed an experiment to test this knowledge and confirmed its accuracy (Nabhan 2001). He suggests that indigenous knowledge can serve to guide scientific research on plant–animal interactions.

Another reason local ecological knowledge is not well known to Western science is that knowledge often resides in local languages, songs, or specialized ritual knowledge. Healers and shamans are important repositories of local plant knowledge and lore, and they may even keep their knowledge secret from other people in their own society. In recent years, ethnobotanists working with pharmaceutical companies have been trying to gain access to the knowledge of traditional healers to identify plants that might be useful for developing new commercial drugs.

One famous example of traditional medicinal knowledge that led to a commercially viable drug is that of the rosy periwinkle plant from Madagascar. Healers there have traditionally used it to treat diabetes, and scientists discovered that it also contains chemicals that are highly effective in treating certain cancers, including Hodgkin's disease. Eli Lilly, a U.S. pharmaceutical company, patented one of these chemicals and markets it as a pharmaceutical drug. Although traditional healers in Madagascar did not necessarily know about the plant's ability to treat cancer, many critics point out that these healers—from whom Western scientists first learned of the plant's healing properties—never received any compensation. As a result, many indigenous

- **Traditional ecological knowledge.** Indigenous ecological knowledge and its relationship with resource management strategies.

Figure 7.5   Maize Biodiversity in Southern Mexico.
Southern Mexico, where maize was domesticated
some 8,000 years ago, has long been a hotspot of maize
biodiversity. People like the Zapotec have developed tens
of thousands of varieties of maize with different flavors,
textures, adaptability to microclimates and soil conditions,
and colors. Each variety reflects the highly specialized
and customized knowledge of its farmers.

healers around the world are becoming increasingly protective of their knowledge in fear that transnational corporations can reap profits from their collective wisdom without their permission.

Because traditional ecological knowledge is customized to particular environments, it can also provide a highly effective basis for managing resources. For example, in the Southern Mexican state of Oaxaca, Zapotec farmers have been growing maize on the same landscape for hundreds of years (Figure 7.5). Farmers have a highly systematic understanding of how soil qualities, weather patterns, lunar phases, plant–plant interactions, and plant–insect interactions affect the growing of maize (Gonzalez 2001). Western scientists have discovered that Zapotec practices of intercropping (planting multiple crops together), building soil mounds for planting maize, letting the land lie fallow, and planting and harvesting by the phases of the moon all contribute to creating a highly productive and sustainable agricultural system (Gonzalez 2001).

Some elements of Zapotec science do not correspond to Western science and beliefs about effective resource management, however. One of the most important differences is that the Zapotec make no distinction between ecological knowledge and other forms of knowledge, such as ideas about morally acceptable behavior. Zapotecs believe that cultivations, especially maize, have a soul that rewards people who share with others. As a result, they believe that the success of a harvest is directly related to the farmer's positive reciprocal exchange relations with other members of the community.

When environmental anthropologists seek to understand how traditional ecological knowledge works to guide human action in particular communities, they have to take into account that the insider's point of view about what is going on in nature—for instance, the Zapotec belief that maize has a soul and if cultivated and shared properly will grow well—is often different from the views of outsiders, such as scientists who would explain that soil and climate conditions are what make maize grow. As we explore in "Classic Contributions: Roy Rappaport's Insider and Outsider Models," one prominent anthropologist argued that both views have relevance to the environmental anthropologist.

The Zapotec case demonstrates that traditional ecological knowledge has allowed communities to thrive for a long time on a landscape without destroying it. Unlike Western sciences, which claim to have universal tools for understanding nature, the Zapotec knowledge of nature is rooted in local cultural traditions and beliefs. The fact that such groups have not destroyed their environments, as many other societies have, has led some researchers to speculate that conservationist principles such as respect for local ecology and nature protection are embedded in traditional ecological knowledge. But do non-Western people actively conserve nature?

● ●

THINKING CRITICALLY ABOUT ENVIRONMENTAL ANTHROPOLOGY

The idea that traditional ecological knowledge provides an effective basis for managing natural resources is often resisted by Western agricultural scientists, who frequently dismiss these knowledge systems as not scientific or rigorous. How should environmental anthropologists respond to these kinds of claims?

● ●

Classic Contributions
Roy Rappaport's Insider and Outsider Models

Roy Rappaport with Maring villagers in Papua New Guinea.

AMERICAN ANTHROPOLOGIST ROY RAPPAPORT (1926–1997) was a major figure in ecological anthropology. He was a pioneer in the use of systems theory for understanding human populations. In his landmark 1968 study *Pigs for the Ancestors: Ritual in the Ecology of a New Guinea People* (1984), Rappaport distinguished between the insider's mental models of human–nature relations, called "cognized models," and models of human–nature relations identified by the observer, called "operational models." He argues that the goal of the anthropologist is to figure out how cognized models guide behavior, and how that behavior helps people adapt to specific environmental conditions:

[T]wo models of the environment are significant in ecological studies, and I have termed these "operational" and "cognized." The operational model is that which the anthropologist constructs through observation and measurement of empirical entities, events, and material relationships. He takes this model to represent, for analytic purposes, the physical world of the group he is studying. . . .

The cognized model is the model of the environment conceived by the people who act in it. The two models are overlapping, but not identical. While many components of the physical world will be represented in both, the operational model is likely to include material elements, such as disease germs and nitrogen-fixing bacteria, that affect actors but of which they may not be aware. Conversely, the cognized model may include elements that cannot be shown by empirical means to exist, such as spirits and other supernatural beings. . . . [T]he important question concerning the cognized model, since it serves as a guide to action, is not the extent to which it conforms to "reality" (i.e., is identical with or isomorphic with the operational model), but the extent to which it elicits behavior that is appropriate to the material situation of the actors, and it is against this functional and adaptive criterion that we may assess it. (Rappaport 1984:237–238; emphasis in the original)

Questions for Reflection

1. What are some reasons Rappaport might advocate a balanced approach between "cognized" and "operational" models of human–nature interactions?

2. Can you identify some elements of the insider's view or "cognized model" of our own society?

Are Industrialized Western Societies the Only Ones to Conserve Nature?

In 1872, when the U.S. government created the world's first national park, Yellowstone, it ushered in a new era of modern nature conservation with global effects. Around the world today, numerous countries, often with the support of influential global organizations like the International Union for Conservation of Nature (IUCN)

Figure 7.6   Stereotypes of Green Indians. In 1971, the "Keep America Beautiful" campaign developed by the U.S. government aired an anti-pollution television ad featuring an American Indian (portrayed by an Italian-American actor with the stage name of "Iron Eyes Cody") who sheds a tear because of pollution. There is usually a large gap between such romantic stereotypes and the real conditions in which indigenous groups relate to the environment.

or the World Wildlife Fund (WWF), have declared the formal protection of hundreds of millions of acres of wilderness landscape and ocean. In many cases, these efforts have stemmed the tide of near-certain destruction from extractive industries, settlement, or uncontrolled exploitation.

At the same time, the dominant cultural model for administering protected areas is based on the separation of humans and nature, emphasizing that nature must be kept uninhabited by people. Around the world, this model has led to forced evictions of indigenous peoples living on protected landscapes, disrupting their customary livelihoods, traditional land rights, and systems of environmental management that emphasize the conservation of resources (Colchester 2003; Chapin 2004). Environmental anthropologists have studied these dynamics closely, because they often generate social conflict in communities with different cultural perspectives on and histories within the natural world, as well as different approaches toward its conservation.

In exploring whether or not non-Western societies have intentionally conserved resources, it is necessary to overcome a powerful stereotype that a lot of Americans and Europeans hold about native peoples, that they are "natural environmentalists" always in tune with the natural world. Environmental anthropologists have documented many examples of destructive indigenous relationships with nature. One such example is that of the Q'eqchi Maya, who live near the Itzaj in Guatemala's Petén region and whose cattle ranching economy is destroying the rainforests of that region. Scholars also point to the "aboriginal overkill" that led to human-caused extinctions of certain animals toward the end of the Pleistocene Era (Ice Age) (Krech 1999). Stereotypes of Indians as "natural environmentalists" are romantic, and they often obscure the real conditions under which a group of people relate to nature (Figure 7.6). The key to answering this section's question is to consider first how indigenous societies have created landscapes that either deliberately or unintentionally have the effect of protecting natural ecosystems and wildlife, and second the ways in which Western societies approach the same objective.

Anthropogenic Landscapes

Upon close examination, many landscapes that appear "natural" to Westerners—sometimes the very landscapes that Westerners want to conserve without people on them—are actually the result of indigenous involvement and manipulation. In other words, they are **anthropogenic landscapes**, or products of human shaping.

A good illustration of an anthropogenic landscape is the North American continent during the early period of European settlement. When British settlers arrived on the East Coast, they found a continent abundant with woodlands and wild game and apparently inhabited by few people, and this discovery confirmed for them a sense that America was an unpeopled wilderness. Most Europeans did not realize that this landscape had been created by indigenous resource management systems, which included regular burning of underbrush to keep shrubs and grasses down and support seasonal migration (Cronon 1983). The intention of these Indian groups was to create environments that were easy to move around and hunt in, though to European eyes they looked like purely natural environments.

Environmental anthropologists have documented numerous examples of the creation of anthropogenic landscapes through human manipulation and management that actively and self-consciously support the conservation of specific plants and animals. For example, the Tohono O'odham of the Sonoran Desert, mentioned

• **Anthropogenic landscape.** Landscapes that are the product of human shaping.

earlier in this chapter, protect rare plants from overharvesting near sacred sites, transplant individual cacti and tubers to more protected sites, and promote the fruiting of certain rare food plants by pruning them (Nabhan 1997:162). The O'odham believe that humans are active participants in the desert ecosystem and that certain animals, plants, and habitats will "degenerate" unless humans care for them (Nabhan 1997:163). An important dimension of the O'odham case is that they recognize certain areas as powerful and sacred, where humans must tread cautiously and lightly. Indeed, many cultures around the world have long conserved resources in similar ways, such as through the designation of "sacred groves" or, as the Marshallese example mentioned earlier suggests, the designation of certain areas and resources as "prohibited" or "taboo."

Another important example of an anthropogenic landscape is the East African savannas of northern Tanzania and southern Kenya. The Maasai, who live there as pastoralists, have extensively modified their environment to support their cattle. They burn scrub brush to encourage the growth of nutritious pasture grass, an act that helps support wildlife biodiversity because these are the same nutritious pastures that the savanna's world-famous wildlife populations of zebras, wildebeest, and other large animals also eat (Igoe 2004). But today, some of these fragile scrublands are in crisis because Maasai pastoralists are undermining them with overgrazing. To understand why they now overgraze, we must look at the clash between Western and Maasai notions of managing and conserving nature.

The Culture of Modern Nature Conservation

To prevent overgrazing and conserve resources for themselves and wildlife populations, Maasai traditionally practiced a form of pastoralism called "transhumant pastoralism" in which they ranged over large territories of commonly held property on regular paths and cycles. During drought years, when pastures are most susceptible to overgrazing, the Maasai would traditionally bring cattle to swamp areas and permanent waterholes. But during the twentieth century, national parks and nature reserves were typically formed around these permanent wet areas (since a lot of wild animals congregate there, too), preventing Maasai access to them. Park administrators and scientists did not understand the delicate balance between people and wildlife that was sustained by the constant movement of people, their herds, and the wild animals. The result is that the Maasai were forced to overgraze areas outside the park during drought periods, producing great resentment among the Maasai and conflicts with park officials (Igoe 2004).

These park officials practice what anthropologist Dan Brockington (2002) calls "Fortress Conservation," an approach to conservation that assumes that people are threatening to nature, and that for nature to be pristine, the people who live there must be evicted. One question for the anthropologist is *Where does this culturally powerful idea that people and conservation of nature are incompatible originate?* The philosophical divide in Western thought between nature and people is one influence. In addition, at least three historical trends came together to create the culture of modern conservation: the enclosure movement in England, westward expansion in the United States, and European colonial expansion.

The English Enclosure Movement

For centuries, England's countryside was characterized by fields and pastures held in common by small farmers. Between the eighteenth and mid-nineteenth centuries, the English Parliament privatized these lands in what is known as the *enclosure movement*. The Napoleonic Wars had driven up the prices of grain and meat, and wealthy landowners saw opportunities to create large commercial farms to take advantage of these markets. Parliament turned over formerly common lands to private ownership, evicting farmers and sending them to work on the new farms or in urban factories. Rural people who tried to continue their lifestyles were branded criminals and sent off to the penal colony of Australia. The resulting depopulation of the English countryside accompanied a shift in how people thought about the landscape. Because the countryside was no longer populated by poor and working people, the wealthy began to idealize it as a place of scenic beauty and leisure (Igoe 2004:81). The connection between landscape appreciation and "civilized tastes" was born.

Westward Expansion in the United States.

During the nineteenth century, the idea of formally preserving wilderness took root in the western United States. With the Louisiana Purchase in 1803, Americans had accepted the doctrine of Manifest Destiny, which presumed that the destiny of the United States was to colonize and civilize the entire North American continent. Always self-conscious about our national identity vis-à-vis Europeans, Americans believed that the spectacular and vast resources and natural beauty of the North American continent could compete with the monuments and civilized arts of Europe. Soon after the turmoil of the Civil War ended, Americans set about showing our own "civilization" by establishing formally protected areas. The Indians who relied on these wilderness areas for their subsistence were branded as uncivilized and unappreciative of nature, and they were forcibly removed. For example, the creation of Yellowstone National Park entailed the removal of six different Indian groups from park lands (Guha 2000).

European Colonial Expansion

European colonial regimes commonly instituted controls on native people's use of natural resources. The main reason was to eliminate native competition against the European businesses exploiting raw materials in the colonies (Grove 1995). British colonial officials took landscape control a step further in East Africa, where they created "Royal Game Reserves" in which English aristocrats and colonial officers could hunt. They forcibly removed people from these areas and criminalized local people (like the Maasai) who continued hunting as "poachers." The Society for the Preservation of the Wild Fauna of the Empire, founded in 1903 and a forerunner of organizations such as the World Wildlife Fund, played a central role in establishing these policies. This was the era of the big-game hunter, and many animal populations—most notably wild elephant and rhinoceros—crashed as a result of overhunting by European elites (Figure 7.7). Many of these parks were later upgraded to national parks where hunting is no longer permitted.

By preventing native peoples in the colonies from engaging in their traditional businesses or gaining access to their commonly held properties, colonial administrators simultaneously eliminated most of the economic opportunities that would have been available had Europeans not come and taken over their territories. Native peoples became dependent on the colonial administration, encouraging the view among Europeans that natives were naturally lazy. To Europeans it seemed that native peoples were unable to look after their own interests, although, as the Malaysian sociologist Syed Hussein Alatas (1977) suggests, most of these native peoples had been quite industrious and able to manage complex businesses with extensive international trade relations until Europeans seized their lands, or banned international

Figure 7.7   Big-Game Hunters and Conservation.
American president Theodore Roosevelt was an avid hunter who went on numerous hunting expeditions in East African Royal Game Reserves. He believed modern life degenerated manhood, and he advocated "getting back to nature" (which for him was hunting) as a way to correct this problem.

shipping, to ensure a government monopoly. Once the native inhabitants of a colony were impoverished from losing control over the best lands and resources, colonizers took on a paternalistic attitude toward native peoples. This view came to be known as the "white man's burden," the so-called duty of white men to look after the interests of their dark-skinned colonial subjects. In fact, however, had local people retained access to the lands and resources they had always made use of, they would not have been anyone's burden.

Is Collaborative Conservation Possible?

Environmental anthropologists recognize that the displacement of local people for the purposes of conserving nature is a powerful cultural idea born of complex historical dynamics. But many also recognize that this approach has been tied closely to colonial power over local natural resources and has tended to ignore subtle histories of how anthropogenic landscapes are produced through active human involvement in a landscape, in ways that can actually support wildlife biodiversity, such as in the Maasai case.

Some conservationists have begun to agree, and during the past several decades, there have been a number of experiments in "co-management" between international conservation groups and indigenous people. In places like Nepal, Alaska, Canada, Panama, Brazil, and Australia, indigenous people have been allowed to continue living in protected areas and have some say in park management. Environmental anthropologists have in turn begun studying these situations. They have found that a collaborative approach creates new kinds of opportunities for dialogue, power-sharing, and relationship-building between conservationists and indigenous communities (Natcher, Hickey, and Hickey 2005). But they can also create new dilemmas for indigenous communities. For example, national and international conservation groups still exercise considerable control, especially over funding, and government scientists often disrespect indigenous knowledge about wildlife and landscape dynamics even though they are supposed to be "co-managing" the resources with the indigenous community (Igoe 2004:158; Nadasdy 2005).

Some critics also assert that the drive to protect nature by creating preserves, even when it is done with the collaboration of indigenous groups, is merely treating a symptom of a deeper problem. Should we not really get to the root of that problem, which is the social practices and ideologies that lead to the destruction of nature in the first place? Who is really to blame for environmental destruction around the world? Anthropologists have a sophisticated understanding of the sociocultural factors and who contributes to environmental destruction, an issue we turn to in the next section.

• •

THINKING CRITICALLY ABOUT ENVIRONMENTAL ANTHROPOLOGY

Americans often assume that people interested in conserving nature tend to be middle-class people who are able to make donations to environmental groups because they have money left over after meeting their basic needs (food, shelter, clothing, and so on). In other words, protecting nature is a luxury, and poor people cannot do it because they need to feed themselves. Based on what we have discussed in this section, why is this view skewed?

• •

How Do Social and Cultural Factors Drive Environmental Destruction?

What are the root causes of environmental destruction? Greed and self-interest tend to rank high on the list, as do poor land-management techniques, overpopulation, and old-fashioned ignorance. Trying to identify a root cause is tempting because it suggests a relatively clear course of action. Were it only as simple as that.

Environmental anthropologists have found that nature's destruction results from a complex interplay of social, cultural, natural, and political-economic factors that always come back to two important questions: How do people consume natural resources in their lifestyles, and what are the social and ecological consequences of that consumption? The concept of ecological footprint and theories of political ecology will help us explore this issue in a later section. But before we review these, let us show how the search for root causes distracts us from understanding the complex interrelationships that produce environmental destruction. We do this by considering population growth, which is one of the most popular explanations as a root cause for environmental destruction.

Population and Environment

Eighteenth-century theologian Thomas Malthus argued that human population grows exponentially (as opposed to arithmetically), quickly overwhelming a limited resource base and leading to famine. Some modern environmentalists, such as Paul Ehrlich, who in 1968 wrote a book with the alarming title *The Population Bomb,* have argued that this is happening on a global scale in the world today. The numbers are stark: in the 72 years from 1927 to 1999, there was a threefold increase in world population, from approximately 2 billion to 6 billion people. Today, that population has grown to nearly 7.5 billion. At these rates of growth, Ehrlich and others concluded that complete environmental collapse is likely. The problem seems self-evident: a small planet cannot indefinitely support a quickly expanding global population, and ecological ruin awaits us if we do not control our population growth.

This is a stark situation, and humanity is charting new territory in facing it. Nevertheless, social scientists have yet to identify any confirmed case of environmental and social collapse because of overpopulation or mass consumption (Tainter 2006). Humans have tended to adapt to the land's **carrying capacity**, which is the population an area can support, by intensifying agriculture (a dynamic we described in Chapter 6, "Foodways"). Sustainable social systems also often respond by adopting new cultural practices to cope with rapid ecological deterioration. In other words, they are resilient, able to absorb change by changing social practices. For example, in the floodplain of the Brazilian Amazon River, attempts to make commercial fisheries more sustainable have focused on how communities can themselves regulate fisheries (de Castro and McGrath 2003). To ensure that overfishing does not take place, communities sign formal fishing accords that regulate who has access to fisheries and the amounts they are allowed to keep. These accords have had some success controlling commercial fishing, and they show that one of the keys to sustainability is to create innovative social institutions that help people collectively deal with changing environmental circumstances; in this case, declining fisheries.

In addition, anthropologists have also shown that the environmental disruptions that lead to famines result from a complex interplay of natural conditions with existing patterns of social inequality. For example, during the 1985 Ethiopian famine, Western aid and relief agencies like the United Nations World Food Programme (WFP)

• **Carrying capacity.** The population an area can support.

and the U.S. Agency for International Development (USAID) argued that Ethiopia's population was too large, resulting in the overconsumption of natural resources, environmental collapse, and famine. Their solution was to implement programs of food relief and land reclamation projects to improve agricultural yield. But these programs failed, because the experts who conceived them misunderstood the complex causes of the famine. The experts based their models on exaggerated data about land degradation and ignored other data, particularly the disastrous effects of the country's civil war and socialist government, which disrupted food distribution channels. Legal barriers that led to insecure access to land also discouraged farmers from investing in traditional soil conservation measures (Hoben 1995). This famine was not a consequence of overpopulation but the result of these other interrelated factors. Not one of these factors by itself would have produced the famine.

The point is that it is impossible to isolate overpopulation as *the* cause of environmental collapse. To do so is a misreading of environmental degradation. In "Doing Fieldwork: James Fairhead and Melissa Leach on Misreading the African Landscape," we examine how one pair of environmental anthropologists has challenged these misreadings using careful ethnographic and historical research methods.

Ecological Footprint

Another problem with overpopulation as a sole explanation for environmental degradation is that it does not address the fact that different societies, as well as people within those societies, consume differing amounts of resources. The concept of an **ecological footprint** addresses this issue by measuring what people consume and the waste they produce. It then calculates the amount of biologically productive land and water area needed to support them. As Figure 7.8 demonstrates, people living in industrialized and post-industrialized countries such as the United States consume much more than people living in less industrialized countries such as India. Of course, these are just averages; some people consume more and others less, usually related to their relative wealth or poverty.

• **Ecological footprint.** A quantitative tool that measures what people consume and the waste they produce. It also calculates the area of biologically productive land and water needed to support those people.

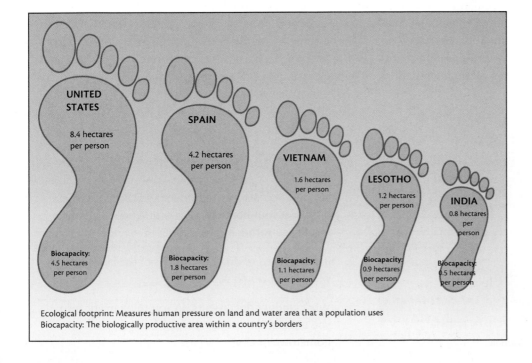

Ecological footprint: Measures human pressure on land and water area that a population uses
Biocapacity: The biologically productive area within a country's borders

UNITED STATES
8.4 hectares per person
Biocapacity: 4.5 hectares per person

SPAIN
4.2 hectares per person
Biocapacity: 1.8 hectares per person

VIETNAM
1.6 hectares per person
Biocapacity: 1.1 hectares per person

LESOTHO
1.2 hectares per person
Biocapacity: 0.9 hectares per person

INDIA
0.8 hectares per person
Biocapacity: 0.5 hectares per person

Figure 7.8   The Ecological Footprints of Five Countries.

Doing Fieldwork
James Fairhead and Melissa Leach on Misreading the African Landscape

IN THE WEST AFRICAN COUNTRY of Guinea, in the prefecture of Kissidougou [kee-see-**doo**-goo], the landscape is a mosaic of forests and savanna lands. From the nineteenth century to the present, French colonial administrators, environmentalists, and development officials have interpreted this landscape as a story of once-extensive forest fragmented by rapid population growth and native mismanagement. As the forest has disappeared, the explanation goes, the savannas have been on the increase.

British anthropologists James Fairhead and Melissa Leach (1996) had heard stories that suggested the opposite was happening—that savannas were retreating and forests were on the increase. So, during the 1990s, they set out to test this counterintuitive claim. Their findings confirmed that forests are in fact increasing and that the real landscape history is a story of savannas being replaced by human-cultivated forests. Even more remarkable, perhaps, is their finding that these processes have intensified *as human populations have grown*. In some cases, forests had grown so successfully that local people no longer had access to useful savanna products, like straw grass for hut roofs. People grow forests for various reasons: forests create protective fortresses around villages, provide hunting grounds by attracting birds and animals, prevent grassland fires from reaching villages, and improve grassland soils for cultivation. The anthropologists' research indicates that elite misreadings of environmental history are not inconsequential. They underestimate how much people modify landscapes in ways that can even *enhance* biodiversity. Development personnel thus risk imposing poorly designed solutions on rural peoples (such as population control programs, instead of, say, technical support for reforestation).

How did Fairhead and Leach learn these things? First, they went to villages with distinct combinations of forest and savanna and listened to local people's own stories of landscape transformation. They recorded oral histories of savanna-to-forest transformation and found that landscape could be converted from savanna to dense forest rapidly, sometimes within a single lifetime. They asked people to show them the process of converting savannas to forest, which starts with the cultivation of useful plants like kola nuts (used to create cooking oil) to break up the dense grassland soils, and follows these with fast-growing tree species. Fairhead and Leach also learned by directly participating in people's agricultural activities, working side by side with them in fields and forests, so that they could understand land-management techniques firsthand.

To complement these insider perspectives, Fairhead and Leach studied different kinds of official documents from government archives. They consulted colonial records that referred to the forests' being used as protective fortresses. They looked at censuses to track population growth. They also consulted aerial photographs and satellite images going back several decades. These images helped them track the establishment of settlements and the resulting growth of forests. By measuring the growth of forest in these images, they could test the claims made by local people, finding support for what people told them.

In isolation, none of these methods would necessarily be sufficient to demonstrate this story: aerial photos can be ambiguous, censuses inaccurate, and oral histories exaggerated. But when combined and carefully executed, they can challenge basic assumptions about environmental degradation.

Questions for Reflection

1. Suppose you wanted to understand the landscape history of your hometown or city. Where and how would you gather information?

2. If you wanted to do oral histories of the landscape, with whom would you speak?

3. What kinds of documents do you think might help you understand the landscape history of your hometown or city?

🌿 **The forest-savanna mosaic in Guinea.**

The distinction between the average Indian and the average North American is the latter's involvement in consumer capitalism. Consumer capitalism promotes the cultural ideal that people will never fully satisfy their needs, so they will continually buy more and more things in their pursuit of happiness. This cultural ideal, that a good life is defined by the accumulation of consumer goods, has enormous ecological consequences. We see these consequences in the production of goods (the extraction of nonrenewable raw materials to make consumer products); the distribution of goods (the reliance on fossil fuels to transport goods to market); and the consumption of goods (the landfills that get filled with trash). As a result, while Americans make up only about 5% of the world's population, they consume roughly 25% of its resources.

Most Americans do not fully appreciate the ecological destructiveness of consumer lifestyles, although signs of it are everywhere: urban sprawl, polluted air and waterways, acid rain, unhealthy forests, global warming, and environmental health problems linked to contamination. In "Thinking Like an Anthropologist: Identifying Hidden Costs," we explore how the simple act of eating a hamburger relates to environmental degradation.

Political Ecology

The kinds of analyses that focus on the linkages between political-economic power, social inequality, and ecological destruction are typical of **political ecology**. Many environmental anthropologists align themselves closely with political ecology, which rejects singular-factor explanations, like overpopulation, ignorance, or poor land use, as explanations for environmental degradation. It asks questions like: *What are the ecological and social consequences of an industrial economy? Who pays the real costs of capitalist development patterns that promote the exploitation, not the replenishment, of natural resources? How do pollution and other problems of environmental degradation reflect and reinforce patterns of social inequality?* Political ecology proposes that capitalism undermines itself over the long term because it exploits the labor and natural resources upon which it relies to produce commodities (O'Connor 1988).

● **Political ecology.** The field of study that focuses on the linkages between political-economic power, social inequality, and ecological destruction.

Social and Economic Inequality: The Case of Small Honduran Farmers

Political ecologists also ask how and why people in desperate poverty overexploit the few natural resources available to them (Peet and Watts 2004). Often, the answer has to do with their marginal position within unequal social and economic systems. Consider, for example, the small farmers in southern Honduras studied by anthropologist Susan Stonich during the 1990s (Stonich 1995). Since the 1950s, large commercial cotton plantations and cattle ranches have encroached on small farmers, pushing them into less productive land on mountain slopes. As commercial farms got larger, the size of small farms declined, causing many farmers to give up and migrate to the cities. Those who remained on their farms shifted from subsistence agriculture to growing cash crops for export. The intense pressure to produce high yields led them to deforest hillsides and abandon soil conservation measures that take more work because they are on steep land, both of which undermine the long-term fertility of their lands. Under these conditions, the farmers found themselves in a spiral of declining environmental quality on their farms.

The dynamics of the decline of small Honduran farmers are connected to political-economic forces operating simultaneously at local, regional, and international levels. Political ecologists explain the environmental degradation as the result of the Honduran government's laws encouraging concentration of land in few hands. To explain why the government creates policies favoring commercial agriculture's

Thinking Like an Anthropologist
Identifying Hidden Costs

ANTHROPOLOGISTS BEGIN THEIR research by asking questions. In this box, we want you to learn how to ask questions as an anthropological researcher. Part One describes a situation and follows up with questions we would ask. Part Two asks you to formulate your own questions based on a different situation.

PART ONE: THE HIDDEN COSTS OF A HAMBURGER

In his popular book *Fast Food Nation*, Eric Schlosser points out that the typical American eats three hamburgers and four orders of French fries every week (2001:6). This meal epitomizes American tastes, but its desirability is also due to its low cost to the consumer—this meal comes in at around $4 or $5, including a soda, at most fast-food restaurants. Why is the price so low? Traditional economists would answer that it is the fast-food industry's technological efficiency and economy of scale that keep costs down. But these facts alone do not explain the low cost, because neither the consumer nor the industry actually pays the real costs for each of the ingredients that go into the meal. Revealing the hidden costs shows who and what bears the actual costs of fast food.

Each ingredient deserves analysis, but in the interest of space, let us consider only the beef that goes into the hamburger. Beef is a notoriously inefficient source of energy and protein. It takes about 2,700 pounds of grain or a couple of acres of pasture to produce a typical 1,050-pound steer

🌱 **A Hamburger with All the Trimmings.**

(Robbins 2005). The amount of land and water it takes to raise beef cattle is much higher than that required for other forms of agriculture. In fact, our "waving fields of grain" are largely destined for livestock, not human, consumption: 80% of grain production in the United States is for livestock forage (Robbins 2005).

Especially in the Western United States, where animals are grazed on public lands, ranchers do not pay the real costs of beef production but transfer those costs to taxpayers and the environment. In arid lands, a typical steer needs as many as 200 to 300 acres to support it. To make so much land available to ranchers, Congress passed the Taylor Grazing Act in 1934, which transferred millions of acres of public land to ranchers if they took responsibility for improving them (Robbins 2005:224). These "improvements" are generally minor and self-interested (such as barbed-wire fences), so taxpayers assume the greater costs of predator control, drought relief, disease control, and the costly reservoir and irrigation projects required to support cattle in arid lands. Ranchers do pay a small grazing fee per animal, but as one recent study indicates, those fees do not even cover the costs of running the grazing program, and the federal government loses $120 million annually (Glazer, Romaniello, and Moskowitz 2015).

But most beef cattle are fed grains and cereals. Grains quickly fatten the steer and have become inexpensive to buy because of chemical fertilizers, herbicides, and pesticides, which keep production costs down and enhance the productivity of grain farmers. To keep grain costs low, the government offers reduced tax rates on agricultural lands and pays farmers direct subsidies to protect them from market variations. And approximately half the water we as a nation consume is used to grow the grain needed to feed cattle (Robbins 2005:217). The amount of water used to produce ten pounds of steak equals the household water consumption of a family for an entire year (Robbins 2005)! It is taxpayers, not grain farmers, who assume the costs of building and maintaining expensive water reclamation and irrigation projects.

Water reclamation projects also have enormous ecological impacts, including flooding to create dams, silting of waterways, diversion of waterways, and effects on fish populations. Use of so many chemical fertilizers, pesticides, and herbicides also carries high ecological costs, damaging soil and groundwater throughout grain-producing areas. Finally, beef has to travel over subsidized highways with subsidized gasoline from where it is produced to where it is eaten.

These costs are not borne exclusively by the people of the United States alone, because Americans produce about 9% of beef in the world but consume about 28% of the world's beef production (Robbins 2005:226). Clearly, our analysis of beef's hidden costs would also have to take into account the ecological and social costs of raising beef in other countries.

What questions does the hidden cost of a burger raise for anthropological researchers?

1. What are the different steps involved in the production, distribution, and consumption of beef, and who is involved in this chain of relationships?
2. Who and what assumes the actual costs of production at each of these steps?
3. Why do some actors in this chain pay the costs more than others?

4. Why are the ecological costs of producing beef not paid by agricultural producers?
5. Does anyone pay those ecological costs?

PART TWO: THE HIDDEN COSTS OF OUR DIGITAL LIVES

The analysis of hidden costs on people and environments can be applied to virtually any aspect of a lifestyle, even the most commonplace. Consider the hidden costs of going online. Many of you know about the toxins in our smartphones and computers, which when not recycled properly contaminate landfills or end up in unregulated "e-waste" markets overseas. But maintaining the Internet itself also has many hidden environmental costs. For example, although we tend to think of the Internet as a "cloud," it is run by vast numbers of servers that draw heavily on nonrenewable energy resources. What questions would you pose as an anthropological researcher in order to explore the hidden environmental and social costs of our digital lives?

expansion, they look to the lending policies of countries like the United States and agencies like the World Bank, both of which have pressured the Honduran government to promote the growth of melons and shrimp for export to pay international debts instead of encouraging the production of food for local consumption (Stonich 1995).

Social and Economic Inequality: Why Poor Neighborhoods and Marginalized People Face the Greatest Environmental Risks

Political ecologists have also observed that environmentally harmful activities disproportionately affect people with little political-economic power. In the United States, it is lower-income people and minority groups, especially African Americans, American Indians, and Latinos, who are unequally exposed to environmental risk. These groups are less able to challenge the powerful economic and political interests behind environmentally harmful activities such as toxic waste dumps and polluting industries (Bullard 1994). In the United States, this issue came to public attention in September 1982, when 400 protesters in Warren County, North Carolina, were arrested at the proposed site of a toxic waste landfill (Figure 7.9). At the time, Warren County was 84% African American and one of the poorest counties in the state. The leaders of the protest, some of them important civil rights leaders, argued that these facts, not the ecological suitability of the site to store toxic waste, motivated the decision to build the waste dump in their county (Sandweiss 1998). This protest marked the start of an **environmental justice** movement, a social movement that addresses the linkages between racial discrimination and injustice, social equity, and environmental quality.

- **Environmental justice.** A social movement addressing the linkages between racial discrimination and injustice, social equity, and environmental quality.

Figure 7.9   The Birth of Environmental Justice. Although the Warren County, North Carolina, protest did not prevent the opening of a highly toxic polychlorinated biphenyl (PCB) landfill site, it inspired others around the country to recognize and challenge situations of environmental discrimination.

Environmental justice is now a global movement, and unlike environmentalist approaches oriented toward creating nature preserves that tend to focus on scenic landscapes and biodiversity, environmental justice tends to be organized around the defense of a people's livelihood and social justice concerns (Guha 2000:105). In the case of the Marshall Islands, for example, which we discussed at the beginning of this chapter, the government and activists there, along with their allies in environmental and human rights groups, have long framed the islanders' situation as rooted in problems of outsider control and domination that undermine local self-determination and livelihoods. From the Marshallese perspective, nuclear fallout, sea-level rise, economic underdevelopment and dependency, and poor public health are intertwined issues, and in their international activism drawing attention to their plight, they emphasize that social and environmental problems are deeply interconnected. Marshallese representatives were present at the first major international environmental justice conference, the People of Color Environmental Leadership Summit in Washington, DC, in 1991. That conference produced a foundational document called the "Principles of Environmental Justice," still important today in struggles around the world, that recognizes that environmental problems often express themselves through the further marginalization of people already struggling with social, political, and economic inequalities (People of Color Environmental Leadership Summit 1991).

Anthropology Confronts Climate Change

In recent years, a number of environmental anthropologists have turned their attention to the social dimensions of climate change, offering important perspectives on the nexus of nature, culture, science, politics, and belief that shapes ideas about climate change's causes, government policies on the environment, and the diverse ways people make sense of climate change in specific cultural circumstances (Crate 2008; Barnes and Dove 2015). At the root of anthropology's approach is the holistic perspective that understands climate change as one of a number of environmental influences on people's social lives, and not the single variable driving environmental change in the world today, as the media sometimes present it. This perspective also brings attention to the ways current patterns of industrial production and consumption related to climate change are already altering people's livelihood strategies and interactions with the economy and the environment (Crate 2008; Barnes and Dove 2015).

A special focus of ethnographic fieldwork on the topic has been the social complexities surrounding the production of knowledge about climate change. Anthropologists have studied the laboratories and international conferences of climate scientists to better understand how their knowledge is created, and in the process they have uncovered complicated social dynamics, cultural patterns, and institutional processes that shape how problems of climate are framed, studied, and communicated in the world of science. Key to these social dynamics are tensions between scientific specialties that use different methods and theories, uncertainties in climate modeling, and funding patterns that prioritize the reductionist perspectives of scientific authorities over the holistic perspectives of social scientists in the construction of public knowledge and policy (Lahsen 2015; Moore, Mankin, and Becker 2015).

Anthropologists have also used ethnography to show that different societies have different ways of conceptualizing climate and climate variability, and more important, that human societies have long dealt with climate variability (Orlove 2005; Crate 2008). For example, as Roderick McIntosh (2015) has described, the Mande people of arid West Africa have long grappled with unpredictable and abrupt changes in precipitation and river patterns. They have developed their own ethnoscience of climate in which certain individuals—so-called "weather machines"—study their society's knowledge of long-term weather patterns and have the cultural authority to help shape community responses, which can include migration, shifts between pastoral and horticultural economies, and modifications of agricultural practices. Flexibility and resilience lie at the heart of the Mande understandings of how to deal with climate variability and change, which suggest broader lessons for the rest of us as we begin to better understand the effects of climate change globally.

●●

THINKING CRITICALLY ABOUT ENVIRONMENTAL ANTHROPOLOGY

Environmental anthropologists reject population growth as a singular cause of environmental degradation around the world. But there are certain conditions in which population growth can play a role in environmental degradation. What kinds of conditions do you think those would be?

●●

Conclusion

Anthropologists agree that we must pay close attention to the social practices and structures that shape the way communities relate to their natural environments. When we do, we can see that nonindustrialized people typically have a deep understanding of their environments, and they routinely understand the behaviors of animals and plants as well as, if not in some cases better than, scientists from other regions. In such communities, the cultural landscape envisions nature differently than do people in the West, often using metaphors that express people's reciprocal ties to the land, or as the Marshallese case that opened this chapter demonstrates, drawing on social, political, and supernatural mechanisms and strategies that protect ecosystems from wanton exploitation.

The cultural landscape of human–nature separation that we see in modern conservation initiatives has only recently begun to appreciate these facts. Historically, Western industrialized countries have designed conservation programs that tend to expel indigenous peoples from landscapes those peoples may have lived on sustainably for many years, even living in ways that support the biodiversity of other species, as in the case of the Maasai.

Environmental anthropologists agree that careful use of natural resources is the basis of a sustainable society. As a result, it is important to look critically at the current causes of the world's ecological crisis, which many prominent scholars and leaders claim is caused by unchecked population growth. However, the causes of today's global ecological crisis—as was the case in past ecological crises—cannot be reduced to any singular cause. We have to consider factors like elite mismanagement of resources, government policy choices, inflexible responses to change, and consumption patterns that extract key resources, create waste, and contribute to changes in climate, ecosystem viability, and so on. We also have to consider who pays the cost of these patterns and realize that questions of unequal access to resources and social patterns of injustice are often at the heart of the world's key ecological crises.

KEY TERMS

Anthropogenic
    landscapes   p. 176

Carrying capacity   p. 180

Cultural landscape
    p. 170

Ecological anthropology
    p. 170

Ecological footprint
    p. 181

Ecosystem   p. 170

Environmental
    anthropology   p. 166

Environmental
    determinism   p. 170

Environmental justice
    p. 185

Ethnobiology   p. 172

Ethnoscience   p. 172

Political ecology   p. 183

Traditional ecological
    knowledge   p. 173

Reviewing the Chapter

Chapter Section	What We Know	To Be Resolved
Do all people see nature in the same way?	Different cultures have different ways of conceptualizing the boundaries between humans and the natural world. Metaphors often play a major role in these conceptualizations.	Anthropologists continue to debate the extent to which general conceptual models and metaphors, or the material forces of nature itself, shape human relations with the environment.

How does non-Western knowledge of nature relate to science?	Different societies have developed highly systematic and sophisticated knowledge systems for classifying the natural world, some of which closely resemble Western science. Unlike Western science, however, which views its methods and findings as universally applicable, these knowledge systems are often highly localized and customized to particular ecosystems and rooted in local moralities.	Anthropologists are still working to understand the specific ways in which traditional ecological knowledge shapes practices of ecological and agricultural management, as well as how it is changing to adapt to new challenges, such as climate change.
Are industrialized Western societies the only ones to conserve nature?	While Western conservation practice is based on the separation of humans and nature, the stewardship traditions of non-Western societies often start from principles that view humans as important and responsible actors in nature. Western nature conservation practices have often disrupted and marginalized local cultures, many of which have had highly successful adaptations to their environments.	As some conservationists have realized new opportunities of co-managing natural resources with indigenous communities, anthropologists are divided over whether these approaches actually benefit indigenous communities.
How do social and cultural factors drive environmental destruction?	The ecological impact of a society depends on its ecological footprint, or the amount of natural resources its people require to live their lifestyles. The negative impacts of environmentally harmful activities tend to fall disproportionately on lower-income people, minority groups, and the colonized.	Anthropologists are still identifying the conditions under which social groups can adopt new cultural ideas and practices that promote resilience and sustainability. One area where anthropological research has future importance is in studying how societies and social groups understand and adapt to climate change.

Readings

For a century, anthropologists have taken a systematic interest in how humans vary in the ways they interact with the environment. There are several good general overviews of the subfield of environmental anthropology, among them Patricia Townsend's book *Environmental Anthropology: From Pigs to Policies* (second edition, Long Grove, IL: Waveland Press, 2008), and Nora Haenn and Richard Wilk's edited reader *The Environment in Anthropology: A Reader in Ecology, Culture, and Sustainable Living* (New York: New York University Press, 2005). The *Routledge Handbook of Political Ecology* (New York: Routledge, 2015), edited by Tom Perreault, Gavin Bridge, and James McCarthy, provides an extensive overview of political ecology's development and themes of current interest.

Two books that explore the complex dimensions of indigenous ways of knowing and interacting with natural environment are Roberto Gonzalez's ethnographic study *Zapotec Science: Farming and Food in the Northern Sierra of Oaxaca* (Austin, TX: University of Texas Press, 2001) and ethnobotanist Gary Paul Nabhan's book *Cultures of Habitat: On Nature, Culture, and Story* (Washington, DC: Counterpoint, 1997).

To explore the differences between insider and outsider understandings of landscapes and how they can lead to sharp conflicts over the conservation of natural resources, read James Fairhead and Melissa Leach's book *Misreading the African Landscape: Society and Ecology in a Forest-Savanna Mosaic* (Cambridge, UK: Cambridge

University Press, 1996) and Jim Igoe's book *Conservation and Globalization: A Study of National Parks and Indigenous Communities from East Africa to South Dakota* (Belmont, CA: Wadsworth, 2004).

Shepard Krech's book *The Ecological Indian: Myth and History* (New York: W. W. Norton, 1999) offers an important and historically rooted challenge to romantic stereotypes of naturally "green" indigenous communities.

For anthropological perspectives on climate change, see the book *Climate Cultures: Anthropological Perspectives on Climate Change*, edited by Jessica Barnes and Michael Dove (New Haven, CT: Yale University Press, 2016).

Economics

Working, Sharing, and Buying

IN RECENT YEARS, China's booming economy has produced a class of wealthy new entrepreneurs, some of whom have grown astonishingly rich from the creation of private businesses. The origins of this situation lie in market reforms introduced after the death of Chairman Mao Tse-tung in 1976, when state leaders began to rethink their policies of collectivization and centralized allocation of resources. Calling the new approach "Socialism with Chinese Characteristics," the state began to allow greater levels of private control of capital, resources, and goods. It also made important changes in state bureaucratic functions to encourage private business, and it opened the country to the capitalist world and foreign investment. These changes ushered in the end of the so-called iron rice bowl, the state system that had provided lifelong social services, employment, and housing and had been a hallmark of China's Communist revolution. As a result, they also produced disruption and uncertainty for tens of millions of people (Osburg 2013).

At the same time, private entrepreneurs began to flourish. By the turn of this century, the government had officially recognized them as making a legitimate contribution to socialism, and it passed a constitutional reform allowing for private property rights. These "new rich" are typically businessmen who have made fortunes in real

The Key to Business Success.   Luxurious nightclubs, such as this one pictured here in Beijing, are critical locations where Chinese businessmen and government officials cultivate *guanxi*, or social networks, and friendships rooted in sentimental bonds. These relationships are believed to be keys to business success.

estate, manufacturing, construction, entertainment, and services. They have gained a new social profile as sought-after marriage partners, trend-setters in fashion and consumption, and patrons of the finest restaurants (Osburg 2013). But the view is not all positive—many are seen as morally suspect profiteers and beneficiaries of illicit activities and corruption, since these successful businessmen typically have close ties to corrupt government officials and managers of state enterprises who provide them with government contracts, licenses, and capital, as well as extralegal protections and favors, in exchange for bribes and kickbacks.

This entrepreneurial sphere is a strongly masculine one, rooted in gendered forms of obligation and the creation of value (Osburg 2013). During any given week, for example, well-connected male entrepreneurs spend many hours and a lot of money in luxurious clubs entertaining state officials, clients, and fellow businessmen through banqueting, drinking, gambling, singing karaoke, receiving massages, and hiring sex workers (Osburg 2013). The reason they give for doing these things is to expand and strengthen *guanxi* [**gwahn**-shee], which are informal webs of social relationships individuals create and use to pursue their own ends. *Guanxi* can help get things done in the slow-moving bureaucracy, or help businessmen get new government contracts. Reciprocity, especially the give-and-take of favors, is a key element of a *guanxi* network, and individuals who can use *guanxi* in ways that benefit others in their network can gain important power and social prestige.

But these networks are not purely about using others to get something, because they also involve sentimental ties and mutual obligation. They are closely associated with *renqing* [**wren**-cheeng], which are affective interpersonal relationships, such as those between kin and close friends. In the new Chinese economy, much is bought and sold to the highest bidder, so building deep relationships among business partners is seen by entrepreneurs as introducing moral values and emotions into their otherwise impersonal and competitive economic activities. Spending many hours together in leisure and entertainment—creating shared experiences of intimacy, vulnerability, and transgression—is one of the ways businessmen can transform the short-term and calculated interests of *guanxi* into the long-term bonds of *renqing* (Osburg 2013). Yet the pressure to spend so much time entertaining, drinking, banqueting, and cavorting with sex workers is exhausting and expensive, and it can generate feelings of being trapped in moral compromises and undesirable obligations. Moreover, as market competition has increased, the cultivation of *guanxi* has intensified, creating pressure to provide even more spectacular experiences for those one is hoping to cultivate (Osburg 2013).

Many Western observers have celebrated the rise of China's new entrepreneurial class as the vanguard of capitalist free enterprise and a liberal democratic opening. But this view misunderstands the complex mixture of capitalism and political authoritarianism that characterizes the Chinese economy, as well

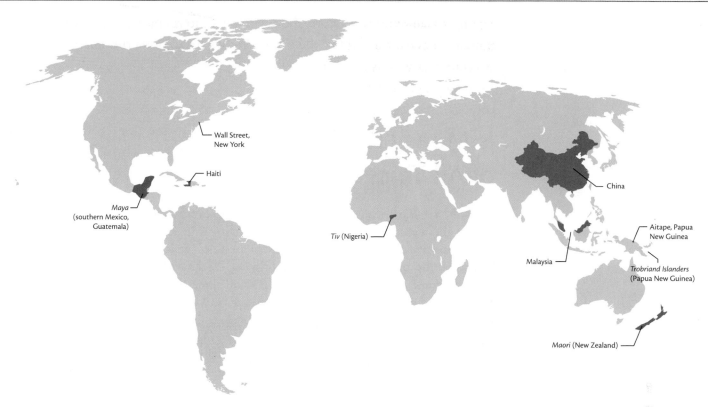

Figure 8.1   Select Peoples and Places Discussed in Chapter 8.

as the heavy dependence of private entrepreneurs on the state. More important, this economy is not a simple transplant of capitalistic practices and beliefs from the West; rather, it is shaped by and embedded in particular Chinese political structures, social relationships, and culturally defined yet dynamic patterns of masculinity, desire, and morality. In fact, *all* economies are shaped by such social and cultural particularities.

At the heart of anthropology's interest in economics is the following question: *How do cultural processes shape what people want and need to live, and how do they shape the work people do to get it?* Embedded in this larger question are the following questions, around which this chapter is organized:

Is money really the measure of all things?

How does culture shape the value and meaning of money?

Why is gift exchange such an important part of all societies?

What is the point of owning things?

Does capitalism have distinct cultures?

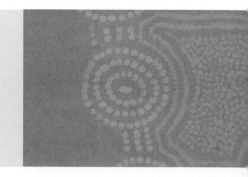

Anthropologists who study economies and economic activities are interested not only in how people satisfy their needs, but in why they want certain things in the first place. Although we have long debated the exact nature of the relationship between economy and culture, the two clearly interpenetrate, and one cannot be fully understood without the other. We begin exploring this relationship by considering the nature of value.

Is Money Really the Measure of All Things?

Many North Americans and Europeans are accustomed, if not also deeply committed, to the idea that money is the measure of all things. We hear all the time that everything has a price and that the price of an object reflects its real value. But what would be the price in dollars of the original Declaration of Independence of the United States? A favorite blanket you have had since childhood? The Wailing Wall, Jerusalem's most sacred Jewish site? An antique gold wedding band that mothers have passed to their daughters for seven generations?

Somebody could try to set dollar values, or even try to buy or sell these things (Figure 8.2). But some objects and relationships carry such sacred or special qualities that they can never really be reduced to a monetary equivalent (Werner and Bell 2004). The awkwardness you might feel thinking about people doing so—as well as the controversies that erupt when someone tries to sell something such as human body parts, virginity, Holocaust memorabilia, and so on—suggests that some deep set of processes defines what is an acceptable economic transaction, what is not, and how we establish monetary values for things. Those processes are cultural. Culture—the collective processes through which people construct and naturalize certain meanings and actions as normal and even necessary—not only shapes what is acceptable to transact, but how and why the transaction will take place, and how the objects or services being exchanged are valued.

Figure 8.2   How Much Is Grandmother's Antique Battle-Axe Worth? In the U.S. television show *Antiques Roadshow*, an expert evaluates the market value of household antiques. The popularity of the show, not to mention the motivation people have to go on it with their antiques, is ultimately less about the money than it is about other factors. What do you think those factors are?

Culture, Economics, and Value

If money is not the measure of all things, where exactly within the processes of culture does **value**—the relative worth of an object or service—come from? **Economic anthropology**, the subfield of cultural anthropology concerned with how people make, share, and buy things and services, has considered this question for a century. Economic anthropologists study the decisions people make about earning a living, what they do when they work, the social institutions that affect these activities, and how these three matters relate to the creation of value (Wilk and Cliggett 2007; Smith 2000).

Although both anthropologists and economists study the origins of value and how economies work, they generally have different goals. Economists typically try to understand and predict economic patterns, often with a practical goal of helping people hold onto and increase their wealth. They also study communities in terms of economic statistics, and they assume that economic transactions in one community or country are like transactions in any other. Anthropologists, on the other hand, do not assume transactions are the same everywhere, as they recognize that cultural particularities shape the character of any transaction. Furthermore, we tend to study how people lead their day-to-day economic lives by means of direct, long-term interaction with them. As a result, we tend to focus more than economists do on understanding the world's diverse **economic systems**, the structured patterns and relationships through which people exchange goods and services, and making sense of how these systems reflect and shape particular ways of life.

Anthropologists rely on four major theoretical approaches to understanding how economies create value: three of these—neoclassical economics, substantivism, and Marxism—are traditional approaches within the social sciences, while the fourth, cultural economics, has been developed by anthropologists. These approaches are summarized in outline form in Table 8.1 and discussed in more detail in the text that follows.

- **Value.** The relative worth of an object or service that makes it desirable.

- **Economic anthropology.** The subfield of cultural anthropology concerned with how people make, share, and buy things and services.

- **Economic system.** The structured patterns and relationships through which people exchange goods and services.

	TABLE 8.1 THEORIES OF CULTURE, ECONOMY, AND VALUE		
Theoretical Approach	What Is the Economy?	How Does the Economic System Work?	How Is Value Created?
Neoclassical Economics	The economy is a division of labor and the exchange of goods and services in a market.	Workers cooperate in the division of labor to produce goods. The market brings together buyers and sellers to exchange those goods.	Value and wealth are created by competition between buyers and sellers.
Substantivism	The economy is the substance of the actual transactions people engage in to get what they need and want.	Economic processes are embedded in and shaped by non-market social institutions, such as the state, religious beliefs, and kinship relations.	Value is relative, created by particular cultures and social institutions.
Marxism	Capitalism, which is a type of economic system, is a system in which private ownership of the means of production and a division of labor produce wealth for a few, and inequality for the masses.	People participate in capitalism by selling their labor. That labor is appropriated by those holding the means of production.	Labor, and especially the exploitation of others' labor, is a major source of value.
Cultural Economics	The economy is a category of culture, not a special arena governed by universal economic rationality.	Economic acts are guided by local beliefs and cultural models, which are closely tied to a community's values.	Value is created by the symbolic associations people make between an activity, good, or service and a community's moral norms.

- **Division of labor.** The cooperative organization of work into specialized tasks and roles.

- **Exchange.** The transfer of objects and services between social actors.

- **Market.** A social institution in which people come together to exchange goods and services.

- **Neoclassical economics.** An approach to economics that studies how people make decisions to allocate resources like time, labor, and money in order to maximize their personal benefit.

- **Capitalism.** An economic system based on private ownership of the means of production, in which prices are set and goods distributed through a market.

- **Formal economics.** The branch of economics that studies the underlying logic of economic thought and action.

The Neoclassical Perspective

Scottish moral philosopher Adam Smith wrote about the creation of value in his influential book *The Wealth of Nations* (1776/1976). Smith observed that in "primitive" societies, individuals did a lot of different kinds of work—growing and preparing food, making their own clothing, building their own homes, and so forth—but in the "civilized" societies of eighteenth-century Europe, such jobs were done increasingly by "the joint labor of a great multitude of workmen" (Smith 1776/1976). This change was due to the **division of labor**, the cooperative organization of work into specialized tasks and roles (Smith 1776/1976). Citing the example of sewing pins, Smith marveled at how dividing the process of making a sewing pin into distinct actions performed by different specialized laborers—one laborer to draw out the wire, a second to cut it, a third to straighten it, and so on—produced exponential growth in the number of pins that could be made in a day.

This change was revolutionary. Before the division of labor, Smith noted, a pin would take a lot of time and effort for an individual to make, so the value of the pin lay in the amount of labor it took to make one. But with the division of labor reducing that time and effort, the value of the pin was now established by its **exchange** (the transfer of objects and services between social actors) in a **market** (a social institution in which people come together to buy and sell goods and services).

For Smith and the economists who follow him, market exchange reflects a natural human propensity to (as Smith famously said) "truck, barter, and exchange." Within the market, individuals pursue their own self-interest, using their capacity for reason and calculation to maximize their individual satisfaction. The world has finite resources ("limited means"), but everybody has unlimited desires ("unlimited ends"), and the result is competition among individuals. Every person's struggle to get the most value theoretically keeps prices, costs of production, profits, and interest rates low while generating great wealth (Wilk and Cliggett 2007). This theory is the foundation of **neoclassical economics**, which studies how people make decisions to allocate resources like time, labor, and money in order to maximize their personal satisfaction (Figure 8.3).

Among anthropologists, this influential theory has provoked a long debate over the nature of the economy. It is, we will see, basically an unresolved debate, but exploring the positions illustrates how anthropologists interested in the relationship between culture, economics, and value have applied—and criticized—neoclassical thought.

The Substantivist–Formalist Debate

In 1944, the Hungarian-American economic historian Karl Polanyi published his book *The Great Transformation* to explain how modern **capitalism**—the economic system based on private ownership of the means of production, in which prices are set and goods distributed through a market—emerged in Europe (Polanyi 1944/1975). Polanyi insisted that the rise of the market in Europe was not inevitable, but a social process that both supported and was supported by the creation of modern nation-states.

In developing that argument, Polanyi proposed that studying economies involves making a distinction between "formal" and "substantive" economics. By **formal economics**, he meant the underlying ("formal") logic that shapes people's actions when they participate in an economy, as we see in the apparently

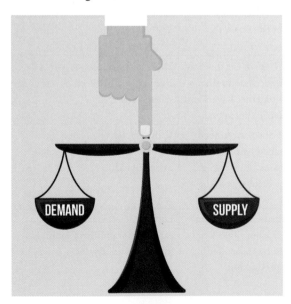

Figure 8.3   An Invisible Hand? Neoclassical economists emphasize that the pursuit of self-interest in markets works like an "invisible hand." In reality, modern markets rarely, if ever, operate so freely, since governments impose regulations and enforce actions to keep markets operating smoothly, and in some cases, fairly.

self-interested and rational decision-makers of neoclassical economic theory. By **substantive economics**, he referred to the daily transactions people actually engage in to get what they need or desire, or the "substance" of the economy. These transactions are embedded in and inseparable from other social institutions, such as politics, religion, and kinship. Anthropologists found this distinction useful for describing issues they were studying in other societies.

The Substantivist Position

Polanyi's own approach to economics was "substantivist." His primary goal was to describe how the production and **redistribution** of goods (collection of goods in a community and then redivision of those goods among members) were embedded in and shaped by non-market social institutions, such as the state, religious beliefs, and kinship relations. Substantivism was relativistic, holding that societies have unique social institutions and processes that influence economics like other aspects of culture; they may not even have a separate category for a domain called "the economy" as we do. From this perspective, the value of goods in an economic system is culturally relative, rooted in particular cultures and social institutions. Substantivism's main unit of analysis was thus not the economy per se, or individual behaviors and actions within it, but a whole society and its institutions (Wilk and Cliggett 2007).

Substantivists felt that the concept of an "economy" did not do justice to the way making a livelihood is inseparably interwoven with customs and social relations in other societies. They argued that research should focus on a broad field of social relations and institutions that provided people with what they needed to live, instead of on any predetermined or limited notion of an economy centered on a market. A major proponent of substantivism in anthropology was University of Chicago anthropologist Marshall Sahlins, as we examine in "Classic Contributions: Marshall Sahlins on Exchange in Traditional Economies."

The Formalist Reaction

By the 1960s, some anthropologists began to criticize substantivism's lack of attention to individual action and behavior, shifting their focus to formal economics. To formalists, individuals in all societies are as rational as neoclassical economics says they are. People everywhere confront limited means and unlimited ends (wants); therefore, they make rational decisions that are appropriate to the satisfaction they desire (Smith 2000). Being anthropologists, the formalists understood that "satisfaction" could be culturally defined and variable, but, they asserted, the decision-making processes people used to achieve satisfaction were basically the same everywhere (Wilk and Cliggett 2007).

By the late 1970s, the debate between substantivists and formalists had fizzled out with no clear winner. The main reason is that the two sides were essentially arguing past each other: one side was talking about societies and their institutions, while the other was talking about individuals, their rationality, and their individual transactions. Both had a point, and both had a role to play in the study of economic behavior.

The Marxist Perspective

The substantivist-formalist debate also fizzled because a number of anthropologists had begun to adopt a Marxist perspective, the political and economic theories associated with German political economist Karl Marx (1818–1883). In his analysis of British capitalism, Marx (1867/1990) characterized the English system as pitting

- **Substantive economics.** A branch of economics, inspired by the work of Karl Polanyi, that studies the daily transactions people engage in to get what they need or desire.

- **Redistribution.** The collection of goods in a community and then the further dispersal of those goods among members.

Classic Contributions
Marshall Sahlins on Exchange in Traditional Economies

SINCE THE 1950s, cultural anthropologist Marshall Sahlins (b. 1930) has been interested in differences and similarities between the economies of small-scale non-Western societies and those of Europe. The following excerpt comes from Sahlins's statement about the nature of the economy in societies with nonindustrial technologies, illustrating substantivist economic theory's emphasis on the social nature of economic transactions. To distinguish it from the modern capitalist economy, Sahlins calls this sort of economic system one of "primitive exchange." Although anthropologists no longer use terminology like "primitive," two important elements of Sahlins's explanation are that (1) nearly every transaction involves a social relationship, and (2) production is organized by families in what he refers to as the "domestic mode of production."

Marshall Sahlins.

What are [in] the received wisdom "noneconomic" or "exogenous" conditions are in the primitive reality the very organization of economy. A material transaction is usually a momentary episode in a continuous social relation. The social relation exerts governance: the flow of goods is constrained by, is part of, a status etiquette. . . .

Yet the connection between material flow and social flow is reciprocal. A specific social relation may constrain a given movement of goods, but a specific transaction suggests a particular social relation. If friends make gifts, gifts make friends. A great proportion of primitive exchange, much more than our own traffic, has as its decisive function this latter, instrumental one: the material flow underwrites or initiates social relations.

Even on its strictly practical side, exchange in primitive communities has not the same role as the economic flow in modern industrial communities. The place of transaction in the total economy is different: under primitive conditions it is more detached from production, less firmly hinged to production in an organic way. Typically it is less involved than modern exchange in the acquisition of means of production, more involved with the redistribution of finished goods. The bias is that of an economy in which food holds a commanding position, and day-to-day output does not depend on a massive technological complex nor a complex division of labor. It is the bias of a domestic mode of production: of household producing units, division of labor by sex and age. (Sahlins 1965:139–140)

Questions for Reflection

1. How do you think Sahlins was being a substantivist?

2. Why do you think transactions in a "primitive" society are oriented more toward redistribution and less toward the production of goods?

the interests of a wealthy class (who owned factories) against those of a poorer working-class (laborers in the factories). At the heart of this system, Marx argued, was a division of labor that produced inequality and conflict.

From the Marxist point of view, the substantivists and formalists had wasted their time debating the nature of exchange and redistribution, while the neoclassicists misunderstood economic activity as individual choice and decision-making. Marxism emphasizes that societies are divided into unequal classes, with a few individuals at the top accumulating wealth and power by appropriating the labor and property of the many below. For them, the real problem is explaining why and how an economy and society based on inequality reproduces itself; in other words, how the production and trade of goods enforces and maintains the social inequality.

Marxists use the concept of **surplus value**, which is the difference between what people produce and what they need to survive, to address this problem. In a capitalist society, workers create greater value than they receive for their labor, generating surplus value. For example, a worker in a widget factory might make $35 of widgets in an hour from $5 of materials, but only get paid $10 per hour. What happens to the $20 of surplus value? The owner of the factory, who controls the **means of production**— the machines and infrastructure required to produce the widget—appropriates it, the Marxists argue, thus exploiting the worker's productivity. This surplus value is the basis of private wealth, but it also creates permanent conflict between the worker and owner classes. The institution of private property and the state, through its social and economic policies, support this inequality.

Marxist analysis introduced issues of power, domination, and the unequal distribution of wealth into anthropology's discussions of culture and economy. But not all attempts to apply Marxist analysis to non-Western societies have been entirely satisfying, because non-capitalist economies work so differently. In particular, such studies do not always adequately address the culturally specific symbolic and moral dimensions of economic interaction, which we turn to next.

- **Surplus value.** The difference between what people produce and what they need to survive.

- **Means of production.** The machines and infrastructure required to produce goods.

The Cultural Economics Perspective

The idea that symbols and morals help shape a community's economy lies at the heart of **cultural economics**. Cultural economics views the economy as a category of culture, not a special arena governed by universal utilitarian or practical reasons (Sahlins 1972, 1976). The roots of this approach lie in substantivism. The cultural economist's goal is to understand, from the "native's point of view," the local beliefs and cultural models that guide and shape economic activities (Gudeman 1986).

To the cultural economist, a close relationship exists between the words "value" (desirability and worth) and "values" (moral norms). Both refer to the symbolic expression of intrinsically desirable principles or qualities. This relationship also implies that moral norms and economic activity influence each other (Sayer 2000).

Anthropologists working in this vein have been especially interested in **prestige economies**, economies in which people seek high social rank, prestige, and power instead of money and material wealth. In indigenous Maya communities of Guatemala and southern Mexico, for example, men have traditionally participated in the Cofradía [ko-fra-**dee**-ah] system, a hierarchical system dating from colonial times that combines civic leadership and Catholic religious authority (Nash 1958) (Figure 8.4). As they enter higher offices with greater responsibilities and power, these men also have the obligation to spend more of their personal money and other wealth on community fiestas and infrastructure. Some will go broke or deep into debt doing so. Underlying this system is a moral philosophy (rather than individual self-interest) emphasizing that the path to status and rank requires an individual to share generously with others whatever material wealth he has.

Recent studies in cultural economics have tended to focus on the dynamism of local economies, recognizing that one society may encompass several local economic models simultaneously, perhaps at different levels or among different institutions (Robben 1989; Gudeman 2001). For example, in the United States, even as dominant cultural models of ideal economic behavior resemble what we

- **Cultural economics.** An anthropological approach to economics that focuses on how symbols and morals help shape a community's economy.

- **Prestige economies.** Economies in which people seek high social rank, prestige, and power instead of money and material wealth.

Figure 8.4   Members of a *Cofradía* in Guatemala. *Cofradías*, which are Catholic civil-religious associations, are a classic example of a prestige economy, since members gain social prestige and authority even as they may go deeply into financial debt to participate.

would expect from Adam Smith's rational economic actors, some religious communities have certain expectations about appropriate economic behavior, such as donating a certain percentage of one's income to the church (tithing), which make explicit connections between economic behavior and morality. Moreover, in our workplaces, homes, and other everyday spaces, most of us rarely ask the neoclassical economics question "What's in it for me?" but we willingly lend a hand, share freely, and offer mutual aid (Graeber 2011). Such a perspective can help us better understand how and why businessmen in China work so hard to build *guanxi* and *renqing* relationships with their business partners, mixing Chinese notions of appropriate and moral economic activity with capitalistic models of economic behavior.

Returning to this section's broader focus on how value is created, it should be clear that none of these theoretical approaches—neoclassical economics, formalism, substantivism, Marxism, or cultural economics—accepts that money is the measure of all things. While the specifics of these theories differ, each nevertheless accepts, at least partially, that cultural processes and social relationships play a central role in establishing value, and that culture and economics are intertwined in complex ways.

THINKING CRITICALLY ABOUT ECONOMICS

Cultural economics argues that a single society can have multiple local cultural models of appropriate economic action and behavior circulating in it. Can you think of at least three different cultural models of economic behavior in the United States?

How Does Culture Shape the Value and Meaning of Money?

If value and its meanings are created through the processes of culture, then it stands to reason that the value and meanings of **money** itself—an object or substance that serves as a medium of exchange, a store of value, or a unit of account—are also created through cultural processes. Money provides a standard measure of value that allows people to compare and trade goods and services. Anything durable and scarce can serve as money. Cowrie (a type of mollusk) shells, rings made of precious metals, brass rods, and even enormous stone disks have been used as money. Some money, known as **commodity money**, has another value beyond itself. Gold or other precious metals, which can also be used as jewelry, are good examples. **Fiat money** is created and guaranteed by a government; an example is our American dollar bills—technically called Federal Reserve Notes—that are backed by promises and not by precious metals. Money interests anthropologists not simply because it is a medium of economic exchange, but also because it has functions and implications beyond our economic lives, affecting important matters like the stability of a society and how people think about personal relationships.

The Cultural Dimensions of Money

Several cultural dimensions of money are of interest to anthropologists, especially the diverse types of money people use and the powerful moral meanings people project onto money and its uses. Together, these dimensions reveal important differences and subtleties in how people use money and establish its value.

Across the world, money is many things to many people, and not everybody wants it for the same reasons. In market-based economies like that in the United States, people want money because it can be used to buy nearly any good or service. Anthropologists call this **general purpose money** because it is money that is used to buy almost anything. Portability and mobility are important features of general purpose money, as we see in our dollar bills, coins, credit cards, checks, and so on.

Another type of money is **limited purpose money**, which refers to objects that can be exchanged only for certain things. For example, the pastoral Tiv people of Nigeria traditionally could purchase cattle and pay a bride price (things of value a groom gives to his bride's father) only with brass rods. In Tiv society, people traditionally did not use money for basic subsistence, but primarily to gain access to goods that give social respectability and prestige, such as a marriage partner, cattle, and other livestock (Bohannon and Bohannon 1968).

In the Tiv case, powerful moral rules regulated the ways in which money was used. The Tiv traditionally had three separate **spheres of exchange**, or bounded orders of value in which certain goods can be exchanged only for others: ordinary subsistence goods, prestige goods, and rights in people, especially women and slaves (Bohannon and Bohannon 1968). To exchange goods across those spheres—such as exchanging subsistence goods for prestige goods—would have been immoral and disallowed. During the British colonial period in Nigeria (1900–1960), the British undermined this traditional system when they introduced general purpose money. Young Tiv men working as laborers and paid in British currency began using it to pay for prestige goods like cattle and bride price. The acquisition of cash value for prestige goods, Bohannon observed, was not just an economic problem: it was a moral problem because it interfered with Tiv notions about what money could be used for and about appropriate ways of creating social status.

- **Money.** An object or substance that serves as a medium of exchange, a store of value, or a unit of account.

- **Commodity money.** Money with another value beyond itself, such as gold or other precious metals, which can be used as jewelry or ornament.

- **Fiat Money.** Money created and guaranteed by a government.

- **General purpose money.** Money that is used to buy nearly any good or service.

- **Limited purpose money.** Objects that can be exchanged only for certain things.

- **Spheres of exchange.** Bounded orders of value in which certain goods can be exchanged only for others.

Figure 8.5 "Dirty Money" and Transactional Orders. One of the reasons people involved in organized criminal enterprises launder money gained from illegal activities is to hide the origins of their wealth from the government. But these people are also moving this money from one symbolic realm or transactional order to another, so once it's been laundered, it is symbolically "clean" and can be shared with intimates, including spouses and children who should be protected from the morally suspect activities through which it was gained. In this case, a Mexican drug cartel leader sought to launder his money through a racetrack in Oklahoma, which the FBI raided.

- **Transactional orders.** Realms of transactions a community uses, each with its own set of symbolic meanings and moral assumptions.

Even general purpose money has cultural and moral dimensions beyond its function as a medium of exchange (Parry and Bloch 1989). We all know, for example, that you cannot simply walk into your university's accounting office, pay a large sum of money, and receive a diploma. Our ideas about getting an education involve a moral obligation to work hard and apply oneself to learn a body of knowledge before the diploma is awarded. If you tried to buy a diploma outright, your money would have no value for this purpose, and one could even imagine that seeking to buy a diploma could feel "dirty," contaminating the purity and goodness we associate with the process of education.

An anthropological explanation for this situation lies in the concept of **transactional orders**, or realms of transactions a community uses, each with its own set of symbolic meanings and moral assumptions (Parry and Bloch 1989). The transactions involved in getting an education, which are steeped in long-term obligations and expectations, are morally distinct from other short-term transactions that have no special moral obligations, such as buying a magazine at your university bookstore (Figure 8.5).

Money and the Distribution of Power

In addition to money's cultural dimensions, different kinds of money reflect and shape the distribution of power in distinctive ways. In his book *Debt: The First 5,000 Years*, anthropologist David Graeber (2011) explores the historical relationship between money and debt cross-culturally. He opens with the observation that when we are in debt to others, we feel great moral pressure to pay it off. This expectation extends to whole countries, so that, for example, when a poor country borrows money from an international financial institution like the World Bank or a rich country to build roads or provide electricity for its people—or even when a dictator borrows money simply to line his pockets—citizens are obligated to pay off the debt, even if doing so means not using that money to address more pressing problems like poverty, disease, and suffering. According to Graeber, many of us recognize that this is an inhumane situation, but we nevertheless accept it and, in doing so, ignore the inequality between the creditor and the debtor, as well as the human suffering that might be involved in paying back the debt.

The origins of this view of debt go back 5,000 years, Graeber writes, to a time when states started creating new kinds of money to promote trade. For long periods of history, commodity money was common because it required no trust to exchange. Indebtedness tends to grow with the rise of commodity money, however, because of its scarcity. Its use also coincides with periods of widespread violence because it can be stolen and is not easily traceable. During periods in which fiat money is used, governments regulate and control the flow of money to a degree and intervene in creditor–debtor relations, including even instituting laws of debt forgiveness, because they recognize the political unrest that grows with high levels of indebtedness. Graeber's broader point here is that these different types of money are related to distinctive kinds of social dynamics and power relations, some of them quite violent and negative. But whatever the type of money, the broader pattern is one in which debtor–creditor relations are full of tension and conflict.

Graeber explains that being in debt to others is not universally viewed as a moral problem or characterized by conflict. He explains that in many societies with what he calls "human" (as opposed to "commercial") economies—in which people's goal is not to acquire money but to create and maintain social relationships—the flow of credit and indebtedness between individuals is a sign of trust and solidarity. In these settings, "money" (which may take the form of yams, pigs, stones, or other objects) is usually used not to acquire goods or gain material wealth, but to provide a unit of account or measure for socially important things—for example, to arrange a marriage, to head off a feud, to console mourners at a funeral, to seek forgiveness for a crime, or to acquire followers (Graeber 2011:130). Sometimes debts incurred in these processes remain unsettled because they are so important socially that they cannot be repaid using money. For much of history, most economies worked this way, and some still do. In the next section, we examine the importance of these kinds of exchanges in many economies.

• •

THINKING CRITICALLY ABOUT ECONOMICS

Do you feel a need to protect certain relationships from money? What is the meaning of money for you in these situations?

• •

Why Is Gift Exchange Such an Important Part of All Societies?

Exchange, which anthropologists understand as the transfer of things and gifts between social actors (Carrier 1996a:218), is a universal feature of human existence and relates to all aspects of life. In many societies, the exchange of gifts is the central defining feature of its economy.

Gift Exchange and Economy: Two Classic Approaches

It may sound strange to think of a gift exchange in economic terms. We tend to think of gifts as personal expressions of **reciprocity**, the give-and-take that builds and confirms relationships. For Americans, the problem is that we distinguish the economy from gift giving, while in the nonindustrial societies anthropologists have traditionally studied, exchanging gifts is at the heart of the local economy. So how are gifts related to economy? Two classic approaches to this question date back to the 1920s.

• **Reciprocity.** The give-and-take that builds and confirms relationships.

Malinowski and the Kula

The exchange of gifts is a central feature of life in Melanesian societies of the Southwest Pacific, a fact Bronislaw Malinowski discovered while he was in the Trobriand Islands. He wrote that, for Trobriand Islanders, "to possess is to give. . . . A man who owns a thing is expected to share it, to distribute it, to be its trustee and dispenser" (1922:97).

He found no better illustration of this phenomenon than the *Kula* [**koo**-la], an extensive inter-island system of exchange in which high-ranking men gave ornamental shell armbands (*mwali*) and necklaces (*soulava*) to lifelong exchange partners on other islands. In the highly structured *Kula*, armbands traveled in one direction and necklaces in the opposite direction (Figure 8.6). For Trobriand Islanders, these shell valuables were about the most valuable things one could possess, even though men typically owned them for only a few months before they gave them to other partners (anthropologists call this **delayed reciprocity**—which involves a long lag time between receiving a gift and paying it back). These shell valuables had no real function, as they were rarely worn, and had no other use. Their value came when they were given away because that is when they brought renown to the man who gave them away.

Malinowski also observed that when men sailed to visit their partners on another island, in addition to the armbands and necklaces, they always brought along many utilitarian goods, such as vegetables, fish, or pots, to exchange for things they could not get on their own island. Malinowski theorized that these ritualized *Kula* exchanges functioned to enhance the status of individual men and distribute goods people could not otherwise get on their home islands. *Kula* is such an important dimension of Trobriand society that colonialism did not undermine it. In fact, it has expanded in recent decades, involving more islands and lower-ranking individuals.

Although Malinowski did not discuss it, Trobriand women also participated in extensive exchange systems: "Thinking Like an Anthropologist: The Role of Exchange in Managing Social Relationships" explores the significance of women's exchange in the Trobriand Islands.

• **Delayed reciprocity.** A form of reciprocity that features a long lag time between receiving a gift and paying it back.

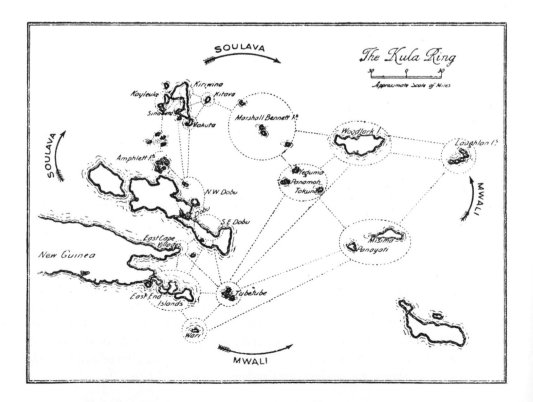

🌱 **Figure 8.6   The *Kula* Cycle with *Mwali* (Armbands) and *Soulava* (Necklaces).**

Thinking Like an Anthropologist
The Role of Exchange in Managing Social Relationships

ANTHROPOLOGISTS BEGIN THEIR research by asking questions. In this box, we want you to learn how to ask questions as an anthropological researcher. Part One describes a situation and follows up with questions we would ask. Part Two asks you to formulate your own questions based on a different situation.

PART ONE: MORTUARY EXCHANGE IN THE TROBRIAND ISLANDS

Since the mid–twentieth century, various scholars have updated Malinowski's picture of the *Kula* and other Melanesian exchange systems. Most notable of these scholars was the American anthropologist Annette Weiner (1933–1997), who conducted fieldwork in the Trobriand Islands during the 1970s and 1980s.

Weiner noted that women rarely participated directly in *Kula*. But she also observed that women participate in their own elaborate exchange system based on delayed reciprocity. This exchange system, called *Sagali*, involves the exchange of grass skirts and bundles made of dried banana leaves, items used almost exclusively in women's exchanges (Weiner 1976, 1988).

Sagali is a mortuary exchange ritual. When someone dies, Trobriand Islanders go through months of mourning during which they shut themselves off from most normal activities. When they eventually emerge from this self-imposed seclusion, their closest relatives give gifts of decorative women's skirts and banana leaf bundles to all the in-laws and other relatives who have helped them out during their months of seclusion. Although the fancy skirts can be worn in traditional dances, the banana leaf bundles have no use whatsoever outside the *Sagali*. Women make them all the time, usually while sitting outside their homes with other women and discussing village news and gossip. Only women give or receive banana leaf bundles or skirts, and men play no role in the exchange except perhaps to help move the huge baskets of bundles from a house to the village plaza for their wives or sisters.

Weiner nevertheless found important similarities between *Sagali* and *Kula*. For example, they both involve delayed reciprocity. That is, just as a man would not receive any *Kula* valuables between visits to his trading partners on other islands, a woman who gave away all her bundles would not receive any back until the next *Sagali*. The significance of both kinds of exchange system lay in the prestige that came from giving away the objects involved, not in accumulating them. If a person hoarded *Kula* valuables or skirts and leaf bundles when called on to exchange them, he or she would be subject to ridicule as a stingy and selfish person.

What questions does this situation raise for anthropological researchers?

1. How can a woman guarantee that *Sagali* exchanges will eventually be repaid at some later exchange?
2. In a *Sagali* ritual, the recipients of bundles and skirts see tangible affirmation of their contributions to the family of the deceased. But what does the deceased's family get out of giving away hundreds of bundles and skirts?
3. How do these transactions build social bonds between the family of a dead person and the people who have supported them during the months of mourning?
4. How does giving and receiving bundles enhance an individual's social status?

In Plain Sight. Malinowski uncritically accepted certain European preconceptions about women's non-economic status, ignoring almost completely *Sagali* exchanges, even though they were going on all around him. Yet we know that he observed them, because he took photographs like this one of women exchanging banana leaf bundles and skirts that they had themselves made.

(continued)

Thinking Like an Anthropologist (continued)

PART TWO: EXCHANGE RELATIONS
SURROUNDING AMERICAN FUNERALS
AND MARRIAGES

Not all American transactions are about acquiring desired goods and services; some exchanges involve delayed reciprocity much as they do in the Trobriand Islands. Two socially based American transactions are best viewed as ritualized exchanges: giving wedding gifts and giving support to family and friends after a death. If you wanted to understand the ritualized aspects of American wedding gifts or mortuary transactions, what questions would you ask as an anthropological researcher?

- **Generalized reciprocity.**
  A form of reciprocity in which gifts are given freely without the expectation of return.

- **Balanced reciprocity.**
  A form of reciprocity in which the giver expects a fair return at some later time.

- **Negative reciprocity.**
  A form of reciprocity in which the giver attempts to get something for nothing, to haggle his or her way into a favorable personal outcome.

Mauss and the Spirit of the Gift

Marcel Mauss (1872–1950), nephew and colleague of French sociologist Émile Durkheim, was the founder of modern French anthropology. In 1924, he published his most influential work, *The Gift*, which compares gift exchange and its functions in a wide range of non-Western societies.

Unlike Malinowski, who viewed gift exchange primarily in terms of how it contributed to an individual's status and identity, Mauss viewed gift exchange in terms of how it builds group solidarity. Gift exchange, Mauss insisted, is steeped in morality and based on obligation, which has three dimensions: (1) *the obligation to give*, which establishes the giver as generous and worthy of respect; (2) *the obligation to receive*, which shows respect to the giver; and (3) *the obligation to return the gift in appropriate ways*, which demonstrates honor. It thus creates and maintains bonds of solidarity between people who, Mauss believed, would otherwise pursue their own personal interests.

For Mauss, gift-giving is so important that the objects people give even take on the identity of the giver. Among the Maori of New Zealand, for example, the gift has a spirit called *hau* that compels the receiver to reciprocate. If this sounds strange, consider that we sometimes believe that objects take on their owner's life force, which is why many collectors buy personal effects of famous persons (Figure 8.7).

Later anthropologists have built on Mauss's insights into how gift exchange lies at the heart of human society. One of the most influential of these was Marshall Sahlins (1972), who argued that gift exchanges help manage group boundaries. Sahlins identified three types of reciprocity involved in gift exchange—generalized reciprocity, balanced reciprocity, and negative reciprocity—each of which defines the social relationship between a giver and a receiver.

Generalized reciprocity refers to giving something without the expectation of return, at least not in the near future. It is uninhibited and generous giving, such as that which takes place between parents and children, married couples, or close-knit kin groups.

Balanced reciprocity occurs when a person gives something and expects the receiver to return an equivalent gift or favor at some point in the future. The *Kula*, *Sagali*, and American exchanges of birthday presents are examples.

Finally, **negative reciprocity**, which economists call "barter," is the attempt to get something for nothing, to haggle one's way into a favorable personal outcome. It exists between the most distant relations, such as between strangers or adversaries.

Figure 8.7   J. K. Rowling's Chair. In 2016, this chair sold at auction for $394,000. The chair by itself is interesting to look at, but it is the fact that J. K. Rowling sat in it when she wrote the first two books in her *Harry Potter* series that makes it so valuable to some collectors.

Sahlins's typology is useful because it suggests that social relationships shape the kinds of reciprocity people practice. But recent studies of gift-giving have focused less on the objective types of reciprocity and more on how people interpret gift exchange. For example, anthropologist Marilyn Strathern (1990) argues that certain Melanesian cultures believe that people acquire their individual identities through gift exchange. These Melanesians do not conceive of people as independent units who *enter into* gift exchange; instead, they see themselves as *made* into people by gift exchange itself. Strathern's broader point is that culturally different concepts of personhood and relationship lead to different understandings of and motivations for gift exchange.

Gift Exchange in Market-Based Economies

Although our cultural models dismiss its economic significance, gift exchange is tremendously important in American and European societies for a lot of the same reasons it is in other societies: it establishes social status, reaffirms relationships, and gives people access to the goods and sometimes influence that they want and need. As in any society, important implicit rules guide our gift exchange.

For example, the gifts we give for holidays and birthdays follow implicit rules. Gifts between siblings or good friends have to be repaid in equal value every bit as much as the *Kula* valuables do. Ideally, gifts should also be personal and embody the relationship between giver and receiver. Yet such gift exchanges among friends are delicate matters. Most Americans feel these gifts should not be cash, for example, in the form of a $20 bill, because it places a concrete value on the relationship. Somewhat less impersonal are **commodities** (mass-produced and impersonal goods with no meaning or history apart from themselves) bought at a store. As commodities, they are equivalent to the money spent to buy them. One solution described by anthropologist James Carrier (1995) is to turn impersonal commodities into personal gifts by wrapping them. This simple action symbolically distances the goods from an anonymous retail environment, suggesting that the giver made a greater effort than simply going to a store (Figure 8.8).

Three points stand out here: (1) Gift exchanges are deeply embedded in the social relations of every society; (2) by personalization we can transform impersonal commodities into personal gifts; and (3) we, like everyone else in the world, invest tremendous symbolic meaning in the things we give, receive, consume, and own. This third point has significant subtleties, which we explore in more detail in the next section.

Figure 8.8   Marketing Celebrities to Sell Goods. Retailers try to help us overcome the impersonality of commodities by creating marketing campaigns that personalize their products. One strategy is to associate a product with a widely recognized celebrity, such as Beyoncé Knowles-Carter, pictured here. Celebrities can generate positive feelings about a product even if they don't actually say anything about its quality.

• **Commodities.** Mass-produced and impersonal goods with no meaning or history apart from themselves.

THINKING CRITICALLY ABOUT ECONOMICS

The way anthropologists think about it, "reciprocity," "exchange," and "sharing" each have different meanings. In what ways do you think these are different from each other?

What Is the Point of Owning Things?

One of the key legacies of anthropological research on gift exchange is that it has helped focus attention on how people relate to each other via things. But these matters go beyond the realm of things moving back and forth between social actors, because people also impose control and exclusive possession over those things, which raises the issue of ownership. Why do people own things, and under what conditions do they maintain dominion over the things they want to control? Why do they even want certain things to begin with? As with all economic systems and transactions, these questions are best addressed through a cross-cultural lens.

Cross-Cultural Perspectives on Property

For anthropologists, owning something is not simply a matter of individual possession or occupation of an object or piece of land—which is the prevailing Western legal view of property—but a matter of interactions between people. The reason for viewing property as social relationships and actions, rather than as a static legal category, has to do with the many cross-cultural variations anthropologists have found in terms of how people actually think about and manage property relationships. Two major issues characterize these processes: (1) They are about the assertion and negotiation of rights in something, many of these rights being held not by individuals but by a group; and (2) they involve declarations and claims that are rooted in culturally specific forms of symbolic communication (Strang and Busse 2011:4).

For example, in the Melanesian and Polynesian societies where the kinds of gift-giving systems described in the previous section are pervasive, anthropologists have observed that some objects cannot be given away or separated from their original owners. Annette Weiner (1992) calls these objects "inalienable possessions," and their inherent value transcends their exchange value. An example Weiner gives is the Maori "Sacred Cloak," which is a cloak made from the feathers of kiwis and other birds and worn traditionally by nobility (Figure 8.9). When a woman wears it, it is said that "she is more than herself—she is her ancestors." The object is understood to be a manifestation of a kin group's cosmological origins, communicating the wearer's nobility and the historical continuity of the lineage. It cannot be given away by any individual because rights in it are held by the kinship lineage.

Weiner observes that in some circumstances, inalienable possessions are transferred to others, but they will never be anything other than temporary loans. She contends that in an economy where the moral code is based on gift-giving, transferring such objects means that the giver, who is still viewed as the owner, has rights over the receiver. She also argues that holding onto an object—that is, keeping it from being exchanged—contributes to the creation of status differences between people and is the basis of maintaining social hierarchy. Importantly, in Polynesia, women often control things associated with the sacred, which can give them power within social groups (Godelier 1999).

Appropriation and Consumption

The other important question about owning things is why people come to want certain things in the first place. Sometimes it has to do with securing access to a critical resource, and then using whatever socially acceptable tools are available

Figure 8.9   Maori Sacred Cloak.

to exclude others from gaining access. But it also often has a lot to do with what a community considers "cool," that is, impressive or trendy. In our own society, marketing and advertising executives work hard to identify and create an image of coolness in ads and commercials—in the clothing we wear, the music we listen to, the foods we eat, the cars we drive, the smartphones we use, and so on—all to get us to buy more things.

Being cool is an important way people in a mass society identify who is and is not a member of their "in-crowd"—their social class, rank, lifestyle, ethnic identity, or other particular grouping (Bourdieu 1984). But objects are not naturally "cool." Whatever symbolic distinctions or qualities they have are culturally constructed. Their meaning results from social and cultural processes that create demand for them, such as the fact that everyone is talking about them or important and respected people own them. People who wish to feel or be thought of as "cool" often seek to satisfy this desire through the act of consumption.

Figure 8.10   Prestige Goods. Although both of these bags are considered prestige goods in their specific cultures, a vast conceptual distance exists between how and why people consume them. String bags (*top*) represent an individual's wealth in social relationships, while Gucci bags (*bottom*) represent an individual's material wealth.

● **Consumption.** The act of using and assigning meaning to a good, service, or relationship.

● **Appropriation.** The process of taking possession of an object, idea, or relationship and making it one's own.

● **Consumers.** People who rely on goods and services not produced by their own labor.

Anthropologists define **consumption** as the act of using and assigning meaning to a good, service, or relationship (see also Chapter 15). Through consumption, people make cultural meaning, build social relationships, and create identities (Douglas and Isherwood 1978; Appadurai 1986). Every culture distinguishes between what is appropriate and what is inappropriate to consume, providing social avenues to consuming culturally accepted goods and limiting consumption of things considered inappropriate.

Consumption begins with an act of **appropriation**, which is a process of taking possession of an object, idea, or relationship and making it one's own (Carrier 1996b; Miller 1995). Consider, for example, the "consumption" of a smartphone. The initial act of appropriation takes place as you shop for it. Shopping entails narrowing your choices on the basis of price, size, look, brand, special features, and your sense of how you want to be seen by others, until you identify the device you want to buy. After paying for it, you continue the appropriation process by personalizing it—by using it in certain ways, such as downloading special apps, putting a particular case on it, or otherwise customizing it to reflect what you want out of a phone. These customizations, as well as how and when you use your smartphone, in turn reflect and define who you are as a person: for example, an informed techie who loves the latest gadgets, a social butterfly who is always networked, a creative and artistic type, or a serious businessperson. Depending on the brand you purchased and how you customize your device, your consumption of this particular smartphone distinguishes your social position in society, as a member of the middle class, or some other grouping based on age, ethnicity, and so on.

In societies where people still make many of the things they consume, people may be just as concerned with wanting cool things—things that identify the owner as worthy of respect—as many Americans are. Of course, other cultures' ideas of what "cool" is may differ greatly from ours. For instance, when people around Aitape on the North Coast of Papua New Guinea exchange food and other subsistence goods with their friends in neighboring villages, they also often give their partners handmade netted string bags with unique designs common to their home villages. String bags are a tangible manifestation of the trader's generosity and commitment to the social and economic relationship between the two exchange partners (Figure 8.10). People are especially proud of the bags that come from very distant villages, because they indicate an extensive network of friends.

Changes in consumption patterns are often visible manifestations of broader cultural changes (Miller 1995). For example, let us return to the Chinese entrepreneurs discussed at the beginning of this chapter. The shift toward a market economy in China made it possible for Chinese people to consume things they could not during the Maoist era. Consumerism itself was not new in China; during the Maoist era, people were **consumers**, that is, people who rely on goods and services not of their own making (Humphrey 2002:40). But consciousness of consumption changed. During the Maoist era, when the state produced and allocated all industrial and agricultural goods, people were encouraged to identify these goods as "their own," because the state presented itself ideologically as an expression of the people.

Now that the state no longer controls the production of many consumer goods, and foreign goods pour in, Chinese people have a bewildering array of choices about how and what to consume. The consumption patterns of new rich entrepreneurs—their choices of fashion, the cars they drive, the foods they eat, and so on—have become important because they help common Chinese people navigate through that variety and shape their sense of what objects and services carry symbolic prestige. As Chinese people negotiate who they are through what and how they consume, we can see that the influx of new consumer goods is the grounds of creating new cultural meanings and social relationships.

Consumption is a key feature of capitalism, but if consumption varies around the globe, does the capitalist system also vary?

●●●

THINKING CRITICALLY ABOUT ECONOMICS

If it is true that changing consumption patterns are visible manifestations of broader cultural changes, what can the massive acquisition of cellular phones and smartphones by millions of people during the past decade tell us about changes in how people communicate?

●●●

Does Capitalism Have Distinct Cultures?

For the better part of the twentieth century, capitalism and socialism/communism existed as opposed forms of economic organization, an opposition that dominated global politics during the Cold War. After the collapse of the Soviet Union and Eastern Bloc (Warsaw Pact) regimes in 1989 and China's shift toward "Socialism with Chinese Characteristics," many economists and political leaders, especially in the United States, asserted that "Capitalism won." But under the influence of local cultures, capitalism can take more varied forms than we might assume.

Capitalism is an economic system based on private ownership of the means of production, in which prices are set and goods distributed through a market. Beyond this generally accepted definition, theoretical approaches to capitalism vary depending on the researcher's philosophical and political persuasions (Blim 2000). For example, followers of influential sociologist Max Weber study the distinct types of capitalism that have existed in different times and places; formalists study capitalism through the actions of individuals and institutions; and Marxists study the changing nature of industrial production, the conditions of workers, and the connection between small-scale economic activities and broader global economic trends.

In spite of their theoretical orientation, however, anthropologists view capitalism as a cultural phenomenon. In fact, its deepest assumptions are cultural: capitalism assumes certain values and ideals to be natural, in the sense that "this is the way things really are." But anthropologists also recognize that the cultural contexts and meanings of capitalist activities take diverse forms. Let us compare two examples—one drawn from Wall Street, the other from Malaysia—to illustrate how capitalist activities and meanings can vary across cultures.

Figure 8.11   The New York Stock Exchange on Wall Street, the Heart of U.S. Capitalism.

Culture and Social Relations on Wall Street

Investment banks on Wall Street, site of the New York Stock Exchange and America's financial capital, are popularly seen as a bastion of individual entrepreneurialism and cold rationalism in pursuit of profits (Figure 8.11). But anthropologists have found that social relationships and cultural processes shape transactions on Wall Street in far more complex ways than our image of Wall Street may suggest.

What interests anthropologists is how, in the context of such social relationships, people construct meanings, and how those meanings shape social action and individual conduct. For example, anthropologist Karen Ho (2009) studied investment banks and the international banking industry on Wall Street using participant observation and open-ended interviews just as an anthropologist working in a foreign village would. She reports that bankers and traders have a conception of Wall Street as an entity that seamlessly mediates vast and anonymous flows of capital throughout the world.

But through her fieldwork, Ho was able to assess the relationship between this concept and actual social practices. She found that these investment banks had transformed the goals of American capitalism since the 1980s, by shifting companies away from traditional corporate goals: producing a quality product in a sustainable way that would provide income for corporate investors, jobs for employees, and useful products for consumers. Instead, investment firms came to stress increasing "shareholder value" as a corporation's mission, a view that justified hundreds of mergers and acquisitions throughout the 1990s and 2000s. The consequence of most mergers and acquisitions was liquidating and breaking up less-profitable firms, selling off their assets at a profit, and firing all their employees. The acquiring hedge fund or investment bank added short-term shareholder profits, but no new production, and many newly unemployed people. The investment banks themselves benefited dramatically from commissions that they received for each step of the process, increasing their own shareholder value and bonuses for individual bankers.

But even the bankers themselves, she discovered, could be laid off at a moment's notice as the banks confronted regular economic crises because of poor investments. She concluded that the structure of the investment bank workplace, a crisis-prone setting in which workers are seen as expendable to protect the profits of the bank itself, has become a powerful cultural model that Wall Street bankers project onto the rest of the economy. Because these bankers control access to money for many corporations, this Wall Street vision of how an economy should work is being imposed on many other businesses.

Throughout her time on Wall Street, Ho also found that strong personal relationships are essential to successful transactions, precisely because the market is so vast and because it is so difficult to decipher with certainty the risks and strengths of any particular global segment. As a result, bankers who tell their clients they have "global reach" and coverage "everywhere in the world"—which is a central part of the image they promote to persuade investors to do business with them—are not being entirely honest. In reality, Ho found, most firms had minimal coverage in most parts of the world, often maintaining empty or barely staffed offices where they only occasionally did business. Their relationships with local banking firms and clients tended to lie nearly dormant, being reactivated only when new investment opportunities arose. Ho's point is that without the personal relationships and knowledge of local conditions and markets, these banks have almost no reach whatsoever, demonstrating that modern financial markets are every bit as dependent on social relationships and local knowledge as any daily transaction anthropologists might study in a rural village setting.

Entrepreneurial Capitalism Among Malays

The southeast Asian nation of Malaysia provides an example of a very different culture of capitalism. During the past several decades, Malaysia has aggressively pursued economic growth through industrialization and the creation of investment opportunities. Malaysia is an Islamic country whose majority are Muslim ethnic Malays. During British colonial times (early 1800s to the mid-1900s), the nation's Chinese minority dominated the economy and remained considerably better off than most of the Malay majority. Since the late 1960s, the Malaysian government's goal for economic growth has been to reduce economic inequality between the country's ethnic Chinese and ethnic Malays by giving Malays preferential treatment and greater control over economic resources through set-aside provisions, government subsidies, special investment programs, and preferential opportunities for university education.

Anthropologist Patricia Sloane (1999) studied the impact of these laws on the culture of Malay entrepreneurs in urban Kuala Lumpur, Malaysia's capital. Few Malay capitalists in her study were extremely wealthy, but they were part of the growing Malaysian middle class. These Malay capitalists' aspirations are not "global" but self-consciously local. The ideology of business was embedded in local values and committed to promoting the economic interests and growth of the Malay ethnic group.

These processes have created a new class of Malay entrepreneurs who think of themselves as the cornerstone of a new, modernized Malaysia. They accept that capitalism is a self-interested enterprise, but they also feel bound by traditional Malay values, insisting on investment and development that serve traditional obligations to family, community, and other Malays. Their idea of capitalism is one in which wealth, social balance, and even salvation are the rewards for those who abide by the moral dictates of social responsibility and obligation. At the heart of these values lie Islamic economic principles—such as the prohibition on charging interest, prohibitions on exploitive or risky activities, and the obligation to share wealth after meeting one's family's needs (Sloane 1999:73).

One effect of these ideals is that few enterprises are economically successful, so business failures are common. But Malays do not view these facts with embarrassment, because for many individuals the primary business goal is not to generate huge profits but to extend and deepen their social networks and to cultivate contacts with powerful people. Entrepreneurship is thus not simply about economic action and profit accumulation; it allows people to show how they are both fully engaged in the modern world of global capitalism and respectful of traditional Islamic and Malay obligations and values.

The challenge for Malays, in other words, has been to pursue a capitalist economy that both improves their material quality of life and conforms to their local cultural values, social practices, and on-the-ground realities. This challenge is not unique to Malaysia. In "Anthropologist as Problem Solver: Jim Yong Kim's Holistic, On-the-Ground Approach to Fighting Poverty," we consider how one anthropologist has sought to create capitalist development that is sensitive to local realities.

Anthropologist as Problem Solver
Jim Yong Kim's Holistic, On-the-Ground Approach to Fighting Poverty

WHEN HE BECAME PRESIDENT of the World Bank in 2012, Jim Yong Kim was not just the first anthropologist and physician to hold such a high position in the world's largest development agency, he was also the first leader to actually have direct work experience in the field of international development. Kim, who was raised in Iowa as the child of Korean War refugees, received an M.D. and a Ph.D. in medical anthropology from Harvard and is a co-founder of Partners in Health, a Massachusetts-based organization that provides high-quality health care for poor people in Haiti, Peru, Mexico, Russia, and parts of Africa. Within the World Bank, which had traditionally been led by economists or businessmen, there has been concern that someone whose career had focused so much on community-level

🌱 **Jim Yong Kim.**

health and humanitarian intervention is not an appropriate leader for an institution that lends money to Third World countries to promote capitalist economic development and fight poverty (Boseley 2012; Rice 2016).

But Kim has a different view on the matter. As an anthropologist, he understands that poor health is a symptom of—and a contributor to—deeper patterns of social inequality, poverty, and lack of economic opportunity. This understanding shaped the work he had done with Partners in Health, which was the first health-care provider in Haiti to provide HIV and tuberculosis treatment for the poor. As Kim explained, "We were trying to make a point. And the point we were trying to make was that just because people are poor shouldn't mean that they shouldn't have access to high quality healthcare. It was always based on social justice, it was always based in the notion that people had a right to live a dignified life" (Boseley 2012). Kim and his colleagues knew that success promoting community health was not just a matter of medical treatment, but required a holistic and on-the-ground approach oriented toward working to remove the causes of poor health in the first place. From this vantage point, there are many factors at work, including specific cultural patterns of disease transmission (see Chapter 14), dirty water, lack of food, political disempowerment, and weak access to jobs and economic opportunity. Partners in Health worked on all these issues, and many of them are the same ones the World Bank works on, especially public infrastructure, political rights, local markets, and economic policy. But the World Bank works on these things from a very different and abstract vantage point, one that involves looking at balance sheets, budget documents, and economic models and charts.

As a profit-driven development bank, the World Bank is a very different kind of institution than Partners in Health. Its lending practices and policies—especially its structural adjustment programs and its economic, not people-centered, orientation—have long been criticized for *deepening* poverty and human suffering. But in the past couple of decades the World Bank has been changing, for example by introducing social and environmental safeguards into projects it funds. Kim, who had long been a staunch critic of the bank, saw an opportunity to help further its evolution.

His presidency has not been without internal controversy, but he has brought a new sensibility to bank leadership informed by his holistic, on-the-ground anthropological background. This sensibility involves a greater appreciation of local development priorities, a deeper understanding of the actual impacts of economic policies on people's lives, and a stronger humanitarian orientation. As he says, "Finance and macroeconomics are complicated, but you can actually learn them. The hardest thing to learn is mud-between-your-toes, on-the-ground development work. You can't learn that quickly. You can't learn that through trips where you're treated like a head of state. You have to have kind of done that before" (Rice 2016).

Questions for Reflection

1. What differences do you think exist between economists and anthropologists in terms of how they think about economic development?

2. What do you think are the advantages and disadvantages of Kim's holistic, on-the-ground perspective for determining economic development plans?

THINKING CRITICALLY ABOUT ECONOMICS

If capitalism can vary across cultures, do you think models of capitalist behavior and thought can also differ within a society? Can you think of any examples drawn from what you know about the different kinds of industries and businesses you would find in the American capitalist economic system? How can you explain the variability of capitalism within a single society?

Conclusion

Most North Americans take for granted that the best way to get the things we need and want is to get a job and begin getting a paycheck. But this is not how people do it everywhere in the world. Whether they are Chinese businessmen gaining access to business opportunities and government contracts through the cultivation of *guanxi* and *renqing*, Trobriand Islanders trading for goods on other islands, or Malaysian entrepreneurs pursuing business practices informed by Islamic values, people differ in their cultural strategies and ideas about appropriate ways to conduct their economic lives. And, when we step back and look at our own economic lives in a consumer capitalist society, we can see that we too have developed distinctive strategies for exchanging goods and money, such as when we symbolically transform commodities into personalized gifts or possessions.

Economic ideas and behaviors never exist independently of culture, morality, and social relationships. Culture shapes what is acceptable to transact, how and why a transaction occurs, and how the goods and services being exchanged are valued. This point is especially important for understanding the complexities of contemporary global economic changes. In an economically interconnected world, the creation of new markets and economic relationships has an impact on whether and how people in a particular place will be able to acquire certain goods and services. But these processes never occur in a cultural and social vacuum, which is why economic processes continue to play out in distinct ways in communities around the world.

KEY TERMS

Reviewing the Chapter

Chapter Section	What We Know	To Be Resolved
Is Money Really the Measure of All Things?	Economies never exist independently of already existing social relationships and culture. Culture shapes what is acceptable to transact, how and why transactions take place, and how the goods or services being exchanged are valued.	Still unresolved is the issue of how to define the category of "economics." Is it a particular logic and decision-making process? Or is it the substance of the economy, meaning the daily transactions of goods and services?
How Does Culture Shape the Value and Meaning of Money?	People's relationships and attitudes toward money depend on factors such as whether their society uses general purpose money or limited purpose money; whether it uses commodity money or fiat money; spheres of exchange; and cultural distinctions between transactional orders.	Anthropologists are still working through the diverse cultural meanings of money, especially the ways money circulates and shifts meanings through distinct transactional orders.

Why Is Gift Exchange Such an Important Part of All Societies?	The exchange of things is a universal feature of human existence. Many societies have met people's material and social necessities through highly organized and principled gift exchanges, but rich subtleties and cross-cultural variations exist in how, when, what, and why people engage in gift exchange.	Although anthropologists accept the central importance of gift exchange in all societies, they continue to embrace distinct theoretical models concerning reciprocity and gift exchange, and debates persist over whether these models adequately capture the complexity of other cultures' approaches to reciprocity.
What Is the Point of Owning Things?	Anthropologists approach ownership and property, not as static legal categories, but as culturally variable matters of social interaction and as bundles of rights. People often want to own things they think are "cool," but the symbolic distinctions and qualities that make objects cool and worthy of respect are always culturally constructed.	People's relationships with objects are more complicated than economic perspectives on consumption suggest. Anthropologists are still documenting and seeking to understand those complexities.
Does Capitalism Have Distinct Cultures?	Capitalism is as much an economic system as it is a cultural phenomenon, whose actual practices and cultural models vary across and within cultures.	The idea that capitalism is not a monolithic economic structure but a variable, culturally diverse set of practices is not universally accepted in anthropology, especially by Marxist anthropologists.

Readings

Since Bronislaw Malinowski's classic monograph on the *Kula* exchange among the Trobriand Islanders (*Argonauts of the Western Pacific*, London: G. Routledge and Sons, 1922), a considerable amount of anthropological research has focused on gift-giving systems around the world. Marcel Mauss's classic 1924 essay *The Gift: The Form and Reason for Exchange in Archaic Societies* (New York: W. W. Norton, 1990) is a necessary starting point. Marilyn Strathern's *The Gender of the Gift: Problems with Women and Problems with Society in Melanesia* (Berkeley, CA: University of California Press, 1988) offers an excellent overview of gift-giving in Melanesia from an anthropological perspective.

For a useful overview of the field of economic anthropology and its primary theoretical debates and orientations, see Richard R. Wilk and Lisa C. Cliggett's book *Economies and Cultures: Foundations of Economic Anthropology* (second edition, Boulder, CO: Westview Press, 2007).

With the fall of the Soviet Union and changes in Communist China, anthropologists working in Russia, China, and other post-socialist countries have found themselves in an interesting position trying to document and analyze the dramatic social transformations playing out in front of them. Three excellent books on this transformation are Caroline Humphrey's *The Unmaking of Soviet Life: Everyday Economies After Socialism* (Ithaca, NY: Cornell University Press, 2002); Katherine Verdery's *What Was Socialism? What Comes Next?* (Princeton, NJ: Princeton University Press, 1996); and John Osburg's *Anxious Wealth: Money and Morality Among China's New Rich* (Stanford, CA: Stanford University Press, 2013), from which the opening of this chapter is drawn.

David Graeber's *Debt: The First 5,000 Years* (New York: Melville House Publishing, 2011) is an ambitious book that draws extensively on ethnographic, historical, and archaeological material to explore the creation and maintenance of debt through state power and violence.

The 2008 financial crisis drew attention to the powerful role Wall Street plays in shaping the economic prospects of people who have nothing to do with investment banking. Karen Ho's *Liquidated: An Ethnography of Wall Street* (Durham, NC: Duke University Press, 2009) provides a detailed and in-depth ethnographic description of how investment banking culture operates.

9

Politics

Cooperation, Conflict, and Power Relations

IF YOU FOLLOW the news much, you'll know that reporting about politics is a major focus of any newspaper or news website. Stories about what the President recently said, conflicts between political parties in Congress, election results here or in another part of the world, or scandals involving local political figures tend to dominate the headlines. But even as these kinds of stories are the lifeblood of important public discourse in any country, they offer a fairly narrow view of what politics actually is. Why do we not find stories like the following?

• In Papua New Guinea, a young woman commits suicide out of protest for being abused by a man, intending to motivate her male relatives to seek justice and reparations.

• In a village in the Venezuelan rain forest, a Yanomami headman scrapes the ground with a machete to shame others into joining him in cleaning the village before a feast.

• In 1930s Italy, government officials concerned with the problem of declining fertility and reproductive rates among the Italian people introduce a census, social insurance programs, housing projects, and social work to support an increase in the size, growth rate, and "vitality" of the population.

• In Cameroon, high-ranking government officials use sorcery to undermine their rivals and impress villagers with their immunity from occult forces.

Revenge Suicide as Politics. This painting (*detail*) represents a suicide performed as a revenge against wrongdoing in Papua New Guinea, by native artist Apa Hugo. See p. 229 for a discussion of the complete image.

• In Hawai'i, a community leader guides disputing adversaries and family members through a healing process in which everyone is expected to share their feelings and grievances openly.

Of course, one reason we do not find such reporting about politics in U.S. news is that these events have little or no bearing on the lives of most of us. But it is easy to come to the conclusion that politics is simply what politicians or political parties said and did in the latest news cycle. Anthropologists take a wider view on **politics**, understanding it to be the relationships and processes of cooperation, conflict, social control, and power that are fundamental aspects of human life. There is considerable variety in how people think about politics and their reasons for engaging in "political" acts. It might be to enrich themselves materially or spiritually; to help their families, friends, or a social group they belong to; to pursue personal power; to resolve a conflict; or to seek dignity or freedom from oppression. It might be to produce relative order in a chaotic situation—or to produce chaos in a relatively ordered situation.

The preceding brief list also suggests that people exert power in diverse ways. Some of these are formal and fairly stable, through institutions and procedures—government offices, armies, codified laws, rituals, or legal proceedings—that are easily identifiable elements of most societies. Others are less formal and more fleeting, such as the creation of temporary alliances, or acts of protest, manipulation, accusation, sorcery, and shame. Political acts may draw attention to the exercise of power, or they may be disguised, hiding the true source of power. Techniques include coercion, oppression, persuasion, and influence, as well as truth-seeking, the collection and sharing of information, and the desire to know intimate details about people's lives.

This approach to politics moves beyond the idea that modern states, which function through elections, bureaucracies, and the like, should be the sole focus of anthropological interest. Even though states are the dominant political form in our contemporary world, the actual practices of modern states are not the same everywhere. More important is the diversity in how people around the world manage power relations at all levels of social life, from the interpersonal to the national and transnational. We can hardly begin to understand this diversity if we focus exclusively on the formal institutions of modern states, because that approach misses the fact that cooperation, conflict, social control, and power are rooted in and emerge from people's everyday social interactions, belief systems, and cultural practices.

At the heart of anthropology's approach to politics is a key question: *How is power acquired and transmitted in a society?* Embedded in this broader question are the following problems, around which this chapter is organized:

• **Politics.** The relationships and processes of cooperation, conflict, social control, and power that are fundamental aspects of human life.

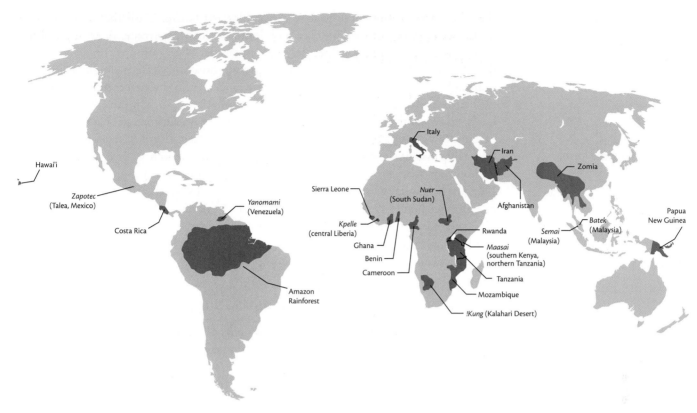

Figure 9.1   Select Peoples and Places Discussed in Chapter 9.

Does every society have a government?

What is political power?

Why do some societies seem more violent than others?

How do people avoid aggression, brutality, and war?

For anthropologists, politics is about how people manage their everyday social relationships through force, influence, persuasion, and control over resources. But before we understand how these processes work in different societies, we need to address the opportunities and pitfalls of thinking about politics solely in terms of how formal political systems work.

Does Every Society Have a Government?

This question might seem strange because the answer seems so obvious. Our society has **government** (a separate legal and constitutional domain that is the source of law, order, and legitimate force) from the federal level down to the most local. We may assume other societies must have something similar. Otherwise, wouldn't they be in the throes of anarchy?

Not necessarily. Consider the !Kung San (also known as Ju/'hoansi), a hunter-gatherer society in the Kalahari Desert of southern Africa. !Kung have historically lived in egalitarian bands of 15 to 20 people and are an **acephalous society**; that is,

- **Government.** A separate legal and constitutional domain that is the source of law, order, and legitimate force.

- **Acephalous society.** A society without a governing head, generally with no hierarchical leadership.

they have no governmental head or hierarchical structure. Until they were brought under the control of the Namibian and South African governments, !Kung did not even have a notion of a distinct political sphere. In !Kung groups, important band decisions have historically been made by group consensus. Life is organized around sharing food, and those who do not share are taunted and shamed mercilessly, or even pushed out of the band (Figure 9.2). The emphasis on sharing and egalitarianism has been a means of keeping people more or less in line without the need for government or **laws** (a set of rules established by some formal authority). Among the !Kung, leadership has been informal, usually one of the senior men guiding the band, but without any formal power over others. In some hunter-gatherer groups, such as the Batek of Malaysia, where relations between men and women are egalitarian, women can also become leaders of a band (Endicott and Endicott 2008).

If governments are not a universal feature of human existence, why do we tend to think of politics primarily in terms of how formal governments work? Part of the reason is historical, the other part philosophical.

- **Laws.** Sets of rules established by some formal authority.

The Idea of "Politics" and the Problem of Order

Our modern notion of politics emerged during the Enlightenment (1650–1800). This was a period of social upheaval in Western Europe in which the rise of industrial capitalism and revolutionary democracies challenged the existing social and political order. Two of the major figures concerned with the problem of disorder caused by these changes were the English philosophers Thomas Hobbes (1588–1679) and John Locke (1632–1704). Hobbes believed that humans are naturally selfish, competitive, and warlike, leading to violence and a chaotic free-for-all as people pursue their own personal interests, a condition avoided only by the absolute rule of a monarch (Hobbes 1909). Locke disagreed, arguing that chaos was avoidable by creating a more limited government based on a "social contract" in which certain basic individual rights are recognized (Locke 2003). This is our modern idea—and justification—for democratic government, and it is what modern politicians refer to when they talk about the "rule of law."

Europeans learned that societies exist around the world that do not have government, written laws, or "social contracts," but they largely dismissed those societies as primitive, uncivilized, and savage. Indeed, one of the central animating ideals

Figure 9.2   The Power of Sharing. In many hunter-gatherer societies, such as the !Kung San pictured here, individuals are obligated to share their goods, especially food. This obligation represents a powerful force for ensuring social stability.

of European colonialism in Africa, Asia, Latin America, and the Pacific was that bringing these people social order created by European forms of government and law would lift them out of their supposed savagery.

Structural-Functionalist Models of Political Stability

During the early twentieth century, the global expansion of British colonialism co-incided with and helped fuel the rise of British anthropology. Colonial authorities often turned to anthropologists to help them make sense of the foreign societies now under British control that did not have forms of government recognizable to the British. This situation presented British anthropologists with important opportunities to study the maintenance of order in societies without formal governments and political leaders. It also allowed these anthropologists to help formalize patterns of indirect rule in which local chiefs were incorporated into the new colonial administration. The theory they used to explain how these societies had maintained order was **structural-functionalism**, which held that the different structures of a society (religion, politics, kinship, etc.) function in an integrated way to maintain social order and equilibrium. In Africa, structural-functionalists identified numerous ways societies maintained order and social control without formal political institutions (Radcliffe-Brown 1952).

For example, kinship could work, as it did among the Nuer pastoralists in southern Sudan, to organize men into lineages that would normally live separately but come together to meet external threats. In "Classic Contributions: E. E. Evans-Pritchard on Segmentary Lineages," on page 226, we find an explanation of the logic of Nuer political organization that maintained social order.

In addition to kinship, various kinds of informal associations (groupings of individuals around nonpolitical matters) can function as a political system. Secret societies, for example, might exercise control over territory, rituals, and the enforcement of certain customs. Many pastoralist societies, like the Maasai of Kenya and Tanzania, divide men from different families into **age-grades**, which are groupings of age-mates, who are initiated into adulthood together, with members of senior grades having some authority over juniors (Kurtz 2001) (Figure 9.3).

Religious rituals can also function politically, integrating a community by bringing people together around common beliefs and activities. Rituals serve political ends by legitimating community authority, ensuring group cohesion, organizing against enemies, and resolving disputes. Beliefs in witchcraft or sorcery, which provoke fear in many societies, can also promote order. Throughout Africa, for example, people who do not behave according to community norms are identified and punished as witches. They might be banished from a village, harassed, or abused physically (Marwick 1952). Without formal courts, structural-functionalists insisted, such practices operated as a rudimentary criminal justice system (Gledhill 2000).

Neo-Evolutionary Models of Political Organization: Bands, Tribes, Chiefdoms, and States

In the 1940s and 1950s, as political anthropology was taking shape in the United States, American anthropologists called "neo-evolutionists" sought to classify the world's diverse political systems and explain how complex political systems, especially states, had evolved from simpler forms of social and political organization. Anthropologists Marshall Sahlins and Elman Service (1960) suggested a typology of societies with different forms of political and economic organization. By considering who controls food and other resources in any given society, they defined four types of society: **bands**, **tribes**, **chiefdoms**, and **states**. This typology was intended both

- **Structural-functionalism.** An anthropological theory that the different structures or institutions of a society (religion, politics, kinship, etc.) function to maintain social order and equilibrium.

- **Age-grades.** Groupings of age-mates, who are initiated into adulthood together.

- **Band.** A small, nomadic, and self-sufficient group of anywhere from 25 to 150 individuals with face-to-face social relationships, usually egalitarian.

- **Tribe.** A type of pastoralist or horticulturist society with populations usually numbering in the hundreds or thousands in which leadership is more stable than that of a band, but usually egalitarian, with social relations based on reciprocal exchange.

- **Chiefdom.** A political system with a hereditary leader who holds central authority, typically supported by a class of high-ranking elites, informal laws, and a simple judicial system, often numbering in the tens of thousands with the beginnings of intensive agriculture and some specialization.

- **State.** The most complex form of political organization, associated with societies that have intensive agriculture, high levels of social stratification, and centralized authority.

Figure 9.3   The Changing Life of the Maasai Warrior. The traditional duties of young Maasai in Kenya whose age-grade is *warrior* are to protect cattle herds from raiders and large cats, and to raid the herds of others. As tourism and wildlife conservation have increasingly disrupted Maasai lives and cattle economy, the duties of these warriors are in transition.

to describe different kinds of society as well as to explain how more complex political forms had developed from simpler ones.

Bands and tribes in this scheme were examples of **non-centralized political systems**, in which power and control over resources are dispersed among members of the society. Chiefdoms and states were examples of **centralized political systems**, in which certain individuals and institutions hold power and control over resources. Although Sahlins and Service (1960) acknowledged that different societies followed different individual evolutionary paths, the tendency was that with increasing population density came more intensive and centralized forms of political organization. Table 9.1 outlines how this classification incorporates politics, economy, size, and population density.

Challenges to Traditional Political Anthropology

Political anthropology's early focus on political systems was valuable for describing the diverse ways humans create and maintain social order, with or without formal governments. But reality hardly ever corresponds to these simple theoretical models. A major problem with the bands-tribes-chiefdoms-states typology is that many cases blur the boundaries between types. For example, the Nuer have tribe-like qualities, such as a lack of central political leadership, but because they have a population of 1.8 million people, they do not have the same kinds of social relations as a "tribe" of 500 people.

In addition, the emphasis on static political systems and order came at the expense of understanding the historical and dynamic nature of political processes. Many early

- **Non-centralized political system.** A political system, such as a band or a tribe, in which power and control over resources are dispersed between members of the society.

- **Centralized political system.** A political system, such as a chiefdom or a state, in which certain individuals and institutions hold power and control over resources.

TABLE 9.1	A NEO-EVOLUTIONARY TYPOLOGY OF POLITICAL ORGANIZATION			
	NON-CENTRALIZED		CENTRALIZED	
	Band	Tribe	Chiefdom	State
Type of Subsistence	Foraging	Horticulture and pastoralism	Extensive agriculture, intensive fishing	Intensive agriculture
Population Density	Low	Low to medium	Medium	High
Type of Economic Exchange	Reciprocity	Reciprocity and trade	Redistribution through chief, reciprocity at lower levels	Markets and trade; redistribution through state based on taxation
Social Stratification	Egalitarian	Egalitarian	Ranked	Social classes
Ownership of Property	Little or no sense of personal ownership	Lineage or clan ownership of land and livestock	Lineage or clan ownership of land, but with strong sense of personal ownership	Private and state ownership of land
Type of Leadership	Informal and situational; headman	Charismatic headman with some authority in group decision-making	Charismatic chief with limited power, usually based on giving benefits to followers	Sovereign leader supported by aristocratic bureaucracy
Law and Legitimate Control of Force	No formal laws or punishments; right to use force is communal	No formal laws or punishments; right to use force is held by lineage, clan, or association	May have informal laws and specified punishments; chief has limited access to coercion	Formal laws and punishments; state holds all access to use of physical force
Some Examples	!Kung San (Southern Africa); Inuit (Canada, Alaska); Batek (Malaysia)	Yanomami (South America); Nuer (South Sudan); Cheyenne (United States)	Kwakiutl (Canada, Alaska); Precolonial Hawaii	Aztec (Mexico); Inca (Peru); Euro-American monarchies and representative democracies

Source: Adapted from Lewellen (1983:20–21).

political anthropologists originally assumed African or Pacific societies were essentially untouched by contact with the West. But many of these "traditional" political systems were not "traditional" at all, as they had been put in place by the British colonial policy of "Indirect Rule," which allowed local rulers to exercise administrative control over their people through whatever existing power structure was in place when the British arrived. Moreover, as British anthropologist Lucy Mair (1969) pointed out, political structures only provide individuals with roles. Within a role, individuals make choices and decisions, manipulate others, and strategize, all in the pursuit of power. From this point of view, the proper focus of political anthropology is political power, an issue we turn to next.

• •

THINKING CRITICALLY ABOUT POLITICS

A complex institution like your college or university has many ways of governing the faculty, staff, and student body. These include formal institutions of governance, such as a faculty senate or president's office, as well as less formal associations and belief structures that help maintain order. What are some of these less formal forms of governance, and how do they contribute to the maintenance of order?

• •

Classic Contributions
E. E. Evans-Pritchard on Segmentary Lineages

E. E. EVANS-PRITCHARD (1902–1973) was a prominent British social anthropologist and a proponent of structural-functionalism. Among the Nuer, Evans-Pritchard could find no central government, central chiefs, or powerful individuals, and he noted that the contentious Nuer were frequently feuding over stolen cattle, their principal form of wealth.

Evans-Pritchard called this situation "ordered anarchy," alluding directly to Hobbes's notion of anarchy. The Nuer are quite independent, tending their herds of cattle in small lineages of several dozen men descended from a single ancestor. These lineages see themselves as having arisen when larger lineage groups broke into smaller groups or segments. Yet, whenever a smaller lineage group faces an external threat, such as aggression from a distantly related lineage, it works together with other closely related lineages to confront the threat. The political unity of the Nuer was thus flexible and non-centralized, allowing them to create larger groups according to need and dismantle those larger groups quickly. Evans-Pritchard described this political system as "segmentary lineages." In this classic quotation, he explains the logic of political organization.

E. E. Evans-Pritchard with Zande boys in Sudan.

A man is a member of a political group of any kind in virtue of his non-membership of other groups of the same kind. He sees them as groups and their members see him as a member of a group, and his relations with them are controlled by the structural distance between the groups concerned. But a man does not see himself as a member of that same group in so far as he is a member of a segment of it which stands outside of and is opposed to other segments of it. This is a fundamental principle of Nuer political structure. Thus a man is a member of his tribe in its relation to other tribes, but he is not a member of his tribe in relation to his segment of it to other segments of the same kind. Likewise a man is a member of his tribal segment in its relation to other segments, but he is not a member of it in the relation of his village to other villages of the same segment. A characteristic of any political group is hence its invariable tendency towards fission and the opposition of its segments, and another characteristic is its tendency toward fusion with other groups of its own order in opposition to political segments larger than itself. (Evans-Pritchard 1940:136–137)

Questions for Reflection

The Nuer live in a region that recently split from Sudan and created itself as the world's newest country, South Sudan (established in 2011). Beginning in 2013, the new country experienced internal strife, and the Nuer engaged in a bloody conflict with other prominent ethnic groups, such as the Dinka, over who should lead the country. By 2015, a peace agreement had been signed, although sporadic violence has continued.

1. Would you expect the lineage dynamics described by Evans-Pritchard to be playing out in the recent conflict? Why or why not?

2. What do you think the leadership structure was like on the Nuer side in this conflict?

What Is Political Power?

The shift from viewing politics as a problem of order to viewing it as a problem of how people gain and wield power began to flourish in the 1960s and continues to the present. "Power" in this sense is typically considered to be the ability to make people think or act in certain ways, through physical coercion or through more symbolic means, such as persuasion (Kingsolver 1996). Beyond this very general definition, however, there are many nuances to political power.

Defining Political Power

Whether it is an exchange of goods, a religious ceremony, or a conversation between a man and a woman, practically all aspects of human existence are imbued with power. But not all power is "*political.*" For anthropologists, **political power** refers to how power is created and enacted to attain goals that are presumed to be for the good of a community, the common good (Kurtz 2001:21).

The exercise of political power requires legitimacy. Legitimacy can come from an independent source—a source outside the individuals that make up a community—such as gods or ancestors, inheritance, some high office, the ability to cure an illness, or the outcome of some legal process, such as an election. Or it can come from a dependent source; that is, power given by other social actors: "granted" from one leader to another, "delegated" from a leader to a follower for a specific purpose, or "allocated" by the community to a leader, such as by election (Kurtz 2001:26).

In addition, political power is tied to control over material resources (territory, money, or other culturally defined goods); human resources (willing followers and supporters); and symbolic resources (flags, uniforms, badges of rank, or other objects that give meaning to political action) (Figure 9.4). There are other important dimensions to political power.

- **Political power.** The processes by which people create, compete, and use power to attain goals that are presumed to be for the good of a community.

Figure 9.4   The Symbolism of Trump's Baseball Hat. As candidate for President of the United States, Donald Trump wore baseball hats bearing his "Make America Great Again" campaign slogan. The message it conveyed was fittingly patriotic, but more important, its presence on a common baseball hat allowed the billionaire Trump to portray himself to his core white, working-class followers as a "man of the people" and thus an appropriate candidate to represent them.

Political Power Is Action-Oriented

People everywhere gain and manage political power through a combination of decision-making, cooperation, opportunism, compromise, collusion, charm, gamesmanship, strategic alliances, factionalism, resistance, conflict, and other processes. A focus on these processes was central to **action theory**, an approach that emerged in the 1960s. Action theorists closely followed the daily activities and decision-making processes of individual political leaders like chiefs in African villages or headmen in Amazonian settlements. They argue that politics is a dynamic and competitive field of social relations in which people are constantly managing their ability to exercise power over others (Vincent 1978). In other words, it is not enough to *be* President of the United States. One has to *act* as the president.

To follow political action, one must be familiar with a society's specific rules and codes about who gets to exercise power and under what conditions. Anthropologist F. G. Bailey (1969) compared these codes to those of playing a game. In politics, as in a game, there are *normative rules,* fairly stable and explicit ethical norms by which players must abide, such as honesty, fairness, and so on. There are also *pragmatic rules,* which are the creative manipulations necessary to win the game itself. For example, in American politics, normative rules require political actors to be open, fair, and honest. But we know based on reading the political news in the newspaper that there are also the pragmatic rules of gaining and holding onto power, which often involve favoritism and even outright lying (Lewellen 2003).

Political Power Is Structural

It became clear to political anthropologists by the 1980s and 1990s that certain power relationships transcend any individual. Political anthropologists began to refer to such power as **structural power**, which is power that not only operates within settings, but also organizes and orchestrates the settings in which social and individual action take place (Wolf 2001:384). "Structure" here means something very different from how the early structural-functionalists understood it. They were interested in social institutions ("structures," as a noun), while this newer perspective focuses on the mix of social processes, relationships, and institutions that shape or "structure" (as a verb) social action.

In this view, power does not lie in a group or individual's exercise of will over others through domination or manipulation, but is dispersed in many shapes and forms, produced and reproduced through the combined actions of important social institutions, science and other knowledge producers, and people living their everyday lives (Foucault 1978). Anthropologist David Horn (1994) used this approach to study how and why Italians of today, for example, accept state intervention in their lives. He traces their acceptance to the rise of social thought, planning, and research around the reproductive health of Italian families after World War I. During this period, the Italian government instituted a census and other programs to measure statistically the population's size, growth rate, and health conditions. Using this information, they instituted new policies of hygiene and family management, including a 1927 tax on bachelorhood and efforts to eliminate contraception and abortion. Although many of these policies failed, Horn observes that these changes had an important effect on Italians, in that they came to accept the idea that the body is not simply the domain of a private individual, but a social problem that requires scientific and state intervention. As a result, they began to willingly accept the idea that they should share intimate details about their reproductive lives with the state and that the state has the right to issue directives intended to manage citizens' lives—all of which are ideas that Italians take for granted today.

Another perspective on structural power emphasizes that under capitalism, relations involved in production have drawn people around the globe into a world system

---

- **Action theory.** An approach in the anthropological study of politics that closely follows the daily activities and decision-making processes of individual political leaders emphasizing that politics is a dynamic and competitive field of social relations in which people are constantly managing their ability to exercise power over others.

- **Structural power.** Power that not only operates within settings, but also organizes and orchestrates the settings in which social and individual actions take place.

(see Chapter 5). These capitalist relationships are the primary source of structural power in the world today, making possible the accumulation of capital based on the sale of labor. They are powerful because they constrain, inhibit, and promote what people can and cannot do in their economic and political lives (Wolf 2001:385). For example, a laborer on a banana plantation in Costa Rica has limited prospects for owning or accumulating wealth because all the arable land where he lives has been turned into plantations by foreign companies (Vandermeer and Perfecto 1995). When global demand for bananas drops, plantations lay off laborers, whose livelihood options are limited because they are landless and often undereducated. One of the few options available to them is to stake out a plot of land in the rainforest to grow crops, contributing to the problem of deforestation.

Political Power Is Gendered

During the past 30 years, feminist anthropologists have observed that while men tend to dominate formal political processes in most societies, relationships between men and women intersect with political power in complex ways. In a number of societies, women exercise formal leadership and political power. In other settings, women may have very little formal power, but they can mobilize to assert informal power in response to events.

In many societies, women may be so disempowered politically and socially that their ability to take direct action lies only in the most dramatic action of all, taking one's own life. For example, on the island of New Britain in Papua New Guinea, some women commit "revenge suicide" in response to abuse or shame (Figure 9.5). Here young women are powerless figures. But a woman's act of suicide shifts the burden of shame to her tormentor (often a husband), and it can even mobilize her male relatives

Figure 9.5   Revenge Suicide in New Guinea. This painting by contemporary Papua New Guinea artist Apa Hugo from 2003 illustrates how suicide can be used as a weapon of the weak. The caption written on the painting in Pidgin English means: "A man fights with his wife and the wife commits suicide. Her parents are distraught and cry in mourning" (*Man krosim meri na – meri i wari na I go sua sait. Na papa mama I wari na karai I stap*).

Figure 9.6   The Politics of Dress. In Iran, there is a rule that women must conceal their hair from the gaze of unrelated men by wearing a headscarf. Some women subvert the rule by draping a big scarf loosely over their heads and slinging the end over their shoulders, making the hair covering an ornament.

and other community members to acknowledge the injustice, forcing them to seek accountability from the offending party (Counts 1980). Although taking such actions may be difficult for many Westerners to comprehend, this situation suggests we must consider forms of political power that are available to those we do not conventionally understand to be "powerful."

This point holds true for an issue that has recently gained widespread public attention in Western Europe and North America: the restrictive rules imposed on Islamic women, such as rules that require women to wear headscarves, restrictions on women mixing with men in public settings, and prohibitions on women driving cars. In many Islamic communities, male clerics justify these rules with *shari'a,* or customary Islamic law.

Anthropologist Erika Friedl (1994) observed that Iranian women found ways to subvert these restrictive rules by using these very rules against repressive male religious leaders. Their acts of protest can be something as simple as wearing a headscarf in a modern stylish way (Figure 9.6). Some women subvert restrictions on attending social gatherings outside the home by making women's pilgrimages to the shrines of local saints. Because these are religious activities, male clerics cannot criticize the women. During these pilgrimages, women can gather to exchange gossip, news, and even political opinions free of the watchful eyes of men.

Political Power in Non-State Societies

To some extent, the exercise of political power differs between state and non-state societies. For example, in non-state societies such as tribal societies of South America and Melanesia, power tends to be temporary and episodic, emerging from personal charisma, not from elections or inheritance from a powerful parent. The Amazon headman, for example, is "a first among equals." He assumes his status as leader by being able to persuade followers, not because he controls power or resources on his own. Such leaders, who are sometimes called "Big Men," cannot transfer their status and power through inheritance when they die.

A Big Man cannot force others to do anything, but he gains influence and authority by giving away wealth and shrewdly persuading others, through a combination of smooth talk and peer pressure, to produce goods they will provide him that he can then redistribute. In their 1970 documentary film *The Feast*, filmmaker Timothy Asch and anthropologist Napoleon Chagnon (1997) show how a Yanomami headman in southern Venezuela sponsored a feast aimed at building an alliance with another community with which his own community had recently been at war. As headman he could not force anyone to help clear the plaza or cook the plantain soup that would be the centerpiece of the feast. His loud haranguing did little to motivate his fellow clan members, but when he led by example, his clansmen started helping and made it a successful feast, forming a new alliance. Persuasion was his most valuable tool.

In contrast to the status leadership of such a Big Man, the kind of political power your hometown mayor has is a quintessential expression of how political power works in a state society. Your mayor is an officeholder, a person who gets power from his or her elected or appointed office. In state societies and chiefdoms, power and authority reside in offices and institutions. Formal rules dictate who can gain an office and the conditions under which it can be gained. Office holders usually have greater access to resources, such as money from taxes and a bureaucracy that can exercise social control over a community. Like Big Men, however, mayors and other American officials often draw on their personal connections to achieve things, as we suggest in "Thinking Like an Anthropologist: The Power of Personal Connections."

The Political Power of the Contemporary Nation-State

Modern states are typically called **nation-states**, independent states recognized by other states and composed of people who share a single national identity. A nation is a population who thinks of itself as "a people" based on sharing—or imagining that they share—a common culture, language, heritage, identity, or commitment to particular political institutions (Robbins 2001:82). The political form of the nation-state originated in Europe several hundred years ago, but it has become so common that now all the world's territory has been claimed by one or another nation-state.

Contrary to Locke's idealizations of the "social contract," membership in a nation-state is not typically voluntary. For many of the world's peoples, conquest and colonialism forced them into nation-states. Leaders of nation-states exercise various forms of political power to assert social control over non-state societies and to ensure the conformity of all their citizens.

These forms of social control include promoting a sense of unity by drawing symbolic lines between those who are included—often it is some version of the "chosen people"—and those who are excluded. Excluded groups may be defined as "enemies" (citizens of competing nation-states, or non-state actors such as "terrorists") or as "inferior" because of racial or ethnic differences. Practically every society makes similar ethnocentric distinctions. But in nation-states, these distinctions often lead to the marginalization of minority groups within the country's boundaries as ethnic or racial "Others." This has been true for American Indians, Australian Aborigines, and indigenous societies in Latin America, among others.

Contemporary nation-states increasingly exercise power over their citizens by creating and managing information about them using institutionalized surveillance. Techniques of surveillance range from the mundane (national identity cards and censuses, for example) to the more secretive and sinister—such as monitoring social media, wiretapping, and hacking computers. Surveillance secures and expands leaders' power and authority, by identifying potential opposition or non-conformity threatening their authority. Many nation-states also use prisons, torture, and violence—even genocide—against citizens who do not conform to dominant values or identities (Figure 9.7). According to Amnesty International (2016), at least 122 of the world's 195 nation-states currently conduct torture on their citizens. And many nation-states kill their own citizens for political misdeeds, including criticism of the state and membership in banned political parties; deeds perceived as immoral; economic offenses (burglary, corruption); or for violent crimes (rape, assault, and murder) (Nagengast 1994:120).

People around the world have long understood the trade-offs of living within nation-states, and not surprisingly, many have resisted or evaded assimilation by states. Political scientist and anthropologist James Scott (2009) has described how, for 2,000 years, disparate groups of people have been living in upland Southeast Asia in basically stateless societies. The region, known to geographers as Zomia, is a rugged and remote mountainous region the size of Europe that consists of parts of seven contemporary nation-states, extending from India and Myanmar (Burma) in the west through China and into Vietnam, Laos, Cambodia, and Thailand in the east. The 100 million or so people who live in this highly ethnically and linguistically diverse region have historically avoided the control of lowland states by living in dispersed, autonomous communities. According to Scott, over time these groups came to the highlands fleeing slavery, conscription, taxes, epidemics, and warfare in the lowlands. They have been mobile, avoiding persecution by pushing deeper into the highlands and developing subsistence patterns of living, such as foraging and shifting

• **Nation-states.** Independent states recognized by other states, composed of people who share a single national identity.

Thinking Like an Anthropologist
The Power of Personal Connections

ANTHROPOLOGISTS BEGIN THEIR research by asking questions. In this box, we want you to learn how to ask questions as an anthropological researcher. Part One describes a situation and follows up with questions we would ask. Part Two asks you to formulate your own questions based on a different situation.

PART ONE: PERSONAL CONNECTIONS IN THE PERSIAN-SPEAKING WORLD

While working for the U.S. State Department in Iran during the 1970s, diplomat Whitney Azoy first encountered the concept of *waaseta*, which in Persian refers to "the power of personal connections." *Waaseta* is based on the cultivation of personal relationships by giving and receiving favors. Individuals at all levels of the government use it, from the local village level up all the way to the president's office. The more extensive one's network of personal connections, the greater one's ability to ask for, offer, and call in favors, all of which translate directly to political power. As a diplomat, Azoy found that cultivating *waaseta* helped him pursue the interests of the United States.

When he later became an anthropologist conducting research among Persian speakers in Afghanistan, Azoy once again encountered *waaseta*. He observed that among Afghans,

> Your family core group was a given; what really mattered were your personal connections beyond home and hearth. You were defined by it: enabled by knowing some people, limited by not knowing others. "Name" or reputation—the currency of old-time, hinterland politics

among both [traditional rulers] and small peasants was ultimately reckoned by whom you knew . . . and whom you could get to do favors for you. (Azoy 2002:A9)

Afghans assumed that Azoy, as an American and a former official in the State Department, had extraordinary personal connections, and they asked him for many favors even long after he left Afghanistan. For instance, after the United States invaded Afghanistan to overthrow the Taliban in 2001 and began developing reconstruction projects, Azoy received a phone call from an Afghan acquaintance with whom he had not spoken in over 20 years. After they caught up on each other's lives, the Afghan asked if Azoy could draw on his *waaseta* in the U.S. government to get money for a reconstruction project.

What questions does this situation raise for anthropological researchers?

1. If *waaseta* encompasses all political relationships in Afghanistan, do Afghans view *waaseta* as corruption, as many Americans are likely to do?
2. What limitations does *waaseta* place on developing a modern-style democracy?
3. Is a Western-style democracy, with its ideological commitment to transparency and avoidance of corruption, the only way to have a democracy?

PART TWO: PERSONAL CONNECTIONS IN U.S. POLITICS

Azoy notes that *waaseta*'s "you-rub-my-back-and-I'll-rub-yours" quality has all the trappings of what we call "corruption." He contrasts it with the rule of law, balance of powers, transparency, and accountability that people in the United States expect of their politicians. But when Azoy made this point to an Afghan acquaintance, the Afghan insisted that American politics is also suffused with *waaseta*. He pointed to the fact that election campaigns are based on the give-and-take of favors between large donors and politicians.

Personal connections are critical to the American government's operations, a fact that very few politicians and bureaucrats hide. In fact, a symbol of a successful, well-connected politician is a smartphone full of phone numbers of other powerful people inside and outside the government with whom he or she has personal connections. If you wanted to understand the role of personal connections in American politics, what questions would you ask as an anthropological researcher?

▼ **Afghan Elders Engaging in *Waaseta* with a British Politician.**

Figure 9.7   Trail of Tears. The 1830 Indian Removal Act in the United States forcibly moved Indians from Georgia to Indian Territory (now Oklahoma). This state-sponsored policy cleared Indians from lands desired by whites, leading to the deaths of thousands of Indians.

cultivation (see Chapter 6), that enable regular movement. Their identities are also flexible, rooted in the maintenance of oral traditions and the reinvention of kinship genealogies as groups move around from country to country. Scott suggests that this long history of autonomy may be coming to an end as contemporary nation-states have begun to assert greater control in these remote areas with the aid of what he calls "distance-demolishing" technologies, such as roads, bridges, airplanes, modern weapons systems, and global positioning systems (Scott 2009:11).

Although nation-states introduce new political dynamics—formalized political parties and bureaucratized elections, greater surveillance and control over groups, and so on—it is important to stress that the political mechanisms that we have explored in non-state societies can also operate in state settings. There is no absolute separation between state and non-state political organization. One illustration is that in a number of West African countries where witchcraft beliefs are common, including Cameroon, campaigning politicians will often seek out and associate with sorcerers. While the Cameroonian government officially rejects witchcraft, some prominent politicians openly accept and perpetuate the idea that they draw on occult powers to defeat their political rivals, because it enhances their power among villagers for whom sorcery remains an important means of social control and authority (Rowlands and Warnier 1988).

It is also common for political leaders to draw on the Big Man logic of material redistribution. For example, in the West African country of Benin, political candidates utilize favors from politicians already established in the government—much like *waaseta* in Iran—to build schools and medical clinics in the communities where they seek election. They also hold political rallies in which they ceremonially offer food, drink, and often money to the local community, again to elicit votes. Local people then pick a leader from different candidates based on which candidate seems likely to offer the most largesse in the future. While the Beninese state enjoys an international reputation for a stable and thriving multi-party democracy, this reputation is due more to calculated public relations than to the realities on the ground (Hedges 2017).

Leaders of nation-states also often co-opt local political actors and their power to serve their own or their nation-state's ends. In post-independence Ghana, for example, where chiefs, headmen, and extended family lineages control village-level resources and political processes, centralized governments have co-opted traditional non-state

Anthropologist as Problem Solver
Maxwell Owusu and Democracy in Ghana

SINCE ITS INDEPENDENCE from Britain in 1957, the West African country of Ghana has alternated between civilian- and military-controlled national governments. When the most recent military government (1981–1992) allowed elections in 1992, the Fourth Republic of Ghana emerged, based on a new constitution with a foundation in democratic principles.

An influential actor in that process was Ghanaian-born political anthropologist Maxwell Owusu of the University of Michigan. Owusu served as a consulting member of the Constitutional Experts Committee, which drafted the 1992 constitution proposals. Owusu has been a staunch critic of autocratic and repressive leadership in post-independence Ghana and other African nation-states. He is an advocate of popular participatory democracy. But as an anthropologist, he understood the problems of imposing foreign political models—such as Western-style democracy with competing political parties—on African societies with different histories and indigenous political traditions. As he has written (Owusu 1992:384), "African democracy may require the integration of indigenous methods of village co-operation with innovative forms of government, combining the power of universal rights with the uniqueness of each district's or nation's own customs and respected traditions."

A viable solution, Owusu insisted, is to create a decentralized state in which local authorities, primarily chiefs, headmen, and lineage heads, participate directly in state processes and decision-making. The advantage is that local leaders can better identify the needs and priorities of villagers, and be more accountable to their communities, than can bureaucrats in a state apparatus. The 1992 constitution of Ghana put this insight to work, creating "District Assemblies" as the basic unit of national government, two-thirds of which are elected and one-third appointed, the latter being mostly traditional leaders or their representatives (Owusu 1992). Owusu observed that, far from making chiefs and other non-state political leaders obsolete, these changes have put traditional leaders at the forefront of political change in the nation-state as a whole (Owusu 1996).

🌱 **Maxwell Owusu.**

Questions for Reflection

1. How does Owusu's notion of participatory democracy, which relies upon decentralization of power toward local traditional leaders, differ from the way local governments at the city, town, or county level work in the United States?

2. Is it likely to be true that local traditional leaders are better able to identify local priorities than national leaders?

leaders by rewarding some with high-level positions in the state bureaucracy. Such an appointment to a governmental position makes the leader responsible at the local level for enforcing national laws and mobilizing support for state-led development programs (Owusu 1996). For several decades, anthropologist Maxwell Owusu has researched how this kind of political power works in post-independence Ghana. He has advocated formally incorporating non-state political leaders into nation-state functions. In "Anthropologist as Problem Solver: Maxwell Owusu and Democracy in Ghana," we examine how his ideas have been put to work.

Except for a brief reference to violence and genocide earlier in the chapter, we have so far discussed the exercise of political power in terms of the cultivation of relationships, persuasion, the collection of information, and the strategic manipulation of others. But violence is also a strategic means of gaining and holding onto political power, and in some societies it seems more common and accepted than in others. In the next section, we explore this issue in more detail.

• •

THINKING CRITICALLY ABOUT POLITICS

As this section shows, different anthropologists have approached political power in different ways. Do you think each of these approaches creates a fundamentally different picture of how political power works? Why or why not?

• •

Why Do Some Societies Seem More Violent Than Others?

By the 1960s, a number of the societies anthropologists studied were experiencing intense post-independence violence, disruption, and conflict related to the end of European colonialism. This situation prompted an urgent concern to understand the relationship between political power and violence, and why political conflicts in some societies seemed to break out in violence more than conflicts did in other societies. What might be done to end and prevent future violence?

In pursuing answers to these questions, anthropologists have learned that violence is a form of power relations rooted in cultural processes and meanings, just as other strategies of political power, such as persuasion and manipulation, are.

What Is Violence?

Violence is typically defined as the use of force to harm someone or something. It is a highly visible and concrete assertion of power, and a very efficient way to transform a social environment and communicate an ideological message (Riches 1986). Violence is also a powerful means of suppressing political dissent and change, and it plays an important role in creating and sustaining social hierarchies and political inequalities.

Yet specifying what violence consists of is not always so straightforward, because violence is different things to different people (Eller 2006). The same person might acknowledge that shoving a person into a vat of boiling water is violent, yet not view placing a lobster, much less a handful of spinach, in that boiling water as violent. Another factor in assessing what is violent is intention. Did the perpetrator mean to do it (violent), or was it an accident (probably not violent)? And rationality: did the perpetrator have control over his or her actions (violent), or was it a case of "losing one's mind" (probably not violent, or at least justified)? And legitimacy: was the act legitimate, such as a boxer beating on another boxer (sports, not violence), or deviant, such as a man beating his wife (violent)? Even the nature of force: was the force personal, as in one person punching another (violent), or structural, as in economic conditions depriving a child of food (open to debate)? And whether you were a victim, perpetrator, or witness, you are likely to have a different perspective on whether or not an act is violent.

• **Violence.** The use of force to harm someone or something.

Even though we might all agree that violence involves some element of harm and an assertion of power over others, people nevertheless have differing opinions on what constitutes violence. Some of these opinions are individually held, but some are related to differences in how we as members of a particular culture define violence and give meaning to it. Culture shapes not only how people think about violence but also how, why, and when they use it as a form of power over others.

Violence and Culture

Since Hobbes, Europeans and Americans have seen violence as a natural condition of humans. But anthropologists offer two major challenges to this view: (1) Neither violence nor its opposite, nonviolence, is an inevitable condition of humanity; both are learned behaviors that express themselves in particular social and historic circumstances; and (2) violence is generally not chaotic and arbitrary, but tends to follow explicit cultural patterns, rules, and ethical codes.

Neither Violence Nor Nonviolence Is Inevitable in Human Societies

In recent years, it has become fashionable to think of aggression and violence as genetically determined. But no animal or human carries genes for dominance, aggression, or passivity. These complex social and psychological conditions and states involve biological processes, such as the production of certain hormones, but they are not fixed properties or traits carried by genes.

So how should we deal with claims—some even made by anthropologists—that some societies are fierce and warlike and others peaceful? The answer, of course, is by demonstrating that neither violence nor nonviolence is universal (Fry 2006). Two famous examples—the Yanomami and the Semai—illustrate our point.

The Yanomami and the Semai

Anthropologist Napoleon Chagnon (1968) described the Yanomami Indians of southern Venezuela whom he has worked with since the early 1960s as the "fierce people." According to Chagnon, the Yanomami have an aggressive style about nearly everything they do. They stage brutal raids against enemy settlements, and they routinely have violent responses to their fellow clansmen (Figure 9.8).

But other anthropologists, including Brian Ferguson (1995) and Jacques Lizot (1985), have seen the Yanomami in a different light, as warm and caring people who from time to time had to defend themselves against enemies. Filmmaker Timothy Asch, who had worked with Chagnon in the field, also produced several films that show a peaceable side of Yanomami life, including images of a father bathing his children and a husband and wife working on projects together (Asch and Chagnon 1968, 1990a, 1990b). Ferguson's research suggests that Yanomami fierceness was not the traditional behavior of these Amazonian Indians, but the result of contact with foreigners: missionaries, prospectors, government officials, and anthropologists such as Chagnon, who has come under fire by Yanomami themselves for disrupting their society (Tierney 2002; see also the "Thinking Like an Anthropologist" box in Chapter 1, on pp. 26–7, in which we discuss controversies surrounding Chagnon's work).

A similar point can be made about a very different case, that of the Semai, egalitarian swidden farmers who live in the Malaysian rainforest. Anthropologist Robert Dentan (1968) characterized the Semai as peaceful and nonviolent because they committed little or no interpersonal violence during his field research.

Figure 9.8   The "Fierce People." In the ethnographic film *The Ax Fight*, from which this image is drawn, the filmmakers represent Yanomami lives as filled with aggression and near-constant violence. But is it really so?

The Semai view themselves as peaceful and reject the idea that violence is a natural condition of human life. At the heart of Semai commitment to nonviolence is their valued concept of *persusah,* referring to the value of not causing trouble for others. Causing *punan,* a condition that makes someone unhappy or frustrated, is unacceptable to Semai. Semai strive to avoid causing *punan,* and emphasize *persusah.* Acts of power or inequality, such as being stingy, refusing a request, or forcing somebody to obey an order, are especially prone to cause *punan.* Arguments do break out from time to time, but people have found other ways of diffusing tensions besides fighting. Anthropologist Clayton Robarchek (1979), who lived with the Semai in the 1970s, argued that almost all aspects of Semai social life emphasize nonviolence, and that Semai children are emotionally conditioned to be nonviolent and peaceful.

But the Semai are not completely nonviolent either. During the Communist insurrection in Malaysia from 1948 to 1960, some Semai became soldiers, and a few were renowned fighters. Anthropologist John Leary (1995) worked with these Semai soldiers during the insurrection and argued that the nonviolent interpretations of Dentan and Robarchek fundamentally misrepresent these men, who were good soldiers. Although Dentan had consistently described the ethos of the Semai as nonviolent and peaceful, he did quote one former soldier who described himself and his comrades in the counterinsurgency as "drunk with blood" (1968:58–59). Robarchek and Dentan (1987) argue that the Semai are indeed socialized to be nonviolent, but when they were brought into the counterinsurgency, they were socialized as soldiers and trained to kill.

The point of these examples is that violence and nonviolence are not absolute or static conditions. They are the result of cultural attitudes and particular social and historical conditions (Fry 2006).

Explaining the Rise of Violence in Our Contemporary World

Anthropologists have long observed that violence and the threat of violence, far from implying chaos, can actually encourage social order. Contrary to stereotypes of violence as chaotic and antisocial, violent acts are ordered because they reflect culturally specific patterns, rules, and ethical codes. These patterns define when and why violence is acceptable, what forms of violence are appropriate, and who can engage in violent acts.

In news reports, pundits routinely explain the rise of violence around the globe as a chaotic outburst of meaningless "tribal" and "ethnic" tensions (Whitehead 2004). Such accounts appear to offer a tidy narrative that seems to explain so much of what is going on in our contemporary world. But they are based on a fundamental misunderstanding of the relationship between violence and culture. Anthropologists have demonstrated that (1) it is not inevitable that people from different ethnic groups will fight, and (2) violence and terror are never meaningless, but highly meaningful and even calculated political strategies.

It Is Not Inevitable That Different Ethnic Groups Will Fight

The countries that made up the former Yugoslavia in Southeast Europe, in a region known as the Balkans, share the stereotype of ethnic and religious tribalism. We even have a word for it—*balkanization*—which refers to the fragmentation of society into hostile factions. During the Bosnian civil war in the 1990s, foreign journalists tended to describe acts of violence by Serbs, Croats, and Muslims as "ethnic violence" based on centuries-old hatreds between these ethnic groups.

Figure 9.9   A Peaceful Balkans. At the time of the 1984 Olympic Games in the Bosnian capital city of Sarajevo, commentators celebrated longstanding peaceful relations between Serbs, Croats, and Muslims in this modern city, challenging any notion of "ancient seething hatreds" portrayed in later years.

But this explanation ignores long histories of coexistence, cultural interchange, and peaceful relations that anthropologists had observed in the region (Lockwood 1975; Bringa 2005) (Figure 9.9). A more complex understanding of the conflict sees violence as a byproduct of a struggle over political power among nationalist leaders after the fall of communist Yugoslavia. Seeking to consolidate their hold over political power and state institutions, nationalists on all sides used the media to broadcast daily doses of fear, hatred, and dehumanizing images of people from the other "ethnic" groups (Bringa 2005). They used targeted violence on people of other ethnic backgrounds. All of these factors created fear and a sense of powerlessness among ordinary people. So when nationalist leaders eventually called on people to attack their neighbors of different backgrounds, some did just that, leading to now well-known incidents of incredible brutality and horror in places such as Srebrenica, the site of a mass killing of Bosnian Muslims by Bosnian Serbs (Oberschall 2000).

At the same time, many people found ways to protect their neighbors of different ethnic backgrounds from being attacked. In other words, even in a period of intense, artificially created ethnic conflict, not everybody participated in the violence, and many did not give in to the ethnic hatred that others promoted. Both points undermine any simplistic story of seething tribalism. Ethnic conflict is not an inevitable condition, and in this case it was manufactured to serve the political and ideological interests of certain leaders.

Violence Is a Meaningful Political Strategy

In the United States, we sometimes hear in the media about events like suicide bombings in Israeli and Iraqi markets and cafés; machete attacks on innocent people in Liberia, Rwanda, and Sierra Leone in Africa; or plane hijackings by some militant group, which of course happened in this country on September 11, 2001. Commentators often call these shocking acts "meaningless" and "barbaric." But such acts are never meaningless. They are meaningful—to both victims and perpetrators—although the different sides interpret the violence very differently (Whitehead 2004). For example, families of suicide bombing victims and families of the suicide bombers themselves comprehend these acts differently. For one side the message is threat and hostility, and for the other it is a message of martyrdom and devotion to a cause.

When people refer to such acts as meaningless and barbaric, they interpret violence as emotional, beyond reason. In fact, violence and the threat of violence are often used as strategic tools for pursuing particular political ends. Consider, for example, the civil war in Sierra Leone (1991–2002), in which at least 50,000 people died. This conflict, waged between the government and a "people's army" called the Revolutionary United Front (RUF), gained widespread notoriety as a barbaric and brutal conflict. According to British anthropologist Paul Richards (1996), the violence was anything but wanton and mindless. He explained that the employment of machete attacks, rape, hand cutting, throat slitting, and other acts of terror by both sides in the conflict were "rational ways of achieving intended strategic outcomes" (Richards 1996:58). For example, during 1995, the RUF frequently cut off the hands of village women. This practice was strategically calculated to communicate a political message to the RUF's own soldiers and to prevent defections. How could this be so? Richards explains that the RUF expanded by capturing young men and turning them into soldiers. Many defected, returning to their villages at harvest time to help their families. RUF leaders reasoned that they could stop defections by stopping the harvest. To stop the harvest, they ordered the hand amputation of women who participated in harvesting grain. As news spread, the harvests stopped, and defections ended because soldiers did not want the same thing to happen to their own mothers and sisters. Richards does not justify these repulsive acts. Rather, his point is that violence is not "meaningless," but highly organized in a systematic if brutal fashion.

Not every conflict leads inevitably to violence. We explore this theme in more detail in our final section.

· ·

THINKING CRITICALLY ABOUT POLITICS

Since the early years of structural-functionalism, anthropologists have recognized that violence or the threat of violence, far from implying chaos, can encourage social integration and social order. How? Why?

· ·

How Do People Avoid Aggression, Brutality, and War?

Whenever we watch the news, unsettling images of aggression, brutality, and war flood our consciousness. Yet millions of people around the world rarely if ever have direct experiences of such things in their daily lives. This does not mean that disputes and conflicts do not arise, because they do everywhere, all the time.

But, as we discussed previously, violence is not an inevitable human response to conflict. People always have creative and peaceful ways to manage or settle their disputes. In every society there are people with the ability to intervene in, negotiate, or settle a dispute, actions that are as much an exercise in political power as the ability to wage war (Rasmussen 1991). Working out the problems that arise from those conflicting accounts inevitably touches on who has access to power and what allows them to hold it.

What Disputes Are "About"

Some disputes are explicitly about who can hold political power. But most disputes are also about other matters that are central to the political life of any community (Caplan 1995). Disputes are about material goods, such as who has the right to land and other forms of property. Disputes are about decision-making, such as who gets to decide important matters. Disputes are about social relations, or who gets to do what to whom. Disputes are about the rules, because disputes tend to arise whenever rules are broken, or when the rules themselves are unclear. And disputes are about dividing people or joining them together in new ways, because when arguments happen, people take sides.

Most North Americans assume that disputes are about winning and losing. We approach a lawsuit pretty much the same way we approach a sporting event, the point being to vanquish the other side. But for many peoples around the world, disputes are not "about" winning and losing. Neither are sporting events. In both cases, the object of a lawsuit or game is to repair a strained relationship.

When Trobriand Islanders play the game of cricket, for example, the goal of the game is to end with a tie, not to win or lose (Kildea and Leach 1975). Sure, the players play hard and even get hurt in the process, but the game is really "about" reaffirming the social relationships that exist among the players and with their communities. Both sides will later claim to have played better and more bravely, but they will have lessened tensions between the two villages. When we look at how people manage disputes around the world, keep in mind that when presented with a dispute, most people prefer to restore harmony by settling the matter to the satisfaction of all parties.

How People Manage Disputes

Legal anthropology, the branch of political anthropology interested in such matters, has identified a number of ways people manage disputes (Nader and Todd 1978). Some strategies are informal, including avoidance, competition, ritual, and play. Others are formal, involving specialized institutions or specialists. The most common of these strategies include adjudication (going to court), negotiation (talking through problems), and mediation (a third party helps resolve the problem).

One of the easiest and most informal ways people handle their disputes is to avoid the matter altogether, which allows tensions to subside. In small-scale communities, people have to get along, and avoiding certain subjects is often the best way of keeping the peace. Even in our society, there are contexts—such as the workplace, dormitories, and families—where some issues are better left untouched, because of the discord they can cause. But people often turn to other informal strategies to handle tensions, such as telling jokes, laughter, gossip, song, duels, sporting contests and other forms of competitive play, ridicule, public humiliation, and even witchcraft accusations (Gulliver 1979; Watson-Gegeo and White 1990; Caplan 1995) (Figure 9.10).

When informal strategies do not work, people usually have more formal means of settling disputes. **Adjudication**, which is the legal process by which an individual or council with socially recognized authority intervenes in a dispute and unilaterally makes a decision, is one possibility. The image of a courtroom with a judge in a robe, a jury, and lawyers comes to mind.

Anthropologist James Gibbs (1963), who conducted fieldwork among the Kpelle [keh-**pay**-lay], rice cultivators of central Liberia, found a different approach to adjudication. Gibbs reported that while Kpelle could take their disputes to government

● **Adjudication.** The legal process by which an individual or council with socially recognized authority intervenes in a dispute and unilaterally makes a decision.

Figure 9.10   Rap Battles and Social Tension. In urban hip-hop culture, "rap battles" involve two individuals engaging in competitive rapping in front of an audience. The individual with greater lyrical prowess—the ability to rhyme, to creatively "diss" (criticize) the opponent, and so on—is the winner. Rap battles are often born from social tensions between individuals or social factions, but they can also provide a creative means to reduce tensions as problems and status differences are publicly aired.

courts, they avoided doing so because they viewed those courts as arbitrary and coercive (Gibbs 1963). Kpelle often turned to their own "moot courts," which are hearings presided over by respected kin, elders, and neighbors. Unlike the government courts, which were slow-moving, allowed only limited testimony, and imposed settlements with harsh penalties for the loser, Kpelle moot courts provided a thorough airing of grievances and a quick treatment of the problem before attitudes hardened. Instead of winner-take-all, their goal was to restore harmony. They often found fault with both parties, avoided harsh penalties when there was a clear loser, and negotiated consensual solutions acceptable to all. Moot courts did not have the same enforcement authority as government courts, but because of their emphasis on reconciliation, they were especially effective for resolving domestic problems, such as quarrels over inheritance or alleged mistreatment of a spouse, where relationships had to continue after the dispute passed.

In a **negotiation**, the parties themselves reach a decision jointly. As with all other strategies for settling disputes, negotiations never take place in isolation. Broader social relationships and circumstances influence the outcome. For example, British legal anthropologist Philip Gulliver (1979)—whose research on negotiation in Tanzania has been influential for explaining the cultural importance of negotiation—observed that in a dispute between two close neighbors over land and water rights that took place in a small district in northern Tanzania in 1957, many factors influenced the ability and willingness of each side to negotiate a settlement. For example, one disputant was more popular and better connected in the community, and he thus had more allies to push his own agenda. But he was willing to negotiate because, like his rival, he was equally worried that the colonial court could intervene and impose a decision. He also worried that if the dispute was not settled, the other side might use witchcraft and further intensify the dispute.

Mediation entails a third party who intervenes in a dispute to aid the parties in reaching an agreement. Native Hawaiians commonly practice a kind of mediation called *ho'oponopono* [**hoh**-oh-poh-no-poh-no], or "setting to right" (Boggs and Chun 1990). This practice is intended to resolve interpersonal and family problems or to prevent them from worsening. It is based on the belief that disputes involve negative entanglements, and that setting things right spiritually will lead directly to physical and interpersonal healing (Boggs and Chun 1990). *Ho'oponopono* usually begins when a leader of high status—a family elder, a leader of a community church, or a professional family therapist—intervenes in a dispute, calling the adversaries and all immediate family members to engage in the process. Group participation is especially important because negative entanglements spread beyond those directly involved in the dispute. After opening with prayers, the leader instructs participants in the process and guides a discussion in which all participants are expected to air their grievances and feelings openly and honestly. They direct them to the leader, not to one another, to avoid possible confrontation. At the end, the leader asks all sides to offer forgiveness and release themselves and each other from the negative entanglements.

- **Negotiation.** A form of dispute management in which the parties themselves reach a decision jointly.

- **Mediation.** The use of a third party who intervenes in a dispute to help the parties reach an agreement and restore harmony.

Is Restoring Harmony Always the Best Way?

It is easy to romanticize dispute settlement traditions whose goal is to restore harmony. Legal anthropologist Laura Nader (1990) observed that harmony and reconciliation are cultural ideologies, and like other ideologies they uphold a particular social order and way of doing things, usually protecting the already powerful.

Nader observed that Zapotec Indians in the southern Mexican village of Talea [tah-**lay**-ah] she studied have a "harmony ideology." Taleans believe "a bad compromise is better than a good fight." They emphasize that people need to work hard to maintain balance and evenhandedness in their relationships with others. They go to local courts frequently, even for very minor disputes, to avoid escalation.

But peace and reconciliation have their price. Nader has seen how these ideologies can prevent a full airing of problems, delay justice, or be used as a form of social control. Harmony ideology sustains a particular power structure, serving the interests of some but not necessarily all.

Since the 1970s, restoring harmony has been a popular strategy in Western countries for conflict-resolution studies and practice. Mediation and negotiated settlements deal with disputes from family and work-related problems to complex international clashes, including civil wars and wars between countries (Davidheiser 2007). These techniques are often called "alternative dispute management."

While some anthropologists welcome the rise of alternative dispute management (Avruch 1998), Nader (1995, 2001) questions its implicit harmony ideology. She observes that many people involved in civil wars and other large-scale conflicts do not necessarily want harmony. They want justice, fairness, and the rule of law. This is a sentiment expressed by many Mozambicans, for example, whose civil war ended in a mediated settlement in 1992. Many Mozambicans believe the settlement, which brought with it the introduction of foreign aid institutions and International Monetary Fund stabilization policies, actually deepened their woes by generating more poverty and inequality than before the war (Hanlon 1996).

Sometimes confrontation and conflict, not harmony, may be a more appropriate way to bring change for the greater good. For example, in the 1970s, Nader (1979) conducted research in collaboration with her brother, the consumer advocate Ralph Nader, on how consumers in industrialized societies deal with faulty products and unscrupulous sellers. What do people do when their washing machine breaks and the manufacturer or retail store they bought it from gives them the run-around? Nader found consumers dissatisfied, even despondent, over fruitless struggles for justice and accountability from corporate giants. Initially Nader recommended that consumer advocates and corporations arrange mediation and negotiated settlements, aiming for a harmonious end to conflicts. Many corporations did just that. But consumer satisfaction is now lower than it was in the 1970s, because these processes have not forced real change in the way corporations make their products. Revising her recommendation, Nader (2007) now believes that conflict, confrontation, a more adversarial relationship in court, and aggressively pushing for stronger laws would have been more effective in bringing beneficial change for consumers.

There is not necessarily a "best way" to solve a dispute. If there were, there would be no more disputes! In addition, dispute settlement is never a neutral act. In handling their disputes, people make ideological assumptions and enact social relationships that uphold—or, as Laura Nader suggests, even challenge—particular power structures.

THINKING CRITICALLY ABOUT POLITICS

Think about the last time you had a nonviolent dispute in your life. How did you handle it? Was one or more of the strategies we discussed—avoidance, adjudication, negotiation, or mediation—involved? How might the outcome have been different if you had pursued a different strategy than the one you did?

Conclusion

If you pay much attention to political news on television or the Internet, you may have the impression that politics is mainly about politicians and their political parties, laws, and bureaucratic institutions. This impression offers only part of the story. Politics always involves some element of state power and bureaucratic processes. Every society has individuals who act a lot like North American politicians. From status leaders such as Big Men and councils of elders who settle disputes, to leaders of armed movements organizing violent acts, leaders everywhere use strategy, manipulation, persuasion, control over resources, and sometimes violence to obtain and maintain power over others.

Yet this view of politics is too narrow to appreciate the diverse forms that political power takes around the world. Not all societies train their young to deal with their problems through violence, and even those that accept violence place limits on its use, encouraging more peaceful ways of handling disputes. People not considered conventionally powerful have ways of challenging the power structure in their societies. And while the nation-state is a common political form worldwide, some post-colonial countries, such as Ghana, have explored ways of integrating traditional political structures based on family lineages and chiefly power into the ways the nation-state functions.

Politics is about relationships of cooperation, conflict, social control, and power that exist in any community and at all levels of social life, from the interpersonal and community levels to the national and transnational. The reason that people around the world have so many ways of managing and thinking about those relationships is the same reason cultural diversity persists in the world today: social processes like those involved in politics are always rooted in and emerge from people's everyday social interactions, belief systems, and cultural practices.

KEY TERMS

Acephalous society p. 221
Action theory p. 228
Adjudication p. 240
Age-grades p. 223
Band p. 223
Centralized political system p. 224
Chiefdom p. 223
Government p. 221
Laws p. 222
Mediation p. 241
Nation-states p. 231
Negotiation p. 241
Non-centralized political system p. 224
Political power p. 227
Politics p. 220
State p. 223
Structural power p. 228
Structural-functionalism p. 223
Tribe p. 223
Violence p. 235

Reviewing the Chapter

Chapter Section	What We Know	To Be Resolved
Does Every Society Have a Government?	Not every society has a government as we know it, or even makes a distinction between those who govern and those who are governed. Some societies organize their political lives on the basis of principles such as egalitarian social relations, reciprocity, and kinship.	Although classical anthropological studies identified many political processes in non-state societies, anthropologists continue to study and debate how successful these processes have been in confronting the transnational forces that affect almost every society today.
What Is Political Power?	Political power operates in multidimensional ways: it is action-oriented, it is structural, and it is gendered. It also tends to operate in particular ways in non-state contexts as well as in modern nation-states.	Anthropologists debate the relative importance of political power wielded by individuals and structural power in shaping fields of social action.
Why Do Some Societies Seem More Violent Than Others?	Neither violence nor nonviolence is an inevitable condition. Both are learned behaviors expressed in particular social and historic circumstances.	Most peoples who have been characterized either as peaceful or as violent are not uniformly peaceful or violent, yet it is not always clear what conditions might have transformed an otherwise peaceful people into a violent one or vice versa.
How Do People Avoid Aggression, Brutality, and War?	Disputes arise in all societies, but they do not necessarily result in aggression, brutality, and war because people everywhere have many peaceful strategies for settling disputes.	Anthropologists continue to debate the effectiveness of the new field of alternative dispute management, especially in cross-cultural and international settings.

Readings

Early twentieth-century anthropologists tended to understand politics in tribal societies as fundamentally an expression of their kinship systems. A classic example is E. E. Evans-Pritchard's 1940 ethnography, *The Nuer: A Description of the Modes of Livelihood and Political Institutions of a Nilotic People* (Oxford, UK: Clarendon Press, 1967). For a comprehensive overview of the field of political anthropology that is as attentive to classic concerns as it is to new research directions, see John Gledhill's book *Power and Its*

Disguises: Anthropological Perspectives on Politics (second edition, Sterling, VA: Pluto Press, 2000).

....

Two books offer a useful overview of how to think anthropologically about violence: David Riches's edited book *The Anthropology of Violence* (Oxford, UK: Basil Blackwell, 1986), which contains a number of classic articles, and Douglas P. Fry's book *The Human Potential for Peace: An Anthropological Challenge to Assumptions*

About War and Violence (New York: Oxford University Press, 2006).

....

Understanding Disputes: The Politics of Argument (Oxford, UK: Berg Publishers, 1995), edited by Pat Caplan, offers a useful introduction to the field of legal anthropology and includes essays by some of the leading figures in the field.

....

James C. Scott has written extensively on the relationships between states and marginalized peoples within states as well those who live beyond state power. His 2009 book *The Art of Not Being Governed: An Anarchist History of Upland Southeast Asia* (New Haven, CT: Yale University Press) provides a cultural and political analysis of the Zomia region of Southeast Asia.

Laura Nader's book *Harmony Ideology: Justice and Control in a Zapotec Mountain Village* (Stanford, CA: Stanford University Press, 1990) offers a detailed ethnographic description of how one community manages disputes to maintain social harmony, but not always to everyone's liking. It pairs well with the film *Little Injustices: Laura Nader Looks at the Law* (Washington, DC: PBS Video, 1981). Though it is now dated, this film offers highly relevant comparative insights into how two societies—Zapotec and American—handle everyday disputes.

Race, Ethnicity, and Class

10

Understanding Identity and Social Inequality

DURING THE LATE NINETEENTH CENTURY, Irish Americans became "white." Before then, other Americans considered them a separate racial group that was not white. Even with their light-colored skin, they were believed to be inferior to immigrants from other Northern European nations (especially England, Germany, France, and the Scandinavian countries) in almost all other respects. The story of their transformation illustrates the fluidity with which racial identities, including whiteness, are culturally constructed.

During the eighteenth century, most Irish were Catholic and spoke Gaelic, a Celtic language. The English, who had conquered and colonized Ireland in the sixteenth century, regarded Irish Catholics as beneath them—a separate and inferior race of people, race being a concept that organizes people into unequal groups based on specific physical traits that are thought to reflect fundamental and innate differences. The English institutionalized this concept of racial inferiority by creating discriminatory laws known as the Penal Codes that denied Irish Catholics the right to vote, to live in incorporated towns, to attend university, and to buy, inherit, or receive gifts of land from Protestants (Ignatiev 1995). This discrimination was based on more than just religious, linguistic, or national differences. It was based on

Irish Lives in New York City. When the Irish first arrived in the United States, many of them moved into tenement buildings, often living side by side with freed slaves. Anglo Americans considered the Irish an inferior race and deserving of their poverty.

247

a racial worldview that emphasized Irish inferiority as part of the "natural order of things."

In the 1840s and 1850s, the Irish Potato Famine forced large numbers of poor Irish to emigrate to the United States, where the Anglo descendants of English settlers also regarded them as an inferior and separate race. They saw Irish and African Americans, or blacks, as closely related, deriding the Irish as "Negroes turned inside out," and African Americans as "smoked Irish" (Ignatiev 1995). In the early years of mass emigration, Irish often lived side by side with freed slaves in segregated neighborhoods in Northeastern cities like New York and Boston. They worked the same low-prestige jobs and even intermarried.

Within a decade, however, the Irish began distancing themselves from blacks and increasingly identifying with whites. Irish workers began monopolizing certain trades and pushing blacks out, sometimes violently. Seeing an opportunity to build its power base in northern cities, the Democratic Party courted Irish voters. Although some Irish leaders rejected the Democratic Party because it supported slavery, a condition they compared to Irish life under English rule, many welcomed the political recognition. In neighborhoods with no black voters, campaigners referred to "the white vote," symbolically redefining the Irish as white. Irish also joined labor organizations, many of which refused to grant black people membership. By the end of the century, although many Irish Americans were still poor and considered lower class than their Anglo counterparts, they had achieved a level of social acceptance as white that would have been unimaginable several decades earlier.

The Irish are not alone in "becoming white" in North America. Jews, Italians, Finns, Greeks, Armenians, and certain Latin Americans—all of whom at one point were considered inferior non-white racial groups—have become white as well. In the process, they have also gone from lower-class status to gaining identification as "middle class."

Most Americans have a worldview that assumes that racial identities are the result of unchanging biological differences. Yet no amount of research into the biological features of these groups will explain how and why those transformations in race and class took place. These changes emerged as a result of the dynamic ways racial and class identities are constructed, symbolized, and institutionalized in the socially stratified society that is the United States. These are cultural, social, and political processes that often serve to create social differences and reinforce social inequalities, and although they have biological dimensions, they are not driven by biology.

At the heart of an understanding of the relationship between identity and inequality is the question around which this chapter is organized: *If differences of identity are not rooted in biology, why do they feel so real, powerful, and unchangeable?* Embedded in this broader question are the following problems, around which this chapter is organized.

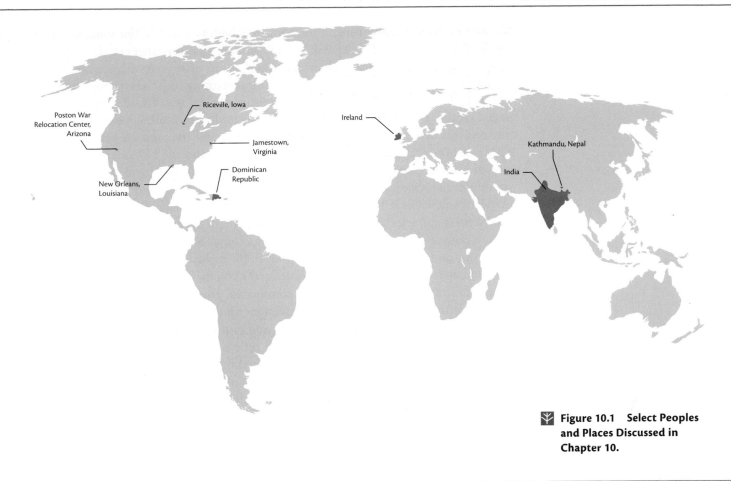

Figure 10.1   Select Peoples and Places Discussed in Chapter 10.

Is race biological?

How is race culturally constructed?

How are other social classifications naturalized?

Are prejudice and discrimination inevitable?

The order represented in the social hierarchy of any society is supported and justified by social institutions, political processes, and powerful symbolism. The categories may feel "natural" or inevitable, even morally necessary, but like all other cultural phenomena, they are constructed and dynamic. In order to show this, we have to begin by dispelling one of the most powerful ideas many Americans hold, that differences of **race** reflect biological differences between groups of people.

• **Race.** A concept that organizes people into unequal groups based on specific physical traits that are thought to reflect fundamental and innate differences.

Is Race Biological?

In 2005, the U.S. Food and Drug Administration (FDA) approved a new drug called BiDil for treatment of congestive heart failure among African Americans. It is the first drug ever intended and approved for a particular racial group, and studies have shown that it has positive benefits for African American patients. For some scientists, medical researchers, and policymakers, this situation confirms that racial groups have specific biological and genetic characteristics that can be treated with specific drugs.

But these claims do not hold up under critical scrutiny, and there is nothing about this situation that proves that African Americans are biologically different from other racial groups. How can this be? The answer lies in the political, economic, and social reasons this drug was developed in the first place, and the processes of its approval (Inda 2014). In recent years, the medical profession and the FDA have been under pressure from Congress and the public to reduce disparities in medical treatment among racial groups. Across the United States, racialized minorities—including African Americans, Latinos, and Native Americans—are more likely than whites to face serious obstacles to treatment, poor treatment, or no treatment at all.

Responding to this pressure and seeing an economic opportunity, the drug manufacturer targeted its efforts in developing BiDil exclusively for African Americans. After demonstrating the success of the drug, the company was able to gain a favorable patent from the FDA, giving it special commercial protection and enabling it to raise capital for the expensive trials among investors who saw the opportunities of marketing to a particular group of people (Brody and Hunt 2006).

But here's the issue: the drug was tested only on African Americans. The drug's manufacturer and various experts have admitted that BiDil will probably work just as well on non–African Americans, but they have not tested it on other groups (Brody and Hunt 2006). At no point have any unique biological or genetic features of African Americans been identified that explain why BiDil works on them in particular. Indeed, all evidence suggests that congestive heart failure does not work differently among blacks than it does among other social groups.

Most solutions to racial inequalities in health have focused on social and environmental problems—better access to health care, better living conditions, better diet, and so on—but in the wake of successful efforts to map the human genome, genetic thinking has come to exercise increasing influence over how such inequalities are imagined (Inda 2014). While the development of pharmaceuticals specifically for racial minorities may be new, attempts to biologize race as part of the natural order of things are not.

The Biological Meanings (and Meaninglessness) of "Human Races"

Since the eighteenth century, European and American scientists have played a key role in the **naturalization** of race—that is, the social processes that make race part of the natural order of things—by producing theories, schemes, and typologies about human differences. Many of these typologies, such as those of nineteenth-century evolutionists, rank races hierarchically (in strata from lower to higher), implying that racial superiority and inferiority are biologically rooted. Other typologies are less ethnocentric and hierarchical. But they all share the same basic flaw. There is no single biological trait or gene unique to any group of people, much less to any group that has been designated "a race." This point is such an important one for anthropologists that we need to examine it in greater detail.

The Problem of Categorizing Humans into "Races"
Historically, scientists have developed four approaches to categorizing humans into racial groups. The first is trait-based, isolating certain physical features, such as head size and shape, bodily structure, facial features, lip shape, eye folds, or skin color, to divide people into races according to what seems physically most typical of the group

• **Naturalization.** The social processes through which something becomes part of the natural order of things.

(Johnston 2004). This approach is closely associated with German taxonomist and anthropologist Johann Friedrich Blumenbach (1752–1840), who identified five racial groups—Mongoloid, Caucasoid, Negroid, Malayan, and American Indian—by isolating physical traits like skin color and facial features like eye folds. American folk classifications do something similar with skin color; for example, making distinctions between white, black, red, and yellow skin to denote certain racial groups. Of course, nobody's skin is really any of these colors; they are just convenient symbolic markers.

A second approach to categorizing races is based on geographic origins. The Swedish taxonomist Carolus Linnaeus (1707–1778) developed such a scheme, dividing humans into four races: African, Asian, American, and European. North American racial models also reflect some elements of this approach, with our division into African-Americans, Asians, Native Americans, Native Hawaiians, Pacific Islanders, and so forth. The obvious weakness of this model is that political designations, such as Hawaiian and Pacific Islander, and vast continents with tremendous ethnic diversity, such as Asia and Africa, are made into racial groups.

Some anthropologists have refined this geographic approach into a third way of categorizing race, called the "adaptational approach" to racial classification, which refers to the notion that people adapt to the environments they live in and pass on those adaptations through inheritance (Coon, Garn, and Birdsell 1950). For example, people who have lived in lower latitudes of the globe for many generations tend to have darker skin than do people dwelling at higher latitudes. They produce more melanin to reflect the ultraviolet rays of the sun, which are stronger near the equator (Figure 10.2). Instead of being seen as an indication of inferiority, this adaptation

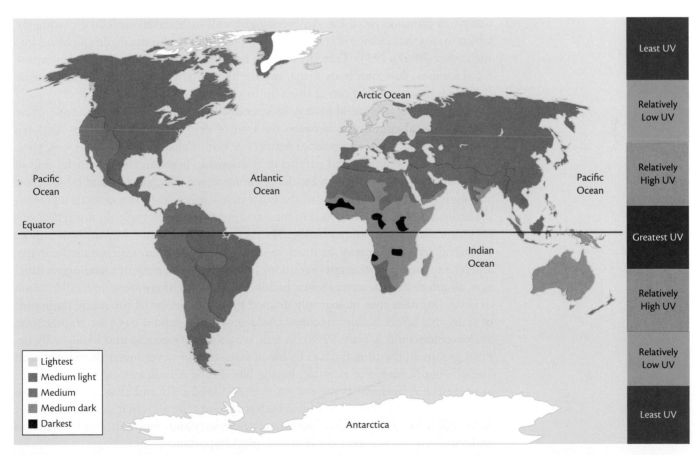

Figure 10.2 The Global Distribution of Skin Pigmentation. This map shows a general correlation between ultraviolet light intensity and skin pigmentation, with people whose families have lived closer to the equator for many generations having darker skin than people whose ancestors have lived farther away from the equator.

indicates fitness and adaptability. Nevertheless, this point suggests only a very general correlation between biology and race, and furthermore, it does not translate neatly to the four or five commonly defined races.

A fourth approach builds on advances in population dynamics since the 1950s, defining races as reproductively isolated breeding populations. This approach focuses on who mates with whom, which allows for the influence of cultural factors, such as religious affiliation or economic status, on the formation of racial groups (Garn 1961). With this approach, the number of races exploded from four or five to hundreds if not thousands, mainly because there are so many breeding populations in the human species. Taken to the extreme, it would also mean that every population qualifies as a race, which blurs the boundary between the two concepts (Long 2003).

Each of these four approaches has specific limitations. But there is a common problem shared by all of them, and for that matter, any attempt to categorize humans into races: these typologies rarely describe an actual individual, and they do not characterize whole groups of people. What look like patently obvious "racial" differences come from a special way of sampling people. This sampling process isolates one or more visible traits, very often skin color or some other arbitrary phenotypical marker, and marks that trait as representative of a whole group of people. More troubling, that one trait can come to be representative of other characteristics, most notoriously, intelligence, aptitude, and personal character.

Biological Variability in Human Populations

Biological traits and genetic features never vary neatly, much less in ways that correspond to the "racial" categories Americans are used to recognizing. Because of historical migration and genetic mixing among human groups, our biological variations occur in a continuous fashion. Anthropologists call such variations "clinal" variations, which means that change is gradual across groups, and that traits shade and blend into each other (Marks 1995). Take any physical trait people use to identify racial groups—facial features, skin tone, body shape, and the like—and you will find that there are no clear lines between variations of that trait in an actual population.

Biological traits also tend to vary independently of each other. For example, there is no biological connection between the trait of skin tone and any other supposed "racial" trait, such as certain facial features or bodily shapes. In a similar way, there is absolutely no physiological parallel or relationship between the superficial trait of skin tone and the biological and social phenomena we call character and intelligence, although this claim tends to be at the heart of many discussions about racial groups.

Finally, visible traits such as skin tone and facial features simply do not reflect important variations in human biological function. Of the many thousands of human biological variations, many are much more consequential than skin tone, nose shape, and hair texture. For example, variations in blood factors, enzymes, and organ function all affect the character of key bodily functions. If there were any valid reason to divide humans into biologically defined groups, any one of the many thousands of traits that affect bodily functions could provide as valid a basis for classification as skin color could (Cohen 1998). In fact, we do classify people into biologically defined groups all the time, such as by blood type, but we never invest these traits with "racial" significance. For example, having blood type A indicates only that a certain antigen (the A antigen) is present on the red blood cells and that the person can donate blood to another person who also has a blood type with that same antigen. But we do not isolate this one characteristic as a necessary and important one by which to make social divisions, even if it is of biological importance.

Thanks to recent research in genetics, we know several important facts about the human genome, which is the sum of all human genetic material. The first is that there is no single gene that encodes race or is unique to any group of people conventionally thought of as a race (Long 2003; Fuentes 2012). The second is that, genetically speaking, humans are a remarkably homogeneous species: there is far greater variation *within* human groups than there is *between* them (Long 2003). In other words, the aggregate sum of variations between the people whose origins lie in Africa is greater than the differences between that group as a whole and all Europeans, Asians, or any other commonly designated "racial" group. But these facts do not imply that race does *not* have biological consequences for people, because it does.

Race *Does* Have Biological Consequences

Even if the origins of racial groups are not genetically or biologically determined, race can *become* biology, by shaping people's biological outcomes due to disparities in access to certain kinds of health care and diets, exposure to certain kinds of diseases, and other factors that can make people either sick or healthy (Gravlee 2009). For example, epidemiological studies in the United States indicate well-defined differences between racial groups in terms of morbidity and mortality, which refer to incidence of disease and life expectancy, respectively. One illustration of this fact is that African Americans and other minority groups such as Latinos and Native Americans have higher rates of many diseases, including hypertension, diabetes, certain cancers, stroke, renal failure, and cardiovascular disease (Gravlee 2009). There is also a gap in black–white life expectancy that has been recognized for many decades. Although the gap has narrowed, from 17.8 years in 1903 to just under five years today, it continues to be a problem (Gravlee 2009).

Race per se is not the *cause* of these health inequalities, however. Rather, these health inequalities are the *result* of race, or more specifically **racism**, which anthropologists define as the repressive practices, structures, beliefs, and representations that uphold racial categories and social inequality. One expression of racism is residential segregation by racial groups, which has been shown to produce inequalities in health because it constrains opportunities such as access to education, certain occupations, and quality health care. This segregation can also create social environments that promote the spread and distribution of disease, diet-related health problems, illegal drug use, and gang violence. All of these problems are linked to poverty and social marginalization, not the biology of the populations affected. **Discrimination**, which is negative or unfair treatment of a person because of his or her group membership or identity, has also been shown to have embodied consequences on individuals, producing a range of effects from hypertension to lower birth weights (Gravlee 2009). The point here is not that different racial groups do not have differences in biology, but that these differences in biology, where they exist, are the result of social inequalities and processes of cultural construction. In the next section, we show how race is culturally constructed.

- **Racism.** The repressive practices, structures, beliefs, and representations that uphold racial categories and social inequality.

- **Discrimination.** The negative or unfair treatment of an individual because of his or her membership in a particular social group or category.

THINKING CRITICALLY ABOUT RACE, ETHNICITY, AND CLASS

The idea that racial differences are genetically and biologically determined is widely accepted by the U.S. public, and the contrary and more complicated view just presented has failed to gain widespread traction even as it offers a more empirically valid understanding of the relationship between race and biology. How do you think anthropologists could communicate these ideas and findings to the broader public?

How Is Race Culturally Constructed?

Like all cultural "realities," the notions that Americans have about race are based on processes that naturalize certain meanings and actions as normal and even necessary. The development of a particular social order nearly always reflects and upholds this confounding of the culturally-constructed and natural. In this case, that social order is one based on systematic patterns of inequality, discrimination, and racism. The key point is that "races" are not self-evident; they are created (Gregory and Sanjek 1994). Scholars refer to the social, economic, and political processes of transforming populations into races and creating racial meanings as **racialization** (Omi and Winant 1996). Racialization always occurs under a particular set of cultural and historical circumstances, and different societies racialize groups differently.

Here we examine two examples of racialization, one drawn from U.S. history, the other from Latin America.

● **Racialization.** The social, economic, and political processes of transforming populations into races and creating racial meanings.

The Construction of Blackness and Whiteness in Colonial Virginia and Beyond

After the English settled Jamestown in 1607, settlers began to raise tobacco as a cash crop. Labor shortages were a problem, so they began to bring indentured servants from England. They also began to rely on African labor. In 1619, for example, a group of African slaves held on a Portuguese ship were captured by an English ship and brought to the Virginia colony as slaves to work. Some English-speaking Africans living in England also began to arrive in the colony as indentured servants (Parent 2003; Smedley 2007a, 2007b). Africans were able to work off their debts and gain freedom from slavery. Some of those men even became prosperous traders and plantation owners and gained rights to vote and serve in the Virginia Assembly, just like any other man with property. Marriages between Africans and non-Africans were not uncommon. Unlike the Irish, whom the English considered racially inferior, Africans were respected because of their success at growing food in tropical conditions, their discipline and intelligence, and their ability to work cooperatively in groups (Morgan 1975; Smedley 2007a; Walsh 2013).

By the mid-1600s, the British began to rely more heavily on enslaved Africans to meet their labor needs and began to impose some restrictions on those slaves, among them restricted access to weapons and the practice of enslaving the children of slaves (Walsh 2013). At the same time, the Virginia colony was entering a period of crisis over land (Smedley 2007a). A few powerful men had taken most of the fertile land, and poor freedmen had difficulty finding any for themselves. Unhappy with their lot, in 1676, thousands of poor freedmen and indentured servants rebelled, in what is known as Bacon's Rebellion. Most were Europeans, but among them were several hundred of African origin. To prevent future unrest, the leaders began passing new laws aimed at gaining more control over laborers. A number of these laws separated out free Africans and their descendants, restricting their rights and mobility, including the ability to vote, own property, and marry Europeans (Parent 2003; Smedley 2007a). These laws took away basic rights that free African settlers had previously held. Within a few years, the colony's labor system was based completely on enslaved African labor, upheld by tight legal restrictions and physical controls over all Africans.

English colonial leaders also promoted a shift in thinking about Africans and their descendants. They began portraying Africans as uncivilized heathens, intellectually incapable of civilization. Such arguments justified African en-slavement. They also began to homogenize all Europeans, regard-less of ethnicity, class, or social status. In early public records, the word "Christian" commonly appeared next to the names of Europeans, but later it was replaced by "white." Poor whites re-ceived land as a way to encourage their identification with the colony's elites, preventing them from siding with Africans. By the end of the seventeenth century, the terms "black" and "white" came to symbolize the differences between the two groups, and the use of this racialized language helped to uphold the artificial lines of difference. Skin color became the chief way of marking status and difference; as Governor William Gooch of Virginia de-scribed, skin color was a "perpetual Brand upon Free Negroes and Mulattos" (Allen 1997:242).

The biologizing of race as a social category became extreme, particularly after the Civil War. In the south, people were defined as "black" if they were believed to have just "one drop" of African blood, meaning a single African ancestor. This notion, called "the one-drop rule," derives from a long-discredited belief that each race had its own blood type, which was believed to correlate with physical appearance and social behavior (Wright 1994:49). Widely promoted in the antebellum South, the rule was a way of enlarging the slave population with the mixed-race children of slaveholders (Figure 10.3).

As in the 1870s, today the vast majority of African Ameri-cans are of mixed ancestry. Over the years, the racialization of African Americans has been used, to a greater or lesser extent, to justify oppression and inequality as the "natural" order of things. The sharp "racial" lines drawn between "blacks" and "whites" upheld a particular social and political order and, more important, served certain economic interests, especially of those who benefited from the cheap labor of racially margin-alized people.

As this example suggests, American racial categories have never been static. Far from it. In "Thinking Like an Anthropologist: Counting and Classifying Race in the American Census," we examine some of this dynamic history in more detail by considering how the U.S. government has classified people in the national census, held every ten years since 1790.

Figure 10.3　The One-Drop Rule. Mark Twain's classic 1894 novel *The Tragedy of Pudd'nhead Wilson* depicts the one-drop rule as a farcical tragedy. In it, Roxy (*pictured here*), a slave who is 1/16 black, switches her baby son, who is 1/32 black, with a white baby, knowing her son will grow up with privileges he would never enjoy if people knew he had even "one drop" of black blood.

Racialization in Latin America

Another powerful demonstration of racialization comes from cross-cultural research in Latin America. In Latin America, the concept of "race" does not exist in many in-digenous societies, but it is well established in societies shaped by European colonial expansion. Yet the distinct history of European conquest and state-building in Latin America has led to the results of racialization in this region being very different from those in the United States. Indeed, the forms and outcomes of racialization differ across many societies colonized by Europeans.

Markers of racial difference are also interpreted differently in Latin American societies than they are in the United States. When dark-skinned, middle-class Latin Americans such as Brazilians, Dominicans, Colombians, Cubans, and Puerto Ricans come to the United States, many are shocked to find themselves referred to and treated as "black." In their home countries, they may think of themselves and be treated as

Thinking Like an Anthropologist
Counting and Classifying Race in the American Census

ANTHROPOLOGISTS BEGIN THEIR research by asking questions. In this box, we want you to learn how to ask questions as an anthropological researcher. Part One describes a situation and follows up with questions we would ask. Part Two asks you to formulate your own questions based on a different situation.

PART ONE: RACE AND THE 1850 CENSUS

Censuses interest anthropologists because they reveal the role of governments in classifying and categorizing groups of people. In addition, over time, census categories change, indicating broader shifts in social categories. The U.S. Census has noted the "color" of American residents from the very first census in 1790, but these categories have changed over time.

The U.S. Constitution requires a census every ten years to determine how many members each state should have in the House of Representatives. The Constitution mentions three kinds of people relevant to the population counted in the allocation of seats in Congress: free persons (each counted as one person), slaves (each counted as two-thirds of a person), and Indians (who were not taxed and not counted until 1860).

The first American census (1790) recorded the head of each household and the number of individuals in each household in basic categories: Whites (by age group and gender), Other Free Persons, and Slaves. From 1800 to 1840, the census expanded the age groupings but used the same basic categories in each household.

In 1850, for the first time, the census recorded the name of every person in the United States and its territories (except American Indians). It also recorded the age, gender, color, occupation, and place of birth of every individual. Color is the most interesting classification because the census form mentions three possible categories: "White," "Black," or "Mulatto." The figure shows a form that was filled out in New Orleans's Fourth Ward.

Few Americans use the word "mulatto" anymore. It refers to mixed-race people, typically those who are part white and part black. Although the 1850 Census doesn't show them, in some parts of the South, people informally used even finer grained terms, such as "quadroon," referring to a person who is one-fourth black and three-fourths white, and "octoroon," a person who is one-eighth black.

All of these terms are obsolete and now considered offensive. But their use in that era suggests some important

points. One is that Americans acknowledged the existence of people who are racially mixed and sought to classify them. Their use also reflects the same ideology that produced the "one-drop rule," in which mixed-race people are categorized as non-white.

After taking the census, the government produced an official summary of what it learned about the population to share with the public (something it still does). Interestingly, the summary never used the terms "Black" or "Mulatto." Instead, it distinguished people in terms of whether they were "White," "Free Colored," or "Slave," despite the fact that the terms "Colored" or "Free Colored" never appeared on the enumeration forms, as we see in the image.

What questions does this situation raise for anthropological researchers?

1. What does the fact that the census forms used one set of categories but the public summary used a different set of categories tell us about American racial categories in the 1850s?
2. Why is it that it wasn't until the 1850s that the government wanted to record who was "mulatto" and "black"?
3. Although the terms "mulatto" and "black" might seem more precise than "colored," do these competing terminologies suggest an (aborted) effort to change public understandings of race?

PART TWO: THE 2000 AND 2010 CENSUSES

Following categorizations first established in the 2000 Census, the 2010 Census asked "What is this person's race?" and indicated that census takers could indicate one or more races. Its list of races includes "White," "Black, African Am., or Negro," and "American Indian or Alaska Native" as well as "Asian Indian," "Chinese," "Filipino," "Japanese," "Korean," "Vietnamese," "Other Asian," "Native Hawaiian," "Guamanian or Chamorro," "Samoan," "Other Pacific Islander," and "Some Other Race" followed by space to print a different option. In contemporary censuses, race is no longer an "either/or" category, and Americans can now check off any number of boxes to reflect the complicated interethnic blending now recognized by Americans. If you wanted to understand the dynamism of racial categories in the contemporary American census, what questions would you ask as an anthropological researcher?

1850: U.S. Census Enumeration Sheet from New Orleans, Louisiana. In southern states like Louisiana, census takers were more sensitive to subtle differences in race than in most northern states. While in northern states people generally understood "color" to mean either black or white, the southern states routinely recognized an intermediary category of mulatto. In this copy of the 1850 enumeration of New Orleans Ward 4, Precinct 3, whites are left blank, blacks are marked "B," and mulattos are indicated with "M." Note that although social status marked by these arbitrary racial categories was clear to everyone, these status differences did not keep whites, blacks, and mulattos from living in the same neighborhoods and even in the same households. (Although residential segregation existed at the time, it was organized not on the basis of race but on the basis of socioeconomic class and wealth.)

Figure 10.4   *Blanquismo* in the Dominican Republic. Between the 1920s and 1950s, the Dominican dictator Rafael Trujillo (1891–1961), pictured here in the center of the photo, promoted an official policy of *"blanquismo"* [blawn-**keys**-moh], or "whitening" of the population. This policy involved a massacre of black Haitians in 1935, invitations for white Europeans to immigrate to the island, and a celebration of European music, dance, and culture. Under *blanquismo*, dark-skinned individuals could be "white," but their whiteness depended on how closely they identified with European culture and attitudes.

either "white" or "mestizo," the latter a hybrid category that recognizes the mixture of European, Indian, and African origins. In either case, it is not common for them to experience the kind of discrimination that is directed toward "blacks" in America or even in their own countries.

Their home countries also have racial inequality and discrimination. Like the English in North America, the Spanish and Portuguese who colonized Latin America controlled African and Indian slaves by defining them as racially inferior and passing laws to control their rights and mobility (Wade 1997). But, unlike the English, they did not place such restrictions on sexual contact between Europeans and these other groups, leading to populations with many shades of skin color. As in the United States, "blackness" symbolizes an inferior and savage condition, while "whiteness" is considered civilized and superior. But these conditions are not firmly attached to skin color or other biological traits. They are linked to social behavior, attitude, and social class. "Blacks" may be people of many different shades of skin color, but they are poor and behave in "unrefined" ways, while "whites" act in a refined and courteous manner (Figure 10.4). "Black" people are still disadvantaged, but it is more obviously for "cultural" rather than "biological" reasons.

Saying "Race Is Culturally Constructed" Is Not Enough

It is not enough to say that race is culturally constructed, because it might give the impression that race is not "real" (Hartigan 2006). Race is very real, of course, because racial groupings come with discrimination, exploitation, stigma, and negative biological outcomes for some and privilege for others.

Put simply, racism is a potent force in making "race" real (Mullings 2005). Racism works through the prejudice that people express against people who are different from them, and through concrete social actions, such as violence or the denial of good wages and access to decent housing, education, and health care. Our point here is to emphasize that the concept of "race" is not a stand-alone concept. It goes hand in hand with prejudicial attitudes and a repressive social order that has real consequences for people's lives.

Of course, race is not the only means by which dominant groups establish and rationalize their social supremacy. In the next section, we consider how categories like ethnicity, class, and caste also operate through processes of naturalization.

• •

THINKING CRITICALLY ABOUT RACE, ETHNICITY, AND CLASS

Racialization is not something that happened a long time ago; it is an ongoing process even in the United States and Latin America today. Can you think of some examples of how it might still be taking place? Can you identify any conditions today that might shape dynamics of racialization differently from, say, during the period of the Virginia colony?

• •

How Are Other Social Classifications Naturalized?

All social hierarchies are rooted in and justified by the notion that social differences are part of the natural order of things rather than arbitrary cultural categories. Yet social hierarchies can be justified and upheld in different ways (Guimarães 1999). While racial ideologies tend to focus on aspects of physical appearance, other systems of classification divide people into groups based on economic status or occupation, behavioral characteristics, common descent, or symbolic purity. What they have in common with racial ideologies is that these divisions are perceived as inevitable and fixed even while in reality they might be quite dynamic. Here we examine three distinct modes of classifying people: ethnicity, which organizes people according to descent; class, which organizes people along lines of poverty and wealth; and caste, which organizes people along lines of symbolic purity.

Ethnicity: Common Descent

Along with race, ethnicity is a salient means of defining group identity and difference in the contemporary world. **Ethnicity** typically refers to membership in a group with a particular history, social status, or ancestry. Members of an ethnic group might be identifiable by any combination of distinctive social characteristics, such as language or dialect, clothing, foodways, etiquette, or bodily modifications such as tattoos or piercings. Americans in particular believe that much can be explained about individuals by knowing their ethnic backgrounds, usually by drawing on common, often negative, stereotypes (Ortner 2006).

The notion of shared "blood" and kinship is generally a central element of ethnicity. Members of ethnic groups often refer to each other as "brothers" and "sisters," might be expected to sacrifice themselves or their interests for the "fatherland" or "motherland," and often believe themselves to be descendants of a common ancestor or ancestral couple (van den Berghe 1999). For these reasons, the ethnicity concept often blends into other terms such as "nation," "nationality," and "tribe." For example, Jews and Muslims, as members of broad "ethnic" communities, not just practitioners of a religion, define themselves—but not members of the other group—as common descendants of Abraham, an important patriarch in both the Old Testament and the Quran (Barth 1969).

By invoking their common descent, ethnic groups establish a distinctive identity and, more important, establish their differences from other groups as part of the natural order of things. A body of scholarship about ethnicity called **primordialism** assumes that ethnicity is largely a natural phenomenon, based on individuals' biological, linguistic, and geographical ties to those with whom they have obvious similarities of appearance, geography, language, or socioeconomic context (Tharoor 1999:2).

Despite an appearance of naturalness, however, ethnic groups do not form for genetic reasons. Some members of ethnic groups may eventually come to justify their identities in biological terms, but they are created for political, economic, and cultural reasons. This argument forms the basis of an alternative theory of ethnicity called **instrumentalism**, which asserts that ethnic groups are not naturally occurring or stable, but highly dynamic groups created to serve the interests of one powerful group or another (van den Berghe 1999).

- **Ethnicity.** A concept that organizes people into groups based on their membership in a group with a particular history, social status, or ancestry.

- **Primordialism.** A social theory that ethnicity is largely a natural phenomenon, because of biological (i.e., "primordial"), linguistic, and geographical ties among members.

- **Instrumentalism.** A social theory that ethnic groups are not naturally occurring or stable, but highly dynamic groups created to serve the interests of one powerful group or another.

The Rise of Latino/a Ethnic Identity

A powerful illustration of how ethnic groups are established has been playing out in the United States in recent decades through the formation of "Hispanic" or "Latino/Latina" ethnic identity. With over 57 million people, Latinos/as now constitute the largest ethnic minority in the United States. The "ethnic" label is applied because Latin Americans do not fit neatly into American racial categories based on skin color and other phenotypic characteristics.

But, as one astute journalist observed, "The theory is that there are no Latinos, only diverse people struggling to remain who they are while becoming something else" (Shorris 2001:9). Most "Latinos" actually think of themselves in terms of national origin—Mexican, Cuban, Puerto Rican, Colombian, Peruvian, and so forth (Fox 1997). There are many reasons for this situation. Different Latin American nations have different customs and identities, and well-developed notions of how they are superior (or inferior) to other Latin American nations. The proximity of Latin America to the United States means that individuals might migrate back and forth between the United States and their Latin American home countries frequently, undermining their sense of common identity with other Latin Americans in the United States. And in cities such as Chicago or New York City, where Mexicans, Dominicans, and Puerto Ricans might live in the same or adjacent neighborhoods, they may see the others as competitors for the same jobs and resources (Fox 1997).

At the same time, however, powerful social forces are driving the construction of a homogeneous ethnic identity out of this diversity. One of these forces is the federal government, which beginning in 1980 included a category for "Hispanic" in the census ("Latino" was added in the 2000 Census), as a way of measuring the quantity of immigrants from Latin America. The federal government was also under pressure from Mexican-American and Puerto Rican civil rights groups, who were beginning to demand political recognition in U.S. society and inclusion in the census (Fox 1997). Government funding began flowing to people in the category, new legislation was developed to address them, and newly labeled politicians emerged with ambitions to gain power for themselves and their new constituencies. Market forces have also helped shape the category. For example, new media have emerged targeting that audience, including radio and television stations, such as Univision, that emphasize a common identity. New consumer products divorced from any single national origin have been created to appeal to a homogeneous group of Latinos (Dávila 2001). A good example of this is the rise of Goya Foods as a Latino food distributor serving the entire United States (Figure 10.5).

- **Class.** The hierarchical distinctions between social groups in society usually based on wealth, occupation, and social standing.

Figure 10.5   Feeding "Latinos." The ethnic group "Latino," referring to a pan–Latin American identity in the United States, is only several decades old. Its emergence is aided by companies like Goya Foods, whose commercial success is based on downplaying national tastes and culinary traditions, and emphasizing ingredients found across a wide spectrum of Latin American cuisines.

Class: Economic Hierarchy in Capitalist Societies

Most Americans think of themselves as "middle class," probably because, as the Declaration of Independence states, "all men are created equal." The result of this notion is that class remains largely hidden in American life. The social theorist Karl Marx saw class as the central organizing principle in capitalist societies, as the distinction between those who control the means of production (factory owners) and those whose labor produces the goods (workers). This definition made sense in the early industrial era but is less relevant to American and European life since the mid–twentieth century. Here we understand **class** to be the hierarchical distinctions between social groups in society, usually based on wealth, occupation, and social standing.

The hiddenness of class in American cultural thought means that class tends to be the last factor introduced as an explanation of social success—as defined by wealth, privilege, and power—and failure, or poverty and social impotence (Ortner 2006:78). As much as they avoid talking about it directly, however, most Americans recognize that people are born into a particular social position due to the economic situations of their families. Indeed, this fact of birth has profound lifelong consequences, since one's class position typically shapes access to educational and occupational opportunities, possibilities for gaining wealth, even the towns and neighborhoods in which one lives.

Being rich or poor is not just a matter of who has or does not have money. There are privileges and exclusions that accompany class hierarchies. Even the rare individuals born into poverty who later become rich can find it difficult, if not impossible, to be accepted by other rich people, who exclude those individuals as *nouveau riche* (the "new rich"), a term that implies lack of civilization and refinement (Figure 10.6).

Several generations ago, Americans regarded class differences as a biological phenomenon. To be wealthy was to be inherently superior, especially in terms of innate intelligence, and to be poor was to be born with inferior intelligence. These ideas have shifted with the growth of the middle class as an intermediary space between the richest and the poorest. Americans now naturalize class in other ways, primarily through the languages of race and ethnicity (Ortner 2006). For example, to be a WASP (white Anglo-Saxon Protestant) implies upper- or upper-middle-class status; to be Jewish implies middle-class status; and to be African American or Latino implies lower- or lower-middle-class status. We all know that these distinctions are little more than crude stereotypes. Nevertheless, these intersections between class and race explain how Americans naturalize apparently neutral categories like middle, upper, or lower class (Ortner 2006).

The concept of class has had much less relevance in anthropology than in other social sciences (Smith 1984). A major reason is that many anthropologists have studied non-capitalist societies where native categories do not correspond with Western economic categories like class (Liechty 2002).

Nevertheless, the spread of capitalism and consumption-oriented lifestyles around the world does create owner and worker classes, as well as middle classes with certain characteristic cultural tendencies that transcend national borders. For example, in his study of urban Kathmandu, Nepal, Mark Liechty (2002) found that the expansion of capitalist markets in recent decades had created a new middle class sandwiched between historically polarized Nepalese elites and commoners. Liechty observed that members of this new middle stratum explicitly distinguish themselves from those above and below them through their consumption of widely circulating consumer goods and mass media, not unlike that of the American middle class. In one passage, he describes a Hindu wedding in the suburbs to which he was invited. Expecting a traditional expression of Nepalese culture, he was surprised at how often a camera crew hired for the occasion interrupted and held up proceedings, even traditional dances. He was especially surprised when an elderly grandmother insisted that the wedding party and camera crew redo a particular bit of the ceremony.

Liechty's broader point is one that many other anthropologists would agree with: the middle class, or any class group for that matter, is not an objective thing "out

Figure 10.6 Portraying the Parvenu in Popular Culture. The French term *parvenu* refers to a person of low origins who has obtained a great fortune. In popular culture, such as film and television, satirizing the "uncultured" ways of the parvenu is a common theme. A prototypical example is the 1960s program *Beverly Hillbillies*, in which the Clampett family from the Ozarks strikes oil and moves to the high-class California city of Beverly Hills. The show plays on stereotypes of poor, rural southerners who misunderstand the ways of their more sophisticated neighbors.

there," shaped by biological imperatives. Rather, people create and re-create social classes in the context of broader historical and economic processes, often by defining themselves in contrast with other groups.

Caste: Moral Purity and Pollution

- **Caste.** The system of social stratification found in Indian society that divides people into categories according to moral purity and pollution.

- **Social stratification.** The classification of people into unequal groupings.

Caste primarily refers to the system of **social stratification** (the classification of people into unequal groupings) found in Indian society that divides people into categories of moral purity and pollution (Sharma 1999). The term derives from the Portuguese word for "pure breed" (*casta*), recognizing that one is born into a caste and should marry only someone of the same caste. Many millions of Indians consider the social divisions associated with their caste system as a "natural" and morally necessary aspect of the human condition.

Just as North Americans "see" race in the subtlest features of somebody's face, hair texture, or skin color, Indians "see" caste in people's occupations, the clothes they wear, how they talk, even their mannerisms. Caste has been described as India's "fundamental institution" (Béteille 1992) because the relationships of inequality upon which it is based are seen by Indians to be so self-evident and are so intertwined with how Indian society works.

Indians actually use two terms for what Westerners have named caste, *varna* [**vahr**-nah] and *jati* [**jah**-tee]. As outlined in classic Hindu religious texts, *varna* refers to the hierarchical division of society into four major groups: Brahmans (priests), Kshatriyas (warriors and rulers), Vaishyas (traders), and Shudras (artisans and servants). Another group outside these four is known as the "Untouchables" (Dalit or, formerly, Harijan). Many occupations and activities are inherently "polluting" in a ritual sense, such as metalworking, leatherworking, street sweeping, or trash collection. The small minority at the top of this system, the Brahmans (10% of the Indian population), are considered the most morally and ritually "pure" and enjoy the highest social status. Relative purity declines and pollution increases as one moves down the hierarchy.

In actual practice, Indians make many finer social distinctions beyond the four major categories of *varna*. They use the term *jati*, which translates in many Indian languages as "kind" or "species," to designate the actual manifestation of *varna* in practice. *Jati* are the actual social groupings, often based on occupation, that exist in a ranked hierarchy in relation to each other. A single village alone may have more than a dozen *jati*. Each has many internal divisions, so what appears like a single *jati* to outsiders may not actually seem that way to its members (Fuller 2004).

Jati and their many subdivisions are upheld by rigid rules that regulate social conduct, especially social and physical contact between groups and subdivisions. Within multicaste villages, for example, people tend to live in residential clusters separated from other castes. Higher castes bar lower castes from using certain village wells and other public facilities, such as restaurants. When people of different castes eat together, such as at a wedding feast, they sit in separate caste and subcaste groups and are served in order of rank (Fuller 2004). Many other aspects of life—including whom an individual can marry, do business with, even have bodily contact with—are governed by the same set of strict rules.

Nevertheless, some Indians have begun to insist that caste no longer exists, because of changing attitudes and the

Figure 10.7   Debating the Indian Census. In recent years, the inclusion of caste categories in the national census of India has sparked a national debate. Many fear that counting caste in the census grants legitimacy to caste-based politics, while others argue that the data obtained can help plan welfare measures.

incorporation of ideals like democracy and the creation of formal government-supported affirmative-action programs (Sharma 1999) (Figure 10.7). This conviction is especially true among some Indians living in urban settings, where everyday contact between members of different castes—sitting next to each other on a city bus, for instance—has weakened rigid rules governing contact between groups (Krishnamurthy 2004). However, while rights of Untouchables now exist, discrimination against them and others of low caste persists.

The social inequality upon which caste is constructed tends to be justified as a natural and inevitable aspect of individuals. However, just saying a particular form of social inequality is "natural" is never quite enough to fully explain its persistence. Social inequality is also upheld by prejudice and discrimination.

●●●

THINKING CRITICALLY ABOUT RACE, ETHNICITY, AND CLASS

The idea that class doesn't exist or is irrelevant in the United States is very powerful, yet social mobility (the ability to change classes) in the United States is restricted. In what ways do you think class mobility is restricted? How is the ideology that Americans have social mobility maintained?

●●●

Are Prejudice and Discrimination Inevitable?

In the aftermath of black civil rights leader Martin Luther King Jr.'s assassination in 1968, Jane Elliott, a teacher in the all-white community of Riceville, Iowa, struggled with how to help her third-grade students understand prejudice and discrimination. She developed an exercise in which she divided the students into two groups, one made up of the blue-eyed kids and the other the brown-eyed kids. She told the blue-eyed kids that they were better and more intelligent than the brown-eyed kids, and treated them with special favors. She ridiculed the brown-eyed kids as less intelligent and unworthy, and shamed them mercilessly. She encouraged the blue-eyed kids to do the same, and they did (Peters 1970, 2005).

The impact of this experience on each group was remarkable. The blue-eyed kids began to feel superior and treated the brown-eyed kids, even those who were their close friends, with disdain. The brown-eyed kids felt humiliated, powerless, and downtrodden. Then, the next day, Elliott reversed the status of each group. Brown-eyed kids were now on top, and the effects on both groups were the same as before: feelings of pain and powerlessness for those in the lower-status group, and a sense of superiority for those in the higher-status group. Over the course of two days, Elliott and her class had constructed and role-played new social categories that closely resembled racial stereotypes in America, with powerful effects on everyone involved.

Elliott's classroom exercise has since become a common technique in anti-discrimination training in schools and organizations. It allows individuals who may never before have experienced **prejudice** (pre-formed, usually unfavorable opinions about people who are different) to experience it firsthand and in a deeply emotional way, to feel what it is like being treated as an inferior minority. It also demonstrates, with tremendous moral force, how the privileged benefit from, and even become

● **Prejudice.** Pre-formed, usually unfavorable opinions that people hold about people from groups who are different from their own.

Figure 10.8   Politically Expedient Scapegoats. One of the ways some politicians advance their careers is to scapegoat certain groups, which means to unjustly blame them for society's problems. In Germany before the Second World War, Hitler and the Nazi Party built the Third Reich by blaming Jews, homosexuals, Communists, and "Gypsies" (Roma) for their country's problems. In the contemporary United States, President Donald Trump has been heavily criticized for his tendency to scapegoat Mexican immigrants and Muslims, which has justified prejudice against and even encouraged mistreatment of people from these groups by Trump supporters.

● **Intersectionality.** The circumstantial interplay of race, class, gender, sexuality, and other identity markers in the expression of prejudicial beliefs and discriminatory actions.

complicit with, these attitudes, especially when people in authority (such as trainers, teachers, politicians, or CEOs) authorize and encourage discrimination (Figure 10.8).

And it raises some questions. Are people naturally disposed to treat humans that are different from them with prejudice? Is discrimination a universal feature of human existence? The answer to both of these questions is *no*. There is nothing in human nature or biology that makes us treat people who are different from us as superior or inferior. Prejudice and discrimination are cultural processes, which is to say, they may feel natural and inevitable, but they are profoundly artificial constructions. Having said that, however, prejudice and discrimination are ubiquitous elements of socially stratified societies, a theme we explore in this next section.

Understanding Prejudice

Prejudice takes many forms and has many sides to it. Prejudice, too, is socially constructed. It is based on taking arbitrary features and assigning qualities of social superiority and inferiority to those qualities. Worldwide, there is a mind-boggling variety of markers upon which prejudices are based. We are most familiar with skin color and hair texture, but other markers include gender behavior, sexual orientation, occupation, family lineage, and religious affiliation. Because people have multiple identities, the markers on which prejudices are based can be multiple and overlapping. Scholars call this phenomenon **intersectionality**, which refers to the circumstantial interplay of race, class, gender, sexuality, and other identity markers in the expression of prejudicial beliefs and discriminatory action. In the United States, for example, black men and women both experience racism, but black women also experience sexism. This intersection of race and gender prejudice can deepen their social marginality (Crenshaw 1989).

Where they exist, prejudices may feel deep, innate, and natural, but they are not static. As attitudes toward groups change, so do accompanying prejudices. There is no better illustration of this than the fact that between 2008 and 2017, the United States was led by a black president, Barack Obama, which would have been unimaginable only 40 years before because of widespread anti-black prejudice. At the same time, the racist and sexist rhetoric surrounding the 2016 presidential elections demonstrated that millions of Americans still hold powerful prejudices against blacks and other groups, among them Muslims, Latinos, and women.

Prejudices tend to express themselves through concrete processes of social rewards and unfair treatment, but they do not always lead to discrimination. In his classic study of prejudice from the 1950s, for example, Gordon Allport (1958) observed that prejudice expresses itself in a continuum from avoidance and non-contact to exclusion, physical aggression, and killing.

Most of us learn prejudices at a young age from people whom we regard as authorities, such as parents and other relatives, community leaders, and teachers. This point explains why our prejudices feel so natural. Drawing on insights gained from her studies of race relations in Mississippi during the 1930s, anthropologist Hortense Powdermaker wrote that prejudices are judgments about a whole group of people based on poor reasoning and insufficient evidence. In "Classic Contributions: Hortense Powdermaker on Prejudice," we examine her point in more detail.

Classic Contributions
Hortense Powdermaker on Prejudice

ANTHROPOLOGIST HORTENSE POWDERMAKER (1896–1970) began studying race relations in Mississippi during the 1930s, making her the first professional anthropologist to conduct ethnographic research in a contemporary American setting. Always interested in issues of social justice (before getting her Ph.D. at the London School of Economics in the 1920s, she was a labor organizer), Powdermaker sought to understand how blacks and whites interacted with each other and the psychological costs of racism.

During the 1940s, she took insights gained from that research to produce the short book *Probing Our Prejudices: A Unit for High School Students*, which was required reading in New York City schools for several decades. In this excerpt from that book, Powdermaker explains how poor reasoning leads to prejudice.

Hortense Powdermaker

Bill plays marbles with a group of boys in his neighborhood, and one of them, John, a Polish boy, cheats. Bill then concludes that all Poles cheat, and he carries this idea with him throughout his life. . . .

When he is older, Bill reads in the paper that two Italians who were drunk got into a fight and one stabbed the other. Bill has never known any Italians but he swiftly jumps to the conclusion that all Italians are drunkards and stab each other in the back.

Or he hears of a Mexican who stole some money from his boss, and so, forever after, he thinks of all Mexicans as thieves.

In all three cases Bill concluded that because one member of a group acted in a certain way, all members of that group will act the same way. This type of poor reasoning is called false generalization. To generalize is to come to a general conclusion as a result of learning particular facts or ideas. For example, if you are a member of a club that functions well at

every meeting and lives up to its standards, you may justifiably say, "We have a good club." This is a true generalization based on observation. If, however, you observe another club during only one of its meetings when nothing is accomplished, and you say, "That club is no good," you are making a false generalization, because you have not based your conclusion on sufficient evidence.

We all suffer from this unfortunate habit of making false generalizations, especially about racial or religious groups or nationalities other than our own. We do not make them as frequently about our own group. If we are white Protestants and a member of our group cheats, we do not condemn all white Protestants. If we are Catholics and one of our members lies, we do not say "All Catholics are liars." In order to be clear-thinking individuals we must realize this inconsistency and avoid making false generalizations. (Powdermaker 1944:29–30)

Questions for Reflection

1. Can you think of other social or political issues beyond race and nationality where people make false generalizations?

2. Why do people accept the logical inconsistencies and poor reasoning that lead to prejudice?

The work of Hortense Powdermaker, Jane Elliott, and others involved in anti-racism education has demonstrated that where individuals have learned prejudices they can also *unlearn* them. Unlearning prejudice, however, does not mean that discrimination automatically goes away. The reason is that discriminatory behaviors, where they exist, tend to be structured into people's social relations and institutions.

Discrimination, Explicit and Disguised

Discrimination may be a very visible feature of a society, upheld by its laws and openly accepted by social convention, as was true throughout the United States, Europe, and South Africa (among other places) for many decades. Or it may be hidden and subtle, operating in disguised but no less insidious ways. We examine both of these modes of discrimination in turn.

Explicit Discrimination

Most of you could quickly name three or four examples of explicit discrimination on the basis of race, ethnicity, class, or religion. In the South, you could name so-called Jim Crow laws, which were laws that prevented blacks from voting and exercising other rights between the end of the Civil War and the 1960s. In other parts of the country, such as the West and Southwest, you could point to the forced resettlement and control of American Indians, and the exploitation of undocumented Mexican labor. Internationally, Nazi Germany's programs to place Jews, homosexuals, and others who did not match "Aryan" ideals into concentration camps where many were killed or died is a classic example.

These examples exhibit a broad range of discriminatory action. What they have in common is that they were practiced openly because they had gained a certain level of social legitimacy and acceptance among members of the higher social strata, and sometimes by the victims themselves. Discriminatory action is often legalized with explicit laws and even bureaucracies to manage and enforce policies of institutionalized coercion and exploitation. It is legitimated because in some way it upholds a social order (blacks as servants to whites, for example) or promotes a new one (a racially homogeneous nation, as in the case of Nazi Germany).

Disguised Discrimination

As plain as these examples of explicit discrimination are, many forms of discrimination can be ambiguous, concealed, and difficult to prove. This fact is especially true where anti-discrimination laws now prohibit the most explicit forms of discrimination, such as in the United States, South Africa, Germany, and other countries once known for open discrimination against racial or ethnic minorities, the poor, or particular religious groups. Where civil rights struggles have succeeded, there may be a misleading sense that the playing field has become level (Mullings 2005).

Discrimination persists because bigotry does not necessarily disappear with changes in formal law, expressing itself in more subtle ways. For example, throughout the United States, blacks, poor people, and members of certain ethnic minority groups who enter shops and malls may be treated with suspicion and experience "racial profiling" or discrimination based on stereotypes. Shopkeepers and security personnel may keep a close eye on them because of stereotypes of these people as thieves. Real estate agents and landlords may steer potential customers away from areas where they do not "fit in," for racial or socioeconomic reasons, even though laws prevent housing segregation and discrimination. Media reports about crime often mention the accused's race or ethnicity, but only when the suspect is non-white, as if their race or ethnicity is the reason for the crime. Immigrants get tagged with labels like "illegal" and "criminal" and tied to the declining economic fortunes of other working people based on the perception that they take those people's jobs. To many people, especially members of higher-status groups, these situations may go unnoticed due to their subtlety or indirectness.

But in the contemporary United States, these disparities extend beyond matters of profiling in everyday life, and there are important differences in how the criminal justice system handles distinct racial groups that are more or less invisible to white middle-class Americans. For members of minority groups, for example, these problems include police violence and extra-judicial killings; higher conviction rates and harsher sentences; and higher incarceration rates (59% of the U.S. prison population is black or Latino, even though these groups make up only 29% of the overall U.S. population; Sakala 2014). Since its emergence in 2013, the Black Lives Matter movement has been fueled by these issues, expressing its indignation on social media and organizing direct-action street protests against police killings of unarmed black people. The movement has demanded reform of police departments and criminal justice systems, and it represents a highly public challenge to the systematic ways black people experience inequality, oppression, and dehumanization (Burton 2015) (Figure 10.9).

Figure 10.9 Race Still Matters. Although it has been heavily criticized by police groups and police supporters for its criticism of the criminal justice system, one of the most powerful effects of the Black Lives Matter movement is to challenge the post–Civil Rights era myth of America as a "colorblind" society, showing that even with legislation protecting equal rights, systemic racial discrimination and inequality persist.

Another proof of discrimination's existence is in the disadvantage that some groups experience that others do not (Rex 1999). For example, we know that in the United States, the educational outcomes of poor white and poor non-white students tend to be much weaker than those of white middle- and upper-middle-class students. There are numerous reasons for this situation, but a crucial one has to do with differences in funding levels for elementary and high schools in poor and middle-class areas. This factor directly affects the quality of teachers, the quality of facilities, and the kinds of programs a school can offer, each of which contributes to student success rates and has long-term consequences for a student's future educational, employment, and income possibilities (Kozol 1992). The underlying forces driving inequality in educational funding could be traced back to the size of the local tax base or employment levels in a community. Nevertheless, the result over the long term is uneven opportunities for different groups, and previously discriminated-against groups rarely end up on top.

What makes this example so loaded is that it is difficult to identify any single culprit for this situation, or even where the explicit racial or class bias lies. Inequality here is not a matter of personal ignorance, which is a common explanation for discrimination. On the contrary, it is clear that certain institutional routines and structural forces create and sustain unfair treatment independent of any particular individuals (Mullings 2005).

Since the early years of the discipline, anthropologists have decried both explicit and hidden forms of discrimination, especially racial discrimination, almost as vigorously as they have provided evidence of inequalities. Yet the powerful effects of racism and discrimination can complicate the conduct of ethnographic fieldwork for minority anthropologists, especially when they are researching their own communities. In "Doing Fieldwork: Tamie Tsuchiyama and Fieldwork in a Japanese-American Internment Camp," we consider the difficulties one minority researcher had working in an environment where racial discrimination was a potent social force.

Figure 10.10   Satirizing White Privilege. In a classic 1980s comedy skit from *Saturday Night Live*, African American comedian Eddie Murphy satirized white privilege. In the skit, he paints his skin with light-colored make-up to create the impression that he is "white," then walks around New York City. He is shocked by the privileges he enjoys: a shopkeeper gives him a free newspaper, he is served a cocktail on a city bus, and when he asks for a loan at a bank, the bank official gives him the money as a gift.

The Other Side of Discrimination: Unearned Privilege

The other side of discrimination is unearned privilege. It is easy for most Americans to recognize how skin color puts an individual at a disadvantage, but it is more difficult for many—especially white Americans—to identify the structural advantages and privileges that accrue to lighter skin.

As Peggy McIntosh (1997) observes, the privilege that comes with having white skin is "like an invisible weightless knapsack of special provisions, assurances, tools, maps, guides, codebooks, passports, visas, clothes, compass, emergency gear, and blank checks." A small sampling of these privileges includes being able to swear, dress in second-hand clothes, or talk with your mouth full and not have people attribute such things to your race; not being hassled by police or have people cross the street at night simply because of your skin color; and being sure that you can receive medical or legal help without your skin color working against you (Figure 10.10). These privileges exist regardless of whether a white individual holds bias against non-white people. The power of white privilege is that

Doing Fieldwork
Tamie Tsuchiyama and Fieldwork in a Japanese-American Internment Camp

DURING WORLD WAR II, President Roosevelt ordered the government to move 110,000 Japanese Americans into concentration camps, ostensibly as a way of protecting them from the rage of white Americans after the Japanese bombing of Pearl Harbor. These camps were bleak and uncomfortable places of imprisonment in isolated areas. The program was based on racial stereotyping and the debatable notion that Japanese Americans would try to undermine the war effort against Japan if they remained free to work and live where they wished like other Americans.

The government hired over 30 anthropologists to conduct research in the camps. They carried out empirical research on Japanese American attitudes and social interactions in the camps, as well as applied research to make the camps run more efficiently, trying to make conditions somewhat more acceptable for the internees. Among these anthropologists was Tamie Tsuchiyama (1915–1984), the first Asian American anthropologist trained in the United States. When the war broke out, Tsuchiyama, a second-generation Japanese American, was a graduate student in anthropology at the University of California at Berkeley.

In 1942, she began working as a staff researcher on a government-funded Berkeley research project at Poston, a camp in Arizona. Tsuchiyama's situation highlights a number of dilemmas about doing fieldwork, especially the fragility of social relationships upon which fieldwork is based and the intersectional complexities of race, gender, and cultural identity confronting minority fieldworkers.

Tsuchiyama was herself a camp resident, suffering hardships similar to those of other internees. But as an anthropologist, she also confronted the difficulties surrounding how one conducts research on one's own social group. The vast majority of anthropologists at the time worked in cultures foreign to their own, where, as outsiders, they could quickly grasp cultural differences. In one's own community, previously formed views of people's behaviors and attitudes can get in the way of a deeper understanding of the culture. Even today, when anthropologists work in

A Japanese-American Internment Camp During World War II.

(continued)

Doing Fieldwork (continued)

their own cultures more than ever, this issue is difficult to resolve.

This dilemma was magnified by the complex relationship between who Tsuchiyama was as an anthropologist working for the government, and who she was as a Japanese American. Camp residents mistrusted her as a government spy. Her research was made more difficult because she was a young woman working in the male-dominated domain of politics (the topic she was told to study), and a Hawaiian, whom mainland Japanese Americans saw as different. So she tried to bring little attention to herself and carried out her research semiclandestinely (Hirabayashi 1999).

Tsuchiyama experienced conflicting emotions about her research subjects. On one hand, she felt great sympathy for their situation, and she complained openly about the discrimination, unfair treatment, and frustration internees experienced. On the other hand, she sometimes experienced feelings of contempt for her informants because they so often treated her with suspicion and resentment (Hirabayashi 1999).

Her advisor at Berkeley claimed all of the credit for her difficult-to-gather research data and findings. By 1944, Tsuchiyama had grown so alienated by what she saw as a colonial situation—the exploitation of her fieldwork and the inequality with her supervisor—that she quit the project.

Although she finished her Ph.D. in 1947, she never held an academic position, and Tsuchiyama's status as a pioneer Asian American anthropologist is largely unrecognized.

Some aspects of Tsuchiyama's situation are not exceptional. In fieldwork, there are always questions about who should receive credit for the work when it is published, especially when field assistants and other helpers are involved in gathering data. These questions get complicated when there are racial inequalities between the anthropologist and field assistants, or when issues of prejudice and discrimination permeate the social environment in which research is being conducted. They highlight how much successful fieldwork relies on a foundation of trust, openness, and fair treatment.

Questions for Reflection

1. How do you think this fieldwork situation might have been different for a white anthropologist?

2. How might this fieldwork situation have been different for Tsuchiyama if she were studying, not a Japanese American internment camp, but a white American suburb?

3. Most anthropologists at some point feel conflicting emotions about their research subjects. How do you think it is possible to overcome these feelings?

it posits whiteness as the norm and being non-white as different, even deviant (Hartigan 2005).

Of course, intersections of class, gender, sexuality, and so on complicate the picture of white privilege. In terms of class, for example, many poor whites would justifiably point to severe social disadvantages not experienced by higher-class whites (Hartigan 2005). But even these poor white individuals experience privileges not accessible to black people. For example, they are rarely pulled over by police because of their "race" in the way many African Americans are for "driving while black," and they rarely experience similar forms of racial profiling.

The broader point here is that social inequality—whether based on racial, class, ethnic, or religious categories—requires the consent of those who benefit from social inequality, who gain unearned privileges simply by being members of a privileged class (Mullings 2005:684). Thus, bringing about real social change requires those who benefit from the inequality to accept the immorality of the situation and support the change (McIntosh 1997).

●●

THINKING CRITICALLY ABOUT RACE, ETHNICITY, AND CLASS

People rarely give up their privileges easily. But, as we have said throughout this chapter, social inequalities and prejudice are cultural processes and thus subject to change. Can you think of any social factors or changes in social relations that might produce a situation in which a group gives up its privileges?

●●

Conclusion

Throughout this chapter, we have consistently argued one central point. In spite of the fact that the social categories most of us take for granted feel real, powerful, and unchangeable, there is nothing fixed or inevitable about them. All social hierarchies appeal to a natural order to justify the rankings and categories they assign to different groups. The markers by which these distinctions are made are arbitrary. If we really want to understand why some people are deemed inferior and others superior, we are better served to explore how belief systems and the dynamics of social power perpetuate prejudice, discrimination, and privilege, rather than searching for any pre-existing biological or moral imperatives.

A final illustration of this point brings us back to where we opened this chapter, with the dynamics of whiteness. Irish Americans today are far less likely to experience discrimination on the basis of their identity than their ancestors did until a century ago. It is now common sense that they are "white." But whiteness has never been a straightforward category. Even today, the meanings and markers of whiteness are in flux. For example, Americans have been dropping ethnic identifications that were so common a generation ago—Irish-American, Italian-American, Polish-American, and so on—and adopting a generic "white" label (Gallagher 1997). This process has had the effect of replacing whatever national and ethnic identities groups sought to maintain during the first generations after immigrating to this country, with a homogeneous racial identity that makes no such distinctions. Moreover, in becoming "white," these groups have come to be thought of as middle class and to share in the privileges of "whiteness," although the dynamics of intersectionality ensure that not all members of any social group are equally privileged or disadvantaged.

What is not in flux here—and this is the unfortunate power of social inequality in American history—is the fact that ideas of race, ethnicity, and class remain a powerful force, even if the individuals and groups assigned to these categories change over time. In hierarchical societies such as ours, inequality is often one of its most enduring features.

KEY TERMS

Caste   p. 262

Class   p. 260

Discrimination   p. 253

Ethnicity   p. 259

Instrumentalism   p. 259

Intersectionality   p. 264

Naturalization   p. 250

Prejudice   p. 263

Primordialism   p. 259

Race   p. 249

Racialization   p. 254

Racism   p. 253

Social stratification   p. 262

Reviewing the Chapter

Chapter Section	What We Know	To Be Resolved
Is Race Biological?	Races are socially, not biologically or genetically, determined. But due to racism and discrimination, race does have consequences for certain people's biological outcomes.	Anthropologists are still working to understand how social dynamics of race and racism express themselves through disparate biological outcomes.
How Is Race Culturally Constructed?	Races are never self-evident; they are culturally constructed through social and historical processes of racialization.	Saying "race is culturally constructed" is not enough, because race has real effects on people's lives, and anthropologists continue to explore the social outcomes and biological dimensions of race.
How Are Other Social Classifications Naturalized?	All social hierarchies appeal to a "natural" order to justify themselves. This "natural" order may feel inevitable, even morally necessary, but like all other cultural phenomena, it is constructed and dynamic.	Race, ethnicity, class, and, in India, caste, interact with each other in complex ways to produce identities, and anthropologists are continuing to work through these complexities.
Are Prejudice and Discrimination Inevitable?	Prejudices are learned attitudes, and as a result they can also be unlearned. Even in the absence of privilege, discrimination may persist because it is structured into social relations in sometimes explicit, but more often than not disguised, ways.	Anthropologists continue to debate the main reasons social hierarchies are upheld. Some emphasize that discrimination and oppression against lower-stratum groups is the key factor, while others emphasize that it is based on the consent of those who gain unearned privileges simply by being members of a dominant group.

Readings

In recent years, the American Anthropological Association (AAA) has sought to provoke a national dialogue on race and racism by sharing anthropological perspectives and research on the connections between race, biology, and culture. To further this aim, it has developed the website *Race: Are We So Different?* (http://www.understandingrace .com/home.html), which is an excellent resource on the latest thinking in anthropology about race.

....

An analysis of the AAA's race website would be usefully paired with the classic text edited by Steven Gregory and Roger Sanjek, *Race* (New Brunswick, NJ: Rutgers University Press, 1994).

....

For ethnographic analysis of the construction of Latino identities, especially in popular culture and consumer capitalism, see Arlene Dávila's book *Latinos, Inc.: The Marketing and Making of a People* (updated edition, Berkeley, CA: University of California Press, 2012).

....

Whiteness, being such a powerful racial category, has recently drawn the attention of anthropologists seeking to understand how it is constructed. For a useful introduction to the anthropology of whiteness, see John Hartigan Jr.'s book *Odd Tribes: Toward a Cultural Analysis of White People* (Durham, NC: Duke University Press, 2005).

....

of corruption and their oppression of the populace. Government propaganda had promoted its soldiers as the country's masculine ideal, so cross-dressing was a protest against the soldiers and the state that supported them (Moran 1997). Cross-dressing also helped identify the rebels as "warriors," a social category of subtle complexity, an alternative masculinity commonly recognized in the villages where rebels operated.

The male warriors' use of feminine symbols was meant to be playful. But it also communicated that true warriors are so powerful that they can overcome the biological and social constraints of maleness. In this society, men derive their special powers as warriors from a deliberate mixing of male and female symbols, thus drawing on the power of both.

Cross-dressing was not to last, however. Two years into the war, cross-dressing became less common as rebels adopted the hyper-masculinized image of Rambo, the macho commando, wearing cut-off sleeves and a headband. The new clothing and bearing continued to differentiate the rebels from government soldiers, this time by tapping into the power and romance of a Hollywood stereotype of strength, an image that brought with it new symbols of power and hypermasculinity.

As wartime Liberia demonstrates, the characteristics people associate with males and females are not set in stone. This point has two important dimensions. First, although all societies distinguish between male and female, the actual boundaries between these categories, and the specific qualities and roles assigned to each, can vary greatly from one society to another. Second, the qualities and roles associated with maleness and femaleness are not static; they can shift, especially in periods of social and political upheaval, and individuals relate to them in fluid ways.

Gender roles always have powerful meanings in any society, leading to the question at the heart of this chapter: *How do relations of gender and sex shape people's lives?* Embedded in this broader question are the following problems, around which this chapter is organized.

How and why do males and females differ?

Why is there inequality between men and women?

What does it mean to be neither male nor female?

Is human sexuality just a matter of being straight or queer?

Gender, sex, and sexuality are at the core of how we define ourselves in contemporary Western culture, shaping individual life conditions in important ways. But what any society associates with one or another gender, how individuals fluidly enact gender, and the circumstances under which gender is important are as constructed as any of the other elements of culture we have explored in this book. As we will explain, many other cultures do not even share our basic notion that humans are either male or female, man or woman, and queer or straight. We begin by offering an anthropological perspective on male and female differences.

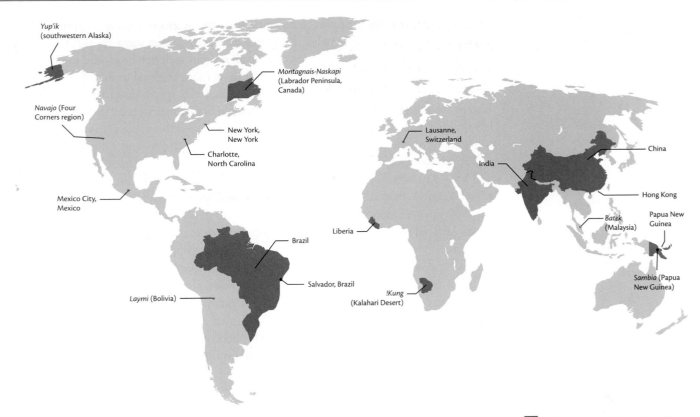

🌱 **Figure 11.1 Select Peoples and Places Discussed in Chapter 11.**

How and Why Do Males and Females Differ?

Walk into any kids' clothing store in a North American mall and the message is clear: boys and girls are fundamentally different. The boys' section is stocked with jeans, cargo pants, and blue or dark-colored t-shirts emblazoned with images of trucks, guns, or sports equipment. The girls' collection is full of frilly dresses and lace-lined shirts and pants in pastel colors like pink and purple, featuring images of butterflies, flowers, or strawberries. Judging by these articles, boys are adventuresome, active, and aggressive, while girls are nurturing, domestic, and sentimental (Figure 11.2).

These clothes convey powerful stereotypes about supposed differences in temperament and personality between males and females. In recent decades, these stereotypes have become topics of intense debate in the United States, as our culture struggles over issues like why women are excluded from certain kinds of jobs and positions of leadership, why men dominate certain professions and positions of power, and even which washrooms transgender individuals should be required to use. The issue is not whether our culture distinguishes males and females. The real issue is to explain why it views gender as a binary of two rigidly fixed options, and why it constructs the differences between males and females in the specific ways it does (Brettell and Sargent 2001). In this section we consider the complex ways that culture and biology interact to shape male and female differences.

Shifting Views on Male and Female Differences

The primary explanation our culture gives for differences between males and females is that they are "hardwired" differently. Differences in **sex**, usually understood in Western cultures as the reproductive forms and functions of the body, are even thought to

🌱 **Figure 11.2 Clothing and Sex/Gender Difference.** North American ideas about sex/gender differences are powerfully expressed through the colors and characteristics of the clothing children are assigned from the earliest ages.

- **Sex.** Understood in Western cultures as the reproductive forms and functions of the body.

produce differences in attitudes, temperaments, intelligences, aptitudes, and achievements between males and females. There is some evidence that supports this belief. For example, some studies have suggested that, in all human societies, boys tend to engage in more rough-and-tumble play, while girls tend to be more engaged in infant contact and care, suggesting that such behaviors are determined at a species level (Edwards 1993). Recent studies also indicate that male and female brains function differently: women's left-brained tendencies provide them with superior verbal skills, while men's right-brained tendencies give them superior visual and spatial skills (McIntyre and Edwards 2009).

But any conclusions about hardwired sex differences grounded in our physiology and anatomy have been muddied by evidence coming out of anthropology and other social sciences that culture and social relationships also shape the preferences and behaviors people associate with maleness and femaleness. For a long time, anthropologists referred to these cultural expectations of how males and females should behave as "gender." For example, the association of girls with pink and boys with blue feels natural and obvious to many Americans. But it is thoroughly artificial: relatively few cultures associate a color with a particular gender, and a century ago in the United States, the colors were reversed, boys wearing pink and girls blue (Kidwell and Steele 1989). American attitudes toward boys and girls did not shift; what changed was the gender association of each color, which had consequences for children's clothing preferences. As we explore in "Classic Contributions: Margaret Mead and the Sex/Gender Distinction," anthropologists have long sought to understand how gender shapes people's identities, preferences, roles, and relationships.

The distinction Mead made between sex (biology) and gender (cultural expectations) was assumed by anthropologists for decades. But in recent years, the distinction has been breaking down because it is difficult to tease apart just how much differences in male and female behavior are caused by "sex," that is, shaped by biology, and how much they are caused by "gender," or cultural expectations (Collier and Yanagisako 1987). Scientists believe that sex-specific biological influences on temperament are strongest during infancy and early childhood. For example, infant boys are more likely to develop their motor skills early, and infant girls are more likely to cry when confronted with unknown people, patterns that are consistent enough to suggest biological differences between the sexes (McIntyre and Edwards 2009). But cultural influences on behavior are strong even very early in a child's life, and these influences get much stronger as they age. As a result, it becomes difficult if not impossible to isolate biological influences on what it means to be male or female.

Another reason the traditional divide between sex and gender is breaking down is that "sex" is not simply a product of nature; it is also mediated and produced in the context of a specific culture. In light of this complexity, anthropologists increasingly reject an either-or perspective—that it's *either* biology *or* culture, *either* sex *or* gender—and accept that ideas and practices associated with male–female differences are shaped by a mix of biology, environmental conditions, individual choices, and most of all sociocultural processes that construct the meanings of the categories of *male* and *female* (Worthman 1995).

- **Gender/sex system.** The ideas and social patterns a society uses to organize males, females, and those who exist between these categories.

- **Gender.** The complex and fluid intersections of biological sex, internal senses of self, outward expressions of identity, and cultural expectations about how to perform that identity in appropriate ways.

Reflecting these intellectual shifts, anthropologists have changed their terminology and commonly refer to the ideas and social patterns a society uses to organize males, females, and those who exist between these categories as a **gender/sex system** (Morris 1995; Nanda 2000). Around the world, gender/sex systems are cross-culturally variable and historically dynamic. As the story of Liberian rebels that opens this chapter suggests, in any particular gender/sex system, a spectrum of possibilities exists for defining and expressing masculinity and femininity, as does a shared understanding of when, how, and why it is important to do so.

It is important to note that **gender** is still a meaningful concept for anthropologists. However, rather than being viewed as a matter of the cultural patterning of sexual

Classic Contributions
Margaret Mead and the Sex/Gender Distinction

FROM THE BEGINNING of her career in the 1920s, anthropologist Margaret Mead (1901–1978) was interested in the differences between males and females, the cultural roles assigned to each, and how sexual differences shaped an individual's life experiences and personality. Mead was possibly the first social scientist to distinguish between biological sex and culturally distinct gender roles (Viswesaran 1997), which she did in her 1935 book *Sex and Temperament in Three Primitive Societies*. This book, which analyzes sex differences in three Papua New Guinea societies (the Arapesh, the Mundugumor, and the Tchambuli), ends with this influential theoretical reflection on the cultural influences on male and female difference.

Margaret Mead.

The material suggests that we may say that many, if not all, of the personality traits which we have called masculine or feminine are as lightly linked to sex as are the clothing, manners, and the form of head-dress that a society at a given period assigns to either sex. When we consider the behavior of the typical Arapesh man or woman as contrasted with the typical Mundugumor man or woman, the evidence is overwhelmingly in favour of the strength of social conditioning. In no other way can we account for the almost complete uniformity with which Arapesh children develop into contented, passive, secure persons, while Mundugumor children develop as characteristically into violent, aggressive, insecure persons. Only to the impact of the whole of the integrated culture upon the growing child can we lay the formation of the contrasting types. There is no other explanation of race, or diet, or selection that can be adduced to explain them. We are forced to conclude that human nature is almost unbelievably malleable, responding accurately and contrastingly to contrasting cultural conditions. The differences between individuals who are members of different cultures, like the differences between individuals within a culture, are almost entirely to be laid to differences in conditioning, especially in early childhood, and the form of this conditioning is culturally determined. Standardized personality differences between sexes are of this order, cultural creations to which each generation, male and female, is trained to conform. (Mead 1935/1963:280–281)

Questions for Reflection

1. Why would an anthropologist study three different societies in New Guinea to demonstrate that gender roles are culturally constructed rather than innately biological?

2. Some scholars have claimed that Mead's New Guinea examples are cultural stereotypes from within the three cultures she studied. If true, would these indigenous stereotypes undermine or support her claim that gender roles are cultural rather than biological?

differences over a biological substrate (as Mead saw it), it now refers to the complex and fluid intersections of biological sex, internal senses of self, outward expressions of identity, and cultural expectations about how to perform that identity in appropriate ways. This approach emphasizes that gender is not an essential or even stable entity, and so it cannot be used to explain behavioral differences between males and females.

Rather, gender is fluid and dynamic, with people actively constructing and enacting gender within a range of culturally bound possibilities, norms, and constraints (McElhinny 2003). Clearly, this view diverges sharply from the male–female binary that dominates Western cultural thought about gender. It is instructive to explore how and why that binary is held up.

Beyond the Male–Female Binary

In the idealized world of science textbooks, human beings are a **sexually dimorphic** species, which means that males and females have a different sexual form. Men have X and Y chromosomes, testes, a penis, and various internal structures and hormones that support the delivery of semen. Secondary effects of these hormones include deep voices, facial hair, and in some cases, pattern baldness. Women have two X chromosomes, ovaries, a vagina, and various internal structures and hormones that support the movement of ova, pregnancy, and fetal development, and the secondary effects of these hormones include breast development and a high voice.

This description is straightforward enough; you already know that nature divides humans into two sexes for the purposes of reproduction. You can probably name some minor exceptions—men with high voices, women with facial hair, individuals who cannot reproduce, and so on—but those variations are not enough to challenge anyone's certainties about the fact of male and female difference. On more systematic inspection, however, what we actually see is not two distinct categories, but a continuum of sexual possibilities in the human species and the important role culture plays in shaping what biological sex means. Chromosomes, gonads, internal reproductive structures, hormones, and external genitalia vary across our species more than you may realize (Fausto-Sterling 2000). Individuals who diverge from the male–female norm are called **intersex**, meaning they exhibit sexual organs and functions somewhere between male and female or including both male and female elements. Some individuals have both ovaries and testes; some have gonad development with separate but not fully developed male and female organs; and some have ovaries and testes that grow in the same organ. Many intersex individuals are infertile, but not infrequently at least one of the gonads functions well, producing either sperm or eggs.

One reputable estimate puts the frequency of intersex in the United States at 1.7% of all live births (Fausto-Sterling 2000). At 1.7 births per 100, intersex is much more common than an unusual but highly recognizable condition like albinism, which occurs in 1 per 20,000 births. This figure of 1.7% is not universal; some populations have higher rates of intersex, and others lower rates. Yup'ik Eskimos in Alaska, for example, have a higher rate of intersex births: 3.5% of births have congenital adrenal hyperplasia, a condition resulting from a genetic mutation that can produce masculine genitalia in girls.

Different societies deal with intersex differently. Many cultures do not make anatomical features, such as genitalia, the dominant factors in constructing gender identities, and some cultures recognize that biological sex is a continuum. A number of gender/sex systems do not see intersex individuals as either male or female, but rather place them in an equivalent third social category, as we discuss later in the chapter. But European and North American societies—which construct sex as either male or female and tend to focus on genitalia as markers of sex—have considered intersexuality abnormal, sometimes immoral, most recently turning it into a medical problem.

With the development of new medical techniques during the late twentieth century, doctors and parents have gained new powers to "correct" what they view as a medical disorder. These days, for example, pregnant women can often know before birth if they will have an intersex child, at which point they may choose to have an abortion. In the United States, most intersex children are treated shortly after birth with "sex-assignment surgery," in which a doctor eliminates any genital ambiguity

- **Sexually dimorphic.** A characteristic of a species, in which males and females have different sexual forms.

- **Intersex.** Individuals who exhibit sexual organs and functions somewhere between male and female elements, often including elements of both.

through surgery, and doctors counsel the parents to raise the child to correspond with that sexual assignment.

The reasons behind parents' decisions to choose sex-assignment surgery for their intersex children are rarely medical; they derive from culturally accepted notions about how a boy's penis or a girl's vagina and clitoris should look. Surgeons work hard to construct culturally "appropriate" genitalia by removing body parts and using plastic surgery. But there is no biological norm for penis or clitoris size or shape, and in fact, many boys are born with very small penises that get larger at puberty, and many girls are born with much larger than average clitorises that present no clinical problems (Fausto-Sterling 2000). The cultural issue surrounding these surgeries is ensuring that the genitals' size and shape will convince others—parents, caretakers, other children, and future sexual partners—that the person is a male or a female.

Sex-assignment surgery shows that "sex" is not simply a biological phenomenon, but is—*quite literally*—constructed upon cultural assumptions: the assumption of a sexual binary in humans, as well as assumptions about what a male or female should look like. These cultural assumptions stand in contrast to the evidence of natural variations that occur in the shape, size, and function of genitalia.

Such surgeries may seem well-intentioned—to help intersex individuals avoid the emotional burdens of being different in a culture that does not accept sexual ambiguity. However, they have become highly controversial, especially among many intersex people themselves, who during the past several decades have spoken out against their treatment, sometimes describing it as mutilation. They have also brought attention to the complex ways that biology and culture intersect to create what we think of as "males" and "females," challenging the injustices they see in our culture's gender/sex system (Figure 11.3).

Do Hormones Really Cause Gendered Differences in Behavior?

The evidence of intersex destabilizes certainties about biologically rooted differences between males and females, but what about hormones? Don't they cause gendered behaviors? Hormones are chemicals our bodies secrete into the bloodstream

Figure 11.3 "Human Rights for Hermaphrodites, Too!" So says this man's t-shirt from a 2009 rally urging the International Olympic Committee (IOC) in Lausanne, Switzerland, to reject discrimination against athletes "suspected" of being intersex (the more common term these days for a hermaphrodite) who participate in international sporting competitions. The IOC has been criticized for supporting forced sexual identification tests and sexual reassignment surgery to "clarify" athletes' sex.

that regulate many of our bodily functions. These days, a lot of people take for granted the power of hormones to shape—and even improve—their lives as males and females. Even minuscule amounts of hormones can have transformative effects on our bodies. Some athletes take anabolic steroids to build muscle mass and improve their performance, and some older men take testosterone injections to enhance their youthfulness and virility. Women take hormones for birth control, and during menopause to moderate hot flashes and mood swings. Individuals receiving sex-assignment surgeries or sex-reassignment surgeries also take hormones to reduce or enhance certain secondary sex characteristics, such as breasts, body hair, and voice pitch. But the transformative effects of many of these administered hormones come with a dark side, including liver damage, fluid retention, heart disease, increased rates of certain cancers, reduced ability to produce sperm in men, and impacts on women's menstrual cycles.

These effects leave us with the impression that hormones play a major role in determining physical and even behavioral differences between males and females. But there is a lot of popular misconception about what hormones do and do not do. One misconception is that certain hormones are linked solely to a specific sex: testosterone to males, and estrogen and progesterone to females. These hormones do play a larger role in one sex than in the other. Estrogen, for example, plays a larger role in women than in men in regulating reproductive cycles. But *both* males and females produce all of these so-called "sex hormones" because they are not connected solely to sexual functions. Hormones are versatile and involved in the growth of several body systems. For example, in addition to producing testosterone, men's testes also produce estrogen, which is involved in bone growth and fertility (Fausto-Sterling 2000).

Popular beliefs in North America hold that sex-specific hormones cause particular behaviors, such as the notion that testosterone causes aggression and the drive to gain social dominance among males. This incorrect belief leads some U.S. states to sentence repeat male sex offenders to "chemical castrations," by the administration of drugs that suppress the male sex drive. The problem is that hormones do not directly cause or trigger any particular behaviors, much less gender-specific behaviors (Worthman 1995). Testosterone by itself does not cause aggression or violence, so efforts to castrate male sex offenders have typically failed to reduce aggressive or violent behaviors (Fausto-Sterling 1992a:126). At best, castration can reduce sexual activity, which is not surprising, since testosterone produced by the testes does regulate sexual potency.

Aggression, dominance, and violence are complex psychological and social states that may involve the production of testosterone, but neither this hormone, nor any other single hormone for that matter, shapes any of these states. Both males and females are capable of aggression and dominance, and societies differ in what they consider to be culturally appropriate levels of aggression expressed by men and women (Brettell and Sargent 2001; Lee 1979). For example, the egalitarian !Kung San (also known as Ju/'hoansi) expect both men and women to be aggressive, although in different ways. !Kung San women engage in verbal abuse, while homicides are usually committed by men. To understand when, why, and how !Kung San men and women express aggression, we have to consider, not just biological factors influencing behavior, but also the immediate social causes of conflict, the availability of weapons, culturally approved expressions of hostility, and the broader conditions, such as political-economic pressures, that drive social conflict (Brettell and Sargent 2001:3).

Related to this whole issue of differences between men and women is yet another enduring question: Are women everywhere subordinate to men because of biological differences between them?

THINKING CRITICALLY ABOUT GENDER, SEX, AND SEXUALITY

In U.S. culture there is a widespread idea that female hormones enable mothers who have given birth to bond with their babies, providing the basis of effective mothering. While birth and the associated lactation do involve elevated production of certain hormones such as oxytocin, mothering is a complex social relationship that must be understood in relation to cultural ideas about effective mothering. What *cultural* ideas do Americans have about effective mothering? Do you think that the production of hormones is necessary to be an effective mother?

Why Is There Inequality Between Men and Women?

Men hold most leadership roles in most societies around the globe. The few exceptions are generally small hunter-gatherer societies, like the Batek of the Malay Peninsula in southeast Asia. This small community lives in bands that anthropologists Kirk and Karen Endicott (2008) report are generally egalitarian in their gender roles, to the extent that the band they lived with during their fieldwork had a woman as its "headman" (Figure 11.4).

But such cases are unusual. In nearly all societies with any degree of social stratification, far more men are in leadership roles than women, not only in political roles, but in economic and social roles involving trade, exchange, kinship relations, ritual participation, and dispute resolution (Ortner 1996:176). For example, in the United States today, only 19% of congressional seats are held by women; in the workplace, women earn on average 81% of what their male counterparts earn; and sex discrimination persists in social expectations, such as the notion that women should do housework. Very few of the privileges men have over women are predicated on physical strength. So why is inequality between the sexes such a common feature of most societies?

Debating "The Second Sex"

In 1949, French existentialist philosopher Simone de Beauvoir published an influential book called *The Second Sex,* in which she argued that throughout history, women have been considered "the second sex," inferior in status and subordinate to men. Even before the publication of this book, during the Victorian era, a handful of women anthropologists had studied women's status and roles in other societies. A few of these anthropologists, animated by the so-called first-wave feminism that was beginning to challenge male domination and win the right to vote, wanted to understand whether all societies treated women as unequally as Euro-American societies did. Nevertheless, it wasn't until the mid-1950s and early

🌱 **Figure 11.4   Batek Headwoman.** This photo, taken in 1976, shows Batek headwoman Tanyogn in the Malaysian rainforest, plaiting a cord out of black fungus rhizomes to make a bracelet.

Figure 11.5   Feminism's First and Second Waves. The first wave of feminism (late 1800s, early 1900s) in Britain and the United States focused on legal obstacles to gender/sex equality, such as laws prohibiting women from voting or owning property. The second wave (1960s and 1970s) focused on issues like unofficial inequalities and reproductive rights. Both had a major influence in anthropology.

1960s that anthropologists—inspired in great part by de Beauvoir's work and the emergence of "second-wave feminism"—began to pay greater attention to the issue of gender/sex inequality (Figure 11.5).

In taking on this issue, most feminist anthropologists rejected the idea that biological differences are the source of women's subordination. Instead, they argued that cultural ideologies and social relations impose lower status, prestige, and power on women than men. But here the agreement ends, and during the 1970s and 1980s, a major debate took place over whether gender inequality is universal, and what causes it.

On one side were those who argued that women's lower status is universal. Sherry Ortner, an influential participant in the debate, observed that the roots of female subordination lay in the distinction all societies make between "nature" and "culture" (Ortner 1974). Women are assigned symbolically to nature because of their role in childbearing, and thus they are viewed as uncultured and uncivilized. Men, on the other hand, are associated symbolically with culture and thus viewed as civilized and superior. Another influential backer of this position was Michelle Rosaldo, who theorized that the subordination of women was due to the distinction all societies make between "public" and "domestic" spheres (Rosaldo 1974). Men are assigned symbolically to the public sphere and thus control political, economic, religious, and other social relations, while women are assigned to the domestic sphere, managing the household and raising children.

On the other side were feminist anthropologists who argued that male domination and female subordination are not inevitable, and that egalitarian relations have existed throughout human history. Inequality exists, they observed, as the result of particular historical processes, especially the imposition of European capitalism and colonization on native peoples who were once egalitarian. For example, Eleanor Leacock (1981) argued that among the Montagnais-Naskapi [mohn-tan-**yay** nahs-**kah**-pee] of the Labrador Peninsula in Canada, women enjoyed equal status with men, held formal political power, exercised spiritual leadership, and controlled important economic activities before the arrival of Europeans. By the 1700s, however, dependence on the fur trade with Europeans undercut the traditional political system and economy, and Jesuit missionaries imposed compulsory Catholic schooling, which was hostile to women's independence and power. Eventually, the Montagnais-Naskapi developed a cultural view of women as inferior and subordinate.

Taking Stock of the Debate

On all sides of the feminist anthropology debate, participants recognized that inequality between men and women is, if not universal, at least pervasive. More important, the debate brought the study of what women say and do to the mainstream of the discipline. The emergence of this so-called "anthropology of women" successfully challenged the discipline's historical bias toward studying males, and it closed a gap in the ethnographic record by producing detailed studies of women's experiences and perspectives (Viswesaran 1997).

But the debate came to an impasse. Some of it had to do with differences of interpretation over the evidence. Some participants also shifted their positions. Ortner, for example, came to recognize that egalitarian relations between men and women can exist, although she also concluded that these relations are fragile and inconsistent (Ortner 1996).

Critics of the debate, including some anthropologists, members of minority groups, and Third World academics, asserted that second-wave feminism, although well intentioned in its concern for women around the world, made ethnocentric assumptions (Mohanty 1991). They pointed out that the mostly white, middle-class feminists involved in the movement had downplayed meaningful differences between women across cultures, assuming that all women viewed the fight for political equality as a singular global priority. In many other countries, women's movements are more local and might be more oriented toward fighting militarism, challenging foreign ideals about beauty and ways of being a woman, or gaining access to local political processes or economic opportunities (Basu 2010).

Critics also emphasized the inappropriateness of using Western models of female inequality to understand male–female relations in other cultures. Other societies' concepts of those relations may differ considerably from ours, and not every culture attaches the same meanings to "oppression" or "exploitation" as we do (Strathern 1988). For example, among the Laymi [**lie**-mee] people of the Bolivian Andes, "male" and "female" are not seen as opposed, dichotomous categories (Harris 1980). Laymi men and women each participate in cultivation, care of livestock, and weaving, and the married couple represents the core of society. Unmarried and young people are seen as wild and undomesticated. The Laymi symbolic order emphasizes age, generation, and marital status, among other factors, over gender for defining one's status and rights.

- **Masculinity.** The ideas and practices of manhood.

Reproducing Male–Female Inequalities

The impasse in the debate also accompanied a shift in how anthropologists studied relations between men and women. A number of anthropologists insisted that understanding inequalities between men and women could not emerge from focusing on the lives of women alone. Rather, it is necessary to focus on women *and* men, especially the dynamic relationships between them that take place in everyday life.

From this vantage point, inequality is not something static that people "possess"; it is something that they "do." For example, patterns of inequality are reproduced in things as basic as everyday language. What American men and women may say may include the same words but mean something different to each gender. As we explored in Chapter 4, such miscommunications happen because our culture has different expectations about how men and women should communicate.

Being a Man

Another influence of focusing on what men and women actually do has involved a rethinking of men. For decades, anthropology involved men studying the lives of other men, but until recently, very few anthropologists had closely examined men *as men*; that is, how men and women collectively view and shape what "being a man" means, and how men actually perform, or act out, manhood (Gutmann 1997). The anthropological study of **masculinity**, the ideas and practices of manhood, has not just opened new avenues of research for understanding how gender identities are constructed; it has also generated new perspectives on the issue of male–female inequality, including the notion that ideals of masculinity are dynamic and do not in themselves necessarily assume male dominance (Figure 11.6).

Anthropologists have observed the existence in many societies of the notion that women are "born" but men are "created"

Figure 11.6 Masculinity in Transition. In recent years, broad social transformations—such as greater numbers of women working outside the home for money, boys and girls in schools being given equal status, and the feminist movement—have contributed to changing perceptions of manhood across the United States, including the acceptance of men's greater involvement in parenting.

(Gutmann 1997). Some of this could be explained by developmental differences: in females, the onset of adult physical characteristics is rapid once menstruation begins, while among males, is it much more gradual. The idea of these differences leads to symbolically assigning women to the category of "nature" and men to "culture," a point that, as Sherry Ortner and other feminists have suggested, provides a basis for women's subordinate status. The idea also explains why male initiation rites are such important events in many societies: when boys are ritually transformed into men—fully entered into the realm of culture that they represent—the social order itself is reproduced and affirmed.

Despite the sometimes static pictures of male–female relations that anthropologists depict for a culture, however, the relationship between masculinity and male dominance does change, as anthropologist Matthew Gutmann has pointed out. During the 1990s, Gutmann studied how men and women define what "being a man" means in a poor neighborhood of Mexico City (Gutmann 1996). He observed that certain ideals and practices of *machismo*—the Mexican stereotype of the dominant, assertive male—contribute to women's subordination, such as when men expect to eat their meals before women and receive better food, abuse alcohol and hit women, or impose decisions on their families. But many men do not behave in these ways, at least, not all the time. Mexican masculinity has always been more subtle and dynamic than the stereotypes of inflexible, domineering *machos* suggest. One reason is that broader social transformations—greater numbers of women are now working outside the home for money, boys and girls in schools are given equal status, and the feminist movement has influenced Mexican life—contribute to changing perceptions of manhood. Gutmann also observed that women play a key role in shaping ideas of masculinity, one of those ways being to challenge men's domination over them. They argue, cajole, and issue ultimatums to men, forcing them to act contrary to *macho* stereotypes.

By focusing on the dynamic nature of male–female inequalities, anthropologists have come to understand that male domination and female subordination are reproduced and performed in complex ways in everyday life. But anthropologists have not studied only "men" and "women." They have also studied people who are not considered, or do not consider themselves, to be either men or women, an issue we deal with in the next section.

THINKING CRITICALLY ABOUT GENDER, SEX, AND SEXUALITY

Inequalities between men and women are reproduced and performed in many different ways in daily life. Can you identify examples in the following: Advertising? Sports? Language? Cooking? Shopping? At the same time, these inequalities are often challenged by both men and women. Can you find examples of such challenges in the same contexts?

What Does It Mean to Be Neither Male Nor Female?

Although it may feel natural to most Americans, the male–female binary taken for granted in Western cultures is as artificial and constructed as the categories and assumptions found in any society's gender/sex system. Many gender/sex systems around the world are less rigid or constraining than our own, including the one that allowed Liberian rebels to adopt feminine clothing and mannerisms to demonstrate their power as warriors.

In many societies, some people live their lives as neither male nor female. They have a culturally accepted, and in some cases prestigious, symbolic niche and social pathway that is distinct from the cultural life plan of males and females (Herdt 1994). Anthropologists use several terms to refer to this situation. One of these terms is **gender variance**, which refers to expressions of sex and gender that diverge from the male and female norms that dominate in most societies. Another term is **third genders**, which recognizes the fact that many societies allow for more than two categories of gender/sex (in actuality ranging anywhere from three to five). Sometimes the terms are used interchangeably, as we do here.

"Third gender" has often been entangled in debates about **sexuality**, which encompasses sexual preferences, desires, and practices. Third gender has been viewed as a form of homosexuality, since some third gender individuals engage in what appear to be same-sex sexual activities (Herdt 1994). But sexual preferences intersect in complex ways with gender variance. People everywhere establish their gender identities, including normative categories like "man" or "woman," not through sexual practices but through social performance: wearing certain clothes, speaking and moving in certain ways, and performing certain social roles and occupations. Performance is central to establishing one's identity as third gender because other markers, such as anatomy, are not always publicly visible. Indeed, in a number of societies, the performance itself—not any essential features of anatomy or sexual preferences—defines an individual as third gender (Whitehead 1981).

Like other aspects of gender/sex systems, such as the inequalities discussed earlier, gender variance is a dynamic phenomenon. In many societies, several different gender/sex systems may even coexist and interpenetrate, especially in societies whose cultural traditions allowed for gender variance when Western nations colonized these societies. To illustrate these points, we consider three examples of gender variance drawn from different contexts: the Navajo, India, and the contemporary urban United States.

- **Gender variance.** Expressions of sex and gender that diverge from the male and female norms that dominate in most societies.

- **Third genders.** A category found in many societies that acknowledge three or more gender categories.

- **Sexuality.** Sexual preferences, desires, and practices.

Navajo *Nádleehé*

Gender variance has been historically documented in over 150 American Indian societies, although it is no longer an important institution except in a few of these societies. Today, where it exists, American Indian gender variance is often called "two-spirit," meaning an individual has both male and female spirits. The phenomenon has been greatly misunderstood, largely because Western culture lacks the conceptual categories to translate the specific beliefs and customs related to gender variance in these societies (Roscoe 1994). For decades, white Americans have used the term *berdache* [burr-**dash**], a derogatory Arabic term that refers to the younger partner in a male–male sexual relationship, to refer to gender variance among American Indians. This term assumes that gender-variant individuals are sexually attracted to individuals of their own sex, which is not always the case (Figure 11.7). Western moral thought also categorizes them as deviants when in fact, in a number of Indian societies, third-gender individuals have held high social status. Furthermore, Western thinking tends to confuse a wide range of beliefs and customs not shared by all societies into a single phenomenon.

The Navajo, who live in the Four Corners area of the Southwest, present an especially subtle and complex example of how one society has defined multiple genders. In Navajo society, *nádleehé* [nahk-**hlay**] are individuals held in high esteem who combine male and female roles and characteristics. They perform both male roles (such as

Figure 11.7   Two-Spirit Singers at a Gathering. Unlike traditional gender variants in American Indian societies, many contemporary two-spirit individuals are gay. Due to anti-gay sentiment, they often experience hostility and discrimination in their home communities. They also feel alienated from white gay and lesbian communities and political activism, which does not acknowledge their unique cultural heritage and the issues of poverty and racism they face as Indians.

hauling wood and participating in hunts and warfare) and female roles (such as weaving, cooking, shepherding, and washing clothes). Some *nádleehé* dress in traditionally female clothing, while others dress in traditionally male clothing. Navajo families have traditionally treated *nádleehé* respectfully, even giving them control over family property. The *nádleehé* participate in important religious ceremonies, and many have become spiritual healers. They also serve as go-betweens in arranging marriages and mediating conflicts.

To understand who becomes a *nádleehé*, it is necessary to understand Navajo ideas about gender (Thomas 1997). The Navajo recognize five genders, two of them being male and female. The term *nádleehé* (in English, "one who changes continuously") refers to intersex individuals whom they consider a third gender. The fourth and fifth genders are also called *nádleehé*, but they are distinct from intersex individuals. The fourth gender is the masculine-female, female-bodied individuals who do not get involved in reproduction and who work in traditional male occupations (hunting and raiding). Today they often serve as firefighters or auto mechanics. The fifth gender is the feminine-male, male-bodied individuals who participate in women's activities of cooking, tending to children, and weaving. Feminine-males may engage in sexual relations with males, although Navajo do not consider these to be same-sex relationships.

The meanings and status of *nádleehé* have changed over the years. For example, the high social status of *nádleehé* became especially pronounced after the 1890s. The U.S. military forced Navajos onto reservations, undermining men's traditional economic activity of raiding (Roscoe 1994). These changes did not affect women's traditional economic pursuits, especially weaving and shepherding, in which *nádleehé* also engaged. *Nádleehé* who took advantage of the opportunities presented by these social changes often became wealthy as shepherds and weavers, such as the famous weaver Hastíín Klah.

Around the same time, however, Christian missionaries on these reservations tried to eliminate the *nádleehé*. Prominent *nádleehé* began to be more discreet about exposing their identities to the outside world, a situation that continues today (Thomas 1997). Although *nádleehé* continue to exist, many young Navajos, especially those raised off reservation, might not identify themselves as *nádleehé* but as "gay" or "lesbian," adopting Western forms of identification that really have nothing to do with traditional Navajo gender notions.

Indian *Hijras*

In India, *hijras* (*hee*-drahs) are members of a third gender who have special social status by virtue of their devotion to Bahuchara Mata, one of many versions of the Mother Goddess worshipped throughout India (Nanda 1994) (Figure 11.8). *Hijras* are defined as males who are sexually impotent, either because they were born intersex with ambiguous genitalia or because they underwent castration. Because they lack male genitals, *hijras* are viewed as "man minus man." They are also seen as "male plus female" because they dress and talk like women, take on women's occupations, and act like women in other ways—although they act as women in an exaggerated, comic, and burlesque fashion.

Individuals from many religious backgrounds—Hindu, Christian, and Muslim— become *hijras*, but their special status emerges from the positive meanings Hinduism attributes to individuals who embody both male and female characteristics and to individuals who renounce normal social conventions. In Hindu thought, males and females exist in complementary opposition. The important Hindu deities Shiva, Vishnu, and Krishna have dual gender manifestations. The female principle is active, both life-giving and destructive, while the male principle is inert and latent. When they become *hijras* by undergoing castration (or, if they are intersex, they can join a *hijra* community), men can become powerful enough to tap into the beneficent and destructive powers of the female principle, as vehicles for the Mother Goddess. *Hijras* are thus viewed as both carrying the ability to bless and inauspicious and stigmatized, and many Indians fear the ability *hijras* have to issue curses.

Hijras live in communes of up to 20 people, led by a *guru* (teacher). They live outside the normal bounds of social convention, having renounced their caste position and kinship obligations. Living marginally like this both stigmatizes them and provides them with social freedom. The primary social role of *hijras* is to provide blessings when a boy is born (a major cause of celebration in India), or to bless a couple's fertility at a wedding. *Hijras* are typically a raucous presence at these events, making crude and inappropriate jokes, performing burlesque dances, and demanding payment for their services. Although it is stigmatized within *hijra* communities, some *hijras* also work as prostitutes, engaging in sex acts with men for pay. *Hijra* prostitutes are not necessarily considered "gay"; Indian society does not consider human sexuality as a dichotomy between gay and straight as ours does, and *hijras* are not considered males anyway.

Figure 11.8 *Hijras* in India. The *hijras* pictured here are protesting against Indian Penal Code Section 377, which criminalizes same-sex relationships. Protestors have sought to overturn the law, alleging that the law, which was created during the British colonial era, is outdated and justifies daily abuse and harassment of members of the gay, lesbian, bisexual, and transgender communities, including *hijras*, by police.

Although British colonialism tried to outlaw *hijras*, they continued to exist largely by conducting their initiation rites (including castration of willing males) in secret. In recent decades, they have had to adapt to a changing Indian society. Government family-planning programs have reduced birth rates, and urban families increasingly live in apartment blocks with security guards who prevent the entrance of *hijras* when they arrive to bless a baby. In response, *hijras* have exploited new economic opportunities, asking for alms of shop owners and expanding prostitution (Nanda 1994:415). They continue to exist mainly because the Indian gender/sex system still considers the combination of male and female as valid and meaningful.

Trans in the United States

Even in the United States, where the culture emphasizes the male–female binary, gender variance exists. Our culture has long recognized the existence of individuals who dress, act, or otherwise present themselves in a manner inconsistent with what the majority of Americans would expect based on their biological sex. Many in the mainstream have stigmatized these people as deviant, immoral, even mentally ill, and some have made them the target of violence and hate crimes.

Beginning in the early 1990s, political activists began challenging the stigma and putting pressure on government and society to recognize formally the existence and rights of gender variants in this country. The term these activists use, *trans*, is shorthand for **transgender**, which refers to someone to whom society assigns one gender who does not perform as that gender but has taken either permanent or temporary steps to identify as another gender (Valentine 2003). *Trans* has become a catch-all term to describe a wide variety of people who had once been seen as separate: transsexuals (people who have had sexual reassignment surgery or strongly desire it), transvestites (people who cross-dress), drag queens (men who wear exaggerated women's clothing, usually for performances), drag kings (women who dress in exaggerated men's clothing), intersex individuals, and people who consider themselves to be neither exclusively male nor exclusively female. It rapidly became a common term in academia, psychiatry, and politics, where trans activists have been effective in promoting legislation on the issue of hate crimes (Figure 11.9). Increasing acceptance of trans terminology has been accompanied by use of another term, **_cisgender_**, which

- **Transgender.** Someone to whom society assigns one gender who does not perform as that gender but has taken either permanent or temporary steps to identify as another gender.

- **Cisgender.** Someone whose gender identity aligns with their biological sex at birth as male or female.

Figure 11.9   Transgender Activism in New York City.

refers to people whose gender identity aligns with their biological sex at birth as male or female. Although some intersexual individuals and others criticize the use of this term as implementing a new binary (trans vs. cis), its use is increasingly widespread in academia and medical fields.

And yet many of the people who occupy the category of "trans" do not necessarily identify themselves as such, suggesting that there is no single community or accepted form of being trans in America. American anthropologist David Valentine has explored this issue in ethnographic research among mostly male-to-female trans-identified people at drag balls, support groups, cross-dresser organizations, clinics, bars, and clubs in New York City. Valentine observed that many individuals resist the trans label because they see it as including them with so many different groups, thus diluting their own issues (Valentine 2007:101). For example, the psychological and social issues confronting people who cross-dress for erotic pleasure are different from the issues of someone who has undergone sexual reassignment surgery and is struggling with the bodily and personal changes involved in that process. Political activists tend to be white and middle class, while many individuals who reject the trans label are racial minorities and poor. This difference suggests that philosophical disagreement is not the only problem confronting the use of the trans label in the United States: class and racial differences play a role, too.

For some people, their uncertainty about the trans label is related to the ongoing hostility in the United States against people who diverge from male and female norms. We explore this issue in more detail in "Thinking Like an Anthropologist: Anthropological Perspectives on American (Non)Acceptance of Trans People."

The meanings of *trans* and *transgender* are still in formation, though it is clear our culture continues to resist accepting people who identify as neither entirely male nor entirely female, because it still does not provide them a legitimate symbolic niche and social pathway. One reason is perhaps that many Americans view trans identities through a moralistic lens, as an expression of a perverse sexuality, a notion anthropologists reject. As we show in the next section, sexuality is also a distinctive issue with its own complexities and cultural variability.

THINKING CRITICALLY ABOUT GENDER, SEX, AND SEXUALITY

Societies in which gender variance is common tend to also be societies that are tolerant toward ambiguity and complexity in other areas of life, such as religious beliefs. How and why might a society develop an acceptance of ambiguity and complexity? Beyond gender and religious beliefs, in what other aspects of social life might one expect to see a tolerance for ambiguity?

Is Human Sexuality Just a Matter of Being Straight or Queer?

Most of us assume that sexuality (sexual preferences, desires, and practices) is an either/or issue, that people are *either* straight *or* queer. We also assume that most humans are heterosexual. The term we use to indicate heterosexuality—"straight"—implies that it is normal and morally correct, while anything else is deviant, bent, or

Thinking Like an Anthropologist
Anthropological Perspectives on American (Non)Acceptance of Trans People

ANTHROPOLOGISTS BEGIN THEIR research by asking questions. In this box, we want you to learn how to ask questions as an anthropological researcher. Part One describes a situation and follows up with questions we would ask. Part Two asks you to formulate your own questions based on a different situation.

PART ONE: TRANS PEOPLE AND PUBLIC BATHROOMS IN PERSPECTIVE

In the past several years, a number of American universities, corporations, and communities have been creating gender-neutral (or "all gender") bathrooms to accommodate people who do not identify themselves as either male or female. The establishment of these bathrooms is rooted in a number of concerns, among them accessibility, personal privacy, inclusion, and preventing discrimination against those who reject gender binaries. Because federal law does not extend nondiscrimination protections to LGBTQ (lesbian, gay, bisexual, trans, and queer) people, each state, county, and city government can enact its own legislation protecting the rights of LGBTQ individuals, including access to gender-neutral bathrooms.

It is in this context that city councilors in Charlotte, North Carolina, in February 2016, passed an ordinance prohibiting discrimination in the city on the basis of sexual orientation or gender identity in public accommodations, including public bathrooms. Conservative politicians and religious leaders around the state denounced Charlotte's law as a moral failing and worried openly that trans people, who they inaccurately stereotyped as sexual predators, would assault innocent bathroom users. In particular, they stoked fears of cross-dressed men entering women's bathrooms to harass or assault women. In response, the state legislature quickly passed a bill called HB 2 (or House Bill 2), which prevented Charlotte and other cities from implementing nondiscrimination provisions for LGBTQ people, and required individuals to use bathrooms that correspond to the sex identified on their birth certificate. The bill is understood to be a direct challenge to trans people in particular.

HB 2 provoked outrage around the country, and many prominent corporations and organizations boycotted North Carolina at the cost of millions of dollars to the state economy. Trans celebrity Caitlyn Jenner even publicly declared that if she found herself in North Carolina she would use a women's bathroom. But other state legislatures, notably that of Texas in early 2017, began preparing their own "bathroom bills" similar to North Carolina's.

Commenting on this situation, anthropologist Elijah Adiv Edelman (2016) observed that characterizations of trans people as sexual predators are inaccurate and often obscure the fact that trans people are at much greater risk of being victims of sexual assault and violence. He observes that anxieties around trans people's access to bathrooms are not about bathrooms themselves, but really anxieties many Americans feel about the "unnaturalness" of sex and gender ambiguity. Importantly, it is this sense of unnaturalness that leads many to justify violence against trans people, explaining why trans people are among the most vulnerable to sexual violence in our society. What worries Edelman is that bills like North Carolina's HB 2 formalize state support for that violence.

This situation raises a number of questions about anthropological research and advocacy on socially vulnerable and marginalized people, including the following:

1. What kinds of symbolic representations of trans people exist in debates over their rights and their use of public facilities?
2. What forms of vulnerability and violence do trans people experience in contemporary American society?
3. How and why have a number of American individuals, corporations, institutions, and state offices

🌱 **Caitlyn Jenner, Trans Celebrity.**

come to accept that LGBTQ individuals should receive state protection from discrimination?

4. What beliefs, political interest groups, and social factors contributed to the creation of North Carolina's HB 2?

5. What role should anthropological researchers take in these acrimonious public debates over public bathrooms, and trans rights more generally?

PART TWO: THE CULTURAL AND SOCIOPOLITICAL MEANINGS OF CAITLYN JENNER'S FAME

In 2015, television personality and former Olympic athlete Bruce Jenner announced a name and gender change, becoming Caitlyn Jenner. Americans had long been fascinated with Jenner—especially as an accomplished Olympian and a participant in the reality show *Keeping Up with the Kardashians*—but since this announcement, interest in Jenner's life has exploded. While some trans activists had hoped that Jenner's fame could help advance their own claims for social legitimacy and legal rights, political and social prejudice against trans people has doubled down in some quarters, as we saw in the North Carolina legislature. What questions might you ask as an anthropological researcher about the cultural meanings and sociopolitical effects of Caitlyn Jenner's fame as a trans woman in American society?

"queer," a term that once had derogatory connotations but in recent years has been appropriated by gay and lesbian communities and given a more positive connotation.

But human sexuality is far more complex and subtle, something that social scientists began to realize after Indiana University biologist Dr. Alfred Kinsey conducted a series of sexuality studies during the 1940s. Kinsey and his colleagues surveyed the sexual lives and desires of American men and women, discovering that sexuality exists along a continuum (Figure 11.10). They found, for example, that 37% of the male population surveyed had had some sexual experience with other men, most of which occurred during adolescence, and at least 25% of adult males had had more than incidental same-sex sexual experiences for at least three years of their lives (Kinsey 1948; Fausto-Sterling 1992b). Many of these men did not think of themselves or lead their lives as gay; this suggests quite clearly that in practice people's sexuality does not fall into absolute categories. More important, Kinsey's research challenged views of same-sex sexuality that consider it a pathological and deviant condition, indicating that psychologically "normal" people may express their sexuality in many ways.

Anthropologists today emphasize that human sexuality is a highly flexible phenomenon that exists along a continuum and is associated with numerous possible expressions of sexual identity. Some of these expressions include lesbian sexuality (sexual attraction between women), gay sexuality (sexual attraction between men), straight sexuality (sexual attraction between men and women), asexuality (non-sexuality, or lack of sexual attraction), bisexuality (sexual attraction to both men and women), demisexuality (sexual attraction only to individuals with whom one has an emotional bond), and pansexuality (sexual attraction to individuals of any gender, including individuals outside the gender binary), among others. Anthropologists reject the notion that sexuality is an essence buried deep in a person's psychological self or genetic make-up

Figure 11.10 Controversial Knowledge. Kinsey's work was highly controversial during a period in American history when same-sex sexual encounters and sexual promiscuity were widely considered to be unacceptable.

(Lancaster 2004), or the notion that sexuality is just a matter of personal preference or individual orientation. Instead they argue that like other forms of social conduct, sexuality is learned, patterned, and shaped by culture and the political-economic system in which one lives (Weston 1993). The central role of culture in shaping sexuality can be seen in two issues we explore here: cross-cultural research on same-sex sexuality, and governments' attempts to shape and control the sexualities of their citizens.

Cultural Perspectives on Same-Sex Sexuality

Anthropological attention to same-sex sexuality goes back to the discipline's early years, when in the 1920s a handful of anthropologists wrote about sexual desires and practices in certain nonindustrialized societies (Lyons and Lyons 2004). Much of that work focused on whether same-sex sexuality was culturally acceptable in non-Western societies. But it was not until the 1960s and 1970s—when the emergence of a gay movement in the United States spurred even greater scholarly attention to issues of sexuality—that anthropologists began paying more consistent attention to issues of sexuality more generally, and the cultural dynamics of same-sex sexuality more specifically (Weston 1993). More recently, the global HIV/AIDS pandemic, the visibility of openly gay celebrities in media and television, and the push for legal rights for gay people have focused even more anthropological attention on issues of same-sex sexuality (Parker 2001; Lewin and Leap 2009).

Motivated by intellectual and personal concerns to gain comparative perspectives on same-sex sexuality, lesbian, gay, and bisexual-identified ethnographers have played a central role in developing cross-cultural studies of same-sex sexuality (Weston 1993). A number of these ethnographers have written about how their own experience of being gay affects their work as anthropologists (Lewin and Leap 1996), a theme we explore in "Doing Fieldwork: Don Kulick and 'Coming Out' in the Field."

One of the difficulties anthropologists studying same-sex sexuality in other societies have faced is the problem of adequately naming what they are studying (Weston 1993). Most North Americans hold the view that people are born straight or gay, implying a fixed and stable condition and identity. This notion originated in the late nineteenth century, when medical science and psychology turned what people had previously considered "perverse" *behaviors* into bio-psychological *conditions* requiring medical intervention. In many other cultures, this idea of same-sex sexuality as a fixed and exclusive condition does not exist. Anthropologists have found in other cultures that same-sex sexual behaviors can exist side by side with heterosexual behaviors, suggesting that sexuality is not an either/or condition in all cultures.

One example comes from the work of anthropologist Gilbert Herdt, who studied the male initiation rituals of the Sambia people of Papua New Guinea. Boys undergo six elaborate stages of initiation that involve behavior he calls "insemination." To be a strong, powerful warrior requires *jerungdu* (the essence of masculine strength), a substance a boy can acquire only from ingesting the semen of a man. Before insemination, the boys must purge harmful feminine essences with a rite that mimics female menstruation: sharp grasses are shoved up the noses of the boys to make them bleed off the lingering essences of their mother's milk. Finally, they receive *jerungdu* in the form of semen directly from young married men on whom they perform fellatio. During the early stages of the initiation, the boys are inseminated orally by the young married men at the height of their sexual and physical powers. When the initiates reach later stages of initiation—after marriage but before they become fathers—younger initiates will fellate them. The final stage of initiation occurs after the birth of their first child. Now in their twenties or thirties, the men have sex only with women, usually their wives, but they can have adulterous trysts with other women in the bush should the opportunity present itself.

Herdt (1981) referred to these initiation activities as "ritualized homosexuality," a term that highlights the homoerotic nature of these rites, since they are sexually

Doing Fieldwork
Don Kulick and "Coming Out" in the Field

IN BRAZIL'S THIRD-LARGEST CITY, Salvador, live nearly 200 *travestis* [trah-**vest**-tees], men who cross-dress and work as prostitutes. *Travestis* adopt female names, clothing styles, hairstyles, make-up, and linguistic pronouns (like "she"). They also ingest hormones and use silicone to acquire feminine bodily features, such as breasts, wide hips, large thighs, and expansive buttocks (Kulick 1998). Such practices might give the impression that these men want to be women or that they consider themselves transgender. But in fact they do not self-identify as women, nor do they desire to undergo sex-reassignment surgery. They consider themselves men—gay men—who desire to have sex with other men—non-gay men—and fashion themselves as an object of desire for those men.

Brazilians are fascinated by *travestis*, several of whom have become national celebrities. But the reality for most *travestis* is that they are discriminated against and poor, living a hand-to-mouth existence, and often dying young from violence, drug abuse, and health problems, particularly AIDS. During the late 1990s, Swedish anthropologist Don Kulick spent a year living among Salvador's *travestis* to understand the day-to-day realities of their lives.

Kulick believes that several factors helped him gain acceptance in the insular *travesti* community. One was that *travestis* were open to his involvement in their lives because they viewed Europeans as more liberal and cultivated than Brazilians, and they thought he would not have the same prejudices against their lives that Brazilians would. Another is that when Kulick started his fieldwork, he spoke very little Portuguese, so he could not communicate very well. *Travestis* came to see him as a nonthreatening presence, someone who would not condemn them.

Kulick believes a third factor played an especially crucial role in his gaining acceptance: he is himself a gay man. The *travestis* asked about his sexual orientation right away, if he was a *viado* (a "fag"). Kulick observes, "Upon receiving an affirmative answer, *travestis* often nodded and relaxed considerably. My status as a self-acknowledged *viado* implied to the *travestis* that I was, in effect, one of the girls, and that I probably was not interested in them as sexual partners. My behavior quickly confirmed that I was not, and after such preliminaries were out of the way, *travestis* realized that they could continue conversing about the topics—boyfriends, clients, big penises, hormone, and silicone—that occupy their time, without having to worry that I might find such topics uninteresting or offensive" (1998:15).

Previous research on *travestis* had been conducted by heterosexual women and a Brazilian male researcher who had presented himself as a potential client. These studies focused on their work as prostitutes, but these researchers had not gained access to the *travestis'* private worlds. Kulick

🔻 **A Travesti Dancing in a Bar in Rio de Janeiro, Brazil.**

(continued)

Doing Fieldwork (continued)

believes that "coming out" to the *travestis* as an openly gay man facilitated access to confidences and discussions that may not have been granted as easily to other researchers.

Questions for Reflection

1. Kulick argues that his access to his informants was benefited by his being gay and being seen as "one

of them." Would this extend to other identities? For example, would female anthropologists be more accepted by female informants, and would male anthropologists be more accepted by male informants? If so, does this mean that women should study women's lives and men should study men's lives?

2. Although Kulick reports his coming out as positive, it was also risky. What kinds of risks might his coming out have had?

arousing for the older men who are fellated. The problem with this terminology is that Western notions of "homosexuality" imply an inborn condition or identity, yet after marriage, Sambia men shift their erotic focus to their wives. Furthermore, the term implies that these acts are intended for erotic pleasure, while for the Sambia, these ritual acts are really intended to develop masculine strength. Herdt and others who study similar rites now refer to them as "semen transactions" or "boy-inseminating rites."

Other contexts raise similar questions about the appropriateness of Western terminology, and also indicate the situational nature of same-sex sexual behaviors. For example, some married Filipina women who migrate to Hong Kong to work as domestic maids consider sexual relationships with other women a "safe" and "moral" alternative to extramarital affairs with men. Affairs with men could end in pregnancy or shame for themselves and their families. So these normally heterosexual women enter into "Hong Kong only" affairs with "tomboys," lesbian women whom they view as sensitive and protective, with whom they can share intimacy while away from their families (Pei-Chia 2008). At no point do these women consider themselves "lesbian," and in fact they work hard to keep such relationships concealed from their families.

Anthropologists have also learned that concepts of same-sex sexuality differ across cultures. In Latin American countries like Mexico (Carrier 1976), Nicaragua (Lancaster 1992; 1997), and Brazil (Parker 1989), a man who engages in same-sex sexual practices is not necessarily identified as, nor would he consider himself, "gay." This notion comes from ideas about passivity and activity in sexual intercourse. For example, Brazilian sexual culture distinguishes being active and being passive participants in sexual intercourse, typically considering the active agent masculine, and the passive agent feminine. The metaphorical language people use to describe sex acts reflects these distinctions: *dar* ("to give") is the passive role of being penetrated during intercourse, while *comer* ("to eat") is the action of penetration (Parker 1989). "Women" and *viados* (a colloquial term meaning "fags" or gay men) are those who "give" (receive penetration), while "men" are the active ones who "eat" (penetrate). The result is that a man who penetrates another man would not consider himself—nor be considered by others—to be gay, yet the man being penetrated would be considered gay.

As Richard Parker (2009), an anthropologist who has studied Brazilian sexual culture, points out, these implicit sexual meanings can have major consequences for designing public health programs. Parker observes that, in the early years of the HIV/AIDS crisis, Brazilians uncritically accepted the notion derived from the

United States and Europe that HIV/AIDS was a "gay disease" transmitted through sex between men and affecting only the gay population. To create effective public health interventions, Parker advised, it was necessary to build programs around the specific Brazilian cultural meanings of sexuality, and not ignore the risky behaviors of men who did not consider themselves susceptible to HIV because they were "not gay."

As these examples suggest, many cultures around the globe do not share the mainstream American view of sexuality as a stable identity, around which cohesive social communities are formed. But as anthropologist Ellen Lewin (1993), who has studied lesbian parents in the United States, has found, even in the United States there is more subtlety to this issue than meets the eye. She writes that lesbian parents focus little energy on policing the boundaries of lesbian sexual identity. Instead of claiming an essential identity that they enforce on others, they negotiate their identities constantly in the face of continuous demands from their children, their lovers, the fathers of their children, and sometimes custody disputes over their children. For example, in custody disputes, they emphasize themselves not in terms of sexuality, but as women who have achieved motherhood and will make "good mothers." As Lewin (1996:107) explains, "Like other people, lesbians and gay men identify themselves along a number of axes, and while sexual orientation is often a salient dimension of their identification, other personal and social characteristics also feed into how they view themselves."

Controlling Sexuality

Long ago, anthropologists observed that every society places limits on people's sexuality by constructing rules about who can sleep with whom. But in the modern world, governments have asserted unprecedented levels of control over sexuality, routinely implementing and enforcing laws that limit the kinds of sexual relations their citizens can have. For example, in dozens of countries around the world, and even in 21 U.S. states, adultery is considered by the law to be "injurious to public morals and a mistreatment of the marriage relationship" and is treated by authorities as a civil offense (subject to fines) or even a crime (subject to jail time). And until the U.S. Supreme Court overturned such laws in 2003, 15 states still outlawed "sodomy," or sex acts considered "unnatural" or "immoral," such as anal sex, oral sex, or same-sex sex acts. In our country, the most contentious public issues—including debates about abortion, gays in the military, and the right to same-sex marriage—involve questions over whether and how the government should control the sexuality of its citizens.

Family-planning programs can also be viewed as another manifestation of government control over sexuality—especially women's sexuality, since such programs tend to focus on women's bodies (Dwyer 2000). China's well-known "One Child Policy," which, until it was phased out in 2015, limited most families to one child, reducing fertility rates and unemployment significantly. But it also involved unprecedented government control over sexuality, including (until 2002, when it was outlawed) forced abortions and sterilizations of women who exceeded their quota or were deemed "unfit" to reproduce.

• •

THINKING CRITICALLY ABOUT GENDER, SEX, AND SEXUALITY

Many queer activists in the United States and Europe have accepted and promote the idea that they were "born" with their sexual identity and that they have no choice in the matter. How do you think anthropologists, who view sexuality as culturally patterned, socially conditioned, and not inborn, should respond to this idea?

• •

Conclusion

The concept of sexuality connects back to concepts we considered earlier in this chapter, namely gender and sex. Although they traditionally have distinct definitions, each of these concepts touches on an issue of central importance to human existence, which is our capacity for sexual reproduction. Yet these concepts are intertwined in complex ways, shaping the ideas and social patterns a society uses to organize males, females, and others who do not fit these neat categories, such as intersexuals and gender variants.

It is important to remember that how we think of sex, gender, and sexuality, as natural as our ideas may feel to us, is not as universal as we may assume. Returning to the Liberian example of cross-dressing warriors that opened this chapter, it would be quite easy—but deeply mistaken—to explain warrior cross-dressing as some kind of perverted erotic fantasy, just because that is how many of us tend to think of cross-dressing in our own culture. But cross-dressing Liberian warriors—both the male rebels who wore women's clothing and the women close to the rebel leadership who donned camouflaged uniforms and matching high heels—were self-consciously engaging with their own traditional notions of sex and gender, specifically mixing male and female symbols to draw on the mystical power of both.

It is also good to remember that matters of sex, gender, and sexuality are not necessarily as stable as they feel to us. Just as Liberian rebels were rather quick to drop cross-dressing in favor of Rambo-style clothing, our own notions of sex, gender, and sexuality are dynamic and fluid as well. Not only does our own society have more diversity and flexibility in sexual practices and gender identification than our cultural categories tend to acknowledge, the very notion of sexuality as an inborn condition is a relatively new one in Western history. The reason these things feel so stable to us in our everyday experience is that they are powerful cultural constructions reproduced and upheld in our everyday lives and most important social institutions.

KEY TERMS

Cisgender   p. 290

Gender   p. 278

Gender variance   p. 287

Gender/sex system
   p. 278

Intersex   p. 280

Masculinity   p. 285

Sex   p. 277

Sexuality   p. 287

Sexually dimorphic
   p. 280

Third genders   p. 287

Transgender   p. 290

Reviewing the Chapter

Chapter Section	What We Know	To Be Resolved
How and Why do Males and Females Differ?	Every society makes a distinction between "male" and "female." But not all societies have the firm binary between males and females we find in Western cultures. Gender/sex systems are cross-culturally variable and historically dynamic, and not all attach the same meanings to apparent biological differences, or even think differences in biology are important for explaining differences between males and females.	Anthropologists continue to work out the relative influences of biological, environmental, and cultural factors on shaping gender.
Why Is There Inequality Between Men and Women?	Biological differences are not the source of women's subordination. Rather, cultural ideologies and social relations impose on women lower status, prestige, and power than men.	The debate over the universality of women's subordinate status was never resolved, and in recent years, new debates have emerged about the extent to which gender inequalities are performed by women and men.
What Does It Mean to Be Neither Male Nor Female?	Many gender/sex systems around the world allow for gender variance and third genders. Gender variants generally establish their unique identities through social performance: wearing certain clothes, speaking and moving in certain ways, and performing certain social roles and occupations.	Western terminology and concepts are not always able to capture the complexity of how other cultures conceive of matters of sex, gender, and sexuality, which raises questions about how to best represent such phenomena.
Is Human Sexuality Just a Matter of Being Straight or Queer?	Human sexuality is variable and patterned by cultural ideologies and social relations. It is also not a fixed or exclusive condition.	Anthropologists continue to work through the complex and subtle ways sexuality interacts with gender, as well as other identities like class, race, and ethnicity.

Readings

The work of biologist Anne Fausto-Sterling, including her book *Sexing the Body: Gender Politics and the Construction of Sexuality* (New York: Basic Books, 2000), offers useful and compelling perspectives on the construction of sex, gender, and sexuality, and especially on the ways societies have dealt with intersex individuals. Caroline Brettell and Carolyn Fishel Sargent's edited reader *Gender in Cross-Cultural Perspective* (sixth edition, New York: Routledge, 2013) offers a range of anthropological arguments and case studies about these issues.

For an overview of feminist anthropology and debates over male–female inequality, see Sherry Ortner's book *Making Gender: The Politics and Erotics of Culture* (Boston, MA: Beacon Press, 1996). Amrita Basu's edited volume *Women's Movements in the Global Era: The Power of Local Feminisms* (second edition; Boulder, CO: Westview Press, 2016) offers a recent assessment of the diversity of feminisms that exist in the world.

Gilbert Herdt's edited book *Third Sex, Third Gender: Beyond Sexual Dimorphism in Culture and History* (New York: Zone Books, 1994) offers a comprehensive overview of gender variance in many cultures. Serena Nanda's book *Neither Man nor Woman: The Hijras of India* (second edition, Boston, MA: Cengage, 1999) is a classic ethnographic study of gender variance in India.

Andrew P. Lyons and Harriet D. Lyons's book *Irregular Connections: A History of Anthropology and Sexuality* (Lincoln, NE: University of Nebraska Press, 2004) examines anthropology's long fascination with the study of sexuality, as well as the dilemmas it has raised. It pairs well with Don Kulick's ethnography of sexuality among transgender prostitutes in Brazil, *Travesti: Sex, Gender, and Culture Among Brazilian Transgendered Prostitutes* (Chicago, IL: University of Chicago Press, 1998).

Kinship, Marriage, and the Family

Love, Sex, and Power

SOAP OPERAS LIKE *General Hospital, The Bold and the Beautiful, Days of Our Lives*, and *The Young and the Restless* are among the world's most popular and enduring television genres. Every day, hundreds of millions of women and men around the globe tune into one or more of them. Although some of these American soaps have enjoyed international popularity, it is Latin American shows—produced and exported by Mexicans, Venezuelans, Argentines, and Brazilians in particular—that have ruled screens worldwide during the past two decades.

One of the most popular Latin American exports of all time is the Mexican *telenovela* [tay-**lay**-noh-**vell**-ah] (as such shows are called in Spanish) *Los Ricos También Lloran* ("The Rich Also Cry"). Produced in 1979, it has enjoyed tremendous popularity and been rebroadcast in dozens of countries throughout the Americas, Europe, Asia, and Africa to the present day. Telenovelas usually run for only a few months and have a clear ending, unlike American soaps, which are long-running and open-ended—*As the World Turns*, for example, the second-longest continuously running TV program in the United States, ran from April 1956 to September 2010, with more than 13,000 episodes.

The basic plot, which many subsequent telenovelas have imitated, is as follows: A beautiful and poor young woman named Mariana becomes a maid for a rich and powerful family. She and the youngest

🌱 **Kinship and the Latin American Telenovela.** Latin American soap operas called telenovelas such as the Mexican show pictured here, *Ni Contigo Ni Sin Ti* ("Neither With You Nor Without You"), have captivated global audiences for decades because of the complicated, if perhaps unlikely, kin relations they present.

IN THIS CHAPTER

What Are Families, and How Are They Structured in Different Societies?
- Families, Ideal and Real
- Nuclear and Extended Families
- Clans and Lineages
- Kinship Terminologies
- Cultural Patterns in Childrearing

How Do Families Control Power and Wealth?
- Claiming a Bride
- Recruiting the Kids
- The Dowry in India: Providing a Financial Safety Net for a Bride
- Controlling Family Wealth Through Inheritance

Why Do People Get Married?
- Why People Get Married
- Forms of Marriage
- Sex, Love, and the Power of Families Over Young Couples

How Are Social and Technological Changes Reshaping How People Think About Family?
- International Adoptions and the Problem of Cultural Identity
- In Vitro Fertilization
- Surrogate Mothers and Sperm Donors

301

son in the family, Luis Alberto, have a scandalous love affair and eventually get married. She has a baby son, Beto, but in a fit of temporary madness, she gives him away to an old woman on the street.

During the next 18 years, Mariana searches desperately for Beto and miraculously finds him when he begins dating Marisabel, who is Mariana and Luis Alberto's adopted daughter (though she doesn't know she's adopted). Mariana tells Marisabel who Beto really is. Marisabel becomes hysterical at the thought of incest with her brother. Mariana does not, however, tell Luis Alberto, fearing he will get angry with her. He gets angry anyway because she spends so much time with Beto that Luis Alberto suspects the two are having an affair. In the final episode, Luis Alberto confronts Beto and Mariana with a gun. In the program's final moments, Mariana screams, "Son!" Luis Alberto goes ballistic. Beto screams, "Father, let me embrace you!" and the family is, against all odds, reunited at long last.

Dark family secrets, suspicious spouses, unruly children, irresponsible parents, and possible incest make for gripping television, to say the least! But to an anthropologist—if not also for many viewers around the world—the fascination this show holds is not due simply to its unlikely storyline, but to its presentation of the complexities of love, sex, and power that are part and parcel of being in any family, anywhere in the world.

Also noteworthy is the show's assumption that blood relations are the central defining relationships in people's lives—after all, Luis Alberto's anger disappears when he realizes Beto is his son, and Marisabel would probably not be so hysterical if she knew Beto wasn't her biological brother. For anthropologists, it is a noteworthy assumption mainly because it reflects one particular culture's way of defining family relationships. Around the world, not all cultures give the same weight to biological relatedness for defining a family.

The biological facts of procreation are only one aspect of what it means to have a family. What is more important is how these biological facts are interpreted, and the special rights and obligations that these facts confer on individuals. At the heart of anthropology's interest in families is the question: *How are families more than just groups of biologically related people?* Embedded within this larger question are the following questions, around which this chapter is organized.

What are families, and how are they structured in different societies?

How do families control power and wealth?

Why do people get married?

How are social and technological changes reshaping how people think about family?

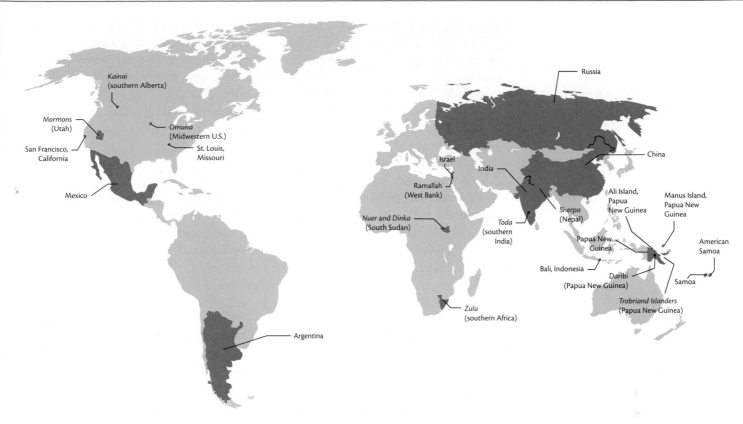

Figure 12.1   Select Peoples and Places Discussed in Chapter 12.

The kinds of influence and control people can exert on their relatives varies widely from one society to another. Yet anthropologists have long recognized that we cannot understand a society until we understand the core relationships of kinship, marriage, and family around which people's social lives are lived. So let us begin by considering what makes a group of relatives a family.

What Are Families, and How Are They Structured in Different Societies?

Families are important in nearly every society. They give members a sense of comfort and belonging and provide them with part of their identity, values, and ideals. They control wealth and the material necessities of life. And, importantly, they assign individuals with basic roles, rights, and responsibilities in relation to other relatives.

It probably feels natural to you that your own family does all (or most) of these things. What is *not* natural is how and why your family is organized and achieves these things in the ways it does. Like other aspects of culture we've explored throughout this book, **kinship**—the social system that organizes people in families based on descent and marriage—is patterned in culturally specific and dynamic ways. We begin by exploring its dynamism, and then we examine the different ways families can be organized cross-culturally.

• **Kinship.** The social system that organizes people in families based on descent and marriage.

Families, Ideal and Real

In every society, a gap exists between that society's ideal family and the real families that exist, the reason being that all families are dynamic. For example, as individuals grow older, they move out of their **natal family**—the family into which they were born and in which they are (usually) raised—to marry and start their own families. In addition, broader social and economic conditions change the composition, size, and character of the ties between family members, as the example of the American family illustrates.

American politicians and religious leaders frequently extol the virtues of the "traditional" family. But just what family do these people have in mind as their model? Most likely, it is some version of the family in the television show *The Adventures of Ozzie and Harriet* (which aired from 1952 to 1966), with a working husband/father who is the head of the household, a loving stay-at-home wife/mother, and two or three children living in a spic-and-span suburban home.

The problem is that the Ozzie and Harriet ideal is not a "traditional" family, but a new pattern—the independent American suburban family—that emerged in the 1950s and lasted for less than 20 years. Only 20 years before then, during the Great Depression of the 1930s, American birth rates had fallen sharply; with limited income, most families refrained from having children. The birth rate remained low from 1942 to 1946 because so many men were serving in the military during World War II. But once these millions of men returned, they began to marry and start families. The 1950s were a time of unprecedented economic growth, and the "baby boom"— 77 million babies in 15 years—encouraged the expansion of new subdivisions filled with these young families. By the late 1950s, around 60% of all Americans lived in such families (Figure 12.2).

During the late 1960s and 1970s, these young post-war families had grown up, children had moved out, and some couples had divorced. These changes paralleled changes in the economy as women began to join the workforce in larger numbers, lowering wages for entry-level jobs. By the 1980s, it was hard for young American families to get by on one salary. Two-income households brought in more wages but put stress on couples, who still needed someone to cook their meals, clean their houses or apartments, and look after their children. Nowadays, families tend to have one or two children rather than three or four. Divorce has become much more common

- **Natal family.** The family into which a person is born and in which she or he is (usually) raised.

Figure 12.2   Which Is the "Traditional American Family"? Is it the TV sitcom family in *Leave It to Beaver* (*left*), or the American farm family in the late nineteenth century (*right*, the extended family of Harold Harding Cunningham of Wilson County, Tennessee)?

than ever before in American life, and today only half of American households are headed by a married couple. When divorced couples with kids get remarried, the composition of a family (with multiple sets of step-parents and step-siblings)—and especially the obligations individuals in it have to each other—can get quite complicated. Such families are sometimes referred to as "blended families," which include full siblings, half-siblings, and step-siblings.

Nuclear and Extended Families

Still, the **nuclear family**—the family formed by a married couple and their children—is the most important family structure in the United States. Ours is not the only society with nuclear families—nuclear family units occur in and are important to nearly every society around the world. Indeed, for many decades, anthropologists wrote of the nuclear family as the most basic unit of kinship (Radcliffe-Brown 1941:2).

Using a basic **kinship chart** (a visual representation of family relationships), we can graph a man's nuclear family easily enough, and we can add another nuclear family for his wife's natal family, and add children (Figure 12.3). Such charts describe biological connections—such as mother–daughter or father–daughter—without expressing the content of these different relationships. For example, when a child is young, the relationship between parent and child may involve teaching and training. But when the widowed mother moves in with her child's family, the content of the relationship is entirely different, even though the biological relationship has not changed. The son or daughter may now look after the finances of the aging parent, but he or she remains the mother's biological child.

One important feature of nuclear and natal families is that they usually function as **corporate groups**, which are groups of people who work together toward common ends, much as a corporation does. The family's goals are not just the goals of one family member, but of the group as a whole. In every society around the world, families are supposed to look after the needs of all members of the family—parents, children, and any other family members who happen to be in residence.

- **Nuclear family.** The family formed by a married couple and their children.

- **Kinship chart.** A visual representation of family relationships.

- **Corporate groups.** Groups of people who work together toward common ends, much as a corporation does.

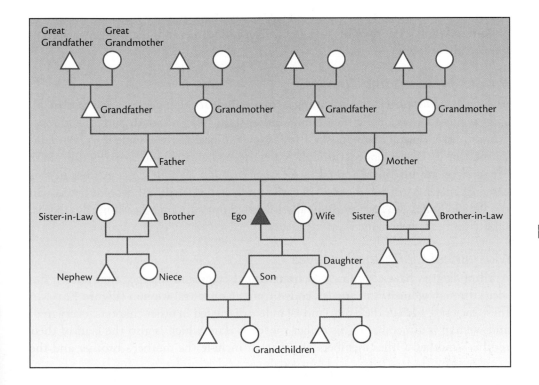

Figure 12.3 A Kinship Chart Plots Out All Sorts of Kin Relations. Here the chart shows members of the extended family from a husband/father's perspective (identified as "Ego" in the chart). Of course, the chart could be drawn from the wife/mother's perspective as well.

Figure 12.4 Extended Families in North America.
(*Top*) An Indian family from the Kainai tribe in the Canadian plains about 1900. (*Bottom*) An American extended family gathers for a reunion in Mt. Carmel, Illinois, in 1904. Everyone in the photo is descended from one deceased couple, parents of seven of the senior women pictured.

- **Extended families.** Larger groups of relatives beyond the nuclear family, often living in the same household.

- **Clan.** A group of relatives who claim to be descended from a single ancestor.

- **Exogamous.** A social pattern in which members of a clan must marry someone from another clan, which has the effect of building political, economic, and social ties with other clans.

- **Lineage.** A group composed of relatives who are directly descended from known ancestors.

- **Patrilineal.** Reckoning descent through males from the same ancestors.

- **Unilineal.** Based on descent through a single descent line, either males or females.

Family groups may also consist of larger groups of relatives beyond the nuclear family, which anthropologists call **extended families** (Figure 12.4). Extended families may live together and function as a corporate group, or they may merely acknowledge ties with one another. In nineteenth-century America, for example, it was common for households to include a nuclear family at its core, as well as some mix of elderly parents, a single brother or sister, the orphaned children of the wife's sister, and perhaps another niece or nephew. Nowadays, for many Americans, only special events like funerals, weddings, and family reunions bring large extended families together.

Clans and Lineages

Sometimes Americans will jokingly refer to their extended family as their "clan." But for anthropologists, the term **clan** refers to something different: a special group of relatives who are all descended (or claim to descend) from a single ancestor. In many societies, links to these ancestors can be quite vague, and in a number of societies, these "ancestors" are animals or humans with distinctive nonhuman characteristics. Clans are often as important as nuclear families in the small-scale societies anthropologists have studied in Oceania, Africa, and the Americas. So much so that in the 1940s, French anthropologist Claude Lévi-Strauss (1969a) challenged the importance of the nuclear family as the basic unit of kinship, arguing instead for the importance of clans as basic units of kinship. Clans typically control land and other resources, as well as any individual member's access to those resources. They are also usually **exogamous**, which means that members of the clan must marry someone from another clan, which has the effect of building political, economic, and social ties with other clans. Clans come in three types: patrilineal, matrilineal, and cognatic. **Lineages** are very similar to clans, but lineages tend to be composed of people who are directly descended from known ancestors, while clan membership is often more vague and assumed rather than empirically known.

Patrilineal Clans and Lineages

The most common clans and lineages in nonindustrial societies are **patrilineal**, such as those found among the Omaha Indians, the Nuer of South Sudan, and most groups in the Central Highlands of Papua New Guinea. In these societies, clan members claim to be descended through males from the same ancestor (Figure 12.5). These clans are **unilineal** (based on descent through a single descent line, in this case, the male). Most Americans will easily understand patrilineal descent because in the United States, we have traditionally inherited our surnames patrilineally; that is, taking on the family name from the father.

Matrilineal Clans and Lineages

Anthropologists have also observed **matrilineal** clans and lineages that reckon descent through women, and are descended from an ancestral woman (Figure 12.6). In these societies, such as the Trobriand Islanders discussed in other chapters, every man and woman is a member of his or her mother's clan, which is also the clan of their mother's mother. Other members of this clan include the mother's brother and the

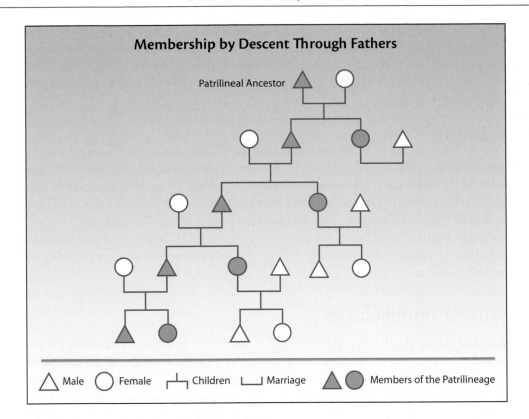

Figure 12.5 Members of a Patrilineage (shaded). Descent is through males.

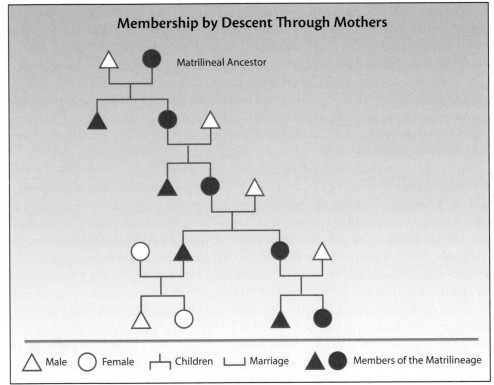

Figure 12.6 Members of a Matrilineage (shaded). Descent is through females.

mother's mother's brother. A person's strongest identity is with his or her relatives in a mother's clan and lineage.

Matrilineality is not the same as matriarchy, in which women hold political power. Matrilineality is only about identity and group membership. In matrilineal societies, land is usually owned by the clan or by a lineage within a larger clan. While women

- **Matrilineal.** Reckoning descent through women, who are descended from an ancestral woman.

may have some say in who uses clan land for gardens or for gathering material for building houses, it is usually the men in the clan who have control over these resources. As such, a young man will look to his mother's brother for guidance and assistance, just as this uncle had looked to his own mother's brother for direction when he was young.

Cognatic Clans

A third kind of clan is the **cognatic** clan (or bilateral clan), such as is found among the Samoans of Central Polynesia. Samoans reckon descent through both the mother and the father, allowing people to be members of both their mother's and their father's clan. The main difference between a cognatic clan and a unilineal clan is that in cognatic clans, one can be a member of any of several clans, and in some societies, multiple membership is possible or even typical. Matrilineal and patrilineal clans, in contrast, are naturally bounded by who a person's mother or father is, respectively.

Kinship Terminologies

Another way to think about the structure of families is to explore terms that people in different societies use to refer to their relatives. Since the 1860s, when American anthropologist Lewis Henry Morgan (1871) collected kinship terminologies from many different languages around the world, anthropologists have collected thousands of different kinship terminologies, but it happens that all of them can be grouped into the six basic patterns Morgan identified (Figure 12.7). Morgan and several other anthropologists from the cultural-evolution school tried to identify some kinship terminologies as more evolved and sophisticated than others. Anthropologist A. L. Kroeber (1909) identified and summarized the basic principles of kinship terminologies by arguing that kinship terminologies are shaped by the kind of clan organization found in a society, not by a group's position on some evolutionary scale. We explore how all kinship systems classify various kin into basic social categories in "Classic Contributions: A. L. Kroeber on Classificatory Systems of Relationship."

This early research on kinship terminologies has been highly influential for two reasons. One of these is the realization that underlying the diversity of terminologies are a few basic systems of organizing people, which we present in Figure 12.6. The second is that anthropologists have come to realize that kinship terminologies do not just provide descriptive names that indicate relationships between individuals, but can also indicate the specific nature of the relationship, rights, and responsibilities that exist between related people. In other words, the term you use to identify a person shapes how you should interact with that person. For example, in many American Indian societies, an individual will use the term *father* to refer, not just to his biological father, but to his father's brothers or even other men of his father's generation with no direct biological ties. The "father" is expected to interact with his "son" in certain culturally accepted ways, such as providing food or other assistance.

Another thing kinship terminologies do is help people keep track of their many relatives by assigning categorical terms. But nobody can keep track of everybody. Each society has kinsmen that are vital to keep track of, while others, usually more distant relatives, are forgotten. Anthropologists refer to this structural process of forgetting whole groups of relatives as **genealogical amnesia**. We explore this phenomenon in more detail in "Thinking Like an Anthropologist: Genealogical Amnesia in Bali, Indonesia, and the United States."

- **Cognatic.** Reckoning descent through either men or women from some ancestor.

- **Genealogical amnesia.** The structural process of forgetting whole groups of relatives, usually because they are not currently significant in one's social life.

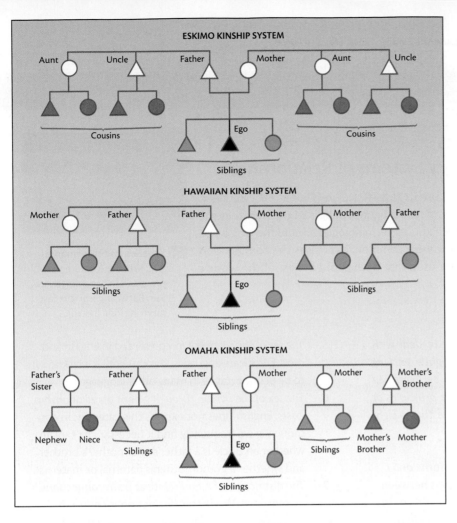

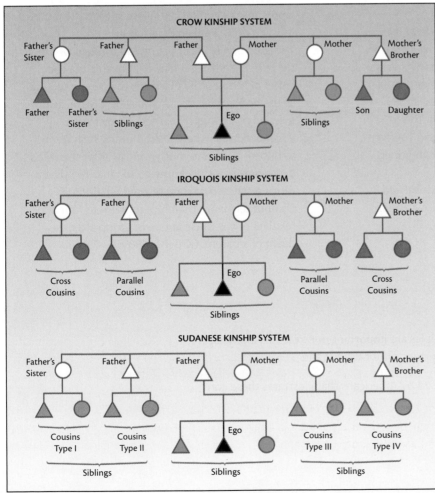

Figure 12.7 The Six Basic Systems of Kinship. Anthropologists have identified six different basic kinship systems, which correspond to the patterns suggested by anthropologist Lewis Henry Morgan in the late nineteenth century. The differences between them can be understood by how people refer to their different cousins.

Classic Contributions
A. L. Kroeber on Classificatory Systems of Relationship

IN 1909, ANTHROPOLOGIST A. L. KROEBER (1876–1960) at U.C. Berkeley, one of early American anthropology's most influential figures, published the view that the key to understanding the differences between kinship terminologies around the world was to understand eight general principles. Most were common, but it was the combination of principles and how completely they were used that distinguished most of the world's different kin terminologies.

Kroeber and Informants. A. L. Kroeber (center) with American Indian informants Sam Batwi and Ishi (the last surviving Yahi Indian).

It is apparent that what we should try to deal with is not the hundreds or thousands of slightly varying relationships that are expressed or can be expressed by the various languages of man, but the principles or categories of relationship which underlie these. Eight such categories are discernible.

1. *The difference between persons of the same and of separate generations.* The distinctions between father and grandfather, between uncle and cousin, and between a person and his father involve the recognition of this category.

2. *The difference between lineal and collateral relationship.* When the father and the father's brother are distinguished, this category is operative. When only one term is employed for brother and cousin, it is inoperative.

3. *Difference of age within one generation.* The frequent distinction between the older and younger brother is an instance. In English, this category is not operative.

4. *The sex of the relative.* This distinction is carried out . . . consistently by English, the one exception being the foreign word cousin. . . .

5. *The sex of the speaker.* Unrepresented in English and most European languages, this category is well known to be of importance in many other languages. . . .

6. *The sex of the person through whom the relationship exists.* English does not express this category. In consequence we frequently find it necessary to explain whether an uncle is a father's or a mother's brother, and whether a grandmother is paternal or maternal.

7. *The distinction of blood relatives from connections by marriage.* While this distinction is commonly expressed by most languages, there are occasional lapses; just as in familiar English speech the father-in-law is often spoken of as father. . . .

8. *The condition of life of the person through whom the relationship exists.* The relationship may be either of blood or by marriage; the person serving as the bond of relationship may be alive or dead, married or no longer married. Many North American Indians refrain from using such terms as father-in-law and mother-in-law after the wife's death or separation. Some go so far as to possess terms restricted to such severed relationship. . . . Distinct terms are therefore sometimes found for relatives of the uncle and aunt group after the death of a parent. (Kroeber 1909:78–79)

Questions for Reflection

1. Which of these eight classificatory principles are important principles in American kin terms, and which are either less important or not used at all?

2. Give an example of a pair of kin terms used by Americans that illustrates these core principles.

Thinking Like an Anthropologist
Genealogical Amnesia in Bali, Indonesia, and the United States

ANTHROPOLOGISTS BEGIN THEIR research by asking questions. In this box, we want you to learn how to ask questions as an anthropological researcher. Part One describes a situation and follows up with questions we would ask. Part Two asks you to formulate your own questions based on a different situation.

PART ONE: GENEALOGICAL AMNESIA AND NAMING PATTERNS ON THE ISLAND OF BALI

In the late 1950s, American anthropologists Hildred and Clifford Geertz (1964, 1975) studied Balinese kinship patterns on the lush, tropical island of Bali in Indonesia. The Balinese have a bilateral kinship system, which means that an individual is related equally to relatives in his or her mother's and father's families (much as Americans are). People are more or less "closely" related, at least in theory, to everyone who is descended from any one of their 16 great-great-grandparents. That is a lot of relatives!

How do the Balinese keep track of them all? The Geertzes found that people don't. While Balinese lived in large extended family groups, the number of relatives they actually interacted with was limited to a few dozen members. Most informants were aware of only a couple hundred kinsmen rather than the thousands that were theoretically possible. The Geertzes referred to this forgetting of relatives as "genealogical amnesia."

🌱 **A Modern Balinese Family Attending a Ceremony.** Most members of this extended family live together in several households inside the same house yard.

Genealogical amnesia was not about how particular individuals literally forgot some of their relatives, but about how features of normal social life encourage people to focus on some relatives so that other relatives gradually drift off their radar screen.

The Geertzes learned that genealogical amnesia was not random, but quite systematic. It is the result of a particular naming system. All Balinese have personal names, and as in the United States and other countries, parents often name their children after grandparents, aunts and uncles, and great-grandparents. But after Balinese men and women marry, they are no longer called by their personal names; they are referred to as "father of so-and-so" or "mother of so-and-so." As their children get older and marry, these parents will begin to be referred to as "grandfather of so-and-so" or "grandmother of so-and-so." (Anthropologists call this naming practice *teknonymy*, a system of naming parents by the names of their children.)

In Bali, the teknonyms assigned to individuals kept changing over time as people got older. The effect of this was that none of the younger people had ever heard the personal names of their grandparents and great-grandparents. The effect of this rather simple naming system was that everyone knew they were related to everyone who was a descendant of a great-grandparent—who would be known as "great-grandfather of so-and-so" or "great-grandmother of so-and-so." But it also obscured relatives, since all the personal names several generations back were no longer used in conversation. Earlier generations were known only by the names of their first-born grandchildren or great-grandchildren, and even these identifications became difficult to pick out of daily conversation after people in those generations had died.

What questions does this situation raise for anthropological researchers?

1. How does being a grandchild of someone with a particular teknonym help you identify other close relatives?
2. What happens to people's knowledge of their common kin ties once their great-grandparents die?
3. How might people be able to identify kin relations more easily if everyone used personal names rather than teknonyms?

(continued)

Thinking Like an Anthropologist (continued)

PART TWO: GENEALOGICAL AMNESIA IN AMERICAN FAMILIES

In the United States, naming practices also produce a systematic pattern of genealogical amnesia. One of the most obvious effects of genealogical amnesia comes from the practice of women dropping their maiden names when they marry. This practice was typical until the 1970s, and it remains fairly common today. What questions would you ask about genealogical amnesia in the United States as an anthropological researcher?

Figure 12.8   Ruth Benedict and *Patterns of Culture.*
An important culture and personality scholar was Ruth Benedict, who was a teacher and close friend of Margaret Mead. Benedict's book *Patterns of Culture* (1934) is a major work in American anthropology and popular in its own right, read by millions of undergraduates and translated into two dozen languages. Benedict argued that particular cultures produce more or less consistent patterns of thought and action in individuals and create a single personality type. By the 1950s, anthropologists had rejected this argument, but Benedict is still considered a major figure in the discipline's early decades.

Cultural Patterns in Childrearing

Nearly a century ago, the anthropologist Margaret Mead began studying how families raised children in different cultures. Between the 1930s and the 1950s, Mead was associated with a loosely connected group of scholars known as the **culture and personality movement**, whose focus was on how patterns of childrearing, social institutions, and cultural ideologies shaped individual experience, personality characteristics, and thought patterns (Hsu 1972) (Figure 12.8). Their assumption was that how a child is bathed, fed, and attended to in the first years of life shapes his or her approach to the world, not only in childhood but in adulthood as well. Most culture and personality studies tried to show that our individual (or collective) psychologies were shaped primarily by our environment (nurture) rather than by our biology (nature). While conducting her first fieldwork project, a detailed study of the kinship system and social organization in American Samoa (Mead 1930a, 1930b), Mead observed how Samoan families were caring for their children. Mead wrote about these things in her popular book *Coming of Age in Samoa* (1928), which looked at the sexual behavior of Samoan adolescents. Mead viewed Samoan adolescent sexuality, which lacked a lot of the psychological distress and anxiety typical of American adolescent sexuality, as a reflection of a culturally distinct childrearing process. Samoan approaches to childrearing involve children in work early in their lives and don't judge maturity by a child's age but according to outward physical changes, such as those associated with puberty.

Throughout the 1930s, Mead continued to study patterns of childrearing cross-culturally. While conducting research with her second husband, Reo Fortune, Mead observed childrearing on Manus Island (a small island located to the northeast of New Guinea) and among three mainland tribes of New Guinea (Mead 1930a, 1930b, 1935). A few years later, she and her third husband, Gregory Bateson, pioneered the use of photographs and motion pictures in their analysis of childrearing on the island of Bali in what is now Indonesia (Sullivan 1999). They used photographs of Balinese parents tending to their children in their book *Balinese Character* (1942), which was an effort to document how childrearing practices influenced the ways Balinese interacted with the world as adults.

Although Mead and Bateson's work receives less attention today, it is clear from a variety of more recent studies by anthropologists and sociologists that parental investment of time and nurturing makes a difference in how much children aspire to achieve as adolescents and adults. Anthropologists in particular have focused on how middle-class and upper-middle-class families have an ideology and the resources to emphasize education and concerted self-improvement, while poor families with fewer resources have less time for nurturing children because they are struggling to keep their families fed and clothed (see, e.g., Stack 1997; Lareau 2003). Mead made a similar point in her 1958 black-and-white film *Four Families*, which showed visually how childrearing in India, France, Japan, and rural Canada led to differences in the ways people interacted as adults (Mead 2001).

We have seen in this section that whether societies place emphasis on small nuclear family groups or on extended kin groups organized as lineages or clans, families organize corporate activities within the group and relationships with people in other groups. Let us turn now to how families control wealth and power.

- **Culture and personality movement.** A school of thought in early and mid–twentieth-century American anthropology that studied how patterns of child-rearing, social institutions, and cultural ideologies shape individual experience, personality characteristics, and thought patterns.

THINKING CRITICALLY ABOUT KINSHIP, MARRIAGE, AND THE FAMILY

Lewis Henry Morgan thought of American kinship as the most rational way of reckoning kin relationships, and he referred to our system as a descriptive rather than classificatory system because relatives on a person's mother's side were called the same thing as those on a person's father's side. But, in fact, terms like "aunt," "uncle," and "cousin" group together very different kinds of relatives under the same label, which makes our system a "classificatory" system. Using your own family as an example, discuss how these terms are classificatory even if "mother," "father," "son," and "daughter" are not.

How Do Families Control Power and Wealth?

Whatever form of family we might find in a society, one of its key functions is controlling and managing its members' wealth. The most obvious way for a family, lineage, or clan group to control its wealth is by defining rights over the productive and reproductive abilities of its women and children, as well as defining the inheritance rights of family members when someone dies. We explore each of these issues in turn next.

Claiming a Bride

In the nonindustrial societies anthropologists studied in the early and mid–twentieth century in Africa, South America, and the Pacific, it was clear that women provided much of the labor needed to plant, weed, and harvest food from their fields and gardens. Even though men performed the most active herding and hunting tasks, women often helped with gathering nuts, fruit, greens, and raw materials for houses, and with fishing. Women's labor is critical in these societies, and when a young woman marries, her family loses her efforts in raising or gathering food for the family.

Every person in such societies is valuable, so to compensate another clan for losing a person, the groom's family gives valuables to the bride's family in what has been called bride wealth, bride price payments, or simply **bride price.** Bride price compensates the woman's natal family for the loss of her productive and reproductive abilities.

- **Bride price (or bride wealth).** Gifts or money given by the groom's clan or family to compensate the bride's clan or family for the loss of one of its women along with her productive and reproductive abilities.

🌱 **Figure 12.9   Bride price.** (*Top*) A Dinka man in East Africa readies his cattle for bride price exchange with his in-laws. (*Bottom*) Cash has replaced traditional shell valuables in many bride price payments in Papua New Guinea.

The patrilineal Zulu tribes of southern Africa, for example, traditionally used cattle for their bride price payments. When a young man had identified a young woman that he was interested in as a wife, his male relatives began negotiations about her bride price, which Zulu call *lobola*. These negotiations marked the beginning of the couple's engagement. Typically the man sought the assistance of male relatives in his patrilineage. The bride price is paid as a series of gifts from the groom to his father-in-law, the first gift of several head of cattle occurring at the time of the marriage. Later the man gives gifts of cattle until the entire bride price has been given. Anthropologist Max Gluckman (1940) reported that the South African government viewed these multiple *lobola* payments as a practice that disrupted the flow of young men to the mines as laborers. It seems that these men wanted to stay in their villages working to assemble the cattle they needed and were not eager to set off as mine workers. The government plan was to limit *lobola* to 11 head of cattle, all of which should be paid at the time of marriage. This plan, together with a tax levied on each Zulu hut, forced young men to work in the mines but disrupted the normal pattern of marriage, since most wives stayed back in their husband's village, and there was no opportunity for the man to build bonds with his father-in-law.

In some tribal societies, other kinds of valuables can be given as bridewealth, including wild game in some Amazon communities, or pigs and shell valuables in many New Guinea societies (Figure 12.9). In other societies, a young man has to work for his wife's family for a year or more, performing what can be called "bride service."

Recruiting the Kids

As with bride price payments aimed at paying for rights in women, "child price" payments are another kind of payment to a woman's family intended to buy rights in the woman's children. Such payments compensate the woman's family for a child who belongs to a different clan, and they allow the father to recruit the child to his clan. This sort of transaction over children is most typical in societies with patrilineal clans, rather than in those with matrilineal clans, where the children belong to their mother's clan and typically live with her. In some societies, child price payments can be paid all at once, but the power of these transactions can best be understood in societies like the Daribi of the Highlands of Papua New Guinea, where payments may take place over many years. Anthropologist Roy Wagner (1967, 1969) described these gifts as countering the rights and claims of the child's uncle (mother's brother) over these children. This uncle could claim the child for his clan if the payments were not made. Because so many transactions between clans are about creating alliances, the ongoing series of payments preserves and perpetuates the relationship between the child's father and the uncle. In this case, the payments in the form of gifts define and bind the two clans, just as they link the two men in an ongoing alliance. Both men get something from the relationship, including assistance from the other when needed.

One significant variation on this pattern occurs when marriage requires that a bride leave her clan and be replaced with another person who goes to live with her natal clan. On Ali Island, just off the north coast of Papua New Guinea, for example, a

2000 household census of some 50 households on the island, conducted by Robert Welsch and Joshua A. Bell, showed that every household had children who were the replacement for a woman who had married out of the clan. People on the island call these children of a married woman sent back to her father and brother's household the woman's "exchange." This pattern meant that, while the clans were clearly identified, every single clan contained people born into another clan and household. These people were adopted into the family and naturalized as small children to become members of the family and clan. Westerners would ordinarily refer to this pattern as adoption, but we usually think of adoption as a rare occurrence, while on Ali it affects every family and every household, as they adopt a sister's children as their own or send their own children to live with the child's mother's brother. Most children are aware of their biological parents and natal families, but they will inherit land and social position from the families who raise them.

The Dowry in India: Providing a Financial Safety Net for a Bride

Another traditional form of marriage payment occurs in the highly stratified communities of India. Here, high-caste families traditionally gave a **dowry** consisting of a large sum of money—or in-kind gifts of livestock, furniture, or even electronics—to a daughter to ensure her well-being in her husband's family. Sometimes the dowry was given, at least in part, to the husband as a way of attracting a prosperous and hard-working husband. The Indian government outlawed the practice of dowry in 1961, but in many parts of the country, the practice continues as before.

In recent years, abuses of dowry have become common, reaching more than 3,000 incidents a year, attracting the attention of the Indian government, state governments, and international human rights groups. In these cases, members of the husband's family threaten the bride if more dowry is not forthcoming. In the most severe cases, the men's families have even killed the bride because her family would not contribute more dowry (Figure 12.10).

- **Dowry.** A large sum of money or in-kind gifts given to a daughter to ensure her well-being in her husband's family.

Controlling Family Wealth Through Inheritance

Families also control wealth, property, and power through rules of inheritance. The death of an individual can create a crisis in a family, because members have to decide how to redistribute land and whatever kinds of wealth that person may have held, which can create conflict. Rules of inheritance typically ensure an orderly process and, more important, ensure that wealth and property stay in the family.

In Western countries, such rules have been codified in law for a long time. For example, centuries ago, Great Britain acknowledged the right of "primogeniture," in which the eldest son inherited a man's entire estate, including all lands and other wealth. Elder brothers might give some allowance to their younger brothers, but these younger sons had no claim to the estate and often went into the Church or the military, or migrated to distant lands. The goal of primogeniture was to preserve large landed estates together with the money and other wealth needed to maintain them.

Figure 12.10   Dowry in Modern India. (*Top*) A woman from Rajasthan shows off part of her dowry. (*Bottom*) Women protest a woman's death in Jammu caused by problems with her dowry.

Inheritance rules also exist in small-scale nonindustrial societies, in spite of the fact that many lack a formal legal code. In many of these societies, the most valuable property is land, but it might also include livestock, locally recognized valuables, vegetables, and rights in people. Not surprisingly, when people die in these societies, land and some forms of durable personal property are the most important things to be inherited. In tribal and chiefly societies, land is typically controlled by clans or some other form of extended family group.

In any society, inheritance usually goes to legitimate heirs—typically the children of a socially recognized married couple. But marriage is such a complicated social institution that we should consider what motivates people to get married in the first place, as well as the less obvious benefits that come to married people.

· ·

THINKING CRITICALLY ABOUT KINSHIP, MARRIAGE, AND THE FAMILY

Although most Americans who get engaged think that the upcoming marriage is about them as a couple, in fact, marriage brings together two sets of families and two sets of friends. Consider the most recent wedding you may have attended, or ask a friend or relative about a wedding he or she attended as a guest. Discuss who paid for different parts of the celebration (reception, officiant, wedding license, flowers, bridesmaids' dresses, groomsmen's tuxes, gifts to bridesmaids and groomsmen, rehearsal dinner, etc.). Now consider who should give gifts and to whom these gifts should be given. How do the dollars and cents of a wedding outline the structure of American families and kin groups?

· ·

Why Do People Get Married?

For at least two centuries, American pastors, priests, and rabbis have preached that sex is reserved for marriage, as it is primarily for procreation. The reality of American life is that sexual behavior is not limited to married couples. At the same time, the study *Sex in America* (Michael, Gagnon, Lauman, and Kolata 1994) found that, on average, married couples (together with unmarried couples who live together) have sex more often and more regularly than single people. But marriage is about a lot more than sex. In this section we explain some of the various reasons people have for getting married, as well as some of the diverse forms that marriage can take.

Why People Get Married

For most Americans, marriage should be about love and sex, and we take for granted our individual right to choose a marriage partner. But in most societies around the world, marriage is about cultivating political and economic relations between families. In such contexts, a common belief is that marriage is too important to be left to the whims of an individual, and so accepted practice is for family members to choose an individual's marriage partner.

Marriage also provides social recognition of the ties between the couple, if not also their families, as well as social legitimacy to the children. The importance of public recognition partially helps explain why same-sex marriage has become a key political issue in the past decade in many societies, including the United States (where it was legalized nationwide in 2015), Canada (where it has been legal since 2005), Mexico (where it is legal in many states but still under debate at the national level), and Argentina (where it has been legal since 2010). Weddings, of course, are important for straight couples as well, which is why so many young brides and their families spend so much time and money staging them. On one hand, weddings proclaim to the world that the couple is united. But, on the other hand, the wedding ceremony brings the two families together in the same spot, where they acknowledge the couple as a unit.

Forms of Marriage

Just as we have seen the definition of marriage widening in the United States and in other countries to allow for same-sex marriage, the tendency around the world has increasingly been to limit the number of partners to a couple. In many traditional societies in Africa, Asia, the Americas, and the Pacific, **polygamy** (or plural marriage) was far more common previously than it is today. The most common form of plural marriage is **polygyny**, in which one man is married simultaneously to two or more women. In parts of Africa and Melanesia, for example, having more than one wife indicates that a man is important, with greater wealth, higher social status, or more importance in the community. From a woman's point of view, being in a polygynous marriage can mean that other wives provide support in conducting household duties, such as raising kids, cooking, and so on. But as these indigenous economies have been drawn into the global system, the number of men with two or more wives has declined, as it is increasingly considered too costly and too old-fashioned (Figure 12.11).

The other form of plural marriage is **polyandry**, in which one woman has two or more husbands at one time. Few societies around the world are known to have allowed polyandry, and the best known are the Toda, one of the hill tribes in India (Rivers 1906; Dakowski 1990), and the Sherpas of Nepal, who formerly used polyandry to keep large estates from being divided into tiny estates (Ortner 1989). Among both the Todas and the Sherpas, a group of brothers marries the same woman, a practice known as "fraternal polyandry" that limits the tensions among co-husbands.

Some anthropologists suggest that polyandry is uncommon because of the dominance of men's roles over women's in most societies. Let's consider some of the power that families have over their members.

Sex, Love, and the Power of Families Over Young Couples

All societies around the world have rules about who can have sex with or get married to whom. Parents and other family members may

- **Polygamy.** Any form of plural marriage.

- **Polygyny.** When a man is simultaneously married to more than one woman.

- **Polyandry.** When a woman has two or more husbands at one time.

Figure 12.11 Polygamy Is Largely in Decline Around the World. (*Top*) A polygamous family in the Palestinian city of Ramallah in the early twentieth century; today, most Palestinian men have only one wife. (*Bottom*) Fundamentalist Mormons, who have broken away from the Mormon Church (formally, the Church of Jesus Christ of the Latter-day Saints) based in Salt Lake City, are the main group that still practices polygyny in the United States.

object to certain possible partners, such as if a woman chooses a partner from the wrong socioeconomic, religious, educational, or ethnic background. And nearly every society has prohibitions against sex and marriage with people who are too closely related.

The Incest Taboo

- **Incest taboo.** The prohibition on sexual relations between close family members.

Many things can happen within a family, but two things that should not happen are sex and marriage. The prohibition on sexual relations between close family members is generally called the **incest taboo**, and this taboo is as close to a universal feature of human societies as anything.

There are two well-known exceptions to the incest taboo, both of which ironically prove this taboo's generality: in ancient Egypt, during the reigns of the pharaohs, and in Hawaii, before Europeans encountered the islands for the first time in 1778. In both societies, ruling monarchs could engage in incest because they were considered living gods, who could preserve the divine essence of their being only by marrying a sibling.

For relationships beyond the nuclear family—such as the marriage of cousins—societies vary in what they allow. In Africa, Southeast Asia, South America, Australia, and New Guinea, the incest taboo includes prohibitions on marriage with some kinds of cousins, particularly in societies with a unilineal clan system. And in most clan-based societies, the prohibition on marriage within the clan suggests that this extension of the incest taboo defines the boundaries of the clan, just as the boundaries of incest define the boundaries of the nuclear family.

Why Is There an Incest Taboo?

Social scientists have suggested two general explanations for the incest taboo. The most common is that incest leads to birth defects, and the incest taboo prevents these birth defects. The main problem with this explanation is that in small-scale societies, only incest within the nuclear family, such as brother–sister pairings, leads to higher rates of birth defects. Even then, higher rates of defects do not mean every birth suffers defects. Within a small community of 300 or 500 individuals, the risk of birth defects from marriages between first cousins is not much different from random mating. Everyone in a small community is already interrelated, and the odds of deleterious (harmful) gene combinations are effectively the same for marriage with a first cousin and for random pairings.

A second explanation, called the "Westermarck Effect," explains the incest taboo as a natural psychological revulsion toward marriage (or sex) with close relatives. First-cousin marriage was common in many places and even in the United States, where it is allowed in more than half of the states. For example, during the century or so before the American Revolution, a surprising number of marriages between first or second cousins were recorded, and it was considered an extremely appropriate match. Recently, evolutionary psychologists like Steven Pinker (1997) have adopted this explanation, arguing that natural selection has selected genes that cause us to feel little sexual attraction for people we have grown up with. There are three critiques of this evolutionary model as an explanation for the incest taboo: (1) No gene (or combination of genes) has been identified as linked to the proposed revulsion; (2) the range of relatives prohibited by the incest taboo varies too widely from society to society to be explained by selection; and (3) there is no reason to assume that the revulsion is the cause of the taboo, when it is equally probable that the incest taboo itself generates the psychological revulsion. That is to say, people are repulsed by sibling marriage because it violates the cultural rules of incest.

Both of these explanations assume that the incest taboo emerges from biology. But anthropologists have suggested that the incest taboo emerges from the context of ordinary life rather than from our biology. They point to the research of Melford Spiro (1958), an anthropologist who studied life in an Israeli kibbutz in the 1950s. Spiro found that the adolescents who lived together in large communal settings avoided marrying or even dating members of their communal group. There was no rule against marriage or sex within the group, but there simply was no sexual attraction because they thought of other members as siblings. This situation is not at all unlike what happens in American college coed dorms, where there is often a similar avoidance of sexual liaisons. Sexual relationships within the same dorm produce so many social complications for both parties that some contemporary college newspapers have warned their readers against the "hallway hookup" and "dormcest" (Sivo 2005).

Coed dorms are a concept that would have shocked most Americans 50 years ago, just as people were shocked by the impact that new methods of birth control had on sexual activity in the 1960s and 1970s. But technology and social attitudes toward it are always changing. As reproductive technologies have changed in important ways over the past few decades, new situations have arisen for families to make sense of and create new kinds of kin relations.

• •

THINKING CRITICALLY ABOUT KINSHIP, MARRIAGE, AND THE FAMILY

Americans often think that marriage is about "love." But marriage is also about economics. Being married and having a family cost money. Recent studies have determined that the average age at marriage in the United States has been rising for several decades as middle-class incomes have declined. Discuss how the economics of modern American life help shape the decision to get married.

• •

How Are Social and Technological Changes Reshaping How People Think About Family?

In the 1960s, the birth control pill allowed women in Western countries like the United States, France, and Great Britain an unprecedented level of direct control over their sexuality. This technological development contributed to a so-called sexual revolution centered around the desire for "casual sex." At first the Pill was available only to married women, but by the end of the 1970s, it became available to single women in most of the United States as well. For all the entanglements of kinship discussed previously, the prospect of having a child does not facilitate casual sex!

By the 1980s, the technological cutting edge shifted away from efforts to prevent pregnancy to efforts to improve fertility and overcome infertility. At the same time, as couples postponed the birth of their first child, infertility was becoming a growing problem, and some couples have sought to create families through adoption, only to find that there are few babies available to be adopted. These families have turned to international adoption, with China, the world's largest country, being the largest source of internationally adopted children. In recent decades, anthropologists interested in matters of kinship have become attuned to the fact that these new social and technological developments have begun to complicate people's understandings of kinship relations. We discuss how this might be in three contexts: international adoption, in-vitro fertilization, and surrogacy, each of which puts stresses and strains on our usual notions of family ties, who is related to whom, and how these relationships should be recognized socially within the community and the American legal system.

International Adoptions and the Problem of Cultural Identity

Adoption has been a human phenomenon for as long as there have been humans. When a parent or both parents have died, often as a result of disease, war, or natural disasters, in traditional small-scale societies, there has always been someone available to look after orphaned children. But until recently, most adoptions were typically local affairs in which a child needing parents was looked after by a neighbor or relative. The mid–twentieth century saw the rise of adoption agencies that could arrange adoptions across the United States, and they did so anonymously. Neither the biological parents nor the adoptive parents knew each other. It was only in the latter part of the last century that intercultural adoptions became common, and in the 1990s a new phenomenon emerged—international adoption, in which a child is adopted across international borders.

Since the 1980s, international adoptions from China, Russia, and Eastern Europe have posed a number of new issues for both the host countries and families in the receiving countries. Not surprisingly, international adoption has political implications for relationships between donor countries and receiving countries. In the context of relationships between the United States and Russia, for example, international adoptions seemed to suggest that Russia could not look after its own children, and many Russians saw the situation as an attack on their national pride. During the decade following the fall of Communism and the breakup of the Soviet Union, many ordinary Russians could not easily look after their newborn children. But as the turbulence of those years calmed and economic stability returned, it was easy for Russian president Vladimir Putin to end international adoptions to the United States.

Two other governmental decisions have played a major role in encouraging international adoption by American couples. The first was the U.S. Supreme Court's *Roe v. Wade* decision in 1973, which effectively declared state laws banning abortion to be unconstitutional; as a result of this decision, there were simply not enough American children available for adoption to satisfy all of the American couples wanting to adopt. The second decision was the People's Republic of China's implementation of its "one-child policy" (1979–2015) as an effort to slow population growth in China. Under this policy, urban families were heavily taxed for having more than one child, and educational and economic opportunities for any second child were limited, discouraging families from having a second child. In addition, Chinese families typically wanted a son to carry on the family name, and when a young family's first child was a girl, many gave the child up for adoption. As a result of these factors, during the 1990s many Americans began adopting Chinese daughters.

Doing Fieldwork
Andrea Louie on Negotiating Identity and Culture in International Adoptions

FOR AMERICAN ADOPTEES, identity has always been an issue, although with anonymous adoptions it was very hard to find information on an adoptee's biological family because state birth records were typically sealed. In recent years, activists have succeeded in gaining some access to these adoptees' files, to find out about their susceptibility to genetic diseases. But with international adoption, "identity" has taken a new form since a growing number of white parents have adopted non-white children who are from diverse ethnic backgrounds.

Adoptions from China have been taking place since the late 1980s or early 1990s. Now these adoptees and their parents confront a new issue: How much should adoptive parents who know little about Chinese culture try to give their Chinese-born children Chinese cultural experiences?

This was the situation studied by anthropologist Andrea Louie, who is herself Chinese American but has limited grasp of Chinese language and culture. Louie turned her attention to the question of how Chinese adoptees and their American families negotiate identity and culture.

To study international adoptions, Louie conducted participant observation and interviews with many dozens of American families with adopted Chinese children. Having a Chinese American son of her own with whom she was confronting many of the same issues of identity and culture gave Louie access to many groups and organizations that were organized around issues of Chinese cultural identity. She conducted her research partly in St. Louis and partly in the San Francisco Bay Area. By conducting interviews and making observations in two different localities, she was able

International Adoption of Children from China.   Adopting children from other countries with quite different cultures presents new inter-cultural challenges for Americans.

(continued)

Doing Fieldwork (continued)

to represent regions where Chinese Americans were unusual and where they were common.

Louie found that adoptive parents of Chinese children regularly confront the problem of the cultural identities of their children. But each family seems to negotiate these identities somewhat differently, depending on where the family lives, the backgrounds of the adoptive parents, and the make-up of the community. From her interviews and participant observation with many of these families and the various organizations they belong to, Louie found that "all Chinese Americans, including Chinese adoptees, craft their own forms of 'Chinese and Chinese American' cultural capital as they negotiate the politics of race, class, and culture in the United States" (Louie 2015:15). She found that negotiating cultural identity in such families is a constant and ongoing issue, even for adoptees now in their twenties or about to begin college. Thus, kinship in these families is not simply about belonging to a family; it becomes a question of intercultural identity in the global world in which we all live today.

Questions for Reflection

1. What problems do Chinese American adoptees in white families face in exploring their Chinese heritage and culture? How would the situation be different for children adopted from Romania or Bulgaria?

2. How are international adoptions similar to and different from white parents adopting African American or American Indian children?

3. To what extent is the discussion of Chinese identity among Chinese American adoptees a striking divergence from the many other kinship and family issues that have captured the attention of anthropologists for a century and a half? Why is this issue so different from many other aspects of kinship studied by anthropologists?

As we can see in "Doing Fieldwork: Andrea Louie on Negotiating Identity and Culture in International Adoptions," modern international adoptions involve issues of cultural identity that rarely arise when adoptions take place within the local community.

In Vitro Fertilization

People often talk about in vitro fertilization (IVF) as a way to produce "test-tube babies." The technique takes eggs from the mother or some other female donor and sperm from the father or a male donor. Fertilization can occur by incubating an egg and sperm in a Petri dish or, if the donor's sperm count is low, one sperm cell can be injected into the egg. After the embryos have reached the 6- to 8-cell stage, they are implanted in the womb of the mother, where some of the embryos can implant in the uterus and lead to a successful pregnancy. Only 25% to 45% of all IVF attempts successfully produce pregnancy. But IVF has become an important procedure, accounting for nearly 1% of all American births annually (Elder and Dale 2000).

The first successful IVF was the birth of Louise Brown in 1978 in England. Since then, the procedure has been used in more than 115,000 live births in the United States, creating a variety of new kinship relationships that people had never had to cope with before. For most couples, the preferred situation was the mother's egg and father's sperm implanted into the mother, based on the belief that blood relations are the most important. But in situations where a man or a woman cannot provide either sperm or an egg, other possibilities present themselves: a mother's egg, donor's sperm; donor's egg, father's sperm; donor's egg and sperm; and any of these in a surrogate uterus. The social relationships between the individuals involved in any of these scenarios do not transfer easily to categories like "mother" and "father," since who provides the biological material may differ from who raises the child or provides the womb to nurture it during pregnancy.

Surrogate Mothers and Sperm Donors

For British anthropologist Marilyn Strathern (1996), the new reproductive technologies offer insights into the ways that ordinary people understand kinship, as these new situations can lead to litigation in the courts where families are being defined, constructed, and dismantled in innovative ways because suddenly there are new parties in the family: surrogate mothers, sperm donors, multiple men claiming to be fathers, and the like. As we have seen herein, both biology and social ties are important for creating links between parents and children. Adoption often separates biology and social ties, so that the biological parent has no social ties with the child, and the adoptive parents have social ties but no biological connection. But the new reproductive technologies introduce new ambiguities into the biological facts.

Traditionally, conception always presented some possible ambiguity about biological paternity, since any number of men besides the husband may have had intercourse with a woman. Paternity tests were perceived as conclusive, but most scientists who work in such fields recognize that blood-typing or the more recent DNA tests are never fully reliable. Even when DNA tests indicate the husband as the biological father, his closest kin cannot always be excluded. And, of course, relatives of both the husband and the wife are often socially present in the couple's life, making sexual contact between the wife and a brother-in-law possible.

The new reproductive technologies—where sperm donors, egg donors, and IVF are involved—introduce new ambiguities about who is the biological mother or even the biological father. Even eggs and semen from a married couple that are intended to be used for IVF can be inadvertently mixed up with specimens from other individuals before fertilization. And, some gay couples wanting a child may request that their semen samples be mixed together intentionally so that one of the men is the biological father, but neither knows whether it is him or his partner. As Strathern suggests, such ambiguities challenge traditional notions that biology and social ties should work together to create kinship bonds between parents and children.

But the most important ambiguity has to do with surrogacy and sperm donors. A surrogate mother is a woman who agrees to have an embryo implanted in her womb. She carries the baby to term, and after the baby is born, the child belongs to the couple who provided the embryo. Quite often, couples choose surrogate mothers when the wife is unable to carry a child to term. Surrogate mothers are rarely related genetically to the children they carry to term. But their body has nurtured the child for nine months, which constitutes some ambiguous link between the surrogate mother and the child. When this procedure was beginning to be common in the United States in the 1990s, for example, TV dramas and soap operas often centered their plots on the surrogate who had formed a bond with the fetus and did not want to give up the baby to the couple who had paid all of her expenses over the preceding nine months. However, studies by anthropologists of surrogate mothers suggest that very few surrogates have any desire to keep the newborns (Ragoné 1996). Most see their role as quite separate from that of the child's mother; their job is to help unfortunate couples by carrying their babies to term, sometimes (but not always) for a fee.

It is not clear where these new technologies will go in the future, or how the courts will apportion rights to claims on the children of surrogacy, sperm and egg donors, and adoption. Rayna Rapp (1992), for example, has suggested that the next advances "in the study of reproduction will be made from inside a critique of the study of science." After several decades of viewing these new reproductive technologies as simple technological advances, it is becoming clear that parental rights are not about biology, but about how people in different cultures choose to interpret and emphasize some biological claims over others.

As we have seen in this chapter, kinship, marriage, adoption, and the family are about claims on people. The courts and the sentiments of the public can easily give some claims more importance than others.

THINKING CRITICALLY ABOUT KINSHIP, MARRIAGE, AND THE FAMILY

Americans have strong feelings that parents have rights over their children, where they can go, what they can participate in, whether they should get vaccines, and so forth. Consider how these parental rights become less clear-cut under the following conditions: (a) the parents have adopted a child, but the birth parents are in the same community; (b) the parents have given up their child for adoption, and they know the family the child lives with; (c) the couple's newborn is the result of the mother's egg and an anonymous sperm donor, who has learned he is the biological father; and (d) the egg was from an anonymous donor, the sperm from the father, and the child was carried to term by a surrogate mother.

Conclusion

Although the tendency in our own culture—if not also in the Mexican telenovela that opens this chapter—is to see kinship and family primarily as matters of blood relationships, anthropologists view the matter rather differently, having seen the great variety of ways different societies construct families and kinship relations. Not only are families imbued with social and cultural expectations, but the very biological acts of sexual intercourse to conceive children are currently being revised with the rise of new reproductive technologies.

Families are at the heart of most systems of social relationship, although the Israeli *kibbutzim* suggest that communal living situations can in some ways overwhelm this most basic social unit. In nonindustrial societies, families are vitally important to most aspects of social life. But industrialization has put pressure on large families and encouraged individual nuclear families rather than large, unwieldy extended families and clans. And families are important to individuals even when, as in our society, the active family units are pared down to parents and a small number of children.

But no matter how dazzling the diverse kinds of families we might find in different societies, whether matrilineal lineages, patrilineal clans, nuclear families, or some other social form, these ways of understanding and working with relatives seem inherently natural. In nearly every society, people look at their families as one of the most natural and biologically based institutions. Just as we saw in the previous chapter, where ideas of sex and gender seem inherently natural, so, too, do the families around which we structure our lives.

KEY TERMS

Bride price   p. 313

Clan   p. 306

Cognatic   p. 308

Corporate groups   p. 305

Culture and personality
    movement   p. 313

Dowry   p. 315

Exogamous   p. 306

Extended families   p. 306

Genealogical amnesia
    p. 308

Incest taboo   p. 318

Kinship   p. 303

Kinship chart   p. 305

Lineage   p. 306

Matrilineal   p. 307

Natal family   p. 304

Nuclear family   p. 305

Patrilineal   p. 306

Polyandry   p. 317

Polygamy   p. 317

Polygyny   p. 317

Unilineal   p. 306

Reviewing the Chapter

Chapter Section	What We Know	To Be Resolved
What Are Families, and How Are They Structured in Different Societies?	Families differ in their composition and structure cross-culturally. But they are also dynamic, and all societies change their understandings of family, kinship, and social relationship as they adapt to new external factors.	It is impossible to predict how any society's system of kinship, marriage, and the family will change without understanding the other social, economic, environmental, and political changes in that society.

Continued

Reviewing the Chapter (continued)

Chapter Section	What We Know	To Be Resolved
How Do Families Control Power and Wealth?	Kin relationships are about social ties between individuals as much as they are about biological ties. All societies have developed ways of ensuring that the family group has some control over collective resources or the labor of its members.	Many anthropologists consider social and cultural factors, such as the desire to control wealth or to exercise power over individuals, to be more decisive in explaining how and why people have kinship relations. Yet some insist that there is a biological basis to kin relations, such as those who promote the idea that the incest taboo is biologically based.
Why Do People Get Married?	Marriage can take on many diverse forms, and our own cultural model of basing marriage on love and sex is not important to all societies, especially those in which marriage is about creating social, economic, and political ties with other groups.	Although we know that economics has an impact on who gets married and who does not, it is not clear what the long-term impact of delayed marriage or the growing number of unmarried couples with children will be.
How Are Social and Technological Changes Reshaping How People Think About Family?	Although international adoptions and new reproductive technologies are changing the biological relationships in families, they are not having much impact on the social roles within families, however they become formed. However, international adoptions, in particular, are raising a new set of questions about the creation of social identities.	It is unclear how new reproductive technologies and international adoptions will change how people think of the expectations, relationships, and meanings of kinship over time.

Readings

The earliest appreciation of the range of variation among the world's societies was published in 1871 by Lewis Henry Morgan, who is otherwise best known for his study of the Iroquois. For a view into how kinship studies became a central problem for anthropologists, see Thomas Trautmann's *Lewis Henry Morgan and the Invention of Kinship* (Lincoln, NE: University of Nebraska Press, 2008).

Detailed studies of kinship and social organization did not really begin to appear until the functionalist British school of social anthropology had emerged in the 1920s. Many students from this theoretical school conducted field research in the British colonies in Africa. The classic collection of ethnographic studies on this topic is the volume edited by A. R. Radcliffe-Brown and Daryl Forde, *African Systems of Kinship and Marriage* (London: Oxford University Press, 1950). Although the essays remain valid as detailed descriptions of kinship in different tribal groups, the most important essay is Radcliffe-Brown's extended discussion, which lays out what was understood of kinship studies at the time.

Two influential texts by American anthropologists on the cultural dynamics of kinship in the United States argue that kinship is never exclusively about biology. These are David Schneider's book *American Kinship: A Cultural Account* (Englewood Cliffs, NJ: Prentice-Hall, 1968), which explores how the study of kinship can reveal fundamental cultural and symbolic meanings Americans hold; and the more recent study by Carol Stack, *All*

Our Kin: Strategies for Survival in a Black Community (New York: Basic Books, 1997), which explores the dynamism and fluidity of "family" relations among urban African Americans.

....

Research on the cultural dimensions of reproductive technologies began exploding during the 1990s. One of the central texts in this vein is Faye Ginsburg and Rayna Rapp's edited volume *Conceiving the New World Order: The Global Politics of Reproduction* (Berkeley, CA: University of California Press, 1995).

....

A discussion of Andrea Louie's work with American families that have adopted Chinese children can be found in her book *How Chinese Are You? Adopted Chinese Youth and Their Families Negotiate Identity and Culture* (New York: NYU Press, 2015).

....

Religion

Ritual and Belief

IT WAS THE SOUTH, in the summer of 1965, the darkest days of the civil rights movement in America. The previous year, Ku Klux Klansmen, members of a white supremacist group, had murdered three voting-rights activists in Mississippi. In March, the black Baptist civil rights leader Reverend Dr. Martin Luther King, Jr., had called on "clergy of all faiths . . . to join me in Selma for a ministers' march to Montgomery." Hundreds marched, but Alabama state troopers launched an unprovoked attack on protesters. Two weeks later, a white Alabama man slew another civil rights worker. During the summer, President Lyndon Johnson signed into law the Voting Rights Act of 1965, but officials in Lowndes County, Alabama, situated between Selma and Montgomery, refused to register any of their non-white citizens to vote, as did those in many other Southern counties with large black majorities (Eagles 1993; Wallace and Wallace 2016).

Into this cauldron of politics, fear, and religion came 26-year-old white seminary student Jonathan Daniels of Keene, New Hampshire. Daniels had marched through Lowndes County with Dr. King in March 1965, and he spent the summer in Lowndes County protesting racial discrimination and trying to register black voters. In August, he participated in a demonstration with Father Richard Morrisroe, a young, white Catholic priest from Chicago, and 27 other activists from the Student Non-violent Coordinating Committee (SNCC). All of them were arrested and held for a week in the Lowndes County Jail in the

---

Selma to Montgomery March. The Rev. Dr. Martin Luther King, Jr., drew heavily on religious symbolism from the biblical Book of Exodus in his civil rights struggles in 1965. Alabama state troopers, who attacked protestors during the march, also felt religious convictions in their actions.

329

quiet little town of Hayneville. After six days, the entire group was abruptly released on their own recognizance.

Outside, it was hot and dusty, so Daniels and Father Morrisroe set off down the street with two young black women who had been especially active with the SNCC, Ruby Sales and Joyce Bailey, to buy soft drinks at the only store in town that regularly served black customers. As Daniels opened the screen door, the store owner, Special Deputy Sheriff Tom Coleman, confronted him, holding a 12-gauge shotgun. Coleman shouted, "This store is closed. Get off this goddam property before I blow your goddam brains out, you black bastards." With that he aimed his gun at Ruby Sales. Seeing what was happening, Daniels pushed Sales to the ground and moved between her and the gun. Coleman fired at point-blank range. The blast threw Daniels out the door and into the street, killing him instantly. Morrisroe grabbed Bailey's hand and ran down the street with her, as Coleman shot him in the back, wounding him critically. Left behind on the ground, Sales now caught up with Bailey, grabbed her by the hand, and ran for cover. News accounts reported that a few minutes after the shooting, Coleman called the Alabama Director of Public Safety to say, "I just shot two preachers. Get on down here" (Eagles 1993; Unsworth 1998).

This incident arose because of a set of conflicting beliefs—those that motivated Tom Coleman versus those that motivated Jon Daniels. Today, we may find Coleman's prejudicial belief in the so-called racial inferiority of blacks even more difficult to understand than Daniels's religiously inspired altruism in his effort to protect Ruby Sales with his own body. Nevertheless, the bigger issue here is how we make sense of the existence of such different beliefs. It leads us to focus on the phenomenon of beliefs and behaviors, which vary so radically among the world's cultures and communities.

At the heart of anthropology's approach to belief and religion is the question: *Why do people believe things that others consider wrong?* Embedded in this broader question are the following problems, around which this chapter is organized:

How should we understand religion and religious beliefs?

What forms does religion take?

How do rituals work?

How is religion linked to political and social action?

Over the past century, anthropologists have come to realize that religious beliefs offer people a roadmap for their behavior: how they should live and how they should understand other people's behaviors, actions, and ideas. At their very heart, religious beliefs create meaning for people through the use of powerful rituals and religious symbols, all of which we discuss in greater depth in this chapter.

Kwakiutl
(Vancouver Island and
mainland, British Columbia)

Inuit
(Northern Canada)

Sioux
(Midwestern U.S.)

Paris, France

Siberia

Seneca
(New York)

Hayneville,
Alabama

Hawai'i

Egypt

Nigeria

Huichol
(Mexico)

Yanomami
(Venezuela)

Punjab,
India

Ningerum
(Papua New Guinea)

Purari
(Papua New Guinea)

Elema
(Papua
New Guinea)

Rio de Janeiro, Brazil

**Figure 13.1   Select Peoples
and Places Discussed in
Chapter 13.**

How Should We Understand Religion and Religious Beliefs?

Western intellectuals and social scientists have historically found the subject of religion problematic. When scholars in the nineteenth century confronted peoples around the world who held mystical worldviews filled with various kinds of spirits, ghosts, and rituals intended to protect families with magic or perhaps kill enemies at a distance with sorcery or witchcraft, most considered these ideas to be non-scientific mumbo-jumbo and evidence that their adherents were of limited intellectual capacity. But by the 1870s, when anthropology was emerging as an academic discipline, scholars began to look systematically for theories that would help them understand the cultural importance of religious beliefs. In this section, we consider four different definitions of religion that anthropologists have suggested, several of which are still commonly used today. Among these is our own approach to religion that builds on the others. In our view, the most effective way to think of **religion** is as a symbolic system that is socially enacted through rituals and other aspects of social life that relate to ultimate issues of humankind's existence.

- **Religion.** A symbolic system that is socially enacted through rituals and other aspects of social life that relate to ultimate issues of humankind's existence.

Understanding Religion, Version 1.0: Edward Burnett Tylor and Belief in Spirits

To make sense of the exotic religious beliefs of non-Western cultures, the British anthropologist Sir Edward Burnett Tylor (1871) suggested that religion had to do with belief in spiritual beings. For him, primitive religions were based on a fundamental error in thinking. He reasoned that people in all societies had dreams, but the

- **Animism.** The belief that inanimate objects such as trees, rocks, cliffs, hills, and rivers are animated by spiritual forces or beings.

so-called primitive peoples had misinterpreted their dreams as reality, transforming the characters in their dreams into souls or spirits. Tylor called such beliefs in spirits **animism**, which refers to the belief that inanimate objects such as trees, rocks, cliffs, hills, and rivers are animated by spiritual forces or beings. For him, the ideas that trees and rocks might have souls and that carved images might contain spirits were just other examples of this same "primitive" misunderstanding. Tylor also reasoned that, as societies evolved and became more complex, the supernatural beings they believed in became more complex as well: spirits gave way to demigods and mythical heroes, which gave way to the gods and goddesses of the ancient Greeks and Romans. Finally, these many gods gave way to a single, all-powerful God—which would eventually, in Tylor's secular way of thinking, yield to science.

Although many anthropologists later rejected Tylor's evolutionary theories, his basic approach to religion remained influential in anthropology for many decades. Some influential scholars, like Sir James Fraser, suggested that ideas about magic had predated ideas about souls and spirits, but there was no more evidence for magic as the origin of religious ideas than there was for dreams. By the Second World War, anthropologists in Great Britain were combining the two theories, writing of "magico-religious" ideas. The main problems with this theory of religion are that it doesn't explain how religion is used to make sense of the world, and it builds on ethnocentric biases that Western cultures are superior to all others.

Understanding Religion, Version 2.0: Anthony F. C. Wallace on Supernatural Beings, Powers, and Forces

- **Rituals.** Stylized performances involving symbols that are associated with social, political, and religious activities.

- **Mana.** Sacred power believed to inhere in certain high-ranking people, sacred spaces, and objects.

By the 1950s, anthropologists in the United States had long abandoned the idea that American Indians and other non-Western peoples were "primitive." They had also come to accept, as Paul Radin argued in his influential book *Primitive Man as Philosopher* (1927), that there was nothing simpleminded in the myths, legends, and religious practices of tribal peoples. When American anthropologists began to look at how American Indian religions had changed—and continued to change—in the context of white expansion and domination, they saw systematic shifts in Indian thinking to make sense of changing times (Figure 13.2).

One of the major figures of this period was Anthony F. C. Wallace, who had studied religious change among the Seneca, one of the Iroquois tribes in upstate New York (1956, 1970). For Wallace, religious change could be observed most easily in the changing religious ceremonies and **rituals** (stylized performances involving symbols that are associated with social, political, and religious activities). While Wallace's focus was on the rituals themselves, he recognized that these performances made sense only in terms of religious beliefs. His definition of religion became standard in anthropology because it linked beliefs with rituals: "beliefs and rituals concerned with supernatural beings, powers, and forces" (Wallace 1966:5).

At the core of Wallace's definition of religion was belief in the supernatural. But in surveying societies around the world, he recognized that some peoples believed in gods or spirits, while others, like the ancient Hawaiians, were concerned with much more amorphous powers and forces that anthropologists had come to call *mana*, which can be understood as raw supernatural power. Just touching things—such as a possession of the chief or even a chief's person—permeated with mana could cause sickness or death for any commoner. High-ranking chiefs, whose bodies were believed

Figure 13.2 The Ghost Dance. The Ghost Dance, which originated among the Sioux around 1890, was an innovative religious movement among various tribes in the Great Plains. It was the Sioux's attempt to recover self-respect and control over traditional resources through ritual, but it led to disastrous consequences at Wounded Knee in 1890, when U.S. Army soldiers misinterpreted the ritual and killed at least 150 Lakota Sioux.

Figure 13.3 Hawaiian Temple Complex (*Heiau*) at Kealakekua Bay on Hawaii's Big Island. This religious center possessed *mana* ("supernatural power"). Ancient Hawaiians believed that *mana* attached to all sacred sites, to persons of noble descent, to ritual carvings of the gods, and to anything the king or nobles touched. For commoners it was dangerous, even deadly, to touch something that possessed *mana*, or even to walk on sacred ground.

to possess mana, could unintentionally cause harm to any commoner who touched the royal body or who sat at a level higher than that of the chief (Figure 13.3). These ideas were about the supernatural, but the powers were not personalized as spirits, demons, or gods. Ultimately, Wallace grouped all forms of the supernatural together.

This approach bounded the field of religion in ways that fit comfortably with traditional European and American views of religion, which also emphasized the supernatural. But Wallace's definition is static, offering little or no direction for understanding how or why religious ideas and practices change. If a society practiced some tribal religion but then converted to Christianity, Islam, or Buddhism, Wallace's definition could help us document what had changed, but little else. It could not tell us what difference the changes in beliefs made in real people's lives. Another problem is that Wallace's definition tends to depict religious people as intellectually limited, or as focused on the mystical rather than the real world of global political, economic, and social processes. Yet perhaps the biggest failing in Wallace's definition is that it does not explain why people hold onto their religious beliefs and practices with such passion, a limitation that was overcome when anthropologists began understanding religion as based on symbols.

Understanding Religion, Version 3.0: Religion as a System of Symbols

Unsatisfied with Wallace's notion of religion as simply belief in the supernatural, American cultural anthropologist Clifford Geertz (1966) proposed another kind of definition that could help explain why beliefs are deeply held and motivational, even to the point of risking harm to oneself, as we saw with the example of Jonathan Daniels at the beginning of this chapter. Geertz argued that religion was a cultural system, or as he put it a "system of symbols," consisting of five elements:

Religion is (1) a system of symbols which act to (2) establish powerful, pervasive, and long-lasting moods and motivations in men by (3) formulating conceptions of a general order of existence and (4) clothing these conceptions with such an aura of factuality that (5) the moods and motivations seem uniquely realistic. (1966:4)

The most important feature of this definition is that it centers on symbols that seem intensely real and factual. For example, one of the central symbols in Christianity generally is the most improbable: the notion that after his execution Christ rose from the dead (called "the Resurrection"). Likely or not, hundreds of millions of people around the world accept Christ's resurrection as a historical fact.

Furthermore, the systems of meaning that these symbols generate can create a sense of moral purpose or meaning in people's lives and move them to action. These conceptualizations of the world offer a set of unquestioned assumptions about the world and how it works, called a **worldview**. The notion of culture adopted in this textbook ultimately derives from this understanding of religion as a cultural system. So when we suggest that culture is about symbolic processes that make the artificial and humanly constructed seem natural, we are arguing that culture consists of symbols that are created and given meaning by social life, not just in religious contexts. People's understandings of the world provided by these symbols, like Geertz's religion, seem uniquely realistic and cloaked in an aura of factuality; the world seems uniquely natural. The symbols describe a "model of" how the world is, as they simultaneously depict a "model for" how the world (morally) should be. When people are confronted with conditions in the world that do not fit with their understanding of how the world should be, they may be moved to effect change, often drawing on the symbols central to their worldview. In the case we discussed at the beginning of this chapter, for example, Jonathan Daniels was moved to action by his belief in racial equality, and his sacrifice was an enactment of a symbol at the heart of his religion—the cross that symbolizes Jesus' sacrifice of his life to give eternal life to all believers.

Most anthropologists continue to find Geertz's approach to religion useful. Following Geertz, they have tried to understand the worldview and ethos of a religion, adopting what is often called an **interpretive approach**, a style of analysis that looks at the underlying symbolic and cultural interconnections within a society.

In spite of its strengths, Geertz's explanation does have limitations. Some scholars, for example, have argued that Geertz's definition of religion as a cultural system assumes that people have a basic need for meaning and for making sense of the world, which may or may not be the case (Frankenberry and Penner 1999). Furthermore, anthropologist Talal Asad (1993) has argued that Geertz's definition of religion as a cultural system does not adequately distinguish religion from the domains of science, aesthetics, common sense, or law. Asad also questions whether we can ever fully understand the emotions people feel during religious experiences, whether rituals, prayers, or social action (Asad 1993). Still others have charged that it does not pay adequate attention to how institutions and power relations within a society create religious meaning (Eickelman and Piscatori 1996; Foucault 1999).

Perhaps the most significant limitation of Geertz's strategy for understanding religious phenomena is that his definition of religion reads as if he were describing a lone believer sitting quietly surrounded only by his own moods and thoughts as company. A key feature of religious beliefs and behavior is that they are rooted in social behavior and social action (Figure 13.4). Beliefs get most of their power from being socially enacted repeatedly through rituals and other religious behaviors. By acting together, the community of believers begins to accept the group's symbolic interpretations of the world as if they were tangible, authentic, and real rather than merely interpretation.

- **Worldview.** A general approach to or set of shared, unquestioned assumptions about the world and how it works.

- **Interpretive approach.** A kind of analysis that interprets the underlying symbolic and cultural interconnections within a society.

Figure 13.4 Expressing Religiosity. Religious rituals are social activities, and many around the world are energetic and boisterous rather than somber, sedate, and pensive as some Americans may assume. On the left is a West African ritual performance that brings the gods into contact with the community, and on the right is a modern mega-church in America in which participants take on a vibrant role in the service.

Understanding Religion, Version 4.0: Religion as a System of Social Action

In July 2013, 3 million Brazilians turned out in Rio de Janeiro to celebrate mass with Pope Francis, the first Roman Catholic pope from Latin America. In this public ritual, we can see that religion is important for these millions of believers, and that it is an intensely exciting and social experience. It is a very different experience from a single nun on retreat praying quietly by herself for days at a time, eating at a communal meal with other nuns, but with no one speaking. Yet both experiences are "religious" in that they deal with worshipers' understandings of the world and how important the supernatural power of God is in people's lives. Both draw power from their social context—being among 3 million worshipers in Rio and with oneself in the convent. And both draw additional power and meaning from being so different from ordinary daily life.

In our view, the social experience of religious practice is what gives the beliefs, the organization of religion in daily life, and the religious symbols meaning for every person present. Most people do not have regular contact with the supernatural. Neither God nor Jesus—to continue with this pair of Catholic ritual experiences introduced here—regularly appears in person to most of the congregants in Rio or to the nuns who devote their lives to the Church. But the personal meaning these Catholics attach to the importance of the intense experiences of the pope's public mass or their private prayers reinforces for them, individually and communally, that God and Jesus are real and present in their lives.

Thus, when we speak of religion in this book, we define it as a symbolic system that is socially enacted through rituals and other aspects of social life that relate to ultimate issues of humankind's existence. This definition implies several elements that earlier scholars have emphasized:

1. The existence of things more powerful than human beings: Although in many societies it takes the form of some supernatural force, we prefer to think of it as a worldview or cosmology that situates the place of human beings in the universe.
2. Beliefs and behaviors surround, support, and promote the acceptance of the underlying idea that things more powerful than humans actually exist.

3. Symbols that make these beliefs and behaviors seem both intense and genuine.
4. Social settings, usually involving important rituals, that people share while experiencing the power of these symbols of belief.

Armed with this sense of religion, let us apply this understanding of religion to one of the great problems of meaning of our time: making sense of why some people willingly put themselves at great risk to promote some greater cause.

Making Sense of the Terrorist Attacks in France: Charlie Hebdo

France has seen various kinds of terrorist attacks for the past two centuries. For the most part, the motivations behind these attacks have been clearly political. In the 1960s, for example, during the Algerian struggle for independence, France experienced a series of attacks conducted by right-wing French nationalist groups opposed to Algerian independence. One of these attacks, the Paris–Strasbourg train bombing of June 1961, killed 28 people and injured over 100 others, making it the deadliest terror attack in the country until 2015 (Pech 2015).

In recent years, France and other European countries have experienced a series of jihadist attacks, much as the United States has. What differentiates these attacks from other terrorist attacks of the past century, however, is that the motivations behind them are largely tied to religious views, and that the attackers seem so willing to put aside their personal safety—and even die—for their cause.

The first high-profile jihadist attack in France came in 2015 at the offices of the satirical magazine *Charlie Hebdo* in Paris. This attack left 12 people dead and another 11 wounded, and it was apparently motivated by the fact that the magazine had published a satirical cartoon on its cover featuring a depiction of the Muslim prophet Muhammad.

Nowhere in the **Quran**, the holy scripture of Islam, is there any overt prohibition on artistic images of the Prophet. However, prohibitions against figural art, especially images of Muhammad, do appear in certain *hadiths*—sayings attributed to the Prophet that were recorded by his followers after his death and have been used as legal precedent where the Quran is silent. Thus, for certain radical jihadist groups, poking fun at Islam by lampooning the Prophet Muhammad with a silly sketch of his face and body offends the believer's sensibility not only by mocking the Prophet and his followers, and in so doing making fun of Islam, but by violating the ban on depicting the figure of the Prophet.

Such prohibitions on what artists, and especially satirists, can depict in their work runs counter to the liberal Western European and American notions of free speech. As in North America, European artists feel that individuals have a right, bestowed on them by their country's constitution and other founding political documents, to freedom of speech, and that no government, political movement, institution, or individual has the right to infringe on this right.

Encouraged by Muslim criticisms of other cartoons depicting Muhammad, the *Charlie Hebdo* staff periodically published satiric cartoons of the Prophet, much as it did of the Pope, Jesus, and political leaders across the globe. No one was immune from *Charlie Hebdo*'s satire, and most people targeted by the magazine ignored the slights. But the jihadist group Al-Qaeda in the Arabian Peninsula (AQAP) responded by publishing in its propagandist magazine *Inspire* a hit list of suitable targets that included a number of the staff of *Charlie Hebdo* (Kapferer 2015; Zagato 2015).

On the morning of January 7, 2015, two jihadist brothers of Arab descent born in Paris to Algerian immigrant parents broke into the *Charlie Hebdo* offices, killing most

● **Quran.** The main body of scripture in Islam, consisting of verses of classical Arabic poetry understood to be revealed to the Prophet Muhammad by Allah, often in dreams or in the midst of other activities. These verses were memorized by Muhammad's followers and written down after his death.

of the magazine's staff and shouting "God is great" in Arabic. Both were killed in a shootout with police two days later. During the armed standoff with French police, one of the brothers said in a telephone interview with a reporter that he was sent by AQAP, and that "We are not killers. We are defenders of the prophet, we don't kill women. . . . If someone offends the prophet, . . . we can kill him. We don't kill women. We are not like you . . . killing women and children in Syria, Iraq and Afghanistan" (Saliba 2015). Despite his claims, several of the victims were in fact women.

The brothers probably knew that French authorities would hunt them down and arrest or shoot them. But they had been radicalized by AQAP jihadists in Yemen, where one of the brothers had visited, and by other radical Islamists they had encountered while serving short prison sentences for robbery. They had framed their justification for the attacks as inspired by Islam, although the political aspects of their actions were obvious.

For their part, European leaders and the public were galvanized into action, holding solidarity marches and rallies in Paris and other cities. The tag phrase *Je suis Charlie* (literally meaning "I am Charlie") appeared on buttons, t-shirts, and banners as a symbol of the anti-terrorist position. Standing with *Charlie Hebdo* was intended to mean standing for Western democratic ideals in which individual freedom of speech is guaranteed, with the same reverence as that given by the jihadists to the defense of Prophet Muhammad and their ban on cartoons.

Anthropologist Angelique Haugerud (2016) suggests that the response to the *Charlie Hebdo* shootings symbolically supported the notion, already common in the West since the September 11 destruction of the World Trade Center in New York City, that liberal democracies were engaged in a "clash of civilizations" between Western Europe, America, and Canada on one hand and the Islamic world on the other. This idea had been the basic ideology behind the medieval crusades. But as Haugerud writes, it started to gain attention again toward the end of the twentieth century, largely in response to political scientist Samuel P. Huntington's (1993, 1996) suggestion that, following the Cold War, the West had become embroiled in a "clash of civilizations" between the Islamic world and the West.

It is true that, in recent times, jihadist groups like Al-Qaeda and the Islamic State have promoted a mix of political and religious justifications for violence against the West. Their goal has been to encourage support among Muslims the world over through anger and outrage over past slights, political powerlessness, economic exploitation, and the violence against civilians that came with the Gulf War, followed by the wars in Afghanistan and Iraq. However, most anthropologists have strongly rejected the view that there is any "clash of civilizations" at all, arguing that the idea that foreign enemies exist and must be overcome allows leaders to take advantage of their own people, their resources, and their free speech (Gusterson 2005; Haugerud 2016).

From an anthropological perspective, the "clash of civilizations" explanation for jihadists attacking *Charlie Hebdo*'s offices misses the point, as it does for other deadly jihadist attacks, such as the November 2015 attack on the Bataclan theatre, or the 2016 Bastille Day attack along the beach in Nice. In each case, the attacks were carried out by individual actors aiming to maim or kill as many people as they could reach. These incidents are evidence not of a clash of civilizations but of tensions that have arisen over discrimination, poverty, limited access to education, and other inequities among Muslims, in contrast to the better financial, social, and political conditions of non-Muslims in many countries around the world. The terrorists' ideas are political acts that have been packaged in religious language and symbols; they are simultaneously religious and political for a small group of actors whose ideas have been reinforced by social activities, conducted both in person and online.

More than a million French men and women marched in solidarity with the Western democratic ideal of freedom of speech. But the most striking and most publicized images were of the 40 world leaders who attended the event, including French President François Hollande, German Chancellor Angela Merkel, European Union President Donald Tusk, Israeli Prime Minister Benjamin Netanyahu, Queen Rania of Jordan, and Malian President Ibrahim Boubacar Keïta. All of these world leaders locked arms in a heavily protected Paris street for a brief photo-opportunity of solidarity, rather than for a political march. Photos of the leaders appeared in newspapers and magazines across the Western world, demonstrating that they stood together in solidarity for freedom of speech (Figure 13.5).

Each of these leaders faced issues of how to deal with Muslim populations in their countries, communities and groups of people these same leaders wanted desperately to integrate into the fabric of a civilized and peaceful society. Indeed, the photo itself suggested the sort of integration and civility they hoped to achieve. But in posing with other leaders, each inadvertently reinforced the view that Islam was at war with Western values, despite the fact that each had previously denied there was any ideological difficulty integrating Muslim citizens into their societies.

Both the jihadists in their violent actions and these world leaders in their arm-in-arm walk in Paris created meaning through social action. Both communities offered a *model of* the world as they had perceived it as well as a *model for* how the world should be. They then rooted those beliefs in social action by attacking their enemies or standing together in solidarity.

Whether in training camps run by ISIS (Islamic State of Iraq and Syria) and Al-Qaeda or among political demonstrations of solidarity in the streets of Paris, both groups create symbolic worlds linked to action. By creating a social world in which sacrifice—even death at the hands of police—strengthened righteous acts, the jihadists constructed a symbolic world where political, religious, and social actions were one. But by marching together in a Paris street, world leaders constructed a symbolic world free of violence and mayhem.

Before taking a closer look at how religious beliefs and behaviors are linked to political and social action in the world, it is necessary to turn to another major preoccupation of the anthropology of religion, the different forms that religion takes around the world.

Figure 13.5 World Leaders March in Solidarity for Freedom of Speech in Paris, January 11, 2015.

THINKING CRITICALLY ABOUT RELIGION

Consider how each of the four definitions or understandings of religion would explain why a religious cult like the Jim Jones cult in Guyana or the early Mormons in Nauvoo, Illinois—where they were attacked by non-Mormons—emerged. Alternatively, use these four explanations or definitions to interpret local reaction in your own community toward people with widely different religions.

What Forms Does Religion Take?

Early anthropologists like Edward Burnett Tylor largely saw all "primitive" societies as having a "primitive" religion. While anthropologists today reject the notion that some peoples are more "primitive" and others more "civilized," it is clear that societies with simple technologies and small populations traditionally had very different religions from those that have formed states with centralized governments and have more sophisticated technologies. But there is no evidence that one form inevitably evolves into another, as the early anthropologists believed.

The variety of human religions that exists seems to correspond to the kinds of social orders that exist in different scales of society. Societies with small populations, for example, developed few governmental institutions larger than the family, clan, or village, and their religious institutions were typically focused on these same primary institutions. Let us begin by considering clan-based religions and totemism common in small-scale societies, and then turn to religions in larger-scale and socially stratified societies, like polytheism, monotheism, and world religions.

Clan Spirits and Clan Identities in New Guinea

Nearly all New Guinea societies are organized around families and groups of families that belong to the same clan, and these clans are typically associated with particular kinds of spirits. The Ningerum of Papua New Guinea, for example, who have a very low population density of seven to 15 people per square mile, are concerned with various clan spirits that inhabit their traditional clan lands. These clan spirits have a full range of human emotions, but they become dangerous when they get jealous or angry, whereupon they can cause sickness or even death to people from other clans or even among the children and elders of their own clans. When they are happy and well attended to by the living with gifts of food, especially pork, they bring good harvest in the gardens, success in hunting, and healthy, prosperous families. All Ningerum rituals, aside from a few specific healing rites, emphasize dealing with all of these clan-based spirits, and at major feasts, pigs are sacrificed to these spirits to honor them with a bit of pork and other gifts made to them.

Among the Elema and Purari tribes of the Papuan Gulf, population densities have been much higher. When these tribes were observed in the early twentieth century, each village had several large longhouses, where men lived with their brothers and sons in rooms belonging to particular clans or subclans (Welsch 2006). These clan and subclan groups had various dances at initiation rituals, and the dance costumes depicted various animals that were associated with the particular clan, such as

Figure 13.6   Eharo Mask from Karama Village, Gulf Province, Collected About 1885. The design of this mask features the face of a gecko on the lower portion, with the body and tail extending upward above the face. A pair of "arms" and "legs" are on the left and right of the body, while the tail extends to the top of the mask. The mask is made of rattan covered with bark cloth that has been painted with traditional pigments in red, black, and white. The gecko was a totemic emblem for one of the clans in the village, and this mask would have been worn along with ten or more other masks in the same design by men of the gecko clan. (Hood Museum of Art, Dartmouth College, Hanover, New Hampshire)

• **Totemism.** A system of thought that associates particular social groups with specific animal or plant species called "totems" as an emblem.

• **Shaman.** A religious leader who communicates the needs of the living with the spirit world, usually through some form of ritual trance or other altered state of consciousness.

crocodiles and geckos (Figure 13.6). These systems of totems are absent among the Ningerum, but they are clearly present in a very simple way among the Elema and Purari tribes.

Totemism in North America

Early anthropologists studying American Indian societies observed that people identified with particular animals, often claiming to be descended from them. These people indicated their clans, lineages, tribes, or other social groups with emblems, usually animals, plants, places, and geographic or meteorological features (Figure 13.7). Anthropologists usually refer to these emblems as totems, and **totemism** as the system of thought that associates particular social groups with specific animal or plant species. Totems help create social cohesiveness by stressing group identity, focusing group and private rituals on totems. Some Native American societies simultaneously employed color symbolism, directional symbols, and species as totems. Until the 1920s, anthropologists interpreted totemism as evidence of a group's limited intellectual capacity, since people could not possibly be descended from eagles, wolves, or pythons.

Anthropologist Ralph Linton (1924) reported that Americans in the military during the First World War adopted a similar reverential attitude toward emblems like the rainbow (for the 42nd or Rainbow Division) without indicating any psychological problems. In American culture today, this phenomenon is widespread, especially in the realm of professional sports. Fans and players alike typically identify with a team's totemic emblems, sometimes enacting behaviors that everyone understands as symbolic of the team emblem, such as the Atlanta Braves' tomahawk chop. These are all examples of American totemism, all of which cultivate a sense of belonging to a social order larger than oneself.

Unlike this sort of American totemism, however, which is largely secular in orientation, traditional tribal societies usually understood their relation to a totemic animal in a supernatural way. Along the Northwest Coast of North America, for example, the Native society is divided into two halves (anthropologists call these halves "moieties"). One belongs to the Eagle totem, while the other belongs to the Raven totem. Within these moieties, each clan is identified with other totems, such as the Salmon, the Frog, the Brown Bear, and so on. These animals were also thought to have a special spiritual connection to the members of their social groups and appeared prominently in the origin myths of each clan. Native peoples carved these totems on memorial totem poles, painted them on clan houses, and decorated their blankets with them. In this way, the totems not only marked the sociopolitical order of clans within a village, but through ceremonies and myths, they linked people with the supernatural realm.

Shamanism and Ecstatic Religious Experiences

As early as the sixteenth century, European travelers from Russia and central Europe encountered tribes in Siberia whose religious rituals involved spiritual leaders called **shamans**, religious leaders who communicate the needs of the living to the spirit world, usually through some form of ritual trance or other altered state of consciousness. These specialists were not political leaders but focused on healing and ensuring

Figure 13.7 Chiefly Totems. Totemic images identified with the clan and social position of a Kwakiutl chief on Vancouver Island, British Columbia. The main images on the two pole are eagles; other elements associated with the eagle moiety are grizzly bears. The figure at the bottom of the left pole holds a ceremonial copper plaque, suggesting the importance of the chief. These poles capture the social identity, the social position, and the accomplishments of the chief, all expressed through the carved memorial pole.

the health and prosperity of the community using drum rituals to connect with the spirits. Anthropologists have observed the role of **trance** (a semiconscious state typically brought on by hypnosis, ritual drumming and singing, or hallucinogenic drugs like mescaline or peyote) as a key element of shamanic practice. The trance appears to allow shamans to accomplish difficult feats that would be impossible in normal circumstances, such as chewing glass or possessing great strength.

Shamanism is found in one form or another on all continents, but especially in North and South America, Africa, and Asia. The details of these shamanic traditions vary widely, but they are often associated with small-scale societies with more or less egalitarian political structures. Anthropologist Napoleon Chagnon and filmmaker Timothy Asch's 1973 film *Magical Death* shows one of the best-known examples of shamanic healing. In this film, the Yanomami shaman heals his family by ingesting hallucinogenic snuff made from a local plant. As in many shamanic traditions, this shaman is assisted by his **spirit familiar** (a spirit that has developed a close bond with the shaman), who helps him see other spirits and heal his children.

The importance of such altered states of consciousness was also explored by anthropologist Barbara G. Myerhoff's (1974) study of the peyote religion of the Huichol [**wee**-choal] Indians of northern Mexico. Myerhoff's key finding is that the rituals of Huichol shamans, including the ritualized hunt for peyote in the Mexican desert, give meaning to the social order of these people. In societies more familiar to Americans, such as some Pentecostal and charismatic Christian traditions, the ecstatic religious experience that has long been associated with shamans is encouraged by members of the congregation through witnessing, singing, and **speaking in tongues** (the phenomenon of speaking in an apparently unknown language, often in an energetic and fast-paced way). Anthropologists have noted that these vocalizations do not correspond to any human language, but symbolically they connect people with God via the Holy Spirit. These individual connections between each participant and the Holy Spirit parallel the egalitarian society they are ritually constructing in their congregations.

Whether it is religions like those of the Ningerum or Elema, totemism among Native American groups, or shamanism, each of these religious systems draws on a

- **Trance.** A semi-conscious state typically brought on by hypnosis, ritual drumming and singing, or hallucinogenic drugs like mescaline or peyote.

- **Spirit familiar.** A spirit that has developed a close bond with a shaman.

- **Speaking in tongues.** The phenomenon of speaking in an apparently unknown language, often in an energetic and fast-paced way.

Figure 13.8   Symbols of Royal Authority in the Benin Kingdom. For the people of the kingdom of Benin, bronze figures and reliefs represented royal connections to the gods. (Hood Museum of Art, Dartmouth College, Hanover, New Hampshire)

• **Polytheism.** Belief in many gods.

mix of the same sorts of elements. All stress group identities and link these identities to various religious symbols. Symbols are also used in the religions of stratified societies, but the groups they highlight are larger entities or social categories that extend beyond the local, face-to-face community.

Ritual Symbols That Reinforce a Hierarchical Social Order

Ritual symbols tend to reinforce the social hierarchy and the political order at the same time as they interact with divine beings and powers. In the former kingdom of Benin, in what is now Nigeria in West Africa, for example, the Oba (king) was believed to be divine. The fiercest animal in the region, the leopard, became a symbol of royal power, projecting an image of the Oba's power over his people. One feature of Benin religious practice was the Igwe Festival, which was a cleansing ritual expelling evil from the entire kingdom led by the Oba. This ritual sequence served to strengthen and renew the Oba's divine powers. Benin bronze sculptures and reliefs often depict members of the royal family, offering another way for the Benin to venerate their Oba (Figure 13.8). By strengthening the Oba, the community felt it was maintaining the well-being of the kingdom. Benin rituals and art together provided a model of the divine nature of the ruler, supporting a social order in which the ruler dominated over all others (Bradbury 1957; Dark 1962, 1982; Eboreime 2003).

Polytheism and Monotheism in Ancient Societies

The kingdoms and dynasties of ancient Egypt provided a similar model of the social order replicated in many of its most important rituals. The pharaoh was a king ruling over a vast empire of people along the Nile and Mediterranean coast and extending into what is now Israel and the Arabian peninsula. Everything about Egyptian ritual—as well as the construction of great pyramids and structures like the Sphinx—celebrated a complex hierarchy of officials and priests, with the pharaoh as a divine figure at the head of the state and its religious organizations. But the pharaoh was not the only divine figure; Egyptians held that there was a host of other, more powerful deities, making their religion one of **polytheism** (belief in many gods). All of these gods demanded the attention of humans, or, it was thought, they might harm the human world with droughts, plagues, locusts, and floods of the Nile River.

Nearly all of the ancient societies in the Middle East and Mediterranean were polytheistic, with complex state rituals that promoted an image of the state and its human leaders as superior to ordinary men. The main exception to polytheism in the ancient world was the ancient Hebrews, whose religion focused on a single god called Yahweh. In all likelihood, Yahweh began as a local deity that was worshiped and venerated by one of the tribes of Israel that became the ancient Hebrews. It seems likely that Yahweh was the deity of Moses' tribe, and after the exodus from Egypt under Ramses the Great of the nineteenth dynasty, his clan or tribal deity gradually pushed out the other gods (Armstrong 1994). When the Hebrews established Yahweh as the

God of Israel, they began a long-term shift to **monotheism**—belief in a single god. Monotheism set the Hebrews apart as distinctive in their region. The key feature of monotheism was that it symbolized a single universal faith because the single God was presented as the deity of all, whereas polytheism encouraged different groups to identify with different local gods, in much the way that totemism works.

- **Monotheism.** Belief in a single god.

World Religions and Universal Understandings of the World

Most of us are more familiar with the universal monotheistic **world religions**— or religions that claim to be universally significant to all people—of Judaism, Christianity, and Islam, than with the small-scale religions discussed previously. All three of these monotheistic world religions provided a general message that was applicable to all people, not just the members of a small clan or social group. For the most part, all three provided a positive, uplifting message for adherents, and all three became identified with the ruling governments. All three also became state religions, whose religious message and ritual supported the government of the state.

- **World religions.** Religions that claim to be universally significant to all people.

Christianity and Islam illustrate the ways a local monotheistic religion can become universalized through a set of beliefs and social order. Christianity began in what is now Israel but spread to communities in Asia Minor and Greece when the apostle Paul began evangelizing. Expanding membership was possible only after the Jewish requirement of circumcision was abolished for new converts. Monotheism encouraged a universal, pan-human approach to faith, and there were many people in the Eastern Mediterranean who wanted a religion that made them part of a new, universal, and growing community.

Five centuries later, Islam emerged in the Arabian peninsula when the prophet Muhammad received holy scripture in the form of poetry from a single, universal god—called Allah in classical Arabic. Most non-Muslim Americans are startled to learn that Muhammed had one Christian wife and lived peaceably among a mix of Muslims, Jews, and Christians in Medina, until members of one of the Jewish tribes attempted to assassinate him. Jesus, Mary, John the Baptist, Moses, Abraham, and Adam, among others, are discussed at some length in the Quran, and all are considered Muslim prophets. From a Muslim point of view, Muslims, Christians, and Jews are all "people of the book," meaning that each has scripture received through prophets from God. But followers of Islam, being the newest of these three religions, feel that God's message was most accurately received by the prophet Muhammad. Thus, they feel that Christians and Jews didn't get the entire message from God, in much the same way that many Christian faiths believe that Jews were not given the full faith until Jesus arrived.

Asia has also produced important world religions that reflect particular histories of social stratification and universalistic belief. Hinduism was a polytheistic religion that emerged in India thousands of years ago. Like the polytheistic religions of the Middle East, Hinduism supported the authority of local princes and kings. Most Hindu ritual was focused on achieving good relations between people and various gods. Sometime in the fourth to sixth centuries BCE, a man named Siddhartha Gautama emerged as a founder of a new faith called Buddhism in reaction to Hinduism. According to Buddhist traditions, having been selfishly pursuing his own pleasure through licentious living, he was mysteriously awakened to his misdeeds and promoted a life of reflection and active commitment to the Buddhist path, accepting the Buddha, the *Dharma* (his teachings), and the *Sangha* (the Buddhist community). Unlike most other religions, Buddhism encourages its members to strive toward greater enlightenment. In this sense, Buddhism is neither monotheistic nor polytheistic, but is as much a moral code of conduct as a religion. The rituals often involve meditation and devotional acts aimed at turning people from this-worldly desires (wealth, sex, power, etc.) to concern for other people and all other creatures, and a state of enlightenment called *Nirvana*.

How Does Atheism Fit in the Discussion?

Finally, we must ask if atheists, agnostics, and nonbelievers have a religion. This question has been a worrisome issue for anthropologists, because traditionally anthropologists have defined religion in terms of a belief in the supernatural, which means that these beliefs have little basis in empirical fact.

But taking a step back, if all humans have some sort of worldview, then everyone has some sort of perspective on life analogous to religion. Secular people must also have symbolic systems that give meaning and purpose to their lives. We saw this secular system of meaning enacted in the solidarity marches in Paris on January 11, 2015, and when the 40 world leaders stood arm in arm on a Paris street to show solidarity in their defense of free speech. For some, secular rituals that celebrate the state or nation, particular occupations, or other identities may achieve many of the same ends as religious rituals. For others, practicing scientific research may construct a worldview similar to that of people with more traditional religious beliefs. Geertz's definition of religion was specifically designed to be as useful for secular worldviews with a rich array of secular symbols as it is for more traditional religions.

• •

THINKING CRITICALLY ABOUT RELIGION

Consider any three different societies we have discussed in this book. Discuss the extent to which the scale of society—measured in terms of population or number of people within the same administrative or governing body—is reflected in complexity of technology and complexity of religious concepts. How do these three measures of complexity—population size, technological complexity, and sophistication of religious ideas—match up? What does this kind of comparison tell us about evolutionary models of society?

• •

How Do Rituals Work?

All rituals have certain key features, including that they are repetitive (happening at set times or before or after certain events) and stylized (following a set order of words or actions). What distinguishes religious ritual from daily habits such as brushing one's teeth (which some of you might think of as a "ritual") is that nobody invests special significance in tooth brushing. Some rituals, such as rites of passage (discussed later), are especially significant in a person's life. But, before we explain why and how they work, it is important to note that anthropologists have long understood that at the heart of all ritual action exists a particular mode of thought that we call "magical." What do we mean?

Magical Thought in Non-Western Cultures

• **Magic.** An explanatory system of causation that does not follow naturalistic explanations, often working at a distance without direct physical contact.

When anthropologists talk of **magic**, they discuss it as an explanatory system of causation that does not follow naturalistic explanations—such as being struck by a weapon or infected by some virus—often working at a distance without direct physical contact. Informants nearly always accept magical explanations as real, and they often believe deeply that such manifestations are frightening or dangerous.

Magic can have many goals, usually goals that are out of reach through an individual taking direct action. The practitioner may want his or her gardens to flourish or his hunt to be successful. She may want the food at her feast to go further than it normally would, or to attract the affections of a handsome young man in a neighboring hamlet. Jealous over another man's abundant successes, a man may want to cause his rival to become ill, or—even more maliciously—he may want his enemy to die. Techniques may involve incantations, spells, unusual behaviors, and the manipulation of any number of special objects, all in an effort to cause some desired event to occur. All of these practices are assumed to occur at a distance with no direct physical contact between the one performing the magic and the object or person upon which he or she wants to act.

For anthropologists, the point is not whether magical practices actually bring about their desired ends or not. It is usually enough to understand that members of a community accept that these processes occur. But why do these puzzling practices make sense to the people who practice magic?

Sympathetic Magic: The Law of Similarity and the Law of Contagion

The English anthropologist Sir James G. Frazer coined the term **sympathetic magic** to refer to any magical rite that relies on supernatural powers to produce its outcome without working through a specific supernatural being such as a spirit, demon, or deity (see "Classic Contributions: Sir James G. Frazer on Sympathetic Magic"). Drawing on dozens of examples from around the world, Frazer showed that sympathetic magic works on two principles that he called the "law of similarity" and the "law of contagion." Both involved sympathetic magic because the person or object acted upon did so "in sympathy" with the magical actions.

• **Sympathetic magic.** Any magical rite that relies on the supernatural to produce its outcome without working through a specific supernatural being such as a spirit, demon, or deity.

The Laws of Magic: Similarities and Contagion

Frazer described the law of similarities as some point of similarity between an aspect of the magical rite and the desired goal. A good illustration is a "voodoo doll," which is an image that represents the maker's enemy. By poking or stabbing the image, they hope to produce pain in the corresponding part of the victim's body. For the Inuit, this principle also applies to charms or fishhooks that represent a seal and allow fishermen or hunters to catch fish as easily as a seal does. Today, anthropologists often speak of these similarities as metaphors, since the charm or fishhook carved as a seal is not really a seal but merely an object that resembles a seal (Figure 13.9). Nevertheless, the thought behind this magical association is that seals are good at catching fish, and so the seal-like charm attached to the hook will attract fish.

Alternatively, a magical rite could follow the law of contagion, in which things that had once been in physical contact with one another could have an effect even when they were no longer in contact. According to the law of contact, mundane objects we've touched or produced as individuals, such as a cigarette butt, a scrap of partly eaten food, hair, nail clippings, sweat, urine, and feces, carry part of our essence, and harmful things done to them by an ill-intentioned magician can by extension hurt us (Figure 13.10).

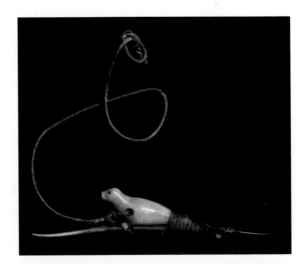

▼ **Figure 13.9 Sympathetic Magic Among the Inuit.** Attached to this fishhook is a charm carved of ivory in the shape of a seal. The charm is meant to ensure that the hook will be successful in catching fish like a seal is successful in catching fish. (Hood Museum of Art, Dartmouth College, Hanover, New Hampshire)

Classic Contributions
Sir James G. Frazer on Sympathetic Magic

SCOTSMAN JAMES G. FRAZER (1854–1941) was one of the earliest anthropologists in Great Britain. He spent his career studying religion in so-called primitive and archaic societies as an armchair anthropologist. He is best known for his multivolume work *The Golden Bough: A Study in Comparative Religion*, first published in two volumes in 1890 and later expanded (Frazer 1911–1915). Although anthropologists draw on very little of Frazer's work today, they still appreciate his insights about magic. Frazer was the first to offer an explanation of the logic that all magic was based upon—the principle of sympathetic magic—which he discusses here.

🌱 **Sir James G. Frazer, the Classic Armchair Anthropologist.**

One of the principles of sympathetic magic is that any effect may be produced by imitating it. To take a few instances. If it is wished to kill a person an image of him is made and then destroyed; and it is believed that through a certain physical sympathy between the person and his image, the man feels the injuries done to the image as if they were done to his own body, and that when it is destroyed he must simultaneously perish. . . .

Magic sympathy is supposed to exist between a man and any severed portion of his body, as his hair or nails;

so that whoever gets possession of hair or nails may work his will, at any distance, upon the person from whom they were cut. This [belief] is world-wide. . . .

Thus we see that in sympathetic magic one event is supposed to be followed necessarily and invariably by another, without the intervention of any spiritual or personal agency. This is, in fact, the modern conception of physical causation; the conception, indeed, is misapplied, but it is there none the less. (Frazer 1890:9–10)

Questions for Reflection

1. Which aspect of sympathetic magic is involved when an athlete wears his or her lucky socks to play a game?

2. Which aspect of sympathetic magic is involved when a boyfriend or girlfriend gives his or her partner something to keep with him or her during a trip?

Applying These Principles to Religious Activities

Although Frazer depicted these two types of magical principles as occurring in separate situations, they often occur together, drawing simultaneously on the similarities and the previous contact. And while Frazer saw magic as distinct and separate from religion, most anthropologists now recognize that magical principles are often invoked in religious rituals.

For example, the Christian ritual of communion embodies both principles of magic simultaneously. The elements used in the rite—the bread and the wine—are consecrated by the priest or pastor and intended to be consumed by the congregation.

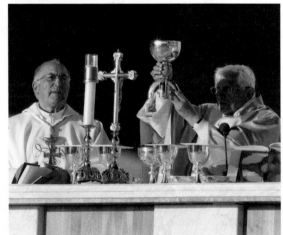

Figure 13.10   Contagious Magic in Papua New Guinea. A Ningerum man in Papua New Guinea prepares for a pig feast by anointing a pig lengthwise with sago flour in the belief that this rite will make the food go farther. When guests eat just a little of the pork, they will quickly feel full. Anointing the pig uses contagious magic.

This ritual imitates the Last Supper, when Jesus is said to have shared bread and wine with his most devoted followers, declaring the bread to be his "body" and the wine to be his "blood." The Last Supper was held at the start of the Jewish feast of Passover, which reenacts the story of the Jewish exodus from Egypt. Because the meal was part of the Passover, the bread was unleavened and flat, similar to the unleavened matzoh bread that is commonly produced today as large flat wafers. Jesus himself is using a metaphor when he announces that the bread "is my body" and that the wine "is my blood." The wine is an appropriate element because it resembles blood in color—law of similarity. The wafer resembles the unleavened bread of the Passover meal, which in turn is a symbol for Jesus' flesh. When congregants each eat a consecrated wafer and drink a sip of wine, they are linked together as a congregation because they have shared the same wafers and wine—law of contact (Figure 13.11).

Magic in Western Societies

Americans tend to believe that modernization has eliminated magical thought in our culture. Yet many of the elements observed in non-Western societies also occur in contemporary America. In his study of baseball players, for example, anthropologist George Gmelch (1978) noted that players often have lucky jerseys, good luck fetishes, or other objects that become charms. For these players, ordinary objects acquire power by being connected to exceptionally hot batting or pitching streaks. These charms follow the law of similarity. For three months during a winning season, one pitcher Gmelch interviewed followed the exact same routine: at lunch he went to the same restaurant, had two glasses of iced tea and a tuna fish sandwich, and for an hour before the game wore the same sweatshirt and jock strap he had worn the first day of the streak. He was afraid that changing anything he had done before the first winning game might produce a bad result.

Figure 13.11   The Christian Eucharist or Communion. The similarity of red wine to blood and wafers to flesh establishes the similarities between the ritual objects and their meaning. Consuming them during the ritual invokes the law of contagion to spread the blessings of God among all the people.

Rites of Passage and the Ritual Process

- **Rite of passage.** Any life cycle rite that marks a person's or group's transition from one social state to another.

The most important type of ritual is a **rite of passage**, a life cycle ritual that marks a person's (or group of persons') transition from one social state to another. In 1909, French sociologist Arnold van Gennep (1960) outlined the structure of rituals that marked the passage of individuals from one status to another. Rites of passage include marriage rituals, in which individuals change status from being single to being married, and rituals that mark the transition from childhood to adulthood. Initiations are common around the world, even in industrial societies such as ours that carry out such rituals in "sweet sixteen parties" for young women, school graduation, and the like. Funerals represent another rite of passage that focuses on the deceased but is largely about the transition survivors will experience. In "Thinking Like an Anthropologist: Examining Rites of Passage," we explore the link between symbols and the construction of meaning in two American rituals: funerals and graduations.

For anthropologist Victor Turner (1967, 1969), all rituals invoke symbols that can convey the underlying meanings of the ritual. Ritual symbols can consist of objects, colors, actions, events, or words. Often symbols point to, suggest, or take meaning from myths or sacred texts known to participants, such as the cross or the wine and wafers in Christian church services. When American brides wear white, they are symbolically expressing their purity, whereas when Chinese wear white at a funeral, they are expressing their grief. What is common throughout these examples is that rituals create solidarity and meaning for participants and represent tradition for a group of people.

• •

THINKING CRITICALLY ABOUT RELIGION

Compare the ritual symbols used in a televised Sunday morning service conducted by a Protestant televangelist with those used in a televised Sunday morning Roman Catholic mass. Although both services are religious rituals for Christian sects, they look very different. How do the different structures in the two services suggest different meanings derived from the same scripture?

• •

How Is Religion Linked to Political and Social Action?

- **Secular worldview.** A worldview that does not accept the supernatural as influencing current people's lives.

Time magazine's cover for April 8, 1966, asked the provocative question, "Is God Dead?" Playing off the nineteenth-century German philosopher Friedrich Nietzsche's famous claim that "God is dead"—suggesting that the **secular worldview**, or a worldview that does not accept the supernatural as influencing current people's lives, had finally overtaken the religious one in Europe—*Time* was asking whether the same secularizing trend was at work in America. Formal church membership in Europe had declined sharply, to fewer than 10% of the population in some countries, and *Time* was suggesting that perhaps religion would no longer play a role in political action, as it had played in the abolition movement and was playing in the civil rights movement. *Time* was so wrong. More than 40 years later, we can see the persistent power of religion in the United States, in politics, in social discourse, in civil rights, and on TV. American church membership has risen gradually since the

Thinking Like an Anthropologist
Examining Rites of Passage

ANTHROPOLOGISTS BEGIN THEIR research by asking questions. In this box, we want you to learn how to ask questions as an anthropological researcher. Part One describes a situation and follows up with questions we would ask. Part Two asks you to formulate your own questions based on a different situation.

PART ONE: STATE FUNERAL FOR PRESIDENT RONALD REAGAN

When former president Ronald Reagan died on June 5, 2004, America began a week of national mourning and state ritual that dominated television and radio. State funerals, like inaugurations, are rites of passage that create a model of the state and become a model for how the state should be. Such secular rituals support and help create a sense of nationalism, American pride, a feeling of belonging to the nation, and a way of linking all Americans to state institutions. All funerals, of course, also have an important personal function: disposing of a dead body, and helping the deceased's friends and relatives adjust to the loss. It was no different when Reagan passed away. Distant relatives and close friends paid their respects to the president's widow and children. But because of his former role as President of the United States, his death became a rite of passage and transition for all Americans.

The former president died in southern California, and the family decided that he would be buried at the Ronald Reagan Presidential Library in Simi Valley, California. The most efficient way to conduct a funeral would be to hold it in California. But most of the ritual occurred in Washington, DC, the center of the government that he had led.

A Public Funerary Ritual.   Mourners file in to view former president Ronald Reagan's flag-draped casket as he lies in state in the Rotunda of the United States Capitol building in Washington, DC, on June 10, 2004.

(continued)

Thinking Like an Anthropologist (continued)

Flown to Andrews Air Force Base, the flag-draped coffin was brought to the Washington Monument, where it was transferred to a horse-drawn caisson, on which it proceeded slowly up Constitution Avenue to the Capitol. The procession was led by a riderless horse with boots pointed backward, symbolic of the dead (former) Commander in Chief. Three pairs of horses pulled the caisson, with riders only on the three left-side horses. When the procession reached Fourth Street, 21 F15 planes made a flyover, and the coffin was carried the rest of the way up to the Capitol by eight-man teams representing each branch of the military. At this point, there was a 21-gun salute, and the band played "Hail to the Chief" and "The Battle Hymn of the Republic." Mrs. Reagan was waiting inside the Capitol to meet the coffin.

After a short ceremony, the former president's body was to lie in state in the Rotunda, at the center of the Capitol building. The flag-draped casket rested on the simple pine frame covered with black cloth that had first held the coffin of Abraham Lincoln in 1865. Present were important politicians who had served in the Reagan administration or in the Bush administration. Only the Reagan family was given seats for the ceremony. After the ceremony, Mrs. Reagan and the dignitaries left, but the public was allowed to file in and around the casket throughout the night. Thousands filed past the casket to pay their respects in solemnity and silence until 7:00 the next morning (Purdum 2004).

The next morning, a motorcade took the body to the National Cathedral for the national funeral service, with eulogies from President George W. Bush, former president George H. W. Bush, former British prime minister Margaret

Thatcher, and former Canadian prime minister Brian Mulroney. After the funeral, a motorcade brought the body back to Andrews, whereupon it was flown to California for a private interment ceremony attended only by the Reagan family and close family friends.

What questions does this situation raise for anthropological researchers?

1. How do the ritual symbols, such as the use of a caisson, riderless horse, 21-plane flyover, 21-gun salute, and so on, add meaning to the ritual?
2. What added meaning was given to the event by holding it in Washington, DC, that could not have been accomplished in the Reagan Library in California?
3. What meaning was created by the particular dignitaries who attended the Rotunda ceremony?
4. What model of social order was conveyed by the particular order in which people viewed the flag-draped casket? What difference did it make that viewing went on for 36 hours that would not have been accomplished if it had lasted for only three hours?

PART TWO: YOUR OWN HIGH SCHOOL GRADUATION

Reflect back on your own high school graduation, which was probably marked by special costumes, processions, music, speeches, and actions (such as shifting the tassel to the other side of the mortarboard) that acknowledged your shift from one status to another. Viewing this graduation as a rite of passage, what questions would you ask about this situation as an anthropological researcher?

late 1940s to about 75% of American adults today. So, why was *Time* magazine so wrong?

The main reason is the magazine's false assumption that as a society "modernizes," it begins to value scientific knowledge and reason over religious values and practices. The *Time* authors assumed that secularization would continue to grow, but American churches responded to social change not by ignoring it but by challenging it. Churches and other religious organizations became increasingly political, often supporting one political party or the other. In nearly every society, political and religious institutions are not only engaged with one another, they are frequently the same institutions.

The broader point here is that religious values, symbols, and beliefs typically either challenge or uphold a particular social order. We illustrate this point by considering the forceful rise of religious fundamentalisms around the world.

The Rise of Fundamentalism

Since the 1960s, the most significant change in U.S. religion has been how much more active religious organizations have become in public life, particularly among the conservative churches that call themselves **fundamentalist**, people belonging to conservative religious movements that advocate a return to fundamental or traditional principles. Fundamentalist TV preachers have expanded their broadcasting since the early 1980s, and conservative religious groups and religious organizations have been as deeply involved in elections and politics as ever. The rise of fundamentalism is not unique to the United States, either. Across the world, conservative groups have turned to fundamentalism to make sense of and to confront changes that are happening all around them. As in the United States, fundamentalist religion and politics are deeply engaged with one another in other societies as well (Berger 1999).

• **Fundamentalist.** A person belonging to a religious movement that advocates a return to fundamental or traditional principles.

Understanding Fundamentalism

Scholars have had difficulty agreeing on a definition of fundamentalism. Traditionally, **fundamentalism** in America has been associated with extremely literal interpretation of scripture, particularly prophetic books in the Bible. Recently, the American media has often associated fundamentalism with Islam, violence, extremism, and terrorism, but both views are far too narrow and biased, because most of the world's religions have their own conservative, "back to fundamentals" branches, and most are not so outwardly violent.

• **Fundamentalism.** Conservative religious movements that advocate a return to fundamental or traditional principles.

To correct these biases, in the 1990s a team of researchers working on the Fundamentalism Project at the University of Chicago studied conservative religious movements within Christianity, Islam, Zionist Judaism, Buddhism, Hinduism, Confucianism, and Sikhism (Marty and Appleby 1991; Almond, Appleby, and Sivan 2003). Not all of these diverse movements rely on literal readings of scripture, and for some groups, sacred writings are of little consequence. Nor do fundamentalist groups necessarily reject everything modern. Most have embraced television, computers, the Internet, and other digital technologies to get the word out. And conservative Arab Muslims celebrate the medieval Islamic origins of modern science and technology.

The Fundamentalism Project (Marty and Appleby 1991:viii–x) found several key themes common to all of these conservative religious movements. These include the following:

- They see themselves as fighting back against the corrosive effects of secular life on what they envision as a purer way of life. They fight for a worldview that prescribes "proper" gender roles, sexualities, and educational patterns. Their interpretation of the purer past becomes the model for building a purer, godlier future.
- They are willing to engage in political, even military, battles to defend their ideas about life and death, including issues that emerge in hospitals and clinics dealing with pregnancy, abortion, and the terminally ill.
- They work against others, whether infidels, modernizers, or moderate insiders, in the process reinforcing their identity and building solidarity within their community.
- They have passion, and the most passionate are those who "are convinced that they are called to carry out God's or Allah's purposes against challengers" (Marty and Appleby 1991:x).

Political action among fundamentalists has sometimes taken a more violent course, as suggested by recent jihadist attacks in the West, and by militant Sikhs' armed combat and insurrection against the government in India. We explore the latter case further in "Doing Fieldwork: Studying the Sikh Militants."

Doing Fieldwork
Studying the Sikh Militants

ANTHROPOLOGIST CYNTHIA KEPPLEY Mahmood, now at the University of Notre Dame, had been studying religion and conflict in the Indian subcontinent for more than a decade, making frequent visits to India, when she became interested in a fundamentalist movement among members of the Sikh religion. From 1980, a militant group of ethnic Sikhs in the northwestern Indian state of Punjab had been engaged in an armed insurgency aimed at forming a sovereign nation called Khalistan ("Land of the Pure"). This insurgency was built on a fundamentalist religious ideology. Khalistanis identify themselves through both their religious and their ethnic identities. This movement, however, does not represent all or even the majority of Sikh people living in Punjab. Other Sikhs support the idea of independence but reject the violence entailed in winning it.

Wanting to study religion and violence, Mahmood turned her attention to the separatist tensions in Punjab, which were as religious as they were political. Studying a violent religious group presented special problems for the anthropologist, because it was impossible for her to live in a community with the militants, targeted as they were by the Indian government they wanted to overthrow. So Mahmood adopted an innovative strategy by conducting research about militant Sikhs and their movement overseas rather than in India.

Over a period of three years in the early 1990s, Mahmood met intermittently with militant Sikhs in various parts of the United States and Canada to understand the motives, rationale, and ideology of this fundamentalist group. Mahmood's interactions with the Sikhs occurred in restaurants, homes, Sikh temples, and even prisons. Many of her informants had come to North America as a way of reinvigorating their movement, which was being suppressed by the Indian government in Punjab. Many informants felt that violent acts were reasonable and acceptable responses to

✤ **A Sikh Temple in India.**   The vast majority of Sikhs are not militant or violent, just as most Christians, Jews, Muslims, Hindus, and Buddhists are nonviolent.

study before the terrorist attacks of 9/11; the tapes of her interviews would have posed a danger for her informants if they had fallen into the hands of various law enforcement agencies, because unlike journalists, anthropologists have no First Amendment rights to protect their sources. Of course, she changed the names of her informants and concealed their identities when she published her book, *Fighting for Faith and Nation: Dialogs with Sikh Militants* (1997).

Questions for Reflection

1. What is lost by conducting research almost entirely through interviews rather than through participant observation?

2. What ethical complications are involved in studying a militant anti-government religious group?

3. How would these complications be different if one conducted research in the Methodist Church?

The broader point here is that fundamentalists are not isolated from the world of politics, but actively engaged in it. Unlike religion in most small-scale societies, fundamentalism does not typically support the existing political order but fights against it. We have seen this in the United States, when the evangelical pastor Jerry Falwell founded a political organization called the Moral Majority in 1979. Members of the

Moral Majority were fundamentalists, and they became active in the presidential elections throughout the 1980s, supporting conservative candidates. In recent decades, fundamentalist Christians have stood in vocal opposition to non-conservative candidates.

What we do see in fundamentalism is that membership and a sense of belonging to a community is an important feature of religious organizations in industrial societies where it is easy for individuals to feel anonymous. Indeed, part of the power of any religious organizations (churches, synagogues, mosques, and other religious centers) is that they bring people together, provide them social support, and give them an identity within a broader secular world. Anthropologists have long understood that this process of belonging and the social action associated with group membership is bolstered by important symbols.

● ●

THINKING CRITICALLY ABOUT RELIGION

Consider the Fourth of July ritual that takes place in your hometown. How do the parades and the speeches and fireworks build symbolic support for the state and federal governments and for the U.S. military? How do the symbols support the existing government?

● ●

Conclusion

A month after Tom Coleman shot Jonathan Daniels in Hayneville, Alabama, an all-white jury found Coleman not guilty of manslaughter. This was a cause of disbelief for many who sympathized with Daniels's worldview. For example, Daniels's hometown newspaper, the *Keene Sentinel*, editorialized that "White Southerners and Northerners who hold [similar] views . . . do not, and apparently cannot, understand why a white man would risk his life to help a Negro register to vote or teach Negro children to read. They simply do not understand that, to men like Jonathan Daniels, all men are brothers, and skin color means nothing. . . . In dying, not only was Jonathan Daniels minding his own business, but he was attending to His business."

When Jonathan Daniels first went to Alabama, he did so with a moral and religious commitment to what he understood as social justice. His actions were driven by a worldview that called him to help create a world suggested by his reading of scripture and his understanding of God. But at the same time, Tom Coleman acted out of his own worldview, one clearly shared by the jury. At that time in America, many people were proud of their prejudices and found many justifications for them, even in their religions. As much as people today may disapprove of Coleman's actions and of those on the jury, these actions were motivated by a shared set of assumptions about what the world should be like. Coleman acted in defense of that ideal world. Just as Daniels's actions made sense in terms of his belief system, Coleman's beliefs and understandings about the world made sense to the large part of his community.

Whether or not we agree with such a perspective, we can never understand the actions of others without understanding a community's worldview and the powerful moods and motivations it creates. These are the benefits of approaching conflicting beliefs from the "native's point of view."

KEY TERMS

Animism   p. 332

Fundamentalism   p. 351

Fundamentalist   p. 351

Interpretive approach
   p. 334

Magic   p. 344

Mana   p. 332

Monotheism   p. 343

Polytheism   p. 342

Quran   p. 336

Religion   p. 331

Rite of passage   p. 348

Rituals   p. 332

Secular worldview
   p. 348

Shaman   p. 340

Speaking in tongues
   p. 341

Spirit familiar   p. 341

Sympathetic magic   p. 345

Totemism   p. 340

Trance   p. 341

World religions   p. 343

Worldview   p. 334

Reviewing the Chapter

Chapter Section	What We Know	To Be Resolved
How Should We Understand Religion and Religious Beliefs?	Anthropologists have long considered the reasons people have religion and how religions work. While some classic approaches emphasized that religion is about the supernatural, more recent approaches emphasize the symbolic and action-oriented character of religious beliefs.	Many anthropologists accept that we can learn a great deal about the worldviews of the peoples we study, but not all anthropologists believe that we can fully understand how any individual sees and feels about his or her world.
What Forms Does Religion Take?	Traditional societies with limited social stratification tend to have simpler religions than the religions of complex societies, but this correlation is not inevitable.	We don't really know what environmental, political, or social conditions produce more complex forms of religious ideas.
How Do Rituals Work?	Rituals use symbols that convey deep meanings about the world and how it should be. All rituals rely on some version of magical thinking. Ritual symbols themselves rely heavily on metaphor and other kinds of resemblances for conveying meaning.	It is not entirely clear why humans in all societies so readily accept ideas and beliefs that can be so easily shown to be incomplete, if not wrong.
How Is Religion Linked to Political and Social Action?	Religions have always been linked to political organizations and the social order. Anthropologists reject the idea that as the world modernized it would become more secular, drawing on the widespread rise of fundamentalism to demonstrate the continuing social and political importance of religion.	There is no real consensus as to how much political institutions can shape religious symbols, rituals, and worldviews, even though it is obvious that groups in power often try to.

Readings

One of the most important early studies of a traditional, non-Western religion is E. E. Evans-Pritchard's 1937 classic ethnography, *Witchcraft, Oracles, and Magic Among the Azande* (abridged edition, Oxford, UK: Clarendon Press, 1976), in which ideas about witchcraft, diviners called "oracles," and magic are described and discussed in their natural context in what is now South Sudan.

....

Two important studies provide examples of symbolic studies of religion. Clifford Geertz's 1966 article "Religion as a Cultural System" (in Michael Banton, ed., *Anthropological* *Approaches to the Study of Religion*, pp. 1–46, ASA Monograph 3, London: Tavistock) explores a symbolic definition of religion that sees religion as a "system of symbols." Victor Turner's book *The Forest of Symbols: Aspects of Ndembu Ritual* (Ithaca, NY: Cornell University Press, 1967) offers a series of explorations of just how such a system of symbols might work in a functioning society in southern Africa.

....

For an anthropological perspective on the interactions between Islam and politics, see Dale F. Eickelman and James P. Piscatori's book *Muslim* *Politics* (Princeton, NJ: Princeton University Press, 1996). Even though it was written before the post-9/11 world, it offers useful analytical tools to understand the complex intersections of religion and political action in the Muslim world.

....

If you want to understand the rise of religious fundamentalisms in recent decades, see Martin Marty and R. Scott Appleby's edited volume *Fundamentalisms Observed* (The Fundamentalism Project, Volume 1, Chicago, IL: University of Chicago Press, 1991).

....

WHAT'S UP WITH LISA'S SMILE?

...ALES OFFERS SOME UNEXPECTED THEORIES. PAGE 11

metro®

...'S #1 FREE DAILY NEWSPAPER

w.metro.us | t: MetroNewYork | f: MetroNewYork

tested for possible a virus at hospital

Mount Sinai

...w York City man who recently visited
...ca was quarantined at Mount Sinai
...ght while awaiting the return of test
...s the Ebola virus. Metro charts
...w the disease is spreading. PAGE 02

...Hospital, where a man was quarantined and is being tested to see if he has the Ebola virus. / GETTY IMAGES

A brand new 'Child' for James Franco
PAGE 13

Toronto has more going for it than Rob Ford
PAGE 16

Wilson calls it a career with Giants after injury
PAGE 21

...all NEW...

MANHATTAN'S HIGHEST DAILY CIRCU...

MAN TEST... EBOLA I...

- Patient had recently travel...
- Docs say unlikely he...

PAGE 3

DAILY...

NEW YORK'S HOMET...

EBOL... SCAR... IN CITY

NEW YORK...
edge Monday...
hospital reve...
ing a man su...
symptoms.
   Officials sai...
man had rec...
West Africa, w...
killed 900 peop...
   "I'm worrie...
man who lives...
center. "It's to...
PAG...

◯ Man tested for dead...
◯ Disease 'unlikely' b...

EBOLA! Man tested for disea...e in NYC

By JAMIE SCHRAM
...ars of an Ebola outbreak
...d City were...

complaining of high fever
and gastrointestinal dis-
tress, was placed in "strict
isolation" at Mount Sinai
...ital (left) while he...

...ng back's career over at 23 SPORTS

14

The Body

Biocultural Perspectives on Health and Illness

DURING THE FALL OF 2014, television screens, newspaper headlines, radio news broadcasts, and social media proclaimed the same terrifying message: an American outbreak of Ebola. The Ebola virus produces fearsome effects in humans, including the hemorrhaging of blood and other bodily fluids, with an average mortality rate of 50%. For several months, the contagious virus had spread across Liberia, Sierra Leone, and Guinea in West Africa, a region that had up to then never seen a single case of Ebola. By the time the first case was diagnosed in America, in late September, thousands of West Africans had died of Ebola, where the virus had reportedly killed as many as eight out of ten infected patients.

The first person to be diagnosed with Ebola in America was a Liberian named Thomas Eric Duncan, who was visiting family in Dallas. Duncan had contracted Ebola before his trip when he helped carry a dying neighbor to a local clinic, where his uncovered hands came in contact with blood seeping through her skin. After noticing that he was running a fever, Duncan went to a Dallas hospital, but the prospect of having to deal with Ebola was so far from the minds of American health workers that they sent him home. Duncan's fever worsened, and he returned to the hospital two days later, when

---

❦ **Cultivating Panic.** When a Liberian man who had contracted Ebola in West Africa died of the disease in Dallas and an American doctor who had been helping Ebola patients in West Africa became sick with the disease soon after returning to New York City in 2014, the tabloids went wild. Media reports, along with the overreactions of public officials such as New Jersey governor Chris Christie and New York governor Andrew Cuomo, intensified public panic around the possibility of an Ebola outbreak in America.

357

doctors began to suspect that he might be infected with the virus. However, the hospital staff had no experience with Ebola, and they were unaware that the protective gear they were using was not adequate to prevent transmission of the virus. In addition, while Duncan had not yet reached the infectious stage of the virus when he first visited the hospital, he had become infectious by the time of his second visit. Two nurses soon came down with fevers, and it was later confirmed that they had become infected through contact with Duncan. One of these nurses had flown to Ohio and back before being diagnosed, and she had developed a fever before boarding her return flight. News of her travel sent the nation into a panic as the media coverage raised the specter of domestic airplane flights spreading the disease around the country.

CNN and other cable news outlets kept Americans' anxieties high, providing round-the-clock updates. Some interviewed missionary health worker Kent Brantly, who had contracted Ebola in Liberia and been transported to Atlanta for treatment earlier in the year. The accompanying footage showed Brantly as he emerged from his jet in a hazmat suit and with assistance hobbled across the tarmac to an ambulance.

Meanwhile, several American volunteer health workers who had been in West Africa got caught up in high-profile situations as public panic around Ebola grew. One of these health workers was Dr. Craig Spencer, who had gone to Guinea to help with the crisis and returned to his home in New York City without symptoms. He eventually developed a fever and checked into a local hospital, where it was confirmed he had contracted Ebola despite wearing heavy protective gear when he was working with Ebola patients. Reporters and cable news commentators heightened the public's fears by documenting and retracing Dr. Spencer's every step since his return from Guinea. Spencer (2015) had followed protocols to ensure he did not spread the virus, and there was no evidence to suggest that he had infected anyone else. But the media unfairly cast him as a villain who had carelessly risked spreading Ebola across the most populous city in America. Under growing pressure from the public, the governors of New York, New Jersey, and Connecticut implemented mandatory quarantine orders for anyone who arrived from West Africa with a fever.

A volunteer nurse named Kaci Hickox, who had worked with Ebola patients in Sierra Leone, arrived at Newark International Airport in New Jersey shortly after the quarantine measures had been established. The new mandatory screening order meant that everyone on a plane traveling from an area in Africa affected by Ebola had to be screened for a fever with a routinely unreliable forehead thermometer that uses a beam of light on the forehead. Hickox's temperature was found to be slightly higher than normal, and she was immediately quarantined in a makeshift facility, a tent in the parking lot of the Newark Airport. Initially, New Jersey governor Chris Christie insisted that Hickox would need to be quarantined for three weeks, a period Hickox and other medical professionals objected to as unnecessarily long. However, after showing no further signs of fever

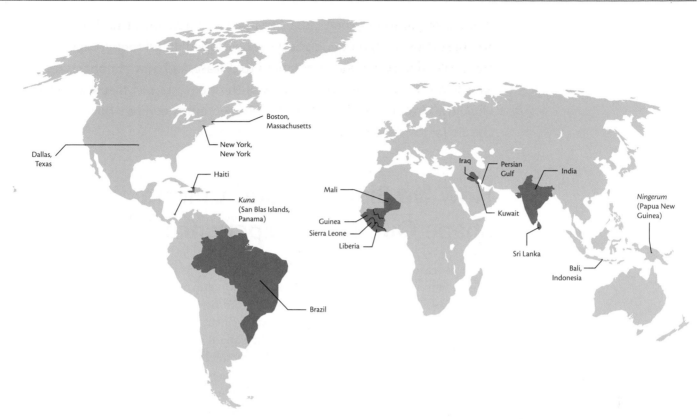

Figure 14.1   **Select Peoples and Places Discussed in Chapter 14.**

or any other symptom of Ebola, Hickox was released a few days later and transported to her home in rural Maine.

The 2014 Ebola outbreak was devastating in West Africa, where it killed more than 10,000 people. Extreme poverty, poor diets, years of armed conflict, broken public healthcare systems, burial practices involving the handling of infected bodies, and inadequate understanding of how the virus could be spread all contributed to this situation. But in spite of the public reaction, Ebola was never a serious risk in America, where the population is healthier and biomedical institutions stronger than in West Africa. Nevertheless, understanding the frenzied reactions of the American media, politicians, and public is not a biomedical problem. It is a cultural one. Cultural beliefs and relationships always shape how people think of the body and its impairment, leading to the question central to this chapter: *How does culture influence our experience of health and illness?* We can answer this question by considering a number of related questions around which this chapter is organized.

How do biological and cultural factors shape our bodily experiences?

What do we mean by health and illness?

How do doctors and other healers gain social authority?

How does healing happen?

What can anthropology contribute to addressing global health problems?

The Ebola epidemic shows how anthropology has a great deal to say about health and illness. Anthropologists have developed useful tools for understanding the links between culture, reactions to disease, and how our bodies respond to disease. This chapter explores how anthropologists put that knowledge to work in addressing real-world health crises. Let us first consider how biology and culture jointly shape the experience of our bodies.

How Do Biological and Cultural Factors Shape Our Bodily Experiences?

Since at least the 1920s, anthropologists have struggled with questions about the relative importance of our human biology as compared with the profound effects that culture has on individuals in any community around the world. In the nineteenth century, anthropologists like Edward Burnett Tylor (1871) and Lewis Henry Morgan (1877) thought that biology could explain why indigenous peoples in Africa, Australia, or the Americas had such modest technologies and tools to work with when compared with those of Europeans and white Americans. Their answer: the bodies and minds of "primitive" people were not as developed as those of people from European stock. For a number of decades after 1920, it looked as if culture could shape who and what people were (e.g., Mead 1928). But in recent years, especially since the emergence of genetics and DNA research as a prominent subfield of biology, it has appeared to many Americans as if it is "all in our genes" or our biological "hardwiring." From this perspective, biology, genes, or hormones can explain sexual orientation, criminality, IQ, wealth, education, and who becomes CEO of a Fortune 500 company.

Today, anthropologists are deeply skeptical of grandiose claims about biological destiny. This sort of "it's-all-in-your-genes-and-hormones" thinking is a cultural idiom our society uses to understand human nature, just as other societies use other idioms and metaphors to understand their own individual and collective selves. This is not to deny that biology plays a role in who we are as individuals, but our biology works with our culture to make us who we are and to determine what we can accomplish and which maladies we will experience. A full appreciation of the human condition requires that we avoid thinking of ourselves as *either* cultural *or* biological (natural) beings, but through a new and emerging paradigm that emphasizes humans as **biocultural** beings in which biological, psychological, and cultural processes interact in complex ways.

The idea of human nature and bodily experience as something fixed in our biology has been central to Western European and American ideas about humanity for more than a century. The fundamental problem with this sort of understanding is that it simply cannot account for who gets sick, who succeeds in school or business, or how many other aspects of our lives and our identities develop. We examine why in the next two sections.

Uniting Mind and Matter: A Biocultural Perspective

One place to mend the divide between biology and culture is in the human **mind**, the emergent qualities of consciousness and intellect that manifest themselves through thought, emotion, perception, will, and imagination. There is increasing biocultural evidence indicating that even our most basic cognition does not happen separately from our bodies. The human nervous system is a complex neurological network that

• **Biocultural.** The complex intersections of biological, psychological, and cultural processes.

• **Mind.** Emergent qualities of consciousness and intellect that manifest themselves through thought, emotion, perception, will, and imagination.

reads and regulates chemical and biological conditions throughout the entire body, not just our thinking brains. Human biology sets certain broad outer limits that all humans share, but the actual character of cognitive processes differs from one individual to the next and across cultures because of the influence of external factors.

These external factors include social context and culture, with which the nervous system interacts through individual cognition. For example, culture shapes some basic aspects of perception. People growing up in societies with little two-dimensional art must learn how to understand photographs after first seeing them (Shore 1996). Cultural differences in perception suggest that mental development varies with cultural practices. Research has also demonstrated that the mental stresses people experience because of rapid social and political-economic change have physical and bodily consequences, including raising blood pressure, affecting our immunity to disease, and creating symptoms of fatigue or feelings of inadequacy (Dressler 2005). These mental stresses may accompany other biological impacts, including changes in diet, nutrition, and general health (Daltabuit and Leatherman 1998). The point is, the mind is not a fixed thing, and manifests itself through the whole person, throughout an individual's lifetime (Toren 1996).

Culture and Mental Illness

Studies of people with psychological problems across the globe have brought into question whether the psychological dynamics observed in Western countries are universal; that is, based purely in human biology. Numerous conditions, among them schizophrenia, anxiety, depression, attention deficit disorders, and narcissistic personality disorders, vary greatly in their incidence in different cultures, suggesting that culture has a profound effect on the ways humans think about their psychology and display mental disorders. Cross-cultural differences in how people from different backgrounds express even the most basic psychological and emotional processes and conditions have an important consequence: we have to approach mental illness in a culturally relative way.

Psychological abnormality is always defined culturally because what is considered abnormal is based on socially accepted norms. Not all societies define the same conditions as psychologically abnormal, nor do they necessarily share the same mental illnesses. A well-known example of a so-called **culture-bound syndrome** (a mental illness unique to a culture) is *koro*, the condition unique to Chinese and Southeast Asian cultures in which an individual believes his external genitalia—or, in a female, nipples—are shrinking and even disappearing.

Societies can even change what they consider a disorder, homosexuality being one such example. Although today few Americans view same-sex sexual attraction as an illness, until 1974 American psychiatrists classified homosexuality as a mental disorder, and until 1990 the U.S. Immigration and Naturalization Service used the classification of homosexuality as "abnormal" as a reason for excluding gay and lesbian immigrants.

Because different societies define mental illnesses differently based on different cultural understandings of individual psychology, treatments differ accordingly. For example, on the Indonesian island of Bali, persons are not conceived of as isolated or indivisible, as we conceive of them in the West. Spirits and deceased ancestors commonly reside in individuals. Madness (*buduh*) can be caused by inherited factors, congenital influences, an ancestral or divine curse, or the blessings of gods (Connor 1982). The task of the village-level healer, called the *balian*, is to identify the specific causes of madness, which are usually related to some kind of social disruption or family conflict. The *balian* then resolves the conflict or disharmony in the family or neighborhood (Connor 1982) (Figure 14.2). Western psychiatry's approach, which often involves isolating the individual through institutionalization or providing

• **Culture-bound syndrome.** A mental illness unique to a culture.

Figure 14.2   Balinese Balians. Balians are ritual specialists and healers who use a mix of traditional herbs, prayers, and other rituals.

Figure 14.3   Candomblé Mediumship. In Brazil, where some two million people practice Candomblé, temples where rituals are carried out are managed by women priests, known as "mothers-of-saint," often with support from men priests ("fathers-of-saint").

pharmaceuticals, would clearly be inappropriate, if not socially disruptive, in these circumstances.

Nevertheless, as documented in Ethan Watters's book *Crazy Like Us: The Globalization of the American Psyche* (2011), Western psychological terms, notions, and illnesses have been globalizing rapidly in recent years. For example, mental illnesses such as depression, anorexia, and post-traumatic stress disorder (PTSD) seem to now exist in places that have never had them before, such as Hong Kong, Sri Lanka, and Tanzania. Watters suggests that much of this is taking place because of the increasingly global flows of Western media and psychiatric practices, as well as the expansion of pharmaceutical companies into new markets throughout the globe. Watters argues that such practices, which are usually based on an assumption of "hyper-individualism," destabilize indigenous notions and ways of treating mental illness in social context.

We can bring these insights about psychological processes and mental illness beliefs even further with a biocultural approach that combines cultural and biological insights. Rebecca Seligman has conducted research on Candomblé, a spirit-possession religion in Brazil (Figure 14.3). Seligman asked a simple question: Why do certain people become spirit mediums and others do not? Biomedicine explains mediumship as a psychological disturbance with a biological basis, but it fails to explain how and why such a disturbance might express itself specifically through mediumship. The cultural approach argues that oppressed and marginalized individuals gravitate toward mediumship, but it fails to explain why not all dispossessed people become mediums (Seligman 2005).

Seligman found that there is no single pathway to mediumship, but the interaction of biological, psychological, and cultural factors plays a crucial role. Among these are a physiological ability to achieve dissociation (trance states); conditions of poverty and oppression that cause emotional distress, which is often experienced through bodily pain; and a cultural outlet and social role that reward people who exhibit the qualities of mediumship. Seligman concludes that, without this holistic perspective on a medium's experience, we cannot appreciate the complexity of how people become mediums.

Now that we have explained how even the most basic matters of human cognition and psychology are not simply the function of our biological hardwiring, we can productively understand more broadly how *all* matters of disease, health, and illness are powerfully shaped by culture.

THINKING CRITICALLY ABOUT THE BODY

If individual psychology differs from one culture to another, what might this suggest about the academic and clinical disciplines of psychology in which most psychologists treat patients who are Americans? What might these psychologists consider when dealing with recent immigrants from Africa or Asia?

What Do We Mean by Health and Illness?

At first glance, "health" and "illness" seem to be straightforward concepts. Dictionaries often define *health* as the "soundness of body and mind" or as "freedom from disease," and *illness* as being "unhealthy" or having a "disease," "malady," or "sickness." The problem is that ideas like "soundness of body" and "malady" do not suggest any objective measure of when we have health and when it has left us. For example, most people feel sore after a hard workout at the gym, and many people have mild seasonal allergies and sinus conditions that rarely impair their daily lives but can be annoying. Are these people healthy?

The borderland between health and illness is more ambiguous than we might have originally assumed. This ambiguity results from two interlaced dynamics: the "subjectivity of illness," which is how people perceive and experience their condition on a personal level, and the "**sick role**," the culturally defined agreement between patients and family members to acknowledge that a patient is legitimately sick. We consider each in turn.

These issues are at the heart of medical anthropology, which is the subfield of anthropology that tries to understand how social, cultural, biological, and linguistic factors shape the health of human beings (Society for Medical Anthropology 2014). Doctors tend to focus on treating sickness and disease, while public health officials have traditionally focused on preventing outbreaks of disease. Medical anthropologists look at the diverse aspects of illness, its prevention, and its treatment. At its core, medical anthropology begins with the fact that, as much as we might like health and illness to be objective categories, health and illness are subjective states.

• **Sick role.** The culturally defined agreement between patients and family members to acknowledge that a patient is legitimately sick, which involves certain responsibilities and behaviors that caregivers expect of the sick.

The Individual Subjectivity of Illness

Illness is a subjective experience, but it is also shaped by cultural and social expectations. This insight is credited to sociologist Earl L. Koos, who in the 1940s conducted a classic study of attitudes toward health and illness in a mainstream American community he called Regionville. In his study, he interviewed thousands of ordinary Americans about being sick. For example, he asked one working-class woman about being sick, to which she replied:

> I wish I really knew what you mean about being sick. Sometimes I've felt so bad I could curl up and die, but had to go on because the kids had to be taken care of, and besides, we didn't have the money to spend for the doctor—how could I be sick? . . . How do you know when you're sick, anyway? Some people can go to bed most any time with anything, but most of us can't be sick—even when we need to be. (Koos 1954:30)

This statement demonstrates both the subjectivity of illness and how health and illness are inherently linked to social behavior and expectations, not to mention social status or social position. When our symptoms impair us so much that we cannot effectively perform the normal social and economic duties expected of us—jobs, school, and, in this case, caring for our family—we can see that our social position within our families and communities affects how we understand and define health.

To understand when a particular symptom is considered significant enough to provoke someone to seek medical care, we have to understand the ordinary expectations of the people involved. In the United States, these expectations are linked to issues like social class, gender, age, the kind of work the person ordinarily performs, and the person's routine lifestyle. The poor and working class routinely work more physically, eat less healthy food, and pay less attention to their health concerns than wealthier people do. It is not that lower-class people do not care about their health, of course.

Figure 14.4 Undernourished Adolescent in Mali. In Mali, undernourishment is caused by a heavy disease load as much as by poor nutrition in the diet.

They simply have less time for doctors' visits, work in jobs they could lose if they miss a day, and eat the least expensive foods, which, as we discussed in Chapter 6 ("Foodways"), are the processed foods made available by the industrial food system. And they often have less adequate health insurance, or no health insurance at all.

Numerous cross-cultural anthropological studies confirm that cultural background also shapes the subjectivity of illness. For example, anthropologist Katherine Dettwyler (2013) conducted research in Mali, a West African nation at the southern edge of the Sahara. There she observed high infection rates of schistosomiasis, a liver and bladder infection caused by a parasitic worm that lives in water. This worm enters the human body through the feet and legs, causing sores on the skin and releasing blood into the urine. Dettwyler found this condition so common in Mali that by puberty, nearly all rural men have blood in their urine. Instead of viewing red urine as a shocking symptom, as Americans would, Malians understood it as a normal condition typical of the transition to adulthood. For these adolescents, it meant they were becoming men, not that they had an infection (Figure 14.4).

Americans might interpret this Malian understanding as ignorance, and perhaps there is some lack of medical knowledge among youth in Mali. But the important point to this example is that people rarely worry about conditions that are very common. Just as manual laborers rarely worry about lower back pain, Malian youth rarely worry about dark urine, generally seeing it as normal and even desirable.

If we think about the example that opens this chapter, we can see that cultural differences led West Africans to react quite differently to the 2014 Ebola outbreak than Americans did. When the outbreak started in West Africa, it took many weeks for people to understand what was happening and even longer before they recognized how dangerous Ebola was, largely because they had never had to deal with an Ebola epidemic before. Americans hadn't seen one of these epidemics either, but the media had been circulating alarming reports about the outbreak in West Africa for some time before the virus was identified in Dallas, and it had made the prospect of a similar outbreak in America sound possible and terrifying. Undoubtedly, the absence of 24-hour news media in West Africa and the presence of it in the United States contributed to the different reactions to Ebola in the two regions. In addition, many younger Americans associated a potential Ebola outbreak with the type of zombie-virus apocalypse depicted in various films that were popular in North America at the time, an association uncommon among West Africans.

The "Sick Role": The Social Expectations of Illness

In all societies around the world, when a person is ill, there are expectations of how that person, as well as friends and family, should behave. For Americans, this typically means the sick person should not go to school or work, should stay in bed and rest, should be given chicken soup, and so on. But these patterns vary cross-culturally. One of this book's authors, Robert Welsch, experienced this kind of cultural difference while conducting field research in Papua New Guinea among the Ningerum people.

One day, Welsch noticed that his body ached all over and his forehead burned with a high fever. It was malaria. At first he retired to his bed to rest, but the fever turned into chills, followed by sweats and an even worse body ache. He took antimalarial pills and aspirin, but the headache became so bad it was unbearable to lay his head on a pillow. Like most Americans, he wanted to be by himself and endure this agony alone.

But Ningerum villagers did not sit idly by. As Welsch's condition worsened, more and more of his friends in the village came by the house to sit and chat and smoke. He later realized that most people in the village attributed his sudden symptoms to sorcery: someone in the area had used magic to hurt him, and people expected him to die. If it was sorcery, there was nothing anyone in the village could really do for him, but nobody wanted to be accused of having caused his death. The only sure way to avoid suspicion of being a sorcerer was to demonstrate concern. Fortunately for everybody, by the eighth day, the fever broke, and the headache and body ache subsided. The villagers who had been keeping vigil for several days went back to their normal activities.

In this instance, the anthropologist and the villagers had very different ideas of how they expect patients and caregivers to behave. Anthropologists refer to these unwritten rules as "the sick role," or the responsibilities and expected behaviors of sick people by their caregivers (Parsons 1951). To be considered legitimately sick—rather than as malingering, or faking sickness—one must accept specific responsibilities and a new social role, which exempts one from one's ordinary daily roles and responsibilities such as school or work. Two key aspects of the sick role are to want to get well, and to cooperate with medical experts.

A great example of this phenomenon comes from many of our own childhoods. During cold and flu season in the winter, many schoolchildren feel under the weather and want to stay home. When a parent agrees to let his or her child stay home, the child may decide later in the day that it would be fun to go out and play in the snow. But "Dr. Mom" steps in with her authoritative zeal to explain that if you are sick enough to stay home, you are too sick to go outside to play. Playing outside does not demonstrate that you want to get well—which is a key aspect of American ideas of the sick role—and slipping out of the house in defiance of Dr. Mom's explicit orders to stay in bed is not compliance with her medical expertise (Figure 14.5).

Both of these responsibilities, wanting to get well and cooperating to do so, may simultaneously come into play in your own college classes. For example, when absent from a class or especially an exam, a student may need to provide a note from a doctor or a clinic to prove that he or she is legitimately sick. This note also demonstrates that the student wants to get better and has sought medical care.

Welsch found that Ningerum people had a different sick role model, believing that if patients still enjoy a minimum of physical strength, they should themselves deal with the illness. For the Ningerum patient to get help with his or her care and treatment, the patient is obliged to display to family and friends precisely how sick and disabled he or she is. Patients convey this information through their actions or visible physical signs of illness rather than through their words. Startling symptoms such as fainting, bleeding, vomiting, shrieking, and sudden weight loss call family members to action. Patients can also display the severity of their condition by using props like a walking stick to limp cautiously across the village plaza, shedding clothing, refusing to eat, or smearing their chests and legs with mud and dirt. All these actions communicate to family and friends that the patient is sick, and (silently) demand that family members show their sincere concern for the patient. Not to do so would suggest that one was not sensitive to a relative's needs—indifference that, to the Ningerum, whose culture prescribes very close kinship ties, would suggest not being fully human.

While culture shapes a community's expectations of the sick role, our medical schools and hospitals have created a culture of medicine that often leads to tensions between the views of professionals and those of lay people. These tensions often have

Figure 14.5 Dr. Mom.
"Dr. Mom" expects her patient to remain in bed when staying home from school.

to do with the social authority given to doctors that makes the relationship asymmetrical, a topic we consider next.

• •

THINKING CRITICALLY ABOUT THE BODY

The "sick role" concept works well for acute diseases like measles, bad colds, and chicken pox, when patients are expected to want to get better and to help in their own care by following medical advice. To meet these expectations, patients are often considered exempt from participating in ordinary social activities, and they are generally not blamed for causing their own sickness. Compare the sick role for an acute infection with that for a chronic condition like diabetes, chronic shortness of breath, or severe arthritis.

• •

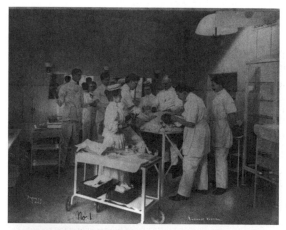

🌱 **Figure 14.6   Improvements in Public Health.** The use of antiseptics in the operating room made surgery much safer in the late nineteenth and early twentieth centuries, as suggested by this photo from 1900 (*top*). However, improvement in life expectancy came from better sanitation and hygiene across the United States, including the use of soaps to promote personal hygiene and the improvement of sewer systems. Large cities also began employing more street cleaners, such as the men shown in this photo from the 1890s (*bottom*). Note that the street cleaners wore white uniforms in an effort to convey a sense of cleanliness to the public.

How and Why Do Doctors and Other Health Practitioners Gain Social Authority?

Medical doctors in the United States have one of the most prestigious, respected, and well-paid occupations. The prestige and social authority doctors enjoy, however, are relatively new. Throughout most of the eighteenth and nineteenth centuries, American doctors had low social status. Medicine was not sophisticated, and doctors often doubled as barbers. During the Civil War, surgeons were little more than butchers who amputated with large, dirty saws, using no antibiotics (the first, penicillin, was discovered in 1928), few painkillers, and no antiseptics (Starr 1982).

Many people assume that doctors gained prestige and authority because new medical discoveries and technologies improved their ability to heal people. Antibiotics like penicillin, for example, have made a huge difference in treating disease. But the major advances in health we take for granted today were mostly improvements in preventing diseases rather than curing them. Clean water, sanitation, and other public hygiene programs saved more lives than doctors' treatments have (Figure 14.6). So how do we explain the social authority of doctors? Medical anthropologists have studied the social authority of healers in many societies. They identify several processes at work, the most important being the social processes that privilege the healers' perspectives over those of their patients, and the designation of otherwise normal conditions as health problems.

The sociologist Eliot Freidson (1970) was among the first to identify the professionalization of the field of medicine as responsible for giving the doctor's perspective privilege over the understandings of ordinary people. It is not that doctors necessarily knew more about what the patient experiences during an illness, but doctors had been trained to treat a wide variety of diseases. Subsequently, medical sociologist Paul Starr (1982) argued that, during the twentieth century, medical doctors in the United States had used their professional status to increase their incomes, the level of respect they received from the public, and the exclusive right to determine the course of treatment for particular patients. American physicians formed professional associations like the American Medical Association, which allowed them to control how many new doctors were being trained. But while American physicians had achieved professional privileges, great respect, and high salaries, few of these perks were enjoyed by doctors in most other countries.

The Disease–Illness Distinction: Professional and Popular Views of Sickness

Around the world, patients often view their illnesses differently from how the doctors or healers who treat them do. In the Western world, patients often feel that their doctors do not understand the intensity of their pain and other symptoms. What frequently emerges is a clash of professional and popular (or lay person's) understandings that we call the "disease–illness distinction," in which doctors focus on **disease**, the purely physiological condition, and patients focus on **illness**, their actual experience of the disease (Eisenberg 1977; and see Figure 14.7).

In our culture, the doctor, not the patient, has the greater authority in identifying and defining health and illness. Sociologist Eliot Freidson (1970:205) explained this authority as the result of a social process: "In the sense that medicine has the authority to label one person's complaint an illness and another's complaint not, medicine may be said to be engaged in the creation of illness as a social state which a human being may assume."

American social structure also upholds the doctor's view as the officially sanctioned one. Because of the doctor's professional training, the hospital, governments, insurance providers, and, in extreme cases, even the courts recognize the diagnosis of the physician as legitimate. At the same time, the patient who has to live with the symptoms generally lacks any ability to authorize a prescription or treatment, or even offer an official diagnosis.

Understanding the distinction between doctors' and patients' perspectives is a key approach in contemporary medical anthropology. In the 1950s and 1960s, anthropologists typically accepted Western medicine as superior and authoritative in much the same ways that Freidson suggests. Anthropologists generally assumed that health problems in developing countries were due to ignorance of medical knowledge and technology. A breakthrough came when Arthur Kleinman, a medical anthropologist who conducted research in Taiwan, argued that the key to understanding such differences in perspective is that healers and patients often have different **explanatory models of illness**, which are explanations of what is happening to the patient's body. Kleinman asserted that the goal of medical anthropology research was not to decide who was right in their explanation, but to accept that different people would come to the illness with different concerns

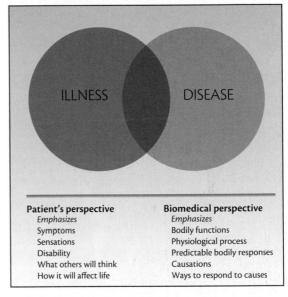

Figure 14.7 The Disease–Illness Distinction. Patients are concerned with the "illness": symptoms, how they feel, and how their activities are affected by these symptoms. Doctors tend to focus on the underlying causes of the symptoms that they speak of as "disease."

- **Disease.** The purely physiological condition of being sick, usually determined by a physician.

- **Illness.** The psychological and social experience a patient has of a disease.

- **Explanatory model of illness.** An explanation of what is happening to a patient's body, by the patient, by the patient's family, or by a healthcare practitioner, each of whom may have a different model of what is happening.

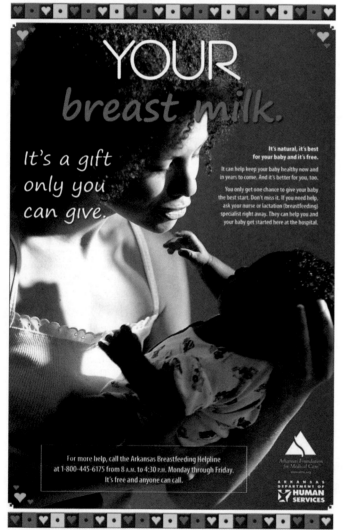

🌱 **Figure 14.8   Changing Views on Infant Formula and Breastfeeding.**
Dr. Benjamin Spock, in his time a highly respected pediatrician, published a series of books beginning in the late 1940s (*top*) that promoted giving baby formula rather than breast milk to infants. Since the 1970s, breastfeeding has had a resurgence in the United States after it became known that a mother's breast milk gives antibodies and partial immunity to infections to her baby (*bottom*).

and different kinds of knowledge. In "Classic Contributions: Arthur Kleinman and the New Medical Anthropological Methodology," we show an example of this approach.

Kleinman's approach also helped medical anthropologists realize the limitations of scientific knowledge, and they began to challenge whether the doctors always had such special and privileged knowledge. Perhaps the patient understood some aspects of his or her body that the physician did not, and perhaps could not, understand. We have already discussed the subjectivity of pain and other symptoms. But in addition, medical knowledge is constantly changing, so how could doctors always have all the answers for how to treat their patients?

For example, consider what the medical profession has advised about breastfeeding for infants. Breastfeeding was universal until the 1950s, when baby formula was developed, and most American pediatricians promoted formula as a technologically superior way to ensure the health of the baby. By the 1970s, new scientific analyses of the contents of breast milk indicated that breast milk contained antibodies that helped the child ward off infections. Rather than viewing breast milk as unsophisticated, the medical world began to see it as nature's way of protecting the child. About the same time in many developing countries, international aid workers were promoting baby formula as a way of producing strong, healthy babies. But by the 1990s, it became clear that this practice was not ideal: babies became malnourished because their poor mothers could not afford enough formula, and where clean drinking water was scarce, mothers often had no choice but to use unsanitary water for their baby formula, resulting in much higher rates of fatal diarrhea (Figure 14.8).

With the spread of AIDS in the developing world, we now know that mothers infected with HIV can give the infection to their infants through breast milk. So, as a result, aid workers are once again, at least in communities where incidences of HIV infection are high, recommending baby formula. Who knows where the science of breast milk will settle in another generation? But as with nearly every other aspect of medicine, few scientific facts have remained, or will remain, static.

Since medical knowledge is constantly changing, it is no wonder that new diseases and drugs to treat them are constantly emerging. One way this knowledge changes is when the professional medical system casts its net of authority out farther, to cover conditions that were not previously understood as medical problems.

Classic Contributions
Arthur Kleinman and the New Medical Anthropological Methodology

IN THE MID-1970s, physician, psychiatrist, and medical anthropologist Arthur Kleinman (b. 1941) published an essay on the history of medical anthropology. In it he added a short appendix where he introduced a new methodology around the concept of explanatory models, highlighting several cases he had come across in his work at the Massachusetts General Hospital in Boston. One case, excerpted here, offers an especially compelling illustration of his point.

For medical anthropologists, identifying the patients' explanatory model (EM) offered a new way of looking at how culture influenced a community's response to symptoms and illness. Rather than seeing an entire community responding uniformly to a set of symptoms, anthropologists now recognized that different individuals in varying relationships to the patient or with different positions in the society held quite varied views, or EMs. Kleinman's approach allowed medical anthropologists to shift the focus of their studies from the society to individuals within the society. And this methodology allowed anthropologists to make sense of how patients in non-Western settings use Western medicine. This new approach allows us to see healthcare decisions as a tension among different explanatory models.

🌱 **Arthur Kleinman.**

Mrs. F. is a 60-year-old white Protestant grandmother who is recovering from pulmonary edema secondary to atherosclerotic cardiovascular disease and chronic congestive heart failure on one of the medical wards at the Massachusetts General Hospital. Her behavior in the recovery phase of her illness is described as strange and annoying by the house staff and nurses. While her cardiac status has greatly improved and she has become virtually asymptomatic, she induces vomiting and urinates frequently in her bed. She becomes angry when told to stop these behaviors. As a result of this, psychiatric consultation is requested.

Review of the lengthy medical record reveals nothing as to the personal significance of the patient's behavior. When queried about this behavior, and asked to explain why she is engaging in it and what meaning it has for her, the patient's response is most revealing. Describing herself as the wife and daughter of plumbers, the patient notes that she was informed by the medical team responsible for her care that she has "water in the lungs." She further reports that to her mind the physiology of the human body has the chest hooked up to two pipes, the mouth and the urethra. The patient explains that she has been trying to be

helpful by helping to remove as much water from her chest as possible through self-induced and frequent urination. She analogized the latter to the work of the "water pills" she is taking, which she has been told are getting rid of the water on her chest. She concludes, "I can't understand why people are angry at me." After appropriate explanations, along with diagrams, she acknowledges that the "plumbing" of the body is remarkable and quite different from what she had believed. Her unusual behavior ended at that time.

This amusing but true case study is but a very striking example of the important role played by alternative explanatory models in health care. I use it because it derives from the still poorly understood and inadequately studied popular culture health-care domain, rather than from the far better appreciated and researched folk medical domain (i.e., that section of the health-care system composed of non-orthodox profession and paraprofessional healers—religious healers, quacks, practitioners of chiropractic and osteopathy, and other specialists). Yet it is the former, family- and community-centered beliefs and practices, which has the greatest impact on all forms of health-care-related behavior. (Kleinman 1975:652–653)

(continued)

Classic Contributions (continued)

Questions for Reflection

1. How might Kleinman's explanatory models methodology help anthropologists understand healthcare choices in non-Western communities?

2. How does Kleinman's explanatory models methodology build on the disease–illness distinction?

The Medicalization of the Non-Medical

Over the past 50 years, the healthcare industry has expanded dramatically, taking over more and more of our individual personal concerns. It has done so by redefining certain social, psychological, and moral problems as medical concerns. This process of viewing or treating as a medical concern conditions that were not previously understood as medical problems is called **medicalization**.

● **Medicalization.** The process of viewing or treating as a medical concern conditions that were not previously understood as medical problems.

Alcoholism is a good example of this phenomenon. Excessive use of alcohol has been a problem throughout the history of the United States, producing opposition to it in the form of the temperance movement in the nineteenth and early twentieth centuries, and Prohibition (with the Eighteenth Amendment to the Constitution outlawing alcohol) in the 1920s. For a long time, alcoholism was seen as a moral failing that caused (usually) men to abandon their jobs and families (Figure 14.9). By the 1980s, psychiatrists, health-maintenance organizations (HMOs), and health insurance companies began to view alcoholism as a disease, defined as "recurrent substance use resulting in failure to fulfill major role obligations at work, school, home" (American Psychological Association 1994). Defining alcohol abuse as a disease, rather than as a crime, socially inappropriate behavior, sinful behavior, or moral failing, reclassifies it as a medical concern.

Three major reasons have been suggested for medicalizing the non-medical. The first is financial: pharmaceutical companies, hospitals, and insurance companies stand to make larger profits when they can define a new disease for which they can provide treatment, care, and coverage. A second explanation is that medicalization enhances the social authority of physicians. A third explanation concerns Americans' current preference for viewing social problems in scientific rather than moral or social terms. In "Thinking Like an Anthropologist: The Emergence of New Disease Categories," we explore how patients and social institutions together created a new disease out of the so-called Gulf War syndrome.

Up to now, we have largely considered how people and their professional healers make sense of and diagnose illness. But a key aspect of the illness experience has to do with how the treatments we get for our illnesses actually help us heal. As with the distinction between health and illness, how the medicines and other treatments we receive help us heal is much more problematic than we might at first assume. It is to the matter of healing that we turn next.

Thinking Like an Anthropologist
The Emergence of New Disease Categories

ANTHROPOLOGISTS BEGIN THEIR research by asking questions. In this box, we want you to learn how to ask questions as an anthropological researcher. Part One describes a situation and follows up with questions we would ask. Part Two asks you to formulate your own questions based on a different situation.

PART ONE: MAKING SENSE OF THE SYMPTOMS OF GULF WAR SYNDROME

In 1990, Iraqi president Saddam Hussein sent his army to invade the independent country of Kuwait. In response, President George H. W. Bush sent some 700,000 American soldiers to the Persian Gulf. During the war, the Iraqi Army set fire to hundreds of oil wells that spewed dark smoke into the atmosphere. Adding to the perception of environmental devastation, many troops worried that American bombing of Iraqi troop positions had released toxic chemicals into the already putrid atmosphere. As it turned out, American bombing did not do this, but anxieties over what the air was doing to soldiers' health ran high.

After returning home, more than 10,000 veterans became ill with medically unexplained symptoms, such as chronic fatigue, loss of muscle control, headaches, dizziness, loss of balance, problems with memory, pain in muscles and joints, shortness of breath, and skin problems of various kinds. Most veterans who reported these symptoms attributed their poor health to their service in the Persian Gulf. Most military doctors who examined them found that their conditions resembled what came to be known during the Vietnam War era as post-traumatic stress disorder (PTSD) (called "battle fatigue" during World War II and "shell shock" in World War I). These war-related conditions are considered anxiety disorders with psychological or psychosomatic roots.

When doctors diagnosed Gulf War veterans' problems as PTSD, most patients objected, claiming that their medical conditions were real and not "in their heads." Veterans had a variety of explanations for their symptoms: long-term contact with nerve agents or chemicals from the burning oil wells or brief encounters with volatile chemical agents. Others interpreted their symptoms as caused by a vaccine for anthrax, which all military personnel were injected with before leaving for the Gulf. Although repeated medical examinations could not confirm the explanatory models these patients had developed, and PTSD seemed the most likely cause, veterans began to refer to all these cases as the "Gulf War syndrome."

From a medical perspective, most of the symptoms the veterans reported were subjective, consisting of diffuse pain, fatigue, malaise, and indigestion. Moreover, the range of symptoms seemed so varied that physicians systematically rejected any single diagnosis as inadequate. In addition, researchers have found the same mortality rates among veterans and other men who never visited the Gulf, suggesting that while the symptoms may be real, they are not causing higher than normal death rates among veterans of the Persian Gulf conflict. Nevertheless, veterans formed advocacy groups to defend their definition of these diverse health issues as Gulf War syndrome.

As we have seen, doctors and patients often have very different ways of understanding and interpreting patients' health concerns. And doctors' more authoritative interpretations are difficult for patients to challenge. But in this case, there were so many vets with self-diagnosed Gulf War syndrome that veterans' groups were able to get congressional attention. The Department of Veterans Affairs formed a study group to investigate the matter, and a federally mandated Research Advisory Committee on Gulf War Veterans' Illnesses (2008) concluded that these illnesses have real biological causes and serious consequences for affected veterans.

The U.S. government now officially recognizes Gulf War syndrome as a disease, even though it has no single cause

⚘ **Gulf War Syndrome, a New Disease Category.** Although the origins of this syndrome are in debate, some have associated Gulf War syndrome with burning oil wells in Iraq and Kuwait.

(continued)

Thinking Like an Anthropologist (continued)

and no common symptoms. And while the official report of the Advisory Committee acknowledged it as a group of real illnesses with genuine effects on veterans, their classification is not a medical classification in the usual sense. But, of course, from the beginning, Gulf War syndrome was no simple health problem.

What questions does this situation raise for anthropological researchers?

1. Why should an environmental explanation—exposure to harmful chemical agents—be more appealing to veterans than PTSD?
2. Why would physicians and researchers initially have rejected Gulf War syndrome as a genuine disorder?
3. What role did political pressure by veterans' advocacy groups play here?

PART TWO: MAKING SENSE OF RESTLESS LEG SYNDROME, ERECTILE DYSFUNCTION, AND OTHER PROBLEMATIC DISEASE CLASSIFICATIONS

Consider any one of the new health conditions that have emerged over the past 30 or 40 years, such as restless legs syndrome, erectile dysfunction, premenstrual syndrome, or acid reflux disease, for which pharmaceutical companies have developed pills, tablets, or capsules as treatments. Today, the American public considers many of these conditions as standard medical diagnoses, even though physicians have not always recognized them. As an anthropological researcher, what questions would you ask about the rise of new health conditions such as these?

Figure 14.9 The Temperance Movement. Alcohol use was condemned as a moral failing by members of this early twentieth-century movement.

THINKING CRITICALLY ABOUT THE BODY

Fifty years ago, alcoholism was considered a moral failing, a behavioral problem found when people have no strong moral code to live by and do bad things to their families and others. Compare this earlier understanding of alcoholism with the now-common view that alcoholism is a disease. How do you think this shift happened?

How Does Healing Happen?

When Robert Welsch was studying healing practices among the Ningerum, one of his informants came down with malaria. Welsch offered him some antimalarial tablets, but his informant could not swallow them because they tasted bad. After several days of lying in bed, the man's nephew performed a traditional ritual, smearing clay on his uncle's painful chest, reciting magic words, and apparently removing a packet consisting of some small object wrapped in a banana leaf from the sick man's chest. Within two hours, the man was up and about with his walking stick, heading for the spring where he showered, a visible sign to everyone in the village, including the anthropologist, that he was feeling better (see Welsch 1983; Figure 14.10).

Figure 14.10 The Power of Non-Medical Healing. A Ningerum healer removes a magical packet from a man's leg by reciting magical words, rubbing magical leaves on the man's body, and sucking to relieve the pain in his leg.

To the Western mind, such examples of traditional healing strain credibility. But anthropologists around the world have observed similar responses to a wide variety of non-medical treatments. We do know that the human body is remarkably resilient. If we cut ourselves superficially while chopping vegetables, the wound will bleed, scab over, and gradually new skin will cover the cut. We do not fully understand how healing works, but we know that healing is more complex than most Americans recognize. Healing is a complex biocultural process: it is not just about pills and surgeries, but about the meaning that the sick person and the healers give to treatments in a specific cultural context. Medical anthropologists generally accept that treatments help our bodies heal in four distinct therapeutic processes: (1) clinical processes, (2) symbolic processes, (3) social support, and (4) persuasion (Csordas and Kleinman 1996). We consider each of these processes next.

Clinical Therapeutic Processes

Most medical professionals working with Western medicine assume that effective treatment comes from **clinical therapeutic processes**, which involve a doctor's observing a patient's symptoms and prescribing a specific treatment, such as a pill. The medicines involved in this treatment have some active ingredient that is assumed to address either the cause or the symptom of a disorder. One example is an antibiotic, which is thought to kill a type of bacterium. Another is a vaccination, which inserts a small amount of the virus or bacterium—usually already dead—into the blood, triggering the body's immune system to react by creating antibodies so the body can fight off the infection in the future.

- **Clinical therapeutic process.** A healing process that involves the use of medicines that have some active ingredient that is assumed to address either the cause or the symptom of a disorder.

Sometimes doctors understand how these physiological processes work; at other times they may not understand the healing process, but assume that it works by some plausible but unproven process. Whatever the case, for medical anthropologists and medical researchers there is still more to understand because these clinical processes do not account for healing such as in the Ningerum case presented earlier.

Symbolic Therapeutic Processes

In most tribal societies that medical anthropologists studied in the twentieth century, there were some treatments that used herbs, teas, and potions. The explanatory models used in these societies sometimes drew on clinical models, but often the herbs and potions were important not so much for their chemical properties as for their symbolic ones. Although the chemical composition of the herb or potion might help the patient heal, people were largely unaware of these properties and used them in rituals for other reasons.

In such cases, healing rituals act as a **symbolic therapeutic process** by virtue of their role in structuring the meanings of the symbols used. The symbolism of healing rituals comes from a number of sources, invoking our olfactory senses and our senses of taste and touch. It can also involve chanting, drumming, singing, and other sounds that create particular moods. Typically, the rituals provide a symbolic temporal progression, as in the form of a mythological story, that the affliction is supposed to follow for the patient to recover and heal.

For example, the French anthropologist Claude Lévi-Strauss (1961) documented a healing ritual among the Kuna [**koo**-nah] Indians of Panama in which, over a period of many hours, the shaman sings, produces smells, and touches a woman in the midst of a difficult birth. The ritual chanting recounts a mythological story in which a child overcomes diverse obstacles to reach its goal. These things relax the mother and her baby so the child can emerge from the womb, just as the hero of the story reaches his final goal. Medical anthropologists Thomas Csordas and Arthur Kleinman (1996) suggest that this kind of ritual is very common around the world because so many societies have found it efficacious.

Social Support

The **social support therapeutic process** involves a patient's social networks, who typically surround the patient, much like Welsch's experience among the Ningerum. Although relatives and friends may perform some (usually) minor treatments on the patient, the major thrust of this therapeutic process comes from the presence of family members who provide comfort and aid to the sick person. Feeling aided and supported by his or her relatives may affect the patient's bodily functions. For example, diabetics often have better control of their blood sugars when they are with supportive family members, but poorer control when feeling isolated.

Persuasion: The Placebo Effect

Persuasion is another powerful therapeutic process. Consider the **placebo effect**, in which a patient is given a non-medicine as if it were a medicine. The classic example of a placebo is a sugar pill given instead of some prescription drug with an active pharmaceutical ingredient. What makes it a placebo is that the sugar pill has a beneficial effect, even though it has no pharmacological or clinically active component. Usually, patients are told that they will receive a powerful medication or procedure, even though they will actually receive the placebo. This strategy, however, worries many people, including doctors, because it amounts to lying to a patient; dispensing placebos challenges professional ethical codes of behavior and even some federal laws in the United States.

Up to now, it has been hard to explain the placebo's effect clinically, since the placebo seems to work through persuading the patient that the drug is effective. Something must be happening within the patient's body, but it seems to lie outside the bounds of ordinary medicine.

A dramatic illustration of the power of the placebo effect comes from a French study conducted in the 1990s. In this study, researchers divided a group of hospitalized cancer patients with mild to moderate cancer pain into four groups to test the effectiveness of naproxen, at the time a new painkiller that many people now know by the brand name Aleve. None of the patients experienced so much pain that they required opiates, and the study put none of the patients in significant distress. First the patients were randomly assigned to one of two groups as they came out of cancer

- **Symbolic therapeutic process.** A healing process that restructures the meanings of the symbols surrounding the illness, particularly during a ritual.

- **Social support therapeutic process.** A healing process that involves a patient's social networks, especially close family members and friends, who typically surround the patient during an illness.

- **Placebo effect.** A healing process that works by persuading a patient that he or she has been given a powerful medicine, even though the "medicine" has no active medicinal ingredient.

surgery. One group was told they would be in a random trial of a powerful new pain reliever and would receive either the test drug or an inert placebo. The second group was told nothing. Members of this second group were unaware they were in a test and would assume that they were receiving standard hospital care. Half of the patients in each group were randomly given either an inert placebo or naproxen, thus creating four groups in all. Nurses, who were unaware of the details of the study, asked patients to evaluate their pain reduction hourly using a pain scale from 1 to 100 that represented the pain they experienced (Bergmann et al. 1994; Kaptchuk 2001).

All the patients given naproxen showed a reduction in pain, confirming that naproxen is an effective painkiller. But patients who were given the placebo and told they were in the study had greater pain relief than those who were given naproxen but were told nothing about their pain treatment regimen. Figure 14.11 illustrates this study's findings. Even more remarkable: this study suggests something that most researchers were not anticipating and had not appreciated. Figure 14.11 shows the large gap in experiences of pain relief between the two groups who were given naproxen. Theoretically, if we assume that naproxen works physiologically, both groups should have experienced similar levels of pain relief. But they did not; the placebo effect enhanced the pain relief in the test group who received naproxen and were told they were in the trial. In other words, those patients in the test group knew they were in the study and expected to get good results from their painkiller. What this tells us is that the placebo effect probably enhances all clinical interventions, whether they are pharmaceuticals, surgeries, or other procedures. When patients *believe* that a pharmaceutical or medical procedure is effective, they regularly see improvements.

The insight that culture and social processes influence the healing process is a powerful insight of medical anthropology. So how do anthropologists put such insights to work? We consider this question in our last section.

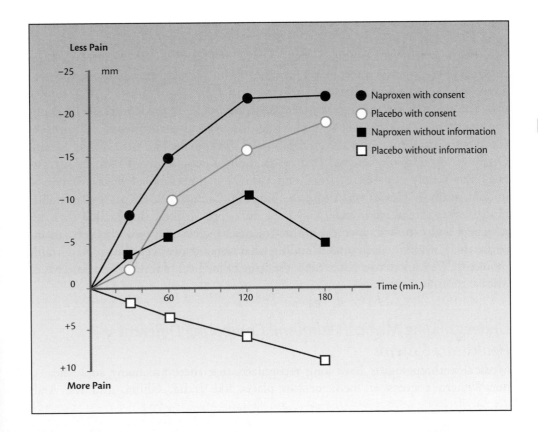

Figure 14.11 Evidence of the Placebo Effect on Pain After Surgery. Everyone in the study who received naproxen experienced pain reduction, but people told about the study who received only the placebo experienced more relief from pain than did patients who received naproxen but were not told about the study. Most strikingly, those given the placebo but told about the study had better pain relief after an hour than those with the Naproxen with no consent, suggesting that the discussion of the drug's effects is more helpful than the drug. (After Bergmann et al. 1994)

THINKING CRITICALLY ABOUT THE BODY

The naproxen study demonstrates the power of the placebo effect. Discuss what this study might mean for a doctor prescribing a "powerful" antibiotic or some brand-new treatment for a condition in a patient he or she sees in his or her clinic.

What Can Anthropology Contribute to Addressing Global Health Problems?

Anthropologists have long recognized that they can contribute to alleviating global health problems by understanding the healthcare systems available to different peoples around the world, how diseases are transmitted within and between communities, and how people use the resources available to them. In recent years, anthropologists have also become more engaged and proactive in trying to improve health conditions in the communities, countries, and regions in which they work. We explore both of these themes—understanding and actively addressing global problems—in the following subsections.

Understanding Global Health Problems

One of the first attempts at addressing global health problems came in the 1950s when medical anthropologists, working through the Institute of Inter-American Affairs, helped design public health programs and rural clinics to promote better health in rural Latin America (Erasmus 1952; Foster 1952; Simmons 1955). Their goal, which they reached with only moderate success, was to find ways for encouraging rural peasants to make better use of newly introduced clinics and improved vaccinations as a way of lowering infant mortality.

By the 1970s, it seemed that Western medicine would fix the world's health problems, and anthropology's role in explaining different cultural systems of healthcare was largely irrelevant. After the eradication of smallpox in 1979, the World Health Organization (WHO) believed that eradication of polio and other infectious diseases was simply a matter of time, and WHO's planners called their program—unrealistically—"Health for All by the Year 2000." But as AIDS and other public health crises spread worldwide, and even polio proved more intractable than researchers had expected, medical anthropologists increasingly saw the need to increase their involvement in understanding what were rapidly becoming global health problems. We explore two issues here: the issue of medical pluralism and patterns of disease transmission.

Understanding Medical Pluralism: Comparing Different Healthcare Systems

Medical anthropologists have long recognized that there are many sophisticated non-Western systems of medicine—in places like India, China, and the Arab world—that had been effective for centuries before the medical systems of the United States and Western Europe had developed antiseptics, antibiotics, and vaccines. As India, China, and the Arab world began to establish modern industrial societies, their healthcare facilities were integrating Western medicine with traditional practices. Medicine was not replacing these ancient traditions, but supplementing them. Nearly all other societies draw on more than one medical tradition simultaneously, a concept called **medical pluralism**, which refers to the coexistence and interpenetration of distinct medical traditions with different cultural roots.

An example of medical pluralism comes from anthropologist Carolyn Nordstrom (1988), who studied Ayurveda, a traditional medical system developed in India and Sri Lanka. Ayurvedic practitioners diagnose health problems using the classical Ayurvedic practice of reading the pulse, and they mix herbs in specified ways. But practitioners also draw upon traditional Sinhalese (referring to the people of Sri Lanka) medical ideas and practices in what Nordstrom refers to as a mediation of Ayurveda and local Sinhala medicine. She learned that practitioners often mix traditional Sinhalese herbal preparations along with those they have learned at an Ayurvedic college, and that many Ayurvedic healers frequently use stethoscopes and thermometers and dispense standard Western medicines along with their herbal preparations. She also observed that some Sinhalese Buddhist monks incorporated Ayurvedic and Buddhist principles in their therapeutic work, sometimes adding Sinhalese preparations as well (Figure 14.12).

The broader point here is that in an increasingly globalized world, medical anthropologists are learning that all medical systems are now plural systems. Successfully addressing global health problems must take this fact into account.

In "Anthropologist as Problem Solver: Nancy Scheper-Hughes on an Engaged Anthropology of Health," we consider another way that anthropologists are becoming increasingly proactive in health problems around the world. These anthropologists and a whole new generation of younger anthropologists are not just observing how healthcare systems work and don't work, they are also active participants trying to make conditions better.

● **Medical pluralism.**
The coexistence and interpenetration of distinct medical traditions with different cultural roots in the same cultural community.

 Figure 14.12   Medical Pluralism. Modern Ayurveda often adopts elements from biomedicine.

Anthropologist as Problem Solver
Nancy Scheper-Hughes on an Engaged Anthropology of Health

MEDICAL ANTHROPOLOGIST NANCY Scheper-Hughes has conducted research in a variety of contexts around the world: in the parched lands and shantytowns of northeast Brazil, in the squatter camps of South Africa, and in the AIDS sanatoria of Cuba. In each of these contexts, she saw structural poverty and blatant examples of what she called "useless suffering." For years, anthropologists have adopted a position of cultural relativism that she feels often puts us in a position of trying to be morally neutral when confronting issues of institutional or state violence against "vulnerable bodies and fragile lives." In her view, to be ethical, anthropologists need to focus critically on the institutions and embedded power relations that shape the health of poor, underserved, and disadvantaged people.

Recently, Scheper-Hughes has been studying the illegal sale of body parts (Scheper-Hughes 2004; Scheper-Hughes and Wacquant 2003). She has interviewed a Brazilian organ-trafficker in his prison cell, people whose kidneys had been sold, and other people involved in this trafficking. In July 2009, Scheper-Hughes assisted authorities in arresting a Brooklyn man accused of selling black-market kidneys. The *New York Daily News* heralded Scheper-Hughes as having an anthropological "'Dick Tracy' moment" when she turned over information to the Federal Bureau of Investigation (FBI) that allowed them to bring this suspected organ-trafficker to justice (Daly 2009). This led to exposing an extensive network that involved people in several countries. She told National Public Radio's (NPR's) Brian Lehrer (NPR 2009), "I had begun to unravel a huge network—a criminal network that really looks like, smells like, a kind of a mafia. The head office of the pyramid scheme originated in Israel; with brokers placed in Turkey; in New York City; in Philadelphia; in Durban; in Johannesburg; in Recife, Brazil; Moldova—all over the place." She went on to say, "And I used my ethnographic investigative skills to just go country-hopping and try to connect the dots. Eventually, it brought me to Isaac Rosenbaum being the head broker for Ilan Peri in Israel, who is the don, basically, of the operation, and who is a slippery guy."

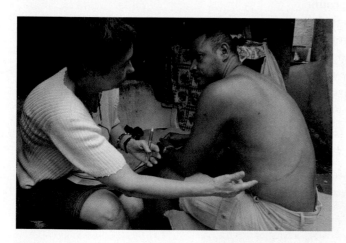

Nancy Scheper-Hughes. Here the anthropologist interviews a man who was trafficked from his home in Recife, Brazil, to Durban, South Africa, so his kidney could be illegally sold. For his kidney he received $6,000, a large sum of money in the slums of Brazil.

Questions for Reflection

1. To what extent is understanding the perspective of people without a voice a contribution to addressing and resolving health issues?

2. Anthropology has become a much more "hands-on" discipline in the past two decades. But does such involvement in shaping policy get in the way of our being able to understand all perspectives holistically?

Understanding Patterns of Disease Transmission

Medical anthropologists have also played a key role in making sense of how infectious diseases spread within a population, which is as much an anthropological or sociological task as it is a medical one. For example, anthropologists have played a key role in helping researchers understand the transmission of HIV, the virus that causes

AIDS. In the United States and Europe, public health officials have promoted the use of condoms to interrupt the spread of HIV. But promoting condoms has not proved so effective in several African countries, Haiti, and certain Southeast Asian countries, each of which had very different cultures of sexuality and patterns of transmission from that in the United States (see also Chapter 11). By studying these patterns of transmission, anthropologists played a central role in helping medical researchers understand how culture was shaping HIV transmission.

In East Africa, for example, HIV was first noticed along major highway routes where long-haul truckers became infected through heterosexual contacts with infected prostitutes, taking the infection to women in the next truck-stop town (Nyamwaya 1993). Truck stops produced ideal conditions for transmission of HIV because they provided a meeting place for truckers and prostitutes who had connections to wide-ranging and international social networks. Anthropologist and geographer Ezekiel Kalipeni (2004) suggests that epidemiologists and medical researchers had completely missed seeing these patterns. He argues that medical researchers explained the observed distribution of cases in terms of traditional patterns of African sexuality, which the medical community assumed was radically different from those of Western Europe. Traditional culture was demonized; the appearance of modern lifestyles, population growth, social inequality, and mounting poverty that was sending villagers in many African countries to urban centers and new forms of employment all went ignored. Anthropologists provided detailed observations of people's ideas about the disease and their explanatory models, as well as specific information about the sexual practices and behaviors of women and men, helping illuminate the patterns of HIV transmission (McGrath et al. 1992; Nyamwaya 1993).

Anthropological insight can also help reveal how patterns of disease transmission differ for infections that might otherwise be assumed to travel along identical pathways. For example, HIV and the Ebola virus are both transmitted through contact with certain bodily fluids, and both are extremely difficult to transmit except under very particular conditions. However, the pathways through which each is most commonly transmitted are very different. For HIV, the most common pathway is through contact with blood, semen, and (perhaps less commonly) vaginal fluids during sexual intercourse. Other possible pathways include needle sharing (such as in a hospital, or in heroin use), blood transfusion, and breastfeeding. In the case of Ebola, the most common pathway is through contact with the blood or feces of an infected person, particularly once the sick person has started bleeding over many parts of his or her body. Transmission requires that the bodily fluid of an infected person enter another person through an open cut, or through the mucus membranes of the eye, nose, or mouth. This disease etiology helps to explain why the family of Eric Duncan (discussed at the beginning of this chapter) never became sick, even though they were quarantined in the same apartment in Dallas together with his dirty clothes, bed sheets, and towels. It also helps explain why Ebola did not spread across the United States as so many Americans had feared. Only two people have (as of this writing) ever contracted Ebola in the United States.

Anthropological Contributions to Tackling the International HIV/AIDS Crisis

As their understanding of global health problems has become more sophisticated, anthropologists have become more assertive in putting their ideas to work. One way they do this is by working with communities to design aspects of the public health system to meet the needs, understandings, and cultural expectations of people in the community. To continue with the example of the HIV/AIDS crisis, we examine the work of Paul Farmer.

Using anthropology's holistic perspective to understand communities and their social problems, anthropologist and physician Paul Farmer (1992) began research for his dissertation in Haiti. As an undergraduate, Farmer had majored in anthropology at Duke University. In 1983, before beginning medical school at Harvard, he spent some time in Cange, a community in the mountainous central plateau of Haiti. In this extremely poor area, he could see firsthand that the social, economic, political, and health problems were interconnected. Farmer saw these connections before HIV/AIDS had been identified and before large numbers of HIV/AIDS cases had been diagnosed in Haiti. When the HIV/AIDS epidemic broke out, the connections between the health of Haitians and socioeconomic and political conditions became even more obvious.

Working with another M.D.-Ph.D. student, Jim Yong Kim, who went on to head the World Bank (see Chapter 8), Farmer helped found an organization in the highland district of Cange in 1987. They called this organization Partners in Health (2010) and developed a small health center. The international health community was initially focused on treating HIV/AIDS patients and on dealing with other public health concerns to slow the spread of HIV/AIDS. But Farmer and Kim had larger goals that they saw as related to health in the Haitian community. They began encouraging local people to plant trees in the once-lush forested region that had been devastated from poverty and rapid population growth, which led to deforestation as poor Haitians turned to their last resource (trees) to make into charcoal. Farmer and Kim put together an integrated program that attacked the causes of poverty and environmental degradation as a way of improving health. After 20 years of execution of this program, Farmer and Kim saw the district returned to something like its lush original environment, along with solid improvements in local health (Kidder 2003).

· ·

THINKING CRITICALLY ABOUT THE BODY

Medical anthropologists have traditionally been involved in public health efforts to vaccinate children, to provide clean drinking water, and more recently to assist with combating HIV/AIDS. Why would such public health efforts be a natural role for anthropologists, rather than involvement in clinical settings that include physicians and their patients in modern urban settings?

· ·

Conclusion

This chapter's focus on issues of our bodies reflects what most of us feel, implicitly, is the most natural part of our beings. But how we understand our bodies and minds and how we make sense of impairments to them are inevitably shaped by the culture we have grown up in and by the concerns and preoccupations people around us have. Whether we are considering chronic pain, psychological issues like PTSD, or infectious diseases like Ebola or HIV, the cultural expectations of the community always shape people's response to any illness condition.

As we saw with the 2014 outbreak of Ebola, discussed in the chapter opener, people living in different cultures, with varying views and cultural expectations, react differently to essentially the same set of facts. In an effort to protect their citizens, each country's leaders approach problems of health and epidemics somewhat differently, because in each case it is not the virus or the epidemiology but the local cultural assumptions that shape these leaders' actions. When individuals become ill in different cultures, they and their families also respond in locally appropriate ways, interpreting the signs, symptoms, and implications in locally meaningful ways.

Recent research even suggests that our bodies respond according to our expectations about the effectiveness of a treatment. Western physicians have dismissed such responses as merely the "placebo effect," but for millennia, societies have looked after their sick with herbs and local rituals that seem to bring relief to the sick.

The research medical anthropologists are conducting today comprises some of the most important applied projects in the discipline. But these research projects have demonstrated that global health concerns and modern epidemics are much more than medical problems. Like everything else in life, health and illness are linked to the kinds of society we live in, our biology, the historic traditions that have motivated and shaped our communities, and the meaning and significance we give to these biological and social facts. These biocultural linkages taken together are what make us human.

KEY TERMS

Biocultural   p. 360

Clinical therapeutic
    process   p. 373

Culture-bound
    syndrome   p. 361

Disease   p. 367

Explanatory model of
    illness   p. 367

Illness   p. 367

Medical pluralism   p. 377

Medicalization   p. 370

Mind   p. 360

Placebo effect   p. 374

Sick role   p. 363

Social support therapeutic
    process   p. 374

Symbolic therapeutic
    process   p. 374

Reviewing the Chapter

Chapter Section	What We Know	To Be Resolved
How Do Biological and Cultural Factors Shape Our Bodily Experiences?	Biocultural perspectives and evidence are breathing new life into classic anthropological interests in cognition, psychologies, and our bodily experiences, suggesting that "human nature" is not a singular condition.	Anthropologists continue to debate how the cultural variability around psychology, emotions, and mental states relates to biological and other psychological processes.
What Do We Mean by Health and Illness?	A person's culture shapes his or her interpretation of symptoms and understanding of the illness condition.	How people in any particular society will interpret the symptoms of illness can be determined only by detailed evidence from illness episodes in a particular society.
How and Why Do Doctors and Other Health Practitioners Gain Social Authority?	By dealing with human concerns as medical or biomedical problems, our society implicitly gives power to health practitioners who can prescribe drugs and other therapies.	It is not entirely clear why some peoples around the world are so ready and willing to give authority to healers, while people in other societies are not willing.
How Does Healing Happen?	Not all healing can be explained by the clinical processes familiar to physicians and medical students. Healing has important social and cultural dimensions.	While the power of the placebo effect is demonstrated, we still don't understand why it can work on our bodies.
What Can Anthropology Contribute to Addressing Global Health Problems?	Clinical solutions to global health problems cannot work effectively without understanding the local culture of the people whose health-related behavior we want to improve, as well as the fact that, due to medical pluralism, most societies combine distinct healing systems.	Up to now, there has been no single solution to a health problem that will work in all societies; it is not clear if there are general strategies applicable to most societies.

Readings

One of the most accessible ways that students can enter the world of medical anthropology is through Katherine Dettwyler's *Dancing Skeletons: Life and Death in West Africa* (second edition, Long Grove, IL: Waveland Press, 2013). Dettwyler's narrative gives students a sense of what it is like to be a medical anthropologist in a developing country. Anne Fadiman's *The Spirit Catches You and You Fall Down: A Hmong Child, Her American Doctors, and the Collision of Two Cultures* (New York: Farrar, Strauss & Giroux, 1997) offers a glimpse into the tensions between American biomedical culture and an Asian immigrant medical culture, which is as religious as it is medical.

....

Arthur Kleinman's classic *Patients and Healers in the Context of Culture: An Exploration of the Borderland Between Anthropology, Medicine, and Psychology* (Berkeley, CA: University of California Press, 1980) provided the first modern formulation of medical anthropology as a systematic branch of anthropology, complete with a methodology that could help us understand interactions between patients and healthcare providers, whether the latter are doctors, traditional healers, New Age consultants, or neighbors. Mary-Jo Delvecchio Good, Paul E. Brodwin, Byron J. Good, and Arthur Kleinman's edited volume *Pain as Human Experience: An Anthropological Perspective* (Berkeley, CA: University of California Press, 1992) explores how medical anthropologists can study the problem of chronic pain using approaches previously suggested by Kleinman.

....

Paul Farmer's book *Pathologies of Power: Health, Human Rights, and the New War on the Poor* (Berkeley, CA: University of California Press, 2004) offers an approach to issues of access to healthcare resources in a variety of contexts around the world, showing how access to healthcare is as important as the way patients and healers understand illness.

....

Materiality

Constructing Social Relationships and Meanings with Things

IN NOVEMBER 1989, the Royal Ontario Museum (ROM) in Toronto, Canada, opened a blockbuster exhibition on the art of Africa called *Into the Heart of Africa*. This was the ROM's first major exhibition of its African collection, and it promised to expose the Canadian public to the delights and charms of African art.

But the curator, cultural anthropologist Jeanne Cannizzo, wanted to do more than just show off the ROM's collection. She wanted to look at how the museum had come to obtain the pieces in this collection in the first place. To that end, she worked with the families of Canadian servicemen who had served in Africa during nineteenth-century British campaigns and World War I. She also contacted families of missionaries who had served in Africa between 1875 and 1925. Much of the ROM's African collection had been donated by these missionaries or servicemen, who had acquired African objects as souvenirs of their travels. Cannizzo also assembled photographs taken by the missionaries and servicemen during their time in Africa, along with statements from their writings, hoping to explore the attitudes of the men and women who had collected the objects in the first place (Cannizzo 1989; Butler 2008).

Her idea was to let the photographs speak for themselves, which was a consequential decision. The catalog released with the show's opening explains that the goal of this approach was to show that the

An object from the *Into the Heart of Africa* exhibit at the Royal Ontario Museum. Chief's stool with figures by unknown Luvale (Lwena) or Mbunda artist, carved wood, c. late 19th-/early 20th century.

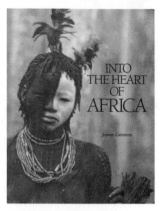

Figure 15.1 Exhibiting African Art. This image shows the cover of the exhibition catalog for *Into the Heart of Africa*, which opened on November 16, 1989, and closed on August 6, 1990, at the Royal Ontario Museum in Toronto, Ontario, Canada.

• **Materiality.** Having the quality of being physical or material.

majority of the Canadians serving in Africa in the early twentieth century would have assumed—like most anthropologists of the day—that Europeans and Canadians were culturally superior to Africans (Cannizzo 1989). Cannizzo hoped to use irony to let the public explore the mindsets and prejudices of the well-meaning Canadians of the early 1900s.

But museum staff quickly realized that different visitors took away quite different meanings from the exhibition, and almost no one in the public saw the perspective of the anthropologist as she had intended it. Worse, Cannizzo's use of irony backfired; using the collectors' own words and images seemed to indicate that Cannizzo and the museum supported the racist attitudes that had predominated in the period between 1875 and 1925, when it was their intention to critique these views.

Soon after the exhibition opened, black community leaders in Toronto wrote critical letters to the Toronto-based newspaper *The Globe and Mail* arguing that the exhibition "infantilize[d] the African peoples depicted" and celebrated a racist view of Africans (quoted in Tator et al. 1998:40). They staged daily protests outside the ROM condemning the museum and its staff as racist. At the same time, the families of the Canadian servicemen and missionaries who had loaned their photographs to the museum read the exhibition differently. They felt that the good intentions of their relatives in the early twentieth century were being ignored. In short, very few people were happy with the exhibition. Although the museum's director stood by the exhibition and its curator, Cannizzo resigned in March 1990, several months before the exhibition closed. The four other museums in Canada and the United States scheduled to receive the exhibition cancelled, wanting none of the tension and controversy that the exhibition had produced.

As anthropologist Simon Ottenberg (1991:81) suggests, "Curating an exhibition is a political act." In this case, his words seem like an understatement. But there is something else going on here, and it is about the objects themselves. The objects and photographs in the exhibition were real objects. They have a concrete, physical presence that we refer to as their **materiality** (having the quality of being physical or material), the theme we will explore in this final chapter. Although the tensions surrounding the ROM's *Into the Heart of Africa* exhibition were not about the material characteristics of the photographs and objects in the show per se, different people nevertheless gave these tangible objects different meanings. This fact raises an important question central to this chapter: *What is the role of objects and material culture in constructing social relationships and cultural meanings?* Embedded within this larger question are several more focused questions around which this chapter is organized.

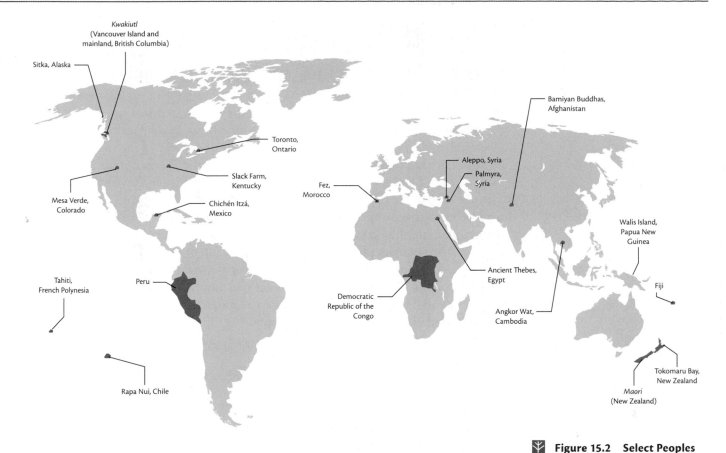

Figure 15.2   **Select Peoples and Places Discussed in Chapter 15.**

Why is the ownership of artifacts from other cultures a contentious issue?

How can anthropology help us understand objects?

How do the meanings of things change over time?

How do objects come to represent our goals and aspirations?

This chapter examines **material culture**, the objects made and used in any society, which is of special interest to anthropologists. Traditionally, the term referred to technologically simple objects made in preindustrial societies, but "material culture" may refer to all of the objects or commodities of modern life as well, including all the latest electronic gadgets, smartphones, and tablets. In previous chapters, we have reflected on the many ways that objects and material culture are important to the material existence of human societies. In this chapter, we look at objects in a different way, how they shape meaning for people and allow us to communicate meaning. When we take objects seriously and consider all the ways people use objects to communicate with others, define themselves through objects, and control others using objects, we can see that anthropology is not "simply" about people, but about the intertwining of people and material things.

• **Material culture.** The objects made and used in any society. Traditionally, the term referred to technologically simple objects made in preindustrial societies, but material culture may refer to all of the objects or commodities of modern life as well.

Why Is the Ownership of Artifacts from Other Cultures a Contentious Issue?

In the United States, the discipline of anthropology began in museums, arising amidst the scramble to put together collections of cultural, archaeological, linguistic, and biological data to document the human story. At first, most of the material culture displayed in museums was from Native Americans in the Western states. From 1850, many of these objects were held in the Smithsonian Institution in Washington, DC.

By the time of the Chicago World's Fair of 1893, the Smithsonian's curators had assembled impressive anthropological exhibits. But rather than rely exclusively on the national collection, the Chicago organizers of the World's Fair appointed anthropologist Frederic Ward Putnam of Harvard's Peabody Museum of Archaeology and Ethnology (established in 1866) to organize its own anthropological exhibits. Putnam competed with the Smithsonian researchers to present the cultures and prehistory of the New World, sending out teams of researchers to acquire new collections from dozens of Indian tribes and to excavate Indian mounds in Ohio, pueblos like Mesa Verde in the Southwest, and ancient sites in Peru (Figure 15.3). At the end of the World's Fair,

Figure 15.3   Kwakiutl Indians with Totem Poles. The totem poles shown here were collected for Frederic Ward Putnam and displayed at the World's Columbian Exposition in Chicago in 1893. Today, they are in the collections of The Field Museum. From *Vistas of the Fair in Color: A Portfolio of Familiar Views* (Chicago, IL: Poole Brothers, 1894). © The Field Museum #GN85650c.

Marshall Field, the wealthy department store merchant, donated a million dollars to help establish a new museum—now known as The Field Museum—on the site of the fairgrounds, which purchased the artifacts and exhibits (Hinsley and Wilcox 2016).

After the World's Fair, the American Museum of Natural History in New York City hired the young Franz Boas, who immediately began building its collections. He organized a series of collecting expeditions to the Northwest coast that brought back many objects for display as well as many volumes of myths and fieldnotes about local customs to help interpret these collections. What followed during the early twentieth century was an international scramble for collections from societies around the world that Western scholars thought of as "primitive" (Cole 1985; Schildkrout and Keim 1998; O'Hanlon and Welsch 2000). These objects documented the lives, economic activities, and rituals of peoples around the globe, and the possession of more of these exotic objects set one museum apart from the others. These objects clearly meant something different to the museums than they did to the native peoples who had used them.

The picture that emerges from all this is that the major American museums were actively competing with one another for objects, in the process employing a lot of anthropologists. For a long time, nobody was concerned about who owned all of these objects, since in a legal sense they belonged to the individual museums. But in recent decades, questions of ownership and control over these objects have become contentious issues. Shouldn't the people whose direct ancestors made or used these objects have some rights over these collections? Who had the right to sell these objects to museums in the first place? Who has the moral right to display and interpret them? Do the museums who own these objects have the right to say whatever they want about another culture's objects, or should the people from whom the objects were collected have a say?

These questions were, of course, at the heart of the ROM's *Into the Heart of Africa* controversy. The museum was in control of the objects, and neither Canadians of African descent nor descendants of white missionaries and servicemen had any say in how their ancestors would be represented. What was so striking was that both white and black Canadians felt that their heritage was being misrepresented, and neither group felt they had a say in the matter. It wasn't the act of showing the objects that either group found problematic; rather, it was that the "wrong" messages were being conveyed about these objects.

Questions of Ownership, Rights, and Protection

Until rather recently, in the United States there have been no special laws protecting the rights of American Indian peoples or their material culture. It has always been assumed that Indian tribes and their members have the right to sell off their possessions to a visiting traveler or anthropologist, or at trading posts developed as places for Indians to sell their handicrafts beginning in the late nineteenth century (Wade 1985). In many tribes today, it is forbidden or controversial to sell off commonly held ritual objects, such as masks and other culturally significant paraphernalia, but a century ago these views varied widely among different tribes. Nevertheless, the assumption was if a museum or a private collector purchased some American Indian object, it belonged to that institution or individual. As suggested previously, however, questions about ownership do not always have such clear answers.

American Indians' Rights and Calls for Repatriation

In the nineteenth century, rights to Indian lands were governed by treaties and later by legislation, particularly the Dawes Act of 1887, which allowed commonly held lands on Indian reservations to be surveyed and divided up into individual lots, which the individual Indian owners could keep, use, or sell as they wished. As a result of the Dawes Act, the majority of land on most reservations was sold off to non-Indian owners by 1950. By the mid-1960s, when civil rights legislation began to protect African Americans,

American Indians began pressing their claims against drilling, mining, pipelines, and agribusiness farming on their reservations. They also protested the ways their peoples and cultures were depicted in movie Westerns, in books, and importantly, in museums. But the claims that seemed to reach the American public's consciousness most directly were those against archaeological excavations of sacred Indian sites and cemeteries.

During the 1970s, activists associated with the **American Indian Movement (AIM)**, a prominent American Indian rights group founded in 1968, began to protest how national, state, and local officials treated Indian remains (Banks 2004). AIM activists asserted that the treatment of Indian remains was an element of a larger pattern of disrespect for Indian cultures. They pointed to histories of forced settlement on reservations; punishment for speaking their native languages in government schools; and pressures on reservations to sell their lands to white Americans. Calls for **repatriation**, or the return of human remains and artifacts to the communities of descendants of the people to whom they originally belonged, came to stand for something much more important than the objects themselves. Repatriating human remains and artifacts became a symbol of respect for Indian identity.

At the time, the United States had only a few basic laws to protect archaeological sites, and these were mostly on government lands. Among these laws were the Antiquities Act of 1906, requiring permission to excavate on government lands, and the National Historic Preservation Act of 1966. The latter act required government agencies to consider the effects of development projects on historical or archaeological sites, because with urban renewal, many historic buildings and structures in urban areas were demolished without consideration of their historic or community significance. This act established the National Register of Historic Places, which protects historically significant sites important to communities across the country. Such sites include archaeological sites and sites of special religious, cultural, or historic significance to all Americans, including Indians.

The Tragedy of Slack Farm and the Passage of NAGPRA

An incident in Kentucky in 1987 led to new state and federal laws that make it a felony to disturb archaeological sites on both government and private lands everywhere. Anthropologists and archaeologists had been aware of an important late-prehistoric site on the property known as Slack Farm near Uniontown, Kentucky, which included an intact cemetery containing more than 1,000 Indian graves, as well as grave goods, like pots, beads, pipes, arrowheads, and ritual artifacts. The owners of the land sold rights to dig on this site for $10,000 to a group of pot hunters, whose sole aim was to make money from the artifacts they could loot from the graves. They dug up the site without any care, losing all meaningful contextual data, and left skeletal material and broken pots all over. Residents complained to the state police, who arrested and fined the looters on the misdemeanor charge of desecrating a venerated object, a charge used primarily when gravestones and cemeteries are damaged (Fagan 1988; Arden 1989). This incident was so offensive to American Indian groups as well as anthropologists and archaeologists that it led the Congress to pass the **Native American Graves Protection and Repatriation Act of 1990**, or **NAGPRA**.

NAGPRA requires the repatriation of human remains and artifacts found with those remains to the families of the dead individuals. The law also requires all museums or other institutions that hold human remains or cultural objects from any native group included in the act to inform tribal representatives of their holdings. If the group feels that an object is of special cultural, religious, or historic significance, they may petition the institution to return or "repatriate" the object. Although many museums own objects from other countries, NAGPRA covers only material from American cultural groups, including American Indians, Hawaiian Islanders, Native Alaskans, and the indigenous peoples of American Samoa and Guam.

- **American Indian Movement (AIM).** The most prominent and one of the earliest American Indian activist groups, founded in 1968.

- **Repatriation.** The return of human remains or cultural artifacts to the communities of descendants of the people to whom they originally belonged.

- **Native American Graves and Repatriation Act (NAGPRA).** The 1990 law that established the ownership of human remains, grave goods, and important cultural objects as belonging to the Native Americans whose ancestors once owned them.

Some archaeologists and anthropologists worried that information about the pre-history of Native Americans, an important part of the heritage of all humans, would be lost if reburial of bones and grave goods became commonplace (Buikstra 1983). They also declared that scientists have a moral and professional obligation to the ar-chaeological data they work with, as well as to the broader public good that can come from such studies (Meighan 1992). Others rejected the Indian position altogether; as one prominent archaeologist was once heard to say, the Indians would "get my bones over my dead body."

Despite such protests and concerns, over the past quarter century, many sets of human remains have been returned to various tribes, along with objects of very special significance to the tribal groups involved. Most important cultural institutions have taken advantage of NAGPRA to establish or reestablish relationships with Native American groups over repatriation concerns. These efforts have involved inviting tribal leaders to visit the museum and study what collections the museum may have from their community. Museums have learned a great deal about their collections by working closely with Indians. But they have also used repatriation to demonstrate their close relationships with the tribes whose objects they display at their museums (Figure 15.4). For their part, tribal groups have used repatriation to celebrate the significance of their traditional culture and to push for greater respect for indigenous peoples. In the process of returning material items to their original communities, both museums and host communities add to the meaning of these objects.

Although NAGPRA has no say over how to deal with objects collected from cultures outside the jurisdiction of the United States, many U.S. institutions have used questions about repatriation to build relationships with native groups in other countries as well. We explore an example of this sort of relationship building in "Anthropologist as Problem Solver: John Terrell, Repatriation, and the Maori House at The Field Museum."

Protection of Historic Sites Around the World

The meaning and importance of historic sites is a problem not limited to the United States, because the meaning of all such sites is frequently contested for political, eco-nomic, religious, and other cultural reasons. Many countries have implemented leg-islation and programs of their own to recognize and protect historic sites, and most governments support UNESCO's **World Heritage Sites program**, which provides financial support to maintain sites of importance to humanity. The majority of the 814 cultural heritage sites currently recognized by UNESCO's program have played a key role in human history. Five of them are sites where early fossil hominids have been found in Africa, China, and Australia. Others are key archaeological sites, such as the pyramids of Giza and the temples and palaces of Ancient Thebes in Egypt, Angkor Wat in Cambodia, Chichén Itzá in Mexico, Mesa Verde in Colorado, and the moai statues on Rapa Nui (Easter Island), all of which are typical of what we often think of as ancient historic and prehistoric sites. Many others are historic cities like Fez in Morocco.

A number of sites have been damaged in recent years because of international con-flicts. These include the site of the ancient city of Palmyra in Syria, which was in-tentionally damaged by ISIS because it predated Islam (Mullen and Elwazer 2015; UNESCO 2015b); the historic city of Aleppo, now largely destroyed by the Syrian government and Russian bombing; and the Bamiyan Buddhas of Afghanistan, in-tentionally destroyed by the Taliban because they represented pre-Islamic religious beliefs (Bearak 2001; Crossette 2001; UNESCO 2015a; Figure 15.5). UNESCO cannot force countries to protect these sites, but it can formally de-list a site if the host country fails to protect it from destruction (UNESCO 2015c). Internationally, there is agreement that such archaeological and historical sites belong to all peoples, not just to the governments that happen to control them at any particular moment.

• **World Heritage Sites program.** A UNESCO-run program that provides financial support to maintain sites of importance to humanity.

Figure 15.4   Repatriating a Chilkat Blanket to the Tlingit at a Memorial Potlatch in Sitka, Alaska, Fall 2002. (*Top*) Tlingit elders who organized the memorial potlatch wearing Chilkat blankets or button blankets: Edwell John, from Dakl'aweidi (Killer Whale) clan; Joe Murray, representing Dakl'aweidi clan; Joe Murray, representing Dakl'aweidi clan, a man from Kaagwaantaan (Wolf) clan; Dan Brown, of Teikweidee (Brown Bear) clan; and Randy Gamble, of Kaagwaantaan clan. They wear headdresses from their respective clans. (*Bottom*) Kellen Haak, registrar of the Hood Museum of Art at Dartmouth College, presents the museum's Chilkat blanket being returned to the Deisheetaan (Beaver) clan in the Raven moiety. To his left are Nell Murphy (from the American Museum of Natural History in New York), anthropologist Sergei Kan (from Dartmouth College, speaking for the group), and Terri Snowball (from the National Museum of the American Indian in Washington, DC). Tlingit leaders in this photo include Alan Zuboff, of L'eeneidi (Dog Salmon) clan, and Garfield George, of Deisheetaan clan.

But destruction can have as powerful a meaning as preservation, depending upon the public attention given to the destruction at the time.

Cultural Resource Management: Not Just for Archaeologists

- **Cultural resource management (CRM).** Research and planning aimed at identifying, interpreting, and protecting sites and artifacts of historic or prehistoric significance.

In response to the legislation introduced in the past few decades, archaeologists in the United States have taken a leading role in managing and preserving our prehistoric and historic heritage. But the need for specialists who can study the architecture and cultural significance of historic sites is increasingly open to people who majored in history and anthropology in college. All of these efforts are often referred to as **cultural resource management (CRM)**, which is a form of applied anthropology. CRM's

Anthropologist as Problem Solver
John Terrell, Repatriation, and the Maori Meeting House at The Field Museum

AT THE HEART of any Maori community in New Zealand is a meeting house where rituals, business, and other important community processes take place. Meeting houses have elaborately carved images on the posts and ridge poles, which not only symbolize a Maori family's ancestry, but embody the spirits of these ancestors as well.

In 1905, The Field Museum in Chicago purchased a nearly complete meeting house named Ruatepupuke [roo-ah-tay-pah-**poo**-kay] that originally came from Tokomaru Bay, New Zealand. The museum bought it from a European curio dealer who had convinced one member of the family to sell

🌿 **John Terrell at the Maori Meeting House at The Field Museum in Chicago.** (*Top*) John Terrell speaking at a workshop held in the meeting house. (*Bottom*) The restored meeting house.

this house. The structure had been quietly and quickly dismantled and shipped overseas. For the Maori family, this was a shameful act that amounted to selling off their ancestors carved in the boards.

When archaeologist John Terrell became The Field Museum's curator of oceanic archaeology and ethnology in 1971, he began researching this Maori meeting house. He brought specialists to the museum to examine the carvings, including Hirini (Sidney) Moko Mead, one of the leading Maori anthropologists. Terrell also visited Tokomaru Bay to confirm what he and other specialists had suspected—that this was indeed their meeting house that had been sold and packed off around 1900.

Terrell then began working with elders at Tokomaru Bay, discussing the future of the structure. Some of the young people wanted their house and their ancestors to come back to the community. But after talking over the matter with Terrell, the elders agreed to keep the house in Chicago, as long as The Field Museum would work with the community to restore the structure. Terrell, in collaboration with Tokomaru elders, chose Maori curators, conservators, and artists to help with the restoration (Hakiwai and Terrell 1994).

The house went on display for the public in 1986 as part of an exhibition called *Te Maori*, and Maori elders were invited to help with the opening. Later, more than 20 elders, both men and women, came to Chicago to perform the rituals that would bring their ancestral spirits from the museum's lower level, where the house had been for many decades, to the second floor, where the house would be reassembled. Elders have been involved with planning and executing all important decisions about Ruatepupuke ever since. They selected their own Maori curator and conservator, as well as a Maori artist who was tasked with carving new pieces missing from the front of the structure. Maori curator Arapata Hakiwai discovered several boards from this meeting house in Te Papa, the National Museum of New Zealand, and Tokomaru elders requested that these carved boards join the house in Chicago where they belonged; the museum complied with this request. One carved houseboard was found in the collections of the Peabody Essex Museum in Salem, Massachusetts, and it, too, was reunited with the other boards from Te Papa in Chicago. The people of Tokomaru Bay are now well known by Maori across New Zealand because their meeting house is so prominently displayed overseas. By working with Terrell and The Field

(continued)

Anthropologist as Problem Solver (continued)

Museum, the people of Tokomaru Bay transformed an embarrassing situation into an object of national pride.

By April 2007, a number of the elders who had been involved with The Field Museum passed away. The younger generation had not been as involved with the museum, and some were talking about bringing Ruatepupuke back to Tokomaru Bay. The Field Museum invited some 50 Maori from Tokomaru Bay, both elders and younger members of the community, to celebrate the meeting house and Maori culture for a week. After this experience, many of those young people recognized that if they want a place for their cultural traditions on the world stage, they can be more successful by working with The Field Museum than they ever could be on their own. As in the 1980s, John Terrell continues to work hard to engage with indigenous communities who made and formerly owned the artifacts his

museum now holds. Together, the curator and the Maori community have found alternative solutions to the question of repatriation of cultural objects that for Maori are the embodiment of their ancestors.

Questions for Reflection

1. What does this example illustrate about the role archaeologists and anthropologists can play in explaining and promoting a community's culture around the world?

2. Many archaeologists have assumed there is a natural tension between them and indigenous peoples. To what extent do you feel this tension is inevitable?

3. Archaeologists and anthropologists have always been the outsiders who most understand the native cultures they study. Why have indigenous peoples so often wanted to challenge their ownership of artifacts?

Figure 15.5   One of the Buddhas of Bamiyan in Afghanistan. This 174-foot-(53-meter-) high figure was carved into the side of a cliff in the sixth or seventh century. It was one of two stone figures known as the Buddhas of Bamiyan that were destroyed by the Taliban in 2001, on the orders of Mullah Omar, after the Taliban government declared that they were idols. (Crossett 2001)

goal is to protect and manage the cultural resources of every community, especially important prehistoric sites and structures. Much of what CRM does is document and interpret historic and prehistoric sites and structures for living communities. The vast majority of archaeological work in the Americas and around the world is done by contract archaeologists, and CRM has become a major focus for those seeking careers in archaeology. But a growing number of applied cultural anthropologists are working in the CRM field with historic and cultural sites and materials. And most communities have a historical society, historic district, or heritage commission that regularly hires consultants to interpret historical and cultural resources in their towns and cities. Many projects are done under the supervision of the National Park Service or a state department of historic resources.

Although many American Indian groups historically criticized archaeologists for doing little to help their communities and for disturbing the bones of their ancestors (Deloria 1969), an increasing number of Indians have earned postgraduate degrees in archaeology and anthropology and use the techniques of CRM to preserve their tribe's cultural heritage. Nearly all tribes that use CRM view heritage management differently than most federal government agencies (Anyon, Ferguson, and Welch 2000:132). One key difference is that non-Indian agencies nearly always see heritage resources as tangible places and things, and scientific study as a way of finding a middle ground between the heritage resource and some other use. Emphasizing their spiritual connections to the past, tribes tend to prefer avoiding the disturbance of the heritage resource altogether, including scientific investigation (Dongoske et al. 1995).

As this section has demonstrated, the social conflicts around objects are complex, suggesting that the meanings and uses of objects are not such straightforward matters. In the next section we deepen this point by pulling back and reviewing what we can learn about societies by looking at objects anthropologically.

THINKING CRITICALLY ABOUT MATERIALITY

How do the meanings of museum collections of American Indian material culture change depending on who is thinking about them? How would these meanings be different if the objects were historical artifacts from a white pioneer community in the National Museum of American History?

How Can Anthropology Help Us Understand Objects?

Until the 1980s, anthropologists tended to look at the study of objects principally as evidence of cultural distinctiveness. They approached cultural and artistic objects as expressions of a society's environmental adaptation or aesthetic sensibilities, or as markers of ethnic identity. Viewed in this way, arts and crafts were considered an expression of a particular tradition, time, or place, but even more so, an expression of the individual creativity of the artist or craftsperson. This way of looking at objects may seem reasonable, but in the mid-1980s, anthropologists began to look at objects in a new way. In particular, they started to recognize that objects were capable of conveying meaning in many different ways simultaneously, many of these ways symbolic.

The Many Dimensions of Objects

The late historian of anthropology George W. Stocking, Jr., edited an influential book called *Objects and Others: Essays on Museums and Material Culture* (1985). Stocking's introduction to this book explained that anthropology's history began with the study of objects in museums decades before anthropologists even began conducting their own field research. Using these collections, they developed crude analyses of how civilized, barbaric, or primitive a society was from the kinds of objects they had or did not have. Later, when anthropologists started conducting fieldwork, they noticed firsthand the importance of objects in rituals, social exchanges, and political activities. Anthropologists began to look at objects to understand the meaning of rituals, the interconnections between people who exchanged particular objects, and the social stratification within a society that could be seen in the presence or absence of objects in a particular household or community. In its most basic sense, this approach has endured until the present.

But the importance of Stocking's work was his argument that objects are multidimensional, and if we really want to understand them, we have to recognize and try to understand not just their three basic physical dimensions—height, width, and depth—but at least four other dimensions as well, among them time (history), power, wealth, and aesthetics, making a total of seven dimensions.

The dimension of *time* or *history* refers to the fact that objects in museums came from somewhere and each had an individual history. In part this asks when, by whom, and how were they produced; how did they get to the museum or their current location; and how have interpretations of them changed over time? The dimension of *power* reveals the relations of inequality reflected in objects, especially why the objects of non-Western people sit in ethnographic museums, while very few non-Western peoples have museums or repositories where local people can view Western objects. During the heyday of colonialism, European and American anthropologists collected thousands of objects from the peoples they studied. Rarely could a community know enough about how these objects might be displayed or studied to be able to give informed consent. *Wealth* reflects the fact that people use objects to establish and demonstrate who has wealth and social status. We have seen how American museum directors saw showy and impressive objects as being quite valuable for their museums and their museums' reputations. Similarly, only the wealthy can typically own original examples of important early artworks. The dimension of *aesthetics* is reflected in the fact that each culture brings with it its own system or patterns of recognizing what is pleasing or attractive, which configurations of colors and textures are appealing, and which are not. These patterns, of course, change over time in the style of artworks, but also in the designs of commonplace objects like pottery (Kubler 1962).

What intrigued Stocking most about objects, especially those now found in museums, was that these things were a historical archive in multiple dimensions that can tell us a great deal about the cultures that made and used these objects, as well as the relationships between the collectors' societies and the communities who originally made them. Furthermore, objects could offer a window for understanding local symbolic systems of meaning. This point was more expansive than just being focused on the objects found in art and ethnographic museums. His insights can actually be applied to any everyday object. Consider, for example, a shiny new bicycle.

A Shiny New Bicycle, in Multiple Dimensions

Picture a shiny new bicycle chained to a bicycle rack on your campus (Figure 15.6). Made of a strong yet lightweight alloy, it is fast, sleek, and an exquisite example of modern technology applied to an object that has been around for more than a century. Like all objects, this bicycle has the physical properties of height, length, and width, dimensions that are quite important for any individual mounting one: think of how difficult it is to ride a bicycle that is too big or small.

Objects are defined by more than their physical traits, however. Objects also embody a temporal dimension of having a past, present, and future. The shape and form of this particular object has emerged from improvements on the functions of generations of bicycles, used by generations of cyclists as a childhood toy, as an inexpensive mode of transport, for racing, or for casual weekend riding. If we think of a bicycle in the abstract, we can choose from among all of these meanings and uses of a bicycle. The particular owner of this bicycle has certain associations that come to mind when he or she thinks of a bicycle, and these associations may be quite different from cyclists who race, from mothers who pedal around the neighborhood with their children, or from bike messengers who spend their days cycling through busy urban traffic. The owner's view of his or her bicycle may be shaped by previous bicycles he or she has owned; it may be influenced by feelings that

Figure 15.6   The Bicycle, Like Anything, Is a Multidimensional Object.

the owner is being ecologically "green" and choosing an environmentally friendly mode of transportation. And such images shape how the owner views himself or herself today or how he or she imagines the future (Vivanco 2013).

This bicycle—like practically every other object North American consumers purchase—is also a commodity that as parts and as a finished product has circulated through a complex economic system, supported by an equally complex set of regulatory rules. As deeply personal as the selection and purchase of an object like a bicycle may be for us as individuals, it was made on an assembly line by dozens of workers, each contributing a small part to the finished effort. If this happened overseas, the bicycle has traveled through a worldwide network of economic linkages, not to mention the complex set of domestic warehouses and shippers, to get to its current owner.

In that process, the manufacturer and the mainstream culture generally have carefully cultivated the current owner's desire to own and use this object. The owner has purchased this particular bicycle and not a more expensive one, and not a beaten-up secondhand one. The owner may even have replaced an older bike with this newer and more efficient one, imagining himself as more of a racer than he really is, or thinking of herself as more environmentally conscious than she might actually be. And our impressions of particular bicycles may be shaped by the images we have seen of them in films, TV programs, advertisements, and shiny brochures advertising a particular brand of bicycle (Vivanco 2013).

Finally, this bicycle, like most other objects we own, is a useful object, not only for where or how far it can take us, not just in how much it can help keep us healthy from the exercise it provides, not simply from the fuel it saves us, but from the impressions of us that it creates in others as they see us ride.

The point of our bicycle example is that *any* mundane object can help us imagine ourselves, our past, and where we are headed. We may use objects to attract the attention and admiration of others. And our objects may be used by others to classify and stereotype us. Although Stocking's seven dimensions do not cover all the aspects or dimensions suggested about our shiny new bicycle, they do offer a simple first glance at how we feel we should look at objects anthropologically.

The Power of Symbols

Now that we have you thinking about objects in multiple dimensions, we can turn to the aesthetic. By studying the art traditions and objects of non-Western peoples, anthropologists have learned that the complex ideas and understandings about the gods, ghosts, spirits, and other supernatural beings who inhabit their cosmologies are embodied in the physical representations we see in carvings. The African carving in Figure 15.7 is a good case in point. The African carver of that sculpture was not trying to depict the human form, but was displaying the distinctive characteristics of supernatural beings by symbolically representing them as anatomical features.

There is every reason to believe that the carvers of such figures, and perhaps others living in their communities when the figures were created, imagined that their spirits and demons looked like the carvings they produced. But when others grow up and the only depiction of a particular spirit is the carving that represents that spirit, they will probably understand the spirit to look just like the

Figure 15.7   Rethinking African Art. When Western audiences were first introduced to objects like the *Nkisi* figure from the Democratic Republic of Congo pictured here, they often responded dismissively and ethnocentrically. They misunderstood African notions of aesthetics. In this *Nkisi* figure, displayed at the Hood Museum of Art at Dartmouth College, each additional element adds meaning and power to the object—the most important here are the nails. Each nail pounded into the carving requested some favor from the spirit in this figure, and it also strengthened the spirit. (Courtesy of Hood Museum of Art, Dartmouth College, Hanover, New Hampshire)

Figure 15.8   An Amulet Depicting an Angel. For some Americans, possessing an image of an angel makes them feel secure and protected. Few of these individuals claim to have ever seen an angel, but they have a shared understanding of what one looks like based on traditional representations.

carvings. In a similar way, although nobody knows what the ancient Hebrew prophet Moses may have looked like, when we hear a discussion of Moses, most of us will immediately imagine an older white man with a long white beard and flowing robes—as Charlton Heston depicted him in the classic 1956 film *The Ten Commandments* (de Mille 1956)—because this is the way Moses appears in nearly all popular images of this ancient figure.

As another example, consider that few of us have seen angels in the flesh, so to speak, yet most of us have images in our minds of what an angel might look like. These images are derived from the images we have seen of angels around the Christmas holidays in stores, in front of churches, surrounding manger scenes, on postage stamps, and the like. All of these images are an American symbolic construction that has its roots in much earlier European notions about the soul, the various angels that appear from time to time in the Bible, both for those who believe in angels and those who do not. Whether they exist or not, angels are a cultural construction that we can see in movies, hear about on certain televangelists' broadcasts and radio programs, and buy as amulets or medallions in shops that sell Christian religious paraphernalia such as the amulet pictured in Figure 15.8. In order to make sense of that amulet, we need to understand the history of angel symbolism in American society and culture in addition to the fact that some Americans believe that possessing these angel amulets will in some supernatural way protect them.

The Symbols of Power

Just as the aesthetic dimensions of objects shape an object's meaning, powerful people use aesthetics in ways to demonstrate and legitimate their social, political, or religious power. Wealthy North Americans and Europeans, for example, may own and display paintings or sculptures by well-known artists to demonstrate their high social position. Others who have taken an art history course or otherwise studied art may use their knowledge of the subject to establish themselves as socially superior to those who have had no such experiences and do not feel comfortable in art museums. In many traditional African kingdoms, such as those whose artworks now get displayed in museums in places like New York or Toronto, the kings and chiefs who ruled these communities distinguished themselves from ordinary people with symbols of rank and authority—staffs, chairs, thrones, clothing, and so forth—artfully carved or woven in a particular local style or aesthetic. Similarly, in many religions, authorities employ aesthetics to indicate that the holder of an item possesses divine power as well as power here on earth.

What sets these objects of power apart is in part their aesthetic style that establishes the objects, and by extension their owners, as important and special. But it is also true that the aesthetic settings and ways in which such objects are used and displayed can also symbolically communicate the power of their owners. An interesting illustration comes from the island of Walis along the north coast of Papua New Guinea, as witnessed by Robert Welsch, one of the authors of this textbook, in 1993. A century earlier, a religious cult leader named Barjani had foretold the coming of Europeans and was believed to be a prophet. After his death, his family's clansmen had erected a shrine for him, where people in need of supernatural assistance could leave a small amount of money or tobacco to ensure Barjani's assistance. When Welsch and his colleague, John Terrell, went to see the shrine, they were mostly interested in the building's historically important architectural style.

The real surprise came when they climbed the small ladder to peer into Barjani's shrine. The interior of the small shrine held a single object in a place of honor on a simple but small platform of palm leaves: an old and well-worn bowler hat, much like the one Charlie Chaplin wore in some of his movies. This was Barjani's hat, an object that possessed its power from Barjani's having worn it, but also from being the only object in the shrine. The meaning of this hat, standing out starkly in such an unexpected place, came partly from its association with Barjani and partly from his association with the foreigners he had predicted would come. In addition, the fact that it was a foreign object that few if any other Walis Islanders could have owned must have made it both exotic and valuable as a relic of this local prophet (Figure 15.9).

Although Barjani's hat is for Walis Islanders a statement about relations between themselves and powerful outsiders, it is also a window into the historical context of both their society and the changing meaning that this bowler hat has had over its century of existence. To pursue this issue further, let us consider the next question around which this chapter is organized, which is how objects change meaning over time.

Figure 15.9   Barjani's Shrine on Wallis Island in Papua New Guinea. Inside, the room was empty except for Barjani's bowler hat and offerings or gifts that had been left in exchange for Barjani's help.

THINKING CRITICALLY ABOUT MATERIALITY

Most people take the objects around them at face value, but anthropologists think about things in more multidimensional ways. Consider some object, statue, artwork, building, or other physical feature on your campus and outline its different dimensions as an anthropologist might. What new insights about your campus, your school's history, or the school's distinctive local culture do you get from this analysis?

How Do the Meanings of Things Change Over Time?

Anthropologists today study some of the very same museum collections that anthropologists studied over a century ago. But we often come to very different conclusions about the people who made and used the objects in those collections. What has changed? Maybe one change is that the objects in the collection have deteriorated over time, but that doesn't really explain the difference. More important is the change in interpretation that we give to the object. This is a key aspect of what Stocking was getting at when he indicated that objects have a temporal dimension: all objects change over time, *if not in their physical characteristics, then in the significance we give to them.*

Around the same time that Stocking was laying out his framework for understanding objects in seven dimensions, another group of anthropologists was developing a set of complementary theories and techniques for analyzing in depth the issue of how objects change over time. Declaring that "things have social lives," they published a book called *The Social Life of Things: Commodities in Cultural Perspective* (Appadurai 1986) in which they laid out some useful concepts and approaches for thinking anthropologically about objects. So how can an *inanimate* object have a *social* life?

The Social Life of Things

The idea that inanimate things have social lives is based on the assumption that things have forms, uses, and trajectories that are intertwined in complex ways with people's lives. Just as people pass through different socially recognized phases of life, objects have "careers" (in the sense of having a course or progression) with recognizable phases, from their creation, exchange, and uses, to their eventual discard. Along the way, it is possible to identify social relationships and cultural ideologies that influence each period in this career. Across cultures, these relationships and ideologies can vary drastically.

Consider a pair of running sneakers sold at a mall. This pair of sneakers may start as cotton fabric and rubber in a Chinese factory. But the shoes mean something quite different there from what they will mean to the mall salesperson, who rings up your purchase, or from what they will mean to you when you first wear them to some social event. The shoes may have aged only a few weeks from the time they were made until you wear them; the change in significance comes not from aging, but from moving from one person to another, some of whom see them as a way to make a living, while others see them as a way to look cool at a party. That pair of shoes has a complicated life, taking on meanings from the contexts it passes through and, to the sensitive observer, revealing a whole range of complex social relations in the process. And throughout it all, the same pair of shoes has changed.

Three Ways Objects Change Over Time

All objects change over time, but they can do so in different ways. Most objects age and are weathered with time, of course, usually becoming less significant because they get old and worn out. But, for understanding the social life of things, there are three major ways that objects change over time:

1. The form, shape, color, material, and use change from generation to generation.
2. An object changes significance and meaning as its social and physical contexts change.
3. A single object changes significance and meaning as it changes hands.

Let us consider a few examples of each of these kinds of changes to illustrate how the social meanings of an object can change over time.

Changing Form from Generation to Generation

Nearly every manufactured product has changed over time as styles and social preferences have changed. While we usually understand these changes as gradual improvements in form or technology, they are just as often due to innovations or differences in style, simply to be different. One of the best examples comes from an anthropological study of women's fashion.

Just before World War II, anthropologists Jane Richardson and Alfred Kroeber (1940) published an analysis of skirt length in women's dresses over the previous 300 years. Studying all sorts of pattern books, sketches, and photographs of women's dresses, they documented how styles of dresses had changed over this period. They found that skirt length had risen and fallen in ways that most women were unaware of. In a more or less predictable way, hem length fluctuated from extremes of long to short over a 50-year period or cycle. Subsequent studies since 1940 have suggested that this cycle has now shortened to about 20 or 25 years (Bernard 2011:355; Figure 15.10).

What is the cause of these cyclical changes? There are actually at least two causes. First, fashionable women want to wear the latest fashion, and this desire encourages many others to follow their lead. Second, the factories and seamstresses that make women's dresses have a vested interest in these garments' changing. They want to sell new dresses, and the best way to sell new dresses is if the styles change so much that everyone's closet is filled with "old-fashioned" dresses. But there is more to it than simply encouraging new sales, because the symbolism of being fashionable relies on constantly changing preferences. And all aspects of the fashion industry are involved in creating long-term changes that involve thousands and thousands of people in the fashion industry as a whole, from the high-end designers to the most inexpensive stores and even the consignment shops, who all rely on—and help produce—those changing preferences.

For over a century, archaeologists have understood the fact that styles and fashions change over time; for example, using pottery styles that were found to have changed over broad regions over decades and centuries to date excavation sites that would otherwise be undateable. As a cooking tool, earthenware pots in the American Southwest became largely obsolete as soon as metal cooking pots became readily available. But, as anthropologist Edwin Wade (1985) shows, the preservation of this traditional style of pottery emerged with the arrival of the Atchison, Topeka, & Santa Fe Railroad to New Mexico after 1880. Pueblo communities that had previously been essentially isolated from the world became directly exposed to outsiders for the first time. Rather than abandoning pottery for metal cooking pots, they began selling their traditional pots to white tourists along the side of the tracks. As time went on, the Pueblo potters adjusted their pottery designs and styles to fit the desires of their tourists. And after the beginning of the Santa Fe Art Market in the 1930s, the changes in pottery styles have been shaped by the changing preferences of fine art collectors rather than tourists.

Changing Meaning with Changing Contexts

Contexts often change as environments and technologies change as well. Tahitians, like other Polynesians, had no knowledge of iron until Europeans first visited their islands (Figure 15.11). On June 18, 1767, the British captain Samuel Wallis was the first Westerner to reach Tahiti, and that day Tahitians learned about the powerful abilities of iron tools for cutting, chopping, and carving. But after learning about iron tools, Tahitian men started plotting ways they could get access to Wallis's steel. The traditionally stodgy and sexually restrained Tahitian society became transformed almost overnight as men

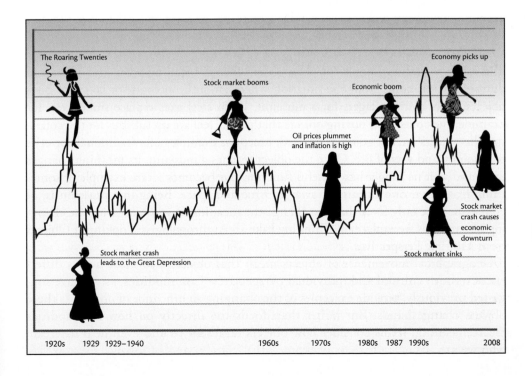

The Roaring Twenties

Stock market booms

Economic boom

Economy picks up

Oil prices plummet and inflation is high

Stock market crash leads to the Great Depression

Stock market sinks

Stock market crash causes economic downturn

1920s   1929   1929–1940   1960s   1970s   1980s   1987   1990s   2008

Figure 15.10   Shifting Dress Styles. Although dress styles in Europe and America have changed in many ways from period to period, they reflect cyclical trends in stylistic and aesthetic innovation (after Richardson and Kroeber 1940; and Bernard 2011).

Figure 15.11   Queen Oberea Welcomes Captain Samuel Wallis at Tahiti. When Wallis and his crew reached Tahiti in 1767, the queen and captain exchanged gifts that included some small iron cutting tools. Tahitians found the iron tools to be far superior to the stone and shell cutting tools they had been using, and they quickly developed a strong desire for iron that transformed their society.

sent their wives, daughters, and sisters out to Wallis's ship, the HMS *Dolphin*, to engage in sex in exchange for any sort of iron tools: knives, axes, or even nails that could be fashioned into cutting tools. The following year, the French captain Louis-Antoine de Bougainville arrived at Tahiti, and a year later British captain James Cook first reached Tahitian shores; they both found Tahitian women to be so sexually promiscuous that the crew nearly dismantled their small lifeboats in a quest for much-desired nails. On his second voyage, Cook brought along quantities of nails and hoop iron to satisfy the local desire for iron. Of course, these interactions with Tahitian women created the stereotype that Polynesians were traditionally very promiscuous, when in fact it was the horny sailors combined with the Tahitian desire for iron that had transformed Tahitian society and introduced sexual license to these islands (Howe 1984). As this example shows, new technologies can have profound impacts on local communities.

Changing Meaning from Changing Hands

The most powerful examples of objects that change meaning when they pass into different hands come from the situation where an anthropologist or collector buys objects from exotic villagers for a museum. Until steel axes replace stone axes, for example, the collector is buying objects that people feel are useful. But for the collector, the objects are not going to be used, except as examples of a traditional society's technology and way of life. Once the object reaches a museum, its meaning changes profoundly; it no longer has a useful function but becomes a rare example of something from an exotic culture far away in time and space. Being in a museum is, of course, not the only force that can change the meaning of an object with the changing of hands, as we explore in "Thinking Like an Anthropologist: Looking at Objects from Multiple Perspectives."

Geographical movements of objects mean that objects also move across differences in both cultural and individual perspectives. Commodities, as we have suggested previously, provide examples of the changing significance of objects as these objects change hands. But rather than focus too directly on how commodities create meaning, let us consider how objects represent us and even help us create who we are.

Thinking Like an Anthropologist
Looking at Objects from Multiple Perspectives

ANTHROPOLOGISTS BEGIN THEIR research by asking questions. In this box, we want you to learn how to ask questions as an anthropological researcher. Part One describes a situation and follows up with questions we would ask. Part Two asks you to formulate your own questions based on a different situation.

PART ONE: NICHOLAS THOMAS ON ENTANGLED OBJECTS IN FIJI

In the 1980s, anthropologist Nicholas Thomas (1989) was studying British museum collections from Fiji that had been acquired in the 1870s, around the time that the British government was annexing the Fiji Islands as a colony. He noticed that there was an extraordinarily large number of weapons brought back by sailors, traders, and people with business interests in the islands. The clubs and the so-called cannibal forks were sought after by wealthy collectors—nearly all of whom were male—probably because such weapons fed their image of tribal societies as vicious and bloodthirsty savages.

Thomas himself did not see these objects as evidence of savagery. He knew that the wooden forks were used by high-ranking chiefs who were prohibited by taboos from touching food with their fingers, as their personal power would in effect poison the food for others. Rarely would these forks have been used for human flesh. Fijian men could be violent, but they also carried clubs mostly in ceremonial situations as a symbol of their strength and masculine power. But for early collectors in England, who had never visited these tropical islands, clubs presented tangible evidence of an aggressive primitive society they imagined living halfway around the world from Victorian England.

In his research, however, Thomas also found that not everybody interested in these objects bought into the idea

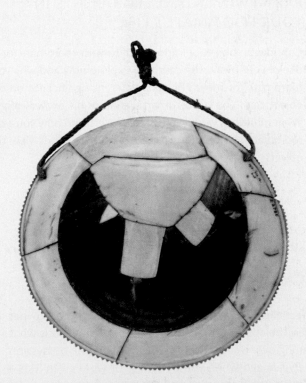

🌿 **Civavonovono (Breastplate) of Whale Ivory, Pearl Shell, and Vegetable Fiber.** This breastplate was collected by Sir Arthur Gordon, first governor of Fiji between 1875 and 1880. It previously belonged to Ratu Seru Cakobau, Vunivalu (war chief) of Bau, who inherited it from his father, Ratu Tanoa Visawaqa. This breastplate is currently at the Museum of Archaeology and Anthropology at the University of Cambridge.

(continued)

Thinking Like an Anthropologist (continued)

that Fijians were bloodthirsty savages. For example, he studied how when the Austrian-Scottish traveler and later collector Anatole von Hügel arrived in Fiji in 1874, he was surprised to find that nobody had attempted to assemble a systematic collection of objects from the islands. Von Hügel was dismissive of the hodge-podge of personal collections he found among the traders and planters in Fiji. For each of them, every object had a personal story: "Every dish was a cannibal dish, every club had been the instrument of some atrocious murder, and every stain on either was caused by blood" (quoted in Thomas 1989:45). Von Hügel went on to assemble a large collection representative of all aspects of Fijian culture. For him, these objects as a collection suggested a complex, socially stratified society with a rich culture. He understood his collection, not in personal terms, but as scientific data.

Thomas also learned that there was yet another set of perspectives on these objects. It happens that von Hügel arrived in Fiji about the same time as the newly appointed colonial governor Arthur H. Gordon. As the first British governor of what became the Crown Colony of Fiji, he viewed Fijian objects very differently from either the traders and planters on one hand or von Hügel on the other. As he was the representative of Queen Victoria and head of the Fijian government, Fijian chiefs gave him gifts in nearly every village he visited. He reciprocated with gifts, usually of British manufacture. As a "chief" himself, Gordon negotiated the political relations with other chiefs using Fijian objects, especially the whale tooth ornaments called *tabua*. *Tabua* were much admired by Fijians, and their possession marked high social status, which was always on the minds of Fijians. For Gordon, Fijian objects were not scientific specimens (as von Hügel viewed them) or evidence of Fijian savagery (as traders and planters viewed them), but tools for promoting government control of the islands and its people.

Thomas concluded that these Fijian objects were "entangled"; that is, taken up in complex ways across cultural boundaries based on differing views about the objects. To understand how different parties viewed Fijian objects differently, Thomas began with a set of anthropological questions:

1. How did Fijians view different kinds of objects differently from Europeans in Fiji?
2. Why did European planters and traders emphasize the bloodthirsty images of Fijians?
3. Why did von Hügel emphasize these objects as scientific specimens rather than as souvenirs?
4. How would the exchange of *tabua* with Governor Gordon enhance his position in the islands?

PART TWO: ENTANGLED OBJECTS IN YOUR ROOMMATE'S LIFE

Consider an object of importance to your roommate (or to one of your friends on campus). Explore how and why your roommate (or friend) places a different significance on this object than you do or other friends of his or hers might. What questions would you ask to understand how you, your roommate (or friend), and perhaps other friends view this object?

THINKING CRITICALLY ABOUT MATERIALITY

The meaning of an object clearly depends on the context in which its owner views it. Over centuries, the change in meaning is often obvious, but what about changes in meaning over a single lifetime? Consider some possession that excited you some years ago when you bought it or were given it as a gift. How do you think about this object today? What has changed to make it more or less valuable to you? Is it valuable to you in a different way today, or has it lost its value altogether?

How Do Objects Come to Represent Our Goals and Aspirations?

When we ask how objects can represent our goals and aspirations, we are really addressing three interconnected issues: (1) Objects express our personal and collective pasts; (2) objects help us express and even formulate our goals and aspirations; and (3) objects can be used in ways that manipulate what our goals and aspirations should be. We consider each of these issues in this final section of the chapter.

The Cultural Biography of Things

To understand how objects help us express our individual pasts, it is helpful to consider an idea first proposed by anthropologist Igor Kopytoff (1986) in an essay included in the book we mentioned before, *The Social Life of Things*. In his essay, Kopytoff begins by observing the problematic fact that in some societies, including pre–Civil War America, some people have been seen as property. By starting with people as property, he was forced to recognize that *all* tangible property has a biography that is profoundly shaped by culture. What Kopytoff meant to communicate to anthropologists is that paying attention to the biography of a thing—its life course from its origins through its distribution, uses, and eventual discard—can uncover important social relationships and cultural dynamics.

As an illustration of this concept, think about this: the objects we choose to keep and display in our rooms, houses, and offices remind us of important things in our lives. But they also communicate important things about us to others. Consider, for example, the posters and other objects you or one of your friends has hung up in a dorm room. A poster featuring a basketball or football player, for instance, highlights an interest in certain sports, teams, or players. Some of these objects suggest events or circumstances that are important in shaping who we are. We knew one first-year student from Texas who proudly displayed the Lone Star flag in his dorm room in a New England college, partly as a reminder of home and partly as a way of expressing his sense of superiority over other students from—in his view—less important states. Flags are often powerful symbols, and his flag was powerful in shaping his identity, too. Fellow students from other states often saw his flag but had less flattering images of him because, in their home communities and social circles, bragging about being from Texas, as the flag's presence implies, was a sign of his not understanding how important other states were. These different perceptions of the same symbol are rooted in the differing cultural biographies of the same symbolic object. These different perceptions, of course, were at the center of the controversy over the ROM's *Into the Heart of Africa* exhibition.

Many objects that remind us of our past, who we are, and how we want others to perceive us are ordinary objects that we have bought in a store or online. When iPads were first released by Apple, some students whose families could afford them rushed to buy them, partly for the new functions that the tablets provided, but often to show off the fact that they could afford such an expensive item. Now that a majority of students have some sort of tablet or portable device, to distinguish themselves and their devices from those of others, students are selecting colorful covers or decorating their cases with images they find pleasing and personally meaningful. By personalizing these objects, as earlier generations of students did to their laptops and three-ring binders, they are making a mass-produced object into an individualized object like no other. People do these things because these objects can express their personal past.

The Culture of Mass Consumption

People do not simply imprint themselves and their pasts *onto* objects. They also formulate who they are and express themselves *through* objects, especially their goals and aspirations about their lives. A useful vantage point from which to observe this dynamic is in the contemporary **culture of mass consumption**—a term that refers to the cultural perspectives and social processes that shape and are shaped by how goods and services are bought, sold, and used in contemporary capitalism—because this culture is so ubiquitous in so many people's lives.

- **Culture of mass consumption.** The cultural perspectives and social processes that shape and are shaped by how goods and services are bought, sold, and used in contemporary capitalism.

Karl Marx and the Commodity Fetish

An influential figure in understanding the culture of mass consumption was the German political-economist Karl Marx. In his masterpiece *Capital*, first published in 1867, Marx (1990) observed that industrial capitalism in England changed people's relationships with everyday objects, and mass-produced commodities in particular gained a peculiar new status in people's lives. Before industrialization, people made the things they needed or wanted, or they acquired them from craftspeople working in small-scale cottage industries. A common craftsman, such as a shoemaker, put a great deal of care into his work, and his workmanship was embodied in the shoes that he made. The shoemaker also developed an important social relationship with the buyer of his shoes, who could come to him to be fitted or to have the shoes repaired if something went wrong after he bought them.

- **Alienation.** The antagonistic detachment between workers and the commodities they produce, as well as between these workers and the buyers of the goods.

But in an industrial factory, a worker makes only part of an object, and he or she has no such relationship with either the fruits of his or her labor or with the buyer. The result, Marx asserted, was the creation of a widespread feeling of **alienation**, or antagonistic detachment, between workers and the commodities they produce, as well as between these workers and the buyers of the goods. As this sense of alienation between people and goods expanded, objects were no longer valued as much for how useful they were, or for the human sweat, ingenuity, and social cooperation that went into them. What held people's attention now were issues like wages, working conditions, and the trading values of the commodities. Divorced from the social relationships in which they were once rooted, Marx argued that commodities began to exercise a strange kind of mystical power over people, controlling their attention and becoming objects of obsessive desire and worship. He called this obsession "the **commodity fetish**."

- **Commodity fetish.** The view of Karl Marx that commodities exercise a strange kind of power over people, controlling their attention and becoming objects of obsessive desire and worship.

If he were alive today, Marx would probably see the commodity fetish as alive and well; for example, in the obsessive hype, fascination, even worship given to the latest iPhone or Nike athletic shoe. For Marx, consumer culture generates a set of goals and aspirations that are fundamentally antisocial, displacing our ordinary social relationships with the aspiration to accumulate fetish-like commodities (Figure 15.12).

The Anthropology of Consumption

Marx's understanding of the culture of mass consumption is influential because it explains the changes in human relations that came with the rise of commodity production. But with his focus on commodity *production*, Marx paid little attention to the process of *consumption* and how people actually acquire, use, and make sense of what they consume. Rather than look at consumption as an antisocial act, many anthropologists who study it have concluded that it is a deeply social, not *anti*-social, act. Seeking out and possessing consumer goods is a key means through which people define and express who they are: their social status, economic means, gender identities, aesthetic sensibilities, individual qualities of taste and discernment, and identification with a certain social class or interest group (Bourdieu 1984; Miller 1987, 1998). In "Classic Contributions: Daniel Miller on Why Some Things Matter," we consider how mass-produced commodities now play such a large role in people's lives.

Figure 15.12   Keeping in Touch. Modern devices such as smartphones allow us to keep in touch with friends, but they are also examples of what Karl Marx called our "commodity fetish"—they control our attention and have become objects of obsessive desire and worship.

Classic Contributions
Daniel Miller on Why Some Things Matter

❦ **Daniel Miller.**

DURING THE LATE 1980s, anthropology saw the emergence of three key figures who have defined current studies of material culture or materiality. The first was historian of anthropology George W. Stocking, Jr. (1985), who suggested that objects have more than three dimensions. The second was anthropologist Arjun Appadurai (1986), whose edited book *The Social Life of Things* encouraged anthropologists to reflect on how objects take on different meanings from their social contexts. The third, and most prolific of the three, was the British anthropologist Daniel Miller (1987), who built on the other two volumes to construct an argument that things matter for understanding the social life of people because things are so important to all human beings in ways they are not for all other animals. In his 1987 volume *Material Culture and Mass Consumption*, Miller introduced the notion that anthropologists should not overlook the commodities of modern cultures, because they mean important things to ordinary people. Even though smartphones, blue jeans, and automobiles are made in distant, impersonal factories, they are meaningful to people because they are so much a part of daily life.

By 1998, Miller had edited a volume called *Material Cultures: Why Some Things Matter*, a few paragraphs of which are excerpted here. In it, he observed that after several decades of ignoring objects (see, e.g., Sturtevant 1969), anthropologists returned to them in the 1990s and made a convincing case that "objects matter." But the question he wanted to answer is why some things matter more than others. The argument he is making here is twofold: (1) that some things in any community matter more than others, and (2) that things are going to matter differently in different cultural settings.

The development of material culture studies may then be seen as a two-stage process. The first phase came in the insistence that things matter and that to focus upon material worlds does not fetishize them since they are not some separate superstructure to social worlds. The key theories of material culture developed in the 1980s demonstrated that social worlds were as much constituted by materiality as the other way around (e.g. Bourdieu 1977; Appadurai 1986; Miller 1987). This gave rise to a variety of approaches to the issue of materiality varying from material culture as analogous with text (e.g. Tilley 1990, 1991) to application of social psychological models (Dittmar 1992).

This book represents a second stage in the development of material culture studies inasmuch as the point that things matter can now be argued to have been made. This volume, by contrast, concentrates on something different and equally important. The volume demonstrates what is to be gained by focusing upon the diversity of material worlds which becomes each other's contexts rather than reducing them either to models of the social world or to specific sub-disciplinary concerns such as the study of textiles or architecture. It will be argued, by example, throughout this volume that studies of material culture may often provide insights into cultural processes that a more literal "anthropology" has tended to neglect. . . .

[I]n using the term "material culture" we believe that there are many ways in which the results can be far less fetishistic than many of those works that do not purport to have such an object focus. At the same time the intention is to focus upon the artefactual world without being founded in any general theory of artefacts or material culture. (Miller 1998:3–4)

(continued)

Classic Contributions (continued)

Questions for Reflection

1. Can you think of an object that you and your friends value as important because it shows that you are important or at least makes you feel important? Why is possession of this object important to you? Is it important to your parents, your teachers, or your roommate?

2. Can you think of an object that one of your parents or grandparents holds in high esteem? Does that person display the object in a place of honor in his or her home? Or, does that person hide the object away, or store it in a safe or a vault? What does that person's treatment of the object say about what the object means to him or her?

How Advertisers Manipulate Our Goals and Aspirations

If large corporations want to survive and expand, they have to persuade consumers to buy their products and not those of one of their competitors. To persuade you to buy their product, they bombard you with advertising that will encourage you to think that their product is necessary for a fulfilling life and that their brand is more likely to help you reach your goals than any other brand. Advertisers proudly announce that they are simply passing on useful information to consumers, but we know that they are really trying to convince us that we need *their* product. We think of this ad-making as part of the process of manipulating our world through a symbolic framing or reframing of their products.

Many TV commercials speak to needs that people already have—from the basics such as food and clothing to those that are less essential such as cars or being attractive to other people. The challenge for advertisers is to get individuals to think that their product is the better one for them. So makers of consumer goods segment their audiences, targeting their products toward particular individuals based on audience demographics, such as gender, socioeconomic class, sexual orientation, and so on.

Most of these ads are fairly obvious about who they are for and what the product does, but they often have other goals that many—perhaps most—Americans do not consciously understand. Consider the ads produced by Budweiser. Any Budweiser ad is aimed at selling their beer. But how are they trying to convince you that their beer is better than other beer, since they provide no comparisons with other brands and never speak about price? The ads are not really about the beer, but about young men's aspirations to be liked by other guys and to have a good time. What they actually present in the commercial is a lot of guys, and usually a bunch of attractive young women, at some sort of party having a good time. If we step back from the ad, we know that nearly any beer in the same setting would create the same party atmosphere, but here Budweiser products are framed as being your link to a great party. The ad constructs what its makers feel are what twenty-something men desire, and symbolically associates their product with this desired goal in order to sell their product. Furthermore, by tapping into preexisting goals and aspirations—the desire to be accepted by others and to have a good time—the beer company presents their product as able to fulfill these desires.

· ·

THINKING CRITICALLY ABOUT MATERIALITY

Consider a store near your campus. What are the characteristics of the consumers this store hopes to sell to? How does this store market specifically to this demographic group? How does the store position certain products to catch the attention of this target demographic? What aspirations is this store emphasizing to get its target audience's attention? Why might some other marketing imagery, or array of commodities in the store or in advertising, be less effective in selling these products?

· ·

Conclusion

Understanding how material objects are given meaning by their social context is central to appreciating how people make sense of their worlds. An important point to keep in mind is that, for the most part, meaning is not intentionally constructed or interpreted; rather, it flows naturally from social patterns that make certain interpretations seem obvious and logical, and others seem foolish, implausible, or simply wrong. In the nineteenth century, most white North Americans and Europeans interpreted native Africans wearing loincloths as less refined and less cultured than themselves because this was the meaning of such clothing in Western culture. The significance that African clothing had for people from these Western communities was that Africans were culturally inferior. At the same time, African villagers probably saw white men—who were trying to demonstrate their cultural refinement and superiority by wearing elaborate suits, ties, vests, and high collars even in tropical Africa—as resembling some of the tribal chiefs who were constantly covered in elaborate robes and ornaments. In each case, people were behaving in their ordinary cultural ways, and they could not interpret the meaning of the other group's costumes any differently. But these meanings were not inherent in the clothes themselves—they had been constructed from years of observing ordinary people in normal social settings.

The issues raised by the materiality of simple objects—whether a piece of clothing, an art object, a photograph, a bicycle, a historic building, or a commonplace object we use in daily life—highlight a broader dynamic that affects the social and cultural construction of meaning in every culture across the globe. The meanings of objects change over time, and the meaning of the past itself changes as social contexts change. Control over the past is a highly contentious issue, but control of the meaning of today's objects, even the significance of a smartphone, is equally contentious. This dynamic has two dimensions. One lies in who has control over access to the resources, both historical and cultural, from which we can document and uncover the story of how things came to be. The other is that interpretations of the material world, whether from the past or the present, differ according to social interests. So the interpretation of objects, artifacts, archaeological sites, and human remains always has a wide variety of legal, moral, and political implications. These implications are constructed by many different people, each with a different set of personal and social agendas. We call this the cultural construction of meaning, whether applied to objects, bodies, practices, or human experiences, and it is this that shows us what cultural anthropology is all about.

KEY TERMS

Alienation   p. 406

American Indian
    Movement (AIM)   p. 390

Commodity fetish   p. 406

Cultural resource
    management (CRM)
    p. 392

Culture of mass
    consumption   p. 406

Material culture   p. 387

Materiality   p. 386

Native American Graves
    and Repatriation Act
    (NAGPRA)   p. 390

Repatriation   p. 390

World Heritage Sites
    program   p. 391

Reviewing the Chapter

Chapter Section	What We Know	Unresolved Issues
Why Is the Ownership of Artifacts from Other Cultures a Contentious Issue?	Ownership of artifacts raises difficult moral, social, and political questions about who has the right to control and display objects. NAGPRA legislation has clarified who should control the bones and artifacts of Indians that archaeologists uncover in their excavations.	NAGPRA does not completely resolve conflicts over who should control archaeological objects, because some museum skeletal collections are themselves poorly documented, so nobody now knows which tribe the remains may have belonged to originally. Archaeologists, museums, and American Indians continue to have to negotiate over what happens to the objects.
How Can Anthropology Help Us Understand Objects?	All objects, old and new, from the most special to the most mundane, have multiple dimensions.	Stocking's original notion of seven dimensions to objects is a useful starting point for analyzing objects. But there is debate over whether these are always the most useful dimensions for analyzing all objects, as well as which dimensions he may have missed.

How Do the Meanings of Things Change Over Time?	All objects change over time, if not in their physical characteristics, then in the significance people give to them. Meanings change because of generational changes, changes in social and technological context, and as objects change hands.	Anthropologists have not yet systematically explored whether the importance of objects has always changed in the same ways, or if different kinds of societies (literate vs. pre-literate; stratified vs. egalitarian, etc.) change the meanings of things in precisely the same ways.
How Do Objects Come to Represent Our Goals and Aspirations?	In order to address this question, three interrelated issues need to be considered: Objects express people's personal and collective pasts; objects help people express and even formulate their goals and aspirations; and objects can be used in ways that manipulate what people's goals and aspirations should be.	Although many anthropologists assume that mass-producing commodities has transformed societies' approach to objects and thus their goals and aspirations, it seems likely that the process of commodification is more complex than recent studies have suggested.

Readings

Regna Darnell's *And Along Came Boas: Continuity and Revolution in Americanist Anthropology* (Amsterdam: John Benjamins, 2000) offers an overview of the early development of anthropology in museums. George W. Stocking, Jr.'s, edited volume *Objects and Others: Essays on Museums and Material Culture* (Madison, WI: University of Wisconsin Press, 1985) remains a classic on the topic of museum anthropology.

....

For a general survey of NAGPRA that emphasizes archaeological material

and its wider implications, see the volume edited by Devon A. Mihesuah, *Repatriation Reader: Who Owns American Indian Remains?* (Lincoln, NE: University of Nebraska Press, 2000). For a more general view of CRM, see Francis P. McManamon and Alf Hatton's edited book *Cultural Resource Management in Contemporary Society: Perspectives on Managing and Presenting the Past* (London: Routledge, 2000).

....

For treatment of objects in cultural anthropology, see Arjun

Appadurai's collection of essays, *The Social Life of Things: Commodities in Cultural Perspective* (New York: Cambridge University Press, 1986), and Daniel Miller's *Material Cultures: Why Some Things Matter* (Chicago, IL: University of Chicago Press, 1998). Luis Vivanco, a coauthor of this book, has applied the social-life-of-things approach to the bicycle in his 2013 book, *Reconsidering the Bicycle: An Anthropological Perspective on a New (Old) Thing* (New York: Routledge).

....

Epilogue
Cultural Anthropology and the Future of Human Diversity

Beginning around the year 2000, people from many countries began traveling to and buying property in a small village called Bugarach (population 189), which is near the Pyrenees mountains in the far south of France. Calling themselves "esoterics," these individuals had identified a nearby mountain peak as a good place to survive what they predicted was going to be a cataclysmic transformation of the world that would take place on December 21, 2012. They had come to this conclusion based on a reading of the Mesoamerican Long Count calendar, one of several calendars used by the ancient Maya that traces back to mythical creation times. They believed that the calendar marked that particular day in 2012 as a special moment of cosmic transformation, provoking the destruction of the world as we know it, but also ushering in a great spiritual awakening for humankind. The mountain near Bugarach, it was thought, was occupied by an alien spaceship that could transport survivors to safety.

Over the next decade, thousands of people poured into the area, many of them to climb the peak and some of them to settle there. As 2012 approached, many locals were growing exasperated with the chaos caused by all the activity, and the village's mayor threatened to call in the army. Not long before that fateful day arrived, police showed up and began limiting access to the mountain. Finally, the day came. . . . And there was no cosmic cataclysm. This fact didn't lead most of the esoterics to ditch their predictions of big changes to come, but only to reassess when these things will occur, and many of them remained in the Bugarach area.

For many of you reading this book, the beliefs and motivations of the esoterics seem strange, exotic, and difficult to understand. And yet there is something deeply human that drove the esoterics to put so much stock in the Maya calendar in their quest to create meaningful lives, something that many of you can probably relate to: the desire to know what the future holds. Wanting to predict the future is a very common human urge. Sometimes it is driven by simple curiosity about how things

---

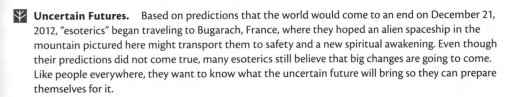

Uncertain Futures. Based on predictions that the world would come to an end on December 21, 2012, "esoterics" began traveling to Bugarach, France, where they hoped an alien spaceship in the mountain pictured here might transport them to safety and a new spiritual awakening. Even though their predictions did not come true, many esoterics still believe that big changes are going to come. Like people everywhere, they want to know what the uncertain future will bring so they can prepare themselves for it.

taken for granted today might differ in the future. But more often than not, there is a pragmatic concern of wanting to know what to do in the present to prepare for what is to come. Across the world, people have developed many esoteric bodies of knowledge to explore and satisfy this urge, and those who can gain access to that special wisdom often carry great social authority. The list includes diviners, oracles, seers, soothsayers, prophets, healers, and fortune tellers. It also includes scientists in disciplines like climatology, physics, and medicine, and a few in social scientific fields like economics, behavioral psychology, and political science. Although we tend to separate the first group from the second because of the latter's use of the scientific method, in the specific cultural contexts in which they operate, all of these actors can make useful and sometimes highly reliable predictions about what is to come. People regularly take action as a result of their pronouncements.

But as Yoda, that iconic source of wisdom in popular culture, once observed, "Difficult to see. Always in motion is the future." Although few anthropologists are likely to consider *The Empire Strikes Back*—the movie in the *Star Wars* franchise in which Yoda makes this observation—to be a source of authoritative and rigorous cultural insight, his observation does align strongly with what we know about human social complexity. It also relates to one of the reasons anthropologists are deeply hesitant to offer predictions about the future, although we as individuals may be as keen as anybody to know what is to come. The human future *is* always in motion. People are not robots, programmed to carry out codes instilled in them by their upbringing and enculturation. One of the things every anthropological fieldworker eventually experiences is that people will *tell* you one thing, only to *do* something different. Usually they are not doing this because they are lying or simply saying what they think the anthropologist wants to hear, or because they are irrational and cannot think straight. They do it because human action is fluid, situational, and context-dependent. Anthropology has developed many strategies—among them the holistic and cross-cultural perspectives (Chapter 2) and a diverse and effective toolkit of fieldwork methods (Chapter 3)—that enable us to understand and contextualize the fluidity of human thought and action.

Moreover, cultures—those collective processes through which we construct and naturalize certain meanings and actions as normal and even necessary—are themselves dynamic, emergent, and changing. As we have explored in this book, no group of people has ever been totally static and homogeneous, not least because different people have different life experiences due to particularities of age, gender, social identity, and other factors, as well as distinct social expectations about how to communicate with others (Chapter 4). Creativity, uncertainty, and social conflict are key aspects of everyday social relations everywhere as people work toward a collective understanding of their individual experiences of the world and with others in community. As humans, we express those understandings through fairly stable forms of symbolic communication, values, behavioral norms, and social traditions. But thanks to the widening scale of social relationships associated with globalization and transnational interconnection (Chapter 5), the processes of cultural dynamism seem to have intensified and manifest themselves in almost all aspects of people's lives in the contemporary world.

This dynamism is present in what we may think of as the material aspects of life: in foodways and environmental relationships (Chapters 6 and 7), and in economic activity and political relationships (Chapters 8 and 9). Even though some aspects of human life seem stable and fixed, no society is entirely static in matters of social identity and gender (Chapters 10 and 11), or even in the most traditional topic that anthropologists have studied, kinship relations (Chapter 12), which have been undergoing change in recent years, driven largely by changing attitudes toward gender, race, ethnicity, and family. Finally, we can see dynamic processes in our religious beliefs and activities (Chapter 13), our interpretations of health and illness (Chapter 14), and our interactions with material objects (Chapter 15).

Two reasons that anthropologists are hesitant to offer predictions about the future are (1) the complexity that characterizes each of these key dimensions of culture, and (2) how each dimension overlaps and intersects with others in a given social and historical context. But there is one thing anthropologists are reasonably certain about as we look to the future, and that is the persistence of human diversity. Diversity, understood by anthropologists as variety and multiplicity, is a basic pattern of nature and the basis upon which natural systems—oceans, forests, mountain ecosystems, and so on—and the species within them thrive.

We can appreciate these patterns among people simply by recognizing the sheer variety of ways of being human in the world. While processes of globalization do appear to contribute to some kinds of cultural convergences around the world—we see it especially in the alignment of certain kinds of economic activity and consumption patterns—the anthropological record of contemporary cultures today is also full of fascinating details about how, through the processes of culture, people everywhere turn alien cultural imports into something more familiar. Although there is still debate in the field about how and why these processes play out as they do, most anthropologists have come to accept that human diversity persists because of, not in spite of, interconnections across cultures.

Anthropology also offers a useful reminder that knowing what to do and making a difference in the present do not require being able to predict the future. Anthropologists are experts at identifying the causes of many different kinds of social problems, and whether it is helping craft a new constitution in Ghana or figuring out ways to address farmworker food insecurity in Vermont (Chapters 9 and 6, respectively), anthropologists have offered effective problem-solving strategies for policymakers and corporations as well as vulnerable communities and social movements struggling to make social change. The variety of practical issues anthropologists have taken on is as diverse as the human condition and reflects engagement with the big issues most of us are worried about in the contemporary world: improving human health and well-being; addressing difficulties of cross-cultural communication; adapting to the challenges of environmental sustainability; handling tensions around international relations, terrorism, and violence; understanding the effects of religious fundamentalism; and moving toward the construction of social justice; among others.

What unites all of these anthropologists are certain shared intellectual commitments. Some of those commitments are very concrete, including appreciation for the persistence of human diversity, the holistic perspective, critical relativism, and a rejection of ethnocentrism. Some are less tangible, but no less critical. Foremost among these is the ability to "think like an anthropologist." To a large extent this has to do with how we pose questions, rooted in recognizing that 99% of a good answer is posing a good question. Doing anthropology means being habitually curious about how and why people do the things they do in their everyday lives, and gaining the skills and confidence to ask useful questions—to ourselves as thought experiments, and to others in empirical research—that help focus attention not just on what is happening but on how to interpret it.

Another key element of anthropological thinking is recognizing that our disciplinary forebears have been asking rigorous questions about human diversity for over a century. Many of those classic questions and the answers to them have constituted anthropology's contributions to knowledge. Anthropologists have learned a great deal about human diversity, and it is often useful to bring those classic examples, debates, and analyses to bear on contemporary problems. At the same time, many debates remain unresolved, new questions emerge all the time, and anthropology's relationships and intersections with many other disciplines in the humanities and natural and social sciences make for a lot of cross-fertilization that brings new issues into consideration. All of these factors contribute to the creation of a dynamic and engaged discipline.

But it is not necessary to be a professional anthropologist to appreciate all these things. With some effort and an open mind, anybody can realize that there is great value and lifelong relevance in learning how to be curious, observe and listen to others, ask meaningful questions, record accurate information, recognize several truths at once, and establish and maintain ethical and collaborative relationships with diverse kinds of people. We feel that there is much to be gained—for a successful career, a meaningful life, or both—for those of you who make the effort to incorporate these activities and approaches into your daily encounters with those around you. While the future of human diversity as a whole does not necessarily depend on *your* doing these things, it will make your understanding of the diverse world in which you live much, much richer.

Glossary

Note: The number at the end of each definition denotes the chapter in which the term is defined.

Accent. A regional or social variation in the way a language is pronounced (e.g., an Alabama accent). (4)

Acephalous society. A society without a governing head, generally with no hierarchical leadership. (9)

Action anthropology. An approach to anthropological research that seeks to study and, at the same time, improve community welfare. (1)

Action theory. An approach in the anthropological study of politics that closely follows the daily activities and decision-making processes of individual political leaders emphasizing that politics is a dynamic and competitive field of social relations in which people are constantly managing their ability to exercise power over others. (9)

Adjudication. The legal process by which an individual or council with socially recognized authority intervenes in a dispute and unilaterally makes a decision. (9)

Age-grades. Groupings of age-mates, who are initiated into adulthood together. (9)

Agroecology. The integration of the principles of ecology into agricultural production. (6)

Alienation. The antagonistic detachment between workers and the commodities they produce, as well as between these workers and the buyers of the goods. (15)

American Indian Movement (AIM). The most prominent and one of the earliest American Indian activist groups, founded in 1968. (15)

Animal husbandry. The breeding, care, and use of domesticated herding animals such as cattle, camels, goats, horses, llamas, reindeer, and yaks. (6)

Animism. The belief that inanimate objects such as trees, rocks, cliffs, hills, and rivers are animated by spiritual forces or beings. (13)

Anthropogenic landscape. Landscapes that are the product of human shaping. (7)

Anthropological linguistics. The study of language from an anthropological point of view. (4)

Anthropology. The study of human beings, their biology, their prehistory and histories, and their changing languages, cultures, and social institutions. (1)

Anthropology of development. The field of study within anthropology concerned with understanding the cultural conditions for proper development, or, alternatively, the negative impacts of development projects. (5)

Applied anthropology. Anthropological research commissioned to serve an organization's needs. (1)

Appropriation. The process of taking possession of an object, idea, or relationship and making it one's own. (8)

Archaeology. The study of past cultures, by excavating sites where people lived, worked, farmed, or conducted some other activity. (1)

Balanced reciprocity. A form of reciprocity in which the giver expects a fair return at some later time. (8)

Band. A small, nomadic, and self-sufficient group of anywhere from 25 to 150 individuals with face-to-face social relationships, usually egalitarian. (9)

Biocultural. The complex intersections of biological, psychological, and cultural processes. (14)

Biological anthropology. The study of the biological aspects of the human species, past and present, along with those of our closest relatives, the nonhuman primates. (1)

Bride price (or bride wealth). Gifts or money given by the groom's clan or family to compensate the bride's clan or family for the loss of one of its women along with her productive and reproductive abilities. (12)

Call systems. Patterned sounds, utterances, and movements of the body that express meaning. (4)

Capitalism. An economic system based on private ownership of the means of production, in which prices are set and goods distributed through a market. (8)

Carrying capacity. The population an area can support. (7)

Caste. The system of social stratification found in Indian society that divides people into categories according to moral purity and pollution. (10)

Centralized political system. A political system, such as a chiefdom or a state, in which certain individuals and institutions hold power and control over resources. (9)

Chiefdom. A political system with a hereditary leader who holds central authority, typically supported by a class of high-ranking elites, informal laws, and a simple judicial system, often numbering in the tens of thousands with the beginnings of intensive agriculture and some specialization. (9)

Cisgender. Someone whose gender identity aligns with their biological sex at birth as male or female. (11)

Clan. A group of relatives who claim to be descended from a single ancestor. (12)

Class. The hierarchical distinctions between social groups in society usually based on wealth, occupation, and social standing. (10)

Clinical therapeutic process. A healing process that involves the use of medicines that have some active ingredient that is assumed to address either the cause or the symptom of a disorder. (14)

Cognate words. Words in two languages that show the same systematic sound shifts as other words in the two languages, usually interpreted by linguists as evidence for a common linguistic ancestry. (4)

Cognatic. Reckoning descent through either men or women from some ancestor. (12)

Colonialism. The historical practice of more powerful countries claiming possession of less powerful ones. (1)

Commodities. Mass-produced and impersonal goods with no meaning or history apart from themselves. (8)

Commodity fetish. The view of Karl Marx that commodities exercise a strange kind of power over people, controlling their attention and becoming objects of obsessive desire and worship. (15)

Commodity money. Money with another value beyond itself, such as gold or other precious metals, which can be used as jewelry or ornament. (8)

Comparative method. A research method that derives insights from a systematic comparison of aspects of two or more cultures or societies. (1)

Consumers. People who rely on goods and services not produced by their own labor. (8)

Consumption. The act of using and assigning meaning to a good, service, or relationship. (8)

Corporate groups. Groups of people who work together toward common ends, much as a corporation does. (12)

Creole language. A language of mixed origin that has developed from a complex blending of two parent languages and exists as a mother tongue for some part of the population. (4)

Cross-cultural perspective. Analyzing a human social phenomenon by comparing that phenomenon as manifested in different cultures. (2)

Cultural anthropology. The study of the social lives of living communities. (1)

Cultural appropriation. The unilateral decision of one social group to take control over the symbols, practices, or objects of another. (2)

Cultural construction. The meanings, concepts, and practices that people build out of their shared and collective experiences. (2)

Cultural determinism. The idea that all human actions are the product of culture, which denies the influence of other factors like physical environment and human biology on human action. (2)

Cultural economics. An anthropological approach to economics that focuses on how symbols and morals help shape a community's economy. (8)

Cultural imperialism. The promotion of one culture over others, through formal policy or less formal means, like the spread of technology and material culture. (5)

Cultural landscape. The culturally specific images, knowledge, and concepts of the physical landscape that help shape human relations with that landscape. (7)

Cultural relativism. The moral and intellectual principle that one should seek to understand cultures on their own terms and withhold judgment about seemingly strange or exotic beliefs and practices. (1)

Cultural resource management (CRM). Research and planning aimed at identifying, interpreting, and protecting sites and artifacts of historic or prehistoric significance. (15)

Culture. The taken-for-granted notions, rules, moralities, and behaviors within a social group. (1)

Culture and personality movement. A school of thought in early and mid–twentieth-century American anthropology that studied how patterns of childrearing, social institutions, and cultural ideologies shape individual experience, personality characteristics, and thought patterns. (12)

Culture-bound syndrome. A mental illness unique to a culture. (14)

Culture of mass consumption. The cultural perspectives and social processes that shape and are shaped by how goods and services are bought, sold, and used in contemporary capitalism. (15)

Culture of migration. The cultural attitudes, perceptions, and symbolic values that shape decision-making processes around, and experiences of, migration. (5)

Customs. Long-established norms that have a codified and law-like aspect. (2)

Delayed reciprocity. A form of reciprocity that features a long lag time between receiving a gift and paying it back. (8)

Descriptive linguistics. The systematic analysis and description of a language's sound system and grammar. (4)

Development anthropology. The application of anthropological knowledge and research methods to the practical aspects of shaping and implementing development projects. (5)

Dialect. A regional or social variety of a language in which the vocabulary, grammar, and pronunciation differ from those of the standard version of the language (e.g., African American vernacular English). (4)

Diffusionists. Early twentieth-century Boasian anthropologists who held that cultural characteristics result from either internal historical dynamism or a spread (diffusion) of cultural attributes from other societies. (5)

Discrimination. The negative or unfair treatment of an individual because of his or her membership in a particular social group or category. (10)

Disease. The purely physiological condition of being sick, usually determined by a physician. (14)

Diversity. The sheer variety of ways of being human around the world. (1)

Division of labor. The cooperative organization of work into specialized tasks and roles. (8)

Dowry. A large sum of money or in-kind gifts given to a daughter to ensure her well-being in her husband's family. (12)

Ecological anthropology. The specific vein with environmental anthropology that studies directly the relationship between humans and natural ecosystems. (7)

Ecological footprint. A quantitative tool that measures what people consume and the waste they produce. It also calculates the area of biologically productive land and water needed to support those people. (7)

Economic anthropology. The subfield of cultural anthropology concerned with how people make, share, and buy things and services. (8)

Economic system. The structured patterns and relationships through which people exchange goods and services. (8)

Ecosystem. Natural systems based on the interaction of non-living factors and living organisms. (7)

Emic perspective. A cultural insider's perspective on his or her culture. (3)

Empirical. Verifiable through observation rather than through logic or theory alone. (1)

Enculturation. The process of learning the cultural rules and logic of a society. (2)

Environmental anthropology. The field that studies how different societies understand, interact with, and make changes to the natural world. (7)

Environmental determinism. A theory that attempts to explain cultural characteristics of a group of people as a consequence of specific ecological conditions or limitations. (7)

Environmental justice. A social movement addressing the linkages between racial discrimination and injustice, social equity, and environmental quality. (7)

Ethics. Moral questions about right and wrong and standards of appropriate behavior. (1)

Ethnicity. A concept that organizes people into groups based on their membership in a group with a particular history, social status, or ancestry. (10)

Ethnobiology. The subfield of ethnoscience that studies how people in non-Western societies name and codify living things. (7)

Ethnocentrism. The assumption that one's own way of doing things is correct, and that other people's practices or views are wrong or ignorant. (1)

Ethnographic method. A research method that involves prolonged and intensive observation of and participation in the life of a community. (1)

Ethnography of speaking. The study of how people actually use spoken language in a particular cultural setting. (4)

Ethnohistory. The study of cultural change in societies and periods for which the community had no written histories or historical documents, usually relying heavily on oral history for data. "Ethnohistory" may also refer to a view of history from the cultural insider's point of view, which often differs from an outsider's view. (3)

Ethnopoetics. A method of recording narrative speech acts—including oral poetry, stories, and ritual use of language—as verses and stanzas in order to capture the format and other performative elements that might be lost in written prose. (4)

Ethnoscience. The study of how people classify things in the world, usually by considering some range or set of meanings. (4, 7)

Etic perspective. An outside observer's perspective on a culture. (3)

Evolution. The adaptive changes organisms make across generations. (1)

Exchange. The transfer of objects and services between social actors. (8)

Exiles. People who are expelled by the authorities of their home countries. (5)

Exogamous. A social pattern in which members of a clan must marry someone from another clan, which has the effect of building political, economic, and social ties with other clans. (12)

Explanatory model of illness. An explanation of what is happening to a patient's body, by the patient, by the patient's family, or by a healthcare practitioner, each of whom may have a different model of what is happening. (14)

Extended families. Larger groups of relatives beyond the nuclear family, often living in the same household. (12)

Fiat money. Money created and guaranteed by a government. (8)

Fieldnotes. Information the anthropologist collects or transcribes during fieldwork. (3)

Fieldwork. Long-term immersion in a community, normally involving firsthand research in a specific study community or research setting where the researcher can observe people's behavior and have conversations or interviews with members of the community. (3)

Food security. Access to sufficient nutritious food to sustain an active and healthy life. (6)

Foodways. Structured beliefs and behaviors surrounding the production, distribution, and consumption of food. (6)

Foraging. Obtaining food by searching for it, as opposed to growing or raising it. (6)

Formal economics. The branch of economics that studies the underlying logic of economic thought and action. (8)

Functionalism. A perspective that assumes that cultural practices and beliefs serve social purposes in any society. (2)

Fundamentalism. Conservative religious movements that advocate a return to fundamental or traditional principles. (13)

Fundamentalist. A person belonging to a religious movement that advocates a return to fundamental or traditional principles. (13)

Gender. The complex and fluid intersections of biological sex, internal senses of self, outward expressions of identity, and cultural expectations about how to perform that identity in appropriate ways. (11)

Gender variance. Expressions of sex and gender that diverge from the male and female norms that dominate in most societies. (11)

Gender/sex system. The ideas and social patterns a society uses to organize males, females, and those who exist between these categories. (11)

Genealogical amnesia. The structural process of forgetting whole groups of relatives, usually because they are not currently significant in one's social life. (12)

Genealogical method. A systematic methodology for recording kinship relations and how kin terms are used in different societies. (3)

General purpose money. Money that is used to buy nearly any good or service. (8)

Generalized reciprocity. A form of reciprocity in which gifts are given freely without the expectation of return. (8)

Globalization. The widening scale of cross-cultural interactions caused by the rapid movement of money, people, goods, images, and ideas within nations and across national boundaries. (5)

Government. A separate legal and constitutional domain that is the source of law, order, and legitimate force. (9)

Green Revolution. The transformation of agriculture in the Third World, beginning in the 1940s, through agricultural research, technology transfer, and infrastructure development. (6)

Headnotes. The mental notes an anthropologist makes while in the field, which may or may not end up in formal fieldnotes or journals. (3)

Holism. Efforts to synthesize distinct approaches and findings into a single comprehensive interpretation. (1)

Holistic perspective. A perspective that aims to identify and understand the whole—that is, the systematic connections between individual cultural beliefs, practices, and social institutions—rather than the individual parts. (2)

Horizontal migration. Movement of a herding community across a large area in search of whatever grazing lands may be available. (6)

Horticulture. The cultivation of gardens or small fields to meet the basic needs of a household. (6)

Human Relations Area Files (HRAF). A comparative anthropological database that allows easy reference to coded information about several hundred cultural traits for more than 350 societies. The HRAF facilitate statistical analysis of the relationship between the presence of one trait and the occurrence of other traits. (3)

Hybridization. Persistent cultural mixing that has no predetermined direction or end-point. (5)

Illness. The psychological and social experience a patient has of a disease. (14)

Immigrants. People who enter a foreign country with no expectation of ever returning to their home country. (5)

Incest taboo. The prohibition on sexual relations between close family members. (12)

Industrial agriculture. The application of industrial principles to farming. (6)

Industrialization. The economic process of shifting from an agricultural economy to a factory-based economy. (1)

Informant. Any person an anthropologist gets data from in the study community, especially a person who is interviewed or who provides information about what the anthropologist has observed or heard. (3)

Instrumentalism. A social theory that ethnic groups are not naturally occurring or stable, but highly dynamic groups created to serve the interests of one powerful group or another. (10)

Intensification. Processes that increase agricultural yields. (6)

Interpretive approach. A kind of analysis that interprets the underlying symbolic and cultural interconnections within a society. (13)

Interpretive theory of culture. A theory that culture is embodied and transmitted through symbols. (2)

Intersectionality. The circumstantial interplay of race, class, gender, sexuality, and other identity markers in the expression of prejudicial beliefs and discriminatory actions. (10)

Intersex. Individuals who exhibit sexual organs and functions somewhere between male and female elements, often including elements of both. (11)

Intersubjectivity. The realization that knowledge about other people emerges out of relationships and perceptions individuals have with each other. (3)

Interview. Any systematic conversation with an informant to collect field research data, ranging from a highly structured set of questions to the most open-ended ones. (3)

Kinship. The social system that organizes people in families based on descent and marriage. (12)

Kinship chart. A visual representation of family relationships. (12)

Lactase persistence. Continuation of lactase production beyond early childhood that allows a person to digest milk and dairy products. (6)

Language. A system of communication consisting of sounds, words, and grammar. (4)

Language ideology. Widespread assumptions that people make about the relative sophistication and status of particular dialects and languages. (4)

Laws. Sets of rules established by some formal authority. (9)

Life history. Any survey of an informant's life, including such topics as residence, occupation, marriage, family, and difficulties, usually collected to reveal patterns that cannot be observed today. (3)

Limited purpose money. Objects that can be exchanged only for certain things. (8)

Lineage. A group composed of relatives who are directly descended from known ancestors. (12)

Linguistic anthropology. The study of how people communicate with one another through language and how language use shapes group membership and identity. (1)

Linguistic relativity. The idea that people speaking different languages perceive or interpret the world differently because of differences in their languages. (4)

Localization. The creation and assertion of highly particular, place-based identities and communities. (5)

Magic. An explanatory system of causation that does not follow naturalistic explanations, often working at a distance without direct physical contact. (13)

Mana. Sacred power believed to inhere in certain high-ranking people, sacred spaces, and objects. (13)

Market. A social institution in which people come together to exchange goods and services. (8)

Masculinity. The ideas and practices of manhood. (11)

Material culture. The objects made and used in any society. Traditionally, the term referred to technologically simple objects made in preindustrial societies, but *material culture* may refer to all of the objects or commodities of modern life as well. (15)

Materiality. Having the quality of being physical or material. (15)

Matrilineal. Reckoning descent through women, who are descended from an ancestral woman. (12)

Means of production. The machines and infrastructure required to produce goods. (8)

Mediation. The use of a third party who intervenes in a dispute to help the parties reach an agreement and restore harmony. (9)

Medical pluralism. The coexistence and interpenetration of distinct medical traditions with different cultural roots in the same cultural community. (14)

Medicalization. The process of viewing or treating as a medical concern conditions that were not previously understood as medical problems. (14)

Migrants. People who leave their homes to live or work for a time in other regions or countries. (5)

Mind. Emergent qualities of consciousness and intellect that manifest themselves through thought, emotion, perception, will, and imagination. (14)

Modes of subsistence. The social relationships and practices necessary for procuring, producing, and distributing food. (6)

Money. An object or substance that serves as a medium of exchange, a store of value, or a unit of account. (8)

Monotheism. Belief in a single god. (13)

Morphology. The structure of words and word formation in a language. (4)

Multi-sited ethnography. An ethnographic research strategy of following connections, associations, and putative relationships from place to place. (5)

Natal family. The family into which a person is born and in which she or he is (usually) raised. (12)

Nation-states. Independent states recognized by other states, composed of people who share a single national identity. (9)

Native American Graves Protection and Repatriation Act (NAGPRA). The 1990 law that established the ownership of human remains, grave goods, and important cultural objects as belonging to the Native Americans whose ancestors once owned them. (15)

Naturalization. The social processes through which something becomes part of the natural order of things. (10)

Negative reciprocity. A form of reciprocity in which the giver attempts to get something for nothing, to haggle his or her way into a favorable personal outcome. (8)

Negotiation. A form of dispute management in which the parties themselves reach a decision jointly. (9)

Neoclassical economics. An approach to economics that studies how people make decisions to allocate resources like time, labor, and money in order to maximize their personal benefit. (8)

Non-centralized political system. A political system, such as a band or a tribe, in which power and control over resources are dispersed between members of the society. (9)

Norms. Typical patterns of actual behavior as well as the rules about how things should be done. (2)

Nuclear family. The family formed by a married couple and their children. (12)

Nutrition transition. The combination of changes in diet toward energy-dense foods (high in calories, fat, and sugar) and declines in physical activity. (6)

Obesity. Having excess body fat to the point of impairing bodily health and function. (6)

Open-ended interview. Any conversation with an informant in which the researcher allows the informant to take the conversation to related topics that the informant rather than the researcher feels are important. (3)

Othering. Defining colonized peoples as different from, and subordinate to, Europeans in terms of their social, moral, and physical norms. (1)

Overweight. Having an abnormally high accumulation of body fat. (6)

Participant observation. The standard research method used by cultural anthropologists that requires the researcher to live in the community he or she is studying to observe and participate in day-to-day activities. (3)

Participatory action research. A research method in which the research questions, data collection, and data analysis are defined through collaboration between the researcher and the subjects of research. A major goal is for the research subjects to develop the capacity to investigate and take action on their primary political, economic, or social problems. (3)

Pastoralism. The practice of animal husbandry. (6)

Patrilineal. Reckoning descent through males from the same ancestors. (12)

Philology. Comparative study of ancient texts and documents. (4)

Phonology. The systematic pattern of sounds in a language, also known as the language's sound system. (4)

Pidgin language. A mixed language with a simplified grammar, typically borrowing its vocabulary from one language but its grammar from another. (4)

Placebo effect. A healing process that works by persuading a patient that he or she has been given a powerful medicine, even though the "medicine" has no active medicinal ingredient. (14)

Political ecology. The field of study that focuses on the linkages between political-economic power, social inequality, and ecological destruction. (7)

Political power. The processes by which people create, compete, and use power to attain goals that are presumed to be for the good of a community. (9)

Politics. The relationships and processes of cooperation, conflict, social control, and power that are fundamental aspects of human life. (9)

Polyandry. When a woman has two or more husbands at one time. (12)

Polygamy. Any form of plural marriage. (12)

Polygyny. When a man is simultaneously married to more than one woman. (12)

Polytheism. Belief in many gods. (13)

Postcolonialism. The field that studies the cultural legacies of colonialism and imperialism. (5)

Practicing anthropology. Anthropological work involving research as well as involvement in the design, implementation, and management of some organization, process, or product. (1)

Prejudice. Pre-formed, usually unfavorable opinions that people hold about people from groups who are different from their own. (10)

Prestige economies. Economies in which people seek high social rank, prestige, and power instead of money and material wealth. (8)

Primary materials. Original sources such as fieldnotes that are prepared by someone who is directly involved in the research project and has direct personal knowledge of the research subjects. (3)

Primordialism. A social theory that ethnicity is largely a natural phenomenon, because of biological (i.e., "primordial"), linguistic, and geographical ties among members. (10)

Proto-language. A hypothetical common ancestral language of two or more living languages. (4)

Push-pull factors. The social, economic, and political factors that "push" people to migrate from their homes and that "pull" them to host countries. (5)

Qualitative method. A research strategy that produces an in-depth and detailed description of social behaviors and beliefs. (1)

Quantitative method. A methodology that classifies features of a phenomenon, counting or measuring them, and constructing mathematical and statistical models to explain what is observed. (1)

Quran. The main body of scripture in Islam, consisting of verses of classical Arabic poetry understood to be revealed to the Prophet Muhammad by Allah, often in dreams or in the midst of other activities. These verses were memorized by Muhammad's followers and written down after his death. (13)

Race. A concept that organizes people into unequal groups based on specific physical traits that are thought to reflect fundamental and innate differences. (10)

Racialization. The social, economic, and political processes of transforming populations into races and creating racial meanings. (10)

Racism. The repressive practices, structures, beliefs, and representations that uphold racial categories and social inequality. (10)

Rapid appraisal. Short-term, focused ethnographic research, typically lasting no more than a few weeks, about narrow research questions or problems. (3)

Reciprocity. The give-and-take that builds and confirms relationships. (8)

Redistribution. The collection of goods in a community and then the further dispersal of those goods among members. (8)

Refugees. People who migrate because of political oppression or war, usually with legal permission to stay in a different country. (5)

Religion. A symbolic system that is socially enacted through rituals and other aspects of social life that relate to ultimate issues of humankind's existence. (13)

Repatriation. The return of human remains or cultural artifacts to the communities of descendants of the people to whom they originally belonged. (15)

Rite of passage. Any life cycle rite that marks a person's or group's transition from one social state to another. (13)

Rituals. Stylized performances involving symbols that are associated with social, political, and religious activities. (13)

Salvage paradigm. The paradigm that holds that it is important to observe indigenous ways of life, interview elders, and assemble collections of objects made and used by indigenous peoples. (1)

Scientific method. The standard methodology of science that begins from observable facts, generates hypotheses from these facts, and then tests these hypotheses. (1)

Secondary materials. Sources such as censuses, regional surveys, or historical reports that are compiled from data collected by someone other than the field researcher. (3)

Secular worldview. A worldview that does not accept the supernatural as influencing current people's lives. (13)

Sex. Understood in Western cultures as the reproductive forms and functions of the body. (11)

Sexuality. Sexual preferences, desires, and practices. (11)

Sexually dimorphic. A characteristic of a species, in which males and females have different sexual forms. (11)

Shaman. A religious leader who communicates the needs of the living with the spirit world, usually through some form of ritual trance or other altered state of consciousness. (13)

Sick role. The culturally defined agreement between patients and family members to acknowledge that a patient is legitimately sick, which involves certain responsibilities and behaviors that caregivers expect of the sick. (14)

Social institutions. Organized sets of social relationships that link individuals to each other in a structured way in a particular society. (2)

Social sanction. A reaction or measure intended to enforce norms and punish their violation. (2)

Social stratification. The classification of people into unequal groupings. (10)

Social support therapeutic process. A healing process that involves a patient's social networks, especially close family members and friends, who typically surround the patient during an illness. (14)

Sociolinguistics. The study of how sociocultural context and norms shape language use, and the effects of language use on society. (4)

Speaking in tongues. The phenomenon of speaking in an apparently unknown language, often in an energetic and fast-paced way. (13)

Spheres of exchange. Bounded orders of value in which certain goods can be exchanged only for others. (8)

Spirit familiar. A spirit that has developed a close bond with a shaman. (13)

State. The most complex form of political organization, associated with societies that have intensive agriculture, high levels of social stratification, and centralized authority. (9)

Structural power. Power that not only operates within settings, but also organizes and orchestrates the settings in which social and individual actions take place. (9)

Structural-functionalism. An anthropological theory that the different structures or institutions of a society (religion, politics, kinship, etc.) function to maintain social order and equilibrium. (9)

Structuralism. An anthropological theory that people make sense of their worlds through binary oppositions like hot–cold, culture–nature, male–female, and raw–cooked. These binary oppositions are expressed in social institutions and cultural practices. (6)

Substantive economics. A branch of economics, inspired by the work of Karl Polanyi, that studies the daily transactions people engage in to get what they need or desire. (8)

Surplus value. The difference between what people produce and what they need to survive. (8)

Sustainable agriculture. Farming based on integrating goals of environmental health, economic productivity, and economic equity. (6)

Swidden agriculture. A farming method in tropical regions in which the farmer slashes and burns a small area of forest to release plant nutrients into the soil. As soil fertility declines, the farmer allows the plot to revert to forest and regenerate nutrients to the soil. (6)

Symbol. Something—an object, idea, image, figure, or character—that represents something else. (2)

Symbolic therapeutic process. A healing process that restructures the meanings of the symbols surrounding the illness, particularly during a ritual. (14)

Sympathetic magic. Any magical rite that relies on the supernatural to produce its outcome without working through a specific supernatural being such as a spirit, demon, or deity. (13)

Syntax. The pattern of word order used to form sentences and longer utterances in a language. (4)

Taste. A concept that refers to the sense that gives humans the ability to detect flavors, as well as the social distinction associated with certain foodstuffs. (6)

Theory. A tested and repeatedly supported hypothesis. (1)

Third genders. A category found in many societies that acknowledge three or more gender categories. (11)

Totemism. A system of thought that associates particular social groups with specific animal or plant species called "totems" as an emblem. (13)

Tradition. Practices and customs that have become most ritualized and enduring. (2)

Traditional ecological knowledge. Indigenous ecological knowledge and its relationship with resource management strategies. (7)

Trance. A semi-conscious state typically brought on by hypnosis, ritual drumming and singing, or hallucinogenic drugs like mescaline or peyote. (13)

Transactional orders. Realms of transactions a community uses, each with its own set of symbolic meanings and moral assumptions. (8)

Transgender. Someone to whom society assigns one gender who does not perform as that gender but has taken either permanent or temporary steps to identify as another gender. (11)

Transnational. Relationships that extend beyond nation-state boundaries but do not necessarily cover the whole world. (5)

Transnational community. A spatially extended social network that spans multiple countries. (5)

Tribe. A type of pastoralist or horticulturist society with populations usually numbering in the hundreds or thousands in which leadership is more stable than that of a band, but usually egalitarian, with social relationships based on reciprocal exchange. (9)

Unilineal. Based on descent through a single descent line, either males or females. (12)

Value. The relative worth of an object or service that makes it desirable. (8)

Values. Symbolic expressions of intrinsically desirable principles or qualities. (2)

Violence. The use of force to harm someone or something. (9)

World culture. Norms and values that extend across national boundaries. (5)

World Heritage Sites program. A UNESCO-run program that provides financial support to maintain sites of importance to humanity. (15)

World religions. Religions that claim to be universally significant to all people. (13)

World systems theory. The theory that capitalism has expanded on the basis of unequal exchange throughout the world, creating a global market and global division of labor, dividing the world between a dominant "core" and a dependent "periphery." (5)

Worldview. A general approach to or set of shared, unquestioned assumptions about the world and how it works. (13)

References

Alatas, Syed Hussein. 1977. *The Myth of the Lazy Native: A Study of the Image of the Malays, Filipinos, and Javanese from the Sixteenth to the Twentieth Century and Its Function in the Ideology of Colonial Capitalism.* London: Routledge.

Allen, Theodore W. 1997. *The Invention of the White Race.* Vol. 2. London: Verso.

Allport, Gordon. 1958. *The Nature of Prejudice.* Abridged edition. New York: Doubleday Anchor Books.

Almond, Gabriel, A., R. Scott Appleby, and Emmanuel Sivan. 2003. *Strong Religion: The Rise of Fundamentalisms Around the World.* Chicago, IL: University of Chicago Press.

Alonso Caamal, Bartolomé. 1997. "Indios, antropologia y descolonization." In Patricio Guerrero, comp., *Antropologia Aplicada* 1997:315–322. Quito, Ecuador: Universidad Politecnica Salesiana.

American Psychological Association. 1994. *Diagnostic and Statistical Manual of Mental Disorders: DSM-IV.* Washington, DC: American Psychological Association.

Ames, Michael. 1999. How to Decorate a House: The Re-negotiation of Cultural Representations at the University of British Columbia Museum of Anthropology. *Museum Anthropology,* 22(3):41–51.

Amnesty International. 2016. *The State of the World's Human Rights. Amnesty International Report 2015/2016.* Accessed on February 17, 2017: https://www.amnesty.org/en/latest/research/2016/02/annual-report-201516/

Amuyunzu-Nyamongo, Mary. 2006. "Challenges and Prospects for Applied Anthropology in Kenya." In Mwenda Ntarangwi, David Mills, and Mustafa Babiker, eds., *African Anthropologies: History, Critique and Practice,* pp. 237–249. Dakar: CODESRIA.

Anderson, Eugene N. 2005. *Everyone Eats: Understanding Food and Culture.* New York: New York University Press.

Anyon, Roger, T. J. Ferguson, and John R. Welch. 2000. "Heritage Management by American Indian Tribes in the Southwestern United States." In F. O. McManamon and A. Hatton, eds., *Cultural Resource Management in Contemporary Society: Perspectives on Managing and Presenting the Past,* pp. 142–159. London: Routledge.

Appadurai, Arjun, ed. 1986. *The Social Life of Things: Commodities in Cultural Perspective.* Cambridge, UK: Cambridge University Press.

Appadurai, Arjun. 1996. *Modernity at Large: Cultural Dimensions of Globalization.* Minneapolis, MN: University of Minnesota Press.

Arden, Harvey. 1989. An Indian Cemetery Desecrated: Who Owns Our Past? *National Geographic* 175:376–392.

Armstrong, Karen. 1994. *A History of God: The 4,000-Year Quest of Judaism, Christianity and Islam.* New York: Ballantine Books.

Asad, Talal. 1993. *Genealogies of Religion: Discipline and Reasons of Power in Christianity and Islam.* Baltimore, MD: John Hopkins University Press.

Asch, Timothy, and Napoleon Chagnon. 1968. *Children Play in the Rain.* Film. Somerville, MA: Documentary Educational Resources.

Asch, Timothy, and Napoleon Chagnon. 1989. *The Ax Fight.* Videocassette. Watertown, MA: Documentary Educational Resources.

Asch, Timothy, and Napoleon Chagnon. 1990a. *A Father Washes His Children.* Videocassette. Watertown, MA: Documentary Educational Resources.

Asch, Timothy, and Napoleon Chagnon. 1990b. *A Man and His Wife Make a Hammock.* Videocassette. Watertown, MA: Documentary Educational Resources.

Asch, Timothy, and Napoleon Chagnon. 1997. *The Feast.* Videocassette. Watertown, MA: Documentary Educational Resources. [Released as 16 mm film, 1970.]

Atran, Scott. 2001. "The Vanishing Landscape of the Petén Maya Lowlands: People, Plants, Animals, Places, Words, and Spirits." In Lisa Maffi, ed., *On Biocultural Diversity: Linking Language, Knowledge, and the Environment,* pp. 157–176. Washington, DC: Smithsonian Institution Press.

Avruch, Kevin. 1998. *Culture and Conflict Resolution.* Washington, DC: United States Institute of Peace.

Azoy, Whitney. 2002. "Waaseta (Personal Connections)." *Bangor Daily News,* Feb. 9–10, 2002, A9–A10.

Bailey, F. G. 1969. *Stratagems and Spoils: A Social Anthropology of Politics.* London: Basil Blackwell.

Banks, Dennis. 2004. *Ojibwa Warrior: Dennis Banks and the Rise of the American Indian Movement,* by Dennis Banks with Richard Erdoes. Norman, OK: University of Oklahoma Press.

Barnes, Jessica, and Michael Dove. 2015. *Climate Cultures: Anthropological Perspectives on Climate Change.* New Haven, CT: Yale University Press.

Barth, Frederick. 1969. *Ethnic Groups and Boundaries: The Social Organization of Culture Difference.* New York: Little, Brown & Co.

Bartlett, Robert. 1982. *Gerald of Wales, 1146–1223.* Oxford, UK: Oxford University Press.

Basch, Linda, Nina Glick Schiller, and Cristina Szanton Blanc. 1993. *Nations Unbound: Transnational Projects, Postcolonial Predicaments, and Deterritorialized Nation-States.* Basel: Gordon and Breach.

Basu, Amitra, ed. 2010. *Women's Movements in the Global Era: The Power of Local Feminisms.* Boulder, CO: Westview Press.

Bates, Daniel G. 1998. *Human Adaptive Strategies: Ecology, Culture, and Politics.* Boston, MA: Allyn and Bacon.

Bauman, Richard, and Joel Sherzer. 1974. *Explorations in the Ethnography of Speaking.* London: Cambridge University Press.

Bearak, Barry. 2001. Over World Protests, Taliban Are Destroying Ancient Buddhas. *New York Times,* March 4, 2001, p. A10.

Benedict, Ruth. 1934. *Patterns of Culture.* Boston, MA: Houghton Mifflin.

Benedict, Ruth. 1946. *The Chrysanthemum and the Sword: Patterns of Japanese Culture.* Boston, MA: Houghton Mifflin.

Bennett, John W. 1996. Applied and Action Anthropology: Ideological and Conceptual Aspects. *Current Anthropology* 37(1):S23–S53.

Berger, Peter L., ed. 1999. *The Desecularization of the World: Resurgent Religion and World Politics.* Washington, DC: Ethics and Public Policy Center.

Bergmann, J. F., O. Chassany, J. Gandiol, P. Deblois, J. A. Kanis, J. M. Segresta, C. Caulin, and R. Dahan. 1994. A Randomized Clinical Trial of the Effect of Informed Consent on the Analgesic Activity of Placebo and Naproxen in Cancer Pain. *Clinical Trials Meta-Analysis* 29:41–47.

Berlin, Brent, and Paul Kay. 1969. *Basic Color Terms: Their Universality and Evolution.* Berkeley, CA: University of California Press.

Berlin, Brent. 1973. Folk Systematics in Relation to Biological Classification and Nomenclature. *Annual Review of Systematics and Ecology* 4:259–271.

Bernard, Russell H. 2011. *Research Methods in Anthropology: Qualitative and Quantitative Approaches.* Lanham, MD: AltaMira Press.

Béteille, André. 1992. Caste and Family in Representations of Indian Society. *Anthropology Today* 8(1):13–18.

Bird-David, Nurit. 1992. Beyond the "Original Affluent Society": A Culturalist Reformulation. *Current Anthropology* 33(1):25–47.

Bird-David, Nurit. 1993. "Tribal Metaphorization of Human-Nature Relatedness: A Comparative Analysis." In K. Milton, ed., *Environmentalism: The View from Anthropology*, pp. 112–125. London: Routledge.

Blim, Michael. 2000. Capitalisms in Late Modernity. *Annual Reviews of Anthropology* 29:25–38.

Boas, Franz. 1889. Die Ziele der Ethnologie. *Gemeinverständliche Vorträge gehalten im Deutsche Gesellig-Wissenschaftlichen Verein* 16:3–30. New York: Herman Bartsch.

Boas, Franz, ed. 1911. *Handbook of North American Indian Languages*. Bulletin of the Bureau of American Ethnology, No. 40. Washington, DC: Government Printing Office for the Smithsonian Institution.

Boas, Franz. 1940. *Race, Language, and Culture*. New York: Macmillan.

Bodley, John. 1999. *Victims of Progress*. 4th edition. New York: McGraw-Hill.

Boggs, Stephen T., and Malcolm Naea Chun. 1990. "Ho'oponopono: A Hawaiian Method of Solving Interpersonal Problems." In Karen Ann Watson-Gegeo and Geoffrey White, eds., *Disentangling: Conflict Discourse in Pacific Societies*, pp. 123–153. Stanford, CA: Stanford University Press.

Bohannon, Paul, and Laura Bohannon. 1968. *Tiv Economy*. Evanston, IL: Northwestern University Press.

Boseley, Sarah. 2012. World Bank's Jim Yong Kim: "I Want to Eradicate Poverty." *The Guardian*. July 25, 2012. Accessed on February 17, 2017: https://www.theguardian.com/global-development/2012/jul/25/world-bank-jim-yong-kim-eradicate-poverty

Boserup, Ester. 1965. *The Conditions of Agricultural Growth: The Economics of Agrarian Change Under Population Pressure*. London: G. Allen & Unwin.

Bourdieu, Pierre. 1977. *Outline of a Theory of Practice*. Cambridge, UK: Cambridge University Press.

Bourdieu, Pierre. 1984. *Distinction: A Social Critique of the Judgement of Taste*. Cambridge, MA: Harvard University Press.

Bourgois, Philippe. 1995. *In Search of Respect: Selling Crack in El Barrio*. New York: Cambridge University Press.

Bradbury, R. E. 1957. *The Benin Kingdom and the Edo-speaking Peoples of South-Western Nigeria*. London: International African Institute.

Brettell, Caroline. 2003. *Anthropology and Migration: Essays on Transnationalism, Ethnicity, and Identity*. Lanham, MD: Rowman and Littlefield.

Brettell, Caroline B., and Carolyn F. Sargent, eds. 2001. *Gender in Cross-Cultural Perspective*. 3rd edition. Upper Saddle River, NJ: Prentice Hall.

Bridges, K., and W. McClatchey. 2009. Living on the Margin: Ethnoecological Insights from Marshall Islanders at Rongelap Atol. *Global Environmental Change* 19(2):140–146.

Bringa, Tone. 2005. "Haunted by Imaginations of the Past: Robert Kaplan's Balkan Ghosts." In Katherine Besteman and Hugh Gusterson, eds., *Why America's Top Pundits Are Wrong: Anthropologists Talk Back*, pp. 60–82. Berkeley, CA: University of California Press.

Brockington, Dan. 2002. *Fortress Conservation: The Preservation of the Mkomazi Game Reserve*. Bloomington, IN: Indiana University Press.

Brody, Howard, and Linda M. Hunt. 2006. BiDil: Assessing a Race-Based Pharmaceutical. *Annals of Family Medicine* 4(6):556–560.

Brown, Michael. 2003. *Who Owns Native Culture?* Cambridge, MA: Harvard University Press.

Brownell, K. D. 2002. "The Environment and Obesity." In C. G. Fairburn and K. D. Brownell, eds., *Eating Disorders and Obesity:*

A Comprehensive Handbook. 2nd edition, pp. 433–438. New York: Guilford Press.

Buikstra, Jane. 1983. Reburial: How We All Lose—An Archaeologist's Opinion. *Council for Museum Anthropology Newsletter* 7(2):2–5.

Bullard, Robert. 1994. *Dumping in Dixie: Race, Class, and Environmental Quality*. 2nd edition. Boulder, CO: Westview Press.

Bulmer, Ralph. 1967. Why Is the Cassowary Not a Bird? *Man* 2:5–25.

Burling, Robbins. 1971. *Man's Many Voices: Language in Its Cultural Context*. New York: Holt, Rinehart and Winston.

Burton, Orisanmi. 2015. "Black Lives Matter: A Critique of Anthropology." *Fieldsites: Hot Spots*, a blog of the Society for Cultural Anthropology. Accessed on February 17, 2017: https://culanth.org/fieldsights/691-black-lives-matter-a-critique-of-anthropology

Butler, Shelly Ruth. 2008. *Contested Representations: Revisiting* Into the Heart of Africa. Peterborough, ON: Broadview Press.

Cannizzo, Jeanne. 1989. *Into the Heart of Africa*. Toronto: Royal Ontario Museum.

Caplan, Pat, ed. 1995. *Understanding Disputes: The Politics of Argument*. Oxford, UK: Berg Publishers.

Carey, Benedict. 2007. Brainy Parrot Dies, Emotive to the End. *New York Times* Sept. 11, 2007. Accessed on July 20, 2010: http://www.nytimes.com/2007/09/11/science/11parrot.html?_r=1

Carrier, James. 1995. *Gifts and Commodities: Exchange and Western Capitalism Since 1700*. London: Routledge.

Carrier, James. 1996a. "Exchange." In Alan Barnard and Jonathan Spencer, eds., *Encyclopedia of Social and Cultural Anthropology*, pp. 218–221. London: Routledge.

Carrier, James. 1996b. "Consumption." In Alan Barnard and Jonathan Spencer, eds., *Encyclopedia of Social and Cultural Anthropology*, pp. 128–129. London: Routledge.

Carrier, Joseph M. 1976. Family Attitudes and Mexican Male Homosexuality. *Urban Life* 5(3):359–375.

Chagnon, Napoleon, and Timothy Asch. 1973. *Magical Death*. Watertown, MA: Documentary Educational Resources.

Chagnon, Napoleon. 1968. *Yanomamö: The Fierce People*. New York: Holt, Rinehart and Winston.

Chambers, Robert. 1997. *Whose Reality Counts? Putting the Last First*. 2nd edition. London: Intermediate Technology Publications.

Chapin, Mac. 2004. A Challenge to Conservationists. *World Watch Magazine* November/December:17–31.

Chossudovsky, Michel. 1997. *The Globalization of Poverty: Impacts of IMF and World Bank Reforms*. Atlantic Highlands, NJ: Zed Books.

Clifford, James, and George Marcus, eds. 1986. *Writing Culture: The Poetics and Politics of Ethnography*. School of American Research Advanced Seminar. Berkeley, CA: University of California Press.

Cohen, Jeffrey. 2004. *The Culture of Migration in Southern Mexico*. Austin, TX: University of Texas Press.

Cohen, Mark Nathan. 1998. *Culture of Intolerance: Chauvinism, Class, and Racism in the United States*. New Haven, CT: Yale University Press.

Colchester, Marcus. 2003. "The Fifth World Parks Congress: Parks for People or Parks for Business?" *World Rainforest Movement Bulletin No. 75*, October 2003. Accessed on February 15, 2005: http://www.wrm.org.uy/bulletin/75/parks.html.

Cole, Douglas. 1985. *Captured Heritage: The Scramble for Northwest Coast Artifacts*. Seattle, WA: University of Washington Press.

Collier, Jane, and Sylvia Yanagisako, eds. 1987. *Gender and Kinship: Essays Toward a Unified Analysis*. Stanford, CA: Stanford University Press.

Connor, Linda. 1982. Ships of Fools and Vessels of the Divine: Mental Hospitals and Madness, a Case Study. *Social Science and Medicine* 16:783–794.

Cooke, Stephanie. 2009. *In Mortal Hands: A Cautionary History of the Nuclear Age*. New York: Bloomsbury USA.

Coon, C. S., S. M. Garn, and J. B. Birdsell. 1950. *Races*. Springfield, IL: Thomas.

Counihan, Carole. 1999. *The Anthropology of Food and Body: Gender, Meaning, and Power*. New York: Routledge.

Counts, Dorothy A. 1980. Fighting Back Is Not the Way: Suicide and the Women of Kaliai. *American Ethnologist* 7:332–351.

Crate, Susan. 2008. Gone the Bull of Winter? Grappling with the Cultural Implications of and Anthropology's Role(s) in Global Climate Change. *Current Anthropology* 49(4):569–595.

Crenshaw, Kimberle. 1989. Demarginalizing the Intersection of Race and Sex: A Black Feminist Critique of Antidiscrimination Doctrine, Feminist Theory, and Antiracist Politics. *The University of Chicago Legal Forum* 140:139–167.

Cronon, William. 1983. *Changes in the Land: Indians, Colonists, and the Ecology of New England*. New York: Hill and Wang.

Crossette, Barbara. 2001. Taliban Explains Buddha Destruction. *New York Times*, March 19, 2001. Accessed on November 26, 2015: http://www.nytimes.com/2001/03/19/world/19TALI.html

Csordas, Thomas, and Arthur Kleinman 1996. "The Therapeutic Process." In Carolyn F. Sargent and Thomas M. Johnson, eds., *Medical Anthropology: Contemporary Theory and Method*, pp. 3–20. Revised edition. Westport, CT: Praeger.

D'Andrade, Roy. 1995. *The Development of Cognitive Anthropology*. Cambridge, UK: Cambridge University Press.

Dakowski, Bruce. 1990. "Everything Is Relatives: W. H. R. Rivers." In *Pioneers of Social Anthropology: Strangers Abroad* (Documentary Film Series). Videorecording. Princeton, NJ: Films for the Humanities and Sciences.

Daltabuit, Magalí, and Thomas Leatherman. 1998. "The Biocultural Impact of Tourism on Mayan Communities." In Alan Goodman and Thomas Leatherman, eds., *Building a New Biocultural Synthesis: Political-Economic Perspectives on Human Biology*, pp. 317–338. Ann Arbor, MI: University of Michigan Press.

Daly, Michael. 2009. Anthropologist's "Dick Tracy Moment" Plays Role in Arrest of Suspected Kidney Trafficker. *New York Daily News*, July 24, 2009. Accessed on August 18, 2009: http://www.nydailynews.com/news/ny_crime/2009/07/24/2009-07-24_seven_year_quest_to_end_rosenbaum_evil_work_pays_off.html

Dark, Philip J. C. 1962. *The Art of Benin: A Catalogue of an Exhibition of the A. W. F. Fuller and Chicago Natural History Museum Collections of Antiquities from Benin, Nigeria*. Chicago, IL: Chicago Natural History Museum.

Dark, Philip J. C. 1982. *An Illustrated Catalogue of Benin Art*. Boston, MA: G. K. Hall.

Darwin, Charles. 1859. *On the Origin of Species by Means of Natural Selection: Or, The Preservation of Favoured Races in the Struggle for Life*. London: J. Murray.

Davidheiser, Mark. 2007. Overview of Peace and Conflict Resolution Study and Practice. *Anthropology News* Oct.:11–12.

Dávila, Arlene. 2001. *Latinos, Inc.: The Marketing and Making of a People*. Berkeley, CA: University of California Press.

de Castro, Fabio, and David McGrath. 2003. Moving toward Sustainability in the Local Management of Floodplain Lake Fisheries in the Brazilian Amazon. *Human Organization* 62(2):123–133.

Delaney, Carol. 1988. Participant Observation: The Razor's Edge. *Dialectical Anthropology* 13(3):291–300.

Deloria, Vine, Jr. 1969. *Custer Died for Your Sins: An Indian Manifesto*. New York: Macmillan.

de Mille, Cecil B., director. 1956. *The Ten Commandments*. Hollywood, CA: Paramount Pictures.

Dentan, Robert Knox. 1968. *The Semai: A Non-Violent People of Malaya*. New York: Holt, Rinehart, and Winston.

Dentan, Robert Knox, K. Endicott, A. G. Gomes, and M. B. Hooker. 1997. *Malaysia and the "Original People": A Case Study of the Impact of Development on Indigenous Peoples*. Boston, MA: Allyn and Bacon.

Dettwyler, Katherine A. 2013. *Dancing Skeletons: Life and Death in West Africa*. 2nd edition. Prospect Heights, IL: Waveland.

Dittmar, Helga. 1992. *The Social Psychology of Material Possessions: To Have Is to Be*. Hemel Hempstead, Hertfordshire, UK: Harvester Wheatsheaf.

Dobrin, Lise M. 2008. From Linguistic Elicitation to Eliciting the Linguistic Lessons in Community Empowerment from Melanesia. *Language* 84(2):300–324.

Dongoske, K., M. Yeatts, T. Ferguson, and L. Jenkins. 1995. Historic Preservation and Native American Sites. *SAA Bulletin* 13(4):13, 39.

Douglas, Mary. 1966. *Purity and Danger: An Analysis of the Concepts of Pollution and Taboo*. New York: Praeger.

Douglas, Mary, and Baron Isherwood. 1978. *The World of Goods*. Harmondsworth, UK: Penguin.

Dressler, William. 2005. What's Cultural About Biocultural Research? *Ethos* 31(1):20–45.

Dreyer, Edward L. 2007. *Zheng He: China and the Oceans in the Early Ming Dynasty, 1405–1433*. New York: Pearson Longman.

Dwyer, Leslie. 2000. "Spectacular Sexualities: Nationalism, Development, and the Politics of Family Planning in Indonesia." In Tamar Mayer, ed., *Gender Ironies of Nationalism: Sexing the Nation*, pp. 25–62. New York: Routledge.

Eagles, Charles W. 1993. *Outside Agitator: Jon Daniels and the Civil Rights Movement in Alabama*. Chapel Hill, NC: University of North Carolina Press.

Eboreime, Joseph. 2003. *The Installation of a Benin Monarch: Rite de Passage in the Expression of Ethnic Identity in Nigeria*. Paper from the ICOMOS 14th General Assembly. Accessed on June 3, 2017: https://www.icomos.org/victoriafalls2003/papers/B3-1%20-%20Eboreime.pdf

Edelman, Elijah Adiv. 2016. Why We Need to Stop Talking About Trans People in the Bathroom. *Anthropology News*. Accessed on February 17, 2017: http://www.anthropology-news.org/index.php/2016/06/22/why-we-need-to-stop-talking-about-trans-people-in-the-bathroom/

Edwards, Carolyn P. 1993. "Behavioral Sex Differences in Children of Diverse Cultures: The Case of Nurturance to Infants." In Michael E. Pereira and Lynn A. Fairbanks, eds., *Juvenile Primates: Life History, Development, and Behavior*, pp. 327–338. New York: Oxford University Press.

Eickelman, Dale F., and James Piscatori. 1996. *Muslim Politics*. Princeton, NJ: Princeton University Press.

Eisenberg, Leon. 1977. Disease and Illness: Distinctions Between Professional and Popular Ideas of Sickness. *Culture, Medicine and Psychiatry* 1(1):9–23.

Elder, Kay, and Brian Dale. 2000. *In Vitro Fertilization*. 2nd edition. Cambridge, UK: Cambridge University Press.

Eller, Jack David. 2006. *Violence and Culture: A Cross-Cultural and Interdisciplinary Approach*. Belmont, CA: Thomson Wadsworth.

Endicott, Kirk, and Karen Endicott. 2008. *The Headman Was a Woman: The Gender Egalitarian Batek of Malaysia*. Long Grove, IL: Waveland Press.

Erasmus, Charles John. 1952. Changing Folk Beliefs and the Relativity of Empirical Knowledge. *Southwestern Journal of Anthropology* 8(4):411–428.

Erlich, Paul R. 1968. *The Population Bomb*. New York: Ballantine Books.

Escobar, Arturo. 1991. Anthropology and the Development Encounter: The Making and Marketing of Development Anthropology. *American Ethnologist* 18:658–682.

Escobar, Arturo. 1995. *Encountering Development: The Making and Unmaking of the Third World*. Princeton, NJ: Princeton University Press.

Escobar, Arturo, Sonia Alvarez, Adusta E. Dagnino. 1998. "Introduction: The Cultural and the Political in Latin American Social Movements." In Arturo Escobar, Sonia Alvarez, and E. Dagnino, eds., *Cultures of Politics/Politics of Culture: Revisioning*

Latin American Social Movements, pp. 1–32. Boulder, CO: Westview Press.

Esteva, Gustavo. 1992. "Development." In Wolfgang Sachs, ed., *The Development Dictionary,* pp. 6–25. London: Zed Books.

Evans-Pritchard, E. E. 1940. *The Nuer: A Description of the Modes of Livelihood and Political Institutions of a Nilotic People.* Oxford, UK: Oxford University Press.

Evans-Pritchard, E. E. 1961. *Anthropology and History: A Lecture Delivered at the University of Manchester with Support of the Simon Fund for the Social Sciences.* Manchester, UK: Manchester University Press.

Fabian, Johannes. 1971. On Professional Ethics and Epistemological Foundations. *Current Anthropology* 12(2):230–232.

Fabian, Johannes. 2001. *Anthropology with an Attitude: Critical Essays.* Palo Alto, CA: Stanford University Press.

Fagan, Brian M. 1988. Black Day at Slack Farm. *Archaeology* 41(4):15–73.

Fairhead, James, and Melissa Leach. 1996. *Misreading the African Landscape: Society and Ecology in a Forest-Savanna Mosaic.* Cambridge, UK: Cambridge University Press.

Farmer, Paul. 1992. *AIDS and Accusation: Haiti and the Geography of Blame.* Berkeley, CA: University of California Press.

Fausto-Sterling, Anne. 1992a. *Myths of Gender: Biological Theories About Women and Men.* 2nd edition. New York: Basic Books.

Fausto-Sterling, Anne. 1992b. Why Do We Know So Little About Human Sex? *Discover Magazine.* June 1992. Accessed on August 19, 2009: http://discovermagazine.com/1992/jun/whydoweknowsolit64

Fausto-Sterling, Anne. 2000. *Sexing the Body: Gender Politics and the Construction of Sexuality.* New York: Basic Books.

Fazioli, K. Patrick. 2014. The Erasure of the Middle Ages from Anthropology's Intellectual Genealogy. *History and Anthropology* 25(3):336–355.

Ferguson, James. 1994. *The Anti-Politics Machine: "Development," Depoliticization, and Bureaucratic Power in Lesotho.* Minneapolis, MN: University of Minnesota Press.

Ferguson, R. Brian. 1995. *Yanomami Warfare: A Political History.* Santa Fe, NM: School of American Research Press.

Field, Les, and Richard G. Fox. 2007. "Introduction: How Does Anthropology Work Today?" In Les Field and Richard G. Fox, eds., *Anthropology Put to Work,* pp. 1–19. Oxford, UK: Berg Publishers.

Finney, Ben R. 1973. *Big Men and Business: Entrepreneurship and Economic Growth in the New Guinea Highlands.* Honolulu: University of Hawaii Press.

Fluehr-Lobban, Carolyn. 2003. *Ethics and the Profession of Anthropology: Dialogue for Ethically Conscious Practice.* Walnut Creek, CA: AltaMira Press.

Food and Agriculture Organization of the United Nations (FAO). 2012. *Undernourishment Around the World.* Accessed on September 11, 2013: www.fao.org/docrep/016/i3027e/i3027e02.pdf

Foster, George M. 1952. Relationships Between Theoretical and Applied Anthropology: A Public Health Program Analysis. *Human Organization* 11(3):5–16.

Foucault, Michel. 1978. *The History of Sexuality: Vol. 1, An Introduction.* Trans. Robert Hurley. New York: Vintage Books.

Foucault, Michel. 1999. *Religion and Culture.* Selected and edited by Jeremy R. Carrette. New York: Routledge.

Fox, Geoffrey. 1997. *Hispanic Nation: Culture, Politics, and the Constructing of Identity.* Tucson, AZ: University of Arizona Press.

Frankenberry, Nancy, and Hans H. Penner. 1999. Clifford Geertz's Long-Lasting Moods, Motivations, and Metaphysical Conceptions. *Journal of Religion* 79(4):617–640.

Fratkin, Elliot. 2003. *Ariaal Pastoralists of Kenya: Surviving Drought and Development in Africa's Arid Lands.* 2nd edition. Boston, MA: Allyn and Bacon.

Frazer, James G. 1890. *The Golden Bough: A Study in Comparative Religion.* 1st edition. 2 vols. London: Macmillan.

Frazer, James G. 1900. *The Golden Bough: A Study in Magic and Religion.* 2nd edition. 3 vols. London: Macmillan.

Frazer, James G. 1911–1915. *The Golden Bough: A Study in Magic and Religion.* 3rd edition. 12 vols. London: Macmillan.

Freidson, Eliot. 1970. *Profession of Medicine: A Study of the Sociology of Applied Knowledge.* New York: Dodd, Mead.

Friedl, Erika. 1994. "Sources of Female Power in Iran." In Mahnaz Afkhami and Erika Friedl, eds., *In the Eye of the Storm: Women in Post-Revolutionary Iran*, pp. 151–168. Syracuse, NY: Syracuse University Press.

Friedman, Jonathan. 1994. *Cultural Identity and Global Process.* London: Sage Publications.

Friedman, Jonathan. 1999. "The Hybridization of Roots and the Abhorrence of the Bush." In Michael Featherstone and Scott Lash, eds., *Spaces of Culture: City-Nation-World,* pp. 230–255. London: Sage.

Fry, Douglas. 2006. *The Human Potential for Peace: An Anthropological Challenge to Assumptions About War and Violence.* New York: Oxford University Press.

Fuentes, Agustín. 2012. *Race, Monogamy, and Other Lies They Told You: Busting Myths About Human Nature.* Berkeley, CA: University of California Press.

Fuller, C. J. 2004. *The Camphor Flame: Popular Hinduism and Society in India.* Princeton, NJ: Princeton University Press.

Gallagher, Charles. 1997. "White Racial Formation: Into the Twenty-First Century." In Richard Delgado and Jean Stefancic, eds., *Critical White Studies: Looking Behind the Mirror,* pp. 6–11. Philadelphia, PA: Temple University Press.

García-Canclini, Nestor. 1995. *Hybrid Cultures: Strategies for Entering and Leaving Modernity.* Minneapolis, MN: University of Minnesota Press.

Gardner, R. Allen, Beatrix T. Gardner, and Thomas E. van Cantfort, eds. 1989. *Teaching Sign Language to Chimpanzees.* Albany, NY: State University of New York Press.

Garn, Stanley. 1961. *Human Races.* Springfield, IL: C. C. Thomas.

Geertz, Clifford. 1963. *Agricultural Involution: The Processes of Ecological Change in Indonesia.* Berkeley, CA: University of California Press.

Geertz, Clifford. 1966. "Religion as a Cultural System." In Michael Banton, ed., *Anthropological Approaches to the Study of Religion,* pp. 1–46. ASA Monograph 3. London: Tavistock.

Geertz, Clifford. 1973. *The Interpretation of Cultures: Selected Essays.* New York: Basic Books.

Geertz, Clifford. 1988. *Works and Lives: The Anthropologist as Author.* Stanford, CA: Stanford University Press.

Geertz, Hildred, and Clifford Geertz. 1964. Teknonymy in Bali: Parenthood, Age-Grading, and Genealogical Amnesia. *Journal of the Royal Anthropological Institute of Great Britain and Ireland* 94(2):94–108.

Geertz, Hildred, and Clifford Geertz. 1975. *Kinship in Bali.* Chicago, IL: University of Chicago Press.

Gellner, Ernest. 1983. *Nations and Nationalism.* Ithaca, NY: Cornell University Press.

Gennep, Arnold van. 1960. *The Rites of Passage.* Trans. by Monica B. Vizedom and Gabrielle L. Caffee. Chicago, IL: University of Chicago Press. [Orig. published 1909 in French.]

Genz, Joseph. 2011. Navigating the Revival of Voyaging in the Marshall Islands: Predicaments of Preservation and Possibilities of Collaboration. *The Contemporary Pacific* 23(1):1–34.

Gibbs, James L., Jr. 1963. The Kpelle Moot. *Africa* 33(1):1–11.

Glazer, Christine, Chuck Romaniello, and Karin Moskowitz. 2015. *Costs and Consequences: The Real Cost of Livestock Grazing on America's Public Lands.* Tucson, AZ: Center for Biological Diversity.

Gledhill, John. 2000. *Power and Its Disguises: Anthropological Perspectives on Politics.* London: Pluto Press.

Global Justice Now. 2016. 10 Biggest Corporations Make More Money Than Most Countries in the World Combined. Accessed on February 17, 2017: http://www.globaljustice.org.uk/news/2016/sep/12/10-biggest-corporations-make-more-money-most-countries-world-combined

Gluckman, Max. 1940. Analysis of a Social System in Modern Zululand. *Bantu Studies* 14:1–30, 147–174.

Gmelch, George. 1978. Baseball Magic. *Human Nature* 1(8):32–39.

Godelier, Maurice. 1999. *The Enigma of the Gift*. Chicago, IL: University of Chicago Press.

Goldschmidt, Walter. 2000. A Perspective on Anthropology. *American Anthropologist* 102(4):789–807.

Gonzalez, Roberto. 2001. *Zapotec Science: Farming and Food in the Northern Sierra of Oaxaca*. Austin: University of Texas Press.

Goodenough, Ward. 1965. Yankee Kinship Terminology: A Problem in Componential Analysis. *American Anthropologist*, New Series, Vol. 67, No. 5, Part 2: Formal Semantic Analysis (Oct., 1965), pp. 259–287.

Gordon, Robert J. 2005. *The Bushman Myth: The Making of a Namibian Underclass*. 2nd edition. Boulder, CO: Westview Press.

Gow, David. 1993. Doubly Damned: Dealing with Power and Praxis in Development Anthropology. *Human Organization* 52(4):380–397.

Graeber, David. 2011. *Debt: The First 5,000 Years*. New York: Melville House Publishing.

Gravlee, Clarence. 2009. How Race Becomes Biology: Embodiment of Social Inequality. *American Journal of Physical Anthropology* 139:47–57.

Gregory, Steven, and Roger Sanjek, eds. 1994. *Race*. New Brunswick, NJ: Rutgers University Press.

Grimm, Jacob. 1822. *Deutsche Grammatik*. Göttingen, Germany: Dieterichsche Buchhandlung.

Grove, Richard. 1995. *Green Imperialism: Colonial Expansion, Tropical Island Edens and the Origins of Environmentalism, 1600–1860*. Cambridge, UK: Cambridge University Press.

Gudeman, Stephen. 1986. *Economics as Culture: Models and Metaphors of Livelihood*. London: Routledge & Kegan Paul.

Gudeman, Stephen. 2001. *The Anthropology of Economy: Community, Market, and Culture*. Oxford, UK: Blackwell.

Guha, Ramachandra. 2000. *Environmentalism: A Global History*. New York: Longman.

Guimarães, Antonio Sérgio Alfredo. 1999. "Racism and Anti-Racism in Brazil." In Roger S. Gottlieb (series ed.) and Leonard Harris (volume ed.), *Key Concepts in Critical Theory: Racism*, pp. 314–330. Amherst, NY: Humanity Books.

Gulliver, Philip H. 1979. *Disputes and Negotiations: A Cross-Cultural Perspective*. New York: Academic Press.

Gusterson, Hugh. 2005. "The Seven Deadly Sins of Samuel Huntington." In Catherine Besteman and Hugh Gusterson, eds., *Why America's Top Pundits Are Wrong: Anthropologists Talk Back*, pp. 24–42. Berkeley, CA: University of California Press.

Gutmann, Matthew C. 1996. *The Meanings of Macho: Being a Man in Mexico City*. Berkeley, CA: University of California Press.

Gutmann, Matthew C. 1997. Trafficking in Men: The Anthropology of Masculinity. *Annual Review of Anthropology* 26:385–409.

Hakiwai, Arapata, and John Terrell. 1994. *Ruatepupuke: A Maori Meeting House*. The Field Museum Centennial Collection. Chicago, IL: The Field Museum.

Hale, Kenneth L. 1992. On Endangered Languages and the Safeguarding of Diversity. *Language* 68(1):1–3.

Hanlon, Joseph. 1996. Strangling Mozambique: International Monetary Fund "Stabilization" in the World's Poorest Country. *Multinational Monitor* 17(7–8):17–21.

Hannerz, Ulf. 1992. "The Global Ecumene." In *Cultural Complexity: Studies in the Social Organization of Meaning*, pp. 217–267. New York: Columbia University Press.

Hansen, Karen Tranberg. 2000. *Salaula: The World of Secondhand Clothing and Zambia*. Chicago, IL: University of Chicago Press.

Harding, Sandra. 1994. "Is Science Multicultural? Challenges, Resources, Opportunities, Uncertainties." In D. Goldberg, ed.,

Multiculturalism: A Critical Reader, pp. 344–370. Oxford, UK: Blackwell.

Harris, Marvin. 1968. *The Rise of Anthropological Theory: A History of Theories of Culture*. New York: Crowell.

Harris, Marvin. 1979. *Cultural Materialism*. New York: Random House.

Harris, Olivia. 1980. "The Power of Signs: Gender, Culture, and the Wild in the Bolivian Andes." In C. P. MacCormack and Marylin Strathern, eds., *Nature, Culture, and Gender*, pp. 70–94. Cambridge, UK: Cambridge University Press.

Hartigan, John, Jr. 2005. *Odd Tribes: Towards a Cultural Analysis of White People*. Durham, NC: Duke University Press.

Hartigan, John, Jr. 2006. Saying "Socially Constructed" Is Not Enough. *Anthropology News*, February 2006, p. 8.

Harvey, L. P. 2007. *Ibn Batuta*. London: I. B. Tauris and Oxford Centre for Islamic Studies.

Hastrup, Kirsten, and Peter Elass. 1990. Anthropological Advocacy: A Contradiction in Terms. *Current Anthropology* 31(3):301–311.

Haugerud, Angelique. 2016. Public Anthropology in 2015: *Charlie Hebdo*, Black Lives Matter, Migrants, and More. *American Anthropologist* 118(3):585–601.

Hedges, Nathan T. 2017. By the Belly Alone: Clientelistic Tensions in Southern Benin. Doctoral Dissertation, University of Virginia, Charlottesville.

Herdt, Gilbert H. 1981. *Guardians of the Flutes: Idioms of Masculinity*. New York: McGraw-Hill.

Herdt, Gilbert H. 1994. Introduction: Third Sexes and Third Genders. In Gilbert Herdt, ed., *Third Sex, Third Gender: Beyond Sexual Dimorphism in Culture and History*, pp. 21–81. New York: Zone Books.

Hill, Jane H. 1978. Apes and Language. *Annual Review of Anthropology* 7:89–112.

Hill, Jane H. 1993. Hasta la vista, baby: Anglo Spanish in the American Southwest. *Critique of Anthropology* 13(2):145–176.

Hill, Jane H. 1998. Language, Race, and White Public Space. *American Anthropologist* 100:680–689.

Hinsley, Curtis M., and David R. Wilcox, eds. 2016. *Coming of Age in Chicago: The 1893 World's Fair and the Coalescence of American Anthropology*. Lincoln, NE: University of Nebraska Press.

Hirabayashi, Lane Ryo. 1999. *The Politics of Fieldwork: Research in an American Concentration Camp*. Tucson, AZ: University of Arizona Press.

Ho, Karen. 2009. *Liquidated: An Ethnography of Wall Street*. Durham, NC: Duke University Press.

Hobbes, Thomas. 1651. *Leviathan, or, the matter, forme, and power of a common-wealth ecclesiaticall and civill*. London: Andrew Crooke.

Hobbes, Thomas. 1909. *Leviathan*. Oxford, UK: Clarendon Press.

Hoben, Alan. 1995. Paradigms and Politics: The Cultural Construction of Environmental Policy in Ethiopia. *World Development* 23(6):1007–1021.

Hobsbawn, Eric, and Ranger, Terence (eds.). (1983) *The Invention of Tradition*. Cambridge, UK: Cambridge University Press.

Hoijer, Harry. 1961. "Anthropological Linguistics." In Christine Mohrmann, Alf Sommerfelt, and Joshua Whatmough, eds., *Trends in European and American Linguistics 1930–1960*, pp. 110–127. Utrecht and Antwerp, The Netherlands: Spectrum Publisher.

Horn, David. 1994. *Social Bodies: Science, Reproduction, and Italian Modernity*. Princeton, NJ: Princeton University Press.

Howe, K. R. 1984. *Where the Waves Fall: A New South Sea Islands History from Its First Settlement to Colonial Rule*. Honolulu, HI: University of Hawaii Press.

Hsu, F. L. K. 1972. "Psychological Anthropology in the Behavioral Sciences." In F. L. K. Hsu, ed., *Psychological Anthropology*, pp. 1–19. Cambridge, MA: Schenkman Publishing Co.

Hubert, Annie. 1997. "Choices of Food and Cuisine in the Concept of Social Space Among the Yao of Thailand." In Helen MacBeth, ed.,

Food Preferences and Taste: Continuity and Change, pp. 157–166. Providence, RI: Berghahn Books.

Humphrey, Caroline. 2002. *The Unmaking of Soviet Life: Everyday Economies After Socialism.* Ithaca, NY: Cornell University Press.

Huntington, Samuel P. 1993. The Clash of Civilizations? *Foreign Affairs* 72(3):22–49.

Huntington, Samuel. 1996. *The Clash of Civilizations and the Remaking of World Order.* New York: Simon and Schuster.

Hymes, Dell H. 1962. "The Ethnography of Speaking." In Thomas Gladwin and William C. Sturtevant, eds., *Anthropology and Human Behavior,* pp. 13–53. Washington, DC: Anthropological Society of Washington.

Hymes, Dell H. 1972. "Toward Ethnographies of Communication." In Pier Paolo Giglioli, ed., *Language and Social Context,* pp. 21–44. Baltimore, MD: Penguin Books.

Hymes, Dell H. 1973. *Toward Linguistic Competence.* Texas Working Papers in Sociolinguistics, No. 16. [Later translated as *Vers la competence de communication,* Paris: Hatier, 1991.]

IANS (Indo-Asian News Service). 2014. Diabetes Can Be Controlled in 80 Percent of Cases in India. Accessed on February 1, 2017: http://news.biharprabha.com/2014/02/diabetes-can-be-controlled-in-80-percent-of-cases-in-india/

Ignatiev, Noel. 1995. *How the Irish Became White.* New York: Routledge.

Igoe, James. 2004. *Conservation and Globalization: A Study of National Parks and Indigenous Communities from East Africa to South Dakota.* Belmont, CA: Wadsworth.

Inda, Jonathan Xavier. 2014. *Racial Prescriptions: Pharmaceuticals, Difference, and the Politics of Life.* Burlington, VT: Ashgate.

Inda, Jonathan, and Renato Rosaldo, eds. 2002. *The Anthropology of Globalization: A Reader.* Malden, MA: Blackwell.

International Obesity Task Force (IOTF). 2013. "The Global Epidemic." World Health Organization Fact Sheet. Accessed on September 10, 2013: http://www.iaso.org/iotf/obesity/obesitytheglobalepidemic/

International Telecommunication Union (ITU). 2016. ICT Facts and Figures 2016. Accessed on February 17, 2017: http://www.itu.int/en/ITU-D/Statistics/Pages/facts/default.aspx

Jetnil-Kijiner, Kathy. 2015. Marshall Islands Poet to the U.N. Climate Summit: "Tell Them We Are Nothing Without Our Islands." *Democracy Now!* Accessed on February 1, 2017: https://www.democracynow.org/2015/12/2/marshall_islands_poet_to_the_un

Johnston, Francis E. 2004. "Race and Biology: Changing Currents in Muddy Waters." Paper presented at the conference Race and Human Variation: Setting an Agenda for Future Research and Education, held September 12–14, 2004, in Alexandria, Virginia. Available at: http://www.understandingrace.com/resources/papers_activity.html

Kalipeni, Ezekiel. 2004. *HIV and AIDS in Africa: Beyond Epidemiology.* Malden, MA: Blackwell.

Kambas, Michele, and Antonio Bronic. 2016. Out of Sight, Out of Mind? Europe's Migrant Crisis Still Simmers. *Reuters,* August 10, 2016. Accessed on February 17, 2017: http://www.reuters.com/article/us-europe-migrants-idUSKCN10L13T?il=0

Kapferer, Bruce. 2015. "Afterward." In Alessandro Zagato, ed., *The Event of* Charlie Hebdo: *Imaginaries of Freedom and Control,* pp. 93–114. Critical Interventions, Vol. 15. Oxford, UK: Berghahn.

Kaplan, David, and Robert A. Manners. 1972. *Culture Theory.* Prospect Heights, IL: Waveland Press.

Kaptchuk, Ted J. 2001. The Double-blind, Randomized, Placebo-controlled Trial: Gold Standard or Golden Calf? *Journal of Clinical Epidemiology* 54:541–549.

Kearney, Michael. 1995. The Local and the Global: The Anthropology of Globalization and Transnationalism. *Annual Review of Anthropology* 24:547–565.

Kearney, Michael. 1996. *Reconceptualizing the Peasantry: Anthropology in Global Perspective.* Boulder, CO: Westview Press.

Khanmohamadi, S. 2008. The Look of Medieval Ethnography: William of Rubruck's Mission to Mongolia. *New Medieval Literatures* 10(1):87–114.

Kidder, Tracy. 2003. *Mountains Beyond Mountains.* New York: Random House.

Kidwell, Claudia Brush, and Valerie Steele, eds. 1989. *Men and Women: Dressing the Part.* Washington, DC: Smithsonian Institution Press.

Kildea, Gary, and Jerry Leach. 1975. *Trobriand Cricket: An Ingenious Response to Colonialism.* DVD. Berkeley, CA: Berkeley Media.

Kingsolver, Ann. 1996. "Power." In Alan Barnard and Jonathan Spencer, eds., *Encyclopedia of Social and Cultural Anthropology,* pp. 445–448. London: Routledge.

Kinsey, Alfred. 1948. *Sexual Behavior in the Human Male.* Philadelphia, PA: W. B. Saunders.

Kleinfield, N. R. 2006. Modern Ways Open India's Doors to Diabetes. *The New York Times,* September 13, 2006. Accessed on September 13, 2006: http://www.nytimes.com/2006/09/13/world/asia/13diabetes.html?ex=1166936400&en=8322bd1c8904e016&ei=5070

Kleinman, Arthur. 1975. "Social, Cultural and Historical Themes in the Study of Medicine in Chinese Societies: Problems and Prospects for the Comparative Study of Medicine and Psychiatry." In A. Kleinman et al., eds., *Medicine in Chinese Cultures: Comparative Studies of Health Care in Chinese and Other Societies. Papers and Discussions from a Conference Held in Seattle, Washington, U.S.A., February 1974,* pp. 589–657. Washington, DC: U.S. Department of Health, Education, and Welfare.

Koos, Earl Lomon. 1954. *The Health of Regionville.* New York: Columbia University Press.

Kopytoff, Igor. 1986. "The Cultural Biography of Things: Commoditization as Process." In Arjun Appadurai, ed., *The Social Life of Things: Commodities in Cultural Perspective,* pp. 64–91. New York: Cambridge University Press.

Korten, David. 1995. *When Corporations Rule the World.* West Hartford, CT: Kumarian Press.

Kozol, Jonathan. 1992. *Savage Inequalities: Children in America's Schools.* New York: Harper Perennial.

Krech, Shepard. 1999. *The Ecological Indian: Myth and History.* New York: W. W. Norton.

Krishnamurthy, Mathangi. 2004. Resources and Rebels: A Study of Identity Management in Indian Call Centers. *Anthropology of Work Review* 25(3–4):9–18.

Kroeber, Alfred L. 1909. Classificatory Systems of Relationship. *Journal of the Royal Anthropological Institute of Great Britain and Ireland* 39:77–84.

Kroeber, Alfred L. 1923. American Culture and the Northwest Coast. *American Anthropologist* 25(1):1–20.

Kubler, George. 1962. *The Shape of Time: Remarks on the History of Things.* New Haven, CT: Yale University Press.

Kulick, Don. 1998. *Travesti: Sex, Gender, and Culture Among Brazilian Transgendered Prostitutes.* Chicago, IL: University of Chicago Press.

Kurtz, Donald V. 2001. *Political Anthropology: Paradigms and Power.* Boulder, CO: Westview Press.

Labov, William. 1990. "Intersection of Sex and Social Class in the Course of Linguistic Change." *Language Variation and Change* 2(2):205–254.

Labov, William, Sharon Ash, and Charles Boberg. 2006. *The Atlas of North American English: Phonetics, Phonology, and Sound Change: A Multimedia Reference Tool.* Berlin: Mouton de Gruyter.

Lahsen, Myanna. 2015. "Digging Deeper into the Why: Cultural Dimensions of Climate Change Skepticism Among Scientists." In Jessica Barnes and Michael Dove, eds. *Climate Cultures: Anthropological Perspectives on Climate Change,* pp. 221–248. New Haven, CT: Yale University Press.

Lakoff, Robin. 1975. *Language and Woman's Place.* New York: Harper and Row.

Lancaster, Roger. 1992. *Life Is Hard: Machismo, Danger, and the Intimacy of Power in Nicaragua.* Berkeley, CA: University of California Press.

Lancaster, Roger. 1997. On Homosexualities in Latin America (and Other Places). *American Ethnologist* 24(1):193–202.

Lancaster, Roger. 2004. The Place of Anthropology in a Public Culture Shaped by Bioreductivism. *Anthropology News* 45(3): 4–5.

Lareau, Annette. 2003. *Unequal Childhoods: Class, Race, and Family Life.* Berkeley, CA: University of California Press.

Larner, John. 1999. *Marco Polo and the Discovery of the World.* New Haven, CT: Yale University Press.

Leacock, Eleanor. 1981. *Myths of Male Dominance.* New York: Monthly Review.

Leary, John. 1995. *Violence and the Dream People: The Orang Asli and the Malaysian Emergency, 1948–1960.* Athens, OH: University Center for International Studies.

Lechner, Frank, and Boli, John. 2005. *World Culture: Origins and Consequences.* Malden, MA: Blackwell.

Lee, Richard. 1969. "!Kung Bushmen Subsistence: An Input-Output Analysis." In Andrew P. Vayda, ed., *Environment and Cultural Behavior,* pp. 47–79. Garden City, NY: Natural History Press.

Lee, Richard. 1979. *The !Kung San: Men, Women, and Work in a Foraging Society.* Cambridge, UK: Cambridge University Press.

Lentz, Carola. 1999. "Changing Food Habits: An Introduction." In Carola Lentz, ed., *Changing Food Habits: Case Studies from Africa, South America, and Europe,* pp. 1–25. Newark, NJ: Harwood Academic Publishers.

Lévi-Strauss, Claude. 1949/1969. *The Elementary Structures of Kinship.* Boston, MA: Beacon.

Lévi-Strauss, Claude. 1961. "The Effectiveness of Symbols." In *Structural Anthropology,* pp. 186–205. New York: Basic Books.

Lévi-Strauss, Claude. 1969a. *The Elementary Structures of Kinship.* Boston, MA: Beacon Press.

Lévi-Strauss, Claude. 1969b. *The Raw and the Cooked.* New York: Harper & Row.

Lewellen, Ted C. 1983. *Political Anthropology: An Introduction.* South Hadley, MA: Bergin & Garvey Publishers.

Lewellen, Ted C. 2003. *Political Anthropology: An Introduction.* 3rd edition. Westport, CT: Praeger.

Lewin, Ellen. 1993. *Lesbian Mothers: Accounts of Gender in American Culture.* Ithaca, NY: Cornell University Press.

Lewin, Ellen. 1996. "'Why in the World Would You Want to Do That?': Claiming Community in Lesbian Commitment Ceremonies." In Ellen Lewin, ed., *Inventing Lesbian Cultures in America.* pp. 105–130. Boston, MA: Beacon Press.

Lewin, Ellen, and William L. Leap, eds. 1996. *Out in the Field: Reflections of Lesbian and Gay Anthropologists.* Urbana, IL: University of Illinois Press.

Lewin, Ellen, and William L. Leap, eds. 2009. *Out in Public: Reinventing Lesbian/Gay Anthropology in a Globalizing World.* Malden, MA: Wiley-Blackwell.

Lieberman, Leslie Sue. 1987. "Biocultural Consequences of Animals Versus Plants as Sources of Fats, Proteins, and Other Nutrients." In Marvin Harris and Eric B. Ross, eds., *Food and Evolution: Toward a Theory of Human Food Habits,* pp. 225–260. Philadelphia, PA: Temple University Press.

Liechty, Mark. 2002. *Suitably Modern: Making Middle Class Culture in Kathmandu.* Princeton, NJ: Princeton University Press.

Linton, Ralph. 1924. Totemism and the A. E. F. *American Anthropologist* 26:296–300.

Little, Peter, and Michael Painter. 1995. Discourse, Politics, and the Development Process: Reflections on Escobar's "Anthropology and the Development Encounter." *American Ethnologist* 22(3):602–609.

Lizot, Jacques. 1985. *Tales of the Yanomami: Daily Life in the Venezuelan Forest.* Trans. by Ernest Simon. Cambridge, UK: Cambridge University Press.

Locke, John. 1690. *Two Treatises on Government: In the Former, the False Principles, and Foundation of Sir Robert Filmer, and his Followers, are Detected and Overthrown. The Latter is an Essay Concerning the True Original, Extent, and End of Civil Government.* London: Awnsham Churchill.

Locke, John. 2003. *Two Treatises on Government: And a Letter Concerning Toleration.* New Haven, CT: Yale University Press.

Lockwood, William G. 1975. *European Moslems: Economy and Ethnicity in Western Bosnia.* New York: Academic Publishers.

Lonely Planet. 2014. "Why Are Hearts the Symbol for a Rustic Toilet in Swedish Countryside?" *Thorn Tree Forum.* Country Forums: Scandinavia and the Nordics: Sweden. Accessed August 2014: https://www.lonelyplanet.com/thorntree/forums/europe-scandinavia-the-nordics/topics/why-are-hearts-the-symbol-for-a-rustic-toilet-in-swedish-countryside

Long, Jeffrey. 2003. *Human Genetic Variation: The Mechanisms and Results of Microevolution.* Paper presented at the American Anthropological Association 2003 annual meeting on November 21, 2003, in Chicago, Illinois. Accessed on May 24, 2007: http://www .understandingrace.com/resources/papers_author.html

Louie, Andrea. 2015. *How Chinese Are You? Adopted Chinese Youth and Their Families Negotiate Identity and Culture.* New York: New York University Press.

Lovgren, Sven. 2003. "Map Links Healthier Ecosystems, Indigenous Peoples." *National Geographic News,* February 27, 2003. Accessed on February 15, 2005: http://news.nationalgeographic.com/news/2003/02/0227_030227_indigenousmap.html

Luntz, Frank. 2007. *Words That Work: It's Not What You Say, It's What People Hear.* New York: Hyperion.

Lyons, Andrew P., and Harriet D. Lyons. 2004. *Irregular Connections: A History of Anthropology and Sexuality.* Lincoln, NE: University of Nebraska Press.

MacBeth, Helen. 1997. *Food Preferences and Taste: Continuity and Change.* New York: Berghahn Books.

Mahmood, Cynthia Keppley. 1997. *Fighting for Faith and Nation: Dialogues with Sikh Militants.* Philadelphia, PA: University of Pennsylvania Press.

Mair, Lucy. 1969. *Anthropology and Social Change.* New York: Humanities Press.

Malinowski, Bronislaw. 1922. *Argonauts of the Western Pacific: An Account of Native Enterprise and Adventure in the Archipelagoes of Melanesian New Guinea.* London: Routledge & Kegan Paul.

Malinowski, Bronislaw. 1948. *Magic, Science and Religion and Other Essays.* Boston, MA: Beacon Press.

Malotki, Ekkehardt. 1983. *Hopi Time: A Linguistic Analysis of the Temporal Concepts of the Hopi Language.* Berlin: Mouton.

Mamdani, Mahmood. 1972. *The Myth of Population Control: Family, Caste, and Class in an Indian Village.* New York: Monthly Review Press.

Marcus, George. 1995. Ethnography in/of the World System: The Emergence of Multi-Sited Ethnography. *Annual Review of Anthropology* 24:95–117.

Marcus, George, and Michael M. J. Fischer. 1986. *Anthropology as Cultural Critique: An Experimental Moment in the Human Sciences.* Chicago, IL: University of Chicago Press.

Mares, Teresa. 2014. "Another Time of Hunger." In *Women Redefining the Experience of Food Insecurity: Life off the Edge of the Table,* ed. Janet Page-Reeves, pp. 45–64. Lanham, MD: Lexington Books.

Mark, Jason 2006. "Will the End of Oil Be the End of Food?" *Alternet.org.* Accessed on March 14, 2007: http://www.alternet.org/envirohealth/41023/

Marks, Jonathan. 1995. *Human Biodiversity: Genes, Race, and History.* New York: Aldine de Gruyter.

Marty, Martin E., and R. Scott Appleby, eds. 1991. *Fundamentalisms Observed.* The Fundamentalism Project, Volume 1. Chicago, IL: University of Chicago Press.

Marwick, M. G. 1952. Social Context of Cewa Witch Beliefs. *Africa* 22:120–135, 215–233.

Marx, Karl. 1867/1990. *Capital: A Critique of Political Economy.* New York: Penguin.

Massey, Douglas, Joaquin Arango, Graeme Hugo, Ali Kouaouci, Adela Pellegrino, and J. Edward Taylor. 1993. Theories of International Migration: A Review and Appraisal. *Population and Development Review* 19(3):431–466.

Mauss, Marcel. 1954. *The Gift: The Form and Reason for Exchange in Archaic Societies.* Trans. W. D. Halls. New York: W. W. Norton & Company.

McCabe, Terrence. 1990. Turkana Pastoralism: A Case Against the Tragedy of the Commons. *Human Ecology* 18(1):81–103.

McDonald, James H. 1993. Corporate Capitalism and the Family Farm in the U.S. and Mexico. *Culture and Agriculture* 45/46:25–28.

McElhinny, Bonnie. 2003. "Theorizing Gender in Sociolinguistics and Linguistic Anthropology." In *The Handbook of Language and Gender*, eds. Janet Holmes and Miriam Myerhoff, pp. 21–42. Malden, MA: Blackwell.

McFate, Montgomery. 2005. Does Culture Matter? The Military Utility of Cultural Knowledge. *Joint Forces Quarterly* 38:42–48.

McGee, R. Jon, and Richard Warms. 2013. *Theory in Social and Cultural Anthropology: An Encyclopedia.* Thousand Oaks, CA: Sage Publishing.

McGrath, J. W., C. B. Rwabukwali, D. A. Schumann, J. Pearson-Marks, R. Mukasa, B. Namande, S. Nakayiwa, and L. Nakyobe. 1992. Cultural Determinants of Sexual Risk Behavior Among Baganda Women. *Medical Anthropology Quarterly* 6(2):153–161.

McIntosh, Peggy. 1997. "White Privilege and Male Privilege: A Personal Account of Coming to See Correspondences Through Work in Women's Studies." In Richard Delgado and Jean Stefancic, eds., *Critical White Studies: Looking Behind the Mirror*, pp. 291–299. Philadelphia, PA: Temple University Press.

McIntosh, Roderick. 2015. "Climate Shock and Awe: Can There Be an 'Ethno-science' of Deep-Time Mande Paleoclimate Memory?" In Jessica Barnes and Michael Dove, *Climate Cultures: Anthropological Perspectives on Climate Change*, pp. 273–288. New Haven, CT: Yale University Press.

McIntyre, Matthew H., and Carolyn Pope Edwards. 2009. The Early Development of Gender Differences. *Annual Review of Anthropology* 38:83–97.

McKenna, James J. 1996. Sudden Infant Death Syndrome in Cross-Cultural Perspective: Is Infant-Parent Cosleeping Protective? *Annual Review of Anthropology* 25:201–216.

Mead, Margaret. 1928. *Coming of Age in Samoa: A Psychological Study of Primitive Youth for Western Civilization.* New York: William Morrow.

Mead, Margaret. 1930a. *Growing Up in New Guinea: A Comparative Study of Primitive Education.* New York: W. Morrow.

Mead, Margaret. 1930b. *Social Organization of Manu'a.* Honolulu, HI: Bishop Museum Press.

Mead, Margaret. 1938. The Mountain Arapesh: I. An Importing Culture. *Anthropological Papers of the American Museum of Natural History* 36:139–349.

Mead, Margaret. 1935/1963. *Sex and Temperament in Three Primitive Societies.* New York: William Morrow.

Mead, Margaret. 2001. *Four Families.* DVD. New York: National Film Board of Canada. [Originally released 1959.]

Meighan, Clement W. 1992. Some Scholars' Views on Reburial. *American Antiquity* 57(4):704–710.

Meigs, Anna. 1997. "Food as a Cultural Construction." In Carole Counihan and Penny Van Esterik, eds., *Food and Culture: A Reader*, pp. 95–106. New York: Routledge.

Menzies, Gavin. 2002. *1421: The Year China Discovered America.* London: Transworld Publishers.

Merry, Sally Engle. 2003. Human Rights Law and the Demonization of Culture. *Anthropology News* 44(2):4–5.

Michael, Robert T., John H. Gagnon, Edward O. Lauman, and Gina Kolata. 1994. *Sex in America: A Definitive Survey.* Boston, MA: Little Brown.

Michaels, Eric. 1994. *Bad Anthropological Art: Tradition, Media, and Technological Horizons.* Sydney: Allen and Unwin.

Miller, Daniel. 1987. *Material Culture and Mass Consumption.* Oxford, UK: Basil Blackwell.

Miller, Daniel, ed. 1995. *Acknowledging Consumption: A Review of New Studies.* London: Routledge.

Miller, Daniel, ed. 1998. *Material Cultures: Why Some Things Matter.* Chicago, IL: University of Chicago Press.

Mintz, Sidney. 1992. A Taste of History. *The Higher Perspective* 8:15, 18.

Mohanty, Chandra Talpade. 1991. "Under Western Eyes: Feminist Scholarship and Colonial Discourses." In Chandra Talpade Mohanty, Ann Russo, and Lourdes Torres, eds., *Third World Women and the Politics of Feminism*, pp. 333–358. Indianapolis, IN: Indiana University Press.

Money, John. 1985. *Destroying Angel: Sex, Fitness, and Food in the Legacy of Degeneracy Theory, Graham Crackers, Kellogg's Corn Flakes, and American Health History.* Buffalo, NY: Prometheus Books.

Moore, Francis, Justin Mankin, and Austin Becker. 2015. "Challenges in Integrating the Climate and Social Sciences for Studies of Climate Change and Adaptation." In Jessica Barnes and Michael Dove, *Climate Cultures: Anthropological Perspectives on Climate Change*, pp. 169–195. New Haven, CT: Yale University Press.

Moran, Mary. 1997. "Warriors or Soldiers? Masculinity and Ritual Tranvestism in the Liberian Civil War." In Louise Lamphere, Helena Ragone, and Patricia Zavella, eds., *Situated Lives: Gender and Culture in Everyday Life*, pp. 440–450. Chicago, IL: University of Chicago Press.

Morgan, Edmund. 1975. *American Slavery, American Freedom.* New York: W. W. Norton.

Morgan, Lewis Henry. 1871. *Systems of Consanguinity and Affinity of the Human Family.* Washington, DC: Smithsonian Institution.

Morgan, Lewis Henry. 1877. *Ancient Society.* Chicago, IL: Charles Kerr & Company.

Morris, Rosalind C. 1995. All Made Up: Performance Theory and the New Anthropology of Sex and Gender. *Annual Review of Anthropology* 24:567–592.

Mullen, Jethro, and Schams Elwazer. 2015. ISIS Destroys Arch of Triumph in Syria's Palmyra Ruins. *CNN*, October 5, 2015. Accessed on November 26, 2015: http://www.cnn.com/2015/10/05/middleeast/syria-isis-palmyra-arch-of-triumph/

Mullings, Leith. 2005. Interrogating Racism: Toward an Antiracist Anthropology. *Annual Review of Anthropology* 34:667–693.

Munson, Barbara. 1999. Not for Sport. *Teaching Tolerance Magazine.* Accessed on July 31, 2010: http://www.tolerance.org/magazine/number-15-spring-1999/not-sport.

Murray, Gerald. 1987. "The Domestication of Wood in Haiti: A Case Study in Applied Evolution." In R. M. Wulff and S. J. Fiske, eds., *Anthropological Praxis: Translating Knowledge into Action*, pp. 223–240. Boulder, CO: Westview Press.

Myerhoff, Barbara G. 1974. *Peyote Hunt: The Sacred Journey of the Huichol Indians.* Ithaca, NY: Cornell University Press.

Nabhan, Gary Paul. 1997. *Cultures of Habitat: On Nature, Culture, and Story.* Washington, DC: Counterpoint.

Nabhan, Gary Paul. 2001. "Cultural Perceptions of Ecological Interactions: An 'Endangered People's' Contribution to the Conservation of Biological and Linguistic Diversity." In Lisa Maffi, ed., *On Biocultural Diversity: Linking Language, Knowledge, and the Environment*, pp. 145–156. Washington, DC: Smithsonian Institution Press.

Nadasdy, Paul. 2005. The Anti-Politics of TEK: The Institutionalizaton of Co-Management Discourse and Practice. *Anthropologica* 47(2):215–232.

Nader, Laura. 1979. Disputing Without the Force of Law. *Yale Law Journal* 88(5):998–1021.

Nader, Laura. 1990. *Harmony Ideology: Justice and Control in a Zapotec Mountain Village.* Stanford, CA: Stanford University Press.

Nader, Laura. 1995. "Civilization and Its Negotiators." In Pat Caplan, ed., *Understanding Disputes: The Politics of Argument,* pp. 39–63. Oxford, UK: Berg Publishers.

Nader, Laura, ed. 1996. *Naked Science: Anthropological Inquiry into Boundaries, Power, and Knowledge.* New York: Routledge.

Nader, Laura. 2001. The Underside of Conflict Management—in Africa and Elsewhere. *IDS Bulletin* 32(1):19–27.

Nader, Laura. 2007. What's Good About Conflict? *Anthropology News* 48(6):14–15.

Nader, Laura, and Harry F. Todd, eds. 1978. *The Disputing Process— Law in Ten Societies.* New York: Columbia University Press.

Nagengast, Carole. 1994. Violence, Terror, and the Crisis of the State. *Annual Review of Anthropology* 23:109–136.

Nagengast, Carole, and Michael Kearney. 1990. Mixtec Ethnicity: Social Identity, Political Consciousness, and Political Activism. *Latin American Research Review* 25(2):61–92.

Nanda, Serena. 1994. "Hijras: An Alternative Sex and Gender Role in India." In Gilbert Herdt, ed., *Third Sex, Third Gender: Beyond Sexual Dimorphism in Culture and History,* pp. 373–417. New York: Zone Books.

Nanda, Serena. 2000. *Gender Diversity: Crosscultural Variations.* Prospect Heights, IL: Waveland Press.

Nash, June. 1981. Ethnographic Aspects of the World Capitalist System. *Annual Review of Anthropology* 10:393–423.

Nash, June. 2007. Consuming Interests: Water, Rum, and Coca-Cola from Ritual Propitiation to Corporate Expropriation in Highland Chiapas. *Cultural Anthropology* 22(4):621–639.

Nash, Manning. 1958. *Machine Age Maya.* Glencoe, IL: Free Press.

Natcher, David C., Susan Hickey, and Clifford G. Hickey. 2005. Co-Management: Managing Relationships, Not Resources. *Human Organization* 64(3):240–250.

National Collegiate Athletic Association (NCAA). 2005. "NCAA Executive Committee Issues Guidelines for Use of Native American Mascots at Championship Events." (Released August 5). NCAA Press Release Archive. Accessed August 2014: http://vNCAA%2BExecutive%2BCommittee%2BIssues%2B Guidelines%2Bfor%2BUse%2Bof%2BNative%2BAmerican %2BMascots%2Bat%2BChampionship%2BEvents.html.

National Public Radio. 2009. Brian Lehrer Interviews Nancy Scheper-Hughes, July 24, 2009. Accessed on May 18, 2017, at: http://www.wnyc.org/shows/bl/episodes/2009/07/24/ segments/137306

Navarro, Z. 2006. In Search of Cultural Interpretation of Power. *IDS Bulletin* 37(6):11–22.

Nederveen Pieterse, J. 2004. *Globalization and Culture: Global Mélange.* Lanham, MD: Rowman & Littlefield.

Nevins, M. Eleanor. 2013. *Lessons from Fort Apache Beyond Language Endangerment and Maintenance.* Chichester, UK: Wiley-Blackwell.

Norberg, Johan. 2006. "How Globalization Conquers Poverty." Accessed on November 19, 2006: http://www.cato.org/special/ symposium/essays/norberg.html.

Nordstrom, Carolyn R. 1988. Exploring Pluralism: The Many Faces of Ayurveda. *Social Science and Medicine* 27(5):479–489.

Nyamwaya, D. O. 1993. Anthropology and HIV/AIDS Prevention in Kenya: New Ways of Cooperation. *AIDS and Society* 4(4):4, 8.

Oberschall, Anthony. 2000. The Manipulation of Ethnicity: From Ethnic Cooperation to Violence and War in Yugoslavia. *Ethnic and Racial Studies* 23(6):982–1001.

O'Connor, James. 1998. *Natural Causes: Essays in Ecological Marxism.* New York: Guilford.

O'Hanlon, Michael, and Robert L. Welsch, eds. 2000. *Hunting the Gatherers: Ethnographic Collectors, Agents and Agency in Melanesia, 1870s–1930s.* New York: Berghahn.

Omi, Michael, and Howard Winant, eds. 1996. *Racial Formation in the United States.* 2nd edition. New York: Routledge.

Ong, Aihwa. 1988. The Production of Possession: Spirits and the Multinational Corporation in Malaysia. *American Ethnologist* 15(1):28–42.

Ong, Aihwa. 1999. *Flexible Citizenship: The Cultural Logics of Transnationality.* Durham, NC: Duke University Press.

Ong, Aihwa. 2006. *Neoliberalism as Exception: Mutations in Citizenship and Sovereignty.* Durham, NC: Duke University Press.

Orlove, Ben. 2005. "Human Adaptation to Climate Change: A Review of Three Historical Cases and Some General Perspectives." *Environmental Science and Policy* 8:589–600.

Ortner, Sherry B. 1971. On Key Symbols. *American Anthropologist* 75:1338–46.

Ortner, Sherry B. 1974. "Is Female to Male as Nature Is to Culture?" In Michelle Rosaldo and Louise Lamphere, eds., *Woman, Culture, and Society,* pp. 67–88. Stanford, CA: Stanford University Press.

Ortner, Sherry B. 1989. *High Religion: A Cultural and Political History of Sherpa Buddhism.* Princeton, NJ: Princeton University Press.

Ortner, Sherry B. 1996. *Making Gender: The Politics and Erotics of Culture.* Boston, MA: Beacon Press.

Ortner, Sherry B. 2006. *Anthropology and Social Theory: Culture, Power, and the Acting Subject.* Durham, NC: Duke University Press.

Osburg, John. 2013. *Anxious Wealth: Money and Morality Among China's New Rich.* Stanford, CA: Stanford University Press.

Ottenberg, Simon. 1991. Review of "Into the Heart of Africa." *African Arts* 24(3):79–82.

Owusu, Maxwell. 1992. Democracy and Africa: A View from the Village. *Journal of Modern African Studies* 30(3):369–396.

Owusu, Maxwell. 1996. Tradition and Transformation: Democracy and the Politics of Popular Power in Ghana. *Journal of Modern African Studies* 34(2):307–343.

Parent, Anthony S., Jr. 2003. *Foul Means: The Formation of Slave Society in Virginia, 1660–1740.* Chapel Hill, NC: University of North Carolina Press.

Parker, Richard. 1989. Acquired Immunodeficiency Syndrome in Urban Brazil. *Medical Anthropology Quarterly* 1(2):155–175.

Parker, Richard. 2001. Sexuality, Culture, and Power in HIV/AIDS Research. *Annual Review of Anthropology* 30:163–179.

Parker, R. G. 2009. *Bodies, Pleasures, and Passions: Sexual Culture in Contemporary Brazil.* 2nd edition. Nashville, TN: Vanderbilt University Press.

Parkin, David, and Stanley Ulijaszek, eds. 2007. *Holistic Anthropology: Emergence and Convergence.* New York: Berghahn Books.

Parry, Jonathan, and Maurice Bloch, eds. 1989. *Money and the Morality of Exchange.* Cambridge, UK: Cambridge University Press.

Parsons, Talcott. 1951. *The Social System.* Glencoe, IL: The Free Press.

Partalidou, M., and Anthopoulou, T. 2016. Urban Allotment Gardens During Precarious Times: From Motives to Lived Experiences. *Sociologia Ruralis.* doi:10.1111/soru.12117.

Partners in Health. 2010. *Partners in Health* web page. Accessed on May 18, 2017, at: http://www.pih.org/

Patel, Raj. 2007. *Stuffed and Starved: The Hidden Battle for the World Food System.* London: Melville House.

Patel, Raj. 2008. *Stuffed and Starved: Markets, Power, and the Hidden Battle for the World's Food System.* New York: Harper Perennial.

Patterson, Penny, director. 2003. *Koko and Friends.* Video recording, produced by the Gorilla Foundation, distributed by Dave West, Utah Film and Video.

Pech, Marie-Estelle. 2015. L'attentat le plu meurtrier depuis Vitry-Le-François en 1961 [The deadliest attack since Vitry-Le-François]. *Le Figaro,* Jan. 8, 2015. Accessed on January 16, 2017: http://www.lefigaro.fr/actualite-france/2015/01/07/01016-20150107ARTFIG00178-historique-des-attentats-en-france-depuis-1994.php

Peet, Richard, and Michael Watts, eds. 2004. *Liberation Ecologies: Environment, Development, Social Movements.* 2nd edition. London: Routledge.

Pei-Chia, Lan. 2008. "Global Cinderellas: Sexuality, Power, and Situational Practices Across Borders." In Stevi Jackson, Lui Jieyu, and Woo Juhyun, eds., *East Asian Sexualities: Modernity, Gender, and New Sexual Cultures,* pp. 33–51. London: Zed Books.

People of Color Environmental Leadership Summit. 1991. "Principles of Environmental Justice." Accessed on February 17, 2017: http://www.ejnet.org/ej/principles.html

Peters, William, producer. 1970. *Eye of the Storm.* Human Relations Film Series. Videocassette. New York: Insight Media.

Peters, William, producer. 2005. *A Class Divided.* PBS Video. (Originally broadcast Mar. 26, 1985, on *Frontline.*)

Pinker, Steven. 1994. *The Language Instinct.* New York: W. Morrow and Co.

Pinker, Steven. 1997. *How the Mind Works.* New York: Norton.

Piot, Charles. 1999. *Remotely Global: Village Modernity in West Africa.* Chicago, IL: University of Chicago Press.

Polanyi, Karl. 1944/1975. *The Great Transformation.* New York: Octagon Books.

Pottier, Johan. 1999. *The Anthropology of Food: The Social Dynamics of Food Security.* Cambridge, UK: Polity Press.

Powdermaker, Hortense. 1944. *Probing Our Prejudices: A Unit for High School Students.* New York: Harper and Brothers Publishers.

Pretty, Jules. 2002. *Agri-Culture: Reconnecting People, Land, and Nature.* London: Earthscan.

Price, David. 2002. Past Wars, Present Dangers, Future Anthropologies. *Anthropology Today* 18(1):3–5.

Purdum, Todd S. 2004. At Rites for Reagan, Soaring Farewells. *New York Times* (Late edition) June 12, 2004, p. A1.

Radcliffe-Brown, Alfred R. 1941. The Study of Kinship Systems. *Journal of the Royal Anthropological Institute of Great Britain and Ireland* 71(1/2):1–18.

Radcliffe-Brown, Alfred R. 1952. *Structure and Function in Primitive Society: Essays and Addresses.* Glencoe, IL: Free Press.

Radin, Paul. 1927. *Primitive Man as Philosopher.* New York: D. Appleton and Co.

Ragoné, Helena. 1996. Chasing the Blood Tie: Surrogate Mothers, Adoptive Mothers and Fathers. *American Ethnologist* 23(2):352–365.

Rahnema, Majid, and Victoria Bawtree. 1997. *The Post-Development Reader.* London: Zed Press.

Ramos, Alcida Rita. 1990. Ethnology Brazilian Style. *Cultural Anthropology* 5(4):452–472.

Ramos, Alcida Rita. 2000. Anthropologist as Political Actor: Between Activism and Suspicion. *Journal of Latin American Anthropology* 4(2)/5(1):172–189.

Rapp, Rayna. 1992. "Anthropology: Feminist Methodologies for the Science of Man." In S. R. Zalk and J. Gordon-Kelter, eds., *Revolutions in Knowledge: Feminism in the Social Sciences,* pp. 79–92. Boulder, CO: Westview Press.

Rappaport, Roy. 1984. *Pigs for the Ancestors: Ritual in the Ecology of a New Guinea People.* 2nd edition. Prospect Heights, IL: Waveland Press.

Rasmussen, Susan. 1991. Modes of Persuasion: Gossip, Song, and Divination in Tuareg Conflict Resolution. *Anthropological Quarterly* 64(1):30–46.

Research Advisory Committee on Gulf War Veterans' Illnesses. 2008. *Research Advisory Council on Gulf War Veterans' Illnesses* web page. Accessed on May 18, 2017: http://www1.va.gov/rac-gwvi/

Rex, John. 1999. "Racism, Institutionalized and Otherwise." In Roger S. Gottlieb (series ed.) and Leonard Harris (volume ed.), *Key Concepts in Critical Theory: Racism,* pp. 141–160. Amherst, NY: Humanity Books.

Rice, Andrew. 2016. Is Jim Kim Destroying the World Bank—Or Saving It From Itself? *Foreign Policy,* April 27, 2016. Accessed on January 17, 2017: http://foreignpolicy.com/2016/04/27/is-jim-yong-kim-destroying-the-world-bank-development-finance/

Richards, Audrey. 1939. *Land, Labor, and Diet in Northern Rhodesia: An Economic Study of the Bemba.* Oxford, UK: Oxford University Press.

Richards, Paul. 1996. *Fighting for the Rainforest.* London: James Currey.

Richardson, Jane, and Alfred L. Kroeber. 1940. Three Centuries of Women's Dress Fashions: A Quantitative Analysis. *University of California Anthropological Records* 5(2):i–iv, 100–53.

Riches, David. 1986. "The Phenomenon of Violence." In David Riches, ed., *The Anthropology of Violence,* pp. 1–27. Oxford, UK: Basil Blackwell.

Ritzer, George. 1996. *The McDonaldization of Society: An Investigation into the Changing Character of Contemporary Social Life.* Thousand Oaks, CA: Pine Forge Press.

Rivers, William H. R. 1906. *The Todas.* London: Macmillan.

Rivoli, Pietra. 2005. *The Travels of a T-Shirt in the Global Economy: An Economist Examines the Markets, Power, and Politics of World Trade.* Hoboken, NJ: John Wiley & Sons.

Robarchek, Clayton A. 1979. Learning to Fear: A Case Study of Emotional Conditioning. *American Ethnologist* 6(3):555–567.

Robarchek, Clayton A., and Robert Knox Dentan. 1987. Blood Drunkenness and the Bloodthirsty Semai: Unmaking Another Anthropological Myth. *American Anthropologist* 89(2):356–365.

Robben, Antonius. 1989. *Sons of the Sea Goddess: Economic Practice and Discursive Conflict in Brazil.* New York: Columbia University Press.

Robbins, Richard. 2001. *Cultural Anthropology: A Problem-Based Approach.* 3rd edition. Itasca, IL: F. E. Peacock Publishers.

Robbins, Richard. 2005. *Global Problems and the Culture of Capitalism.* 3rd edition. Boston, MA: Pearson/Allyn and Bacon.

Rosaldo, Michelle Zimbalist. 1974. "Woman, Culture, and Society: A Theoretical Overview." In Michelle Rosaldo and Louise Lamphere, eds., *Woman, Culture, and Society,* pp. 17–42. Stanford, CA: Stanford University Press.

Rosaldo, Renato. 1989. *Culture and Truth: The Remaking of Social Analysis.* Boston, MA: Beacon Press.

Roscoe, Will. 1994. "How to Become a Berdache: Toward a Unified Analysis of Gender Diversity." In Gilbert Herdt, ed., *Third Sex, Third Gender: Beyond Sexual Dimorphism in Culture and History,* pp. 329–372. New York: Zone Books.

Rouse, Roger. 1991. Mexican Migration and the Social Space of Postmodernism. *Diaspora: A Journal of Transnational Studies* 1(1):8–23.

Rowlands, M. and J. P. Warnier. 1988. Sorcery, Power and the Modern State in Cameroon. *Man* (n.s.) 23:118–132.

Sahlins, Marshall. 1965. "On the Sociology of Primitive Exchange." In M. Banton, ed., *The Relevance of Models for Social Anthropology,* pp. 123–236. ASA Monographs, 1. London: Tavistock.

Sahlins, Marshall. 1972. *Stone Age Economics.* Chicago, IL: Aldine-Atherton.

Sahlins, Marshall. 1976. *Culture and Practical Reason.* Chicago, IL: University of Chicago Press.

Sahlins, Marshall. 1999. Two or Three Things That I Know About Culture. *Journal of the Royal Anthropological Institute* 5(3):399–421.

Sahlins, Marshall, and Elman Service, eds. 1960. *Evolution and Culture.* Ann Arbor, MI: University of Michigan Press.

Said, Edward. 1978. *Orientalism.* New York: Pantheon Books.

Sakala, Leah. 2014. Breaking Down Mass Incarceration in the 2010 Census: State-by-State Incarceration Rates by Race/Ethnicity. *Prison Policy Initiative.* Accessed on February 17, 2017: https://www.prisonpolicy.org/reports/rates.html

Saliba, Emmanuelle. 2015. Paris Killer Cherif Kouachi Gave Interview to TV Channel Before He Died. *NBC News,* January 9, 2015. Accessed on January 16, 2017: http://www.nbcnews.com/storyline/paris-magazine-attack/paris-killer-cherif-kouachi-gave-interview-tv-channel-he-died-n283206

Sandweiss, Stephen. 1998. "The Social Construction of Environmental Justice." In David E. Camacho, ed., *Environmental Injustices, Political Struggles: Race, Class, and the Environment,* pp. 31–57. Durham, NC: Duke University Press.

Sanjek, Roger. 1990. "Vocabulary for Fieldnotes." In Roger Sanjek, ed., *Fieldnotes: The Making of Anthropology,* pp. 71–91. Ithaca, NY: Cornell University Press.

Sapir, Edward. 1921. *Language: An Introduction to the Study of Speech.* New York: Harcourt, Brace.

Sapir, Edward. 1929. The Status of Linguistics as a Science. *Language* 5(4):207–214.

Saussure, F. de. 1916. *Cours de linguistique générale.* Paris: Payot.

Saussure, F. de. 1986. *Course in General Linguistics.* LaSalle, IL: Open Court.

Sayer, Andrew. 2000. Moral Economy and Political Economy. *Studies in Political Economy* Spring:79–103.

Scheper-Hughes, Nancy. 1995. The Primacy of the Ethical: Propositions for a Militant Anthropology. *Current Anthropology* 15:227–283.

Scheper-Hughes, Nancy. 2004. Parts Unknown: Undercover Ethnography of the Organs-Trafficking Underworld. *Ethnography* 5:29–73.

Scheper-Hughes, Nancy, and Loïc Wacquant, eds. 2003. *Commodifying Bodies.* Thousand Oaks, CA: Sage Publications.

Schildkrout, Enid, and Curtis A. Keim. 1998. *The Scramble for Art in Central Africa.* Cambridge, UK: Cambridge University Press.

Schlosser, Eric. 2001. *Fast Food Nation: The Dark Side of the All-American Meal.* Boston, MA: Houghton Mifflin Company.

Scott, James. 2009. *The Art of Not Being Governed: An Anarchist History of Upland Southeast Asia.* New Haven, CT: Yale University Press.

Segal, Daniel A., and Sylvia J. Yanagisako, eds. 2005. *Unwrapping the Sacred Bundle: Reflections on the Disciplining of Anthropology.* Durham, NC: Duke University Press.

Seligman, Rebecca. 2005. Distress, Dissociation, and Embodied Experience: Reconsidering the Pathways to Mediumship and Mental Health. *Ethos* 33(1):71–99.

Sharma, Devinder. 2004. *Farmer's Suicides.* ZeeNet. Accessed on December 20, 2006: http://zcomm.org/znetarticle/farmers-suicides-by-devinder-sharma/

Sharma, Ursula. 1999. "Caste." In Frank Parkin (series ed.), *Concepts in the Social Sciences.* Buckingham, UK: Open University Press.

Sheridan, Michael. 2006. "Linguistic Models in Anthropology 101: Give Me the Cup." In P. Rice and D. McCurdy, eds. *Strategies in Teaching Anthropology,* pp. 54–56. 4th edition. Upper Saddle River, NJ: Prentice Hall Professional.

Shore, Bradd. 1996. *Culture in Mind: Cognition, Culture, and the Problem of Meaning.* New York: Oxford University Press.

Shorris, Earl. 1992. *Latinos: A Biography of the People.* New York: W. W. Norton.

Shorris, Earl. 2001. *Latinos: Biography of a People.* New York: W. W. Norton.

Sillitoe, Paul. 2002. Contested Knowledge, Contingent Classification: Animals in the Highlands of Papua New Guinea. *American Anthropologist* 104(4):1162–1171.

Silverblatt, Irene. 1988. "Political Memories and Colonizing Symbols: Santiago and the Mountain Gods of Colonial Peru." In Jonathan Hill (ed.), *Rethinking History and Myth: Indigenous South American Perspectives on the Past,* pp. 174–194. Urbana, IL: University of Illinois Press.

Simmons, Ozzie G. 1955. Popular and Modern Medicine in Mestizo Communities of Coastal Peru and Chile. *Journal of American Folklore* 68(1):57–71.

Sivo, Ellen. 2005. The DOs and DON'Ts of College Romance. *The Vermont Cynic* Nov. 29, 2005. Website accessed on June 3, 2017: https://vtcynic.com/36166/life/the-dos-and-donts-of-college-romance/.

Sloane, Patricia. 1999. *Islam, Modernity, and Entrepreneurship Among the Malays.* New York: St. Martin's Press.

Small, Meredith. 1998. *Our Babies, Ourselves: How Biology and Culture Shape How We Parent.* New York: Anchor Books.

Smedley, Audrey. 2007a. *The History of the Idea of Race . . . And Why It Matters.* Paper presented at the conference Race, Human Variation and Disease: Consensus and Frontiers, Warrenton, Virginia, March 14–17, 2007. Accessed on May 18, 2017, at: http://www.understandingrace.com/resources/papers_author.html

Smedley, Audrey. 2007b. *Race in North America: Origin and Evolution of a Worldview.* 3rd edition. Boulder, CO: Westview Press.

Smith, Adam. 1776/1976. *An Inquiry into the Nature and Causes of the Wealth of Nations.* Chicago, IL: University of Chicago Press.

Smith, M. Estellie. 2000. *Trade and Tradeoffs: Using Resources, Making Choices, and Taking Risks.* Long Grove, IL: Waveland Press.

Smith, Raymond T. 1984. Anthropology and the Concept of Social Class. *Annual Review of Anthropology* 13:467–494.

Society for Medical Anthropology. 2014. What Is Medical Anthropology? Accessed on June 1, 2014: http://www.medanthro.net/9/ comment-page-1/#comment-36

Spencer, Craig. 2015. Having and Fighting Ebola: Public Health Lessons from a Clinician Turned Patient. *New England Journal of Medicine* 372:1089–1091.

Spencer, Herbert. 1874. *The Principles of Sociology.* London: Williams and Norgate.

Spielmann, Katharine A., and James F. Eder. 1994. Hunters and Farmers: Then and Now. *Annual Review of Anthropology* 23:303–323.

Spiro, Melford E. 1958. *Children of the Kibbutz.* Cambridge, MA: Harvard University Press.

Spittler, Gerd. 1999. "In Praise of the Simple Meal: African and European Food Culture Compared." In Carola Lentz, ed., *Changing Food Habits: Case Studies from Africa, South America, and Europe,* pp. 27–42. Newark, NJ: Harwood Academic Publishers.

Spitulnik, Debra. 1998. "Mediating Unity and Diversity: The Production of Language Ideologies in Zambian Broadcasting." In Bambi B. Shieffelin, Katharyn A. Woolard, and Paul V. Kroskrity, eds., *Language Ideologies: Practice and Theory,* pp. 163–188. New York: Oxford University Press.

Stack, Carol B. 1997. *All Our Kin.* New York: Basic Books.

Starr, Paul. 1982. *The Social Transformation of American Medicine.* New York: Basic Books.

Steward, Julian. 1955. *Theory of Culture Change: The Methodology of Multilinear Evolution.* Urbana, IL: University of Illinois Press.

Stiles, Daniel. 1993. Nomads on Notice. *Natural History* 102(9):51–56.

Stocking, George W., Jr., ed. 1985. *History of Anthropology: Vol. 3. Objects and Others: Essays on Museums and Material Culture.* Madison, WI: University of Wisconsin Press.

Stoffle, Richard, Rebecca Toupal, and Nieves Zedeño. 2003. "Landscape, Nature, and Culture: A Diachronic Model of Human-Nature Adaptations." In H. Selin, ed., *Nature Across Cultures: Views of Nature and the Environment in Non-Western Cultures,* pp. 97–114. London: Kluwer Academic Publishers.

Stonich, Susan. 1995. "Development, Rural Impoverishment, and Environmental Destruction in Honduras." In M. Painter and W. Durham, eds., *The Social Causes of Environmental Destruction in Latin America,* pp. 63–99. Ann Arbor, MI: University of Michigan Press.

Strang, Veronica, and Mark Busse, eds. 2011. *Ownership and Appropriation.* New York: Berg.

Strathern, Marilyn. 1988. *The Gender of the Gift: Problems with Women and Problems with Society in Melanesia.* Berkeley, CA: University of California Press.

Strathern, Marilyn. 1990. *The Gender of the Gift: Problems with Women and Problems with Society in Melanesia.* Reprint. Berkeley, CA: University of California Press.

Strathern, Marilyn. 1996. "Enabling Identity? Biology, Choice and the New Reproductive Technologies." In S. Hall and P. du Gay, eds., *Questions of Cultural Identity,* pp. 37–52. London: Sage.

Strong, Pauline. 1996. Animated Indians: Critique and Contradiction in Commodified Children's Culture. *Cultural Anthropology* 11(3):405–424.

Sturtevant, William. 1964. "Studies in Ethnoscience." In A. Kimball Romney and Roy G. D'Andrade, eds., *Transcultural Studies of Cognition,* pp. 99–131. Menasha, WI: American Anthropological Association.

Sturtevant, William C. 1969. Does Anthropology Need Museums? *Proceedings of the Biological Society of Washington* 82:619–649.

Sullivan, Gerald. 1999. *Margaret Mead, Gregory Bateson, and Highland Bali: Fieldwork photographs of Bayung Gedé.* Chicago, IL: University of Chicago Press.

Sutton, David. 2011. Eating in Times of Financial Crisis. *Food Anthropology: A Blog of the Society for the Anthropology of Food and Nutrition.* June 27, 2011. Website accessed on February 17, 2017: https://foodanthro.com/2011/06/27/eating-in-times-of-financial-crisis/

Tainter, Joseph. 2006. Archaeology of Overshoot and Collapse. *Annual Review of Anthropology* 35:59–74.

Tannen, Deborah. 1990. *You Just Don't Understand: Men and Women in Conversation.* New York: Morrow.

Tator, Carol, Frances Henry, and Winston Mattis. 1998. *Challenging Racism in the Arts: Case Studies of Controversy and Conflict.* Toronto: University of Toronto Press.

Tedlock, Dennis. 1972. "Pueblo Literature: Style and Verisimilitude." In Alfonso Ortiz, ed., *New Perspectives on the Pueblos,* pp. 219–242. Albuquerque, NM: University of New Mexico Press.

Tedlock, Dennis. 1988. "Ethnography as Interaction: The Storyteller, the Audience, the Fieldworker, and the Machine." In Regna Darnell and Michael K. Foster, eds., *Native North American Patterns,* pp. 80–94. Papers of the Canadian Ethnology Service 112. Hull, Quebec: Canadian Museum of Civilization.

Tedlock, Dennis. 1993. *Breath on the Mirror: Mythic Voices and Visions of the Living Maya.* San Francisco, CA: HarperSanFrancisco.

Teeter, Karl V. 1964. "Anthropological Linguistics" and Linguistic Anthropology. *American Anthropologist* 66(4), Part 1:878–879.

Tharoor, Shashi. 1999. The Future of Civil Conflict. *World Policy Journal* 16(1):1–11.

Thomas, K. 1983. *Man and the Natural World: Changing Attitudes in England, 1500–1800.* New York: Oxford University Press.

Thomas, Mark. 2008. *Belching Out the Devil: Global Adventures with Coca-Cola.* London: Ebury Publishing.

Thomas, Nicholas. 1989. Material Culture and Colonial Power: Ethnological Collecting and the Establishment of Colonial Rule in Fiji. *Man* 24(1):41–56.

Thomas, Wesley. 1997. "Navajo Cultural Constructions of Gender and Sexuality." In Sue-Ellen Jacobs, Wesley Thomas, and Sabine Lang, eds., *Two-Spirit People: Native American Gender Identity, Sexuality, and Spirituality,* pp. 156–173. Urbana, IL: University of Illinois Press.

Thomson, Rob, Tamar Murachver, and James Green. 2001. Where Is the Gender in Gendered Language? *Psychological Science* 12:171–175.

Tibon, Jorelik. N.d. "What is 'Mo'? Traditional Conservation Sites in the Marshall Islands." *Republic of the Marshall Islands Biodiversity Clearinghouse Mechanism.* Accessed on February 17, 2017: http://biormi.org/index_navmap.shtml?en/community.html

Tierney, Patrick. 2000. *Darkness in El Dorado: How Scientists and Journalists Devastated the Amazon.* New York: W. W. Norton.

Tilley, Christopher. 1990. *Reading Material Culture.* Oxford, UK: Blackwell.

Tilley, Christopher. 1991. *Material Culture and Text: The Art of Ambiguity.* London: Routledge.

Toren, Christina. 1996. "Psychological Anthropology." In Alan Barnard and Jonathan Spencer, eds., *Encyclopedia of Social and Cultural Anthropology,* pp. 456–461. London: Routledge.

Trevor-Roper, Hugh R. 1983. "The Invention of Tradition: The Highland Tradition of Scotland." In Eric Hobsbawn and Terence Ranger, Eds., *The Invention of Tradition,* pp. 15–41. Cambridge, UK: Cambridge University Press.

Trubek, Amy. 2008. *The Taste of Place: A Cultural Journey Into Terroir.* Berkeley, CA: University of California Press.

Truman, Harry S. 1949. Inaugural Address, January 20, 1949. Accessed on June 3, 2014: http://www.bartleby.com/124/pres53.html

Tsing, Anna Lowenhaupt. 2000. The Global Situation. *Cultural Anthropology* 15(3):327–360.

Tsing, Anna Lowenhaupt. 2005. *Friction: An Ethnography of Global Connection.* Princeton, NJ: Princeton University Press.

Tuhiwai Smith, Linda. 2012. *Decolonizing Methodologies: Research and Indigenous Peoples.* 2nd edition. London: Zed.

Turner, Victor. 1967. *The Forest of Symbols: Aspects of Ndembu Ritual.* Ithaca, NY: Cornell University Press.

Turner, Victor. 1969. *The Ritual Process: Structure and Anti-Structure.* Chicago, IL: Aldine.

Two Bears, Davina R. 2006. Navajo Archaeologist Is Not an Oxymoron: A Tribal Archaeologist's Experience. *American Indian Quarterly* 30(3–4):381–387.

Tylor, E. B. 1871. *Primitive Culture: Researches into the Development of Mythology, Philosophy, Religion, Art, and Custom.* London: John Murray.

Ulijaszek, Stanley. 2007. "Bioculturalism." In David Parkin and Stanley Ulijaszek, eds., *Holistic Anthropology: Emergence and Convergence,* pp. 21–51. New York: Berghahn Books.

Ulijaszek, Stanley J., and Hayley Lofink. 2006. Obesity in Biocultural Perspective. *Annual Reviews of Anthropology* 35:337–360.

UNESCO. 2015a. Cultural Landscape and Archaeological Remains of the Bamiyan Valley. *World Heritage List,* No. 208. Accessed on November 26, 2015: http://whc.unesco.org/en/list/208

UNESCO. 2015b. Site of Palmyra. *World Heritage List,* No. 23. Accessed on November 26, 2015: http://whc.unesco.org/en/list/23

UNESCO. 2015c. *World Heritage List, Delisted Sites.* Accessed on November 26, 2015: http://whc.unesco.org/en/list/?&&&delisted=1

Underhill, Paco. 2005. *Call of the Mall: A Walking Tour Through the Crossroads of Our Shopping Culture.* New York: Simon and Schuster.

United Nations. 2016. *International Migration Report 2015.* Department of Economic and Social Affairs. United Nations, New York. Accessed on February 17, 2017: http://www.un.org/en/development/desa/population/migration/publications/migrationreport/docs/MigrationReport2015_Highlights.pdf

Unsworth, Tim. 1998. Murder in Black and White. *U.S. Catholic* 63(3):35–38.

U.S. Census Office, J. D. B. DeBow, superintendent. 1853. *The Seventh Census of the United States: 1850.* Washington, DC: Robert Armstrong, Public Printer.

Valentine, David. 2003. "The Calculus of Pain": Violence, Anthropological Ethics, and the Category Transgender. *Ethnos* 68(1):27–48.

Valentine, David. 2007. *Imagining Transgender: An Ethnography of a Category.* Durham, NC: Duke University Press.

Van den Berghe, Pierre. 1999. "Ethnicity as Kin Selection: The Biology of Nepotism." In Roger S. Gottlieb (series ed.) and Leonard Harris (volume ed.), *Key Concepts in Critical Theory: Racism,* pp. 50–73. Amherst, NY: Humanity Books.

Vandermeer, John, and Ivette Perfecto. 1995. *Breakfast of Biodiversity: The Truth About Rainforest Destruction.* Oakland, CA: Food First.

Veseth, Michael. 2005. *Globaloney: Unraveling the Myths of Globalization.* Lanham, MD: Rowman & Littlefield.

Vincent, Joan. 1978. Political Anthropology: Manipulative Strategies. *Annual Review of Anthropology* 7:175–194.

Viswesaran, Kamala. 1997. Histories of Feminist Ethnography. *Annual Review Anthropology* 26:591–621.

Vivanco, Luis. 2006. *Green Encounters: Shaping and Contesting Environmentalism in Rural Costa Rica.* New York: Berghahn Books.

Vivanco, Luis. 2013. *Reconsidering the Bicycle: An Anthropological Perspective on a New (Old) Thing.* New York: Routledge.

Voegelin, C. F. 1965. Sociolinguistics, Ethnolinguistics, and Anthropological Linguistics. *American Anthropologist* 67(2):484–485.

Vournelis, Leo. 2011. Strained Yogurt and People in Greece. *Food Anthropology* blog. Accessed on January 22, 2016: https://foodanthro.com/2011/10/12/strained-yogurt-and-people-in-greece/

Wade, Edwin L. 1985. "The Ethnic Art Market in the American Southwest, 1880–1980." In Richard Handler (series ed.) and George W. Stocking, Jr. (volume ed.), *History of Anthropology: Vol. 3, Objects and Others: Essays on Museums and Material Culture,* pp. 167–191. Madison, WI: University of Wisconsin Press.

Wade, Peter. 1997. *Race and Ethnicity in Latin America.* London: Pluto Books.

Wagner, Roy. 1967. *The Curse of Souw: Principles of Daribi Clan Definition and Alliance.* Chicago, IL: University of Chicago Press.

Wagner, Roy. 1969. "Marriage Among the Daribi." In R. M. Glasse and M. J. Meggitt, eds., *Pigs, Pearlshells, and Women: Marriage in the New Guinea Highlands,* pp. 56–76. Englewood Cliffs, NJ: Prentice Hall.

Wagner, Roy. 1975. *The Invention of Culture.* Englewood Cliffs: Prentice-Hall.

Wallace, Anthony F. C. 1956. Revitalization Movements: Some Theoretical Considerations for Their Comparative Study. *American Anthropologist* 58:264–281.

Wallace, Anthony F. C. 1966. *Religion: An Anthropological View.* New York: Random House.

Wallace, Anthony F. C. 1970. *The Death and Rebirth of the Seneca.* New York: Knopf.

Wallman, Joel. 1992. *Aping Language.* Cambridge, UK: Cambridge University Press.

Walsh, Lorena. 2013. Development of Slavery in the 17th-century Chesapeake. Website accessed on June 2, 2017: http://www.historyisfun.org/video/development-slavery/.

Warren, Kay. 1998. *Indigenous Movements and Their Critics: Pan-Maya Activism in Guatemala.* Princeton, NJ: Princeton University Press.

Watson, James L., and Melissa L. Caldwell, eds. 2005. *The Cultural Politics of Food and Eating: A Reader.* Malden, MA: Blackwell Publishing.

Watson-Gegeo, Karen Ann, and Geoffrey White, eds. 1990. *Disentangling: Conflict Discourse in Pacific Societies.* Stanford, CA: Stanford University Press.

Watters, Ethan. 2011. *Crazy Like Us: The Globalization of the American Psyche.* New York: Free Press.

Wax, Murray, and Felix Moos. 2004. Anthropology: Vital or Irrelevant. *Human Organization* 63(2):246–247.

Weiner, Annette B. 1976. *Women of Value, Men of Renown: New Perspectives in Trobriand Exchange.* Austin, TX: University of Texas Press.

Weiner, Annette B. 1988. *The Trobrianders of Papua New Guinea.* Fort Worth, TX: Harcourt Brace Jovanovich College Publishers.

Weiner, Annette. 1992. *Inalienable Possessions: The Paradox of Keeping-While Giving.* Berkeley, CA: University of California Press.

Welsch, Robert L. 1983. "Traditional Medicine and Western Medical Options Among the Ningerum of Papua New Guinea." In Lola Romanucci-Ross, Daniel E. Moerman, and Laurence R. Tancredi, eds., *The Anthropology of Medicine: From Culture Toward Medicine,* pp. 32–53. New York: Praeger.

Welsch, Robert L. 2006. "Coaxing the Spirits to Dance." In Robert L. Welsch, Virginia-Lee Webb, and Sebastine Haraha, *Coaxing the Spirits to Dance: Art and Society in the Papuan Gulf of New Guinea,* pp. 4–44. Hanover, NH: Hood Museum of Art at Dartmouth College.

Welsch, Robert L. 2013. "Exploring Linguistic Diversity Along the North Coast of New Guinea." In J. Forbes Farmer, ed., *The Social Sciences: Understanding Inquiry and Analysis,* pp. 17–29. Buford, GA: LAD Custom Publishing.

Welsch, Robert L., Luis A. Vivanco, and Augustin Fuentes. 2017. *Anthropology: Asking Questions About Human Origins, Diversity, and Culture.* New York: Oxford University Press.

Werner, Cynthia, and Duran Bell, eds. 2004. *Values and Valuables: From the Sacred to the Symbolic.* Lanham, MD: Rowman Altamira.

Westermark, George D. 1998. History, Opposition, and Salvation in Agarabi Adventism. *Pacific Studies* 21(3):51–71.

Weston, Kath. 1993. Lesbian/Gay Studies in the House of Anthropology. *Annual Review of Anthropology* 22:339–367.

White, Leslie. 1949. *The Science of Culture: A Study of Man and Culture.* New York: Farrar, Strauss.

Whitehead, Harriet. 1981. "The Bow and the Burden Strap: A New Look at Institutionalized Homosexuality in Native North America." In Sherry Ortner and Harriet Whitehead, eds. *Sexual Meanings: The Cultural Construction of Gender and Sexuality,* pp. 80–115. Cambridge, UK: Cambridge University Press.

Whitehead, Neil L. 2004. "Cultures, Conflicts, and the Poetics of Violent Practice." In Neil Whitehead, ed., *Violence,* pp. 3–24. Santa Fe, NM: School of American Research.

Whorf, Benjamin Lee. 1956. *Language, Thought, and Reality: Selected Writings,* edited by John B. Carroll. Cambridge, MA: Technology Press of Massachusetts Institute of Technology.

Wiley, Andrea. 2004. "Drink Milk for Fitness": The Cultural Politics of Human Biological Variation and Milk Consumption in the United States. *American Anthropologist* 106(3):506–517.

Wiley, Andrea. 2011. *Reimagining Milk.* New York: Routledge.

Wilk, Richard, and Lisa Cliggett. 2007. *Economies and Cultures: Foundations of Economic Anthropology.* 2nd edition. Boulder, CO: Westview Press.

Wolf, Eric. 1984. *Europe and the People without History.* Berkeley, CA: University of California Press.

Wolf, Eric. 2001. *Pathways of Power: Building an Anthropology of the Modern World.* Berkeley, CA: University of California Press.

Woolard, Kathryn A. 1998. "Introduction: Language Ideology as a Field of Inquiry." In Bambi B. Shieffelin, Kathryn A. Woolard, and Paul V. Kroskrity, eds., *Language Ideologies: Practice and Theory,* pp. 3–47. New York: Oxford University Press.

Worthman, Carol M. 1995. Hormones, Sex, and Gender. *Annual Review of Anthropology* 24:593–616.

Wright, Lawrence. 1994. One Drop of Blood. *New Yorker,* July 25, pp. 46–55.

Yardley, Jim. 2012. Malnutrition Widespread in Indian Children, Report Finds. *New York Times,* January 10, 2012. Accessed on August 12, 2013: http://www.nytimes.com/2012/01/11/world/asia/malnutrition-in-india-is-widespread-report-finds.html.

Zagato, Alessandro, ed. 2015. *The Event of* Charlie Hebdo: *Imaginaries of Freedom and Control.* Oxford, UK: Berghahn.

Zurayk, Rami. 2011. Use Your Loaf: Why Food Prices Were Crucial in the Arab Spring. *The Guardian.* July 16, 2011. Accessed on February 17, 2017: https://www.theguardian.com/lifeandstyle/2011/jul/17/bread-food-arab-spring

Credits

CHAPTER 1

Chapter 1 opening photo (p. 2): Private Collection/The Stapleton Collection/Bridgeman Images; **Figure 1.1 (p. 5):** OUP; **Figure 1.2 (p. 7):** Bain Collection, Prints and Photographs Division, Library of Congress, LC-USZ62-99609; **Figure 1.3 (p. 9):** OUP; **Classic Contributions (p. 11):** Pitt Rivers Museum, Oxford, UK/Bridgeman Images; **Figure 1.4 (p. 12):** Nina Raingold/Getty Images; **Doing Fieldwork (p. 15):** Courtesy of Robert L. Welsch; **Figure 1.5 (p. 16):** OUP; **Figure 1.6 (p. 18):** Photo by Luis A. Vivanco; **Figure 1.7 (p. 19):** Courtesy of Robert L. Welsch; **Figure 1.8 (p. 21):** © FAO/ Alessandra Benedetti; **Figure 1.9 (p. 21):** Andrew Curry; **Figure 1.10 (p. 22):** James McKenna; **Figure 1.11 (p. 22):** Marybeth Nevins; **Figure 1.12 (p. 24):** National Archives and Records Administration; **Thinking Like an Anthropologist (p. 26):** cover of *Darkness in El Dorado,* by Patrick Tierney

CHAPTER 2

Chapter 2 opening photo (p. 30): AP Photo/Scott Boehm; **Figure 2.1 (p. 33):** OUP; **Figure 2.2 (p. 35):** Peters, J.M. 1977. *Pictorial Communication.* Capetown, South Africa: David Philip. p. 90; **Figure 2.3 (p. 36):** Alexander Atack/Alamy Stock Photo; **Figure 2.4 (p. 37):** PATRICK KOVARIK/ AFP/Getty Images; **Classic Contributions (p. 40):** Negative MNH 8301, National Anthropological Archives, Smithsonian Institution; **Figure 2.5 (p. 42):** Transportstyrelsen, public domain via Wikimedia Commons; **Figure 2.6 (p. 44):** mikecranephotography.com/Alamy Stock Photo; **Figure 2.7 (p. 46):** from *The Silent Friend* by R. and L. Perry & Co. (1847), via Archive.org; **Figure 2.8 (p. 47, top):** Bain Collection, Prints and Photographs Division, Library of Congress, LC-DIG-ggbain-15053; **Figure 2.8 (p. 47, bottom):** www.healthexhibits.com; **Thinking Like an Anthropologist (p. 48):** imageBROKER/Alamy Stock Photo; **Anthropologist as Problem Solver (p. 50):** University of British Columbia Archives, Photo by Frank Nowell [UBC 1.1/1643]; **Figure 2.9 (p. 51):** "Ninth Session of the UN Permanent Forum on Indigenous Issues" by Broddi Sigurðarson is licensed under CC BY-SA 2.0 from Wikimedia Commons

CHAPTER 3

Chapter 3 opening photo (p. 55): Lara Jo Regan/Gallery Stock; **Figure 3.1 (p. 57):** OUP; **Thinking Like an Anthropologist (p. 59):** AP Photo/Brian Kersey; **Figure 3.2 (p. 61):** London School of Economics and Political Science, MALINOWSKI/3/ARG/1; **Classic Contributions (p. 62):** Library of the London School of Economics and Political Science, MALINOWSKI/3/B/18/1; **Figure 3.3 (p. 64):** Courtesy of Robert L. Welsch; **Figure 3.4 (p. 66):** Courtesy of Luis A. Vivanco; **Figure 3.5 (p. 67):** Courtesy of Luis A. Vivanco; **Figure 3.6 (p. 68):** http://hraf.yale.edu/; **Figure 3.7 (p. 69, top):** Reproduced by permission of University of Cambridge Museum of Archaeology & Anthropology, N.22900.ACH2; **Figure 3.7 (p. 69, bottom):** Cambridge University Library; **Figure 3.8 (p. 71):** AP Photo; **Figure 3.9 (p. 72):** Smithsonian Institution, National Anthropological Archives; **Figure 3.10 (p. 73):** Bateson Idea Group; **Anthropologist as Problem Solver (p. 74, top):** © Fiona Watson/ Survival; **(bottom):** © Survival International; **Figure 3.11 (p. 75):** Photo by Candace Di Carlo. Used with permission of Philippe Bourgois

CHAPTER 4

Chapter 4 opening photo (p. 80): PeteSherrard/iStockphoto; **Figure 4.1 (p. 83):** OUP; **Figure 4.2 (p. 84):** University of Buffalo News; **Figure 4.3 (p. 86):** Gorilla Foundation; **Figure 4.4 (p. 87):** OUP; **Figure 4.5 (p. 88):** OUP; **Figure 4.6 (p. 91):** Tsuji/Getty Images; **Figure 4.7 (p. 91):** Jake Warga/Getty Images; **Figure 4.8 (p. 92):** AP Photo/Pablo Martinez Monsivais; **Figure 4.9 (p. 92):** Zoe Cormack; **Classic Contributions (p. 94):** Archives and Special Collections, Vassar College Library, Benedict 123.15; **Figure 4.10 (p. 95):** Photo by © Historical Picture Archive/CORBIS/ Corbis via Getty Images; **Figure 4.11 (p. 96):** underlying image WCS Data Archives, http://icsi. berkeley.edu/wcs/data.html; **Figure 4.12 (p. 98):** Courtesy of Robert L. Welsch; **Figure 4.13 (p. 98):** Megapress/Alamy Stock Photo; **Doing Fieldwork (p. 99):** Photo by Ira Bashkow; **Thinking Like an**

Anthropologist (p. 101, left): Kate Duerr/flickr; **Thinking Like an Anthropologist (p. 101, right):** NoDerog/iStockphoto

CHAPTER 5

Chapter 5 opening photo (p. 108): Photo by Ashley Cooper/Corbis via Getty Images; **Figure 5.1 (p. 111):** OUP; **Figure 5.2 (p. 113):** public domain via Wikimedia Commons; **Figure 5.3 (p. 114):** Photo by Alberto Buzzola/LightRocket via Getty Images; **Figure 5.4 (p. 115, top and middle):** Redrawn from Segal, A. (1993) *An Atlas of International Migration*. London: Hans Zell Publishers. Copyright remains with the estate of Aaron Segal; **Figure 5.4 (p. 115, bottom):** OUP; **Thinking Like an Anthropologist (p. 117):** Lynsey Addario; **Classic Contributions (p. 120):** By permission of Sydel Wolf; **Figure 5.5 (p. 121):** Courtesy of Luis A. Vivanco; **Figure 5.6 (p. 123):** Per-Anders Pettersson/Getty Images; **Figure 5.7 (p. 125):** © Paul Jeffrey; **Figure 5.8 (p. 128):** AP Photo/Mark Humphrey; **Figure 5.9 (p. 129):** Paw Media; **Doing Fieldwork (p. 131):** Photo by Qilai Shen/ Bloomberg via Getty Images

CHAPTER 6

Chapter 6 opening photo (p. 136): STR/AFP/Getty Images; **Figure 6.1 (p. 139):** OUP; **Figure 6.2 (p. 140, top):** Christer Fredriksson/Getty Images; **Figure 6.2 (p. 140, bottom):** Tim E White/ Getty Images; **Figure 6.3 (p. 141):** Photo by Found Image Holdings/Corbis via Getty Images; **Classic Contributions (p. 143):** 400.28014. Audrey Richards and harvesters, Mwamba. Photographed by Bronislaw Malinowski?, 1930s © RAI; **Figure 6.4 (p. 144):** Universal History Archive/UIG via Getty Images; **Thinking Like an Anthropologist (p. 146, top):** Rido/Shutterstock; **Thinking Like an Anthropologist (p. 146, bottom):** © Jamie Grill/Tetra Images/Corbis; **Figure 6.5 (p. 148):** REUTERS/Alamy Stock Photo; **Figure 6.6 (p. 150):** Survival International; **Figure 6.7 (p. 151):** Robert L. Welsch; **Figure 6.8 (p. 152):** ERIKA LARSEN/National Geographic Creative; **Figure 6.9 (p. 154):** © Ocean/Corbis; **Figure 6.10 (p. 156):** Tom Pietrasik; **Anthropologist as Problem Solver (p. 157, top):** courtesy of Teresa Mares—used with permission; **Anthropologist as Problem Solver (p. 157, bottom):** Design Pics Inc/Alamy Stock Photo

CHAPTER 7

Chapter 7 opening photo (p. 164): ISAAC MARTY/AFP/Getty Images; **Figure 7.1 (p. 167):** OUP; **Figure 7.2 (p. 168):** Drawn after "Pueblos Indígenas y Ecosistemas Naturales en Centroamérica y el Sur de México," National Geographic/Center for the Support of Native Lands; **Figure 7.3 (p. 169):** Photo by: Education Images/UIG via Getty Images; **Figure 7.4 (p. 170):** ART Collection/Alamy Stock Photo; **Figure 7.5 (p. 174):** Courtesy of Luis A. Vivanco; **Classic Contributions (p. 175):** Roy Rappaport Papers, Special Collections & Archives, UC San Diego; **Figure 7.6 (p. 176):** no known rights holder could be located; **Figure 7.7 (p. 178):** Gilder Lehrman Collection, New York, USA/ Bridgeman Images; **Figure 7.8 (p. 181):** OUP; **Doing Fieldwork (p. 182):** Rainer Wendt; **Thinking Like an Anthropologist (p. 184):** Image Source/Alamy Stock Photo; **Figure 7.9 (p. 186):** Bettmann/ Getty Images

CHAPTER 8

Chapter 8 opening photo (p. 190): Sim Chi Yin/VII/Redux; **Figure 8.1 (p. 193):** OUP; **Figure 8.2 (p. 194):** Spontoon Pipe Tomahawk from ANTIQUES ROADSHOW (http://www.pbs.org/ wgbh/roadshow/season/18/anaheim-ca/appraisals/spontoon-pipetomahawk-ca-1840--201303A07l) © 1997–2016 WGBH Educational Foundation; **Figure 8.3 (p. 196):** © Alexander Kovalenko | Dreamstime.com; **Classic Contributions (p. 197):** Photo by Ulf Andersen/Getty Images; **Figure 8.4 (p. 200):** richardmcguire.ca; **Figure 8.5 (p. 202):** AP Photo/Brett Deering, File; **Figure 8.6 (p. 204):** from *Argonauts of the Western Pacific* by Bronislaw Malinowski (1922); **Thinking Like an Anthropologist (p. 205):** London School of Economics and Political Science, Malinowski/3/5/19; **Figure 8.7 (p. 206):** PA Images/Alamy Stock Photo; **Figure 8.8 (p. 207):** AP Photo/Peter Kramer; **Figure 8.9 (p. 209):** Photo Lot 97 DOE Oceania: Poly: New Zealand: New Zealand Gov't 05097700, National Anthropological Archives, Smithsonian Institution; **Figure 8.10 (p. 210, top):** Daderot/Wikipedia; **Figure 8.10 (p. 210, bottom):** Photo by James Leynse/Corbis via Getty Images;

Figure 8.11 (p. 212): AP Photo/Richard Drew; **Anthropologist as Problem Solver (p. 214):** Debby Wong/Shutterstock

CHAPTER 9

Chapter 9 opening photo (p. 218): art by Apa Hugo, photo courtesy of Robert L. Welsch; **Figure 9.1 (p. 221):** OUP; **Figure 9.2 (p. 222):** © Anthony Bannister/Gallo Images/Corbis; **Classic Contributions (p. 224):** Pitt Rivers Museum; **Figure 9.3 (p. 225):** Photo by J. Carrier/Getty Images; **Figure 9.4 (p. 227):** Patrick T. Fallon/Bloomberg via Getty Images; **Figure 9.5 (p. 229):** art by Apa Hugo, photo courtesy of Robert L. Welsch; **Figure 9.6 (p. 230):** © Michel Setboun/Corbis; **Thinking Like an Anthropologist (p. 232):** AP Photo/Murad Sezer; **Figure 9.7 (p. 233):** WOOLAROC MUSEUM, BARTLESVILLE, OKLAHOMA; **Anthropologist as Problem Solver (p. 234):** Courtesy of Maxwell Owusu, photo by Shafica Ahmed; **Figure 9.8 (p. 236):** courtesy of Documentary Educational Resources; **Figure 9.9 (p. 238):** AP Photo; **Figure 9.10 (p. 240):** Photo by Craig Barritt/Getty Images for Electus Digital/WatchLOUD

CHAPTER 10

Chapter 10 opening photo (p. 246): North Wind Picture Archives via AP Images; **Figure 10.1 (p. 249):** OUP; **Figure 10.2 (p. 251):** after Agustín Fuentes, *Core Concepts in Biological Anthropology*, McGraw Hill 2007: 310, Figure 10.4; **Figure 10.3 (p. 255):** from *Pudd'nhead Wilson and Those Extraordinary Twins* by Mark Twain (1894) via HathiTrust; **Thinking Like an Anthropologist (p. 257):** Courtesy of Robert L. Welsch; **Figure 10.4 (p. 258):** Bettmann/Getty Images; **Figure 10.5 (p. 260):** Patti McConville/Alamy Stock Photo; **Figure 10.6 (p. 261):** Pictorial Press Ltd/Alamy Stock Photo; **Figure 10.7 (p. 262):** RAVEENDRAN/AFP/Getty Images; **Figure 10.8 (p. 264):** Library of Congress Prints and Photographs Division Washington, D.C. 20540 USA; **Classic Contributions (p. 265):** New York World-Telegram and the Sun Newspaper Photograph Collection (Library of Congress); **Figure 10.9 (p. 267):** Genna Martin/seattlepi.com; **Figure 10.10 (p. 268):** screenshot from *Saturday Night Live*; **Doing Fieldwork (p. 269):** Photographer: Lange, Dorothea. UC Berkeley, Bancroft Library

CHAPTER 11

Chapter 11 opening photo (p. 274): PASCAL GUYOT/AFP/Getty Images; **Figure 11.1 (p. 277):** OUP; **Figure 11.2 (p. 277):** © Iris Images; **Classic Contributions (p. 279):** Photo by George Rose/Getty Images; **Figure 11.3 (p. 281):** FABRICE COFFRINI/AFP/Getty Images; **Figure 11.4 (p. 283):** Courtesy of Kirk and Karen Endicott; **Figure 11.5 (p. 284, top):** Schlesinger Library, Radcliffe Institute, Harvard University/Bridgeman Images; **Figure 11.5 (p. 284, bottom):** Photo by Keystone/Getty Images; **Figure 11.6 (p. 285):** Jonatan Fernstrom/Getty Images; **Figure 11.7 (p. 288):** Photo by David Victor; **Figure 11.8 (p. 289):** INDRANIL MUKHERJEE/AFP/Getty Images; **Figure 11.9 (p. 290):** HECTOR MATA/AFP/Getty Images; **Thinking Like an Anthropologist (p. 292):** Photo by Jason Kempin/Getty Images for The Point Foundation; **Figure 11.10 (p. 293):** Photo by Arthur Siegel/The LIFE Images Collection/Getty Images; **Doing Fieldwork (p. 295):** AP Photo/Silvia Izquierdo

CHAPTER 12

Chapter 12 opening image (p. 300): Photo by Edgar Negrete/Clasos.com/LatinContent/Getty Images; **Figure 12.1 (p. 303):** OUP; **Figure 12.2 (p. 304, left):** Michael Ochs Archives/Getty Images; **Figure 12.2 (p. 304, right):** Prints and Photographs Division, Library of Congress, LC-DIG-ppmsca-08768; **Figure 12.3 (p. 305):** OUP; **Figure 12.4 (p. 306, top):** Collection 10: James Willard Schultz Photographs, 1859-1947, Merrill G. Burlingame Special Collections at Montana State University Libraries; **Figure 12.4 (p. 306, bottom):** Courtesy of Robert L. Welsch; **Figure 12.5 (p. 307):** OUP; **Figure 12.6 (p. 307):** OUP; **Figure 12.7 (p. 309):** OUP; **Classic Contributions (p. 310):** UC Berkeley, Hearst (Phoebe A.) Museum of Anthropology; **Thinking Like an Anthropologist (p. 311):** Trevor Thompson/Alamy Stock Photo; **Figure 12.8 (p. 312):** Library of Congress Prints and Photographs Division Washington, D.C. 20540 USA; **Figure 12.9 (p. 314, top):** © Irene Abdou Photography; **Figure 12.9 (p. 314, bottom):** Courtesy of Robert L. Welsch; **Figure 12.10 (p. 315, top):** Rolf Lunheim; **Figure 12.10 (p. 315, bottom):** REUTERS/Adnan Abidi; **Figure 12.11 (p. 317, top):** Photograph Collection, Prints and Photographs Division, Library of Congress,

LC-DIG-ppmsca-13196; **Figure 12.11 (p. 317, bottom):** GEORGE FREY/AFP/Getty Images; **Doing Fieldwork (p. 321):** AP Photo/The Salt Lake Tribune, Scott Sommerdorf

CHAPTER 13

Chapter 13 opening image (p. 328): AP Photo/BH; **Figure 13.1 (p. 331):** OUP; **Figure 13.2 (p. 332):** from *The Ghost-Dance Religion and the Sioux Outbreak of 1890* by James Mooney (1896), via Archive.org; **Figure 13.3 (p. 333):** Photo by SSPL/Getty Images; **Figure 13.4 (p. 335, left):** Photo by Dan Kitwood/Getty Images; **Figure 13.4 (p. 335, right):** AP Photo/Jessica Kourkounis; **Figure 13.5 (p. 338):** AP Photo/Michel Euler; **Figure 13.6 (p. 340):** Hood Museum of Art; **Figure 13.7 (p. 341):** Curtis (Edward S.) Collection, Prints and Photographs Division, Library of Congress, LC-USZ62-47016; **Figure 13.8 (p. 342):** Hood Museum of Art; **Figure 13.9 (p. 345):** Hood Museum of Art; **Classic Contributions (p. 346):** © National Portrait Gallery, London; **Figure 13.10 (p. 347):** Courtesy of Robert L. Welsch; **Figure 13.11 (p. 347):** AP Photo/Chris Clark; **Thinking Like an Anthropologist (p. 349):** Photo by Mario Tama/Getty Images; **Doing Fieldwork (p. 352):** Photo by Frank Bienewald/LightRocket via Getty Images

CHAPTER 14

Chapter 14 opening photo (p. 356): Richard Levine/Alamy Stock Photo; **Figure 14.1 (p. 359):** OUP; **Figure 14.2 (p. 362):** Hemis/Alamy Stock Photo; **Figure 14.3 (p. 362):** YASUYOSHI CHIBA/AFP/Getty Images; **Figure 14.4 (p. 364):** AP Photo/Jerome Delay; **Figure 14.5 (p. 365):** Image Source/iStockphoto; **Figure 14.6 (p. 367, top):** Prints and Photographs Division, Library of Congress, LC-USZ62019404; **Figure 14.6 (p. 367, bottom):** Bain Collection, Prints and Photographs Division, Library of Congress, LC-DIG-ggbain-09893; **Figure 14.7 (p. 368):** OUP; **Classic Contributions (p. 369):** Courtesy of Pan Tianshu; **Figure 14.8 (p. 370, top):** Photo by Jay Colton/The LIFE Images Collection/Getty Images; **Figure 14.8 (p. 370, bottom):** Breastfeeding promotion campaign poster developed by Arkansas Foundation for Medical Care, www.afmc.org, under contract with the Arkansas Department of Human Services, Division of Medical Services. Image copyright 2014 by Getty Images. All rights reserved; **Thinking Like an Anthropologist (p. 371):** AP Photo/Matt Dunham; **Figure 14.9 (p. 372):** Minnesota Historical Society; **Figure 14.10 (p. 373):** Courtesy of Robert L. Welsch; **Figure 14.11 (p. 375):** adapted from Bergmann et al. 1994; **Figure 14.12 (p. 377):** Jochen Tack/Alamy Stock Photo; **Anthropologist as Problem Solver (p. 378):** © Organs Watch

CHAPTER 15

Chapter 15 opening photo: With permission of the Royal Ontario Museum © ROM; **Figure 15.1 (p. 386):** With permission of the Royal Ontario Museum © ROM; **Figure 15.2 (p. 387):** OUP; **Figure 15.3 (p. 388):** Photo by The Field Museum Library/Getty Images; **Figure 15.4 (p. 392):** Courtesy of Kellen Haak; **Anthropologist as Problem Solver (p. 393, top):** The Field Museum, GN91326_119d, Photographer John Weinstein; **Anthropologist as Problem Solver (p. 393, bottom):** The Field Museum, GN92047_062_65d, Photographer John Weinstein; **Figure 15.5 (p. 394):** robertharding/Alamy Stock Photo; **Figure 15.6 (p. 396):** Courtesy of Luis A. Vivanco; **Figure 15.7 (p. 397):** Hood Museum of Art; **Figure 15.8 (p. 398):** Penalope/iStockphoto; **Figure 15.9 (p. 399):** Courtesy of Robert L. Welsch; **Figure 15.10 (p. 401):** Paradigm PR; **Figure 15.11 (p. 402):** Private Collection/The Stapleton Collection/Bridgeman Images; **Thinking Like an Anthropologist (p. 403, left):** Photo by Noam Galai/Getty Images for GIFF; **Thinking Like an Anthropologist (p. 403, right):** Tanoa, King of Ambau. Drawn by A.T. Agate. Engd. by Rawdon, Wright & Hatch. (Philadelphia: Lea & Blanchard. 1845); **Classic Contributions (p. 407):** Photo by Noam Galai/Getty Images for GIFF; **Figure 15.11 (p. 408):** CREATISTA/Shutterstock

EPILOGUE

Epilogue opening photo (p. 412): Tim Sambrook/Alamy Stock Photo

List of Boxes

Index